Handbook of Research on Cloud Computing and Big Data Applications in IoT

B. B. Gupta
National Institute of Technology Kurukshetra, India

Dharma P. Agrawal
University of Cincinnati, USA

A volume in the Advances in Computer and
Electrical Engineering (ACEE) Book Series

Published in the United States of America by
    IGI Global
    Engineering Science Reference (an imprint of IGI Global)
    701 E. Chocolate Avenue
    Hershey PA, USA 17033
    Tel: 717-533-8845
    Fax: 717-533-8661
    E-mail: cust@igi-global.com
    Web site: http://www.igi-global.com

Library of Congress Cataloging-in-Publication Data

Names: Gupta, B. B., 1982- editor.
Title: Handbook of research on cloud computing and big data applications in
  IoT / B.B. Gupta and Dharma P. Agrawal, editors.
Description: Hershey, PA : Engineering Science Reference, , an imprint of IGI
  Global, [2019] | Includes bibliographical references.
Identifiers: LCCN 2018053032| ISBN 9781522584070 (hardcover) | ISBN
  9781522584087 (ebook)
Subjects: LCSH: Cloud computing. | Big data. | Internet of things.
Classification: LCC QA76.585 .H3628 2019 | DDC 004.67/82--dc23 LC record available at https://lccn.loc.gov/2018053032

This book is published in the IGI Global book series Advances in Computer and Electrical Engineering (ACEE) (ISSN: 2327-039X; eISSN: 2327-0403)

British Cataloguing in Publication Data
A Cataloguing in Publication record for this book is available from the British Library.

The views expressed in this book are those of the authors, but not necessarily of the publisher.

For electronic access to this publication, please contact: eresources@igi-global.com.

Advances in Computer and Electrical Engineering (ACEE) Book Series

Srikanta Patnaik
SOA University, India

ISSN:2327-039X
EISSN:2327-0403

MISSION

The fields of computer engineering and electrical engineering encompass a broad range of interdisciplinary topics allowing for expansive research developments across multiple fields. Research in these areas continues to develop and become increasingly important as computer and electrical systems have become an integral part of everyday life.

The **Advances in Computer and Electrical Engineering (ACEE) Book Series** aims to publish research on diverse topics pertaining to computer engineering and electrical engineering. **ACEE** encourages scholarly discourse on the latest applications, tools, and methodologies being implemented in the field for the design and development of computer and electrical systems.

COVERAGE

- Computer Hardware
- Analog Electronics
- Sensor Technologies
- Power Electronics
- VLSI Design
- Qualitative Methods
- Computer Science
- Chip Design
- Applied Electromagnetics
- VLSI Fabrication

IGI Global is currently accepting manuscripts for publication within this series. To submit a proposal for a volume in this series, please contact our Acquisition Editors at Acquisitions@igi-global.com or visit: http://www.igi-global.com/publish/.

Titles in this Series

For a list of additional titles in this series, please visit: www.igi-global.com/book-series

Code Generation, Analysis Tools, and Testing for Quality
Ricardo Alexandre Peixoto de Queirós (Polytechnic Institute of Porto, Portugal) Alberto Simões (Polytechnic Institute of Cávado and Ave, Portugal) and Mário Teixeira Pinto (Polytechnic Institute of Porto, Portugal)
Engineering Science Reference • copyright 2019 • 288pp • H/C (ISBN: 9781522574552) • US $205.00 (our price)

Global Virtual Enterprises in Cloud Computing Environments
N. Raghavendra Rao (FINAIT Consultancy Services, India)
Engineering Science Reference • copyright 2019 • 281pp • H/C (ISBN: 9781522531821) • US $215.00 (our price)

Advancing Consumer-Centric Fog Computing Architectures
Kashif Munir (University of Hafr Al-Batin, Saudi Arabia)
Engineering Science Reference • copyright 2019 • 217pp • H/C (ISBN: 9781522571490) • US $210.00 (our price)

New Perspectives on Information Systems Modeling and Design
António Miguel Rosado da Cruz (Polytechnic Institute of Viana do Castelo, Portugal) and Maria Estrela Ferreira da Cruz (Polytechnic Institute of Viana do Castelo, Portugal)
Engineering Science Reference • copyright 2019 • 332pp • H/C (ISBN: 9781522572718) • US $235.00 (our price)

Advanced Methodologies and Technologies in Network Architecture, Mobile Computing, and Data Analytics
Mehdi Khosrow-Pour, D.B.A. (Information Resources Management Association, USA)
Engineering Science Reference • copyright 2019 • 1857pp • H/C (ISBN: 9781522575986) • US $595.00 (our price)

Emerging Innovations in Microwave and Antenna Engineering
Jamal Zbitou (University of Hassan 1st, Morocco) and Ahmed Errkik (University of Hassan 1st, Morocco)
Engineering Science Reference • copyright 2019 • 437pp • H/C (ISBN: 9781522575399) • US $245.00 (our price)

Advanced Methodologies and Technologies in Artificial Intelligence, Computer Simulation, and Human-Computer Interaction
Mehdi Khosrow-Pour, D.B.A. (Information Resources Management Association, USA)
Engineering Science Reference • copyright 2019 • 1221pp • H/C (ISBN: 9781522573685) • US $545.00 (our price)

Optimal Power Flow Using Evolutionary Algorithms
Provas Kumar Roy (Kalyani Government Engineering College, India) and Susanta Dutta (Dr. B. C. Roy Engineering College, India)
Engineering Science Reference • copyright 2019 • 323pp • H/C (ISBN: 9781522569718) • US $195.00 (our price)

701 East Chocolate Avenue, Hershey, PA 17033, USA
Tel: 717-533-8845 x100 • Fax: 717-533-8661
E-Mail: cust@igi-global.com • www.igi-global.com

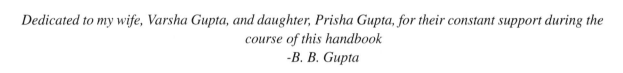

Dedicated to my wife, Varsha Gupta, and daughter, Prisha Gupta, for their constant support during the course of this handbook
-B. B. Gupta

Dedicated to my wife, Purnima Agrawal, for her constant support during the course of this handbook
-Dharma P. Agrawal

Editorial Advisory Board

List of Contributors

Table of Contents

Detailed Table of Contents

Chapter 1
Muhammed Tawfiqul Islam, The University of Melbourne, Australia
Rajkumar Buyya, The University of Melbourne, Australia

This chapter presents software architectures of the big data processing platforms. It also provides in-depth knowledge on resource management techniques involved while deploying big data processing systems in the cloud environment. It starts from the very basics and gradually introduce the core components of resource management which are divided into multiple layers. It covers the state-of-art practices and researches done in SLA-based resource management with a specific focus on the job scheduling mechanisms.

Chapter 2
Sanjay P. Ahuja, University of North Florida, USA

The proliferation of public cloud providers and services offered necessitate that end users have benchmarking-related information that help compare the properties of the cloud computing environment being provided. System-level benchmarks are used to measure the performance of overall system or subsystem. This chapter surveys the system-level benchmarks that are used for traditional computing environments that can also be used to compare cloud computing environments. Amazon's EC2 Service is one of the leading public cloud service providers and offers many different levels of service. The research in this chapter focuses on system-level benchmarks and looks into evaluating the memory, CPU, and I/O performance of two different tiers of hardware offered through Amazon's EC2. Using three distinct types of system benchmarks, the performance of the micro spot instance and the M1 small instance are measured and compared. In order to examine the performance and scalability of the hardware, the virtual machines are set up in a cluster formation ranging from two to eight nodes.

Chapter 3

Nag Nami, San Jose State University, USA
Melody Moh, San Jose State University, USA

Intelligent systems are capable of doing tasks on their own with minimal or no human intervention. With the advent of big data and IoT, these intelligence systems have made their ways into most industries and homes. With its recent advancements, deep learning has created a niche in the technology space and is being actively used in big data and IoT systems globally. With the wider adoption, deep learning models unfortunately have become susceptible to attacks. Research has shown that many state-of-the-art accurate models can be vulnerable to attacks by well-crafted adversarial examples. This chapter aims to provide concise, in-depth understanding of attacks and defense of deep learning models. The chapter first presents the key architectures and application domains of deep learning and their vulnerabilities. Next, it illustrates the prominent adversarial examples, including the algorithms and techniques used to generate these attacks. Finally, it describes challenges and mechanisms to counter these attacks, and suggests future research directions.

Chapter 4

Nitigya Sambyal, Punjab Engineering College (Deemed), India
Poonam Saini, Punjab Engineering College (Deemed), India
Rupali Syal, Punjab Engineering College (Deemed), India

The world is increasingly driven by huge amounts of data. Big data refers to data sets that are so large or complex that traditional data processing application software are inadequate to deal with them. Healthcare analytics is a prominent area of big data analytics. It has led to significant reduction in morbidity and mortality associated with a disease. In order to harness full potential of big data, various tools like Apache Sentry, BigQuery, NoSQL databases, Hadoop, JethroData, etc. are available for its processing. However, with such enormous amounts of information comes the complexity of data management, other big data challenges occur during data capture, storage, analysis, search, transfer, information privacy, visualization, querying, and update. The chapter focuses on understanding the meaning and concept of big data, analytics of big data, its role in healthcare, various application areas, trends and tools used to process big data along with open problem challenges.

Chapter 5

Shaurya Gupta, Amity University Rajasthan, India
Ramesh Chandra Poonia, Norwegian University of Science and Technology, Norway
Vijander Singh, Amity University Rajasthan, India
Linesh Raja, Amity University Rajasthan, India

The need for data outsourcing or database as a service (DaaS) is extremely important for any organization. In addition, data storage or data retrieval cost high especially for small companies. This chapter aims to study the various challenges in cloud computing communication issue. The chapter on multi-tiering a cloud emphasizes security enhancement due to the application of tiers in the cloud such that services availability is also improved. Cloud computing is a recent network trend for advanced communication systems. A lot of research led to the advancements in the areas of newer modes but multi-tiering a cloud is still an embarking issue for the researchers.

This chapter proposes a security framework for achieving secure and privacy-preserving mobile social networks named ASPP. Based on the cooperative neighbor, reactive routing protocol, and short signatures technique, the proposed scheme can not only detect and avoid but also can preserve the message privacy against elemental attacks and compound attacks. In addition, ASPP is robust against eavesdropping attack, wormhole attack, packet analysis attack, packet tracing attack, and replay attack. Extensive analyses and experiments are given to demonstrate its high detection rate and practicability under various scenarios.

Machine learning has found its immense application in various cybersecurity domains owing to its automated threat prediction and detection capabilities. Despite its advantages, attackers can utilize the vulnerabilities of machine learning models for degrading its performance. These attacks called adversarial attacks can perturb the features of the data to induce misclassification. Adversarial attacks are highly destructive in the case of malware detection classifiers, causing a harmful virus or trojan to evade the threat detection system. The feature perturbations carried out by an adversary against malware detection classifiers are different from the conventional attack strategies employed by an adversary against computer vision tasks. This chapter discusses various adversarial attacks launched against malware detection classifiers and the existing defensive mechanisms. The authors also discuss the challenges and the research directions that need to be addressed to develop effective defensive mechanisms against these attacks.

Big data analytics is one of the key research areas ever since the advancement of internet technologies, social media, mobile networks, and internet of things (IoT). The volume of big data creates a major challenge to the data scientist while interpreting the information from raw data. The privacy of user data is an important issue faced by the users who utilize the computing resources from third party (i.e., cloud environment). This chapter proposed a data independent reusable projection (DIRP) technique for reducing the dimension of the original high dimensional data and also preserves the privacy of the data in analysis phase. The proposed method projects the high dimensional input data into the random low dimensional space. The data independent and distance preserving property helps the proposed method to reduce the computational complexity of the machine learning algorithm. The randomness of data masks the original input data which helps to solve the privacy issue during data analysis. The proposed algorithm has been tested with the MNIST hand written digit recognition dataset.

Cloud computing provides resources using multitenant architecture where infrastructure is created from one or more distributed datacenters. Scheduling of applications in cloud infrastructures is one of the main research area in cloud computing. Researchers have developed many scheduling algorithms and evaluated them using simulators such as CloudSim. Their performance needs to be validated in real-time cloud environments to improve their usefulness. Aneka is one of the prominent PaaS software which allows users to develop cloud application using various programming models and underline infrastructure. This chapter presents a scheduling API developed for the Aneka software platform. Users can develop their own scheduling algorithms using this API and integrate it with Aneka to test their scheduling algorithms in real cloud environments. The proposed API provides all the required functionalities to integrate and schedule private, public, or hybrid cloud with the Aneka software.

Chapter 10

To conquer medical carelessness, a novel framework will be created on the grounds that daily medicinal services are essential. This framework conveys equipment, and Android application, the pulse, temperature of body, dampness rate are detected by the sensor in equipment. There is a Raspberry pi over which this detected information is transferred. The system dependent on internet of things (IOT) is utilized for remotely getting to information. With the end goal to get to the information universally, IOT used to keep all refreshed data on pages, a great opportunity to put information on mists. There is an Android-based application that can get to information from server through wi-fi to give us a chance to see the detected information. On the off chance that any of the anomalies are discovered, those must be settled, so it will send message to tolerant and individual specialists.

Chapter 11

Over the last two decades, the science has come a long way from relying on only physical experiments and observations to experimentation using computer simulators. This chapter focuses on the modelling and analysis of data arising from computer simulators. It turns out that traditional statistical metamodels are often not very useful for analyzing such datasets. For deterministic computer simulators, the realizations of Gaussian process (GP) models are commonly used for fitting a surrogate statistical metamodel of the simulator output. The chapter starts with a quick review of the standard GP-based statistical surrogate model. The chapter also emphasizes on the numerical instability due to near-singularity of the spatial correlation structure in the GP model fitting process. The authors also present a few generalizations of the GP model, reviews methods, and algorithms specifically developed for analyzing big data obtained from computer model runs, and reviews the popular analysis goals of such computer experiments. A few real-life computer simulators are also briefly outlined here.

Cloud-based reliable and protected data storage technique is proposed in this chapter. The proposed technique encrypts and protects data with less time consumption. Power consumption of storage is dependent upon capacity of storage and physical size of storage. Time analysis is presented graphically in this chapter. Reliable data storage is represented in cloud based proposed approach. Data is encrypted with minimum time complexity due to usage of proposed cloud-based reliable data storage. The competent ratio of time complexity is graphically observed in proposed data storage technique. Power consumption of storage has been typically dependent on the basis of capacity of storage and amount of storage. A ratio of power consumption and capacity of storage is presented in cloud-based approach. An efficient usage of energy is shown depending on current consumption and voltage in proposed reliable approach.

Chapter 13

The internet of things (IoT) is a fast-growing paradigm gaining position in the modern scenario of communication. It targets to provide interconnection among different objects at any time, and anywhere on the earth, under the leverage of internet. IoT has exhibited the promising enhancement in almost all dimensions of the everyday human life scenarios. The IoT applications are smart energy systems, manufacturing services, industrial automation, healthcare, education, smart city, transportation, and security and surveillance. However, there are several issues associated with IoT objectives such as data traffic, security and privacy, data analytics, device localization, and scalability. In addition to this, the IoT objects are resource constrained in terms of memory, computing power, energy, storage, and networking capability. Hence, IoT systems need enabling technologies to overcome these challenges by means of cloud computing, big data, cyber physical systems, and block chain. This chapter discusses how these enabling technologies can be integrated with IoT and its challenges.

Chapter 14

In this chapter, the authors present their system, which can use natural language query to interact with heterogeneous information networks (HIN). This chapter proposes a solution combining the GraphFrames, recurrent neural network (RNN) long short-term memory (LSTM), and dependency relation of question for generating, training, understanding the question-answer pairs and selecting the best match answer for this question. The RNN-LSTM is used to generate the answer from the facts of knowledge graph. The authors need to build a training data set of question-answer pairs from a very large knowledge graph by using GraphFrames for big graph processing. To improve the performance of GraphFrames, they repartition the GraphFrames. For complicated query, they use the Stanford dependency parser to analyze the question and build the motif pattern for searching GraphFrames. They also develop a chatbot that can interact with the knowledge graph by using the natural language query. They conduct their system with question-answer generated from DBLP to prove the performance of our proposed system.

Fog computing is an extension to cloud computing that inhibits its limitations and enhances its amenities. Being similar to cloud computing, it has some more fascinating features that escalate the overall performance of the system. It faces many new disputes besides those already inherited from cloud computing. Fog computing is actually a paradigm that provides services at the network's edge as it serves the end-users with data, applications, storing, and computing capabilities. Fog computing is a new breed in services and applications to the end-users by enabling the above features, hence making its security and privacy aspects much more challenging then the cloud computing. Further, in this chapter, the basic concepts of fog computing are discussed with its applications as a high lighting feature. In addition, discussion about the attacks that could setback the advantages of fog computing and some defense mechanisms to overcome the effects of these attack have been discussed, giving a comprehensive study of fog computing.

Chapter 16

Analyzing the evolution of new generation peripherals can affirm that the next decade will be characterized by the exponential increase in the number of "objects" interconnected to the internet that will be more able to communicate with each other independently and will lead to the affirmation of the paradigm internet of things (IoT), which will revolutionize everyday life on a global level. This evolution will concern not only the business realities, interested in the development of applications and systems necessary to emerge and be competitive on the market but also the ordinary citizens who will be surrounded by interconnected objects able to facilitate their everyday life. This aspect implies particular attention to the implementation of solutions oriented to cyber security necessary to guarantee an efficient and effective level of protection against the threats coming from the "world" internet, known by the term cyber space.

Chapter 17

Cloud computing involves storing data using a third party that ensures that confidential data cannot be accessed even by the cloud itself. Thus, security is one major issue in cloud computing. Recent advancements in exploiting chaotic systems' sensitivity to initial conditions, and their ability to extract strings of random numbers for confusion and diffusion have helped enhance security. They can provide resistance from statistical attack and protection against reconstruction dynamics. However, the concept of chaos for security is still in its emerging stages. This chapter presents how chaos theory can be used for random number generation to further secure data in the cloud. The authors have discussed and compared some popular methods for authentication and encryption of data, images, and videos. The overview of chaos engineering discusses the discipline of experimenting on multi-server systems to ensure its ability to tackle glitches.

Cloud computing has become one of the most important technologies in our day-to-day lives. The computing resources are delivered to the customers based on subscription basis via internet. Big data storage and processing are main application of cloud. Furthermore, the development of internet of things provides the platform for interconnecting devices over internet. This includes everything from mobile phones, washing machines, lamps, headphones, wearable devices, and everything else we never think of. This enables machine-to-machine communication, also applies to the components of the machine. The main objective of this chapter is to give an overview of cloud computing, big data, and internet of things and the advance research topics.

Chapter 19

Due to the momentous growth in the field of Internet of Things (IoT), various commercial and government organizations are exploring possibilities of mass issuance of smart cards in different applications. Widespread deployment of smart card-based systems in heterogeneous environment would facilitate card holders to participate in these applications in a personalized manner. Despite the security features, valuable data and access to decisive services make these systems prime target for attackers. These systems can be subjected to a range of security attacks – from hardware exploitation to exploitation of software bugs, from unauthorized data access to social engineering, and so forth. In the future, where many sectors will be trying to adopt the concept of Blockchain, it will create new opportunities for benefiting citizens with enhanced security over their data. In this chapter, the author performs in-depth analysis over the role of Blockchain in securing the smart card ecosystem.

Chapter 20

Opportunistic networks are one of the emerging evolutions of the network system. In opportunistic networks, nodes are able to communicate with each other even if the route between source to destination does not already exist. Opportunistic networks have to be delay tolerant in nature (i.e., able to tolerate larger delays). Delay tolerant network (DTNs) uses the concept of "store-carry-forward" of data packets. DTNs are able to transfer data or establish communication in remote area or crisis environment where there is no network established. DTNs have many applications like to provide low-cost internet provision in remote areas, in vehicular networks, noise monitoring, extreme terrestrial environments, etc. It is therefore very promising to identify aspects for integration and inculcation of opportunistic network methodologies and technologies into delay tolerant networking. In this chapter, the authors emphasize delay tolerant networks by considering its architectural, routing, congestion, and security issues.

The number of devices operating on IoTs has exceeded billions globally. This chapter aims to examine the cyber security risks of such systems with widespread use and investigate some IoT vulnerabilities. It examines the effects of these vulnerabilities on business life and personal life, and the precautions to be taken to eliminate them. In addition, the regulations and measures to be applied at the state level is discussed. The safe use of IoT systems cannot be achieved solely by individual awareness. An awareness and sense of responsibility in the manufacturing layer is also a must. This chapter investigates the reasons behind the lack of security precautions taken in the manufacturing phase of IoT devices and suggests solutions. It also discusses the details of malwares such as Mirai, whose targets are mainly IoT vulnerabilities.

Chapter 22

The advent of social networking and internet of things (IoT) has resulted in exponential growth of data in the last few years. This, in turn, has increased the need to process and analyze such data for optimal decision making. In order to achieve better results, there is an emergence of newly-built architectures for parallel processing. Hadoop MapReduce (MR) is a programming model that is considered as one of the most powerful computation tools for processing the data on a given cluster of commodity nodes. However, the management of clusters along with various quality requirements necessitates the use of efficient MR scheduling. The chapter discusses the classification of MR scheduling algorithms based on their applicability with required parameters of quality of service (QoS). After classification, a detailed study of MR schedulers has been presented along with their comparison on various parameters.

Chapter 23

Software-defined networks (SDN) are a new paradigm shift in the world of network centralized command and control, providing network omniscience and separates control and data planes. Most of the research work till date focuses on increasing efficiency and manageability of computational and storage resources which results in emergence of current virtualization technologies. The feasibility and applications of SDN in current datacenters and network infrastructures is being studied by academia, industry, and the standardization bodies. This chapter explains SDN concepts and its difference from legacy networking, interrelated terminologies, protocols, programming languages, benefits, and shortcomings. Moreover, exploration of current research areas and techniques along with in-depth analysis and future research directions will be presented.

Foreword

In the past decade, business and research organizations across the world switched towards digital transformations and scientific innovations to grow in the competitive era of information and communication technology (ICT). These organizations are adopting latest technologies like Cloud computing, big data analytics, the Internet-of-things (IoT) as also other innovative strategies to move forward in the business and science processing. The convergence of these technologies can be seen with increasing adoption and development.

Cloud computing provides on-demand computational and storage resources to individuals or organizations without any requirement of building and maintaining in-house computational infrastructures, with the delivery of information technology (IT) services including software, infrastructure, and platform through Internet-based applications which users can access remotely. Thus, Cloud computing is characterized as a technology owing dynamicity, provisioning and cost-saving potential, and indeed a viable alternative for big businesses and collaborations across the globe.

Big data is a term which signifies large datasets coming from a myriad of resources and characterized by its volume, variety, and velocity. Big data analytics involves mapping the structured and unstructured data to gain better insights, thus providing a completely different dimension to the field of data analytics. Cloud-based applications are significantly contributing to the bulk of data generation while at the same time, provide a powerful abstraction for scalable big data processing systems with enhanced reliability and availability.

IoT establishes an ecosystem of smart and inter-connected devices having the capability of communicating and transferring data over the Internet with minimal or no human intervention. This idea of inter-connected things has empowered businesses and consumers by providing them with enhanced control and better solutions. IoT devices generate a massive amount of data, in turn can be fed to the data processing tools and applications to create logic workflows for these devices to work in a smart fashion.

I believe that *Handbook of Research on Cloud Computing and Big Data Applications in IoT* is a valuable addition to existing literature and serving as a source of recent researches in this unceasingly developing area, turning out significant to readers for a valuable contribution to the current subject matter and impressive work. This handbook serves as a handy reference for practitioners and application developers also provides an opportunity for researchers and academicians to explore and understand advanced computing technologies and their impact to conduct more sophisticated studies.

Kuan-Ching Li
Providence University, Taiwan
Taichung, Taiwan

Preface

Today, Cloud Computing based services, Big data models and Internet-of-things (IoTs) are becoming significant parts of modern information and communication technology (ICT) systems. They cover storage and communication innovations, as well as a wide range of frameworks, including business, finance, manufacturing, management, and so forth. Although, these have developed separately over time as distinct and sophisticated disciplines, but increasing business demand is making them more intertwined. Cloud computing has ended up being an unbelievable innovation which ensures provisioning of easily deployable and versatile information technology (IT) solutions at decreased infrastructure and maintenance costs with reduced time. Moreover, Cloud computing configurations encourage the processing of huge amount of data and intelligent decision making process involved in big data analysis by cutting down the requirement of massive machines for the purpose. IoT establishes an association between the physical world and the Internet through numerous technologies and standards, and creates a network of smart devices that produce enormous amount of data. To streamline the applications with the convergence of these paradigms, it has become inevitable to understand the advance researches in these three domains.

This book contains chapters dealing with latest empirical research findings in the area of Cloud computing, big data and IoT. These include security and privacy in cloud computing, cyber-security issues in Clouds, information revelation and privacy in Cloud computing, multi-party online gaming on Clouds-risk, threat and security solutions, Cloud computing security data analysis tools and services, secured handling of extra-scale computational loads on Clouds, anonymous authentication for privacy preserving in Cloud, privacy concepts and applications in Cloud platforms, user behaviour and modelling on cyberspace, Cloud forensics, security and privacy of cloud user's data, evolutionary algorithms for privacy analysis in Cloud computing, evolutionary algorithms for mining Cloud computing for decision support, security and privacy in Internet-of-things (IoTs), optimization of dynamic processes in Cloud computing, computational intelligence solutions to security and privacy issues in mobile cloud computing, chaos theory and chaotic systems for cloud content security, artificial neural network and neural system applied to cloud computing and mitigating the privacy risks of cloud networking, Cloud databases built to be highly scalable and robust against hardware failures, Cloud storage resilience designed to run over distributed file systems providing data replication and automatic failover capabilities, cyber-attacks and solutions for high fidelity Cloud storage, security and privacy in heterogeneous IoT, secure and privacy preserving data mining and aggregation in IoT applications, cross-domain trust management in smart networks, secure authentication of IoT devices, MAC layer security protocols for the IoT applications, IoT security mechanisms targeting application layer protocols, resource-savvy intrusion detection for networks of things, security and privacy of big data, privacy in big data end-point input validation and filtering, privacy in big data integration and transformation, privacy in parallel and distributed computation, privacy in big data storage management, privacy in big data access control mechanisms, privacy in big data mining and analytics, and privacy in big data sharing and visualization.

Specifically, the chapters contained in this handbook are summarized as follows:

In Chapter 1, authors present software architectures of the big data processing platforms, and provides in-depth knowledge on resource management techniques involved while deploying big data processing systems in the cloud environment. The chapter starts from the very basics and gradually introduces the core components of resource management which have been divided into multiple layers. It covers the state-of-art practices and researches done in SLA-based resource management with a specific focus on the job scheduling mechanisms.

In Chapter 2, authors survey the system-level benchmarks that are used for traditional computing environments that can also be used to compare cloud computing environments. Amazon's EC2 Service is one of the leading public cloud service providers and offers many different levels of service. The research in this chapter focuses on system level benchmarks and looks into evaluating the memory, CPU, and I/O performance of two different tiers of hardware offered through Amazon's EC2. Using three distinct types of system benchmarks, the performance of the micro spot instance and the M1 small instance are measured and compared. In order to examine the performance and scalability of the hardware, the virtual machines are set up in a cluster formation ranging from two to eight nodes.

In Chapter 3, authors aim to provide concise, in-depth understanding of attacks and defense of deep learning models. The chapter first presents the key architectures and application domains of deep learning and their vulnerabilities. Next, it illustrates the prominent adversarial examples, including the algorithms and techniques used to generate these attacks. Finally, it describes challenges and mechanisms to counter these attacks, and suggests future research directions.

Chapter 4 focuses on understanding the meaning and concept of big data, analytics of big data, its role in healthcare, various application areas, trends and tools used to process big data along with open problem challenges.

Chapter 5 aims to study the various challenges in cloud computing communication issue. Proposed Chapter on multi-tiring a cloud emphasizes security enhancement due to the application of tiers in the cloud such that services availability is also improved. Cloud computing is a recent network trend for advanced communication systems. A lot of research led to the advancements in the areas of newer modes but multi-tiring a cloud is still an embarking issue for the researchers.

In Chapter 6, authors propose a security framework for achieving secure and privacy-preserving in mobile social networks, named ASPP. Based on the cooperative neighbor, reactive routing protocol, and short signatures technique, the proposed scheme can not only detect and avoid but also can preserve the message privacy against elemental attacks and compound attacks. In addition, ASPP is robust against eavesdropping attack, wormhole attack, packet analysis attack, packet tracing attack, and replay attack. Extensive analyses and experiments are given to demonstrate its high detection rate and practicability under various scenarios.

Chapter 7 discusses various adversarial attacks launched against malware detection classifiers and the existing defensive mechanisms. It also discusses the challenges and the research directions that need to be addressed to develop effective defensive mechanisms against these attacks.

In Chapter 8, authors propose a data independent reusable projection (DIRP) technique for reducing the dimension of the original high dimensional data and also preserves the privacy of the data in analysis phase. The proposed method projects the high dimensional input data into the random low dimensional space. The data independent and distance preserving property helps the proposed method to reduce the computational complexity of the machine learning algorithm. The randomness of data masks the original input data which helps to solve the privacy issue during data analysis. The proposed algorithm has been tested with the MNIST hand written digit recognition dataset.

Chapter 9 presents a scheduling API developed for the Aneka software platform. Users can develop their own scheduling algorithms using this API and integrate it with Aneka to test their scheduling algorithms in real cloud environments. The proposed API provides all the required functionalities to integrate and schedule private, public or hybrid cloud with the Aneka software.

Chapter 10 presents a Cloud based Patient Health Monitoring System using the Internet of Things. This framework conveys equipment and Android application, the pulse, temperature of body, dampness rate is detected by the sensor in equipment. There is a Raspberry pi over which this detected information is transferred. The System dependent on Internet of Things (IOT) is utilized for remotely getting to information. With the end goal to get to the information universally, IOT used to keep all refreshed data on pages' a great opportunity to time and put away information on mists. There is an Android based application that can get to information from server through Wi-Fi to give us a chance to see the detected information. On the off chance that any of the anomalies are discovered those must be settled, so it will send message to tolerant and individual specialist.

Chapter 11 focusses on the modelling and analysis of data arising from computer simulators. It turns out that traditional statistical metamodels are often not very useful for analyzing such datasets. For deterministic computer simulators, the realizations of Gaussian Process (GP) models are commonly used for fitting a surrogate statistical metamodel of the simulator output. The chapter starts with a quick review of the standard GP based statistical surrogate model. The chapter also emphasizes on the numerical instability due to near-singularity of the spatial correlation structure in the GP model fitting process. The authors also present a few generalizations of the GP model, reviews methods and algorithms specifically developed for analyzing big data obtained from computer model runs, and reviews the popular analysis goals of such computer experiments. A few real-life computer simulators are also briefly outlined here.

In Chapter 12, Cloud based reliable and protected data storage technique is proposed. The proposed technique encrypts and protects data with less time consumption. Power consumption of storage is dependent upon capacity of storage and physical size of storage. Time analysis is presented graphically in this chapter. Reliable data storage is represented in cloud based proposed approach. Data is encrypted with minimum time complexity due to usage of proposed cloud based reliable data storage. The competent ratio of time complexity is graphically observed in proposed data storage technique. Power consumption of storage has been typically dependent on the basis of capacity of storage and amount of storage. A ratio of power consumption and capacity of storage is presented in cloud based approach. An efficient usage of energy is shown depending on current consumption and voltage in proposed reliable approach.

Chapter 13 discusses enabling technologies for IoT along with issues, challenges and research opportunities. The Internet of Things (IoT) is fast growing paradigm gaining position in the modern scenario of communication. It targets to provide interconnection among different objects at any time, and anywhere on the earth, under the leverage of Internet. IoT has exhibited the promising enhancement in almost all dimensions of the everyday human life scenarios. The IoT applications are smart energy systems, manufacturing services, industrial automation, health care, education, smart city, transportation and security and surveillance. However, there are several issues associated with IoT objectives such data traffic, security and privacy, data analytics, device localization and scalability. In addition to this, the IoT objects are resource constrained in terms of memory, computing power, energy, storage and networking capability. Hence, IoT systems need enabling technologies to overcome these challenges by means of

Cloud computing, Big Data, Cyber Physical Systems, and Block chain. This chapter discusses how these enabling technologies can be integrated with IoT, and its challenges.

Chapter 14 presents a system which can use natural language query to interact with Heterogeneous Information Network (HIN), and proposes a solution combining the GraphFrames, Recurrent Neural Network (RNN)- Long Short Term Memory (LSTM) and dependency relation of question for generating, training, understanding the question-answer pairs and selecting the best match answer for this question. The RNN-LSTM is used to generate the answer from the facts of knowledge graph.

In Chapter 15, authors discuss Fog Computing concepts, applications and countermeasures against security attacks. Fog Computing is an extension to cloud computing which inhibits its limitations and enhances its amenities. Being similar to cloud computing it has some more fascinating features which escalate the overall performance of the system. It faces many new disputes besides those already inherited from cloud computing. Fog computing is actually a paradigm which provides services at the network's edge as it serves the end-users with data, applications, storing and computing capabilities. Fog computing is a new breed in services and applications to the end-users by enabling the above features. Hence making its security and privacy aspects much more challenging then the cloud computing. Further in this chapter, the basic concepts of fog computing are discussed with its applications as a high lighting feature. In addition, discussion about the attacks that could setback the advantages of fog computing and some defense mechanisms to overcome the effects of these attack have been discussed, giving a comprehensive study of fog computing.

Chapter 16 presents a survey on Industrial Internet of Things (IoT) threats and security. By analyzing the evolution of new generation peripherals, we can affirm that the next decade will be characterized by the exponential increase in the number of "objects" interconnected to the Internet which will be more and more able to communicate with each other independently and will lead to the affirmation of the paradigm " Internet of Things (IoT) "or" Internet of Things "which will revolutionize everyday life on a global level. This evolution will concern not only the business realities, interested in the development of applications and systems necessary to emerge and be competitive on the market but also the ordinary citizens who will be surrounded by interconnected objects able to facilitate their everyday life. This aspect implies particular attention to the implementation of solutions oriented to Cyber Security, necessary to guarantee an efficient and effective level of protection against the threats coming from the "world" Internet, known by the term Cyber Space.

Chapter 17 presents how chaos theory can be used for random number generation to further secure data in the cloud. It also discusses and compares some popular methods for authentication and encryption of data, images, and videos. The overview of Chaos Engineering discusses the discipline of experimenting on multi-server systems to ensure its ability to tackle glitches.

Chapter 18 presents a study on recent trends in Cloud based data processing for IoT era. Cloud computing has become one of the most important technology in our day today life. The computing resources are delivered to the customers based on subscription basis via internet. Big data storage and processing are main application of cloud. Furthermore, the development of Internet of Things provides the platform for interconnecting devices over internet. This includes everything from mobile phones, washing machines, lamps, headphones, wearable devices and everything else we never think off. This enables machine to machine communication, also applies to the components of the machine. The main objective of this chapter is to give an overview of cloud computing, big data and Internet of Things and the advance research topics.

Chapter 19 discusses the perspective on using Blockchain for ensuring security in smart card systems. Due to momentous growth in the field of Internet of Things (IoT), various commercial and government organizations are exploring possibilities of mass issuance of smart cards in different applications. Widespread deployment of smart card based systems in heterogeneous environment would facilitate card holders to participate in these applications in a personalized manner. Despite the security features, valuable data and access to decisive services make these systems prime target for attackers. These systems can be subjected to a range of security attacks – from hardware exploitation to exploitation of software bugs, from unauthorized data access to social engineering, and so forth. In future, where many sectors will be trying to adopt the concept of Blockchain, it will create new opportunities for benefiting citizens with enhanced security over their data.

Chapter 20 emphasizes on Delay tolerant networks by considering their architectural, routing, congestion and security issues. Opportunistic networks are one of the emerging evolutions of the network system. In opportunistic networks, nodes are able to communicate with each other even if the route between source to destination is not already exists. Opportunistic networks have to be Delay tolerant in nature i.e. able to tolerate larger delays. Delay Tolerant Network (DTNs) uses the concept of 'store-carry-forward' of data packets. DTNs are able to transfer data or establish communication in remote area or crisis environment where there is no network established. DTNs have many applications like to provide low-cost internet provision in remote areas, in vehicular networks, noise monitoring, extreme terrestrial environments etc. It is therefore very promising to identify aspects for integration, and inculcation of opportunistic network methodologies and technologies into Delay Tolerant Networking.

Chapter 21 investigates the reasons behind the lack of security precautions taken in the manufacturing phase of IoT devices; and suggests solutions. It also discusses the details of malwares such as Mirai; whose target are mainly IoT vulnerabilities.

In Chapter 22, authors discuss the classification of MR scheduling algorithms based on their applicability with required parameters of Quality of Service (QoS). After classification, a detailed study of MR schedulers has been presented along with their comparison on various parameters.

Chapter 23 explains SDN concepts and its difference from legacy networking, inter related terminologies, protocols, Programming languages, benefits and shortcomings. Moreover, exploration of current research areas and techniques along with in-depth analysis and future research directions will be presented.

By covering latest advances in Cloud computing, big data, and IoT, this handbook will be a significant asset for understanding all the dimensions of cutting edge innovations in these domains. The subject matter of this book is exceptionally invigorating, useful, and simple to pursue for students ranging from novice to advanced levels. It contains an impressive and up-to-date collection of Cloud, big data and IoT related issues, different arrangements, and open research challenges. The target audience of this book will be composed of professionals, developers, faculty members, scientists, graduate students, research scholars and software developers who are seeking to carry out research/develop software in the field of Cloud computing, big data, and the IoT. This handbook is likely to have global reader since the said subjects are taught almost by every university worldwide by computer science and engineering and information technology departments.

Acknowledgment

Many people have contributed greatly to this *Handbook of Research on Cloud Computing and Big Data Applications in IoT*. We, the editors, would like to acknowledge all of them for their valuable help and generous ideas in improving the quality of this handbook. With our feelings of gratitude, we would like to introduce them in turn. The first mention is the authors and reviewers of each chapter of this handbook. Without their outstanding expertise, constructive reviews and devoted effort, this comprehensive handbook would become something without contents. The second mention is the IGI Global staff, especially Ms. Jordan Tepper, assistant development editor and her team for their constant encouragement, continuous assistance and untiring support. Without their technical support, this handbook would not be completed. The third mention is the editor's family for being the source of continuous love, unconditional support and prayers not only for this work, but throughout our life. Last but far from least, we express our heartfelt thanks to the Almighty for bestowing over us the courage to face the complexities of life and complete this work.

B. B. Gupta
National Institute of Technology Kurukshetra, India

Dharma Agrawal
University of Cincinnati, USA
January 12, 2019

Chapter 1

Resource Management and Scheduling for Big Data Applications in Cloud Computing Environments

Muhammed Tawfiqul Islam
https://orcid.org/0000-0003-4922-7807
The University of Melbourne, Australia

Rajkumar Buyya
The University of Melbourne, Australia

ABSTRACT

This chapter presents software architectures of the big data processing platforms. It also provides in-depth knowledge on resource management techniques involved while deploying big data processing systems in the cloud environment. It starts from the very basics and gradually introduce the core components of resource management which are divided into multiple layers. It covers the state-of-art practices and researches done in SLA-based resource management with a specific focus on the job scheduling mechanisms.

INTRODUCTION

Cloud Computing is an emerging platform which can provide infrastructure, platform, and software for storing and computing of data. Nowadays Cloud Computing is used in many small and large organizations like a utility (Buyya et al. 2009) as it is more affordable to go for the pay per use service of cloud service providers instead buying and maintaining own computing resources. While registering in any Cloud Service, both the cloud service customer and the cloud service provider must agree on some predefined policies which are called the Service Level Agreement (SLA). Violation of SLAs may affect the proper execution and performance of an application of any customer, so it poses a significant threat on a cloud service provider's business reputation. Therefore, it is essential to manage the cloud resources in such a way that it guarantees SLA.

DOI: 10.4018/978-1-5225-8407-0.ch001

Big Data (Assunção et al. 2015; Kune et al. 2016) is the recent hype in information technology. Scientific applications generate a large amount of data which is used for discoveries and explorations. Besides, social media data analysis, sentiment analysis, and business data analysis are crucial for business organizations to adopt customer needs and gain more profits. Cloud computing can be an appropriate solution to host big data applications, but many challenges need to be addressed to use the existing cloud architectures for big data applications. This chapter discusses the challenges of hosting big data processing platforms in the cloud. Moreover, it also gives a comprehensive overview of cloud resource management for big data applications. Resource management is a broad domain that contains many complex components. However, to make it easier to understand, we divide it as a layered architecture and discuss the critical elements from each layer. Our focus will be on resource allocation and scheduling mechanisms and how the existing research tried to incorporate SLA in these components. We will also point out the limitations of the current approaches and highlight future research directions.

The contents of this chapter are organized as follows. Sections 2 provides background on cloud computing, big data, big data processing platform systems and their architectures and some popular cluster managers. Section 3 gives a layered overview of the overall resource management process for big data applications on the cloud. Section 4 shows a taxonomy of resource allocation for big data applications. Section 5 exhibits a taxonomy of job scheduling mechanisms for big data applications. Section 6 discusses the research gaps and future research directions towards SLA-based resource management. Finally, section 7 concludes the chapter.

BACKGROUND

In this section, we briefly discuss the key features of cloud computing. Moreover, we explain the architectures of the popular open-source software systems for processing big data applications. Also, we provide an overview of some popular cluster managers. Finally, we conclude with explaining why the cloud is a viable alternative to deploy a big data processing software and how cluster managers can be used for efficient management of the system.

Cloud Computing

Cloud computing delivers a shared pool of on-demand computing resources on a pay-per-use basis. The main features of cloud computing are:

- **Resource Elasticity:** Cloud resources can be easily scaled up or down to meet application or user demands.
- **Metered Service:** Users are billed based on what resources they used and how long they have used them.
- **Easy Access:** The resources of cloud can be easily accessed and can be provisioned as a self-service manner.

There are three different types of cloud. These are:

- **Public Cloud:** There are many public cloud service providers who offers computing resources as a pay-per-use basis. Organizations can hire resources from these service providers to deploy their own applications. It greatly reduces the cost of buying computing hardware and removes the burdens of managing local resources.
- **Private Cloud:** Many organizations setup an on-premise computing resource facility which is known as the private cloud. The main reason for setting up a private cloud is to reduce the data transfer overhead to the public cloud. In addition, it also ensures that private and sensitive data are kept on the organization's premises to reduce security threats.
- **Hybrid Cloud:** It is mix of both public and private cloud. Sometimes organizations need to scale up their resources in public cloud to be processed in the public cloud.

Cloud provides computing as a service, and we can divide cloud services in three ways:

- **Software as a Service (SaaS):** SaaS can be used from any devices through the Internet and typically these services are accessed via a web browser. The required software needed by the user for any specialized task are already developed and provided thorough different interfaces. Users just define the task, input data and collect the results. Example: Google Apps[1]
- **Platform as a Service (PaaS):** A platform is provided for developing distributed, scalable cloud-based programs. It greatly reduces the hassle for managing the underlying resources. Example: IBM Cloud[2]
- **Infrastructure as a Service (IaaS):** Computing and storage resources are provided to setup a user's own infrastructure to build platform and services. Reduces the hassle of buying and managing own physical hardware, provides a scalable on demand pool of resources. Example: Windows Azure[3], Amazon EC2[4].

Big Data

In today's world, huge amount of data is being generated through social media, scientific explorations and many other emerging applications like Internet of Things (IoT). The term "Big data" is not about the size of data; rather it covers many other aspects. For simplicity, we can define it in terms of the 3V as shown in Figure 1.

The volume of data can be small or large, from a few Megabytes to thousands of Terabytes. Each day we are generating so much data that recently (in 2015) we have moved into a Zettabyte era. Velocity represents the speed of incoming data. For example, some applications need real-time or near real-time processing and comes with great speed. These types of applications can be categorized as streaming applications. In contrast, applications that need offline processing of huge volume of static data are called batch applications. Finally, data can have many varieties such as structured, unstructured etc. Storing and processing of data is often not possible by the traditional Database Management Systems (DBMS) and NoSQL has greatly replaced SQL in many domains. There are many other aspects of big data (many other Vs) depending on the specific domain.

Figure 1. Big data 3V

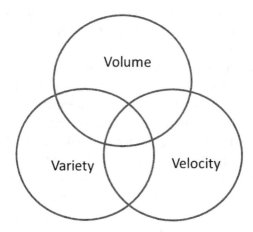

Big Data Processing Platforms

Processing big data is a difficult task, and it is not possible in a centralized system. Therefore, distributed computing solutions are used for parallel processing of big data. Many big data processing platforms have emerged over the last decade. Figure 2 shows a taxonomy on big data processing platforms. As it shows, previously only batch-based platforms like Hadoop was mostly used. However, due to the discovery of many scientific, business and social streaming applications, real-time processing became more influential and dedicated stream processing platforms like Strom, S4 were invented. However, applications became more complex, and often organizations need to have both batch and stream-based processing. Hence, some hybrid processing platforms like Apache Spark, Apache Flink are being used in the industry.

In this chapter, we only focus on batch and hybrid-based processing platforms and briefly discuss about some of the most popular ones.

Figure 2. A Taxonomy of big data processing frameworks

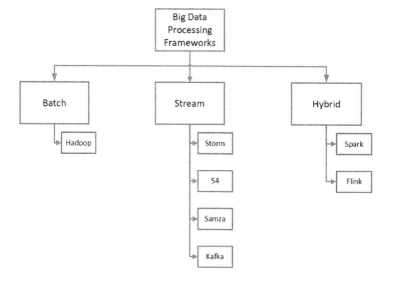

Apache Hadoop

Apache Hadoop, introduced by Yahoo in 2005, is the open source implementation of the MapReduce programming paradigm. The main feature of Hadoop is to use primarily distributed commodity hardware to parallel processing of batch-based jobs. The core of Hadoop is its fault-tolerant file system Hadoop Distributed File Systems (HDFS) (Shvachko et al. 2013) that can be explicitly defined to span in many computers. In HDFS, the block of data is much larger than a traditional file system (4KB versus 128MB). Therefore, it reduces the memory needed to store the metadata on data block locations. Besides, it reduces the seek operation in big files. Furthermore, it greatly enhances the use of the network as only a fewer number of network connections are needed for shuffle operations. In the architecture of HDFS, there are mainly two types of nodes: Name node and Data node. Name node contains the metadata of the HDFS blocks, and the data node is the location where the actual data is stored. By default, three copies of the same block are stored over the data nodes to make the system fault tolerant. The resource manager of Hadoop is called Yarn (Vavilapalli et al. 2013). It is composed of a central Resource Manager who resides in the master node and many Node Managers that live on the slave nodes. When an application is submitted to the cluster, the Application Master negotiates resources with the Resource Manager and starts container (where actual processing is done) on the slave nodes.

The main drawback of Hadoop was that it stored intermediate results in the disk, so for shuffle-intensive operations like iterative machine learning, a tremendous amount of data is stored in the disk and transferred over the network which poses a significant overhead on the whole system.

Figure 3. Apache hadoop architecture

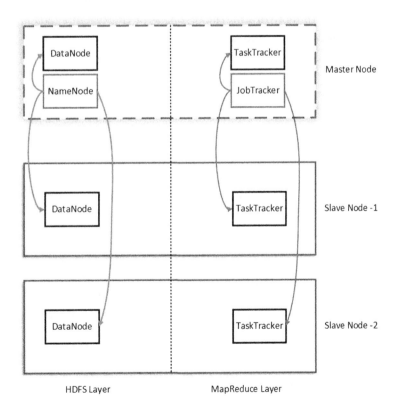

Apache Spark

Apache Spark (Zaharia et al. 2016) is one of the most prominent big data processing platforms. It is an open source, general-purpose, large-scale data processing framework. It mainly focuses on high-speed cluster computing and provides extensible and interactive analysis through high-level APIs. Spark supports batch or stream data analytics, machine learning and graph processing. It can also access diverse data sources like HDFS, HBase (George 2011), Cassandra (Lakshman and Malik 2010), etc. and use Resilient Distributed Dataset (RDD) (Zaharia et al. 2012) for data abstraction.

As compared to the Hadoop system tasks, Apache Spark allows most of the computations to be performed in memory and provides better performance for some applications such as iterative algorithms. When the results do not fit on the memory, the intermediate results are written to the disk. Spark can run locally in a single desktop, in a local cluster, and on the cloud. It runs on top of Hadoop Yarn, Apache Mesos (Hindman et al. 2011) and the default standalone cluster manager. Jobs/applications are divided into multiple sets of tasks called stages which are inter-dependent. All these stages make a directed acyclic graph (DAG), where each stage is executed one after another.

Apache Flink

Apache Flink (Katsifodimos and Schelter 2016) is an open-source stream processing platform. It executes data-flow programs in data-parallel pipelines. Flink is fault-tolerant and treats batch data as a form of a stream, therefore, it is a hybrid framework. Programs can be written in Java, Scala, Python, and SQL. Flink does not provide any data storage mechanism. Instead, it uses other data sources like HDFS, Cassandra, etc. During the execution stage, Flink programs are mapped to streaming dataflows. Every dataflow starts with one or more origins (input, queue or file system) and ends with one or more sinks (output, message queue, database or file system). An arbitrary number of transformations can be done on the stream. These dataflow streams are arranged as a directed acyclic dataflow graph, allowing

Figure 4. Apache spark architecture

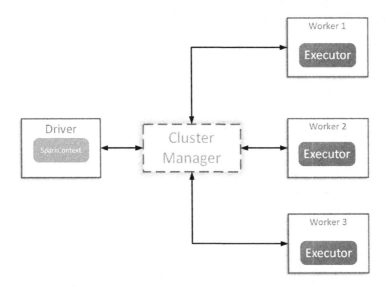

the flexibility for the applications to branch and merge dataflows. Flink is relatively new and unstable as compared to the matured frameworks like Hadoop and Spark. It is yet to be seen whether Flink can be scalable like Spark in a production-grade cluster.

CLUSTER MANAGERS

Apache Hadoop Yarn

Apache Hadoop Yarn (Vavilapalli et al. 2013) is the resource manager for Apache Hadoop. The core idea of Yarn is to split up the mechanisms for resource management such as job scheduling, monitoring, etc. into separate daemons. There is a global Resource-Manager in the master node and Node Managers in each of the worker/slave nodes. Resource Managers and Node Managers form the whole data-computation framework. Resource Manager is the ultimate co-ordinate that can dictate resource provisioning and scheduling in the entire system. Node Managers are responsible for running containers and monitor resource usages and reporting the resource usage statistics to the Resource Manager. Furthermore, per-application Application-Manager negotiates with the Resource Manager to reserve resources and collaborates with the Node Manager to run containers and monitor the tasks.

The Resource Manager has two main components: Scheduler and Applications-Manager. Scheduler tracks and maintains a queue of jobs set the order of the jobs and allocate resources to each of the jobs before execution. The scheduler functions are based on the implemented policies and SLA requirements of the applications. The scheduler has a pluggable policy which makes it extendable to different scheduling policies. For example, CapacityScheduler and FairScheduler are the example plugins implemented and available with Yarn. Applications-Manager accepts job submission requests and provides the service to restart failed jobs.

Figure 5. Apache hadoop yarn architecture

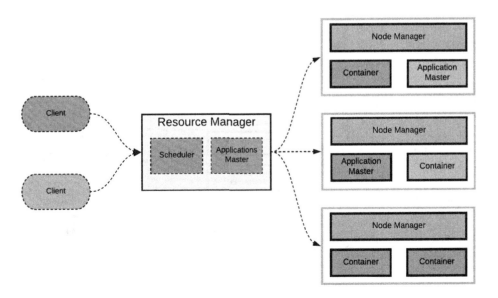

Apache Mesos

Apache Mesos (Hindman et al. 2011) is said to be the data-center level cluster manager. Mesos was built primarily to support multiple different big data processing frameworks to be running in the same cluster. Mesos isolates the resources (e.g., CPU, Memory and disk) shared by different framework tasks/ executors and run them in the same physical/ virtual machine. Schedulers from different frameworks negotiate with Mesos to reserve resources for running tasks. Moreover, each application (of any big data processing system like Spark, Hadoop, Storm) is called a framework and can have a custom implemented scheduler that can negotiate with Mesos to set the required resources for that application.

Mesos send resource offers to each framework by using the Dominant Resource Fairness (DRF) (Ghodsi et al. 2011) resource allocator which tries to distribute the resources among multiple frameworks equitably. However, Mesos has an advanced scheduler and operator HTTP APIs and supports Dynamic Resource Reservation for any application. Therefore, by using the scheduler/operator APIs, it is possible to build custom pluggable scheduler with specific SLA requirements. Frameworks can also be assigned with particular roles and set resource quotas to make the resource management flexible.

Google Kubernetes

Kubernetes[5] is an open source container management platform which is designed to run at production scale. It was built upon the foundations laid by Google. The architecture of Kubernetes supports loosely-couped mechanism for service discovery. There are a master and one or more computing nodes in a Kubernetes cluster. The master exposes APIs, schedules workloads and controls the cluster. Each node runs a container runtime like Docker or rkt an agent that communicates with the master. A node also has additional components responsible for logging, monitoring, service discovery and optional add-ons. A pod is a collection of containers that serve as a core unit of management. It acts as logical isolation for containers sharing same context and resources. Replica sets provide the required scale and availability of services by maintaining a pre-defined set of pods. The deployment of an application can be scaled

Figure 6. Apache mesos architecture

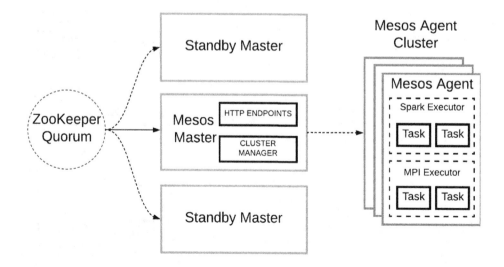

by using replica sets which ensures an application has its desired number of pods running to meet the requirements. The master node has etcd, which is an open-source distributed key-value database and acts as the single point of truth for all components in a Kubernetes cluster. When an application gets enough pods to run, the nodes pull images from the image registry and works with the local container runtime to launch the container in each pod. Kubernetes is flexible and provides a rich set of APIs for building custom container management modules which are particularly useful in deploying efficient, large-scale IoT/Fog based applications.

RESOURCE MANAGEMENT FOR BIG DATA APPLICATIONS

In this section, we will provide a brief overview of the significant components of resource management for Big Data applications. Many steps or components can be included. However, the overall process of managing resources for big data applications is a complex task, and many parts are inter-dependent thus it is hard to distinguish them. Therefore, as shown in Figure 7, we have simplified the categorization in three different layers and only discuss the key elements from each of these categories.

RESOURCE MANAGEMENT LAYERS

Setup Layer

The first layer of resource management is the Cluster Setup. In this layer, hardware or virtualized resources are selected depending on the applications. Additionally, a cluster manager is deployed to manage the resources and jobs from different big data processing frameworks. Lastly, one or more big data processing frameworks are used.

Figure 7. Key components of resource management in a big data cluster

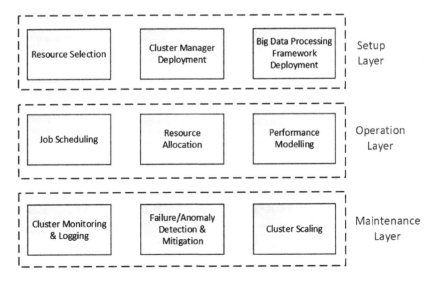

Resource Selection

Both physical or virtualized resources can be used to build a cluster. Generally, depending on the applications and analytics demands of any business organization, the hardware resources are chosen. The setup can be done on-premise (local cluster or private cloud), deployed on cloud resources (public cloud) or a hybrid deployment (some local resources with a pay-as-you-go subscription from a cloud provider) can also be made. The actual underlying hardware resources might vary with applications. However, CPU, RAM, Storage, and Network are the must no matter where the cluster is deployed. Nowadays, GPU resources are gaining popularity due to the widespread use in sophisticated machine learning (deep learning) algorithms running in platforms like TensorFlow.

Cluster Manager Deployment

The next step is to choose a cluster manager to manage both the jobs and the resources. A cluster manager also balances the workloads and resource shares in a multi-tenant environment. For containerized applications, Kubernetes or Docker Swarm can be deployed to provide container management platform. Kubernetes excels as a complete management system featuring scheduling, dynamic on-the-fly updates, auto-scaling, and health monitoring. However, Docker Swarm features a system-wide view of the whole cluster from a single Docker engine. Apache Hadoop Yarn is the cluster manager of choice if all the applications of the cluster are only MapReduce or Hadoop-based. In contrast, Apache Mesos is a better choice than Yarn as it supports efficient resource isolations for multiple different big data processing frameworks and provides strong scheduling capabilities.

Big Data Processing Framework Deployment

Many big data processing frameworks are available which can run distributed applications across one or more clusters. The applications can be real-time, stream or batch and for each type of applications, there are some frameworks which are capable of handling the requirements efficiently. It is not possible to say which is the best possible framework to deploy in general. Instead, each one has its own merits and suits a group of applications. For example, in the last decade, Hadoop was the most prominent platform to process MapReduce based static batch jobs. However, due to the increasing popularity of real-time systems and streaming applications; Apache Spark, Apache Flink, and Apache Storm have become the standard choice to tackle them. Apache Storm is particularly useful for stream-based applications. Apache Spark is vastly replacing both Hadoop and Strom, and it is a hybrid platform that supports both batch and stream processing. Apache Flink is new a hybrid platform that needs to be more stable to compete with the likes of Spark or Storm.

Operation Layer

The second layer of resource management is the operation layer. Here, performance models are built to determine the set of resources to be allocated that is enough to meet user SLA and schedule multiple jobs in a multi-tenant setup. Moreover, the overall cluster utilization is maximized, and each job's performance is enhanced without interfering with any other job's SLA.

Performance Modelling

The performance of a job might vary depending on various aspects like allocated resources, workload size, task placement, etc. Hence, before a complete deployment of a job, performance models can be established which will be used in resource allocation and job scheduling phase to choose an optimized set of resources to run the job without sacrificing any performance constraints. Generally, performance modeling can be done in two ways. First, running the job with different resource configurations and workloads to build job profiles. Second, collecting historical data of jobs running in the cluster. Both job profiles or historical data can be used to perform statistical analyses, training machine learning algorithms or build mathematical models. These models are then used to select optimal resource configurations and efficient scheduling strategies. There are many existing researches that tried to model the performance of different types of jobs running in both Spark or Hadoop based platforms. (Zhuoyao Zhang, Cherkasova, and Loo 2013) modeled the performance of MapReduce workloads in a heterogeneous cluster (where resources are different types, or the performance varies). This model is then used to predict the job completion times. (Wang and Khan 2015) proposed a simulation-based approach where they have used different Apache Spark configuration parameters and modeled different stages of a job to predict its completion time.

Resource Allocation

Resource allocation means reserving a set of resources for a job which will be used by that job to run its tasks up to a specific period. Generally, resource allocation is of two types.

- **Static:** Manual resource allocation for each job by the user if the user has enough knowledge on the application behavior on the cluster environment.
- **Dynamic:** The job is started with a few sets of resources. Based on the utilization and to meet the SLA constraints, more resources might be allocated or deallocated over time.

   Choosing the right amount of resources to meet user SLA is crucial as improper resource allocation might lead to either under-utilization or over-utilization problem. Therefore, as mentioned in the previous step, performance models are used to determine the optimal set of resources for each job. Resource allocation can be done from both big data processing framework or cluster manager side. (Islam, Karunasekera, and Buyya 2017) modeled Spark jobs based on different parameters such as input size, iteration, resource requirements to predict the job runtime. Then an optimized resource configuration parameter is suggested based on the models which is enough for that job to meet its deadline. (Sidhanta, Golab, and Mukhopadhyay 2016) also suggested a deadline-aware model to perform resource allocation which is also cost-effective. The model is called OptEx and it estimates job runtime before resource allocation by using the job profiles. (Verma, Cherkasova, and Campbell 2011) proposed a resource provisioning framework for MapReduce jobs which also uses job profiles from jobs to estimate the required resources for jobs.

Job Scheduling

It is the most critical component of resource management. Job scheduling means settings the order of the jobs in which they will run on the cluster. Additionally, the resources can also be ordered before running any jobs. Both job and resource ordering depend on the scheduling policy. The most straightforward scheduling policy that is used in all the cluster managers and big data frameworks is the FIFO (First in First Out). Here, jobs are ordered according to their arrival time; that means the job that comes first is executed first in the cluster. If there are not enough resources in the cluster to run all the jobs, then the remaining jobs are placed in a queue which is sorted based in increasing order of their arrival time. In most cases, the FIFO scheduler underperforms with complex SLA requirements in a multi-tenant cluster setup. Therefore, a vast amount of research exists in this area that proposes efficient schedulers with optimal scheduling policies. However, most of the scheduling algorithms are either application or the SLA-demand specific. Also, the parameters that are considered vary greatly depending on the application or cluster setting. The more sophisticated schedulers tackle both resource allocation and scheduling together to make it more efficient. First, these schedulers use some pre-existed performance models for the jobs at hand or build it dynamically then decide the resource configuration for a job before scheduling it. Moreover, the resource usages of the currently executing jobs are tracked, and further resources will be reallocated or deallocated to make it optimally achieve the SLA requirements. Job scheduling is a massively broad and explored topic in both big data and cloud computing. We will provide a detailed discussion and compare the existing works in section 4.

MAINTENANCE LAYER

It is the final layer of resource management for big data applications. The components of this layer are responsible for maintaining an already deployed big data cluster.

Cluster Monitoring and Logging

Cluster Monitoring is crucial as it plays a vital role in the resource management lifecycle. The cluster monitoring data can be logged and saved in persistent storage. This data can be used to validate the performance of the resource allocation and scheduling policies. Besides, if a feedback-based system is used (can be both feedback-based resource reprovisioning/ scheduling and machine learning models that are updated and improved by using the current system status), it needs to use the cluster monitoring data to improve the system performance. Popular big data processing frameworks like Hadoop, Spark, and Storm provide cluster-wide monitoring data and web-UI to visualize the health of the cluster. Besides, cluster monitoring data can also be found from cluster/container management systems like Kubernetes, Mesos and Yarn. Sometimes while building sophisticated application/user-specific resource management modules, data from the underlying platform might not be enough. In those cases, the administrator or developer might need fine-grained resource usage and health data which is possible by using tools such as Collectd[6] or Prometheus[7]. A cluster monitoring system like Prometheus not only provides cluster monitoring data, but it can also offer a time-series database to store the monitoring data. The database is particularly useful for applying advanced machine learning algorithms or performing time-series analysis on the monitoring data.

Failure/Anomaly Detection and Mitigation

When a cluster is deployed, and in operation, jobs might fail due to an anomaly in the system, hardware/ software failure, resource over-utilization, resource-scarcity, etc. By analyzing cluster-wide monitored log data, it is possible to detect the root cause of failures in the system. It is important to solve the issue to keep the cluster healthy so that the jobs can meet their SLAs. The most trivial way to solve the failure is to restart the failed jobs. In the case of resource scarcity, jobs might fail due to a shortage of resource or interference of co-located jobs. This problem can be solved by throwing more resources in the cluster so that the jobs can run properly. In case of hardware or software failures, the affected hardware that might be prone to failure can be avoided in scheduling to avoid any further failures. Chronos (Yildiz et al. 2015) is a Hadoop-based failure-aware scheduler that uses pre-emption on failed jobs. Then it recovers from failure by reallocating the failed jobs with pre-empted resources to meet the SLA objectives. Fuxi (Zhuo Zhang et al. 2014) is fault-tolerant resource management and scheduling system that can predict and prevent failures in large clusters to satisfy user performance needs.

Cluster Scaling

A big data processing cluster might need to be scaled up and down based on the current usage. In a high-load hour, the currently running VMs might not be enough to run all the jobs while satisfying all the users' SLAs. Therefore, in this situation, the cluster needs to be scaled up to satisfy the peak surge of resource demands. In contrast, in a light-load hour, a cluster might go under-utilized. In this scenario, the existing cluster jobs can be consolidated in fewer VMs so that the underutilized VMs can be freed and turned off. Dynamically scaling up or down the cluster is possible by using elastic cloud services offered by Amazon AWS or Azure. (Gandhi et al. 2016) is a model-driven autoscaler for Hadoop clusters. It uses novel gray-box performance models to predict job runtimes and resource requirements to dynamically scale the cluster so that SLA is satisfied.

A TAXONOMY ON SCHEDULING OF BIG DATA APPLICATIONS

Many types of research have been done in the task and resource scheduling in the cloud computing environment. Researchers are trying to adapt existing scheduling approaches to facilitate the needs of big data applications. However, many challenges are posed due to the different characteristics of big data applications. In this section, different scheduling policies will be discussed. We have divided job scheduling approaches for big data applications based on four aspects. Figure 8 exhibits a taxonomy of big data job scheduling in the cloud.

Based on the taxonomy, Table 1 shows a summary of comparison between the existing studies on Job scheduling for big data. In the following subsections, a detailed comparison will be provided between all these works regarding the critical aspects of scheduling. When referring to a paper, we will follow the serial number of the corresponding paper from Table 1.

Figure 8. A taxonomy of scheduling of big data applications on cloud

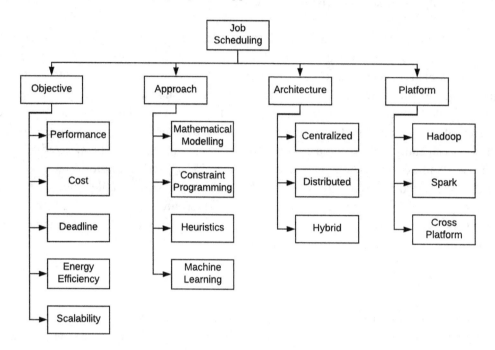

Objective

The target of a scheduling algorithm to achieve is called the objective. A scheduler can be single-objective or multi-objective, and it depends on the application scenario. Most of the scheduling algorithms focus on improving application performance. Besides, monetary cost reduction, handling soft or tight deadlines of jobs, energy-efficient placement of jobs and scalability of the overall system are also important objectives. Generally, the more objective is added to a scheduler, the more complex the decision-making progress becomes. Sometimes, the overhead of the scheduling solution could be a bigger issue rather than achieving the objects. Therefore, in real systems, different trade-offs are made on the objectives to design fast schedulers with fewer overheads.

Now, each of the following subsections will provide a detailed study on the existing literature from the perspective of the scheduling objectives.

Performance-Oriented Scheduling

Performance improvement in scheduling can be achieved from two levels. First one is from the application/job level; where the target is to minimize the execution time of a job. The second one is from the cluster level; where a cluster scheduler has a global goal to improve the performance of the whole cluster. The most optimized way of scheduling is doing both. First, the job performance can be modeled by building mathematical models, machine-learning models, using monitoring data, etc. to set the appropriate resource requirement and configuration parameters for a job which is enough to maintain its SLA. Then, while each job is submitted, the cluster level scheduler improves the performance of the job

Table 1. Comparison between the existing scheduling algorithms

SL No.	Literature	Objective	Approach	Architecture	Platform
1	(Mashayekhy et al. 2015)	Deadline, Cost, Energy-efficiency	ILP, Heuristic	Centralized	Cross-Platform
2	(Ousterhout et al. 2013)	Performance, Scalability	Sampling, Late bind	Distributed	Spark
3	(Ren et al. 2015)	Performance, Scalability	Sampling, SRPT	Hybrid	Cross-Platform
4	(Sandhu and Sood 2015)	Cost, Scalability	AKNN, Naive Bayes	Hybrid	Cross-Platform
5	(Zhao et al. 2015)	Deadline, Cost	Greedy Heuristics, ILP	Centralized	Cross-Platform
6	(Kaur and Chana 2014)	Cost, Scalability	Prediction-based	Centralized	
7	(Alrokayan, Vahid Dastjerdi, and Buyya 2015)	Deadline, Cost	Prune Tree, Greedy Heuristics	Centralized	Cross-Platform
8	(Lim, Majumdar, and Ashwood-Smith 2014)	Performance, Deadline	Constraint Programming	Centralized	Hadoop
9	(Maroulis, Zacheilas, and Kalogeraki 2017a)	Deadline, Energy-efficiency	EDF, Periodic-DVFS	Centralized	Spark
10	(Lu et al. 2016)	Performance	Genetic algorithm	Centralized	Hadoop
11	(Rasooli and Down 2012)	Performance, Scalability	Multiplexing	Hybrid	Hadoop
12	(Fonseca Reyna et al. 2015)	Performance	Reinforcement learning	Centralized	Hadoop
13	(Nayak et al. 2015)	Performance, Deadline	Greedy, Negotiation	Centralized	Hadoop
14	(Zacheilas and Kalogeraki 2016)	Performance, Deadline, Cost	Pareto-Frontier	Centralized	Hadoop
15	(Yildiz et al. 2015)	Performance	Task pre-emption	Centralized	Hadoop
16	(Zeng et al. 2017)	Performance, Cost, Deadline	Greedy Heuristics	Centralized	Hadoop
17	(Sidhanta, Golab, and Mukhopadhyay 2016)	Performance, Cost, Deadline	Mathematical model, Prediction	Centralized	Spark
18	(Cheng et al. 2017)	Performance	Reservation aware, Dependency-aware	Centralized	Cross-Platform
19	(Chen, Lin, and Kuo 2014)	Performance, Deadline	Graph Modelling	Centralized	Hadoop
20	(Kim et al. 2016)	Cost, Energy-efficiency	Reinforcement Learning	Centralized	Cross-Platform
21	(Imes, Hofmeyr, and Hoffmann 2018)	Performance, Energy-efficiency	Machine Learning Classifiers	Centralized	Hadoop
22	(F. Zhang et al. 2014)	Performance, Cost	Evolutionary algorithm	Centralized	Cross-Platform
23	(Maroulis, Zacheilas, and Kalogeraki 2017b)	Performance, Energy-efficiency	Time-series prediction, DVFS	Centralized	Spark
24	(Zong, Ge, and Gu 2017)	Performance, Energy-efficiency	Power profiles	Centralized	Cross-Platform
25	(W. Zhang et al. 2014)	Performance, Deadline	Interference-aware	Centralized	Hadoop
26	(Hwang and Kim 2012)	Deadline, Cost	Pricing List, Bin Packing	Centralized	Hadoop
27	(Jyothi et al. 2016)	Performance, Deadline, Scalability	Job Profiles, Task Packing, Resource Reprovision	Centralized	Hadoop
28	(Guo et al. 2017)	Performance, Scalability	Slot Management, Speculative Execution	Centralized	Hadoop
29	(Orhean, Pop, and Raicu 2018)	Performance	Reinforcement Learning	Centralized	Cross-Platform
30	(Polo et al. 2011)	Performance, Scalability	Job Profiles, Slot reconfiguration	Centralized	Hadoop
31	(Kc and Anyanwu 2010)	Deadline	Greedy Heuristic	Centralized	Hadoop

by various techniques such as task consolidations in the same node to reduce network transfers, placing tasks close to data, order jobs based on their priority or deadline, etc.

Cost-Efficient Scheduling

The monetary cost of running a big data processing cluster in a cloud environment is crucial. Improper resource selection and resource scheduling might lead to resource wastage which intern increases the monetary cost of the cluster. If using VMs as the worker nodes of a big data cluster, it is often useful to turn-off unused or underutilized VMs to save cost if it does not affect performance/SLA of the jobs. Saving cost is mostly comes with a sacrifice of performance guarantee as cost can be saved by using a smaller number of resources in a cluster which might impact performance. Therefore, when both cost and performance is considered, resources are saved/consolidated only after ensuring a satisfying performance for all the jobs. In extremely scalable or fast scheduling systems, improving performance is the only goal and cost saving is mostly ignored.

Deadline-Oriented Scheduling

Some jobs are associated with deadlines, and some job is time-critical or real-time and needs to be scheduled as soon as they arrive. Therefore, the deadline is an SLA parameter, and many schedulers try to minimize deadline violations. There are several techniques to achieve this — first, the pre-emption mechanism where non-priority jobs are killed when priority jobs need to be scheduled. Second, reserving some resources that can be dedicated to time-critical or deadline-constrained jobs only. Lastly, ordering the jobs beforehand based on their deadlines. However, maintain the job deadline while handling other SLA constraints for jobs is difficult due to the presence of stragglers (large periodic jobs that might hold a considerable chunk of resources), job inter-dependency (a deadline-constrained job might wait for other critical or non-priority jobs), etc. When multiple objects such as cost, deadline and performance are considered together, generally there are strict priorities between the objectives. For example, the first objective is always ensuring a satisfiable performance of a job so that it meets its given deadline. When these objectives are satisfied, only then cost-saving is considered.

Energy-Efficient Scheduling

One of the significant challenges of running big data applications in cloud deployed cluster is minimizing their energy costs. Electricity used in the data centers in the USA accounted for about 2% of the total electricity usage of the whole country in 2010. Furthermore, each year, the energy consumption by data-centers is increasing at over 15%. Lastly, the energy costs can take up to 42% of a data-centers total operational cost. It is predicted by IDC (Internet Data Corporation) that by the year 2020, big data analytics market will surpass $200 billion. Therefore, more and more data-centers are made, and these data-centers will consume a tremendous amount of energy soon. Consequently, it is crucial to make the scheduling techniques energy-efficient from both the application and the cluster side. Furthermore, from both the cluster and application side, consolidating resources to save cost leads to energy saving as it helps to reduce the number of active physical machines from the infrastructure side.

Scalable Scheduling

Scalable scheduling means that the resource management or scheduling algorithms are scalable to large clusters and can perform in the presence of high number of scheduling requests in a heterogeneous environment. Although the centralized approach of scheduling is less complicated to handle the complex steps of scheduling at one place, it is not as scalable as a distributed/hybrid approach of scheduling. It can be observed that scheduler scalability is addressed in only a few works (2, 3, 4, 6, 11, 28, 30) which mostly have distributed/hybrid architecture. However, as the existing cluster systems are growing massively on size and scale to handle massive amounts of analytics demands, future research should focus on the distributed or hybrid deployment of schedulers to make them scalable.

Approach

The solution method towards the scheduling problem varies. Generally, a complete and sophisticated scheduler has separate performance prediction and resource assignment modules. The performance models are built from mathematical models to predict the runtime of a job, cost of running a job, deadline violation, etc. in advance which helps to make accurate scheduling decisions. Constraint programming-based approaches try to minimize or maximize an objective by satisfying the constraint parameters set by the job and the restrictions of resources on the cluster. However, for both resource assignment/allocation and scheduling, the optimization problem is always modeled as an NP-Hard problem. Therefore, even if exact algorithms or constraint solving approach can find optimal scheduling decisions, it is not feasible in most of the case and only applicable in small-scale clusters. In contrast, heuristics or meta-heuristics approaches are faster, less-complicated and provided acceptable near-optimal solutions and can be scalable to large clusters. Nowadays, machine learning approaches are also becoming popular to build sophisticated and intelligent schedulers.

Architecture

Some scheduling designs are centralized, some are distributed. Recently, some hybrid approaches have also been proposed which uses both a distributed or local scheduler and a global scheduler. Generally, there are two levels in scheduling. One is at the cluster manager level which manages and schedules all the jobs submitted from multiple users. Another one is on the application level that schedules the tasks of a job to the allocated resources by the cluster-level scheduler. A centralized cluster-level scheduler design is less complicated as it controls all the jobs. However, for a massive cluster, a centralized scheduler could be a single point of failure. This limitation is solved with either having backup master nodes with the cluster manager (using tools like ZooKeeper) or by designing a distributed scheduler where the worker nodes co-ordinate with each other to manage the tasks from different jobs.

Platform

Most of the researches have tried to design efficient scheduling algorithms for Hadoop MapReduce based clusters as it was the mostly used distributed data processing platform in the last decade. However, as Apache Spark, Apache Storm, etc. are becoming more popular and vastly replacing Hadoop these days, the researchers are focusing on these platforms now to devise scheduling algorithms. Lastly, due to the popularity of the cluster managers that support multiple different big data frameworks at the same time (Apache Mesos), or container-based platforms (Docker, Kubernetes); research has been going on building cross-platform cluster-level schedulers that can work with a cluster manager to effectively handle jobs from different platforms.

To summarize, it is always a hard challenge to provide a general scheduling strategy for all types of big data applications. To design a sophisticated scheduling algorithm, the type of big data application needs to be detected. Furthermore, depending on the user SLAs, the objectives should be chosen carefully. Then after setting the priority between different objectives, a suitable scheduling strategy can be devised.

FUTURE RESEARCH DIRECTIONS

Energy-Efficient Fog/IoT Deployment

Fog/IoT is going to become the most investigated area in the next decade because of the availability of a vast number of wearable devices, smartphones, smart sensors, etc. Therefore, the distributed deployment of data processing applications will be typical. However, it is not efficient to send all the data to process in the cloud data-centers as it might impose excessive network/transmission/bandwidth overhead in the whole system and increase the energy consumption of the data-centers. Therefore, energy-efficient software systems need to be developed that can process and analyze data on the edge/fog level to reduce energy consumption and boost the performance of time-critical applications. Also, it will help to meet the SLA requirement through multi-tiered resource management over the cloud data-center, fog nodes, and mobile devices.

Intelligent Resource Management

Machine learning algorithms are becoming more accurate and suitable for solving complex problems. Specifically, it is useful in resource management across all the different components. The resource usage statistics, system status, and the configuration parameters can be used to predict the system performance. Additionally, machine learning can be used for predicting anomaly, resource demand, peak usage period which will help to build sophisticated scheduling, resource scaling, and load-balancing algorithms. Lastly, small applications focusing on resource monitoring, performance analysis, local scheduling can be packaged as containers in a system that runs through a containerized management system to push small resource management components on the fog/edge level for achieving faster and flexible services.

Shared-Sensing in IoT

As the number of IoT and mobile devices is increasing, a vast amount of resources from multiple users can be underutilized which neither energy-efficient nor cost-effective. Therefore, fog/IoT devices from various service providers and customers can be used collaboratively to provide efficient services. However, the software architecture should be made in such a way that it is both secure and beneficial for the collaborating partners. Besides, new protocols need to be designed on how to set the monetary cost and discount in a shared IoT infrastructure.

SUMMARY

In this chapter, we have discussed the basics of cloud computing, the emergence of big data, processing platforms and tools used to handle big data applications and an overall view of resource management for big data applications in the cloud. We have specifically focused on the job scheduling aspect of resource management and provided a detailed taxonomy of job scheduling for big data applications. Furthermore, we have discussed the relevant research in scheduling and showed comparisons of various approaches regarding different aspects of scheduling. Lastly, we have highlighted some new research directions that need to be investigated to cope with the advanced resource management requirements in the modern era.

REFERENCES

Alrokayan, M., Dastjerdi, A. V., & Buyya, R. (2015). SLA-Aware Provisioning and Scheduling of Cloud Resources for Big Data Analytics. *2014 IEEE International Conference on Cloud Computing in Emerging Markets, CCEM 2014*, 1–8.

Assunção, M. D., Calheiros, R. N., Bianchi, S., Netto, M. A. S., & Buyya, R. (2015). Big Data Computing and Clouds: Trends and Future Directions. *Journal of Parallel and Distributed Computing, 79–80*, 3–15. doi:10.1016/j.jpdc.2014.08.003

Buyya, R., Yeo, C. S., Venugopal, S., Broberg, J., & Brandic, I. (2009, June). Cloud Computing and Emerging IT Platforms: Vision, Hype, and Reality for Delivering Computing as the 5th Utility. *Future Generation Computer Systems, 25*(6), 17. doi:10.1016/j.future.2008.12.001

Chen, C. H., Lin, J. W., & Kuo, S. Y. (2014). Deadline-Constrained MapReduce Scheduling Based on Graph Modelling. *IEEE International Conference on Cloud Computing, CLOUD*, 416–23. 10.1109/CLOUD.2014.63

Cheng, D., Zhou, X., Lama, P., Wu, J., & Jiang, C. (2017). Cross-Platform Resource Scheduling for Spark and MapReduce on YARN. *IEEE Transactions on Computers, 66*(8), 1341–1353. doi:10.1109/TC.2017.2669964

Gandhi, A. (2016). Autoscaling for Hadoop Clusters. *Proceedings - 2016 IEEE International Conference on Cloud Engineering, IC2E 2016: Co-located with the 1st IEEE International Conference on Internet-of-Things Design and Implementation, IoTDI 2016*, 109–18. 10.1109/IC2E.2016.11

George, L. (2011). *HBase: The Definitive Guide*. Retrieved from http://books.google.com/books?hl=en&lr=&id=nUhiQxUXVpMC&pgis=1

Ghodsi, A. (2011). Dominant Resource Fairness : Fair Allocation of Multiple Resource Types Maps Reduces. *Ratio*, 24–24. Retrieved from http://www.usenix.org/events/nsdi11/tech/full_papers/Ghodsi.pdf

Guo, Y., Rao, J., Jiang, C., & Zhou, X. (2017). Moving Hadoop into the Cloud with Flexible Slot Management and Speculative Execution. *IEEE Transactions on Parallel and Distributed Systems, 28*(3), 798–812. doi:10.1109/TPDS.2016.2587641

Hindman, B. (2011). *Mesos: A Platform for Fine-Grained Resource Sharing in the Data Center*. Retrieved from http://static.usenix.org/events/nsdi11/tech/full_papers/Hindman_new.pdf

Hwang, E., & Kim, K. H. (2012). Minimizing Cost of Virtual Machines for Deadline-Constrained MapReduce Applications in the Cloud. *Proceedings - IEEE/ACM International Workshop on Grid Computing*, 130–38. 10.1109/Grid.2012.19

Imes, C., Hofmeyr, S., & Hoffmann, H. (2018). Energy-Efficient Application Resource Scheduling Using Machine Learning Classifiers. In *Proceedings of the 47th International Conference on Parallel Processing - ICPP 2018* (pp. 1–11). New York: ACM Press. doi:10.1145/3225058.3225088

Islam, M. T., Karunasekera, S., & Buyya, R. (2017). DSpark: Deadline-Based Resource Allocation for Big Data Applications in Apache Spark. In *2017 IEEE 13th International Conference on E-Science (e-Science)* (pp. 89–98). Auckland, New Zealand: IEEE. doi:10.1109/eScience.2017.21

Jyothi, S. A. (2016). Morpheus: Towards Automated SLOs for Enterprise Clusters. *12th USENIX Symposium on Operating Systems Design and Implementation (OSDI 16)*, 117–34. Retrieved from https://www.usenix.org/conference/osdi16/technical-sessions/presentation/jyothi

Katsifodimos, A., & Schelter, S. (2016). Apache Flink: Stream Analytics at Scale. *2016 IEEE International Conference on Cloud Engineering Workshop (IC2EW)*, 193–193. Retrieved from http://ieeexplore.ieee.org/document/7527842/

Kaur, P. D., & Chana, I. (2014). A Resource Elasticity Framework for QoS-Aware Execution of Cloud Applications. *Future Generation Computer Systems*, 37, 14–25. doi:10.1016/j.future.2014.02.018

Kc, K., & Anyanwu, K. (2010). Scheduling Hadoop Jobs to Meet Deadlines. *Proceedings - 2nd IEEE International Conference on Cloud Computing Technology and Science, CloudCom 2010*, 388–92. 10.1109/CloudCom.2010.97

Kim, B.-G., Zhang, Y., van der Schaar, M., & Lee, J.-W. (2016). Dynamic Pricing and Energy Consumption Scheduling With Reinforcement Learning. *IEEE Transactions on Smart Grid*, 7(5), 2187–2198. doi:10.1109/TSG.2015.2495145

Kune, R., Konugurthi, P. K., Agarwal, A., Chillarige, R. R., & Buyya, R. (2016). The Anatomy of Big Data Computing. *Software, Practice & Experience*, 46(1), 79–105. doi:10.1002pe.2374

Lakshman, A., & Malik, P. (2010). Cassandra. *Operating Systems Review*, 44(2), 35. doi:10.1145/1773912.1773922

Lim, N., Majumdar, S., & Ashwood-Smith, P. (2014). A Constraint Programming-Based Resource Management Technique for Processing Mapreduce Jobs with SLAs on Clouds. *Proceedings of the International Conference on Parallel Processing*, 411–21. 10.1109/ICPP.2014.50

Lu, Q., Li, S., Zhang, W., & Zhang, L. (2016). A Genetic Algorithm-Based Job Scheduling Model for Big Data Analytics. *EURASIP Journal on Wireless Communications and Networking*, 152(1), 152. doi:10.118613638-016-0651-z PMID:27429611

Maroulis, Zacheilas, & Kalogeraki. (2017a). A Framework for Efficient Energy Scheduling of Spark Workloads. *Proceedings - International Conference on Distributed Computing Systems*, 2614–15.

Maroulis, S., & Zacheilas, N. (2017b). ExpREsS: EneRgy Efficient Scheduling of Mixed Stream and Batch Processing Workloads. *Proceedings - 2017 IEEE International Conference on Autonomic Computing, ICAC 2017*, 27–32. 10.1109/ICAC.2017.43

Mashayekhy, L., Nejad, M. M., Grosu, D., Zhang, Q., & Shi, W. (2015). Energy-Aware Scheduling of MapReduce Jobs for Big Data Applications. *IEEE Transactions on Parallel and Distributed Systems*, *26*(10), 2720–2733. doi:10.1109/TPDS.2014.2358556

Nayak, D. (2015). Adaptive Scheduling in the Cloud - SLA for Hadoop Job Scheduling. *Proceedings of the 2015 Science and Information Conference, SAI 2015*, 832–37. 10.1109/SAI.2015.7237240

Orhean, A. I., Pop, F., & Raicu, I. (2018). New Scheduling Approach Using Reinforcement Learning for Heterogeneous Distributed Systems. *Journal of Parallel and Distributed Computing*, *117*, 292–302. doi:10.1016/j.jpdc.2017.05.001

Ousterhout, K., Wendell, P., Zaharia, M., & Stoica, I. (2013). Sparrow : Distributed, Low Latency Scheduling. *ACM Symposium on Operating Systems Principles (SOSP)*, 69–84. Retrieved from http://dl.acm.org/citation.cfm?doid=2517349.2522716

Polo, J. (2011). Resource-Aware Adaptive Scheduling for MapReduce Clusters. Lecture Notes in Computer Science, 7049, 187–207. doi:10.1007/978-3-642-25821-3_10

Rasooli, A., & Down, D. G. (2012). A Hybrid Scheduling Approach for Scalable Heterogeneous Hadoop Systems. *Proceedings - 2012 SC Companion: High Performance Computing. Networking Storage and Analysis, SCC, 2012*, 1284–1291.

Ren, X., Ananthanarayanan, G., Wierman, A., & Yu, M. (2015). Hopper : Decentralized Speculation-Aware Cluster Scheduling at Scale. Sigcomm 2015, 379–92.

Reyna, César, Martínez Jiménez, Bermúdez Cabrera, & Méndez Hernández. (2015). A Reinforcement Learning Approach for Scheduling Problems. *Investigación Operacional, 36*(3), 225–31. Retrieved from http://0-search.ebscohost.com.mercury.concordia.ca/login.aspx?direct=true&db=a9h&AN=108651151&site=ehost-live&scope=site

Sandhu, R., & Sood, S. K. (2015). Scheduling of Big Data Applications on Distributed Cloud Based on QoS Parameters. *Cluster Computing*, *18*(2), 817–828. doi:10.100710586-014-0416-6

Shvachko, Kuang, Radia, & Chansler. (2013). *The Hadoop Distributed File System*. Academic Press.

Sidhanta, S., Golab, W., & Mukhopadhyay, S. (2016). OptEx: A Deadline-Aware Cost Optimization Model for Spark. *Proceedings - 2016 16th IEEE/ACM International Symposium on Cluster, Cloud, and Grid Computing, CCGrid 2016*, 193–202. 10.1109/CCGrid.2016.10

Vavilapalli, V. K. (2013). Apache Hadoop YARN. *Proceedings of the 4th annual Symposium on Cloud Computing - SOCC '13, 13*, 1–16. Retrieved from http://dl.acm.org/citation.cfm?doid=2523616.2523633

Verma, A., Cherkasova, L., & Campbell, R. H. (2011). Resource Provisioning Framework for MapReduce Jobs with Performance Goals. Lecture Notes in Computer Science, 7049, 165–86. doi:10.1007/978-3-642-25821-3_9

Wang, K., & Mohammad, M. H. K. (2015). Performance Prediction for Apache Spark Platform. *Proceedings - 2015 IEEE 17th International Conference on High Performance Computing and Communications, 2015 IEEE 7th International Symposium on Cyberspace Safety and Security and 2015 IEEE 12th International Conference on Embedded Software and Systems, H*, 166–73. 10.1109/HPCC-CSS-ICESS.2015.246

Yildiz, O., Ibrahim, S., Phuong, T. A., & Antoniu, G. (2015). Chronos: Failure-Aware Scheduling in Shared Hadoop Clusters. *Proceedings - 2015 IEEE International Conference on Big Data, IEEE. Big Data, 2015*, 313–318.

Zacheilas & Kalogeraki. (2016). ChEsS: Cost-Effective Scheduling Across Multiple Heterogeneous Mapreduce Clusters. In *2016 IEEE International Conference on Autonomic Computing (ICAC)*. IEEE. Retrieved from http://ieeexplore.ieee.org/document/7573117/

Zaharia, M., Chowdhury, M., Das, T., & Dave, A. (2012). Resilient Distributed Datasets: A Fault-Tolerant Abstraction for in-Memory Cluster Computing. *Nsdi*, 2–2. Retrieved from https://www.usenix.org/system/files/conference/nsdi12/nsdi12-final138.pdf

Zaharia, M., Franklin, M. J., Ghodsi, A., Gonzalez, J., Shenker, S., Stoica, I., ... Venkataraman, S. (2016). Apache Spark. *Communications of the ACM, 59*(11), 56–65. doi:10.1145/2934664

Zeng, X. (2017). Cost Efficient Scheduling of MapReduce Applications on Public Clouds. *Journal of Computational Science*. Retrieved from https://www.sciencedirect.com/science/article/pii/S1877750317308542

Zhang, F., Cao, J., Tan, W., Khan, S. U., Li, K., & Zomaya, A. Y. (2014). Evolutionary Scheduling of Dynamic Multitasking Workloads for Big-Data Analytics in Elastic Cloud. *IEEE Transactions on Emerging Topics in Computing, 2*(3), 338–351. doi:10.1109/TETC.2014.2348196

Zhang, W., Rajasekaran, S., Wood, T., & Zhu, M. (2014). MIMP: Deadline and Interference Aware Scheduling of Hadoop Virtual Machines. *Proceedings - 14th IEEE/ACM International Symposium on Cluster, Cloud, and Grid Computing, CCGrid 2014*, 394–403. 10.1109/CCGrid.2014.101

Zhang, Z. (2014). Fuxi: A Fault-Tolerant Resource Management and Job Scheduling System at Internet Scale. *Proc. VLDB Endow., 7*(13), 1393–1404. 10.14778/2733004.2733012

Zhang, Z., Cherkasova, L., & Loo, B. T. (2013). Performance Modeling of MapReduce Jobs in Heterogeneous Cloud Environments. *2013 IEEE Sixth International Conference on Cloud Computing*, 839–46. Retrieved from http://ieeexplore.ieee.org/document/6740232/

Zhao, Y. (2015). SLA-Based Resource Scheduling for Big Data Analytics as a Service in Cloud Computing Environments. *2015 44th International Conference on Parallel Processing*, 510–19. Retrieved from http://ieeexplore.ieee.org/document/7349606/

Zong, Z., Ge, R., & Gu, Q. (2017). Marcher: A Heterogeneous System Supporting Energy-Aware High Performance Computing and Big Data Analytics. *Big Data Research, 8*, 27–38. Retrieved from http://linkinghub.elsevier.com/retrieve/pii/S221457961630048X

ENDNOTES

[1]   https://gsuite.google.com.au/intl/en_au/

[2]   https://www.ibm.com/cloud/

[3]   https://azure.microsoft.com/en-au/

[4]   https://aws.amazon.com/ec2/

[5]   https://kubernetes.io/

[6]   https://collectd.org/

[7]   https://prometheus.io/

Chapter 2
On the Use of System-Level Benchmarks for Comparing Public Cloud Environments

Sanjay P. Ahuja
University of North Florida, USA

ABSTRACT

The proliferation of public cloud providers and services offered necessitate that end users have benchmarking-related information that help compare the properties of the cloud computing environment being provided. System-level benchmarks are used to measure the performance of overall system or subsystem. This chapter surveys the system-level benchmarks that are used for traditional computing environments that can also be used to compare cloud computing environments. Amazon's EC2 Service is one of the leading public cloud service providers and offers many different levels of service. The research in this chapter focuses on system-level benchmarks and looks into evaluating the memory, CPU, and I/O performance of two different tiers of hardware offered through Amazon's EC2. Using three distinct types of system benchmarks, the performance of the micro spot instance and the M1 small instance are measured and compared. In order to examine the performance and scalability of the hardware, the virtual machines are set up in a cluster formation ranging from two to eight nodes.

INTRODUCTION

The cloud is an emerging platform that is taking shape as more vendors offer services and researchers delve deeper into how to use it and how to measure it. Currently, reliance is placed upon the specifications that each cloud vendor publishes to judge price and performance comparisons. With more widely accepted benchmarking, these specifications may become easier to compare in a more direct manner. Performance is the one of the key factors for any enterprise when determining the true benefits of cloud computing. Cloud providers promise many services with corresponding service quality attributes to end user.

DOI: 10.4018/978-1-5225-8407-0.ch002

End users however require a vendor neutral means to assure that a certain level of performance will be achieved before they commit to hosting their applications and services in the cloud provided by a specific cloud provider. This is where benchmarks play a vital role. Benchmarking would allow enterprises to perform transparent and insightful comparisons to see how various types of applications run on different clouds with various kinds of instance configurations.

When examining the performance of cloud computing, it is worthwhile to note the many different varieties of performance testing that can be done. The evaluation of a cloud environment can vary widely depending on the hardware, hypervisor, guest operating systems, and applications used in the configuration (Ahuja & Sridharan, 2012). Policies set in place by the cloud provider can also have an effect in relation to how much of a priority over the system resources a virtual machine has. Each vendor that offers a cloud service will inarguably use a different setup and configuration that may lead to changes in performance.

The contents of this paper detail the benchmarking of the Amazon Elastic Compute Cloud using the STREAM benchmark for memory bandwidth, IOR benchmark for disk input and output, and NPB-EB benchmark for communication speed. Section two examines some example cloud platforms. Section three identifies previous work in cloud benchmarking, section 4 provides a sampling of system level benchmarks, and section five focuses on the benchmarking performed and its results. Section six draws conclusions.

PLATFORM

Current cloud computing offerings come from a number of service providers ranging from small local companies running 3rd party cloud OS software to offer up their hardware resources to other local businesses to some of the world's largest companies running massive services running their own proprietary software to serve clients across the entire globe. The smaller providers are typically more focused on local business clients as their hardware infrastructure isn't large enough to scale for the needs of large national or international companies. For this reason we will focus on a subset of services offered by the three largest providers; Amazon Web Services (AWS) Elastic Compute Cloud (EC2) which was used in testing for this paper, as well as Microsoft Windows Azure (Azure) VM Roles, and Google Cloud Platform (GCP) App Engine (AE).

The Elastic Compute Cloud (EC2) by Amazon is an Infrastructure as a Service (IaaS) public cloud. EC2 is available, for an hourly fee, to the public. As an IaaS product, EC2 offers users a virtual machine and options of OS to be installed on it. This is to contrast against the Platform as a Service (PaaS) product, where an OS with middleware is rented to the user, or Software as a Service (SaaS), which provides an end-product or application for use. This makes EC2 flexible for use during peak hours or as a full time enhancement or replacement of the existing server infrastructure of a business.

The VM Roles from Windows Azure are very similar to the EC2 instances and are also IaaS services but are a less mature product and as such offer far fewer sizing options. AppEngine (AE) from Google in contrast is a PaaS and offers no options of operating system and even restricts the programming languages to Java (and others that compile to java byte code), Python, and currently experimentally, the Google Go language.

RELATED WORK

The paper by Folkerts, Alexandrov, Sachs, Iosup, Markl, and Tosun (2012) is one of the earliest systematic studies on the topic of cloud benchmarking. Based on general benchmark requirements, the authors describe what cloud benchmarking should or should not be. The paper points out the main challenges in building scenario-specific benchmarks for the cloud. The goal of cloud benchmarking is to help developers to predict the behavior of the targeted application and help users to know the performance offered by the target applications for comparison with other offerings. Benchmarking in the cloud computing world can help establishing a baseline of user's application ability to support business requirements. Many vendors/cloud providers do not reveal the details about the implementations of the services provided by them. So it helps organizations or end user to review the benchmarks and decide who (cloud provider) suites better to their needs.

With the increasing commercialization and use of the cloud, more research goes towards the benefits of the cloud, such as the operational and financial advantages of the cloud (Ahuja & Rolli, 2011). It has become a greater priority to accurately depict the performance of cloud services. To this end, benchmarking methodologies and benchmark comparisons across clouds has become a more common topic of concern. Another experiment was conducted between Amazon's EC2 platform and Microsoft's Windows Azure platform that analyzed the differences between the IaaS and PaaS environments with similar methodologies (Ahuja & Mani, 2013).

Salah, Al-Saba, Akhdhor, Shaaban, and Buhari (2011) examined benchmarking of EC2, Elastic Hosts, and BlueLock. The authors made use of the Simplex benchmark to measure CPU execution time, the STREAM benchmark for memory bandwidth, and FIO benchmark to determine average disk input and output. EC2 was benchmarked as having the lowest CPU performance, which the authors attribute to the limit EC2 imposes on how many cycles can be used by an instance, despite its CPU's faster clockrate. EC2 does, however, maintain the same performance when the benchmark is run across two virtual machines, indicating use of the second core made available. EC2 ranked lowest in the memory bandwidth benchmark, except its low standard deviation indicates that the bandwidth is predictable. In the FIO benchmark, EC2 was tested by a sequential read and write of one gigabyte without cache; EC2 outperformed the other two cloud platforms in both the read and the write categories.

Lenk, Menzel, Lipsky, Tai, and Offermann (2011) sought to determine if the performance indicators provided by cloud providers are accurate and comparable. They performed tests with the following benchmarks: Crafty, dcraw, eSpeak, HMMer, JTR, OFMM, OpenSSL, OSVD, OSVSP, OVSP, and Sudokut. The authors never directly indicate what each benchmark measures; however the units of measure and if the higher values or lower values are better are provided. The benchmarks were run across small, medium, and large EC2 instances, Flexiscale, and Rackspace. The direct comparisons are never made by the authors; however the paper indicates that the cloud providers' actual statistics varied from what would have been expected given the publicity materials. The authors did specifically point out that EC2's performance varied according to the architecture beneath the instances, which the user has no control over, therefore this impact is not completely known until the instance is spun up. Also, time of day did not seem to impact the performance of one virtual running without outside communications. Lenk, Menzel, Lipsky, Tai, and Offermann also pointed out that these benchmarks are synthetic, and therefore may not be completely indicative of a true business application's performance in the cloud.

The experiment to be described in this research is different from these previous two examples of other work in cloud benchmarking. While the experiment in Salah, Al-Saba, Akhdhor, Shaaban, and Buhari (2011) uses the STREAM benchmark, like our research, it uses alternatives to the IOR and NPB-EB that we put in use. The work by Lenk, Menzel, Lipsky, Tai, and Offermann (2011) uses the benchmarking as a means to an end to determine how accurate cloud provider publicized details are, while our work seeks to benchmark EC2 for its own purpose. Also, neither of these experiments looked at the EC2 micro instance which we take advantage of in our benchmarking.

TRADITIONAL SYSTEM LEVEL BENCHMARKS

This section provides a sampling of existing system level benchmarks from traditional computing environments that could be leveraged for use in cloud environments. These benchmarks typically aim to capture CPU, memory, and I/O performance.

Unixbench Benchmark

The purpose of Unixbench benchmark is to measure the overall performance of UNIX-like system at system-level (Github, byte-unixbench). It measures the performance of the system running single threaded and multi-threaded tasks. Unixbench runs series of individual tests, aggregates the scores and produces final indexed score which is the geometric mean of individual test scores. The testing factors that are included in the benchmark include Dhrystone, Whetstone, throughput, process creation, shell scripts, system call overhead etc. The results of this benchmark depend on hardware, operating system and compiler version. Higher Unixbench score indicates better performance.

Bonnie++

Bonnie++ is a disk I/O performance benchmark that conducts tests to derive performance relating data read and write speeds, maximum number of seeks per second, and maximum number of file metadata operations/second (Coker.com. Bonnie++). Read in (Read, 2010) used Bonnie++ and IOZone for benchmarking disk IO performance in the cloud.

IOZone

This benchmark is used to test the file system performance to measures variety of file operations. It is known for its broad analysis of file system of vendor's computer platform. It is portable and also runs on many operating systems. It offers tests for following operations: Read, write, re-read, re-write, read backwards, read strided, fread, fwrite, random read, pread, mmap, aio_read, aio_write (IOZone.org).

Cachebench

This benchmark suite evaluates the performance of memory hierarchy of computer systems, particularly multiple levels of cache present on or off the processor. It incorporates 8 benchmarks of which the first three benchmarks Cache Read, Cache Write and cache Read/Write/Modify provide information about the compiler. The remaining benchmarks are hand tuned Cache Read, hand tuned Write and hand tuned Cache Read/Write/Modify, memcpy() and memset(). This benchmark suite was used by Ostermann et al in (Osterman, 2008) to evaluate cloud computing services for scientific computing.

IOR Benchmark

Interleaved or Random (IOR) benchmark tests the performance of parallel file system using various interface and access patterns (Nserc.org, IOR). System performance is measured focusing on Parallel/ Sequential read/write operations. The drawback of this benchmark it needs MPI installed on the system for process synchronization. This benchmark has been used by Ghoshal et al to evaluate the IO performance of virtualized cloud environments (Ghoshal, 2011).

Blogbench

This is a file system benchmark for UNIX systems (Denis, blogbench). It stresses the file system with multiple threads of random reads, writes, and rewrites. It mimics the behavior of a blog by creating blogs with content and pictures, modifying blog posts, adding comments to these blogs, and then reading the content of the blogs. It has been used to benchmark a virtual machine of an OpenStack cloud (Openstack.org, blogbench).

Iperf

Iperf is a reliable benchmarking tool to measure maximum TCP bandwidth, allowing tuning of various parameters and UDP characteristics (iperf.fr). Iperf using TCP streams measures network throughput whereas Iperf in UDP measures packet loss, jitter, delay. Advantage of this benchmark is that the server can handle multiple connections at a time. The benchmark can be run for user specified time (default run time is 10 seconds) rather than the set of amount of data to transfer. It has been used by Cloud Spectator to test the internal network throughput capability of largest cloud IaaS providers.

Dbench

Dbench is a popular open source benchmark that used to test the disk I/O performance (Github.org, dbench). It uses file system calls to measure the disk performance. It generates only file system load. Throughput result is expressed in MB/sec. Dbench benchmark has been used by Cloud Spectator group to analyze disk I/O performance of cloud providers.

RESULTS AND COMPARASIONS

Test Bed

Amazon's EC2 offers a wide variety of hardware to be used for virtual machines (http://aws.amazon. com/ec2/). In this experiment, the three types of benchmarks were executed on micro-sized and small-sized virtual machines on Amazon's EC2 platform. The micro instance (t1.micro) utilizes a low amount of resources to provide for a short burst of computing capacity. The micro instance has 613 Megabytes of memory and up to two EC2 Compute Units usable for short periodic bursts. The M1small instance (m1.small) is similar to the micro instance in terms of resources. The small instance has 1.7 Gigabytes of memory but is limited to only one EC2 Compute Unit. An EC2 Compute Unit provides an equivalent CPU performance of a 1.0-1.2 GHz 2007 Opteron or 2007 Xeon processor (Perry, 2009).

To create the Amazon EC2 nodes and to manage the virtual machines, a program called StarCluster was utilized. StarCluster is a cluster-computing toolkit that allows the user to remotely spin up multiple virtual machines on Amazon's EC2 and have them automatically configured in a cluster. StarCluster is written in Python 2.7 and was released open-source under the LGPL license. StarCluster has several preset AMIs that define the operating system environment on the virtual machines (http://star.mit.edu/cluster). In this experiment, the ami-999d49f0 image was used to create a Linux environment using Ubuntu 11.10 64-bit.

Benchmarks and Metrics

Three types of benchmarks were used in this experiment. The benchmarks STREAM, IOR, and NPB-EP tested aspects in memory, I/O, and CPU performance respectively.

The STREAM Benchmark examines the performance of memory bandwidth within high performance computers. It performs four different operations that occur in memory (McCalpin, 1995). These operations are Copy, Scale, Add, and Triad. Each of the operations reported their results in terms of MB/s. The STREAM benchmark was written in C and FORTRAN and was created by John McCalpin (http://www.cs.virginia.edu/stream/ref.html).

The IOR benchmark was created to examine the I/O capabilities of a high performance computer. It performs two operations, Read and Write, and reports the results of them in MiB/s. The MiB/s metric is measuring the throughput of data when the virtual machine is either reading from or writing to a file. An important detail to observe when measuring I/O is to examine how performance is affected when multiple nodes are trying to read or write to the same file at the same time. The IOR benchmark is available for download on the SourceForge website (http://sourceforge.net/projects/ior-sio/).

The NAS Parallel Benchmarks (NPB) are a set of several different benchmarks that are targeted at evaluating the performance of high performance computers. The Embarrassingly Parallel (NPB-EP) benchmark used in this project measured the performance of the CPU by generating a large quantity of random numbers. The collected results were reported in the operation time in seconds and the total number of millions of operations per second (Mop/s). This benchmark program can be downloaded from NASA's open-source software website, or a preconfigured version is available on Github's website at (https://github/com/moutai/hpc-medley).

Research Methodology

To be able to use StarCluster, Python 2.7 must be installed on the host computer. StarCluster is necessary to create the nodes on Amazon's EC2 in a preconfigured cluster. It is critical that the configuration file for StarCluster is edited to have the correct information. The configuration file holds information on connecting to the AWS account, the proper encryption key to use, the type and number of nodes to create, and any of services needed to be used by the nodes on the cluster. Once the file has been properly configured, open a command prompt, navigate to the folder where StarCluster was installed, and use the following command to create the cluster:

starcluster start [name]

After this command is invoked, StarCluster will create the cluster and properly configure all of the nodes. One node will be assigned as the master and communicates with all of the other nodes within the cluster. Using either the StarCluster command or another program, like WinSCP, connect to the master node of the cluster and transfer all of the benchmark files over to /home/ec2-user folder. This folder is shared amongst all of the nodes, which is important when compiling the benchmarks.

To compile and run the STREAM benchmark, use the following commands from the STREAM-MPI folder:

Compile:

mpicc -DPARALLEL_MPI -03 -o stream_mpi stream_mpi.c

Run:

mpiexec -host master, node001, node002, node003./stream_mpi > output/c1.m_n4.1.txt

To compile and run the IOR benchmark, use the following commands from the IOR/src/C folder:
Compile:

make

Run:

mpiexec -host master,node001, node002, node003./IOR -b 4m -t 4m > output/c1.m_n4.1.txt

To compile and run the NPB-EP benchmark, use the following commands from the NPB-MPI folder:
Compile:

make EP NPROCS = 4 CLASS = A

Run:

mpiexec -host master, node001, node002, node003 bin/ep.A.4 > output/ep.A.4_3.txt

Each benchmark should be run ten times to acquire uniform results in the event of a result appearing to be skewed. Once all of the benchmarks have been processed, move all of the output files off of the master node. The cluster can be terminated from the same command prompt using the following command:

starcluster terminate [name]

This methodology should be repeated multiple times using 1, 2, 4, 6, 8 nodes and t1.micro & m1.small instance types. These parameters are specified in the StarCluster configuration file previously mentioned.

Results

After taking the data from the output files, the mean value for each metric was generated and used to create the eight figures on the next page. The figures display the results of 1, 2, 4, 6, 8 node clusters benchmarked on the micro instance type and small instance type. The figures can be used to find whether or not there are any patterns present as the number of nodes are scaled up in the cluster. Overall, the figures show that each benchmark has its own unique behavior.

The STREAM benchmark tested the bandwidth capability of the memory. Figure 1 [Copy], Figure 2 [Scale], Figure 3 [Add], and Figure 4 [Triad] all present the data results from this benchmark. Figure 1 shows a drop in performance on the small instance type whenever more nodes are added; however, the micro instance type cluster fluctuates around the same value. This fluctuating behavior can be observed on the other graphs as well for both the micro and small instance types. This behavior is probably attributed to the processing speed and not the actual memory. Both instance types must handle some form of overhead when more nodes are added, but the micro instance type is able to achieve bursts in performance to overcome the performance of the small instance type. Also, for this benchmark, the total capacity of the memory most likely does not matter as much as the speed of the memory. Nodes utilizing a faster memory module and processor will probably show increased performance over simply adding more nodes to the cluster.

The IOR benchmark was supposed to measure the average read and write times when testing the I/O functionality. Figure 5[Write] and Figure 6[Read] show the averages of all of the tests ran using this benchmark. However, due to the nature of the graphs, it is unlikely that they properly reflect the real performance of I/O on these clusters. When using only a single node, the average read and write times seemed standard; but on all of the multi-node clusters, the results plummeted and stagnated at very low levels. It is not likely that these results were mere coincidence. These results were consistent for both micro and small instance types even running the benchmark on newly configured clusters during different times of the day and on multiple days. It is speculated that either the benchmark was not properly set up for this experiment and therefore is not running properly, or the overhead for utilizing more than one node in the cluster is so high for this benchmark that it negatively affects overall performance drastically. It would be worthwhile to attempt the testing of the I/O metric again using a different benchmark to see if these results are truly false.

Lastly, the NPB-EP benchmark shows promising results when testing the performance of the CPU. Figure 7 and Figure 8 respectively show the operation time of the benchmark in seconds and the total number of million operations per second. Here it is very clear that the increased nodes positively affect the performance of the benchmark. As more nodes are added, the time it takes to complete the benchmark decreases for both the micro and small instance types as shown in Figure 7. Likewise, Figure 8 shows that the total number of operations completed increases gradually as well. It is important to note that the micro instance is utilizing its second EC2 Compute Unit to perform better than the small instance for this benchmark. The micro instance can gain a burst in performance when needed, whereas the small instance type is limited to its single EC2 Compute Unit.

Services

The services from AWS used for this paper include the EC2 compute service that gives customers the use of Virtual Machines on demand with nearly any operating system. EC2 instances can be created in a variety of sizes from the Micro which includes a single virtual core up to 2 ECU and only 613MiB of ram to the Eight Extra Large which offers 88 ECU and 244GB of ram. Also offered are cluster compute instances that give access to GPU compute as well as dedicated SSD storage for speed or a complete physical hard drive array of 24, 2TB HDD for massive storage capacity.

Windows Azure VM Roles offer an equivalent to the AWS Micro called an Extra small that includes shared compute capacity and 768MB of ram. However, they top out an Extra Large role that only has 8 cores and 14GB of ram (http://www.windowsazure.com/en-us/).

Google App Engine on the other hand is a platform service designed to scale horizontally automatically as needed and doesn't offer Virtual Machines to manage (https://developers.google.com/appengine/).

Economic Model

The EC2 service is part of the overall IaaS offering that AWS is built upon. The economic model around this service is pay for usage where that usage is computed based upon a combination of the instance size and the geographic location it is created/running in per hour or part thereof. The per hour usage cost can be reduced by computing your minimum usage requirements and reserving instances to meet that need. For batch processing that can be run at different times Amazon also offers spot instances where unused capacity is bid upon and becomes available for the bidders use when they are the highest bidder for the current time period and the capacity is available for their use. Other services offered by AWS vary from IaaS to PaaS type services and pricing models vary as well from the per usage hour type model the EC2 service has to pay per request or transaction (http://aws.amazon.com/ec2/pricing/).

This is a similar economic model to Azures Web, Worker, and VM Roles in which they can be used in an IaaS capacity and are paid for in a per hour of usage where the user determines the size of instance needed. Some of the other services offered in Azure similar to AWS have pay per request or transaction models as well.

In contrast to the usage per hour models of EC2 and VM Roles Google App Engine charges based on exact resources used. This means if your application is sitting idle there are no charges and when your application is processing the platform monitors exact compute cycles, network bandwidth, and other resources consumed and bills by the monitored amount used.

CONCLUSION

Our system level performance testing of the micro and small instances within the Elastic Compute Cloud shows that EC2 is a viable option for the hosting of distributed applications that may make use of multi node clusters. It can also be a viable solution for companies, or individuals, which wish to have dedicated virtual machines, with or without clustering, but do not want to invest in their own hardware.

Figure 1. Data Transfer Rate of the Copy Operation in the Stream Benchmark across multiple cluster configurations

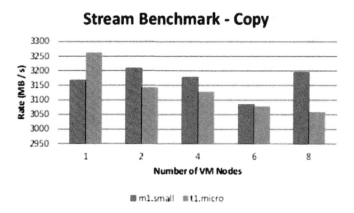

Figure 2. Data Transfer Rate of the Scale Operation in the Stream Benchmark across multiple cluster configurations

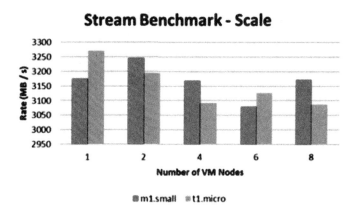

Figure 3. Data Transfer Rate of the Add Operation in the Stream Benchmark across multiple cluster configurations

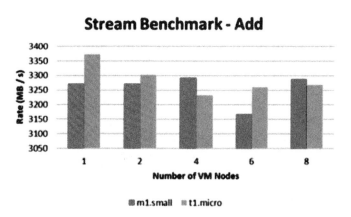

Figure 4. Data Transfer Rate of the Triad Operation in the Stream Benchmark across multiple cluster configurations

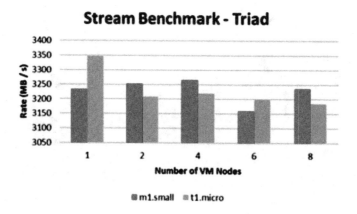

Figure 5. Average Speed of the Write Operation in the IOR Benchmark across multiple cluster configurations

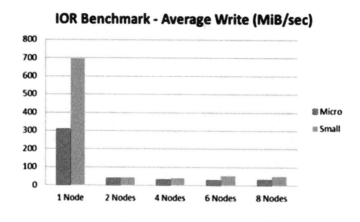

Figure 6. Average Speed of the Read Operation in the IOR Benchmark across multiple cluster configurations

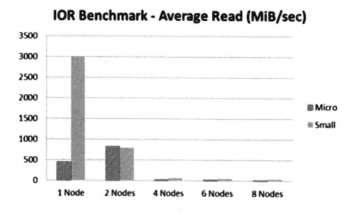

Figure 7. Operation Time (in seconds) of the NPB-EP Benchmark across multiple cluster configurations

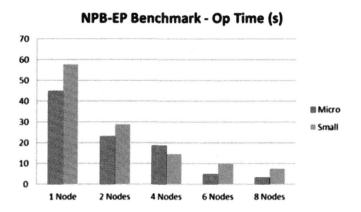

Figure 8. Million Operations per Second of the NPB-EP Benchmark across multiple cluster configurations

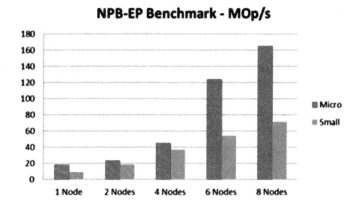

The variability in performance from run to run on the same instance type running in the same data center from a single Cloud provider leads us to conclude that there are many factors that can affect the performance of your application in different ways at different times but can be, depending on the nature of your application, mitigated by scaling your cluster.

This set of benchmarks, testing memory, CPU, and disk input and output, was run on only a single service from one provider and only a very small subset of that service's options. We leave it up to future researchers to both verify our results and to expand our testing and hypothesis to more services and providers to gain a better understanding of whether or not the variability we experienced was due to temporary conditions, the provider we selected, or to the cloud service paradigm as a whole.

ACKNOWLEDGMENT

This research has been supported in part by the FIS Distinguished Professor in Computing Sciences Award to Dr. Sanjay P. Ahuja.

REFERENCES

Ahuja, S., & Mani, S. (2013). Empirical performance analysis of HPC benchmarks across variations of cloud computing. *International Journal of Cloud Applications and Computing, 3*(1), 13–26. doi:10.4018/ijcac.2013010102

Ahuja, S., & Rolli, A. (2011). Survey of the state-of-the-art of cloud computing. *International Journal of Cloud Applications and Computing, 1*(4), 34–43. doi:10.4018/ijcac.2011100103

Ahuja, S., & Sridharan, S. (2012). Performance evaluation of hypervisors for cloud computing. *International Journal of Cloud Applications and Computing, 2*(3), 26–67. doi:10.4018/ijcac.2012070102

Amazon.com. Inc. (n.d.a). *Elastic Compute Cloud.* Retrieved from http://aws.amazon.com/ec2/

Amazon.com. Inc. (n.d.b). *EC2 Pricing.* Retrieved from http://aws.amazon.com/ec2/pricing/

Amazon.com. Inc. (n.d.c). *EC2 Instance Types.* Retrieved from http://aws.amazon.com/ec2/instance-types/

Coker.com. (n.d.). *Bonnie++.* Retrieved from http://www.coker.com.au/bonnie++/

Denis, F. (n.d.). *blogbench - manned.org.* Retrieved from http://manned.org/blogbench/fbdee406

Folkerts, E., Alexandrov, A., Sachs, K., Iosup, A., Markl, V., & Tosun, C. (2012). Benchmarking in the cloud: What it should, can, and cannot be. *4th TPC Technology Conference (TPCTC),* 173-188.

Ghoshal, D., Canon, R., & Ramakrishnan, L. (2011). IO Performance of Virtualized Cloud Environments. *Proceedings of the DataCloud-SC '11 Proceedings of the Second International Workshop on Data Intensive Computing in the Cloud,* 71-80. 10.1145/2087522.2087535

Github.com. (n.d.). *byte-unixbench - A Unix benchmark suite.* Retrieved from https://github.com/kdlucas/byte-unixbench

Github.org. (n.d.). *Dbench.* Retrieved from https://github.com/sahlberg/dbench

Google Inc. (n.d.). *App Engine.* Retrieved from https://developers.google.com/appengine/

Icl.cs.utk.edu. (n.d.). *Cachebench Home Page.* Retrieved from http://icl.cs.utk.edu/llcbench/cachebench.html

IOR Benchmark on SourceForge. (n.d.). Retrieved from http://sourceforge.net/projects/ior-sio/

IOzone.org. Retrieved from http://www.iozone.org/

Iperf. (n.d.). Retrieved from https://iperf.fr/

Lenk, A., Menzel, M., Lipsky, J., Tai, S., & Offermann, P. (2011). What are you paying for? Performance benchmarking for infrastructure-as-a-service offerings. *Cloud Computing (CLOUD), 2011 IEEE International Conference on,* 484-491.

Massachusetts Institute of Technology. (n.d.). *StarCluster.* Retrieved from http://star.mit.edu/cluster/

McCalpin, J. D. (1995). *Memory bandwidth and machine balance in current high performance computers. In IEEE Computer Society Technical Committee on Computer Architecture (TCCA)* (pp. 19–25). IEEE.

Microsoft. (n.d.). *Windows Azure.* Retrieved from http://www.windowsazure.com/en-us/

Mucci, P. J., & London, K. (1998). *The CacheBench report.* Retrieved from http://www.cs.surrey.ac.uk/BIMA/People/L.Gillam/downloads/publications/Fair%20Benchmarking%20for%20Cloud%20Computing%20Systems.pdf

Nersc.gov. (2013). *IOR.* Retrieved from https://www.nersc.gov/users/computational-systems/cori/nersc-8-procurement/trinity-nersc-8-rfp/nersc-8-trinity-benchmarks/ior/

OpenStack Cloud Software. (n.d.). *blogbench.* Retrieved from https://review.openstack.org/#/c/97030/

Ostermann, S. (2008). *An Early Performance Analysis of Cloud Computing Services for Scientific Computing.* Delft University of Technology Parallel and Distributed Systems Report Series, report number PDS-2008-006. Retrieved from http://www.st.ewi.tudelft.nl/~iosup/PDS-2008-006.pdf

PassMark Software Inc. (n.d.). Retrieved from http://www.passmark.com/

Perry, G. (2009). *What are Amazon EC2 compute units? Thinking out cloud.* Retrieved from http://gevaperry.typepad.com/main/2009/03/figuring-out-the-roi-of-infrastructureasaservice.html

Read, J. (2010). Disk IO Benchmarking in the Cloud. *Cloud Harmony.* Retrieved from http://blog.cloudharmony.com/2010/06/disk-io-benchmarking-in-cloud.html

Salah, K., Al-Saba, M., Akhdhor, M., Shaaban, O., & Buhari, M. I. (2011). Performance evaluation of popular cloud IaaS providers. *Internet Technology and Secured Transactions (ICITST), 2011 International Conference for,* 345-349.

Taifi, M. (2012). *NPB Benchmark.* Retrieved from https://github.com/moutai/hpc-medley/

University of Virginia. (n.d.). *Stream Benchmark.* Retrieved from http://www.cs.virginia.edu/stream/ref.html

KEY TERMS AND DEFINITIONS

Benchmarking: The process of measuring the performance of an application, platform, or communication medium.

Cloud Computing: The practice of hosting services on a remote server(s) which are accessible through the Internet. Connected users are able to access, store, manage, and process data utilizing the resources of the remote server instead of their local computer.

Cluster: A group of computers networked together so that they are able to share resources and function as a single, distributed entity.

Computing Services: Availability of resources to perform computational work via a third party. Typically in the form of data processing or application hosting through Cloud providers.

Infrastructure as a Service: The hosting of various hardware and hardware configurations by a third party in a remote location accessible over the Internet. Oftentimes highly scalable in terms of resources which can be adjusted on-demand for dynamic utilization.

Instance Type: Refers to the specifications of a virtual machine. The computational resources allocated to a virtual machine will determine its instance type. Large instance types will have more dedicated resources for the virtual machine to utilize.

Virtualization: Simulating the environment of a computer hardware platform, operating system, or application. To the end-user, the virtualized environment should be indistinguishable from a similar real environment.

Chapter 3

Adversarial Attacks and Defense on Deep Learning Models for Big Data and IoT

Nag Nami
San Jose State University, USA

Melody Moh
 https://orcid.org/0000-0002-8313-6645
San Jose State University, USA

ABSTRACT

Intelligent systems are capable of doing tasks on their own with minimal or no human intervention. With the advent of big data and IoT, these intelligence systems have made their ways into most industries and homes. With its recent advancements, deep learning has created a niche in the technology space and is being actively used in big data and IoT systems globally. With the wider adoption, deep learning models unfortunately have become susceptible to attacks. Research has shown that many state-of-the-art accurate models can be vulnerable to attacks by well-crafted adversarial examples. This chapter aims to provide concise, in-depth understanding of attacks and defense of deep learning models. The chapter first presents the key architectures and application domains of deep learning and their vulnerabilities. Next, it illustrates the prominent adversarial examples, including the algorithms and techniques used to generate these attacks. Finally, it describes challenges and mechanisms to counter these attacks, and suggests future research directions.

INTRODUCTION

Smarter and efficient methods to collect, process and store massive amount of data has facilitated the research to automate tasks which was not possible earlier. One of the biggest beneficiaries of the Big Data revolution is the concept of deep learning, which encompasses the more complicated architectures of artificial neural networks (ANN). Deep learning builds its foundation upon the large volumes of

DOI: 10.4018/978-1-5225-8407-0.ch003

available data to learn new representations which could not be determined by traditional algorithms. The vast amount of available data has facilitated the advancements in the field of computer vision and natural language processing, which in turn has created new applications for IoT.

Global research in academia and industry has revolutionized the adoption of IoT devices in every aspect of life. From smart home devices like Amazon echo, Google Home and Facebook portal to industrial applications like deliveries by drone, warehouse automation, medical imaging and self-driving vehicles. The inception of these devices in both personal and industrial setting has been accelerated by the advancements in the field of deep learning. Transforming perception into smart responses/action in real time is possible only due to faster and more accurate models. For instance, smartphones use face detection and recognition to authenticate the correct user. Tesla uses deep learning to design self-driving features such as object detection, semantic segmentation, lane detection, pedestrian detection, traffic sign recognition, etc., to help it make smart decisions in real-time situations. Artificial assistants like Siri, Bixby, Alexa, and Google assistant extensively use deep learning for effective natural language processing and speech recognition. Smart surveillance security cameras are equipped with face and activity recognition which identify and record any abnormal activity or entry. Hence in a modern-day setting, Big Data, Deep Learning and IoT devices make a close-knit cycle in the research and development arena.

But, with the wide-scale adoption of IoT devices, the systems are exposed to a multitude of vulnerabilities. One such vulnerability is adversarial examples, which are carefully crafted inputs, aimed at fooling the model and bringing down its accuracy and real-world performance. These attacks are not easy to detect as they are usually imperceptible to humans, yet they can easily degrade the model's accuracy. The adversaries are asymmetric in nature and are created in specific ways to compromise the integrity of deep learning models. These have posed major risks in implementing deep learning in safety-critical applications, such as home security, medical imaging, and autonomous vehicles.

The purpose of this chapter is to introduce the concept of adversarial examples and their prominent attack methodologies which are widely successful. Defense strategies and countermeasures are also discussed which showcase how the research for making robust models that can withstand an adversarial attack have evolved over the years. New methods of attack and their countermeasures are being actively explored to make deep learning models secure and resilient. Yet, because of the black-box nature of the deep learning models, securing them directly against these attacks is not an easy problem to solve. This chapter aims at presenting some of the important attacks and defenses.

CHAPTER OBJECTIVE

This chapter aims to provide a concise, in-depth understanding of adversarial attacks on deep learning models and defense against such attacks. This is achieved by presenting (1) the key architectures and application domains of deep learning and their vulnerabilities, (2) prominent adversarial examples, including the algorithms and techniques used to generate these attacks, and (3) challenges and mechanisms to counter these attacks, and future research directions.

CHAPTER ORGANIZATION

The chapter first provides an overview of deep learning models, its prominent architectures and its applications in different domains of big data and IoT. The chapter next discusses how these different domains of deep learning applications can be exposed to an adversarial example attack. Then, it delves into the concept and details of the adversarial examples, different techniques and algorithms to generate them. And how these crafted attacks expose the vulnerabilities of popular applications of deep learning models. This is followed by challenges of securing the models against these attacks, and a description of the existing security measures in place to prevent such attacks. Finally, the chapter ends with some concluding remarks and suggestions for future research direction.

OVERVIEW OF DEEP LEARNING AND ITS APPLICATIONS

In this section, the authors briefly introduce the concepts of deep neural networks and its prominent architectures such as feed-forward neural networks, convolutional neural networks (CNN), Recurrent Neural Networks (RNN), Generative Adversarial Networks (GAN) and Reinforcement Learning (RL). Different components that constitute a model and few state-of-the-art models are also discussed.

Major Concepts in Deep Learning

Artificial intelligence systems use machine learning models to perform specific tasks like a human. Machine learning models are mathematical or statistical algorithms that are used to train machines on data extracted from various sources. Deep learning is a form of machine learning concept which breaks complex problems into simpler modules. It creates a hierarchical graph of cascading layers which collectively represents the overall problem. This graphical structure is termed as an artificial neural network, as it functionally resembles an organism's neural system.

Given sufficient training data, deep learning models can identify relationships and patterns in the raw data with minimal inputs from a programmer/researcher. When contrasted with traditional machine learning algorithms, the uniqueness of deep learning models is further highlighted. For example, most of the traditional machine learning algorithms cannot handle large amounts of data both analytically and computationally (Storcheus, Rostamizadeh, & Kumar, 2015). Their objective is to learn the underlying function which represents the overall problem. It becomes increasingly difficult to learn meaningful representations from the data due to the curse of dimensionality (Bengio & LeCun, 2007). Moreover, domain expertise plays a huge role in sampling the data which further adds to the challenge of learning new patterns from a research perspective. Deep learning is agnostic to these problems of high dimensionality and domain expertise, as it focuses on building a hierarchy of simple graphs which collectively represent the whole complex problem (Yuan, He, Zhu, & Li, 2017). For example, word embedding's are used to transform a large language corpus into smaller groups of adjacent words which in turn are used for text generation, convolutional neural networks are used to generate edge, fabric and attention filters to describe an image into simpler components. Hence deep learning is conceptually and architecturally built to train upon a huge amount of data. Widely used architectures are discussed next.

Feed-Forward Neural Network

Neural network is a versatile technique using which a function can be decomposed into a sequence of linear and non-linear transformations. This sequence of linear or non-linear transformations are built into the network at each layer and it constitutes the overall network design. Non-linearity can be introduced at any layer by using an activation function. Sigmoid, tanh, and RELU are few of the more popular activation functions in use today.

Let's consider a function where x denotes a set of n input parameters $\{x_1, x_2, x_3, ..., x_n\}$. This function can be represented using a sequence of transformations, where the number of transformations denote the number of layers in the network:

where {} are the weight matrices and {} are the activation functions. Layers in a neural network consists of one input layer, one output layer and any number of hidden layers.

Recurrent Neural Network (RNN)

Unlike feed-forward neural network where data is transferred either in forward or backward direction (backpropagation), in RNN the neurons in the hidden layers have a recurrent connection to themselves, which helps in transferring information within the network to the next iterations. The neurons act like memory cells which are capable of retaining and forwarding some information to the subsequent time steps (Funahashi & Nakamura, 1993). Hence, internal computation of hidden neuron acts on the current input value and previous hidden state to update the current state of the neuron. They are used to process sequence of data which can even be of variable length. Unfortunately, RNNs suffer from the problem of vanishing gradient which means this architecture cannot handle a long sequence of data (Hochreiter, 1998). But Long Short-Term Memory (LSTM) has a more robust memory unit which can retain information for longer time steps and also choose to forget irrelevant information (Hochreiter & Schmidhuber, 1997). Similarly Gated Recurrent Unit (GRU) comprise of gated logic to control the flow of information from past and current time steps (Chung, Gulcehre, Cho, & Bengio, 2014). These flavors of RNN are more robust and are used extensively in language modeling, DNA sequencing, signal processing, and malware detection.

Convolutional Neural Network (CNN)

Convolutional neural networks use the mathematical concept of convolutions instead of the general concept of matrix multiplication which is used in the feed-forward neural network. This architecture is well suited for grid-like input, which is the main reason why it works so well with images. The multi-dimensional input is multiplied with a kernel matrix in a sliding window fashion, which produces a new feature map (Krizhevsky, Sutskever, & Hinton, 2012). Multiple feature maps in each layer represent various simpler representations of the input n-dimensional matrix. CNNs are one of the most successful architectures of deep learning that have shown significant success in the field of computer vision.

Generative Adversarial Network (GAN)

GAN aims at training two models instead of one in an adversarial setting. There is one generator model (G) which aims at creating a better synthetic sample of the original data. And there is a discriminator model (D) which trains to better identify real input samples from synthetic ones generated by the generator. This architecture is set up in form of a two-player minimax game, where both the models are pitched against each other (Goodfellow, Ian et al., 2014). At the end of sufficient training iterations, the generator model (G) could be used to create realistic synthetic samples equivalent to the training data, and the discriminator model (D) could identify real from synthetic data with high accuracy. GANs are one of the emerging concepts in the field of deep learning and are used in style transfer, image transposition, transforming low-resolution images to high resolution, text to image and text generation.

Reinforcement Learning (RL)

RL is a novel concept which is based on the idea of an agent learning about its environment on its own. The programmer needs to set up the environment and specify the rules of the environment. It does not tell/teach the agent about how to operate in the environment. The agent needs to explore all the possible options and take the necessary actions on its own. It learns which actions are good vs which are bad based on the numerical reward score at the end of a training cycle (Sutton, Barto, & Bach, 1998). Hence, instead of the commonly used loss function to train a model, RL uses a reward function that rewards the agent whenever its action leads to positive results. A good agent tries out multiple actions to find the best possible overall reward. RL is being widely used in robotics and autonomous systems across industries.

Prominent Architectures in Deep Learning

There are several deep learning architectures which are used in the field of computer vision, natural language processing, cyber-security, robotics and more. In computer vision, 2010 Imagenet Challenge paved the way for advancements in the field of image recognition and object detection. For image recognition, AlexNet (Krizhevsky et al., 2012), VGG (Simonyan & Zisserman, 2014), GoogLeNet (Szegedy, Vanhoucke, Ioffe, Shlens, & Wojna, 2016; Szegedy, Ioffe, Vanhoucke, & Alemi, 2017), and Inception-v4 (Szegedy et al., 2017)models are few of the famous models. Faster R-CNN (Ren, He, Girshick, & Sun, 2015), a single shot detector (Liu, W. et al., 2016), YOLOv2 (Redmon & Farhadi, 2017) and Mask R-CNN (He, Gkioxari, Dollár, & Girshick, 2017) are state of the art object detection models.

Applications in Big Data and IoT

The abundance of data is a boon for creating deep learning models since the models require large volumes of data to explore and understand complex data patterns. Since Volume is one of the characteristic Vs of big data, deep learning has a strong association with it (Najafabadi et al., 2015). In Big Data Analytics, information retrieval and efficient storage are of paramount importance (Council, 2013). But with the exponential growth of semi-structured data, the task of information retrieval and storing structured information becomes challenging.

In the case of images or videos, data is collected from multiple sources and is often of various formats. Extracting information from such sources cannot be done using traditional methods. Instead, deep learning can aid in gathering information from the content of the image (i.e., image recognition), objects present in the image (object detection), activity happening in the image (action detection), etc. Such operations will help in efficient storage, indexing and facilitate fast data processing and information retrieval. Another important application of deep learning could be in large-scale storage of natural language texts. Deep learning concepts like word embedding can help in the transformation of natural text in the form of a vector comprising of numbers. This, in turn, will help in logical indexing of multiple texts based on their similarity which will help in efficient data storage and retrieval. In practice, it is difficult to imagine a deep learning solution without big data analytics.

A similar trend is worth noticing when it comes to the wide-scale adoption of deep learning models in IoT devices. Increased network speed, better availability, and advancements in processor chips has ushered a new race to automate a variety of tasks across industries and home. Especially smart home devices, video surveillance, medical equipment, unmanned aerial vehicles (drones), recreational robots and autonomous driving, are a few of the widely-used applications where deep learning is deployed on IoT devices (Gupta, Agrawal, & Yamaguchi, 2016). Smarter and slim deep learning frameworks like Tensorflow Lite (Abadi et al., 2016) and Intel Openvino have facilitated the deployment of these models onto the resource-constrained IoT devices. From home assistants conversing with humans to smart security systems, deployment of deep learning models in IoT devices will only increase with time. As deep learning touches more lives through IoT devices, it is of utmost importance that the models are secure against attacks.

ADVERSARIAL ATTACKS ON DEEP LEARNING MODELS

(Szegedy et al., 2013) discovered an interesting property of deep neural networks which generated some skepticism around the security of the state-of-the-art models. It was demonstrated that deep neural networks can be forced to produce incorrect results by using a perturbed version of the input, which is not perceptible to the human eye but adversely affects the accuracy of any deep learning model.

Overview of Adversarial Attack

Though adversarial attacks have been prevalent since a couple of decades, their applications were limited to conventional machine learning methods. Variable length of extra padding bits at the end of a malware to mask its signature (Barreno, Nelson, Joseph, & Tygar, 2010), defeating spam filters by appending additional text at end of spam messages are few of the many adversarial attacks which were used against machine learning methods (Biggio, Fumera, & Roli, 2010a; Lowd & Meek, 2005).

The idea of adversarial examples attack which works like a game between an adversary and a machine learning model was first proposed by (Dalvi, Domingos, Sanghai, & Verma, 2004). The approach for attack and defense of the adversarial samples was to play an iterative game which prepared the adversarial examples in an incremental manner. (Biggio, Fumera, & Roli) (2010), used a gradient-based approach for the first time to construct adversarial samples. They experimented on multiple models ranging from linear regression, SVM to neural networks.

The general concept of adversarial examples, in the context of deep learning, can be represented in form of an optimization problem where the aim is to minimize the objective function which constructs the adversarial examples as close as possible to a genuine input. This adversarial example is almost imperceptible to the human eye but can fool the deep learning model. This concept can be summarized in form of the following equation:

$$Given: f\left(x\right) \to y$$

$$where\ x \in \left[0,1\right] is\ the\ input,$$

$$y \in \left\{y_1, y_2, y_3, \ldots, y_k\right\} are\ the\ k\ outcome\ labels$$

$$Let\ f\left(x_j\right) = y_j$$

$$r = \left\|x_j - x_j'\right\| such\ that\ 0 < r < \epsilon\ and\ x_j' \in \left[0,1\right]$$

$$Objective\ is\ to\ minimize \left|r\right|$$

$$\therefore f\left(x_j'\right) = y_j'\ and\ y_j \neq y_j'$$

Assuming an example of image classification where the images are made up of normalized x pixels and belong to k different categories. $f\left(x\right) \to y$ is the function which represents the deep neural network which correctly classifies a sample input image x_j as y_j category. The objective is to create a new input x_j' which is like x_j. Distance measure can be used to quantify the closeness of the two images which is denoted by r. The new image x_j' is constructed by solving the optimization problem of finding out the minimum value of r which is lower bounded by 0 and upper bounded by a constant $\in$. This $\in$ controls the overall structural and geometric composition of the synthetic image. A successfully constructed x_j' should be able to produce an output of $f\left(x_j'\right)$ as y_j' which is not the correct result. For a human, the adversarial sample x_j' is still similar to the original sample x_j. Hence a robust neural network should also classify it as y_j, but it fails in doing so. This describes a successful creation of an adversarial example and a demonstration of how a simple attack can look like in real world.

TAXONOMY OF ADVERSARIAL THREAT MODELS

Adversarial examples have been widely researched in the past decade and the research has picked pace after the exposed vulnerabilities in the deep learning models. In this section, the authors have categorized the different adversarial threat models into four categories: objective-based, knowledge-based, modes of attack and closeness to the original data.

Objective-Based

The adversarial examples can be segregated into four broad categories based on the objective of the attack.

- **Type I Error Attack:** The adversarial examples can be created in a manner such that, the sample resembles closely to one class, but when fed to the deep learning model, it triggers an incorrect class, that is, the model classifies it as another class. If such a sample belongs to the negative class, it will trick the model into classifying it as a positive class (false positive). For example, adding a few pieces of tape or physical perturbations to "Stop" sign can create an adversarial example that will be identified as "Speed Limit 45" sign by a traffic sign recognizer model (Eykholt et al., 2018). In the case of malware detection, a benign sample can be modified such that the model classifying benign samples vs malware samples identifies it as a malware. This increases the false positive rate, which in practice is aimed to be kept at a minimum in case of malware detection.
- **Type II Error Attack:** When the adversarial example belongs to the positive class, but the model misclassifies it as a negative class (in case of a binary classification problem) then the attack is called a Type II error attack. Such adversarial examples trigger false negatives in the model's outputs. For example, in the case of malware detection, the adversarial example can be a slightly perturbed version of the malware, but the model recognizes it as a benign sample. Doing so will enable the malware to bypass the security protocol and infect the target system.
- **One-Class Target Attack:** In this attack, the adversarial samples are prepared with the goal of tricking the model to output only one class irrespective of the input. In the case of multi-class classification, like facial recognition, the intruder can create such adversarial samples which always identifies the attacker as a genuine user (Sharif, Bhagavatula, Bauer, & Reiter, 2016). The same attack can be done in the opposite direction where the attacker can construct samples such that the model never identifies one specific label class. For example, in the case of traffic sign detection model, the attacker can construct adversarial samples such that the model is never able to recognize the stop sign (Papernot et al., 2017).
- **Reduced Predicted Probability Attack:** Deep neural network models are capable of classification with high accuracy. Some Adversarial samples have an effect where the predicted probability of classes is reduced significantly, this forces the model to make a less confident prediction.

Knowledge-Based

Attacks on deep neural networks could be done through multiple setups. Attackers knowledge of the system being attacked plays a crucial role in the design of the adversarial samples. The concepts of creating different attacks based on knowledge of the system were used by (Biggio et al., 2013) and (Carlini & Wagner, Nov 3, 2017). A knowledge-based adversarial example can fall under one or more categories mentioned below.

- **White Box Attack:** Deep neural network architecture is complicated and consists of multiple components. Given a scenario where the attacker has complete knowledge of all components of the neural network architecture under attack, such an attack can be classified as white box attack. This is a common attack in the research field as the adversarial examples are constructed against publicly available state-of-the-art models. In this setup, the attacker has access to the training data, test data, the hyper-parameters used in model training, layers topology, number of nodes used, activation functions used, model weights, the algorithm used for optimizing the loss function, etc. The attacker can use internal information of the deep neural network architecture to identify its weak spots in feature space. Most importantly, access to the internal model weights of the neural network helps the attacker in creating a very effective adversarial attack.

- **Black Box Attack:** On the contrary to white box attacks, the black box attacks are constructed with no information about the deep neural network architecture. The adversary in this case only has the information about the purpose of the target model and the list of results it can produce. This attack is preferred while attacking the commonly available deep learning solutions provided by Google, IBM, Amazon, Facebook, etc. (Papernot et al., 2017). There are multiple ways an adversary can choose to conduct a black box attack. The concept of a chosen plaintext attack from the field of cryptography could be used, such that, the attacker can choose the input samples and run it through the network to obtain corresponding labels. The attacker can use this information to understand the functioning of the deep learning model and construct adversaries to attack it. In another approach, the adversary can create a new model by observing the target model as a black box and searching the weak spots by conducting hard-negative example mining. Hard-negative example mining is the technique of identifying the training samples which are given low probability score by the target model but intuitively should have received a high score.
- **Zero-Knowledge Attack:** Much like the black box attack where the adversary does not have any knowledge about the model under attack, zero-knowledge attack also does not know if the model is protected by any detector module (D). A detector (D) represents any security scheme or module or trained network that is capable of identifying an adversarial attack on the target model. This is one of the most difficult attacks and if the attacker succeeds in this attack, then defending against it is considered extremely challenging.
- **Limited-Knowledge Attack:** This type of attack is similar to a white box attack. But, in a limited-knowledge attack the adversary does not know if the model is protected by a detector scheme (D).
- **Perfect-Knowledge Attack:** In this setup, the adversary has complete knowledge of the model under attack, including all details of the defense mechanism incorporated in the model.

Modes of Attack

Adversarial attacks can be implemented during any step of the data pre-processing pipeline (Biggio, Fumera, & Roli, 2014). Attacks can also be implemented during other phases of model creation such as model training, model testing, etc.

- **Evasion Attack:** Evasion attacks on models can take place during the testing phase, where the adversary tries to fool the system by tuning the adversarial sample. This attack is commonly used when zero-information is available about the model to be attacked. The attacker can use either a non-adaptive approach or an adaptive approach to create adversarial examples by running multiple iterations of predict cycles on the model under attack. The attacker does not have access to the training phase of the model.
- **Poisoning Attack:** This type of attack is done during the training phase where training data is contaminated with malicious data. To contaminate training data, adversarial samples are mixed into the training samples. Another method is to manipulate a subset of training data into malicious

samples. This method is largely used when limited information is available about the model under attack. And finally, the most lethal method of poisoning the model is by corrupting the logic of the model. By doing this the attacker is able to compromise the training phase of the model which will render the model vulnerable to future attacks against adversarial samples.

- **Exploratory Attack:** Exploratory attacks are performed when no information is known about the target model and access to training and test dataset is restricted. The attacker resorts to exploring the model as a black box and tries to understand the purpose and results that the model can produce. With enough experimentations, the attacker should be able to identify the weak spots of the target model.

Closeness to Original Data

Fundamentally the adversarial examples are built to be as close as possible to the original data. Adversarial samples are constructed through a min-max game where the malicious samples must be different enough to fool the model, and at the same time they should be close enough to the normal data so that no suspicions are raised. Supporting this fundamental construct of the adversarial samples, (Rozsa, Rudd, & Boult, 2016) proposed a new metric named Psychometric perpetual Adversarial Similarity Score (PASS) to evaluate the closeness of the sample which was consistent with human perception. Discussed below is another common class of perturbations of adversarial samples:

- **Individual Sample Attack:** In this attack, the attacker creates multiple perturbations from a clean input to attack the model. This approach is more compute intensive and is applicable when the attacker is trying to conduct a very specific attack.
- **Universal Sample Attack:** This attack focuses on analyzing the model structure and input data with a vision to create a generalized perturbation which can be used to create adversarial samples from any number of clean samples.

ALGORITHMS TO GENERATE ADVERSARIAL EXAMPLES (H)

Since (Szegedy et al., 2013) discovered the intriguing characteristics of neural networks in relationship with perturbations, a lot of research has been done in the field of generating adversarial examples. This section lists and describes some of the significant algorithms used for the creation of adversarial examples. Even though many of the mentioned techniques have been defeated by a counter defense mechanism, the algorithms below showcase the chronological advancements in the logic of preparing adversarial examples.

Limited-Memory Broyden-Flecher-Goldfarb-Shanno (L-BFGS)

(Szegedy et al., 2013) argued that due to multiple non-linear layers between the input and output, the neural networks efficiently assign a non-generalization prior over the various input feature space. In the case of image recognition, it can assign a non-significant probability to regions which do not contain input and high probability to the area of pixels which contains inputs affecting the output. They further extended the argument by stating it was expected by the neural network to identify images with small perturbations in the areas of high probability since local generalization is supported by other computer vision algorithms. But their hypothesis was proved wrong as the neural networks failed to identify images with small perturbations, which were imperceptible to the human eye. They termed such perturbed samples as adversarial examples.

They constructed the problem in form of box-constrained optimization problem where the adversarial sample was created by minimizing the perturbation (r).

$$minimize \left\| r \right\|$$

$$where\, f\left(x + r\right) = l\, and\, x + r \in D\left(input\, domain\right)$$

Here, x is the original input and is perturbed using r, such that x + r also belongs to the input domain. The minimizer r might satisfy multiple values and x + r denotes one specific value from the solution space. Finding the value of r such that $f\left(x + r\right) = l$ is a hard problem because neural networks are non-convex in general. Hence, they used a line-search method to find out an approximate solution. Their method gave good performance attack wise but was computationally expensive.

Fast Gradient Sign Method (FGSM)

For many problems, the precision of an individual input feature is limited. Due to this, a classifier can classify an input x and its adversarial example $\tilde{x} = x + \eta$ to the same class if η is smaller than the precision of the features. Let us consider the following for weight *w* and the adversarial example $\tilde{x}$:

$$w^T \tilde{x} = w^T x + w^T \eta$$

The adversarial perturbation makes the activation grow by $w^T \eta$. $\| \eta \|_\infty$ does not change with the increase in the number of dimensions. But, if the weight vector w has n dimensions and the average magnitude of the weight vector is m, then the activation will grow linearly with $\in nm$. For higher dimensions, an infinitesimal number of small changes can be made to the input that results in one large change to the output. This has been called "accidental steganography" and it is a linear and faster way to create adversarial examples.

(Goodfellow, Ian J., Shlens, & Szegedy, 2014) proposed the Fast Gradient Sign Method of generating adversarial examples. They hypothesize that it is easy to create adversarial examples for inputs with high dimensions. They also hypothesize that neural networks use linear techniques for faster optimization and hence are prone to linear adversarial attacks.

$$\eta = \in sign\left(\nabla_x J\left(\theta, x, y\right)\right)\left(i\right)$$

Here, θ is the parameter of the model, x is the normal input to the model, y is the target output for the input, and $J\left(\theta, x, y\right)$ is the cost function for the model. The gradient of the cost function ∇_x with respect to the input is calculated. $\in$ is used to control the amplitude of the perturbation.

Fast Gradient Value Method

(Rozsa et al., 2016) extends the work from previous paper to create a Fast Gradient Value (FGV) method for creating adversarial examples. In FGSM, only the sign of the gradient of cost function was used, whereas in FGV method, Rozsa *et al.* proposed using the raw gradient of the cost function after scaling it. This changed the equation from (i) to:

$$\eta_{grad} = \nabla_x J(\theta, x, y)$$

Both the methods, FGSM and FGV, apply a one-time small modification to the input. This makes the generation of adversarial examples faster and easy. But, as the modifications are done one-time, protecting the models from such attacks also becomes easy.

Another variant of the model was proposed by (Kurakin, Goodfellow, & Bengio, 2016a), where they describe an iterative FGSM, where a small step size α is applied to the fast gradient at each iteration. This method is called Iterative Fast Gradient Sign Method (I-FGSM). This method creates strong white-box adversaries as compared to one-time methods. The method uses below equation

$$x_0^* = x, x_{t+1}^* = x_t^* + \alpha sign\left(\nabla_x J\left(x_t^*, y\right)\right)$$

$where, x : benign\ input$

$x_t^* : t^{th} adversary$

$\alpha : step\ size$

This method stabilizes optimization and prevents getting stuck in poor local maxima by using the gradient of the cost function from each iteration. This understanding led to the creation of iterative approaches of FGSM which utilized the concept of momentum by (Dong et al., 2018).

One-Step Target Class Method (OTCM)

(Kurakin, Goodfellow, & Bengio, 2016b) improved upon their previous work and proposed a new approach which maximizes the probability of a target class, which usually is not the true class of the input.

$$x^{adv} = x - \alpha sign\left(\nabla_x J\left(x, y\right)\right)$$

$where, x^{adv} : adversarial\ sample$

$x : benign\ sample$

$\alpha : step\ size$

They extended their logic from targeted class to any random class.

Basic Iterative Method (BIM)

(Kurakin et al., 2016a) demonstrated with the use of a smartphone how adversarial examples can fool a deep learning model in real life example. They extended the concept of FGSM and proposed the algorithm BIM which created samples in an iterative manner with a small step size and it clipped the pixel values of intermediate results whenever it exceeded the maximum perturbation threshold of ϵ.

$$x_0^{adv} = x, x_{n+1}^{adv} = Clip_{x,\epsilon}\left\{x_n^{adv} + \alpha sign\left(\nabla_x\ J\left(x_n^{adv}, y_{true}\right)\right)\right\}$$

$Clip_{x,\in} : Clip\ values\ when\ x^{adv} > \in, s.t. \in > 0$

The final adversarial examples were generated after multiple iterations of the algorithm.

Iterative Least-Likely Class Method (LL Class)

(Kurakin et al., 2016a) also proposed an algorithm to attack the model by tricking the model into selecting the least-likely class of a prediction to be its final result. The argument behind this attack was to create a more interesting attack where the adversarial sample was able to trigger a completely unrelated and absurd output. This technique is derived from BIM.

$$x_0^{adv} = x, x_{n+1}^{adv} = Clip_{x,\epsilon}\left\{x_n^{adv} - \alpha sign\left(\nabla_x J\left(x_n^{adv}, y_{LL}\right)\right)\right\}$$

$where, x : benign\ input$

$y_{LL} : label\ of\ least\ likely\ class$

$x_n^{adv} : n^{th} adversarial\ sample$

$\alpha : step\ size$

$Clip\ values\ when\ x^{adv} > \epsilon, s.t. \epsilon > 0$

Jacobian-Based Saliency Map Attack (JSMA)

This attack was proposed by (Papernot et al., 2016), where a greedy approach to finding the most informative pixels was used based on L_0 distance. This algorithm used the Jacobian-based method to find the gradient of pixels to compute the saliency map of the input. The values indicate the pixels which contribute significantly to the output of the model, which in turn can be modified to create an adversarial example.

$$J_F\left(x\right) = \left[\frac{\partial F\left(x\right)}{\partial x_1}, \frac{\partial F\left(x\right)}{\partial x_2}\right]$$

where J : Jacobian matrix,

F : Function learned by Neural Network

The Jacobian matrix $J_F\left(x\right)$ is a vector of partial derivatives of the neural network function F over the individual input components (x_1, x_2). The authors used the output of the second-to-last layer to obtain the saliency map from gradients calculated from the Jacobian method. This approach is computationally expensive and relatively slow, but the authors claim to have achieved a 97% adversarial success rate with a mean modification rate of 4.02% to input features per sample. (Carlini & Wagner, 2017b), modified the above algorithm to use the output of the final softmax layer instead of the actual logits.

DeepFool

(Moosavi-Dezfooli, Fawzi, & Frossard, 2016), proposed a method to generate minimal perturbations which is sufficient to mislead the model using iterative linearization approach. Starting with binary classification problem with affine classifiers: $f\left(x\right) = w^T x + b$, (Moosavi-Dezfooli et al., 2016), proved that it is possible to create an adversarial example by using ℓ_2 norm in an iterative manner until the $sign(f\left(x\right)) \neq sign(f\left(x + r\right))$ where r is the minimum perturbation required. They extended the algorithm to multi class classification and claimed that this approach works with ℓ_∞ norm as well. DeepFool was able to create adversarial samples by using smaller perturbations, compared to (Szegedy et al., 2013), the average perturbations was five times less.

C&W's Attack

After (Papernot, McDaniel, Wu, Jha, & Swami, 2015), published their work, where they claimed that defensive distillation increased the robustness of deep learning models which resulted in the drop of the success rate of adversarial examples from 95% to 0.5%, (Carlini & Wagner, 2017b), challenged the claim by introducing new white-box attack methodology which was 100% successful against both undistilled and distilled models. They introduced three new attacks based on different distance measures named L2 attack, L0 attack, and L∞ attack. Using the L2 attack, they constructed adversarial examples which successfully attacked distilled models. L0 attack is not differentiable and hence is conducted in an iterative manner where the gradient of L2 distance is taken after each round to identify and remove trivial pixels. They claimed that this algorithm is more effective and efficient compared to JSMA attack. Finally, L∞ attack is also iterative in nature and only penalizes the largest perturbation value. Instead of L_2 distance, it uses a custom distance measure as the objective measure which penalized all large values simultaneously.

Zeroth Order Optimization (ZOO)

(Chen, Zhang, Sharma, Yi, & Hsieh, 2017), proposed a new black-box attack which was as effective as a C&W attack by (Carlini & Wagner, 2017b), and was better than other black-box attacks. The core idea of the attack lies on the zero-order stochastic coordinate descent problem, where the challenge is to compute the approximate gradient using the difference between the predicted probability of the target model y' and the desired class label. The zeroth order optimization aims at solving the following hinge-like loss function:

Solving the optimization problem is computationally expensive and they proposed a ZOO-ADAM algorithm for random selection of variables to create adversarial samples.

Universal Perturbation

Existence of universal image-agnostic perturbations which can attack state of art deep learning models was proposed by (Moosavi-Dezfooli, Fawzi, Fawzi, & Frossard, 2017). They claimed that perturbations calculated using a small set of training samples can create adversarial examples from new samples successfully. The adversarial examples were universal in terms of the dataset and deep learning model. In other words, the universal perturbations were able to create adversarial samples from new unseen data and it was used to attack multiple deep learning models. Based on their findings they extended their study on the geometric relationship between high dimensional class boundaries. They demonstrated the results of their attacks on CaffeNet (Jia, Y. et al., 2014), VGG-F(Chatfield, Simonyan, Vedaldi, & Zisserman, 2014), VGG-16 (Simonyan & Zisserman, 2014), VGG-19 (Simonyan & Zisserman, 2014), GoogLeNet and ResNet-152 (He, Zhang, Ren, & Sun, 2016) using L_2 and L_∞ norms, which proved the universality of the attacks on models.

VULNERABILITIES OF DEEP LEARNING APPLICATIONS

Deep learning has applications in a wide array of domains. Though image recognition has been the most researched application, vulnerabilities of these networks have been exposed in object detection, reinforcement learning, natural language processing, malware detection, etc. In this section, the authors describe the different applications of deep learning where adversarial examples have successfully attacked a model.

Facial Recognition

Many smartphone manufacturers have been using facial recognition for user authentication, it is also used in multiple security application across the world. Deep learning models have been the backbone

Table 1.

Attack Method	Dataset	Targeted models	Papers
L-BFGS	MNIST	DNN	(Szegedy et al., 2013)
FGSM	MNIST	DNN	(Goodfellow, Ian J. et al., 2014)
Fast Gradient Value	MNIST ImageNet	LeNet GoogLeNet ResNet	(Rozsa et al., 2016)
OTCM	ImageNet	Inception v3	(Kurakin et al., 2016b)
BIM	MNIST CIFAR10	DNN	(Kurakin et al., 2016a)
ILLC	MNIST CIFAR10	DNN CNN	(Kurakin et al., 2016a)
JSMA	DREBIN MNIST CIFAR	DNN LeNet-5 CNN	(Papernot et al., 2016)
DeepFool	MNIST CIFAR10 ILSVRC 2012	LeNet CaffeNet GoogLeNet	(Moosavi-Dezfooli et al., 2016)
C&W	MNIST CIFAR10 ImageNet	CNN	(Carlini & Wagner, 2017b)
ZOO	MNIST CIFAR10 ImageNet	Inception-v3 CNN	(Chen et al., 2017)
Universal Perturbation	ILSVRC 2012 MNIST	CaffeNet VGG-19 GoogLeNet ResNet-152	(Moosavi-Dezfooli et al., 2017)

of this feature because of its high accuracy and performance. But, this mode of authentication is not completely secure. (Sharif et al., 2016), demonstrated that the facial recognition system (FRS) can be fooled by using a colorful eyeglass frame around the eyes. They used the softmaxloss score, initially used by (Parkhi, Vedaldi, & Zisserman, 2015), as the objective function to quantify the attack success.

Given an input x of class c_x classified as $f(x)$ (vector of probabilities)

$$softmaxloss\left(f(x), c_x\right) = -\log\left(\frac{e^{h_{c_x}.f(x)}}{\sum_{c=1}^{N} e^{h_c.f(x)}}\right)$$

where $,.,.$ denotes dot product of two vectors,

h_c : one − hot vector of class c,

$f\left(x\right):Predicted\ probability,$

$N:number\ of\ classes$

Sharif et.al used L-BFGS method to generate adversarial examples, which was used to demonstrate both impersonation and dodging attack. These attacks significantly increased the fault rate and insult rate but were ineffective against Faster R-CNN (Ren et al., 2015) model which is more popularly used.

Object Detection and Semantic Segmentation

Another application of deep neural network in the field of images is semantic segmentation and object detection. In semantic segmentation, every pixel in the image is classified as either a target class or non-class. In the case of object detection, all known instances of a target class are classified and bounding-boxes are drawn around them. Xie et al. (2017) explain that as both semantic segmentation and object detection are dependent on classification, they are also prone to adversarial attacks. They created generative adversarial perturbations by optimizing cost function over pixels or proposals. This method, called the Dense Adversary Generation (DAG) is used to generate adversarial examples for object detection and semantic segmentation models.

Natural Language Processing (NLP)

Making machines capable of understanding language as efficiently as a human has always been a huge motivation for AI. NLP models are now able to read comprehensions and answer questions about these comprehensions with good accuracy. There are also models that can convert speech to text with great accuracy. Even such models can be susceptible to adversarial attacks; hence it is important to understand how adversarial examples can affect the NLP models and whether they can be utilized to make more robust models.

Jia, R. & Liang (2017), uses adversarial examples to test their question answering model based on the Stanford Question Answering Dataset (SQuAD). Automatically generated sentences are synthetically inserted into the paragraphs. These sentences are formed in a way such that the answers to the questions do not change and humans are not misled by these changes, although these changes do distract the models from the correct answers. The adversarial examples resulted in accuracy reduction by more than 30%. NLP models need to be trained and tested using adversarial examples to ensure security and robustness against such attacks.

Speech Recognition

Automatic speech recognition (ASR) model is another application of NLP that can be attacked using adversarial examples. Carlini & Wagner (2018), show that creating small perturbations to existing waveforms that are inaudible to humans can trick the ASR models into giving incorrect solutions. Gradient-based single-step methods, which were used to attack images, did not work in case of audio. Modified Connectionist Temporal Classification (CTC) loss function was used in a white box setup to construct adversarial examples which by default changed the decibel (dB) scale of the modified audio signals. These adversarial examples have a success rate of 100%, but their effectiveness in a practical setting is doubtful.

Malware Detection

Machine learning and deep learning techniques are used in various security applications. Models are trained on benign and known malware samples; these models are later used to score every new file and classify them as benign or malware. Machine learning and deep learning models are also used for intrusion detection in the networks (Javaid, Niyaz, Sun, & Alam, 2016) and anomaly detection (Garcia-Teodoro, Diaz-Verdejo, Maciá-Fernández, & Vázquez, 2009; Ryan, Lin, & Miikkulainen, 1998). But in these applications also models are prone to be affected by adversarial examples.

Grosse, Papernot, Manoharan, Backes, & McDaniel (2017) show that adversarial examples can be used to fool malware detection models by 63% by adding small but meaningful perturbations to the input files. Xu, Qi, & Evans (2016) use adversarial attacks on PDF malware classifiers, PDFrate and Hidost. The malware samples are modified to appear like a benign sample, although they still act maliciously. Such adversarial examples are then used as input to the classifiers and they are able to fool the classifiers with high accuracy.

Where previous works have relied on using gradient-based methods to create adversarial examples Hu & Tan (2017), use Generative Adversarial Networks to create adversarial examples of malware called MalGAN. The adversarial examples generated using MalGAN are better at fooling malware classification models than traditional methods.

Table 2.

Application	Dataset	Model	Method	Papers
Face Recognition	PubFig image Kumar, Berg, Belhumeur, & Nayar, 2009 LFW (Huang, G. B., Mattar, Berg, & Learned-Miller, 2008)	DNN VGG_Face	L-BFGS	(Kumar, Berg, Belhumeur, & Nayar, 2009; Sharif et al., 2016)
Object Detection	Cityscapes PascalVOC-2007	FCN-Alex FCN-VGG	DAG	(Xie et al., 2017)
Semantic Segmentation	LISA Cityscapes	DNN	ILLC	(Xie et al., 2017)
NLP	SQuAD	LSTM BiDAF	AddSent AddAny	(Jia, R. & Liang, 2017)
Speech Recognition	Feature Adversary	Mozilla Common Voice	CTC-loss	(Carlini & Wagner, 2018)
Malware Detection	DREBIN malwr	DNN	JSMA GAN	(Javaid et al., 2016) (Xu et al., 2016) (Grosse et al., 2017)

CHALLENGES OF SECURING DEEP LEARNING MODELS AGAINST ADVERSARIAL ATTACKS

The existence of adversarial examples that can trick a deep learning model into performing poorly is an intriguing concept in itself. It is an open topic of research which is of interest for both attackers and researchers who intend to make resilient deep learning models. But, due to the intrinsic nature of deep neural networks, it has not yet been conclusively proven why does such samples exist. And, no universal detection or defense mechanism exists which can protect a model from any attack. Based on these facts, there are a few challenges pertaining to the adversarial examples which currently restrict the researcher's community to make better attacks or defense mechanisms. In this section, the authors discuss few of the factors which offer challenges towards defending against adversarial examples.

Szegedy et al. (2013), found that adversarial examples created from one dataset were able to attack the same deep neural network trained using a different dataset. This was an interesting observation because it hints at the transferable nature of the adversarial examples attack. Later Papernot, McDaniel, & Goodfellow (2016), experimented with adversarial examples that were constructed using one deep neural network architecture to attack a different neural network architecture. The results confirmed the transferability property of the adversarial examples. It also empowered the attackers to attack systems with limited or no knowledge using adversarial examples trained on a different model. Liu, Y., Chen, Liu, & Song (2016), further explored this characteristic of adversarial examples and proposed that non-targeted attacks are more transferable compared to the targeted attacks.

The question of why adversarial examples exist is an open topic of research. One possible explanation is that exhaustively covering all possible test cases and corner cases would make models extremely complex. As a result, most models cover only high probability test cases ignoring these examples (Szegedy et al., 2013), (Pei, Cao, Yang, & Jana, 2017).

For linear models that take inputs with high dimensions, the chances of creating adversarial examples become infinitesimal. Even slight changes to the input can result in adversarial examples that the model had not seen before. Goodfellow, Ian J. et al. (2014), pointed out that this issue is not limited to just neural networks but other linear models as well.

No universal method exists to defend against adversarial attacks; all these attacks and defense are application specific and most of them are based on some specific characteristic of neural networks. Though there is some research which claims to provide universal security but recently they have been shown to fail given a small change in attack strategy (Carlini & Wagner, 2017a). Hence as of today, it is not possible to have a 100% secure deep neural network which can resist any adversarial example attack.

DEFENSE AGAINST ADVERSARIAL ATTACKS

In this section, the authors provide a brief overview of recent research done towards protecting deep neural networks against adversarial attacks. The defenses can be classified in terms of how they are implemented in practice. These strategies work in a reactive manner to defend the target models from adversarial examples (Gong, Wang, & Ku, 2017; Song, Kim, Nowozin, Ermon, & Kushman, 2017). There is also a proactive approach where the defense strategy is to make the model more robust during the training phase, even before it is attacked using an adversarial sample.

Detecting Adversarial Examples

This is one of the more researched reactive approaches towards protecting deep learning networks against adversarial attacks. In this strategy, a separate detector module or network that works with the target network is created to identify an adversary in real time and prevent it from affecting the targeted network.

Lu, Issaranon, & Forsyth (2017), proposed an architecture named SafetyNet which uses SVM with RBF kernel to distinguish an adversarial sample from a normal sample. It relies on the inner states of the later layers of the targeted neural network to detect adversarial examples. If the detector module marks an input sample as adversarial, then it is rejected and is not fed to the original network. This approach is claimed to be resilient to attack types generated using Fast sign method, Iterative methods, DeepFool architecture, and transfer methods.

Another study conducted by Metzen, Genewein, Fischer, & Bischoff (2017), also advocates a similar idea of using a detector module to identify adversarial samples from normal samples. They proposed to train the original network with only normal data and then freeze the model weights. Then, the adversarial samples are prepared for each training record and the new dataset of twice the size is used to train the binary classification model to identify adversarial samples from normal samples. They also propose to use a dynamic approach to protect against adversaries that possess knowledge of the detector module.

Feinman, Curtin, Shintre, & Gardner (2017), claimed that since the uncertainty in adversarial samples is more as compared to normal input samples using a Bayesian neural network to identify adversarial examples gives better results. Meng & Chen (2017), used Jensen-Shannon divergence to calculate the probabilistic dissimilarity amongst the normal and adversarial samples. Hendrycks & Gimpel (2016), used principal component analysis (PCA) to demonstrate that standard adversarial samples have different signatures compared to normal samples.

Attacking Adversarial Examples

Since adversarial examples are created using small perturbations upon genuine data, it could be possible to identify and remove those anomalous perturbations from the adversarial sample and make it benign. This too is a reactive approach as it aims at turning adversarial examples harmless. Gu & Rigazio (2014), proposed three approaches to transform adversarial examples into benign samples or make them easier for models to identify. They argued that if adding small noise to the normal data created the adversarial example, if more noise is added to the adversarial examples then they would not be able to fool the model, especially in case of Type I attacks. In the other two approaches, they used a 3-layer auto-encoder and a denoising auto-encoder to transform the adversarial samples into benign and to remove the small perturbations respectively.

Applying a similar approach in case of image recognition, Song et al. (2017), restructured adversarial images back into normal images using PixelCNN (Salimans, Karpathy, Chen, & Kingma, 2017).

Deep Neural Network Verification

Network verification aims at preparing a defense mechanism against adversarial examples in a reactive manner such that the network itself should be able to identify and reject adversarial samples.

Katz, Barrett, Dill, Julian, & Kochenderfer (2017), proposed a network verification method(ReluPlex) applicable only to ReLU activation function (Nair & Hinton, 2010). Their technique involved the simplex method that handles non-convex ReLU activation. They showed that a neural network verified using Satisfiability Modulo Theory (SMT) is immune to adversarial attacks that use samples with small perturbations. Carlini, Katz, Barrett, & Dill (2017), extended Katz et.al work on ReLU and proposed that the same logic would work on max operator using ReLU activation. This helped in encoding max-pooling layers in ReluPlex where L_1 and L_∞ norms could be calculated. However, both the methods involve large computations and are inherently slow, hence its utility is restricted to smaller networks.

Another idea was proposed by Gopinath, Katz, Pasareanu, & Barrett (2017), which involved identifying safe spots in input images by analyzing the neural network. These safe spots are characterized by special areas of input space where small perturbations do not affect the model's evaluation result. Then the model is trained to emphasize those spots in order to make better predictions. Hence, the neural network becomes immune to adversarial data as the model determines its output through safe spots which are unperturbed.

Defensive Network Distillation

Based on the concept of distillation within neural networks initially proposed by (Hinton, Vinyals, & Dean, 2015), Papernot et al. (2015) proposed the use of network distillation for making deep neural networks robust enough to resist any adverse effect from adversarial examples. This is one of the proactive approaches which involves a modified way of training the network. The initial application of the concept was to create smaller networks by using transfer learning from previous networks. The initial target value called hard class was replaced by the result of the final Softmax layer which gave the probability of each class based on the set temperature value.

$$q_i = \frac{e^{z_i/T}}{\sum_j e^{z_j/T}}$$

where z_i is the calculated probability of class i,

T is the Temperature

q_i is the final probabilty of class i

Ideally, the temperature value is 1, but in the case of distilled networks, it is some value greater than 1. The result of this function produces soft classes in terms of class probabilities, which are later used to train other networks of similar configuration. Such a network is arguably more robust and resilient to adversarial attacks. This approach was tested on MNIST and CIFAR-10 datasets and it reduced the success rate of JSMA attack by 0.5% and 5% respectively.

Adversarial Retraining

Proactively generating adversarial examples and using them in the training phase helps in creating more generalized and robust networks (Goodfellow, Ian J. et al., 2014). Huang, Xu, Schuurmans, & Szepesvári (2015), followed this approach and used adversarial samples in the training phase. They showcased that this process added more robustness to the model and the model was able to handle adversarial examples during the test phase with more precision. But this success was only limited to one-step attack and the approach could not protect the model from iterative attacks like BIM. Tramèr et al. (2017), demonstrated using the ImageNet dataset that the approach is more robust to white-box attacks compared to transferred black-box attacks.

Defense-GAN

Samangouei, Kabkab, & Chellappa (2018), proposed the use of Wasserstein Generative Adversarial Network (WGAN) to defend against both white-box and black-box type of adversarial attacks (Arjovsky, Chintala, & Bottou, 2017). The generator module of the GAN generated new data distributions and the discriminator network classified the genuine inputs from the adversarial inputs. The purpose of this architecture is to project input image onto the generator output, ensuring that the output image has minimal reconstruction error. This helped the network to learn the original and slightly perturbed representation of the source image. Defense-GAN is a highly non-linear process where two adversarial networks train in the min-max game setting. To obtain impressive results longer training durations are required which increases the computational costs.

CONCLUSION AND FUTURE RESEARCH DIRECTION

Deep Leaning has revolutionized the application of artificial intelligence in security critical applications by creating highly accurate and precise models. Its vulnerability to adversarial examples, however, has raised serious concerns in its full-fledged adoption. In this chapter, the authors have discussed the vulnerabilities of the deep learning models with respect to adversarial example attacks. Recent research in securing the deep learning models against the attacks and possible future research directions and best practices have been outlined.

Table 3.

Defense	Mode	Papers
Detecting Adversarial Examples	Reactive	(Lu et al., 2017) (Metzen et al., 2017) (Feinman et al., 2017)
Attacking Adversarial Examples	Reactive	(Gu & Rigazio, 2014) (Song et al., 2017)
DNN Verification	Reactive	(Katz et al., 2017) (Carlini et al., 2017) (Gopinath et al., 2017)
Defensive Network Distillation	Proactive	(Hinton et al., 2015) (Papernot et al., 2015)
Adversarial retraining	Proactive	(Tramèr et al., 2017)
Defense-GAN	Proactive	(Arjovsky et al., 2017)

Even though some research has been conducted to construct adversarial examples and to defend deep learning models against them, the core idea behind the existence of adversarial examples is still elusive to the research community. Most of the proposed attacks work on a specific model configuration and countermeasures for these are prepared to protect against the corresponding attacks. Carlini & Wagner (2017), showcased that the recent existing defense strategies are rigid in structure and can be defeated by using a new loss function in existing attack strategies. Hence, as of now, no universal defense strategy exists for different kinds of adversarial example attacks.

After researching upon the subject, some observations may be derived to guide the future research direction. Firstly, most researchers have chosen to showcase their work on the MNIST dataset, which is a considerably small and basic dataset. As a best practice, the attack strategies must be showcased on multiple datasets to prove the effectiveness of the adversarial attacks. Next, quantifying the robustness of attacks by publishing the upper bounds for perturbation would help in comparing different attacks. In addition, there exists a need for a standard platform where different attacks can be performed and evaluated on a large scale.

It would be helpful if researchers conduct their experiments to defend the model in a white-box fashion, where it must be assumed that the defense strategy itself can be attacked. In the case of adversarial examples detector, the effectiveness of the model must be judged based on both false positives and true positives. Hence, it is better to present the receiver operator characteristics (ROC) of the model (Carlini & Wagner, Nov 3, 2017). Finally, an important future research work should be to create defense strategies based on generalized concepts that prevent transferability of attacks.

REFERENCES

Abadi, M., Barham, P., Chen, J., Chen, Z., Davis, A., Dean, J., . . . Isard, M. (2016). Tensorflow: A System For Large-Scale Machine Learning. *Osdi, 16,* 265-283.

Arjovsky, M., Chintala, S., & Bottou, L. (2017). *Wasserstein Gan.* Arxiv Preprint Arxiv:1701.07875

Barreno, M., Nelson, B., Joseph, A. D., & Tygar, J. D. (2010). The Security Of Machine Learning. *Machine Learning, 81*(2), 121–148.

Bengio, Y., & Lecun, Y. (2007). Scaling Learning Algorithms Towards AI. *Large-Scale Kernel Machines, 34*(5), 1–41.

Biggio, B., Corona, I., Maiorca, D., Nelson, B., Šrndić, N., Laskov, P., ... Roli, F. (2013). (2013). Evasion Attacks Against Machine Learning At Test Time. Paper Presented At The *Joint European Conference On Machine Learning And Knowledge Discovery In Databases*, 387-402.

Biggio, B., Fumera, G., & Roli, F. (2010a). Multiple Classifier Systems For Robust Classifier Design In Adversarial Environments. *International Journal of Machine Learning and Cybernetics, 1*(1-4), 27–41. doi:10.100713042-010-0007-7

Biggio, B., Fumera, G., & Roli, F. (2014). Security Evaluation Of Pattern Classifiers Under Attack. *IEEE Transactions on Knowledge and Data Engineering, 26*(4), 984–996. doi:10.1109/TKDE.2013.57

Carlini, N., Katz, G., Barrett, C., & Dill, D. L. (2017). *Ground-Truth Adversarial Examples*. Arxiv Preprint Arxiv:1709.10207

Carlini, N., & Wagner, D. (2017). *Adversarial Examples Are Not Easily Detected*. Retrieved From Http:// Dl.Acm.Org/Citation.Cfm?Id=3140444

Carlini, N., & Wagner, D. (2017a). Adversarial Examples Are Not Easily Detected: Bypassing Ten Detection Methods. *Proceedings Of The 10th ACM Workshop On Artificial Intelligence And Security*, 3-14.

Carlini, N., & Wagner, D. (2017b). Towards Evaluating The Robustness Of Neural Networks. *2017 IEEE Symposium On Security And Privacy (SP)*, 39-57. 10.1109/SP.2017.49

Carlini, N., & Wagner, D. (2018). *Audio Adversarial Examples: Targeted Attacks On Speech-To-Text*. Arxiv Preprint Arxiv:1801.01944

Chatfield, K., Simonyan, K., Vedaldi, A., & Zisserman, A. (2014). *Return Of The Devil In The Details: Delving Deep Into Convolutional Nets*. Arxiv Preprint Arxiv:1405.3531

Chen, P., Zhang, H., Sharma, Y., Yi, J., & Hsieh, C. (2017). Zoo: Zeroth Order Optimization Based Black-Box Attacks To Deep Neural Networks Without Training Substitute Models. *Proceedings Of The 10th ACM Workshop On Artificial Intelligence And Security*, 15-26.

Chung, J., Gulcehre, C., Cho, K., & Bengio, Y. (2014). *Empirical Evaluation Of Gated Recurrent Neural Networks On Sequence Modeling*. Arxiv Preprint Arxiv:1412.3555

Dalvi, N., Domingos, P., Sanghai, S., & Verma, D. (2004). (2004). Adversarial Classification. *Proceedings Of The Tenth ACM SIGKDD International Conference On Knowledge Discovery And Data Mining*, 99-108.

Dong, Y., Liao, F., Pang, T., Su, H., Zhu, J., Hu, X., & Li, J. (2018). (2018). *Boosting Adversarial Attacks With Momentum. The IEEE Conference On Computer Vision And Pattern Recognition (CVPR)*.

Eykholt, K., Evtimov, I., Fernandes, E., Li, B., Rahmati, A., Xiao, C., ... Song, D. (2018). Robust Physical-World Attacks On Deep Learning Visual Classification. *Proceedings Of The IEEE Conference On Computer Vision And Pattern Recognition*, 1625-1634.

Feinman, R., Curtin, R. R., Shintre, S., & Gardner, A. B. (2017). *Detecting Adversarial Samples From Artifacts*. Arxiv Preprint Arxiv:1703.00410

Fischer, V., Kumar, M. C., Metzen, J. H., & Brox, T. (2017). *Adversarial Examples For Semantic Image Segmentation*. Arxiv Preprint Arxiv:1703.01101

Funahashi, K., & Nakamura, Y. (1993). Approximation Of Dynamical Systems By Continuous Time Recurrent Neural Networks. *Neural Networks*, 6(6), 801–806.

Garcia-Teodoro, P., Diaz-Verdejo, J., Maciá-Fernández, G., & Vázquez, E. (2009). Anomaly-Based Network Intrusion Detection: Techniques, Systems And Challenges. *Computers & Security*, 28(1-2), 18–28. doi:10.1016/j.cose.2008.08.003

Gong, Z., Wang, W., & Ku, W. (2017). *Adversarial And Clean Data Are Not Twins*. Arxiv Preprint Arxiv:1704.04960

Goodfellow, I., Pouget-Abadie, J., Mirza, M., Xu, B., Warde-Farley, D., Ozair, S., . . . Bengio, Y. (2014). Generative Adversarial Nets. *Advances In Neural Information Processing Systems,* 2672-2680.

Goodfellow, I. J., Shlens, J., & Szegedy, C. (2014). *Explaining And Harnessing Adversarial Examples.* Retrieved From Https://Www.Openaire.Eu/Search/Publication?Articleid=Od_____18:2bc05c2b2e 804ef575988e1726ae8a5b

Gopinath, D., Katz, G., Pasareanu, C. S., & Barrett, C. (2017). *Deepsafe: A Data-Driven Approach For Checking Adversarial Robustness In Neural Networks.* Arxiv Preprint Arxiv:1710.00486

Grosse, K., Papernot, N., Manoharan, P., Backes, M., & Mcdaniel, P. (2017). Adversarial Examples For Malware Detection. *European Symposium On Research In Computer Security,* 62-79.

Gu, S., & Rigazio, L. (2014). *Towards Deep Neural Network Architectures Robust To Adversarial Examples.* Arxiv Preprint Arxiv:1412.5068

Gupta, B., Agrawal, D. P., & Yamaguchi, S. (2016). *Handbook Of Research On Modern Cryptographic Solutions For Computer And Cyber Security.* IGI Global.

He, K., Gkioxari, G., Dollár, P., & Girshick, R. (2017). Mask R-Cnn. *Computer Vision (ICCV), 2017 IEEE International Conference On,* 2980-2988.

He, K., Zhang, X., Ren, S., & Sun, J. (2016). Deep Residual Learning For Image Recognition. *Proceedings Of The IEEE Conference On Computer Vision And Pattern Recognition,* 770-778.

Hendrycks, D., & Gimpel, K. (2016). *Early Methods For Detecting Adversarial Images.* Arxiv Preprint Arxiv:1608.00530

Hinton, G., Vinyals, O., & Dean, J. (2015). *Distilling The Knowledge In A Neural Network.* Arxiv Preprint Arxiv:1503.02531

Hochreiter, S. (1998). The Vanishing Gradient Problem During Learning Recurrent Neural Nets And Problem Solutions. *International Journal of Uncertainty, Fuzziness and Knowledge-based Systems,* 6(2), 107–116.

Hochreiter, S., & Schmidhuber, J. (1997). Long Short-Term Memory. *Neural Computation,* 9(8), 1735–1780. doi:10.1162/neco.1997.9.8.1735

Hu, W., & Tan, Y. (2017). *Generating Adversarial Malware Examples For Black-Box Attacks Based On GAN.* Arxiv Preprint Arxiv:1702.05983

Huang, G. B., Mattar, M., Berg, T., & Learned-Miller, E. (2008). Labeled Faces. In *The Wild: A Database Forstudying Face Recognition In Unconstrained Environments. Workshop On Faces In'real-Life' Images: Detection.* Alignment, And Recognition.

Huang, R., Xu, B., Schuurmans, D., & Szepesvári, C. (2015). *Learning With A Strong Adversary.* Arxiv Preprint Arxiv:1511.03034

Javaid, A., Niyaz, Q., Sun, W., & Alam, M. (2016). A Deep Learning Approach For Network Intrusion Detection System. *Proceedings Of The 9th EAI International Conference On Bio-Inspired Information And Communications Technologies (Formerly BIONETICS),* 21-26.

Jia, R., & Liang, P. (2017). *Adversarial Examples For Evaluating Reading Comprehension Systems.* Arxiv Preprint Arxiv:1707.07328

Jia, Y., Shelhamer, E., Donahue, J., Karayev, S., Long, J., Girshick, R., ... Darrell, T. (2014). Caffe: Convolutional Architecture For Fast Feature Embedding. *Proceedings Of The 22nd ACM International Conference On Multimedia,* 675-678.

Katz, G., Barrett, C., Dill, D. L., Julian, K., & Kochenderfer, M. J. (2017). Reluplex: An Efficient SMT Solver For Verifying Deep Neural Networks. Paper Presented At The *International Conference On Computer Aided Verification,* 97-117.

Krizhevsky, A., Sutskever, I., & Hinton, G. E. (2012). Imagenet Classification With Deep Convolutional Neural Networks. *Advances In Neural Information Processing Systems,* 1097-1105.

Kumar, N., Berg, A. C., Belhumeur, P. N., & Nayar, S. K. (2009). Attribute And Simile Classifiers For Face Verification. *Computer Vision, 2009 IEEE 12th International Conference On,* 365-372.

Kurakin, A., Goodfellow, I., & Bengio, S. (2016a). *Adversarial Examples In The Physical World.* Arxiv Preprint Arxiv:1607.02533

Kurakin, A., Goodfellow, I., & Bengio, S. (2016b). *Adversarial Machine Learning At Scale.* Arxiv Preprint Arxiv:1611.01236

Liu, W., Anguelov, D., Erhan, D., Szegedy, C., Reed, S., Fu, C., & Berg, A. C. (2016). Ssd: Single Shot Multibox Detector. *European Conference On Computer Vision,* 21-37.

Liu, Y., Chen, X., Liu, C., & Song, D. (2016). *Delving Into Transferable Adversarial Examples And Black-Box Attacks.* Arxiv Preprint Arxiv:1611.02770

Lowd, D., & Meek, C. (2005). Adversarial Learning. *Proceedings Of The Eleventh ACM SIGKDD International Conference On Knowledge Discovery In Data Mining,* 641-647.

Lu, J., Issaranon, T., & Forsyth, D. A. (2017). Safetynet: Detecting And Rejecting Adversarial Examples Robustly. *Iccv,* 446-454.

Meng, D., & Chen, H. (2017). Magnet: A Two-Pronged Defense Against Adversarial Examples. *Proceedings Of The 2017 ACM SIGSAC Conference On Computer And Communications Security,* 135-147.

Metzen, J. H., Genewein, T., Fischer, V., & Bischoff, B. (2017). *On Detecting Adversarial Perturbations.* Arxiv Preprint Arxiv:1702.04267

Moosavi-Dezfooli, S., Fawzi, A., Fawzi, O., & Frossard, P. (2017). *Universal Adversarial Perturbations.* Arxiv Preprint.

Moosavi-Dezfooli, S., Fawzi, A., & Frossard, P. (2016). Deepfool: A Simple And Accurate Method To Fool Deep Neural Networks. *Proceedings Of The IEEE Conference On Computer Vision And Pattern Recognition,* 2574-2582.

Nair, V., & Hinton, G. E. (2010). Rectified Linear Units Improve Restricted Boltzmann Machines. *Proceedings Of The 27th International Conference On Machine Learning (ICML-10),* 807-814.

Najafabadi, M. M., Villanustre, F., Khoshgoftaar, T. M., Seliya, N., Wald, R., & Muharemagic, E. (2015). Deep Learning Applications And Challenges In Big Data Analytics. *Journal Of Big Data, 2*(1), 1. doi:10.118640537-014-0007-7

Papernot, N., Mcdaniel, P., & Goodfellow, I. (2016). *Transferability In Machine Learning: From Phenomena To Black-Box Attacks Using Adversarial Samples.* Arxiv Preprint Arxiv:1605.07277

Papernot, N., McDaniel, P., Goodfellow, I., Jha, S., Celik, Z. B., & Swami, A. (2017). Practical Black-Box Attacks Against Machine Learning. *Proceedings Of The 2017 ACM On Asia Conference On Computer And Communications Security*, 506-519.

Papernot, N., Mcdaniel, P., Jha, S., Fredrikson, M., Celik, Z. B., & Swami, A. (2016). (2016). The Limitations Of Deep Learning In Adversarial Settings. *Security And Privacy (Euros&P), 2016 IEEE European Symposium On*, 372-387.

Papernot, N., Mcdaniel, P., Wu, X., Jha, S., & Swami, A. (2015). *Distillation As A Defense To Adversarial Perturbations Against Deep Neural Networks.* Arxiv Preprint Arxiv:1511.04508

Parkhi, O. M., Vedaldi, A., & Zisserman, A. (2015). Deep Face Recognition. *Bmvc, 1*(3), 6.

Pei, K., Cao, Y., Yang, J., & Jana, S. (2017). Deepxplore: Automated Whitebox Testing Of Deep Learning Systems. *Proceedings Of The 26th Symposium On Operating Systems Principles,* 1-18.

Redmon, J., & Farhadi, A. (2017). *YOLO9000: Better, Faster, Stronger.* Arxiv Preprint.

Ren, S., He, K., Girshick, R., & Sun, J. (2015). Faster R-Cnn: Towards Real-Time Object Detection With Region Proposal Networks. *Advances in Neural Information Processing Systems*, 91–99.

Rozsa, A., Rudd, E. M., & Boult, T. E. (2016). Adversarial Diversity And Hard Positive Generation. *Proceedings Of The IEEE Conference On Computer Vision And Pattern Recognition Workshops*, 25-32.

Ryan, J., Lin, M., & Miikkulainen, R. (1998). Intrusion Detection With Neural Networks. *Advances In Neural Information Processing Systems,* 943-949.

Salimans, T., Karpathy, A., Chen, X., & Kingma, D. P. (2017). *Pixelcnn: Improving The Pixelcnn With Discretized Logistic Mixture Likelihood And Other Modifications.* Arxiv Preprint Arxiv:1701.05517

Samangouei, P., Kabkab, M., & Chellappa, R. (2018). *Defense-GAN: Protecting Classifiers Against Adversarial Attacks Using Generative Models.* Arxiv Preprint Arxiv:1805.06605

Sharif, M., Bhagavatula, S., Bauer, L., & Reiter, M. K. (2016). Accessorize To A Crime: Real And Stealthy Attacks On State-Of-The-Art Face Recognition. *Proceedings Of The 2016 ACM SIGSAC Conference On Computer And Communications Security*, 1528-1540.

Simonyan, K., & Zisserman, A. (2014). *Very Deep Convolutional Networks For Large-Scale Image Recognition.* Arxiv Preprint Arxiv:1409.1556

Song, Y., Kim, T., Nowozin, S., Ermon, S., & Kushman, N. (2017). *Pixeldefend: Leveraging Generative Models To Understand And Defend Against Adversarial Examples.* Arxiv Preprint Arxiv:1710.10766

Storcheus, D., Rostamizadeh, A., & Kumar, S. (2015). A Survey Of Modern Questions And Challenges In Feature Extraction. *Feature Extraction: Modern Questions And Challenges*, 1-18.

Sutton, R. S., Barto, A. G., & Bach, F. (1998). *Reinforcement Learning: An Introduction*. MIT Press.

Szegedy, C., Ioffe, S., Vanhoucke, V., & Alemi, A. A. (2017). Inception-V4, Inception-Resnet And The Impact Of Residual Connections On Learning. *Aaai, 4* 12.

Szegedy, C., Vanhoucke, V., Ioffe, S., Shlens, J., & Wojna, Z. (2016). Rethinking The Inception Architecture For Computer Vision. *Proceedings Of The IEEE Conference On Computer Vision And Pattern Recognition*, 2818-2826.

Szegedy, C., Zaremba, W., Sutskever, I., Bruna, J., Erhan, D., Goodfellow, I., & Fergus, R. (2013). *Intriguing Properties Of Neural Networks* Retrieved From Https://Www.Openaire.Eu/Search/Publication?Articleid=Od_____18:5d22d165a1409152d22f2f7e03072187

Tramèr, F., Kurakin, A., Papernot, N., Goodfellow, I., Boneh, D., & Mcdaniel, P. (2017). *Ensemble Adversarial Training: Attacks And Defenses* Retrieved From Https://Www.Openaire.Eu/Search/Publication?Articleid=Od_____18:5fc0601651346f3f957eedba1c1435ad

Xie, C. A. W., Zhang, J. A., Zhou, Z. A., Xie, Y. A., & Yuille, L. A. (2017). Adversarial Examples For Semantic Segmentation And Object Detection. *2017 IEEE International Conference On Computer Vision (ICCV)*. 10.1109/ICCV.2017.153

Xu, W., Qi, Y., & Evans, D. (2016). Automatically Evading Classifiers. *Proceedings Of The 2016 Network And Distributed Systems Symposium*.

Yuan, X., He, P., Zhu, Q., & Li, X. (2017). *Adversarial Examples: Attacks And Defenses For Deep Learning*. Retrieved From Https://Www.Openaire.Eu/Search/Publication?Articleid=Od_____18:F09505f95ca22264d0b6a5700fb27f84

Chapter 4
Big Data Analytics:
Applications, Trends, Tools, and Future Research Directions

Nitigya Sambyal
Punjab Engineering College (Deemed), India

Poonam Saini
Punjab Engineering College (Deemed), India

Rupali Syal
Punjab Engineering College (Deemed), India

ABSTRACT

The world is increasingly driven by huge amounts of data. Big data refers to data sets that are so large or complex that traditional data processing application software are inadequate to deal with them. Healthcare analytics is a prominent area of big data analytics. It has led to significant reduction in morbidity and mortality associated with a disease. In order to harness full potential of big data, various tools like Apache Sentry, BigQuery, NoSQL databases, Hadoop, JethroData, etc. are available for its processing. However, with such enormous amounts of information comes the complexity of data management, other big data challenges occur during data capture, storage, analysis, search, transfer, information privacy, visualization, querying, and update. The chapter focuses on understanding the meaning and concept of big data, analytics of big data, its role in healthcare, various application areas, trends and tools used to process big data along with open problem challenges.

INTRODUCTION

Data nowadays is available in wide variety of forms ranging from *structured* which has a high degree of organization; *semi-structured* which is a form of structured data but does not conform with the formal structure of data models as seen in relational databases; *unstructured* which lacks any uniform structure and *sensor data* which is an output obtained from device that detects changes in the physical environment. However due to increase in digitization, the amount of data created every day is huge which in

DOI: 10.4018/978-1-5225-8407-0.ch004

turn increases the complexity to manage and analyse the data. Management of such data essentially includes three main functions:

1. **Data Acquisition:** It involves capturing data from various locations by defining sources of data, type, templates, configurations etc. It can be from texts, documents, tables (relational databases), audio, image, video etc.
2. **Data Preparation:** It deals with data storage, cleaning, enrichment and validation with primary focus on ensuring accountability and trustworthiness.
3. **Data Distribution:** It deals with both sharing and protection of data, ensuring data privacy, security etc.

Big data which is an emerging topic has attracted the attention of many researchers and practitioners from agriculture industry, banking sector, business corporations, healthcare and cybernetics fields. Big Data is characterized by 5 V_s (Kulkarni, Bhartiya, Kishore & Gunturi, 2016) as shown in Figure 1.

- **Variety**: Varied type of structured dataphone numbers, address, name etc; unstructured like photos, videos, tweets etc and semi-structured data like HTML, XML, JSON documents etc.
- **Velocity:** High speed at which vast amount of data is being generated, transmitted, collected and analysed.
- **Volume:** Incredible amount of data generated each second from disparate sources like social media, credit cards, online transactions, sensors, videos, photographs etc.
- **Veracity:** This indicates the trustworthiness of data *i.e.* degree to which data is accurate, precise and reliable.
- **Value:** It mainly signifies the worth of the data in terms of cost and benefits of collecting and analysing a particular data.

Big data analytics aims to computationally analyse large data sets to discover hidden patterns, correlations, market trends, customer preferences, behaviour, opinion, associations and other useful information that can help organizations make better informed business decisions.

Figure 1. 5 V_s of big data

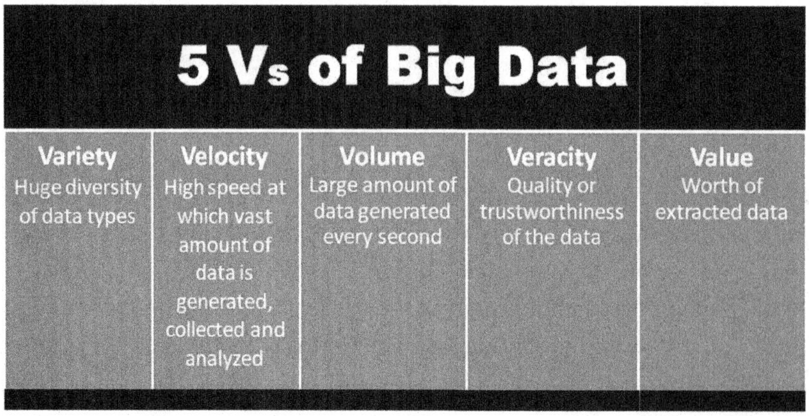

5 Vs of Big Data				
Variety	**Velocity**	**Volume**	**Veracity**	**Value**
Huge diversity of data types	High speed at which vast amount of data is generated, collected and analyzed	Large amount of data generated every second	Quality or trustworthiness of the data	Worth of extracted data

Table 1. Types of data analytics

Type	Description	Application Examples
Descriptive Analytics	• Preliminary stage of data processing to create a concise description of historical data. • Provides useful information that can be used for further analysis	• Summarize and represent data in various forms. • Making reports concerning company's production, inventory, financials, operations, sales and customers.
Predictive Analytics	• Advanced analytics to make predictions about future events. • Uses combination of data mining, statistics, modelling, machine learning, and artificial intelligence.	• Sales forecast. • Prediction of group of items purchased together. • Prediction of input demand from the supply chain or inventory levels forecast. • Text mining, data mining, media mining.
Diagnostic Analytics	• Finds dependencies and patterns to determine the cause of an event. • Provides in-depth insight of a problem. • Characterized by techniques: drill down, data mining, data discovery and correlations.	• Medicine prescription in healthcare industry. • Selection of high potential employees. • Determining the reasons for success of past campaigns, events etc.
Prescriptive Analytics	• Analytics devoted to find best plan of action to be followed during a given event. • Deals with both descriptive and predictive analytics	• Optimize production, scheduling and inventory in the supply chain. • Optimize customer experience.

There are mainly four types of analytics that can be performed on big data namely: Descriptive analytics, Predictive analytics, Diagnostic analytics and Prescriptive analytics (Delen & Demirkan, 2013). *Descriptive analytics* involves interpretation of historical data to understand the various changes that have happened overtime. This enables analysis of trends, clusters, correlations and variations. *Predictive analytics* consist of pattern examination in current data to predict future outcomes or event. *Diagnostic analytics* is an advanced analytics which examines data to determine the reason for occurrence of an event. *Prescriptive analytics* automates complex decisions to make predictions and then actively updates recommendation based on changing scenarios.

The description and examples of all four discussed analytics techniques have been elaborated in the Table 1.

The book chapter is divided into following sections: Section 2 discusses the role of big data analytics in healthcare, Section 3 gives a brief outline of various application areas of big data, Section 4 elaborates upon benefits of healthcare analytics. Section 5 describes the various trends in big data along with varied tools available to analyze it, Section 6 lists out the challenges and barriers to big data analytics and section 5 consist of conclusion along with future scope.

BACKGROUND: BIG DATA ANALYTICS AND HEALTHCARE

This section provides description and overview of big data in general with special focus on healthcare. Nowadays data is generated at such a faster rate from heterogeneous sources. Various tools and techniques have been developed for managing such vast datasets to effectively uncover hidden patterns, unknown correlations, market trends, customer preferences etc.

Maniyaka et. al. (2011) reviewed various techniques and models for big data analytics. Some of these are *association rule mining,* which finds relationship among various datasets; *classification,* which provides a label to a new data point based on already categorised data; *cluster analysis,* which assigns same group to data points having common properties; *crowd sourcing,* that generates repository of knowledge from group; *data mining,* which uses combination of various techniques to uncover meaningful patterns; *ensemble learning,* which uses combination of machine learning and statistics modelling to make predictions etc. Hermann et al. (2015) has discussed the various application areas of visual analytics such as in geo special research, climate research, financial market research etc. The main goal of visual analytics as discussed by González-Torres et al. (2016) is to provide meaningful insights from large datasets like stock exchange rates, supply chain management, population distribution, disease trends, forensics, academic, web pages etc. Statistical analytics requires iterative collection of data followed by pre-processing before decision making. A study by Vatrapu et al. (2016) focussed on Sentiment analysis used in social media analysis. The author grouped the sentiments into three categories namely positive, negative and neutral. Customer's sentiments about a product or organisation were uncovered based on the extracted social media data for it. This ensured better sales and product planning strategies.

Big Data analytics finds application in various fields like scientific research, agriculture, social administration, business, social media, commerce, marketing, banking etc. Healthcare analytics is one of the most prominent area for research as it can not only reduce the morbidity and mortality but can even predict potential complications associated with diseases, identify various biomarkers and their correlations etc. This not only lowers significant burden on both family and society but also ensures healthy lifestyle by prevention of many health risks.

In neuro-degenerative research, many studies have focussed on collection of patient data to predict presence of a disease. Tang et al. (2017) applied chi square on data collected through questionnaire to determine the fear of getting alzheimer disease (AD) or dementia, Likelihood of agreeing to be screened or tested for AD or dementia and concern about sharing AD or alike diagnostic information. It was observed that women were most afraid of getting AD as compared to men and caregivers. About 47.1% of respondents were likely to get screened of which most of them belonged to 60+ age group. 30.8% respondents were concerned about getting AD as their family and friends will treat them differently. However, the main drawback of this study is the self supported information with limited response categories for respondents.

Vartharajan et al. (2017) used human motion recognition to detect early stage of AD. Various shapes of gait signals of healthy individuals and alzheimer patients were obtained through sensor device using Dynamic Time Warping (DTW) algorithm. The comparison of gait signals obtained from two groups was done using middle level cross identification function. The research study reports DTW sensitivity and specificity as 95.9% and 94.5% respectively.

Aich et al. (2018) collected voice measurements of 31 people among which 23 were diagnosed with Parkinson disease. Principal Component Analysis (PCA) was used for selection of 11 features from original feature set. These features were used to compare performance of various classification approaches. It is concluded that PCA based feature sets perform better with random forest classifier in terms of accuracy (96.83%), sensitivity (0.9975), specificity (0.9985), Positive predicted value (PPV) (0.9912), Negative Predicted Value (NPV) (0.994) in comparison to original feature sets.

In 2018, Papa et al. (2018) conducted an empirical study on 273 respondents using Partial Least Square Structured Equation Modeling (PLS – SEM) to determine their attitude towards adoption of smart healthcare devices in India. The relationship has been analysed with respect to four main parameters namely, intrusiveness, comfort, perceived usefulness and perceived ease of use of smart wearable health devices. The study shows existence of a strong correlation of IOT application on healthcare industry with performance parameters values as 0.904, 0.906, 0.922 and 0.892 respectively.

In diabetes research, Sandesara et al. (2017) examined the significance of diabetes and microvascular complications in patients having heart failure with preserved ejection fraction (HFpEF). The data was collected from 3385 patients (49% male & 89% white) with HFpEF from the treatment of Preserved Cardiac Function Heart Failure with an Aldosterone Antagonist Trial (TOPCAT). The results of the cox regression illustrated that patients with diabetes and microvascular complications have an increased risk of re-hospitalization because of heart failure and the risk of cardiovascular death increases manifold in comparison to diabetic patients without any complications.

Park et al. (2018) browsed various libraries like PubMed, Web of Science and Cochrane for meta analysis of 14 selected clinical studies. The data was pooled with random effect model to assess the association between urinary or blood microRNA expression level and diabetic nephropathy. The results suggested that hsa-miR-126 family is significantly down regulated in blood for patients suffering with diabetic kidney disease. On the contrary their urinary level was up regulated. It was also noted that hsa-miR-770 family microRNA were significantly up regulated in both blood and urine from patients with diabetic nephropathy. Thus, it is inferred that miR-126 and hsa-miR-770 family microRNA have significant diagnostic and pathogenic implications for diabetic neuropathy.

Machine learning algorithms like Support Vector Machines (SVMs), decision trees, Artificial Neural Network (ANN), Deep Neural Network (DNN) etc. have been extensively used in the literature. Apart from statistical data, image data is also widely used by healthcare professionals to provide better services. A few of the recent research work in diabetic retinopathy has been discussed below.

Pal et al. (2017) evaluated various data mining techniques for prediction of diabetic retinopathy symptoms at an early stage using 18 data attributes based on UCI repository imageset. It was observed that among various classifiers, SVM with linear kernel gives the highest accuracy for both Python and Weka tool as 74.65% and 67.85% respectively.

Wan et al. (2018) evaluated the performance of AlexNet, VggNet, GoogleNet and ResNet models along with parameter tuning and transfer learning for classification of DR. The result shows that overall classification is improved with transfer learning with VggNet-S giving the best accuracy of 95.68% among all classifiers. The remaining classifiers exhibit overfitting due to complex architecture, more training parameters and less training data.

Cao et al. (2018) focused on detection of subtle signs of DR *i.e.*, microaneurysms by using Random forest (RF), NN and SVM. Principal component analysis and RF feature importance are used for feature dimensionality reduction of 25x25 patch size from DIARETDB1 and ROC data before feeding as input to classifiers. RFs with 25 trees, single hidden layer NNs with 10-100 neurons and SVMs with radial basis function kernel have been used as classifiers. For DIARETDB1, SVM outperforms RF and NN using principal component and RF feature importance. For ROC dataset, SVM outperforms RF and NN with AUC 0.870 with 40% PCA. Also, AUC of 0.810 is achieved. Using DIARETDB1 as training data and ROC as testing data, the proposed method can be generalized across different dataset.

Hemanth et al. (2018) proposed a Modified Hopfield Neural Network (MHNN) for DR classification in human retinal images. Six textural features namely mean, energy, standard deviation, entropy, variance and contrast were selected from 256x256 images, thereby reducing its size to 1x6. A modified Hopfield network consisting of 1 input layer, 1 output layer, one set of weight matrix between input-output layer and 6 neurons representing each feature in input-output layer is proposed. 3-Cross validation with 0.01 as predefined energy value is used along with this architecture. The detection of normal images using modified HNN gives accuracy, sensitivity and specificity as 99.25%, 99% and 99% respectively. For detection of DR images, the accuracy specificity and sensitivity values are 99.25%, 99% and 99% respectively. Also, modified HNN shows better accuracy as compared to HNN and other neural network approaches such as feed forward NN, back propagation NN, CNN and Bayesian NN.

Table 2 outlines the techniques and tradeoffs of above discussed data analytics research studies in healthcare.

Application Areas

Big data is a very powerful tool which has led to intelligent decision making in various fields like banking, agriculture, marketing, healthcare etc. Many new technologies and techniques have been developed as conventional systems are inadequate to store and process big data. Such techniques can be applied in some of the fields listed below (Khan & Alam, 2016):

1. **Mass Media:** Analysis of this data has revolutionized the way mass media organizations operate and plan audience involvement strategy.
   a. Identification of exact content with which a customer engages on regular basis has provided new avenues to capitalize on customer's media interests.
   b. Business models namely on-demand and scheduled viewing have been mastered through big data.
   c. Analytics helps in drawing audience attention essentially to gain a competitive edge which further helps to reach target audience in an effective manner.
   d. Analytics can help in behavioural analytics, tastes prediction and affinity of users to specific channels and programs.
2. **Social Data Analytics:** (also known as social big data analytics) helps in gaining meaningful location aware social media insights by analysing facebook, twitter and other social media posts or comments (Gandomi & Haider, 2015). It has also helped in tracking audience behaviour and opinion towards a product or campaign. The insights obtained through such analysis has helped companies adjust their pricing, promotion and campaign placement strategies accordingly.
3. **Text Analytics:** This involves extraction of unstructured textual information to analyse words, cluster of words and documents to gather valuable information. Text analytics can help in spam filtering, predict customer needs and improve long term strategic decision through sentiment analysis, determine opinion of audiences in election polls etc.
4. **Digital Forensics:** It involves capturing, recording and analysing any suspicious activity on the network to locate attack sources and prevent future threats. This requires identification, collection, organization, preservation and presentation of data or evidences collected from internet or local intranets. This further requires employing appropriate measures like server isolation or traffic rerouting etc (Saxena & Kishore, 2016).
5. **Healthcare:** Predictive analytics in healthcare and medical fields can help in timely and reliable prognosis of a disease along with estimating survivability and patient's risk profiles (Verma, Jhajharia & Kumar, 2016). Electronic Health Records (EHRs) that have been adopted in hospitals have helped in deeper understanding of patient disease pattern, associated complications and drug efficacy. This has led to improved patient care and better management of patients.
6. **Call Data Records:** Multiple databases of call data records can be analysed using big data technologies to find links between suspects by identifying phone numbers, call durations, locations etc. This can be used for criminal investigations (Khan, Ansari, Dhalvelkar & Sabiqua, 2017).

Table 2. Data analytics techniques, description and limitation along with future scope of selected healthcare studies

Authors [Ref.]	Technique	Description	Limitation and Future Scope
Tang et al.(2017)	• Chi-Square	The study analyses: • Fear of getting AD or dementia. • Likelihood of agreeing to be screened or tested for AD or dementia. • Concern about sharing AD or diagnostic information.	• Self supported information. • Response categories limited respondents options. • Determine the extent to which a factor influence willingness to be screened and patient worry about getting AD or dementia.
Vartharajan et al.(2017)	• Dynamic time warping	• DTW algorithm compares the various shapes of gait signals collected from AD patients and warps to align them in time. • Gait signal shapes of healthy and alzheimer patients compared using middle level cross identification function.	• Various IOT devices can be used to collect more physiological signals to detect early stage of the diseases.
Aich et al. (2018)	• PCA • Non-linear classifiers	• Feature selection using PCA. • PCA based feature reduction perform better with random forest classifier.	• Use other feature reduction and classification techniques to compare the performance of all the parameters of the performance metrics.
Papa et al. (2018)	• PLS-SEM	• Empirical study on 273 respondents about attitude towards adoption of smart healthcare devices in India.	• Validation of generated insights by investigating other countries through longitudinal analysis.
Sandesara et al. (2017)	• χ^2 test • Student's t-test • Kaplan-Meier • Cox regression	• Examines the prognostic significance of diabetes and microvascular complications in patients with HFpEF. • Observation: increase risk of cardiovascular death over various diabetes and microvascular complications categories.	• Small sample size. • Baseline characteristics are self-reported. • Biomarkers such as HbA_1c have not been collected. • No explanation of mechanism that links diabetes and microvascular complications with adverse events in patients with HFpEF.
Park et al. (2018)	• log odds ratio • SElnOR • I^2 for hetrogenity analysis	• Meta analysis to establish blood and urine-incident microRNAs hsa-miR-126 and hsa-miR-770 as an accurate, stable and reproducible biomarker for diabetic nephropathy.	• Studies examining similar microRNAs are limited. • Quantification variation of qPCR experiments between studies. • Limited studies on evaluation of urine hsa-miR-126.
Pal et al. (2017)	• SVM • KNN • Decision tree • Naive bayes classifier	• Comparison of classifiers accuracy to predict presence of DR.	• Deep neural networks can be applied on image dataset to enhance the accuracy.
Wan et al. (2018)	• CNN	• Performance evaluation of AlexNet, VggNet, GoogleNet, ResNet models along with parameter tuning and transfer learning for DR classification.	• Overfitting problem in AlexNet, GoogleNet and ResNet due to complex architecture, more training parameters and less training data.
Cao et al. (2018)	• Random Forest(RF), NN, SVM • PCA • RF feature importance	• Detection of microaneurysms by Random forest (RF), NN and SVM. • PCA and RF feature importance for feature space reduction	• Generation of two dimensional classifier confidence map based on features captured from all locations in eye and application of RX anomaly detector to improve accuracy of method
Hemanth et al. (2018)	• MHNN	• Modified HNN for detection of DR in retinal images. • Mean, entropy, standard deviation, energy, variance and contrast features were selected from 256x256 images	• Different features and their combinations can be used to improve system performance. • Reduction in size of network architecture by use of optimization techniques. • Development of modified networks with an emphasis on training time for retinal image classification.

7. **Behavioural Analytics***:* Digital data (emails, phone calls, text messages etc), non-digital data (documents, handwritten notes, newspaper cuttings etc), web digital trail (record of pages that have been viewed while surfing, metadata of emails etc) and social media data can be analysed to determine the behaviour of an individual (Baig & Jableen, 2016).

8. **Banking:** Analytics is used in banking industry to differentiate fraudulent transactions from legitimate transactions based on customers past history. Customer segmentation based on customer demographics, daily transactions and interactions has also been employed by banks to plan better promotion, marketing campaigns and provide personalized assessment.

9. **Agriculture:** Biotechnology firms can employ analytics on the sensor data to optimise crop efficiency. Various simulations can be run to measure the effect of environmental changes, water level, soil composition, gene sequencing etc to determine optimal parameters for plant growth.

10. **Marketing:** Business firms analyse customer data to identify reasons why their advertising failed to stimulate interest in a specific product. This also helps marketers to improve sales by developing ads that are more likely to go viral.

Big Data and Healthcare

Big data in healthcare refers to huge amount of data collected from sources like electronic health records (EHRs), medical imaging, genomics sequencing, pharmaceutical research and wearable medical devices. Analytics of such healthcare data, also known as *healthcare analytics*, helps in cost reduction of healthcare facilities including diagnosis, treatment, medication and predicts outbreak of endemic and epidemic diseases. Following are some of the advantages of healthcare analytics:

1. Finds association among factors which influence willingness of patients to be screened for a specific disease (Tang et al., 2017).

2. Develops better communication strategies to increase the likelihood of screening and early detection of heterogeneous disorders (Tang et al., 2017).

3. Identifies relationship between various biomarkers that cause the onset of a disease (Barboza & Ghisi, 2018).

4. Assess temporal disease aspects like changes in outcomes over time in relation to associated biomarkers, timing of disease onset and exploring individual and group patterns caused by the disease (Garcia & Marder, 2017).

5. Internet of Things (IOT) devices can be used to collect patient's physiological signals to detect early stages of neurodegenerative disorders like alzheimer, parkinson, huntington etc (Varatharajan, Manogaran, Priyan & Sundarasekar, 2017).

6. Pervasive computer technologies like eHealth, telehealth etc, along with ubiquitous information and ICT can provide consumer-oriented healthcare services anytime and anywhere (Haluza & Jungwirth 2016).

7. Health guidance through ICT applications can help to reduce body weight, blood pressure and assist long term medical care requirements at considerably lower cost (Haluza & Jungwirth, 2016).

8. Develops training system which can overall improve the physical, mental and cognitive performance of dementia patients (Unbehaun et al., 2018).

9. Machine learning coupled with data analytics can improve accuracy and reliability of disease diagnosis (Aich et al., 2018).

10. Physiological signals that reflect the electrical activity of specific parts of body, can be used to make important decisions regarding diagnosis, treatment monitoring, drug efficacy and assess quality of life (Faust et al., 2018).

Despite various advantages of healthcare analytics, it is difficult to merge big healthcare data into conventional databases due to its diversity in format. This makes it enormously challenging to process and harness its full potential.

TRENDS AND TOOLS IN BIG DATA

This section discusses the major trends and industrial tools being used in recent years to analyse large and wide variety of data.

Trends

The way of collecting and storing data dates back to 1950 when first commercial mainframe computer was introduced. Since 90s, big data and big data analytics has evolved from three main stages: *Big data 1.0* from 1994-2004, *Big data 2.0* from 2005-2014 *and Big data 3.0* from 2015 onwards (Lee, 2017). The various developments associated with big data have been summed up in the Table 3.

Tools

Big data due to its five characteristics namely, volume, variety, velocity, value and veracity cannot be analysed by traditional analytics tools. Big Data analytics tools enable collection and storage of large datasets to analyse them in order to provide new valuable insights. Various tools which can be used in diverse application areas have been discussed in this section (Barua & Mishra, 2016).

1. **Security:** Apache sentry, a big data tool is used to tackle the issue of protecting data from hackers. It is a granular role based authorization module for Hadoop that establishes privileges on data for authenticated users. It consist of (Kulkarni, Bhartiya, Kishore & Gunturi, 2016):

Table 3. Trends in big data analytics

Year	Name	Developments

1994-2004	Big Data 1.0	• e-commerce
		• web mining techniques:
		   o web usage mining
		   o web structure mining
		   o web content mining

2005-2014	Big Data 2.0	• Social media content mining, usage mining, structure mining • Sentimental analytics, natural language processing, computational linguistics • Social network analysis to measure social network structure
2015 Onwards	Big Data 3.0	• IOT applications generating huge image audio and video data • Streaming analytics

a. **Sentry Server:** It manages the authorization to access metadata and supports interface to securely retrieve and manipulate metadata.

b. **Data Engine:** It loads the sentry plugin and routes all client requests to sentry plugin for validation.

c. **Sentry Plugin:** It runs in the data engine and offers interfaces to manipulate metadata and evaluates the requests using the data retrieved from server.

2. **Data Warehousing:** These are central repositories of integrated data from one or more disparate resources. Two major data warehouse systems are:

a. Snowflake is a data warehouse system to safely store, transform and analyse business data. It has data warehouse built on the cloud which can satisfy the modern needs of the customer.

b. BigQuery is a fully managed, petabytes scale and low cost enterprise datawarehouse for big data analytics. It can scan terabytes and petabytes of data in minutes. It can even encrypt and replicate the data to ensure the security, availability and durability.

3. **NoSQL Databases:** Also known as "non SQL" or "non relational" database provides a mechanism for storing and retrieving data which is modelled by means other than the tabular relations used in relational databases. These scale upward for cloud computing e.g. MongoDB, DataStax, Redislabs etc.

4. **Hadoop:** Fast data exploration can take place through Hadoop distributed systems. clouderaImpala is an open source massively parallel processing (MPP) SQL query engine for data stored in computer cluster running Apache Hadoop.

5. **AtScale:** It is a business intelligence tool which allows users to query data as it lands in the hadoop cluster. It involves no data movement therefore; the cost of moving or gathering data into costly hardware is eliminated. It provides virtual cubes which deliver a single semantic layer for consistency, fast performance and data governance.

6. **JethroData:** It is an indexed based SQL engine for Hadoop which enables real time business intelligence work on big data. Initially a onetime Jethro-indexed version of data set is created and stored in hadoop. As new data arrives, it is passed to Jethro to perform incremental indexing every minute. It is mainly used when there are dozens of internal and external customer expecting quick response.

7. **KNIME:** It uses visual programming to manipulate, analyse and model big data. It uses combination of data mining and machine learning to analyse data. Instead of writing programming codes, one has to just drag and drop connection points between activities.

8. **Tableau:** It is a big data analytic tool which allows publishing of interactive data visualizations to web for free. Tableau visualizations can be embedded into blogs and web pages.

9. **OpenRefine:** It is a data cleaning software which operates on rows of data. It offers functionality like: data cleaning, data transformation and parsing data from websites. However it is unsuitable for very large datasets.

10. **R Programming:** It allows statistical computing through a wide variety of statistical tests. R programming comes with inbuilt features like collection of big data tools, graphical facilities, operator suite for dealing with arrays etc.

11. **Splice Machine:** The main advantage of this tool is portability of its architecture across public clouds like Google, AWS, Azure etc. It is dynamically scalable and employs machine learning models to evaluate every querry.

Some of the latest big data analytic tools are SKYTREE, talend, Microsoft HDInsight, Apache spark, plotly, lumify, IBM SPSS modeller etc.

Table 4 shows the process of Big Data Analytics tool that consist of collection of data from large datasets, storage, processing and visualization to provide valuable insights for intelligent decision making (Sahu, Jacintha & Singh, 2017).

Challenges

One of the most obvious challenge associated with big data is management of such large volume of data generated each second. To deal with huge amount of data growth, many enterprises have resorted to use of different tools and technologies like compression, deduplication etc to reduce the amount of storage space required for data storage and analysis. Despite various benefits discussed in previous sections, there still exist some challenges and barriers to big data analytics. Some of the major challenges have been discussed as follows.

1.   **Lack of Data Interoperability:** There is lack of any global standards or naming conventions and metadata (Kulkarni, Bhartiya, Kishore & Gunturi, 2016).

Table 4. Process of big data analytics tool

Step	Description	Tool and Description

Collection	Collection of data from varied sources like
	  • Social media data generated from twitter, facebook, linkedin, google etc.
	  • Machine data generated from enterprise resource planning, weblogs, global positioning systems etc.
	  • Transactional data generated from flipkart, amazon, walmart, ebay.
	  • Clinical data.
		• **Import.io:** Data extraction from web pages.
		• **Octoparse:** Powerful website crawler.
		• **Scrapper:** Free web crawler tool that auto generates smaller XPaths for defining URLs to crawl.
		• **Parsehub:** Web crawler that extracts data from websites using AJAX technologies, cookies, Java Script etc.

Storage	Selection of appropriate file system which scales to large capacity and allows linkage of datasets together across locations.	• **Hadoop:** Distributed storage of large datasets on computer clusters. • **Cloudera:** Data management and analysis. • **MongoDB:** Data management for frequently changing unstructured and semi-structured data. • **Talend:** Real time data integration and master data management for business innovation.

Processing	Transformation of large datasets into valuable formats by
	  • Categorization
	  • Summarization
	  • Matching up
	  • Advanced algorithm and functions
		• **Qubole:** Cloud based Hadoop platform for both structured, semi-structured and unstructured data
		• **BigML:** Dominant machine learning examination for predictive analytics
		• **Statwing:** Simple to very complex visual analysis.

Visualization	Intelligent decision making through accurate and valuable insights of data obtained through new in memory data visualization tools.	• **Tableau:** Generate bar charts, scatter plots, maps and supports live data visualization by database or API linkage. • **Silk:** Creates interactive maps and charts without extra programming. • **CartoDB:** Location data visualization and manage numerous data files and types.

2. **Data Integration:** Data comes from varied sources and reconciling this data so that it can be used for making reports and summaries is very difficult. Despite availability of many ETL tools, this is still one of the biggest challenge in managing big data.

3. **Data Validation:** Data integration and data validation are closely related concepts. Data obtained from disparate sources may sometimes fail to agree leading to data inconsistency problems.

4. **Lack of Data Trustworthiness:** Since data is processed to make critical decisions, there is unavailability of proper auditing or governance to ensure its trustworthiness.

5. **Technical Fragmentation:** This includes failure of internet to function consistently at all points and lack of compatibility in the systems to fully interoperate.

6. **Governmental Fragmentation:** Presence of government policies that prevent use of internet to create, distribute or access resources.

7. **Commercial Fragmentation:** Some business practices prevent the use of the internet to create, distribute or access information.

8. **Inconsistency and Lack of Interoperability in IOT:** This prevents customers from buying IOT products and services due to integration inflexibility.

9. **Erroneous Collection of Data:** There are chances of collection of erroneous or worthless data which can result in transmitting of error to next processing phase and ultimately leading to faulty conclusions (Saxena & Kishore, 2016).

10. **Socio-Demographic Bias:** Bias in the quantity, frequency and quality of tweeting behaviour over gender, age, ethnic and socio- economic group can result in incorrect conclusions (Gruebner et al., 2017).

11. **Digital Divide:** There exist digital divide between rich and low income groups due to difference in frequency of access to computers resulting in under representation of low income group in research studies.

12. **Contextual Bias**: This occurs in social data analysis and exist due to local social norms such as those defined by immediate friends, local trends or national regulations.

13. **Organizational Resistance**: Apart from various technical issues, there may be presence of management issues like lack of understanding, communication and cooperation among employees. This causes difficulty in procurement of big data.

14. **Lack of Skilled Staff**: In order to extract, analyse and generate insights professionals with big data skills are required. To cope with such shortage of talent, many companies have started using machine learning and statistical tools to make intelligent decisions.

Some other challenges may be related to privacy, security issues, information consent, underlying technology used, storage, data mining techniques, technical complexity, obsolete tools, unavailability of regular staff training and technical expert knowledge required for data enabled analytical framework etc.

CONCLUSION

Big data analytics refers to the process of analyzing large volumes of data sets to discover patterns and connections that can provide valuable insights. It is captured from heterogeneous sources including social networks, digital images, sales records, videos, sensors etc. Various application areas of big data analytics include medical data analysis, journalism, social media analysis, behavioural analysis, security, digital forensics etc. Healthcare analytics is one of the most prominent areas of research. It has helped in timely and reliable prognosis of disease by merely analysing patients clinical data. Analysis of EHRs from hospitals can help in estimating patient's survivability, predict future complications, evaluate drug efficacy. This in turn has reduced significant morbidity and mortality due to diseases, thereby promoting better management of risk patients and improved patient care. One of the most challenging problem associated with big data is large data growth per second. Processing of such voluminous data can be done through non conventional tools like apache sentry, snowflake datawarehouse system, BigQuery, NoSQL databases, hadoop, JethroData etc. Healthcare analytics is one of the major areas that have harnessed the maximum potential of big data. It has led to early disease diagnosis along with reduction in cost of healthcare facilities. However, there still exist barriers to big data analytics like lack of interoperability, data integration, validation, trustworthiness, technical, government and commercial fragmentation, erroneous data collection, unavailability of skilled big data professionals etc. These challenges can be overcome by devising and adopting advanced machine learning and statistical analytic tools and techniques employing deduplication, compression etc that can collect, preserve and analyse big data evidences in secured and efficient manner.

REFERENCES

Aich, S., Younga, K., Hui, K. L., Al-absi, A. A., & Sain, M. (2018). A Nonlinear Decision Tree based Classification Approach to Predict the Parkinson ' s disease using Different Feature Sets of Voice Data. In *International Conference on Advanced Communication Technology*. IEEE.

Baig, A. R., & Jabeen, H. (2016). Big data analytics for behavior monitoring of students. *Procedia Computer Science*, *82*, 43–48. doi:10.1016/j.procs.2016.04.007

Barua, K., & Mishra, B. S. P. (2016). Trends in big data. *CSI Communications*, *40*(8), 18-19.

Cao, W., Czarnek, N., Shan, J., & Li, L. (2018). Microaneurysm detection using principal component analysis and machine learning methods. *IEEE Transactions on Nanobioscience*, *17*(3), 191–198. doi:10.1109/TNB.2018.2840084 PMID:29994317

Delen, D., & Demirkan, H. (2013). Data, information and analytics as services. *Decision Support Systems*, *55*(1), 359–363. doi:10.1016/j.dss.2012.05.044

Faust, O., Hagiwara, Y., Hong, T. J., Lih, O. S., & Acharya, U. R. (2018). Deep learning for healthcare applications based on physiological signals: A review. *Computer Methods and Programs in Biomedicine*, *161*, 1-13.

Gandomi, A., & Haider, M. (2015). Beyond the hype: Big data concepts, methods, and analytics. *International Journal of Information Management*, *35*(2), 137–144. doi:10.1016/j.ijinfomgt.2014.10.007

Garcia, T. P., & Marder, K. (2017). Statistical approaches to longitudinal data analysis in neurodegenerative diseases: Huntington's disease as a model. *Current Neurology and Neuroscience Reports*, *17*(14), 1–9. doi:10.100711910-017-0723-4 PMID:28229396

González-Torres, A., García-Peñalvo, F. J., Therón-Sánchez, T., & Colomo-Palacios, R. (2016). Knowledge Discovery in Software Teams by Means of Evolutionary Visual Software Analytics. *Science of Computer Programming*, *121*(C), 55–74. doi:10.1016/j.scico.2015.09.005

Gruebner, O., Sykora, M., Lowe, S. R., Shankardass, K., Galea, S., & Subramanian, S. V. (2017). Big data opportunities for social behavioral and mental health research. *Social Science & Medicine*, *189*, 167–169. doi:10.1016/j.socscimed.2017.07.018 PMID:28755794

Haluza, D., & Jungwirth, D. (2016). ICT and the future of healthcare: Aspects of pervasive health monitoring. *Informatics for Health & Social Care*, *43*(1), 1–12. doi:10.1080/17538157.2016.1255215 PMID:28005444

Hemanth, D. J., Anitha, J., & Indumathy, A. (2018). Diabetic Retinopathy Diagnosis in Retinal Images Using Hopfield Neural Network. *Journal of the Institution of Electronics and Telecommunication Engineers*, *62*(6), 893–900. doi:10.1080/03772063.2016.1221745 PMID:30382410

Hermann, M., & Klein, R. (2015). A Visual Analytics Perspective on Shape Analysis: State of the Art and Future Prospects. *Computers & Graphics*, *53*, 63–71. doi:10.1016/j.cag.2015.08.008

Khan, S., & Alam, M. (2016). The changing face of journalism and mass communications in the big data era. *CSI Communications*, *40*(8),16-17.

Khan, S., Ansari, F., & Dhalvelkar, H. A. (2017). Computer. Criminal investigation using call data records (cdr) through big data technology. In *International Conference on Nascent Technologies in Engineering Field (ICNTE)*. Mumbai, India: IEEE. 10.1109/ICNTE.2017.7947942

Kulkarni, A., Bhartiya, V., Kishore, G.H., & Gunturi, S.B. (2016). Data management: backbone of digital economy. *CSI Communications*, *40*(8), 7-13.

Lee, I. (2017). Big data: Dimensions, evolution, impacts, and challenges. *Business Horizons*, *60*(3), 293-303.

Manyika, J., Chui, M., Bughin, J., Brown, B., Dobbs, R., Roxburgh, C. & Byers, A.H. (2017). *Big Data: The Next Frontier for Innovation, Competition, and Productivity*. McKinsey Global Institute.

Pal, R., Poray, J., & Sen, M. (2017). Application of Machine Learning Algorithms on Diabetic Retinopathy. In *2nd IEEE International Conference on Recent Trends in Electronics Information and Communication Technology*. IEEE. 10.1109/RTEICT.2017.8256959

Papa, A., Mital, M., Pisano, P., & Giudice, M. D. (2018). E-health and wellbeing monitoring using smart healthcare devices: An empirical investigation. *Technological Forecasting and Social Change*, 1–10. doi:10.1016/j.techfore.2018.02.018

Park, S., Moon, S. R., Lee, K., Park, I. B., & Nam, S. (2018). Urinary and Blood MicroRNA-126 and -770 are Potential Noninvasive Biomarker Candidates for Diabetic Nephropathy: A Meta-Analysis. *Cellular Physiology and Biochemistry*, *46*(4), 1331–1340. doi:10.1159/000489148 PMID:29689545

Sahu, S. K., Jacintha, M. M., & Singh, A. P. (2017). Comparative Study of Tools for Big Data Analytics: An Analytical Study. In *International Conference on Computing, Communication and Automation*. Greater Noida, India: IEEE. 10.1109/CCAA.2017.8229827

Sandesara, P. B., O'Neal, W. T., Kelli, H. M., Samman-Tahhan, A., Hammadah, M., Quyymi, A. A., & Sperling, S. S. (2017). The prognostic significance of diabetes and microvascular complications in patients with heart failure with preserved ejection fraction. *Diabetes Care*, *41*(1), 150–155. doi:10.2337/dc17-0755 PMID:29051160

Saxena, S., & Kishore, N. (2016). Big data:challenges and opportunities in digital forensics. *CSI Communications*, *40*(8), 20.

Tang, W., Kannaley, K., Friedman, D. B., Edwards, V. J., Wilcox, S., Levkoff, S. E., ... Belza, B. (2017). Concern about developing Alzheimer's disease or dementia and intention to be screened: An analysis of national survey data. *Archives of Gerontology and Geriatrics*, *71*, 43–49. doi:10.1016/j.archger.2017.02.013 PMID:28279898

Unbehaun, D., Vaziri, D., Aal, K., Li, Q., Wieching, R., & Wulf, V. (2018). MobiAssist - ICT-based Training System for People with Dementia and their Caregivers: Results from a Field Study. In *Proceedings of the 2018 ACM Conference on Supporting Groupwork – GROUP*. Sanibel Island, FL: ACM. 10.1145/3148330.3154513

Varatharajan, R., Manogaran, G., Priyan, M. K., & Sundarasekar, R. (2017). Wearable sensor devices for early detection of Alzheimer disease using dynamic time warping algorithm. *Cluster Computing*, 1–10. doi:10.100710586-017-0977-2

Vatrapu, R., Mukkamala, R. R., Hussain, A., & Flesch, B. (2016). Social Set Analysis: A Set Theoretical Approach to Big Data Analytics. *IEEE Access: Practical Innovations, Open Solutions*, *4*, 2542–2571. doi:10.1109/ACCESS.2016.2559584

Verma, S., Jhajharia, S., & Kumar, R. (2016). Prognosis on wheels: Administrative effort and scope for data science for cancer treatment. *CSI Communications*, *40*(8), 28-30.

Wan, S., Liang, Y., & Zhang, Y. (2018). Deep convolutional neural networks for diabetic retinopathy detection by image classification. *Computers & Electrical Engineering*, *72*, 274–282. doi:10.1016/j.compeleceng.2018.07.042

Chapter 5
Tier Application in Multi–Cloud Databases to Improve Security and Service Availability

Shaurya Gupta
Amity University Rajasthan, India

Ramesh Chandra Poonia
Norwegian University of Science and Technology, Norway

Vijander Singh
Amity University Rajasthan, India

Linesh Raja
https://orcid.org/0000-0002-3663-1184
Amity University Rajasthan, India

ABSTRACT

The need for data outsourcing or database as a service (DaaS) is extremely important for any organization. In addition, data storage or data retrieval cost high especially for small companies. This chapter aims to study the various challenges in cloud computing communication issue. The chapter on multi-tiering a cloud emphasizes security enhancement due to the application of tiers in the cloud such that services availability is also improved. Cloud computing is a recent network trend for advanced communication systems. A lot of research led to the advancements in the areas of newer modes but multi-tiering a cloud is still an embarking issue for the researchers.

DOI: 10.4018/978-1-5225-8407-0.ch005

INTRODUCTION

The need for Data outsourcing or database as a service (DaaS) is significant for any organization. Besides, data storage or data retrieval cost high, especially for small companies. This chapter aims to study the various challenges in cloud computing communication issue. Proposed Chapter on multi-tiering in cloud emphasizes security enhancement in the application of tiers in the cloud and improve services availability.

Motivation and Objective

Cloud computing is a recent network trend for advanced communication systems. Much research led to the advancements in the areas of newer modes but multi-tiering a cloud is still an embarking issue for the researchers. The purpose of the proposed new model by applying tier is to address the security and the privacy risks issues in a cloud computing environment. There are three security factors that h examined in the proposed model, namely data integrity, data intrusion and service availability.

Literature Survey

Mentioned below is the schematic block diagram of a cloud system in Figure 1. It describes how communication is achieved in the cloud paradigm.

Part A is the client side, which sends data inquiries to server or instance such as in Amazon in the cloud service provider (CSP) in part B.

Mohammed A. AlZain, Ben Soh and Eric Pardede in 2011 argued that the data source in part B stores the data in the cloud side which is a trusted cloud, additional to ensuring the privacy of any query that the client has made and for the security of the client stored data.

MCDB provides cloud with database stored in a multi-cloud service provider which is different than Amazon cloud service. MCDB model does not preserve security by a single cloud; rather security and privacy of data preserved by applying multi shares technique (Jijun Lu, Swapna S. Gokhale, 2012) on multi-cloud providers. It avoids the adverse effects of a single cloud, reduces the security risks from a malicious insider in the cloud computing environment, and reduces the negative impact of encryption techniques.

Figure 1. Overview of cloud model

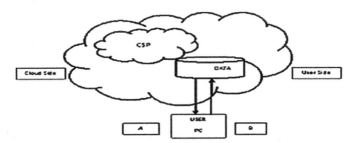

MCDB preserves security and privacy of user's data by replicating data among several clouds and by using the secret sharing approach. Mohammed A. AlZain, Ben Soh and Eric Pardede in 2011 observed that it deals with the database management system DBMS (data source) to manage and control the operations between the clients and the cloud service providers (CSP).

MCDB has three layers the presentation layer, the application layer, and the data management layer. The presentation layer contains the end user's browser and the HTTP server. The management layer consists of the Database Management System (DBMS) and the database service provider. DBMS communicates with the Servlet Engine through the JDBC protocol. According to Mohammed A. AlZain, Ben Soh and Eric Pardede in 2011 communication between components are through a secured private high-speed network that uses secure protocols.

Veluru, S., Rahulamathavan, Y., Gupta, B. B., & Rajarajan, M. in 2015 given an idea to preserve privacy in text analytics applying data mining in several fields of e-mail addresses. They presented a survey of text mining and privacy preserving techniques strategies and challenges in e-mail analysis.

Gupta, S., & Gupta, B. B. in 2017 given an analysis between web application and available development platforms.

Gupta, B. B. (Ed.) in 2018 in his book provided the details about Security and privacy in cloud computing, ad-hoc networks, e-services, mobile systems, WSNs, distributed system, grid systems and many more.

Stergiou, C., Psannis, K. E., Kim, B. G., & Gupta, B. in 2018 presented a survey of IoT and Cloud Computing with a focus on the security issues of both technologies. Authors combine the two aforementioned technologies i.e. Cloud Computing and IoT, to examine the standard features and to discover the benefits of their integration. They also provided the contribution of Cloud Computing to the IoT technology. They surveyed the security challenges of the integration of IoT and Cloud Computing.

TIER IN CLOUD

Cloud Computing

Economic computing resources and advanced network technology is referred to as cloud computing. The security of Cloud computing is considered to be the most critical issue in cloud computing environment due to the valuable stored information for users in the cloud. The opinion of Mohammed A. AlZain, Ben Soh and Eric Pardede in 2011 is that cloud providers should address privacy and security issues. Cloud computing offers dynamically scalable resources provisioned as a service over the Internet. Jens-Matthias Bohli, Nils Gruschka and Meiko Jensen in 2013 explained that the third party, on-demand, self-service, pay-per-use, and seamlessly scalable computing resources and services offered by the cloud paradigm promise to reduce capital as well as operational expenditures for hardware and software.

Tiers in Cloud

Tier in MCDB provides cloud with database stored in a multi-cloud service provider which is different than Amazon cloud service i.e. single cloud service provider. MCDB model does not preserve security by single cloud rather security and privacy of data preserved by applying tiers in multi shares technique on multi-cloud providers. By doing so, it avoids the adverse effects of single cloud, reduces the security risks from a malicious insider in the cloud computing environment, and reduces the negative impact of encryption techniques (Mohammed A. AlZain, Ben Soh and Eric Pardede, 2011). Tier in MCDB preserves security and privacy of user's data by replicating data among several clouds and by using the secret sharing approach. It deals with the database management system DBMS (data source) to manage and control the operations between the clients and the cloud service providers (CSP). The basic idea is to use multiple distinct clouds at the same time to mitigate the risks of malicious data manipulation, disclosure, and process tampering. Jens-Matthias Bohli, Nils Gruschka and Meiko Jensen in 2013 observed that by integrating distinct clouds, the trust assumption could be lowered to an assumption of non-collaborating cloud service providers. Implementing Multi tiers in cloud environment offers security to the application to execute via shared manner. If the application fails, it needs not to be restarted only the previous state needs to resend the data. This feature envisages the fault tolerance mechanism of the multitier cloud system.

Multi Tiering in Cloud

Cloud Communication in Multi-Tier Database

The effective cloud communication is an integration of the following:

- Replication of applications allows to receive multiple results from one operation performed in distinct clouds and to compare them within the own premise. It enables the user to get evidence on the integrity of the result.
- Partition of application System into tiers allows separating the logic from the data. This gives additional protection against data leakage due to flaws in the application logic.
- Partition of application logic into fragments allows distributing the application logic to distinct clouds. This has two benefits. First, no cloud provider learns the complete application logic. Second, no cloud provider learns the overall calculated result of the application. Thus, this leads to data and application confidentiality.
- Partition of application data into fragments allows distributing fine-grained fragments of the data to distinct clouds. None of the involved cloud providers gains access to all the data, which safeguards the data's confidentiality. The architecture of a multi-tiered Web application consists of three tiers namely presentation, business, and data tiers.

Heng WU, Wenbo Zhang, Jianhua Zhang, JunWEI, Tao HUANG in 2013 explained that the multi-tiered architecture extends the standard, two-tiered client-server model by placing a multithreaded application server between the client and the database tiers. In this architecture, the presentation tier consists of a front-end Web server the application tier resides in the second tier which is the home of the business logic, and the back-end database resides in the data tier. The clients consume the services offered by a multi-tiered Web application through high-level and platform-independent calls. The Web server intercepts the calls and redirects them to the application server which performs the processing. Jijun Lu, Swapna S. Gokhale in 2012 observed that the application server makes calls as needed to the back-end database and responds to the client as appropriate.

Figure 2. Partition of application system into tiers.
Reprinted from Jijun Lu, Swapna S. Gokhale "Hierarchical availability analysis of multi-tiered Web applications", Published online: 28 March 2012_ Springer Science+Business

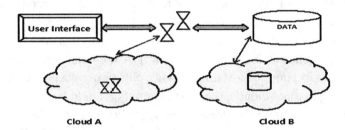

Figure 3. Partition of application layers into partitions.
Reprinted from Jijun Lu, Swapna S. Gokhale "Hierarchical availability analysis of multi-tiered Web applications", Published online: 28 March 2012_ Springer Science+Business

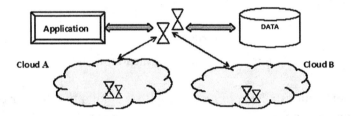

Figure 4. Architecture of a multi-tiered Web application.
Reprinted from Jijun Lu, Swapna S. Gokhale "Hierarchical availability analysis of multi-tiered Web applications", Published online: 28 March 2012_ Springer Science+Business

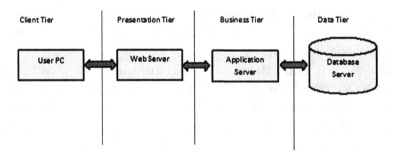

Analysis Methodology

The clients consume the services offered by a multi-tiered Web application through high-level and platform-independent calls. The Web server intercepts the calls and redirects them to the application server which performs the processing. The application server makes calls as needed to the back-end database and responds to the client as appropriate (Jijun Lu, Swapna S. Gokhale, 2012). Multi-tiered Web applications must be systematically assessed for their availability starting from the early phases of their life cycle to enable them to meet the stringent availability expectations imposed on them. Such an assessment should identify availability bottlenecks.

Figure 5. Hierarchical analysis methodologies.
Reprinted from Jijun Lu, Swapna S. Gokhale "Hierarchical availability analysis of multi-tiered Web applications", Published online: 28 March 2012_ Springer Science+Business

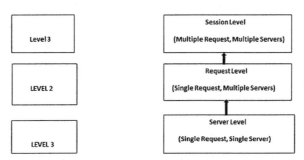

The methodology partitions the analysis into three levels, namely server, request, and session levels.

- **Server-Level Analysis:** A server is a basic unit which lies at the heart of a multi-tiered Web application. Thus, the server-level analysis focuses on the availability of a single server when serving a request.
- **Request-Level Analysis:** A request is a fundamental unit of interaction between a user and the site. A request may visit one or more tiers of a multi-tiered Web application. Thus, at the second level, the availability of a multi-tiered Web application when serving a single request is analyzed.
- **Session-Level Analysis:** A Web user typically interacts with the application through a series of consecutive and related requests. A sequence of such related requests is termed as a session. Since a user's experience will depend on the availability over the entire session, at this level, session characteristics are considered into the availability analysis.

Definition of Three-Tier Application

A three-tier application is a specific type of n-tier architecture. Here three-tier architecture is followed:

Figure 6. Overview of Multi Clouds
Adapted from Mohammed A. AlZain, Ben Soh and Eric Pardede, "MCDB: Using Multi-Clouds to Ensure Security in Cloud Computing", 2011 Ninth IEEE International Conference on Dependable, Autonomic and Secure Computing.

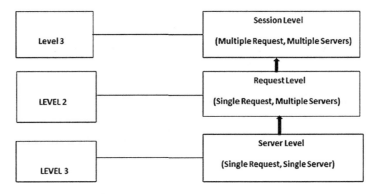

- Presentation tier (also called as the user interface or the client application)
- Business logic tier (also called as the application server)
- Data storage tier (also called as the database server)

Three-Tier Application Architecture

N-tier denotes a software engineering concept used for the design and implementation of software systems using client/server architecture divided into multiple tiers. It decouples the design and implementation complexity, therefore allowing for the scalability of the deployed system.

In a three-tier application, the user interaction is managed by the presentation tier, which provides an easy-to-operate front end. The business rules are managed by the business tier, which controls and separates the entire application framework. The underlying data is stored and served by the data storage tier, which is called data persistence.

The three tiers are loosely coupled to each other, with predetermined and stable interfaces. This decoupling allows for significant changes to occur within the design, implementation and scale of each tier, without impacting the other tiers.

The business rules are removed from the client and are executed in the application server, also known as the middle tier. The application server ensures that the business rules are processed correctly. It also acts as an intermediary between a client application and database server.

The advantage of a three-tier application over a two-tier application is the added modularity. This allows the replacement of any tier without affecting the other tiers and the separation of business-related functions from database-related functions. Finally, a three-tier application significantly increases a system's load balancing, scalability for performance and maintainability (Cachin, Keidar & Shraer, 2009).

Benefits of Middle-Tier Servers

A middle-tier server plays a vital role in a three-tier application. It handles requests from clients, shielding them from the complexity involved in dealing with back office systems and databases (Abu-Libdeh, Princehouse & Weatherspoon, 2010). The middle-tier server might support a variety of clients, such as Web browsers, Java applications, and handheld devices. The clients handle the user interface. They do not query databases, execute complex business rules, or connect to legacy applications. They let the middle-tier server do these jobs for them transparently.

Figure 6 illustrates a three-tier application. Tier 1 is composed of multiple clients, which request services from the middle-tier server in tier 2. The middle-tier server accesses data from the existing systems in tier 3, applies business rules to the data, and returns the results to the clients in tier 1.

Middle-tier servers provide business services to clients. For instance, a middle-tier server in an online shopping application may provide a variety of services: catalog lookup, order entry, and credit verification. Middle-tier servers also provide system-level services:

1. Remote access to clients and back-office systems
2. Session and transaction management
3. Security enforcement
4. Resource pooling

Figure 7. Three-tier client/server application

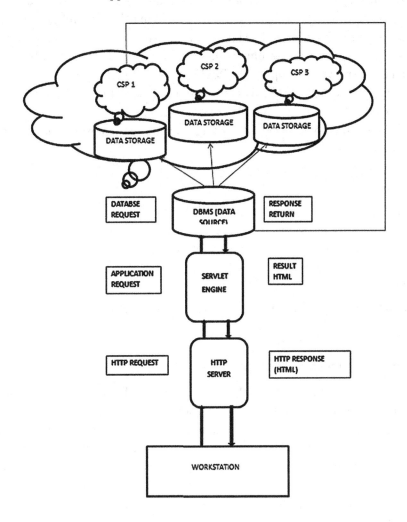

Because the middle-tier provides these services, the clients can be thin, simple, and rapidly developed. You can integrate new clients with existing applications and databases, protecting your investment in legacy systems.

Middle-tier servers enable you to create large-scale distributed applications for the enterprise. The architecture of the J2EE platform makes it the ideal choice for developing middle-tier servers.

The RFC 2060

AlZain et al. give this document in 2011 specify an Internet standards track protocol for the Internet community. The Internet Message Access Protocol, Version 4rev1 (IMAP4rev1) allows a client to access and manipulate electronic mail messages on a server. It permits manipulation of remote message folders, called "mailboxes", in a way that is functionally equivalent to local mailboxes. IMAP4rev1 also provides the capability for an offline client to resynchronize with the server.

IMAP4rev1 includes operations for creating, deleting, and renaming mailboxes, checking for new messages, permanently removing messages, setting and clearing flags, searching and selective fetching of message attributes, texts. Messages in IMAP4rev1 are accessed by the use of numbers. These numbers are either message sequence numbers or unique identifiers. Thus accessing emails from the mailboxes area way easy and efficient when compared to POP3 protocol where the emails are to be downloaded into the host machines before reading them. This is not the case in the IMAP protocol where the messages can be viewed from the server without being downloaded.

IMAP4rev1 does not specify a means of posting mail this function is handled by a mail transfer protocol such as SMTP.

Message Attributes

This topic gives the details of Message Attributes of the mail provided by the IMAP4rev1 in addition to message text each message has several attributes associated with it. These attributes may be retrieved individually or in conjunction with other attributes or message texts.

Message Numbers

Messages in IMAP4rev1 are accessed by one of two numbers, the unique identifier and the message sequence number.

Unique Identifier (UID) Message Attribute

A 32-bit value assigned to each message, which when used with the unique identifier validity value forms a 64-bit value that is permanently guaranteed not to refer to any other message in the mailbox. Unique identifiers are assigned in strictly ascending fashion in the mailbox as each message is added to the mailbox it is assigned a higher UID than the messages which were added previously.

Unlike message sequence numbers, unique identifiers are not necessarily contiguous. Unique identifiers persist across sessions. This permits a client to resynchronize its state from a previous session with the server Associated with every mailbox is a unique identifier validity value, which is sent in a UID-VALIDITY response code in an OK untagged response at mailbox selection time. If unique identifiers from an earlier session fail to persist to this session, the unique identifier validity value must be higher than the one used in the earlier session.

Flags Message Attribute

A list of zero or more named tokens associated with the message. A flag is set by its addition to this list and is cleared by its removal. There are two types of flags in IMAP4rev1. A flag of either type may be permanent or session-only.

A system flag is a flag name that is pre-defined in this specification. All system flags begin with "\". The currently-defined system flags are:

```
\Seen          Message has been read
\Answered      Message has been answered.
\Flagged       Message is "flagged" for urgent/special attention.
\Deleted       Message is "deleted" for removal by later EXPUNGE.
```

```
\Draft           Message has not completed composition (marked as a draft).
\Recent          Message is "recently" arrived in this mailbox.  This session
is the first session to have been notified about this message.
\Recent set for this message. This flag cannot be altered by the client.
```

A flag may be permanent or session-only on a per-flag basis. Permanent flags are those which the client can add or remove from the message flags permanently; that is, subsequent sessions will see any change in permanent flags. Changes to session flags are valid only in that session.

Internal Date Message Attribute

The internal date and time of the message on the server. This is not the date and time in the header, but slightly date and time which reflect when the message was received. This should be the internal date and time of the source message.

Installations Survey

The users attempt to access their emails via insecure networks, Compromise their password, and thus give malicious users a point of entry to the system. M. A. AlZain and E. Pardede, (2011) concluded that as the number of users grows, the risk increases, as there are now more potential access points to the system. So IMAP server that allows creating email-only users who are entirely separate from the local system account database seems to be a more secure answer to the problem mentioned above.

The Imail presents a decent solution to this. It is a higher performance IMAP server that could handle huge mailboxes or mailboxes with a large number of messages. It uses a pseudo-database format. User authentication can be managed through Cache level 2, which integrate with Database to use authentication to allow remote users.

SMTP- the protocol used to transfer messages from one host to another. First, the users interact with the mail reader when they compose file, search and their emails. There is a mail daemon running on each host, and the daemon uses SMTP running over TCP to transmit the message to a daemon running on another machine and daemon puts incoming messages into the Users mailbox. The Sendmail program on the sender's machine establishes an SMTP/TCP connection to the Sendmail program on the recipient's machine, and the mail traverses one or more gateways on its route from the sender host to the receiver host. Like the end hosts, these gateways also run a Sendmail process. Independent of how many mail gateways are in the path, an independent SMTP connection is used between each host to move the message closer to the recipient. Each SMTP session involves a dialogue between two mail daemons, with one acting as a client and the other as a server. Multiple messages might be transferred between two hosts during a single session.

DESIGN OF THE TIERED MODEL

- The browser clients have an email account. The authentication of the users is verified by the server and the valid users are allowed to read their mailboxes.

- They can send emails with the Sendmail as the MTA. Thus the job of Sendmail is to transport mails and is not concerned about the messages inside the body.
- The incoming emails are sent into the respective mailbox of the users.
- Users can read emails from their mailboxes. They can send emails and can delete the unnecessary ones.
- The user details are stored in the MYSQL Database which can retrieve them as needed.
- **JavaMail:** It is one of the most popular Java-based implementations of SMTP (Sendmail Transfer Protocol).
- **IMAP:** Cyrus IMAP (Internet Message Access Protocol) server provides access to personal mail through the IMAP protocol. It uses a pseudo-database format. This provides email only users who are entirely separate from the local account database. The mailbox database is stored in parts of the file system that is private to the IMAP.

CONCLUSION

In this chapter tiered communication has been discussed which communicates with remote clients acting as a middle tier to communicate with servers to provide real-time data as equivalent to a simple two-tier web service. However, here application of tiers introduces more flexibility and improves fault tolerance and thus reliability of the system.

Multi-tier cloud systems are thus efficient enough as upon communication failure entire transaction would not be restarted but only data needs to be resent from the immediately previous tier. This improves the quality of performance of the system.

The system could be deployed with enhancements as a multi-location central communication service as a multi-tier communication channel. Real-time systems such as the operation of railway traffic which demand efficient communication delivery could be deployed as such kind of network infrastructure to provide better systems management and fault tolerance.

Figure 8. Overview of the system

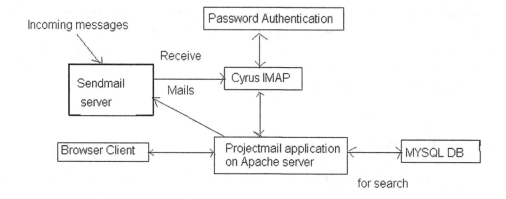

REFERENCES

Abu-Libdeh, H., Princehouse, L., & Weatherspoon, H. (2010, June). RACS: a case for cloud storage diversity. In *Proceedings of the 1st ACM symposium on Cloud computing* (pp. 229-240). ACM. 10.1145/1807128.1807165

Alzain, M. A., & Pardede, E. (2011, January). Using multi shares for ensuring privacy in database-as-a-service. In *2011 44th Hawaii International Conference on System Sciences* (pp. 1-9). IEEE. 10.1109/HICSS.2011.478

AlZain, M. A., Soh, B., & Pardede, E. (2011, December). MCDB: Using multi-clouds to ensure security in cloud computing. In *Dependable, autonomic and secure computing (DASC), 2011 IEEE Ninth International Conference on* (pp. 784-791). IEEE.

Amazon, Amazon Web Services. (2010). *Web services licensing agreement*. Author.

Bohli, J. M., Gruschka, N., Jensen, M., Iacono, L. L., & Marnau, N. (2013). Security and privacy-enhancing multi-cloud architectures. *IEEE Transactions on Dependable and Secure Computing*, *10*(4), 212–224. doi:10.1109/TDSC.2013.6

Cachin, C., Keidar, I., & Shraer, A. (2009). Trusting the cloud. *ACM Sigact News*, *40*(2), 81–86. doi:10.1145/1556154.1556173

Gupta, B. B. (Ed.). (2018). *Computer and Cyber Security: Principles, Algorithm, Applications, and Perspectives*. CRC Press.

Gupta, S., & Gupta, B. B. (2017). Detection, avoidance, and attack pattern mechanisms in modern web application vulnerabilities: Present and future challenges. *International Journal of Cloud Applications and Computing*, *7*(3), 1–43. doi:10.4018/IJCAC.2017070101

Lu, J., & Gokhale, S. S. (2013). Hierarchical availability analysis of multi-tiered Web applications. *Software Quality Journal*, *21*(2), 355–376. doi:10.100711219-012-9176-9

Shamir, A. (1979). How to share a secret. *Communications of the ACM*, *22*(11), 612–613. doi:10.1145/359168.359176

Singh. (2018). *Source Redundancy Management and Host Intrusion Detection in Wireless Sensor Networks*. Recent Patents on Computer Science.

Stergiou, C., Psannis, K. E., Kim, B. G., & Gupta, B. (2018). Secure integration of IoT and cloud computing. *Future Generation Computer Systems*, *78*, 964–975.

Veluru, S., Rahulamathavan, Y., Gupta, B. B., & Rajarajan, M. (2015). Privacy preserving text analytics: research challenges and strategies in name analysis. In *Standards and standardization: concepts, methodologies, tools, and applications* (pp. 1415–1435). IGI Global. doi:10.4018/978-1-4666-8111-8.ch066

Wu, H., Zhang, W., Zhang, J., Wei, J., & Huang, T. (2013). A benefit-aware on-demand provisioning approach for multi-tier applications in cloud computing. *Frontiers of Computer Science*, *7*(4), 459–474. doi:10.100711704-013-2201-8

Chapter 6
Achieving Secure and Privacy-Preserving in Mobile Social Networks

Mohamed Amine Ferrag
https://orcid.org/0000-0002-0632-3172
Guelma University, Algeria

Abdelaziz Amara korba
Badji Mokhtar-Annaba University, Algeria

ABSTRACT

This chapter proposes a security framework for achieving secure and privacy-preserving mobile social networks named ASPP. Based on the cooperative neighbor, reactive routing protocol, and short signatures technique, the proposed scheme can not only detect and avoid but also can preserve the message privacy against elemental attacks and compound attacks. In addition, ASPP is robust against eavesdropping attack, wormhole attack, packet analysis attack, packet tracing attack, and replay attack. Extensive analyses and experiments are given to demonstrate its high detection rate and practicability under various scenarios.

INTRODUCTION

A mobile social network fueled with heterogeneous wireless infrastructures (e.g., cellular/ WiFi) and mobile devices (e.g., smartphones, tablets), which can facilitate multimedia services by providing ubiquitous connections between service providers and users in a mobile environment (Zhang et al., 2014). Mobile social networks still face many security and privacy challenges, including private information leakage, cheating detection, Sybil attacks, DDoS attacks and so on (Liang et al., 2014). Based on spoofed identities, pseudonyms, locations, and profiles, an adversary can launch active or passive attacks (deliberately delays, drops, corrupts, or modifies messages) in order to steal the social data as well as to damage P2P communications (Ferrag et al., 2016). According to the work (Ferrag et al., 2017), the privacy preserva-

DOI: 10.4018/978-1-5225-8407-0.ch006

tion models for mobile social networks can be divided into location privacy, identity privacy, anonymity, traceability, interest privacy, backward privacy, and content-oriented privacy.

In this chapter, to address both security and performance challenges in ad hoc social networks, we propose a security framework for achieving secure and privacy preserving in mobile social networks, called ASPP, for ad hoc social communications. With the proposed ASPP scheme, each node user can be privacy-preserving authenticated before joining other nodes using routing protocol. The contributions of this chapter are fourfold.

- First, we formalize the system model where we consider the social characteristics, i.e., human mobility, human group and preferences in a typical MANET which consists of trusted authority (TA), some stationary social unit (SU) deployed at the social space, and a large number of mobile equipped with WiFi technology moving on a social space. Next, we improve the AODV routing protocol basing on some concepts of social theory to be suitable for ad hoc social communications, i.e., degree centrality, closeness centrality, and betweenness centrality.

- Second, we propose an efficient certificate scheme, where the TA issues the private key SK_{n_i} and certificate $Cert_{TA,n_i}$ using the Schnorr signature algorithm (Schnorr, 1991). The node n_i can verify the certificate $Cert_{TA,n_i}$ by the procedure $S.check$ and cannot use these certificates directly in ad hoc social communication. Based on the proxy re-signature cryptography technology (Toshiyuki et al., 2013), the node request N_y resignature key from S_x and then re-signs the certificates issued by the TA to be the same as those issued by S_x itself. With this method of key distribution, the proposed ASPP scheme guarantees the node identity confidentiality.

- Third, we provide conditional privacy preservation to the nodes with demand response. Although the SU act as certificate issuers in ASPP, they do not know what certificates are held by a node. Therefore, the adversaries cannot trace the interested nodes although they had compromised all SU. Then, to detect and verify the attack against routing protocol, based on three control messages $\{Detectreq, Detectrep, Notifreq\}$, each node initiates a response request and send $Detectreq$ signed to nodes in its routing table at 1-hop, and waits the response of his request for runs the notification phase. After receiving a request response, the node checks its signature. If valid and $TDetect_{n_i} < 0$, it considers that the link with the node is proved. Otherwise, it returns suspicious and starts the notification phase.

- Finally, to validate the efficiency and effectiveness of the proposed ASPP, we integrate in the AODV implementation, being the modified protocol designated AODV-ASPP. Extensive simulation results in the first scenario show that the proposed ASPP scheme can detect the black hole attack more in the configuration where attack is launched on a number of more hops. Thus, in the second scenario, we focus on the transmission delay of ASPP at the node with extensive performance evaluation, which further convinces its practicality.

This work extends our previous work that introduced a new security mechanism for ad hoc on-demand distance vector in ad hoc social network (Ferrag et al., 2013a). In our previous work, we have provided the taxonomy of attacks and their influence on the security property using the AODV as routing protocol. Then, we have presented a security mechanism based on use of two messages $Detectreq$ and digital signatures *Champ _ sig* to detect malicious links. In this chapter, we focus on investigating the privacy of node under the routing attacks.

The remainder of this chapter is organized as follows: Section 2 surveys some related research work. Section 3 presents the system model, the routing improvements, and the research objectives. Section 4 gives some preliminaries, including the secure hash function, bilinear pairings, and the short signatures technique. Then, Section 5 presents the proposed ASPP scheme, followed by the security analysis and performance evaluation in Sections 6 and 7, respectively. Finally, Section 8 draws our conclusion.

RELATED RESEARCH WORK

In this section, we review some of these existing works (Deng, 2003; Deng, 2006; Jian, 2007; Kamat, 2005; Ozturk, 2004; Yipin, 2010; Lu, 2012a, 2012c; Gupta, 2016; Chaudhary, 2017; Stergiou, 2018; Li, 2018;Ferrag, 2018). Generally, to achieve contextual privacy, the existing approaches can be categorized into two types: one is by source location privacy, and the other is by destination location privacy.

- By source location privacy, Kamat et al. (2005) describes two techniques for location privacy: 1) fake packet generation technique in which a destination creates fake sources whenever a sender notifies the destination that it has real data to send; 2) the phantom single-path routing, which achieves location privacy by making every packet generated by a source walk a random path before being delivered to the destination. Another technique to protect the source location privacy is presented by Ozturk et al. (2004) where it requires a source node to send out each packet through numerous paths to a destination to make it difficult for an adversary to trace the source.
- By destination location privacy, Deng et al. (2003) describes a technique to protect the locations of destinations from a local eavesdropper by hashing the identification fields in packet headers, then in (Deng et al., 2006) presents four techniques to protect the location privacy of destination from a local eavesdropper who is capable of carrying out time correlation and rate monitoring. Another technique to protect the destination location privacy is presented in (Jian et al., 2007) proposed the location privacy routing protocol (LPR) for destination location privacy. The LPR algorithm provides privacy to the destination with help of redundant hops and fake packets when data is sent to the destination.

The privacy-preservation scheme has been improved for different types of network. Yipin et al (2010) propose an efficient pseudonymous authentication scheme with strong privacy preservation (PASS), for vehicular communications. Unlike traditional pseudonymous authentication schemes, the size of the certificate revocation list (CRL) in PASS is linear with the number of revoked vehicles and unrelated to how many pseudonymous certificates are held by the revoked vehicles. For achieving vehicle user's privacy preservation while improving key update efficiency of location based services in vehicular ad hoc networks, Lu et al. (2012c) propose a dynamic privacy-preserving key management scheme, called DIKE. Another privacy-related study but for smart grid communications, where Lu et al. (2012a) propose an efficient and privacy-preserving aggregation scheme, named EPPA. EPPA uses a super increasing sequence to structure multidimensional data and encrypt the structured data by the homomorphic paillier cryptosystem technique, and to reduce authentication cost, it adopts the batch verification technique.

Our proposed ASPP is a privacy-preservation scheme with response requested and demand response. Compared with previously reported privacy-preservation schemes, cannot only satisfy the security and privacy requirements of ad hoc but also can detect, prevent and notify the elemental attacks and composed attacks. More importantly, ASPP is the first study on privacy preservation against the routing attacks, i.e., the elemental attacks and composed attacks in this chapter.

SYSTEM MODEL, ROUTING IMPROVEMENTS, AND RESEARCH OBJECTIVES

In this section, we formalize the system model, including routing improvements, and research objectives. We provide an overview of the architecture, and highlight several interesting properties.

System Model

Mobile Ad hoc NETworks (MANETs) have a wide range of applications. In fact, they are robust, inexpensive and adaptable to both urban as rural areas. Among the applications, we include: military applications, operations of rescue, commercial applications, vehicular networks (VANET) or Social Network (VSN) (Lu, 2012). In our work, we consider the social characteristics (human mobility, human group and preferences) in a typical MANET which consists of trusted authority (TA), some stationary social unit (SU) deployed at the social space, and a large number of mobile equipped with WiFi technology moving on a social space, as shown in Figure 1. Furthermore, we use the abbreviation ADSocial in this chapter for ad hoc social network (Ferrag et al., 2013b).

- The TA is fully trusted by all parties in the system and in charge of the registration of SUs and mobile device. The TA can divide its huge precinct into several domains and deploy SUs at the boundary between these domains. The domain information is available to all entities. In addition,

Figure 1. System model

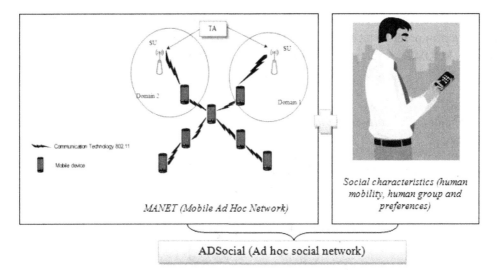

the TA is assumed powered with sufficient storage capability and is infeasible for any adversary to compromise (Calandriello et al, 2007).

- The SU connect with the TA by wired links in the system. They provide service for information dissemination and certificate updating. The certificates issued by a SU can only be used in the domain where the SU is located.

- Formally, such a wireless ad hoc network, as shown in Figure 2, ADSocial can be represented as an undirected graph $\mathcal{G} = (\mathcal{V}, \varepsilon)$, where $\mathcal{V} = \{v_1, v_2, ...\}$ is the set of all node $\mathcal{N} = \{n_1, n_2, ...\}$, and $\varepsilon = \{(v_i, v_j) \mid v_i, v_j \in \mathcal{V}\}$ is the set of edges. Let $d(v_i, v_j)$ denote as the distance between v_i and v_j, the each e_{ij}, which indicates whether there exists a communication edge between two nodes v_i and v_j or not, is defined as

$$e_{ij} = \begin{cases} 1, d(v_i, v_j) \leq R; \\ 0, d(v_i, v_j) > R; \end{cases} \tag{1}$$

ROUTING IMPROVEMENTS

In our work, we use the AODV (Ad hoc On demand Distance Vector) (Perkins et al., 2003) which is a reactive routing protocol by distance vector. We consider a typical wireless ad hoc network which consists of links created by AODV and large number of mobile nodes $\mathcal{N} = \{n_1, n_2, ...\}$ randomly deployed at a certain interest region of social with the area S. In ADSocial with AODV, when a source node $n_i \in \mathcal{N}$ needs a route to a certain destination, and no path is available (the path may be non-existent, have expired or be faulty). The node source broadcasts a route request message RREQ (Route REQuest). Then it records the identifier of RREQ ([RREQ_ID, @ SRC]) in its history (buffer) and associates it with a timer which will count down his life beyond which this entry will be deleted. However, when an intermediate node has no valid path to the destination, it receives the RREQ and then adds or updates the neighbor from which the packet was received. The node finds that the RREQ is already covered; he abandons and does not rebroadcast. Otherwise, it updates its routing table with the information contained in the application in order to reconstruct the reverse path to the source later. To ensure the absence of routing loops, AODV uses the principle of sequence numbers. Upon receipt of a RREQ packet, the

Figure 2. ADSocial under consideration $\mathcal{G} = (\mathcal{V}, \varepsilon)$

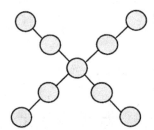

destination adds or updates its routing table in a path to the neighboring node from which it received the packet and a path to the source. The destination then generates a route reply RREP and it sends in unicast to next hop toward the source. When the route reply reaches the source, a bidirectional path is established between the source and the destination and the transmission of data packets can begin.

We improve the AODV routing protocol basing on some concepts of social theory presented in (Batallas and Yassine, 2006; Kamat, 2005; Opsahl, 2010). We consider the following three measures for AODV:

- **Degree Centrality:** In ADSocial, a central node is one that relates to a large quantity of other nodes in the network. Therefore, we propose that groups are formed around the nodes with the densest neighborhood; the node that has the largest number of neighbor's symmetrical hop is considered the center of group. In this way, we are sure that the center of the group is the node that covers the largest number of nodes in group. Thus, the degree of node n_i is equal to sum of RREQ messages received, the centrality of node n_i is calculated by:

$$C_D(n_i) = d(n_i) = \sum_{\forall i \neq j} e_{ij} \tag{2}$$

where $C_D(n_i)$ is the degree centrality of node i; $d(n_i)$ is the degree of node i; e_{ij} is 1 if a route request message RREQ sent by j to node i; and 0 otherwise. However, we distinguish three states:

  - **State (1):** $C_D(n_i) = 0$, node n_i has happened, or he just left his group and has no neighbor in its neighborhood.
  - **State (2):** $C_D(n_i) \neq 0$ and with low density, node n_i part of group members.
  - **State (3):** $C_D(n_i) \neq 0$ and with highest density, node n_i is the center of a group.
- **Closeness Centrality:** A node which is the center of a group can reach the other nodes or groups using paths available in ADSocial. Therefore, the classical definition of centrality proximity is modeling the dissemination of information through the use of shortest paths. Assuming that the network is fully connected, the proximity of a center node n_i can be measured by:

$$C_c(n_i) = \left[\sum_{\forall i \neq j} dr(n_i, n_j) \right]^{-1} \tag{3}$$

where $C_c(n_i)$ is closeness centrality of node n_i and $dr(n_i, n_j)$ is the path between node n_i and node n_j. In AODV routing protocol, $dr(n_i, n_j)$ is calculated by the information in routing table.

- **Betweenness Centrality:** This measure was introduced by Freeman (1978) as a measure to quantify the control of a human being in communication between human beings. In ADSocial, betweenness is focusing on nodes that lie in the path between other nodes, is another one to measure the centrality. The node communicates in AODV with another node uses its routing table to send messages on the shortest path using routing table. Hence, we suggest that if other paths are available in the AODV routing protocol, nodes that have a high probability to occur on a shortest path selected at random between two nodes chosen at random have a high betweenness. More precisely, the formula betweenness centrality of a node can be defined by:

$$C_b\left(n_i\right) = \sum_{i \neq j \neq k \in G} \frac{g_{jk}\left(n_i\right)}{g_{jk}} \tag{4}$$

where $C_b\left(n_i\right)$ is the betweenness centrality of node n_i, $g_{jk}\left(n_i\right)$ is total number of shortest paths from node n_j to node n_k and g_{jk} is the number of those paths that pass through n_i.

Research Objectives

Since the ad hoc social is a large-scale wireless network scenario for public service, it faces serious security and privacy challenges. In the ASPP scheme, we aim to achieve the following security and privacy objectives.

- **Availability:** This property implies that the services or resources requested are available in a timely manner, even if there is a problem or a malfunction in the system. In our context, it is necessary to ensure access to the routing service at any time.
- **Authentication:** This includes user authentication and message integrity. All accepted messages should be from legal members and delivered unaltered.
- **Content Oriented Privacy:** Ensure this property is achieve the following three properties:
  - **Immutability**: This property says that it must be impossible to change a part of the message designated as unmodifiable by the signer, while maintaining a valid signature.
  - **Transparency (Privacy):** It should be infeasible to decide whether a message has been sanitized or not. This may be desirable in applications where one should not be able to discriminate against messages produced by the sanitizer. This property implies privacy. If the adversary against privacy exists, it is able to recover the original message from messages changed. So, it will be possible to use this adversary for construct an adversary against transparency.
  - **Accountability:** It should be impossible to produce, for a person other than the signer, an original signature or a modified signature. So, in case of problems on the origin of a signature, it must be able to properly find that is the origin of the signature.

PRELIMINARIES

In this section, we introduce some preliminaries, including secure hash chains (Mao, 2003), bilinear pairing technique (Grewalet et al., 2013), and short signatures technique (Boneh and Boyen, 2008), which are the bases of our proposed ASPP scheme. In addition, the notations used throughout this chapter are given in Table 1.

Hash Chains

A hash function is a one-way function in particular allowing to reduce a bit string of any size $\{0,1\}$ in a digest of fixed size $\{0,1\}^{\lambda}$ with λ a security parameter.

Table 1. Notations

Symbol	Notation
ADSocial	Ad hoc Social Network
n_i	The node i in ADSocial
$Detectreq$	The message of response requested
$Detectrep$	The message of demand response
$Notifyreq$	The message of notification
T	The current timestamp
$TNormal_{Detectreq}$	Time to send the message $Detectreq$
K	The temporary key
H_1, H_2	A hash function
$S.Init$	Generates an environment bilinear
$S.GenK$	Generates the secret key
$S.Sign\left(K, SK_{n_i}, Detectreq\right)$	Signing the message $Detectreq$ with the temporary key K and secret key SK_{n_i}
$S.Check\left(Detectreq, \sigma_{n_i,Detectreq}, K\right)$	Verifying the signature $\sigma_{n_i,Detectreq}$ of the message $Detectreq$ with the temporary key K
$Enc_s\left(.\right)$	A secure symmetric encryption algorithm with the secret key s
$\|$	The concatenation
Send_Request (C)	Send the message C
PID_{n_i}	The pseudo identity of n_i
SK_{n_i}	The secret key of n_i
PK_{n_i}	The public key of n_i
σ_{TA,n_i}	A signature signed by TA for n_i
$Cert_{TA,n_i}$	A certificate of n_i issued by TA
ΔT	The privacy requirement on the validity period length of a certificate
S_x	The x-th SU
$TDetect_{n_i}$	The attack detection time of n_i
R	The maximum transmission
SD	The speed of light
$SIMS$	Short Inter-Message Space

Definition 1 (Cryptographically Secure Hash Function $\mathcal{H}$): *A hashing function $\mathcal{H} : \{0,1\}^* \rightarrow \{0,1\}^\lambda$, with λ a security parameter, is cryptographically secure if it satisfies the following three security properties. 1) Preimage-resistance, given $y \in \{0,1\}^\lambda$, regardless the adversary, the probability of finding x as $\mathcal{H}(x) = y$ is negligible. This corresponds to the definition of a one-way function; 2) Second pre-image resistance, given $x \in \{0,1\}^*$, regardless the adversary, the probability of finding $x' \neq x$ as $\mathcal{H}(x) = \mathcal{H}(x')$ is negligible. 3) Collision-resistance, regardless the adversary, the probability of finding a couple (x,x') as $\mathcal{H}(x) = \mathcal{H}(x')$ and $x' \neq x$ is negligible.*

Supposing that $\mathcal{H}^i(x) = \mathcal{H}\left(\mathcal{H}^{i-1}(x)\right)$, a hash chain of length L , i.e., $\{S_i\}$, is constructed by recursively applying $\mathcal{H}$ to an initial seed value SD, where $S_i = \mathcal{H}^i(SD), i \in [1,L]$. Obviously, given S_i , it is easy to compute $S_j = \mathcal{H}^{j-i}(S_i)(j > i)$ but infeasible to obtain S_{i-1} .

BILINEAR PAIRING TECHNIQUE

Let $\mathbb{G}_1, \mathbb{G}_2, \mathbb{G}_T$ be three cyclic groups of prime order q . Coupling is an application $e : \mathbb{G}_1 \times \mathbb{G}_2 \rightarrow \mathbb{G}_T$ with the following three properties. 1) Calculable, for all $(x,y) \in \mathbb{G}_1 \times \mathbb{G}_2$, there is an efficient algorithm to compute $e(x,y)$; 2) Bilinear: for all $(x,y) \in \mathbb{G}_1 \times \mathbb{G}_2$, and all $(a,b) \in \mathbb{Z}_q^2, e(x^a, y^b) = e(x,y)^{ab}$; 3) Non-degenerate: there exists g_1 generator of $\mathbb{G}_1$ and g_2 generator of $\mathbb{G}_2$ such as $e(g_1,g_2) \neq 1_{\mathbb{G}_T}$.

Definition 2 (The Strong Diffie-Hellman Problem (SDH)): *Let $\left(q, \mathbb{G}_1, \mathbb{G}_2, \mathbb{G}_T, e, g_1, g_2\right)$ an environment bilinear of prime order q . Given $\left(g_1, g_2, g_2^x, g_2^{x^2}, \dots, g_2^{x^q}\right)$ with x randomly chosen in $\mathbb{Z}_q$, the strong Diffie-Hellman problem is to find a couple $\left(c, g_1^{\frac{1}{x-c}}\right)$ with $c \in \mathbb{Z}_q$.*

SHORT SIGNATURES TECHNIQUE

The technical short signature is defined by the following four algorithms:

- **$S.Init\left(1^\lambda\right)$:** This algorithm generates an environment bilinear $\left(q, \mathbb{G}_1, \mathbb{G}_2, \mathbb{G}_T, g_1, g_2, e, \psi\right)$. $\mathbb{G}_1, \mathbb{G}_2$ two groups of prime order q with g_1 a generator of $\mathbb{G}_1$ and g_2 a generator of $\mathbb{G}_2$. ψ is an isomorphism such as $g_2 = \psi(g_1)$. We note $S.param = \left(\lambda, q, \mathbb{G}_1, \mathbb{G}_2, \mathbb{G}_T, g_1, g_2, e, \psi\right)$.
- **$S.GenK\left(S.param\right)$:** This procedure randomly selects r and r' in $\mathbb{Z}_q^*$ and computes $u = g_1^r \in \mathbb{G}_1$ and $v = g_2^{r'} \in \mathbb{G}_2$. We note $z = e(g_1, g_2) \in \mathbb{G}_T$. The secret key of the signer is:

$$SK = \left(S.param, u, v, z\right) \tag{5}$$

- **$S.Sign\left(PK, SK, m\right)$**: Is the signature algorithm. It takes as input the signing key pair $\left(PK, SK\right)$ and a message m. The signer randomly chooses $r \in \mathbb{Z}_q^*$ such as $x + m + yr \neq 0 \bmod q$ and computes:

$$A = g_1^{\frac{1}{x+m+yr}} \tag{6}$$

The signer obtains signature $\sigma = \left(A, r\right)$ of message m.

- **$S.check\left(m, \sigma, PK\right)$**: With this procedure, the verifier ensures that $\sigma = \left(A, r\right)$ is a signature of the signer, designated by the public key $PK = \left(S.param, u, v, z\right)$, of message m checking the following equality:

$$e\left(A, u \cdot g_2^m \cdot v^r\right) = z \tag{7}$$

If equality (7) is valid, it returns true, otherwise it returns false.

OUR PROPOSED ASPP SCHEME

In this section, we will present our ASPP scheme, which mainly consists of six phases: 1) system initialization; 2) pseudo identity, private key and certificate issued by the TA; 3) node certificate updating; 4) message signature and verification; 5) response requested; and 6) demand response.

System Initialization

Assume that there exists a TA in the system, which initializes the whole system. For side routing, the AODV initializes three control messages $\left\{Detectreq, Detectrep, Notifreq\right\}$, which have the same message format of a route request message RREQ and includes three parts, namely, message signing cost, verification cost, and communication overhead, (including the certificate and the signature, as shown in Table 2). The TA initializes the system by running the following steps.

1. The TA initializes the security settings by running $S.Init\left(1^\lambda\right)$ to generate an environment bilinear $\left(q, \mathbb{G}_1, \mathbb{G}_2, g_1, g_2, e, \psi\right)$, where $\left(\lambda, l_1\right)$ is the security parameters.
2. The TA selects r and r' in $\mathbb{Z}_q^*$ and computes $u = g_1^r \in \mathbb{G}_1$ and $v = g_2^{r'} \in \mathbb{G}_2$, and picks up a random number $s \in \mathbb{Z}_q^*$ as the master-key. TA also chooses two secure cryptographic hash func-

tions H_1, H_2, where $H_1 : \{0,1\}^* \rightarrow \mathbb{G}_1$, $H_2 : \{0,1\}^* \times \mathbb{G}_2 \rightarrow \{0,1\}^{l_1}$, and a secure symmetric encryption algorithm $Enc_s(.)$.

3. The TA chooses ΔT according to the privacy requirements of most nodes and sets the validity period of the certificate equal to ΔT. Then, the TA estimates the number of certificates that a node has to update from a SU once according to the SU density in each domain (Lu, 2012).

4. The TA publishes in ADSocial the public system parameters $\left(q, \mathbb{G}_1, \mathbb{G}_2, g_1, g_2, e, \psi, H_1, H_2, Enc_s(.), \Delta T\right)$ and keeps the master-key s secretly.

PSEUDO IDENTITY, PRIVATE KEY, AND CERTIFICATE ISSUED BY THE TA

When a new node n_i desire to communicate with other nodes, for an SU S_x in the domain D_y, the TA issues the private key SK_{n_i} and certificate $Cert_{TA,n_i}$ as shown in the list that follows.

1. The TA starts to compute the pseudo identity $PID_{n_i} = Enc_s\left(ID_{n_i}\right)$ with the master-key s.

2. The TA chooses a random number $r \in \mathbb{Z}_q^*$, sets the secret key $SK_{n_i} = H_1\left(PID_{n_i}\right)$ and the public key $PK_{n_i} = rg_1$.

3. The TA generates the signature σ_{TA,n_i} using the Schnorr signature algorithm (Schnorr, 1991), where $\sigma_{TA,n_i} = S.Sign\left(s, PK_{n_i}\right)$.

4. The TA securely delivers PID_{n_i}, SK_{n_i} and $Cert_{TA,n_i}$ to n_i where $Cert_{TA,n_i}\left(PK_{n_i}, \sigma_{TA,n_i}\right)$. Then, it stores the mapping between the real ID_{n_i} and $Cert_{TA,n_i}$.

The node n_i can verify the certificate $Cert_{TA,n_i}$ by the procedure $S.check\left(\sigma_{TA,n_i}, g_{1pub}, PK_{n_i}\right)$. With this method of key distribution, the ASPP guarantees the node identity confidentiality.

Table 2. Format of the signed message $Detectreq$

0										1										2							
0	1	2	3	4	5	6	7	8	9	0	1	2	3	4	5	6	7	8	9	0	1	2	3	4	5	6	7
Type								J	R	G	D	U		Reserved										Hop Count			
$Detectreq$ ID																											
Destination IP Address																											
Destination Sequence Number																											
Originator IP Address																											
Originator Sequence Number																											
Certificate														Signature													

Node Certificate Updating

ASPP adopts a restore strategy, wherein each node can obtain a large set of certificates from the TA. But it cannot use these certificates directly in ad hoc social communication. In the domain D_y, only the certificates issued by an SU S_x belonging to this domain are valid. However, ASPP adopts the proxy re-signature cryptography technology (Toshiyukiet al, 2013), it only needs to request N_y resignature key from S_x and then re-signs the certificates issued by the TA to be the same as those issued by S_x itself. Given that the current time window is TW_k, the node n_i can submit the signing certificates $Scert$ to request the corresponding re-signature keys from the S_x.

Figure 3. The flowchart for certificate updating

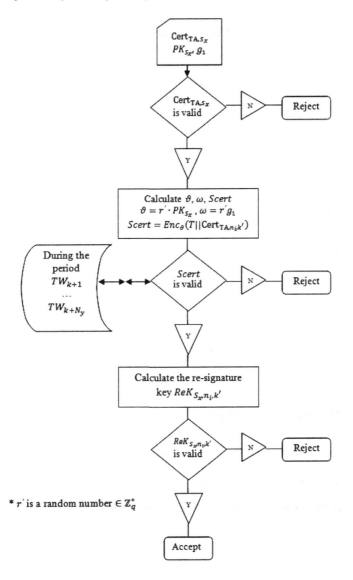

The whole process of certificate updating is shown in figure 3 and the list that follows.

1. The S_x broadcasts its certificate $Cert_{TA,S_x}$ periodically, e.g., every 3 s.
2. The node n_i verify the certificate $Cert_{TA,S_x}$. If $Cert_{TA,S_x}$ is valid, the node n_i selects a random number $r' \in \mathbb{Z}_q^*$ and calculates the shared secret key $\vartheta = r' \cdot PK_{S_x}$ and the hint $\omega = r'g_1$.
3. The node n_i calculates the signing certificates

$$Scert = Enc_{\vartheta}\left(T \parallel Cert_{TA,n_i,k'}\right)$$

where $k' \in \left[k+1, k+N_y\right]$ and T is the time stamp, then sends the request message $(\omega, Scert)$ to S_x.

4. To decrypt the request message and checks whether T is fresh, the social unit S_x calculates the shared secret key $\vartheta' = \omega \cdot SK_{S_x}$, then verify the signing certificates $Scert$ during the period from TW_{k+1} to TW_{k+N_y}. If the verification is valid, S_x calculates the re-signature key

$$ReK_{S_x,n_i,k'} = \left(\frac{1}{SK_{S_x}}\right) \cdot PK_{TA,n_i,k'}$$

for each $Cert_{TA,n_i,k'} \in Scert$.

5. The social unit S_x sends $\{ReK_{S_x,n_i,k'}\}$ back to the node n_i.
6. The node n_i verifies each re-signature key in $\{ReK_{S_x,n_i,k'}\}$ by checking that

$$\left(ReK_{S_x,n_i,k'}, PK_{S_x}\right) = e\left(\left(\frac{1}{SK_{S_x}}\right) \cdot PK_{TA,n_i,k'}, PK_{S_x} \cdot g_1\right).$$

Message Signature and Verification

To sign the three messages $\{Detectreq, Detectrep, Notifreq\}$, the node n_i should use Schnorr signature algorithm, i.e., $S.Sign\left(K, SK_{n_i}, Detectreq\right) \parallel \sigma_{n_i,Detectreq}$ where $K = H2\left(T \cdot Cert_{S_x,n_i}\right)$ is the temporary key, $Cert_{TA,n_i}$ is the certificate of n_i issued by the TA, and SK_{n_i} is the secret key of n_i. After receiving the message $Detectreq$ from n_i, the other nodes first verify whether $Cert_{S_x, n_i}$ is valid and then accept

the message if $S.Check\left(Detectreq, \sigma_{n_i, Detectreq}, K\right)$ is true.

Based on the transmit power, the time of sending the message $Detectreq$, and environmental conditions, the attack detection time $TDetect_{n_i}$ of n_i can be then defined as follows:

$$TDetect_{n_i} = TNormal_{Detectreq} - \frac{R}{SD} \tag{8}$$

where R the maximum transmission of node transmitter, SD is the speed of light, and $TNormal_{Detectreq}$ is time to send the message $Detectreq$. $TDetect_{n_i}$ must be calculated carefully to avoid erroneous decisions. If $TDetect_{n_i} < 0$, there's probably an attack. (See algorithm 1, line 10)

Response Requested

The adversary can delete, modify or copy the control messages to send false messages. However, to detect and verify the attack, each node $n_i \in$ ADSocial initiates a response request (runs algorithm 1) to nodes n_j in its routing table at 1-hop, and waits the response of his request for running the notification phase.

This phase of response request is summarized in the following steps:

1. The node n_i first signs the message with the private key SK_{n_i} and the temporary key $K = H2\left(T \cdot Cert_{S_x, n_i}\right)$. To avoid collisions, he waits the exhaustion of $SIMS$ time. Then, it sends to all nodes at 1-hop in its routing table and continues to the next step. (See algorithm 1, line 1 to 6)

2. After receiving a request response sent by n_j, the node n_i retrieves from R the encrypted control message $Detectrep$. Then, it checks its signature. If valid and $TDetect_{n_i} < 0$, it considers that the link with the node n_j is proved. Otherwise, it returns suspicious and starts the notification phase. (See algorithm 1, line 7 to 19)

3. If the node n_i determines that the link with the node n_j is suspicious. The notification phase (See algorithm 2) is summarized in the following steps:

   a. The node n_i prepares a notification message $Notifyreq$. Then, it removes the adversary node n_j in its routing table 1-hop.

   b. The node n_i sends a notification message to its neighbors. When the neighbor node receives the notification request, it removes the node adversary in its routing table. In the end, the neighbor node broadcasts the notification message to all nodes in its routing table. (See Figure 4)

Algorithm 1. Response_requested

```
    Input: The control message  Detectreq
    Output: The link is proved or suspicious
1:    Begin
2:      Obtain the current timestamp;
```

3:      Compute the temporary key $K = H2\left(T \cdot Cert_{S_x, n_i}\right)$;

4:      Compute $C = S.Sign\left(K, SK_{n_i}, Detectreq\right) \| \sigma_{n_i, Detectreq}$;

```
5:      Obtain the short time  SIMS  (Short Inter-Message Space);
6:      Send_Request ( C );
   7:      When node receive the encrypted control message  Detectrep,
                 recover  Detectrep  from  D ;
```

8:      Compute $\gamma = S.Check\left(Detectrep, \sigma_{n_j, Detectrep}, K\right)$;

```
9:      if   γ = true  then begin
```

10:          Compute $TDetect_{n_i} = TNormal_{Detectreq} - \dfrac{R}{SD}$;

11:          if $TDetect_{n_i} < 0$ then begin

```
12:
return suspicious;
13:
end;
14:                                  else return proved;
15:                          end;
16:   else Begin
17:           return suspicious;
18:         end;
19:  End;
```

Remarks*:*

- In ASPP, a node takes a large number of certificates, but each certificate validates in different time slots. It can restrict the credential misuse.
- With the adopted re-signature cryptography technology (Toshiyuki et al, 2013), the node cannot generate a correct signature for the forged certificate.
- The notification phase (Algorithm 2) is executed after the verification of response message *Detectrep*.

Algorithm 2. Notify

```
    Input: The control message   Notifyreq , the adversary node  n_x
    Output:  R  ready for transmission
1:   Begin
2:      Compute  R = S.Sign(K, SK_{n_i}, Notifyreq) || σ_{n_i,Detectreq} ;
3:      if   n_x ∈ (1 - hop of n_i)  then
4:                 begin
5:                      remove  n_x  in the routing table of  n_i  at 1-hop;
6:                      return;
7:                   end;
8:      else return;
9:   End;
```

Figure 4. Response requested and demand response

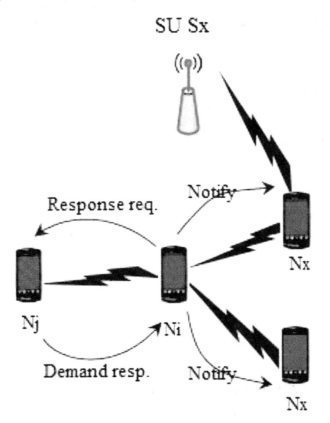

Demand Response

When the node n_j receives request detection, it executes Demand_Reponse () (Algorithm 3).

This phase of demand response is summarized in the following steps:

1. When the node n_j receives the encrypted control message $Detectreq$, it retrieves C and checks its signature $S.Check\left(Detectrep, \sigma_{n_i, Detectreq}, K\right)$.

2. If the signature is valid, the node n_j signs the response $S.Sign\left(K, SK_{n_j}, Detectrep\right) \| \sigma_{n_j, Detectreq}$ back to n_i. Otherwise, the node n_j sends response requested to the node n_i.

SECURITY ANALYSIS

In this section, we first describe the oracles, and then we prove that the proposed ASPP has the content oriented privacy, and conditional privacy for certificate. Finally, we discuss the robustness of the ASPP against elemental attacks and compound attacks.

The Oracles

The semantic security of $S.Sign\left(PK, SK, m\right)$ in ASPP is defined using a game between a challenger and an adversary. Let a polynomial adversary $\mathcal{A}$ trying to gain experience against challenger $\mathcal{C}$. In ASPP, the adversary can use the following four oracles:

Algorithm 3. Demand_Reponse

```
    Input:  C  the encrypted control message  Detectreq
    Output:  D  the encrypted control message  Detectrep
1: Begin
2:     Obtain the current timestamp  ;
3:     Compute the temporary key  K = H2(T · Cert_{S_x,n_j})  ;
4:     Compute D = S.Sign(K, SK_{n_j}, Detectrep) ‖ σ_{n_j,Detectreq}  ;
5:     When node receive the encrypted control message  Detectreq,
               recover  Detectreq from  C  ;
6:      Compute  γ = S.Check(Detectreq, σ_{n_i,Detectreq}, K);
7:      if   γ = true  then Send_reponse  (D, n_i)  ;
8:                          Else Response_requested ()  ;
9:    End;
```

- $\mathcal{O}.\boldsymbol{Sign}\left(\boldsymbol{m},\boldsymbol{PK},\boldsymbol{VAB}\right)$ allows the adversary $\mathcal{A}$ to obtain an original signature on a message m of his choice with the signer's public key PK and the variable VAB that the adversary has set.

- $\mathcal{O}.\boldsymbol{Modify}\left(\boldsymbol{m},\boldsymbol{\sigma},\boldsymbol{ALT}\right)$ allows the adversary $\mathcal{A}$ to modify a pair of message-signing $\left(m,\sigma\right)$ choice with the changes ALT that it wishes. The oracle returns a modified signing valid if changes are eligible and $\perp$ when error.

- $\mathcal{O}.\boldsymbol{Prove}\left(\boldsymbol{m},\boldsymbol{\sigma},\boldsymbol{DB}\right)$ allows the adversary $\mathcal{A}$ to obtain proof of the origin of a pair message-signing $\left(m,\sigma\right)$ according a database $DB = \left\{\left(m_k, \sigma_k\right)\right\}_{k\in[1,q]}$.

- $\mathcal{O}.\boldsymbol{Sign}\,/\,\boldsymbol{Modify}_b\left(\boldsymbol{m},\boldsymbol{VAB},\boldsymbol{MOD}\right)$ allows the adversary $\mathcal{A}$ to take as input a message m, VAB and MOD. The oracle returns $\perp$ if MOD does not match with VAB. If $b = 0$, it returns an original signature of signatory on m' (m' is the corresponding message to the message m modified by MOD). And if $b = 1$, it performs an original signature of signatory on the message m by VAB and modify it by MOD.

Content Oriented Privacy

In our proposed ASPP, the content-oriented privacy can be guaranteed by the security of $S.Sign\left(PK,SK,m\right)$. If the ciphertext $S.Sign\left(PK,SK,m\right)$ is provably secure, so does the content oriented privacy in ASPP. Therefore, we will prove the semantic security property of $S.Sign\left(PK,SK,m\right)$ by using the techniques from provable security proved by Brzuska et al. (2009).

Theorem 1: Let $\left(q,\mathbb{G}_1,\mathbb{G}_2,\mathbb{G}_T,e,g_1,g_2\right)$ *be an environment bilinear of prime order,* λ *a security parameter and* $\mathcal{A}$ *be a polynomial adversary in ASPP seeking to gain experience against challenger* $\mathcal{C}$. *This adversary can access to the four oracles:*

$\mathcal{O}.Sign\left(m,PK,VAB\right),$

$\mathcal{O}.Modify\left(m,\sigma,ALT\right),$

$\mathcal{O}.Prove\left(m,\sigma,DB\right)$

$\mathcal{O}.Sign\,/\,Modify_b\left(m,VAB,MOD\right).$

The ASPP scheme is secure, i.e., it is immutable, transparent, and accountable.

Proof: We stepwise go through the properties. Most times we describe each property for ASPP.

Immutability

Definition 3 (ASPP Immutability): *Let λ be a security parameter, $S.Init\left(1^{\lambda}\right)$ an initialization algorithm and $S.GenK$ a key generation algorithm of signer $\left(PK, SK\right)$. Let $\mathcal{A}$ an adversary with access to the signing oracle $\mathcal{O}.Sign\left(m, PK, VAB\right)$ and the oracle of prove $\mathcal{O}.Prove\left(m, \sigma, DB\right)$. We consider the following random experiment:*

Experiment $EXP_{\operatorname{Im} m, \mathcal{A}}^{ASPP}\left(\lambda\right)$

$S.param \leftarrow S.Init\left(1^{\lambda}\right)$

$\left(PK, SK\right) \leftarrow S.GenK\left(S.param\right)$

$\left(m^{*}, \sigma^{*}, PK^{*}\right) \leftarrow \mathcal{A}^{Sign, Prove}\left(S.param, PK\right)$

if $S.check\left(m^{*}, \sigma^{*}, PK^{*}\right) =$ true then $b \leftarrow 1$ else $b \leftarrow 0$

return b

We define the success of the adversary polynomial $\mathcal{A}$ in the experiment $EXP_{\operatorname{Im} m, \mathcal{A}}^{ASPP}\left(\lambda\right)$ via:

$$Succ_{\operatorname{Im} m, \mathcal{A}}^{ASPP}\left(\lambda\right) = \Pr\left[1 \leftarrow EXP_{\operatorname{Im} m, \mathcal{A}}^{ASPP}\left(\lambda\right)\right] \tag{9}$$

The ASPP is said to be $\left(\lambda, t, \epsilon\right)$ immutable secure, if no adversary $\mathcal{A}$ running in time t has a success $Succ_{\operatorname{Im} m, \mathcal{A}}^{ASPP}\left(\lambda\right) < \epsilon$, with ϵ negligible.

Transparency (Privacy)

Definition 4 (ASPP Transparency): *Let λ be a security parameter, $S.Init\left(1^{\lambda}\right)$ an initialization algorithm and $S.GenK$ a key generation algorithm of signer $\left(PK, SK\right)$ and b one bit chooses randomly. Let $\mathcal{A}$ an adversary with access to the four oracles: $\mathcal{O}.Sign\left(m, PK, VAB\right)$, $\mathcal{O}.Modify\left(m, \sigma, ALT\right)$, $\mathcal{O}.Prove\left(m, \sigma, DB\right)$ and $\mathcal{O}.Signe / Modify_{b}\left(m, VAB, MOD\right)$. If $b = 0$, the oracle of challenge returns a signature ; or a signature changed if $b = 1$. We consider the following random experiment:*

$Experiment\ EXP_{Transp,\mathcal{A}}^{ASPP}\left(\lambda\right)$

$S.param \leftarrow S.Init\left(1^{\lambda}\right)$

$\left(PK.SK\right) \leftarrow S.GenK\left(S.param\right)$

$b \leftarrow \left\{0,1\right\}$

$b^{*} \leftarrow \mathcal{A}^{Signe,Modify,Prove,Signe/Modify_{b}}\left(S.param,PK\right)$

if $b^{*} = b$ then $a \leftarrow 1$ else $a \leftarrow 0$

return a

We define the advantage of the adversary polynomial $\mathcal{A}$ in the experiment $EXP_{Transp,\mathcal{A}}^{ASPP}\left(\lambda\right)$ via:

$$Adv_{Transp,\mathcal{A}}^{ASPP}\left(\lambda\right) =\mid \Pr\left[1 \leftarrow EXP_{Transp,\mathcal{A}}^{ASPP}\left(\lambda\right)\right] - \frac{1}{2} \tag{10}$$

The ASPP is said to be $\left(\lambda,t,\epsilon\right)$ transparent secure, if no adversary $\mathcal{A}$ running in time t has an advantage $Adv_{Transp,\mathcal{A}}^{ASPP}\left(\lambda\right) < \epsilon$, with ϵ negligible.

Accountability

Definition 6.3 (ASPP Accountability): *Let λ be a security parameter, $S.Init\left(1^{\lambda}\right)$ an initialization algorithm and $S.GenK$ a key generation algorithm of signer $\left(PK,SK\right)$. Let $\mathcal{A}$ an adversary with access to the oracle of change $\mathcal{O}.Modify\left(m,\Sigma,ALT\right)$ and returns a quadruplet $\left(SK^{*},\pi_{or/ALT}^{*},m^{*},\sigma^{*}\right)$. We consider the following random experiment:*

$Experiment\ EXP_{Acc,\mathcal{A}}^{ASPP}\left(\lambda\right)$

$S.param \leftarrow S.Init\left(1^{\lambda}\right)$

$\left(PK.SK\right) \leftarrow S.GenK\left(S.param\right)$

$$\left(PK^*, \pi^*_{or/ALT}, m^*, \Sigma^*\right) \leftarrow \mathcal{A}^{Modify}\left(S.param, PK\right)$$

Let $\left(m'_k, \sigma'_k\right)_{k \in [1,n]}$ the response of the oracle modified

if $S.check\left(m^*, \sigma^*, PK^*\right) = \text{tru}$

and $(PK^*, m^*) \neq (PK^*_k, m^*_k)$ where $k \in \left[1, n\right]$

then $a \leftarrow 1$ else $a \leftarrow 0$

return a

We define the success of the adversary polynomial $\mathcal{A}$ in the experiment $EXP^{ASPP}_{Acc,\mathcal{A}}\left(\lambda\right)$ via:

$$Succ^{ASPP}_{Acc,\mathcal{A}}\left(\lambda\right) = \Pr\left[1 \leftarrow EXP^{ECPDR}_{Acc,\mathcal{A}}\left(\lambda\right)\right] \tag{10}$$

The ASPP is said to be $\left(\lambda, t, \epsilon\right)$ accountable secure, if no adversary $\mathcal{A}$ running in time t has a success $Succ^{ASPP}_{Acc,\mathcal{A}}\left(\lambda\right) < \epsilon$, with $\in$ negligible

This completes the proof.

Conditional Privacy for Certificate

In ASPP, conditional privacy for certificate is preserved by re-signature technology where SU S_x acts as the certificate issuer for the node n_i and only the certificates issued by an SU S_x belonging to this domain are valid. With adopts the proxy re-signature cryptography technology (Toshiyukiet al, 2013), SU S_x has no idea about infringing on n_i's privacy.

Robustness

In this subsection, we discuss the robustness of ASPP. Specifically, we show how the ASPP prevents known attacks against the routing protocols, as elementary attacks and compound attacks. Both types of attacks affect the privacy of messages and the performance of routing protocols in ad hoc social communications.

- **Resistance Against Elemental Attacks:** An adversary could make the following four basic actions on messages:
  ○ Deleting a message, the adversary does not participate in routing, it's like he is not part of the social network.

    ◦   Modification of a message, the adversary can play the sequence number of the destination and / or the number of hops in control messages by increasing the first and decreasing the second.

    ◦   Manufacture of a message, the adversary can be made operational without being picked on the path. Like making a route reply even if no valid path to the destination.

    ◦   Reduce the time, the adversary can reduce the processing time for control messages and re-transmit faster so they reach the destination more quickly. This will ensure for the adversary a place on the path.

These attacks do not affect ASPP proposed because the node checked the validity of received message with $S.Check$. If message is not valid, it will be directly eliminated.

- **Resistance Against Compound Attacks**: An adversary can combine elemental attacks to perform compound attacks potential to achieve more advanced goals. As insertion into an already established route or not yet established, the creation of a routing loop or tunnel. However, the ASPP can detect and check the compound attacks and then notify other nodes, by use of control messages($Detectreq$, $Detectrep$, $Notifyreq$) and authentication of this messages based on pseudo identity, the private key and certificate issued by the TA have been integrated in the proposed ASPP.

PERFORMANCE EVALUATION

To evaluate the proposed ASPP, we conducted simulations in two different scenarios. Our proposals were integrated in the AODV implementation, being the modified protocol designated AODV-ASPP. In this section, we first introduce the used simulation environment and afterwards present our simulation results for each scenario.

Scenario 1

In the first scenario, we evaluate the effectiveness of ASPP against black hole attack (Kamatchi et al., 2013) on reactive routing AODV using the simulator Ns-2 (Information Sciences Institute, 2007) configured with the standard IEEE 802.11 (11 Mbps and 2 Mbps were used to transmit unicast and broadcast traffic, respectively). We generated a number of random topologies with N nodes on a square field, where N is between 30 to 80 square field size varies of 600x600m to 1500x1500m depending on the size of ADSocial. The maximum transmission range is πR^2 and traffic model is CBR.

Let $P_{k.neigh.adversary}$ denote the probability that there are at least k neighbors in the transmission range πR^2 of an adversary node with the area S, then

$$P_{k.neigh.adversary} = P(N \geq k \mid \pi R^2)$$

$$= 1 - P\left(N < k \mid \pi R^2\right)$$

$$= 1 - \sum_{i=0}^{k-1} P\left(N = i \mid \pi R^2\right) \tag{11}$$

$$= 1 - \sum_{i=0}^{k-1} \binom{|\mathcal{V}|}{i} \left(\frac{\pi R^2}{S}\right)^i \cdot \left(1 - \frac{\pi R^2}{S}\right)^{|\mathcal{V}|-i}$$

And the black hole detection rate D_r

$$D_r = \frac{1}{T_{detect}} \tag{12}$$

where T_{detect} is the detection time of black attack.

Figure 5 shows the probability of k neighbors of an adversary $P_{k.neigh.adversary}$ in a parameterized wireless ad hoc social network with different k, ($1 \le k \le 20$). It can be seen the expected high probability of black hole attack can be achieved when choosing a proper k, i.e., $k \le 5$.

Figure 6 (a,b,c) shows the black hole detection rate D_r varies with the tunnel length which is the number of hops between the adversary nodes, where $k = 5$ and $R = 10m, 15m, 20m$. As seen in Figure 6, the black hole detection rate D_r rises with the increase of R on the whole. For the same R, the black

Figure 5. Probability of k neighbors of an adversary $P_{k.neigh.adversary}$ with $S = 200 \times 200\,m^2$, $R = 5m, 10m, 15m, 20m$, $|\mathcal{V}| = 100$, and $1 \le k \le 20$

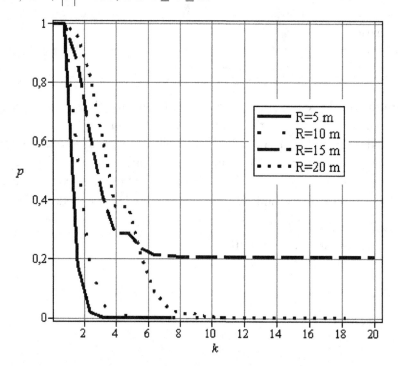

Figure 6. The black hole detection rate D_r varies with the tunnel length

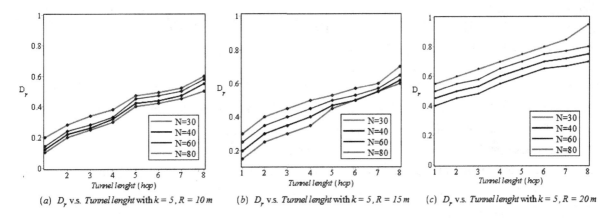

(a) D_r v.s. *Tunnel lenght* with $k = 5, R = 10\,m$ (b) D_r v.s. *Tunnel lenght* with $k = 5, R = 15\,m$ (c) D_r v.s. *Tunnel lenght* with $k = 5, R = 20\,m$

Figure 7. The black hole detection rate D_r varies for different HELLO emission interval T_{Hello} (s) and different the black hole attack duration

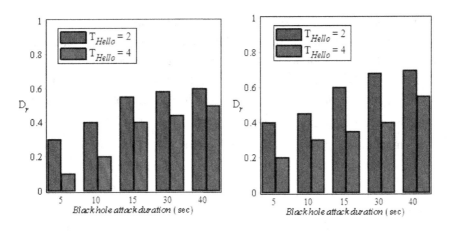

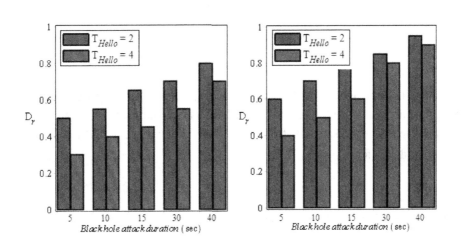

hole attack is detected more in the configuration where attack is launched on a number of more hops. That is obvious fact, as through the link of hole, packets are encapsulated. In addition, from Figure 6, we can also roughly observe the relation between D_r and the number of node N, i.e., with the increase of N, the black hole detection rate will also increase.

To further discuss on the black hole detection rate, Figure 7 (a,b,c,d) shows the black hole detection rate D_r varies for different HELLO emission T_{Hello} interval and different the black hole attack duration, where $k = 5$ and $R = 10m, 15m, 20m, 25m$. As seen in Figure 7, if the black attack duration is shorter than black hole detection rate D_r becomes poor (i.e., less than 0.55). This is due to the fact that there are some nodes that do not perform the algorithm 1 and algorithm 2. As seen in Figure 6, also in Figure 7, the black hole detection rate D_r rises with the increase of R on the whole. This result demonstrates the impact of T_{Hello} on the detection time. If T_{Hello} emission interval is long enough, then it takes more time to detect. Therefore, the ECDPR scheme needs to use small message emission intervals. In addition, the earlier the black hole attacks are detected, the more energy can be saved in the whole network.

Scenario 2

An important performance metric in ADSocial systems is how long it takes for a node sends the message, i.e., *Detectreq* to reach its neighboring nodes. Thus, in the second scenario, we focus on the transmission delay of ASPP at the node. Roughly, the computation costs of ASPP include, detection, verification and notify of attack, which mainly involve the following cryptographic operations: authentication, genk, encrypt, decrypt, multiplication in Z_q^* and hash operations. We implement the Tate pairing with an embedding degree k = 2 Cocks-Pinch (CP-80) curve. CP-80 is over $\mathbb{F}_p$ with 512 bit prime p. Then, we implement the Ate paring with an embedding degree k = 6 Miyaji-Nakabayashi-Takano curve (MNT-80). MNT-80 is $\mathbb{F}_{p^3}$ with 160 bit prime p. Benchmarks for the selected pairing were running on a modern workstation, where the processor is 64-bit Intel i5 520M, clocked at 2.4GHz. The measured results are given in Table 3. Based on these benchmark numbers and the adopted Inner-Product Predicate Encryption (IPE) (Park, 2011), we can estimate the computation costs in ASPP, and the relevant results are given in Table 4 (Scott, 2011).

Then, we have

$$\mu = \begin{cases} 169.3 \ / \ s, w \ / \ o \ pairing \ precomputation; \\ 377.3 \ / \ s, with \ pairing \ precomputation. \end{cases}$$

Next we evaluate the transmission delay of ASPP. Based on the M/D/1 process (Donald, 2008), we consider the average arrival of *Detectreq* at the node is a Poisson process with arrival Rate λ, departure rate μ, and move the process from state i to $i + 1$. The average delay time of Detectreq before being put into the node buffer is t_v,

$$t_v = \frac{1}{\mu} \cdot \frac{2 - \rho}{2 - 2\rho} \text{ , where } \rho = \frac{\lambda}{\mu} \tag{13}$$

Table 3. Time costs of required operations

Curve	CP-80		MNT-80	
G_2 type	$\mathbb{F}_p$		$\mathbb{F}_{p^3}$	
k	2		6	
Modulus (bits)	512		160	
Paring	Tate		Ate	
with/without precomp.	w	w/o	w	w/o
GenK	0.207ms	1.020ms	0.663ms	2.239ms
Encrypt	0.366ms	1.695ms	0.194ms	0.767ms
Decrypt 2	1.213ms	2.360ms	1.392ms	3.788ms
Decrypt *	0.834ms	1.991ms	1.043ms	3.383ms

2: 2 pairings / *: multi-pairing

Table 4. Time costs of required operations in ASPP

Curve	CP-80		MNT-80	
With/Without Precomp.	w	w/o	w	w/o
Detectreq authentication				
Encrypt $\left(t_e \right)$	0.207ms	1.020ms	0.663ms	2.239ms
	0.366ms	1.695ms	0.194ms	0.767ms
Decrypt $\left(t_d \right)$	1.213ms	2.360ms	1.392ms	3.788ms

By broadcasting *Detectreq*, encrypt and decrypt can be reduced. However, this mechanism will incur the transmission delay. In addition, the black hole attack will also cause the transmission delay. Let the invalid probability of a *Detectreq* arriving at node be p due to the black hole attack. We study the average delay time in buffer of the node as follows. We first consider how long it takes the i-th *Detectreq* in the node to wait for the arrival of the next $i+1$-th Detectreq. Since the invalid probability of a *Detectreq* is p, when a valid *Detectreq* is put into buffer of the node, the number of *Detectreq* authentications at the node is a geometrically distributed random variable:

$$P(\text{ number of authentication } = k) = p^{k-1}\left(1-p\right) \tag{14}$$

where $= 1, 2, \cdots$. We define $t_{i(i+1)}$ to be the average waiting time,

$$t_{i(i+1)} = \sum_{k=1}^{\infty} \frac{k}{\mu} \cdot p^{k-1}\left(1-p\right) = \frac{1}{\mu\left(1-p\right)} \tag{15}$$

For $i = 1, 2, \cdots, n-1$. Also, for the trivial case $i = n$, $t_{ii} = t_{nn} = 0$. Thus, before *Detectrep* is sent, the waiting time for each *Detectreq* in buffer of the node is

$$T_i = \begin{cases} \dfrac{n-i}{\mu(1-p)}, & i = 1, 2, \cdots, n-1; \\ \\ 0, & i = n. \end{cases} \tag{16}$$

And the average waiting time is

$$t_w = \sum_{i=1}^{n} \frac{1}{n} T_i = \frac{1}{n} \cdot \frac{1}{\mu(1-p)} \cdot \left(1 + 2 + \cdots + (n-1)\right)$$

$$= \frac{1}{n} \cdot \frac{1}{\mu(1-p)} \cdot \frac{n(n-1)}{2}$$

$$= \frac{1}{n} \cdot \frac{n(n-1)}{2\mu(1-p)}$$

and the transmission delay t_r of ASPP at the node in status the receiver node is

$$t_r = t_v + t_w + t_d = \frac{2-\rho}{2\mu(1-\rho)} + \frac{n-1}{2\mu(1-p)} + t_d, \ \rho = \frac{\lambda}{\mu} < 1 \tag{18}$$

Fixing the parameters n and p, Figure 8 (a,b,c,d,e,f) shows the transmission delay t_r varies with the average arrival rate λ, where $1 \leq \lambda \leq 100$. As seen in Figure 8, the transmission delay t_r rises with the increase of λ on the whole. Also, the transmission delay t_r with Cocks-Pinch curve (CP-80) is less than that Miyaji-Nakabayashi-Takano curve (MNT-80). This result indicates that CP-80 the transmission delay could be reduced when the performance of the mobile device (the node) is improved. In addition, from Figure 8, we can also roughly observe the relation between t_r and p, n, i.e., with the increase of p and n, the transmission delay t_r will also increase.

To further discuss the relation subtly, we plot t_r varies with p and n in Figure 9, where λ is fixed as 100. It can be seen that for small p, the transmission delay increases very slowly with n. However, for large p, the transmission delay increases quickly. This indicates that the parameter p due to the black hole attack is the dominant factor for the transmission delay. Therefore, for small, the proposed scheme can gain a good performance in terms of transmission delay. Also, the difference between Figure 9(a), Figure 9(b), Figure 9(c) and Figure 9(d) demonstrates that the precomputation of CP-80 can reduce the transmission delay. In addition, the implementation of cryptographic methods used by ASPP on another type of processor, such as ARM-M series and Intel Atom, is underway.

Figure 8. Average transmission delay t_r varies with the average arrival rate λ, where $1 \leq \lambda \leq 100$

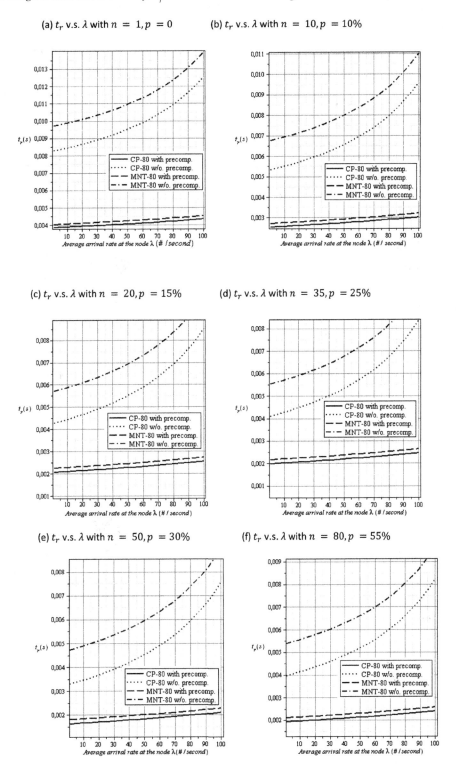

(a) t_r v.s. λ with $n = 1, p = 0$

(b) t_r v.s. λ with $n = 10, p = 10\%$

(c) t_r v.s. λ with $n = 20, p = 15\%$

(d) t_r v.s. λ with $n = 35, p = 25\%$

(e) t_r v.s. λ with $n = 50, p = 30\%$

(f) t_r v.s. λ with $n = 80, p = 55\%$

Figure 9. Average transmission delay t_r varies with p and n, where $1\% \leq p \leq 80\%$ and $1 \leq n \leq 100$

(a) t_r v.s. n and p with $\lambda = 100$

w/o pairing precomput. (CP-80)

(b) t_r v.s. n and p with $\lambda = 100$

with pairing precomput. (CP-80)

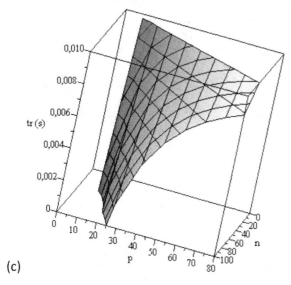

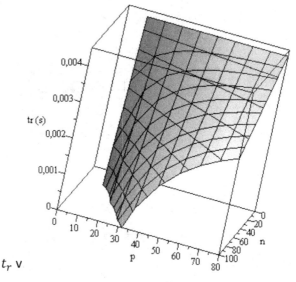

(c)

t_r v

w/o pairing precomput. (MNT-80)

with pairing precomput. (MNT-80)

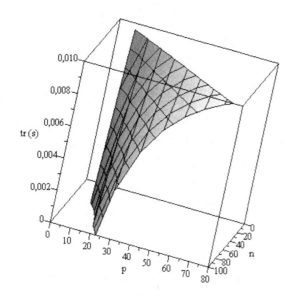

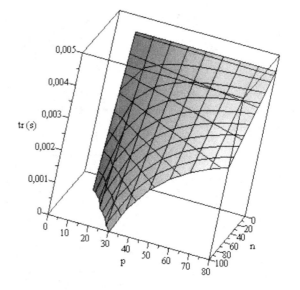

CONCLUSION

In this chapter, we have proposed ASPP for secure ad hoc social communications. ASPP cannot only satisfy the security and privacy requirements of ad hoc but also can detect, prevent and notify the elemental attacks and composed attacks. In addition, through the extensive performance evaluation, the ASPP has been demonstrated to be disinfected and effective for AODV routing protocol against the black hole attack and efficient in terms of transmission delay. Our future work will focus on investigating the relation between user mobility and privacy under the black hole attack.

REFERENCES

Ad, I., Hubaux, J., & Edward, K. (2008). Impact of denial of service attacks on Ad Hoc networks. *IEEE/ACM Transactions on Networking*, *16*(1), 791–802. doi:10.1109/TNET.2007.904002

Awerbuch, B., David, H., Cristina, N., & Herbert, R. (2002). An on-demand secure routing protocol resilient to byzantine failures. In *Proceedings of the 1st ACM workshop on Wireless security* (pp. 21-30). Atlanta, GA: ACM. 10.1145/570681.570684

Azarderakhsh, R., Longa, P., Hu, S., & Jao, D. (2013). Efficient implementation of bilinear pairings on ARM processors. *Springer Selected Areas in Cryptography*, 149-165.

Batallas, D., & Yassine, A. (2006). Information leaders in product development organizational networks: Social network analysis of the design structure matrix. *IEEE Transactions on Engineering Management*, *53*(4), 570–582. doi:10.1109/TEM.2006.883706

Bender, A., Adam, B., Neil, S., Bobby, B., & Daniel, S. (2009). Persona: an online social network with user-defined privacy. In *Proceedings of the ACM SIGCOMM 2009 conference on Data communication* (pp. 135-146). Barcelona, Spain: ACM.

Boneh, D., & Boyen, X. (2008). Short signatures without random oracles and the SDH assumption in bilinear groups. *Journal of Cryptology*, *21*(2), 149–177. doi:10.100700145-007-9005-7

Brzuska, C., Fischlin, M., Freudenreich, T., Lehmann, A., Page, M., Schelbert, J., ... (2009). Security of sanitizable signatures revisited. In *Proceeding of the 12th International Conference on Practice and Theory in Public Key Cryptography* (pp. 317-336). Springer-Verlag Berlin.

Calandriello, G., Papadimitratos, P., Hubaux, J. P., & Lioy, A. (2007). Efficient and robust pseudonymous authentication in VANET. In *Proceeding of 4th ACM International Workshop VANET* (pp. 19–28). Montréal, QC, Canada: ACM. 10.1145/1287748.1287752

Chaudhary, P., & Gupta, B. B. (2017). A novel framework to alleviate dissemination of XSS worms in online social network (OSN) using view segregation. *Neural Network World*, *27*(1), 5–25. doi:10.14311/NNW.2017.27.001

Clausen, T., & Jacquet, P. (2003). *Optimized link state routing protocol. RFC 3626*. IETF.

Deng, J., Han, R., & Mishra, S. (2003). *Enhancing base station security in wireless sensor networks. CU-CS-951-03: University of Colorado*. Department of Computer Science Technical Report.

Deng, J., Richard, H., & Shivakant, M. (2006). Decorrelating wireless sensor network traffic to inhibit traffic analysis attacks. *Elsevier Pervasive and Mobile Computing Journal*, *2*(2), 159–186. doi:10.1016/j. pmcj.2005.12.003

Donald, G., John, F. S., James, M. T., & Carl, M. H. (2008). *Fundamentals of queueing theory* (4th ed.). Wiley.

Emre, S., Riva, O., Stuedi, P., & Alonso, G. (2009). Enabling social networking in ad hoc networks of mobile phones. *Proceedings of the VLDB Endowment International Conference on Very Large Data Bases*, *2*(2), 1634–1637. doi:10.14778/1687553.1687611

Ferrag, M. A. (2012a). *Study of attacks in ad hoc networks*. LAP Lambert Academic Publishing.

Ferrag, M. A., Derdour, M., Mukherjee, M., Derhab, A., Maglaras, L., & Janicke, H. (2018). *Blockchain Technologies for the Internet of Things: Research Issues and Challenges. IEEE Internet of Things Journal*.

Ferrag, M. A., Maglaras, L., & Ahmim, A. (2017). Privacy-preserving schemes for ad hoc social networks: A survey. *IEEE Communications Surveys and Tutorials*, *19*(4), 3015–3045. doi:10.1109/ COMST.2017.2718178

Ferrag, M. A., Nafa, M., & Ghanemi, S. (2012b). OlsrBOOK: a privacy-preserving mobile social network leveraging on securing the olsr routing protocol. In *Proceeding of The 8 th International Scientific Conference eLearning and Software for Education* (pp. 133-139). Bucharest, Romania: Editura Universitara.

Ferrag, M. A., Nafa, M., & Ghanemi, S. (2013a). A new security mechanism for ad-hoc on-demand distance vector in mobile ad hoc social networks. In *Proceedings of the 7th Workshop on Wireless and Mobile Ad-Hoc Networks (WMAN 2013) in Conjunction with the Conference on Networked Systems NetSys/KIVS*. Stuttgart, Germany: WMAN.

Ferrag, M. A., Nafa, M., & Ghanemi, S. (2013b). Security and privacy in mobile ad hoc social networks. In D. B. Rawat, B. B. Bista, & G. Yan (Eds.), *Security, Privacy, Trust, and Resource Management in Mobile and Wireless Communications* (pp. 223–244). IGI Global.

Ferrag, M. A., Nafa, M., & Ghanemi, S. (2016). EPSA: An efficient and privacy-preserving scheme against wormhole attack on reactive routing for mobile ad hoc social networks. *International Journal of Security and Networks*, *11*(3), 107–125. doi:10.1504/IJSN.2016.078390

Freeman, L. C. (1978). Centrality in social networks: Conceptual clarification. *Elsevier Social Networks*, *1*(3), 215–239. doi:10.1016/0378-8733(78)90021-7

Guha, S., Tang, K., & Francis, P. (2008). NOYB: privacy in online social networks. In *Proceedings of the first workshop on Online social networks* (pp. 49–54). Seattle, WA: ACM. 10.1145/1397735.1397747

Gupta, B., Agrawal, D. P., & Yamaguchi, S. (Eds.). (2016). *Handbook of research on modern cryptographic solutions for computer and cyber security*. IGI Global. doi:10.4018/978-1-5225-0105-3

IETF MANET group. (n.d.). Retrieved June 01, 2013, from http://datatracker.ietf.org/wg/manet/

Information Sciences Institute. (2008). Retrieved June 01, 2013, from http://www.isi.edu/nsnam/ns/

Jian, Y., Shigang, C., Zhan, Z., & Liang, Z. (2007). Protecting receiver-location privacy in wireless sensor networks. In *Proceedings of 26th IEEE International Conference on Computer Communications* (pp. 1955-1963). Anchorage, AK: IEEE Computer Society. 10.1109/INFCOM.2007.227

Kamatchi, V., Rajeswari, M., & Raja, K. (2013). Securing data from black hole attack using aodv routing for mobile ad hoc networks. In *Proceedings of the Second International Conference on Advances in Computing and Information Technology* (pp. 365-373). Chennai, India: Springer Berlin Heidelberg. 10.1007/978-3-642-31552-7_38

Lee, J., & Hong, C. S. (2011). A mechanism for building Ad-hoc social network based on users interest. In *Proceedings of the 13th Asia-pacific Network Operatens and Management Symposium* (pp. 1-4). Taipei, Taiwan: IEEE Computer Society.

Li, H., Bok, K., & Yoo, J. (2013). Mobile P2P social network using location and profile. In Ubiquitous Information Technologies and Applications (Vol. 214, pp. 333-339). Springer Netherlands. doi:10.1007/978-94-007-5857-5_36

Li, T., Gupta, B. B., & Metere, R. (2018). Socially-conforming cooperative computation in cloud networks. *Journal of Parallel and Distributed Computing, 117*, 274–280. doi:10.1016/j.jpdc.2017.06.006

Liang, X., Li, X., Luan, T., Lu, R., Lin, X., & Shen, X. (2012). Morality-driven data forwarding with privacy preservation in mobile social networks. *IEEE Transactions on Vehicular Technology, 61*(7), 3209–3221. doi:10.1109/TVT.2012.2202932

Liang, X., Zhang, K., Shen, X., & Lin, X. (2014). Security and privacy in mobile social networks: Challenges and solutions. *IEEE Wireless Communications, 21*(1), 33–41. doi:10.1109/MWC.2014.6757895

Lin, X., Lu, R., Shen, X., Nemoto, Y., & Kato, N. (2009). SAGE: A strong privacy-preserving scheme against global eavesdropping for ehealth systems. *IEEE Journal on Selected Areas in Communications, 27*(4), 365–378. doi:10.1109/JSAC.2009.090502

Lu, R. (2012). *Security and privacy preservation in vehicular social networks*. University of Waterloo.

Lu, R., Liang, X., Li, X., Lin, X., & Shen, X. (2012a). EPPA: An efficient and privacy-preserving aggregation scheme for secure smart grid communications. *IEEE Transactions on Parallel and Distributed Systems, 23*(9), 1621–1631. doi:10.1109/TPDS.2012.86

Lu, R., Lin, X., Liang, X., & Shen, X. (2012c). A dynamic privacy-preserving key management scheme for location based services in VANETs. *IEEE Transactions on Intelligent Transportation Systems, 13*(1), 127–139. doi:10.1109/TITS.2011.2164068

Lu, R., Lin, X., Zhu, H., Liang, X., & Shen, X. (2012b). BECAN: A bandwidth-efficient cooperative authentication scheme for filtering injected false data in wireless sensor networks. *IEEE Transactions on Parallel and Distributed Systems, 23*(1), 32–43. doi:10.1109/TPDS.2011.95

Mao, W. (2003). *Modern Cryptography: Theory and Practice*. Prentice Hall.

Nait-Abdesselam, F., Bensaou, T., & Taleb, T. (2008). Detecting and avoiding wormhole attacks in wireless ad Hoc networks. *IEEE Communications Magazine, 46*(4), 127–133. doi:10.1109/MCOM.2008.4481351

Opsahl, T., Agneessensb, F., & Skvoretzc, J. (2010). Node centrality in weighted networks: Generalizing degree and shortest path. *Elsevier Social Networks*, *32*(2), 245–251. doi:10.1016/j.socnet.2010.03.006

Ozturk, C., & Zhang, Y. (2004). Source-location privacy in energy-constrained sensor network routing. In *Proceedings of the 2nd ACM workshop on Security of ad hoc and sensor networks* (pp. 88-93). Washington, DC: ACM. 10.1145/1029102.1029117

Park, J. H. (2011). Inner-product encryption under standard assumptions. *Springer Designs. Codes and Cryptography*, *58*(3), 235–257. doi:10.100710623-010-9405-9

Perkins, C., Belding-Royer, E., & Das, S. (2003). *Ad hoc On-Demand Distance Vector Routing*. Retrieved June 01, 2013, from http://tools.ietf.org/html/rfc3561

Sanguankotchakorn, T., Shrestha, S., & Sugino, N. (2012). Effective Ad Hoc Social Networking on OLSR MANET Using Similarity of Interest Approach. In *Proceedings of 5th International Conference IDCS*, (pp. 15-28). Wuyishan, Fujian, China: Springer Berlin Heidelberg. 10.1007/978-3-642-34883-9_2

Sanzgiri, K., Dahill, B., Levine, B. N., Shields, C., & Belding-Royer, E. M. (2002). A secure routing protocol for ad hoc networks. In *Proceedings of 10th IEEE International Conference on Network Protocols* (pp. 78-87). Paris, France: IEEE Computer Society. 10.1109/ICNP.2002.1181388

Schnorr, C. (1991). Efficient signature generation by smart cards. *Journal of Cryptology*, *4*(3), 161–174. doi:10.1007/BF00196725

Scott, M. (2011). On efficient implementation of pairing-based protocols. In *Proceedings of 13th IMA International Conference IMACC* (pp. 296-308). Oxford, UK: Springer Berlin Heidelberg.

Shirey, R. (2007). *Internet security glossary*. Retrieved June 01, 2013, from http://tools.ietf.org/html/rfc4949

Stergiou, C., Psannis, K. E., Kim, B. G., & Gupta, B. (2018). Secure integration of IoT and cloud computing. *Future Generation Computer Systems*, *78*, 964–975. doi:10.1016/j.future.2016.11.031

Toshiyuki, I., Nguyen, M., & Tanaka, K. (2013). Proxy re-encryption in a stronger security model extended from CT-RSA2012. In *Proceedings of The Cryptographers' Track at the RSA Conference* (pp. 277-292). San Francisco, CA: Springer Berlin Heidelberg.

Yanyong, Z., & Celal, O. (2005). Enhancing source-location privacy in sensor network routing. In *Proceedings of the 25th IEEE International Conference on Distributed Computing Systems* (pp. 599-608). Genova, Italy: IEEE Computer Society.

Yeung, C. A., Liccardi, I., Lu, K., Seneviratne, O., & Berners-lee, T. (2009). Decentralization: The future of online social networking. *W3C Workshop on the Future of Social Networking Position Papers*.

Yipin, S., Lu, R., Lin, X., & Shen, X. (2010). An efficient pseudonymous authentication scheme with strong privacy preservation for vehicular communications. *IEEE Transactions on Vehicular Technology*, *59*(7), 3589–3603. doi:10.1109/TVT.2010.2051468

Zhang, K., Liang, X., Shen, X., & Lu, R. (2014). Exploiting multimedia services in mobile social networks from security and privacy perspectives. *IEEE Communications Magazine*, *52*(3), 58–65. doi:10.1109/MCOM.2014.6766086

Chapter 7
Adversarial Attacks and Defenses in Malware Detection Classifiers

Teenu S. John
Indian Institute of Information Technology and Management, India

Tony Thomas
Indian Institute of Information Technology and Management, India

ABSTRACT

Machine learning has found its immense application in various cybersecurity domains owing to its automated threat prediction and detection capabilities. Despite its advantages, attackers can utilize the vulnerabilities of machine learning models for degrading its performance. These attacks called adversarial attacks can perturb the features of the data to induce misclassification. Adversarial attacks are highly destructive in the case of malware detection classifiers, causing a harmful virus or trojan to evade the threat detection system. The feature perturbations carried out by an adversary against malware detection classifiers are different from the conventional attack strategies employed by an adversary against computer vision tasks. This chapter discusses various adversarial attacks launched against malware detection classifiers and the existing defensive mechanisms. The authors also discuss the challenges and the research directions that need to be addressed to develop effective defensive mechanisms against these attacks.

INTRODUCTION

Machine learning (ML) has been widely used in applications such as pattern recognition, natural language processing (Akter, and, & 2018, n.d.), intrusion detection, facial recognition, and malware detection processes. ML comprises of two phases: - a training phase in which the model is given large data to learn and make predictions and a testing phase in which the model is evaluated with a new dataset that is independent of the training set to assess its performance. A validation set is used to tune the parameters of the ML model for better accuracy before finalizing the model. Generally, machine learning can be

DOI: 10.4018/978-1-5225-8407-0.ch007

categorized as supervised, unsupervised, semi-supervised and reinforcement learning (RL). Supervised learning technique such as SVM trains the classifier with associated labels while in unsupervised learning, like clustering, the classifier works with no knowledge about the labels. In cybersecurity, a supervised learning technique like decision tree, neural networks and SVM can be used in malware detection and spam detection, since these applications acquire a large set of labelled data instances. For intrusion detection, a semi-supervised learning method outperforms the other two for its ability to detect unknown attacks. An unsupervised learning like self-organizing maps is used for effectively detecting anomalies in the network. The reinforcement learning, on the other hand, utilizes the feedback of the environment for learning with the help of agents. Reinforcement learning is found to be effective when there are high false positives, especially in the case of anomaly detection. Here a reinforcement agent helps to adjust the parameters of the detection model by adjusting the weights of the algorithm. An important challenge in cybersecurity is the amount of data that needs to be analyzed by security analysts to detect the attacks. For a cyber-threat management system, a security analyst has to analyze a large number of data such as firewall logs, and user activities (Big Data) to detect all possible attacks (Bhushan & Gupta, 2017) (Bhushan & Gupta, 2018) (Hossain, Muhammad, Abdul, 2018, n.d.). Hence security vendors are equipping themselves with ML techniques to automatically detect malwares and vulnerable executables from a large volume of data. This is why major cybersecurity threat management systems like Sophos's Invincea and Radware's Seculert technology are acquiring ML capabilities to detect and prevent sophisticated cyber-attacks. Among the ML classifiers, deep learning has attracted researchers due to its increased classification accuracy and its ability to learn from unlabelled data (Thomas, John & Uddin, 2017, n.d.). Deep learning has gained its popularity especially with Google's AlphagoAI, an intelligent player modelled to play the game of Go using deep learning. The main advantage of deep learning is its ability to generate new features from limited or existing features which makes it extremely useful in malware detection and biometrics.

The accuracy of the classifier is highly significant in ML, especially in security-sensitive applications. This is because if a threat management system fails to detect an adversary, a data breach may occur damaging the valuable cyber-assets of the enterprise. There are various factors that influence the accuracy of a classifier. The amount of data that is provided to the classifier for training and the effectiveness of feature selection directly impacts the model accuracy. In addition to that, a critical problem encountered by the classification models that deteriorates the accuracy is the overfitting problem(Pham & Triantaphyllou, 2008). Overfitting is a problem in which the model learns the outliers and noise in the training instances as features rather than learning the true features. Besides all these, an attack can be launched against an ML model that can degrade the accuracy, leading to erroneous model outputs called adversarial attacks. Adversarial attacks can be defined as inputs that are intentionally crafted by an attacker to undermine the performance of the classifier(Zantedeschi, Nicolae, & Rawat, 2017). An adversarial attack is launched by gathering the information about the data and the training algorithm implemented by the ML model or by crafting test data to evade the detection. In cybersecurity applications, the goal of the attacker can be either to access the system assets with false negatives (integrity attacks) or to disable the filtering mechanism with high false positives (availability attacks) (L. Chen, Ye, & Bourlai, 2017) (Gupta, and, & 2018, n.d.). In malware detection classifiers, the integrity attacks systematically construct malware variants that appear to be benign (W. Yang, Kong, Xie, & Gunter, 2017). The availability attack in-turn creates a denial of service in which the benign samples are classified incorrectly as malicious. Machine learning is widely applied in Android malware detection since sophisticated malwares can easily evade

Google Play's defense by various obfuscations. However, adversarial attacks on (Internet of Things) IoT malwares are yet to be explored. There are only a few IoT specific malwares available to analyse and the recent study focuses on IoT related Android malwares.

Adversarial attacks on mobile malware detection systems are really threatening. It can make an attacker gain unauthorized access to the device without the user's consent (Ouaguid, 2018). In malware detection, feature values are extremely important since a slight change in the values can influence the output of the classifier. In addition to that, it is seen that these adversarial attacks are transferable. This means that the attacks targeting a specific classifier can also cause misclassification on other classifiers. There are simple techniques to perform feature manipulations such as injecting bytes or appending bytes at the end of the file(Anderson, Kharkar, Filar, & Roth, 2017). Simply injecting some bytes in the file does not require complex feature manipulations and can be easily detected by monitoring the file structure. However, if an adversary adopts fine-grained modifications of features, the above technique does not work.

There are many data manipulation methods that can be employed by an adversary other than simple feature removal and deletion. The authors will be discussing various such techniques employed by an adversary to evade detection in the upcoming sections. The first part of the chapter provides a deep insight into the various types of attacks adopted by adversaries to evade ML- based malware detection classifiers. The authors discuss how feature perturbations are carried out by attackers to evade the detection and also the transferability of these adversarial attacks. The second part of the chapter discusses the existing defensive methods and their effectiveness in detecting these attacks. The third and final part of the chapter discusses the challenges and research directions that need to be addressed to develop effective defensive mechanisms against these attacks.

BACKGROUND

The first work that discussed the learning in the presence of malicious errors was proposed by Valiant(Valiant, n.d.). Later Kearns and Li (Kearns & Li, 1993)proposed an extension of this work by proposing algorithms for designing an error-tolerant learning model. In cybersecurity, the study of the behavior of ML under adversarial attack has been widely discussed in the case of spam detection, where the classifier is poisoned with malicious training instances. Defense against adversarial machine learning is an interesting area that needs to be explored more. Adversarial defensive methods so far can be extensively divided into two:-reactive and proactive defense. In reactive defense the role of the attacker is to find the vulnerabilities of the model and launch the attack. On the other hand, the role of the defender is to analyze and implement proper countermeasures against the attack. The attack and defense are performed alternatively in reactive defense and is regarded as a race between the two. In proactive defense, the defender takes the adversarial model and launches penetration testing to explore the vulnerabilities and then proposes proper defensive mechanisms against the attack. There exist several adversarial perturbation techniques. Each of these works models the attackers with different capabilities and knowledge. The following section will discuss the different types of attackers with different knowledge levels that are targeting ML classifiers.

TYPES OF ADVERSARIES AND ATTACK TYPES

The attacker's knowledge in adversarial settings can be classified into perfect knowledge, limited knowledge and zero knowledge (Biggio et al., 2013). In a perfect knowledge attack, the attacker has complete knowledge about the feature space and the trained model including the type of classifier. In a limited knowledge attack, the attacker knows the feature space and the classifier but has no knowledge about the training data of the classifier. In that case, the attacker can choose a surrogate dataset that is constructed from the same underlying distribution. In the case of e-mail spam detection, the attacker can collect the features by carrying out some network attacks. In a zero-knowledge attack, the attacker has little or no knowledge about the type of the classifier and the model parameters used by the detector. These attacks are called black box attacks.

Ling et al. (L. Huang, Joseph, Nelson, Rubinstein, & Tygar, 2011) proposed a taxonomy of attacks based on attack influence, security violation and specificity. The attack influence can be exploratory or causative depending upon the attack conducted at test time and training time. The exploratory attack alters the test samples to evade detection while causative attack manipulates the data at the training time to induce misclassification. The security violation attack can be either availability attack, privacy attack or integrity attack. Availability attack induces denial of service that causes the legitimate sample to be classified as malicious, thus rejecting it. The privacy attack in turn, retrieves confidential and sensitive data from the system. In the case of integrity attacks, the aim of the adversary is to classify a malicious sample as legitimate. The attack specificity categorizes adversarial attacks into targeted and indiscriminate. Targeted attack manipulates a specific data instance while indiscriminate attack conducts attacks in general, not targeting a specific instance.

The adversarial malware detection can be classified into three(Anderson, Filar, & Roth, 2017):-gradient based attacks, score based attacks and black box attacks A comparison of various attacks are given in Table 1.

1. **Gradient Based Attacks:** In gradient based approaches the model under attack should be fully differentiable and in addition to that the model parameters like weights and biases must be known to the attacker.
2. **Black Box Attacks:** In this type of attack, the adversary does not have any knowledge about the target classifier and its parameters. The only knowledge the adversary has is the label that is generated by the classifier that indicates whether the given sample is malicious or not.
3. **Score Based Attacks:** In score based technique the attacker monitors the score of the ML model by prompting the classifier using queries. A score of the classifier is actually its predicted value which indicates whether the corresponding sample is malicious or not.

There are many adversarial attacks and defenses proposed in the literature (Figure 1). The authors will be discussing about various attacks against malware detection classifiers in the upcoming section.

Gradient Based Attacks

In gradient based attacks, the attacker utilizes the gradient information of the classifier for perturbing the sample to evade detection. The gradient information of the classifier provides information about the optimal points where the error is low, where the classifier accurately classifies the samples.

Figure 1. Adversarial attacks and defenses in malware detection

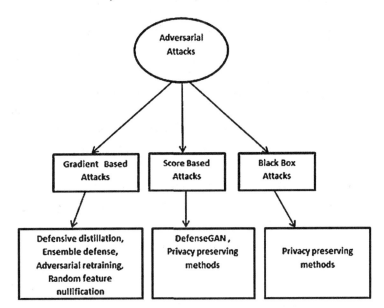

Fast Gradient Sign Method Attack (FGSMA)

In machine learning, gradient descent algorithms are used to minimize the error incurred during the classification. Let X and Y be the original sample and its corresponding class, θ be the parameters of the network and $J\left(\theta, X, Y\right)$ be the loss function. When an ML model is trained, it actually traverses over the surface defined by $J\left(\theta, X, Y\right)$ with respect to θ and the objective is to reduce the error of the model by finding the optimal point where the error is low at each step. Let θ be the parameters of the model. The parameter is updated by:

$$\theta = \theta - \epsilon \nabla_{\theta} J(X, Y, \theta)$$

where ϵ represents a small value that is chosen. In gradient based attacks, the attacker's intention is to change Y w.r.t X. Here θ is considered as a fixed parameter and the attacker will compute a sample $\hat{X} = X + \epsilon \nabla_{X} J(X, Y)$ that will increase the loss by a value ϵ. There are many gradient based attacks employed in the literature. Fast Gradient Sign Method Attack (FGSMA) attack is one such method(Goodfellow, Shlens, & Szegedy, 2014). FGSM computes the sign of the slopes to increase or decrease the input values to induce successful misclassification. Since FGSMA requires continuous features, it cannot be used to perturb the malware samples that uses sparse binary features(Stokes, Wang, Marinescu, Marino, & Bussone, n.d.). But the adversaries can employ an adaptation to FGSMA when the malware detection classifier is using binary features for classification(A. Huang, Hemberg, & Reilly, n.d.). There are many refinements of FGSMA attacks (Kurakin, Goodfellow, & Bengio, 2016). However to generate malware samples that evade detection using these methods is yet to be explored.

Jacobian Based Saliency Map Attacks (JSMA)

The method was introduced by Papernot et al.(Papernot, McDaniel, Jha, et al., 2016) that states that small feature perturbations of the input obtained using the forward derivative can significantly induce large variations in the neural network output. Gross et al.(Grosse, Papernot, Manoharan, Backes, & McDaniel, 2016) proposed an attack based on jacobian matrix perturbation called Jacobian based Saliency Map (JSMA) to generate adversarial malware samples. This type of attack needs information about the network architecture and parameters of the model. Adversaries who are well aware of the architecture of the model can find this perturbation by slightly performing heuristics on the input data. Their technique is described below.

Let $F : X \rightarrow Y$ be the classification algorithm, where $X \in \{0,1\}^m$ represents the input sample with m features (0 if present 1 otherwise) and Y represents the label indicating whether the sample is malicious or benign. Then the adversary finds a small feature permutation δ_x on X, to manipulate the classification result such that $F(X + \delta)$ results in misclassification.

The steps involved in Jacobian based adversarial perturbation are as follows:

The first step is computing the gradient of F with respect to X. This is to find the direction in which X is perturbed to induce misclassification and is given by:

$$
J_F = \frac{\partial F(X)}{\partial X} = \left[\frac{\partial F_i(X)}{\partial X_j} \right]_{i \in 0,1, j \in [1,m]}
$$

Then the adversary chooses the perturbation δ_x with maximum positive gradient to induce misclassification.

Since $X \in \{0,1\}^m$ is a binary indicator vector, the adversary increases one component in X by exactly 1 to induce misclassification. Here the adversarial sample crafting process is iterative ie: after finding out the gradient, the attacker selects a feature whose gradient is the largest for the target class that the adversary wants to classify. He then changes its value in X to obtain a new input vector $X(1)$. The adversary then recomputes the gradient under this newly crafted input $X(1)$ and computes the next feature to change. This process continues until the maximum allowable limit is reached or the crafted input sample can successfully cause a misclassification. This helps to find the input features that lead to significant changes in the network output. The authors generated the samples bounded by L1 constraints that added some extra features while keeping the original features same. Since the proposed attack is carried out only in the feature space by adding features, applications are not generated and there is no oracle to test whether the applications are malicious or not. Their method produced evasion efficacy from 50% to 84%, by changing different model parameters of the neural network architecture. However the computational complexity associated for perturbing the sample is so high because for each iteration, JSMA computes the derivative of the classifiers output probability with respect to the perturbed sample.

Blackbox Attacks

Gradient based attacks such as FGSMA and JSMA require complete knowledge about the architecture and parameters of the targeted classifiers. However, a black box attack can be carried out by the above perturbation algorithms against a target model with unknown architecture(Papernot et al., 2017) The idea is to misclassify the data instances utilizing the transferability of the attacks. A substitute detector can be used to obtain the label rather than scores in the case of black box attacks so that the attacker can craft the malicious instance to evade detection. This is because machine learning based malware detection algorithms are usually unified with antivirus software or employed in the cloud environment, and hence acts as a black-box system to an adversary. It is practically difficult for an adversary to know the architecture and the parameters of the classifier. However, it is possible to know which features a malware detection algorithm uses by feeding some carefully designed data instances to the black-box algorithm. This means that if a malware detection algorithm uses static DLL or API features, an adversary can modify a benign program's DLL or API features to malware's DLL or API features. If the detection results change for most of the modifications, the adversary can conclude that the malware detection algorithm uses DLL or API features. Thus the adversary can launch an attack without knowing the architecture of the model.

Wei et al. (Hu & Tan, 2016) proposed a generative adversarial network (GAN) based adversarial malware generation algorithm called MALGAN that can evade the windows malware detection system. MALGAN employs a substitute detector to the black box malware detection system. It first approximates the targeted model by querying it for output labels to train a substitute model, which is then used to craft adversarial samples which were misclassified by the originally targeted model. Black box attacks are not only launched against deep neural networks (DNN) but also against graph-based clustering. The attack was demonstrated against Pleides(Antonakakis et al., 2012) a botnet detection system. The bot malware uses a domain generation algorithm (DGA) to generate a large number of domains and select only a few for establishing botnets. Pleides use clustering to group the generated domains. This is based on the assumption that the bots from the same botnet with the same DGA would generate similar NXDomain (Nonexistent Domain) traffic. In this case an attacker can launch attack against the clustering algorithm by injecting some unwanted domains into the network to mislead the clustering approach. Chen et al.(Y. Chen et al., 2017) demonstrated two types of attacks adversarial attacks called target noise injection attacks and small community attacks against Pleides. Here the nodes and the connected domains should be known to the adversary. These attacks change the structural equivalence and homophily assumptions used by the graph based clustering. In noise injection attacks, the attacker injects some additional domains thus misleading the clustering. In small community attacks, the attacker exploits the information loss in graph embedding. This is by removing nodes or edges in so that the single attack graph is split into multiple clusters without making much change in the original graph.

Score Based Attacks

In score based attacks, attackers make use of the target model's confidence scores to launch the attacks. The confidence score indicates how confident the system is about that prediction. In this case, the attacker crafts malware samples, and presents it to the ML system for measuring the confidence score of the classifier. Thus the attacker can directly measure the efficacy of any perturbation. Here the attacker does not have any detailed information about the model parameters or features. In score based attacks, and chooses a malicious sample that is correctly classified by a target classifier as malicious. Then the adversary tries to craft a sample with the same malicious behavior, but that is misclassified as benign by the ML. The attacker can choose any method to manipulate the malicious sample to force misclassification and have knowledge about the samples that are classified as benign. Even though the attacker has a black box access, the adversary can submit many variants of the same samples to obtain the confidence score of the classifier. A confidence score is typically a number between 0 and 1 that indicates the classifier's prediction of maliciousness about the submitted sample, where the values above some predefined threshold are considered malicious.

In (Xu, Qi, & Evans, 2016a), the authors employed a fitness function to evaluate the effectiveness of the generated malware variants. The generated variant with a positive fitness score is said to be evasive. The proposed method found nearly 17K evasive variants from 500 malicious seeds, and also achieved 100% evasion rate against the PDFrate classifier. An oracle or a detector is used to evaluate the efficiency of evasive variants so that an attacker can generate more effective malicious samples.

Another effective method adopted by the adversary to launch score based attacks is the reinforcement learning method. Hyrum et al.(Anderson, Filar, et al., 2017) proposed a reinforcement learning approach called deep Q-learning to evade Windows malwares. Figure 2 illustrates this.

The model consists of an agent and an environment. The agent chooses the actions and action changes the state of the environment. The agent learns the lessons through exploration and exploitation. The agent is the one who crafts the adversarial malware samples and the action state consists of the type of modifications applied for crafting the malware. The environment will be an antimalware engine and the agent will get a reward if the malware sample bypasses the engine. The state information that is emitted by the antimalware will be the current feature vector of the malware. This state information is used to further craft the malware if it is detected by the antimalware engine. The agent will get a reward '1' if the malware sample becomes successful in bypassing the antimalware engine and '0' otherwise. In addition to this, a score will be provided by the classifier to generate more evasive variants.

The adversaries use a variety of feature manipulation techniques to evade gradient based, score based and black box attacks. The authors will be providing a detailed description of how the features are manipulated adopted by the adversary to evade detection.

Figure 2. Adversarial attacks using reinforcement learning

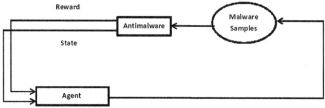

Table 1. Comparison of various attacks

Gradient Based Attacks	Black Box Attacks	Score Based Attacks
Utilizes the gradient information of the adversary.	Utilizes the label obtained from the classifier to launch the attack.	Utilizes the confidence score obtained from the classifier.
Needs to know the architecture or the parameters of the model.	The attacking model is completely a blackbox model.	The attack requires a rough knowledge of the likely features used by the classifier.
The attack uses the gradient information to craft the samples and is efficient.	The attack utilizes the substitute model's gradient information to craft samples or can randomly inject bytes.	The attacker uses an oracle to craft the samples.

ADVERSARIAL FEATURE MANIPULATION TECHNIQUES

Feature extraction is one of the most important tasks in ML since its effectiveness can influence the generalization of the classifier and can reduce the overhead by selecting the relevant features. ML assumes that the training and the test set follow the same distribution, which is violated in adversarial attacks. There are many feature perturbation techniques employed by an adversary to evade image classification models (Yuan, He, Zhu, Bhat, & Li, 2017). In the case of malware detection, many of these techniques cannot be employed as it can destroy the malicious functionality of the program or the application. In addition to that, the robustness of the application or the program should be maintained in such a way that it should not crash during the installation. Inducing random mutations may destroy the application functionality. Hence, careful perturbations are applied in such a way that a malicious program is classified as legitimate. This section provides various feature manipulation mechanisms adopted by the adversary to evade malware detection classifiers.

Gradient Descent Attack

Gradient descent attacks can be applicable to the classifiers with differentiable discriminant function. In the case of e-mail spam detection, the adversary's goal is to manipulate the messages by bounding some constraints on the words without altering the semantics. In that case, a gradient descent attack can be launched to produce more effective perturbations that evade detection (Biggio et al., 2013). The method is described below:

Let $F : X \rightarrow Y$ be the classification algorithm, where X represents the input sample and $y \in Y = \{+, -\}$ denotes a label indicating whether the sample is benign or malicious. The given classifier F is trained on a dataset $D = \{X_i, Y_i\}_{i=1}^n$ which is sampled from a distribution P(X, Y). The label $Y_c = f(X)$ assigned by the classifier is acquired by thresholding a continuous discriminant function $g : X \rightarrow \mathbb{R}$. The label Y_c refers to the label assigned by the classifier that may or may not be different from the true label Y assuming that $F(X) = -1$ if $g(x) < 0$ and +1 otherwise.

Perfect Knowledge Attack

In perfect knowledge attack, as the attacker has complete knowledge about the classifier, the adversary's goal is to minimize $g(X)$. The adversary tries to transform the attack points in the test data, perturbing the sample bounded by a maximum distance of d_{max} from the original attack sample. The distance measure $d : X \times X \longmapsto \mathbb{R}$ is dependent on the type of application. A Hamming distance can be used to calculate the number of feature values that are changed from X to X'. In email spam detection, a Manhattan distance measure can be used to alter the features. Usually, L1 norm is preferred over L2 norm when a few features are manipulated.

Limited Knowledge Attack

In a limited knowledge attack, the attacker knows the feature representation and the type of the classifier but does not know the trained classifier f and its training data D. Thus the adversary cannot directly compute $g(X)$. But the attacker chooses a surrogate dataset $D' = \{\hat{X}_i, \hat{Y}_i\}_{i=1}^{n_q}$ and can take n_q samples drawn from the same distribution $P(X, Y)$ from which D was taken. Then the adversary approximates the discriminant function $g(X)$ to $\hat{g}(X)$ as the discriminant function of a surrogate classifier. An attacker can query f with the samples of D' and then manipulate the training data obtained by the score provided by the classifier. Based on this, for a sample X^0, the attacker calculates a sample X^* to minimize $\hat{g}(X)$, subject to a bound on its distance from X^0 and is given by:

$$X^* = \arg\min_X \hat{g}(X) \text{ subject to } d(X, X^0) \leq d_{\max}$$

which is a non-linear optimization problem. A gradient descent or quadratic techniques such as Newton's method, L- BFGS, or BFGS can be employed to solve this. To make his evasion successful, the attacker chooses attack points from densely populated regions of the legitimate points that are closer to $g(x)$ that tends to become negative in value. An additional component is added that acts as a penalizer for x in low density regions which is weighted by a parameter $\lambda \geq 0$ and the optimization problem becomes

$$\arg\min_X F(X) = \hat{g}(X) - \frac{\lambda}{n} \sum_{i|y_i^c = -1} k\left(\frac{X - X_i}{h}\right) \text{ subject to } d(X, X^0) \leq d_{\max},$$

where h denotes the bandwidth parameter for a kernel density estimator (KDE), k denotes the kernel and n is the number of benign samples ($y_c = -1$) available to the adversary. The authors performed perfect knowledge and limited knowledge attack in PDF malware detection classifiers. The experiments showed that SVM and neural networks can be easily evaded even if the adversary can learn the target classifier only from a small set of surrogate dataset. The experiments suggest that PDF malware detection can be easily evaded if the classifier employs the logical structure of the file as the features of the classifier since the attack is launched by feature additions.

Feature Additions and Removal Attacks

A malware can inject additional system calls or API features to evade detection. One can induce dead codes into the application to mislead antivirus systems. (Calleja, Mart\'\in, Menéndez, Tapiador, & Clark, 2018) proposed a feature addition attack in which the attacker injects unused permissions to mislead the classifier. In Android applications, this can be achieved easily since many of the applications are over privileged ie. they contain more number of permissions than required. Feature removal is not an easy task for the adversary since the semantics and intrusive functionality should not be altered. In Android, an attacker can remove the features of the dexcode in a variety of ways to force misclassification. Eg: by hiding the IP addresses using encryption. Even if the attacker cannot randomly remove malware features, he can balance between feature additions and removal to launch attacks. Sen et al.(Calleja et al., 2018) proposed a two-step attack utilizing the above technique by removing some unused permissions and injecting some sensitive API's to craft a malicious sample that is classified as benign by the classifier. The experiments showed that RevealDroid, a static Android malware detection classifier can be misled by injecting static API calls. Their method carefully manipulated API calls while maintaining its intrusive functionality. The authors experimented the attack on Drebin dataset and took 29 malware families to test the efficiency of the attack. Their experiments showed that out of 29 malware families, 28 of them were misclassified.

Feature Evolution and Confusion Attacks

Wei et al (W. Yang et al., 2017) introduced a new method of evading Android malware detection classifiers by constructing malwares that evade detection using mutations. They proposed a feature evolution attack and a feature confusion attack. A feature evolution attack is carried out by mimicking the evolution of malware families. A phylogenetic analysis of malware families was carried out to know the difference between different malware families so that an adversary can mimic similar way to generate malware variants. Here a pairwise distance computation is done to find the similarities between the feature vectors. The method is as follows. Let p_i represents the API calls of an application i and let p_j be the API calls of an application j. The similarity is computed by (need to correct the equation)

$$S_{i,j} = \left| \frac{p_i \cap p_j}{p_i \cup p_j} \right|.$$

If $S_{i,j}$ lies above a particular threshold value, each application is further analysed to build mutants of the applications to evade detection. This is as follows:

Let $(f_i^k)_1, (f_i^k)_2 \ldots \ldots (f_i^k)_m$ denotes the m feature vector of API call k in app i and let $(g_j^k)_1, (g_j^k)_2 \ldots \ldots (g_j^k)_n$ denotes the n feature vectors of API call k in app j. To mutate the API call k, in app j, the problem is modeled as a matching problem in a bipartite graph where $(f_i^k)_1, (f_i^k)_2 \ldots \ldots (f_i^k)_m$ denotes the first disjoint set and $(g_j^k)_1, (g_j^k)_2 \ldots \ldots (g_j^k)_n$ denotes the second disjoint set and the edges represent the maximum matching pairs. Each $(f_i^k)_r$ will be a binary value either 1 or 0 indicating whether the feature exists or not. The distance between the two applications w can be defined as the number of equivalent bits to the number of all feature bits and is given by:

$w((f_i^k)_r, (g_j^k)_t = \text{shared feature vectors of } (f_i^k)_r \text{ and } (g_j^k)_t \text{ Feature vector length}$

where $(f_i^k)_r$ and $(g_j^k)_t$ representing the feature value of API method k between the two applications i and j. After the pairwise distance calculation, the output is fed into the phylogenetic tree algorithm called Unweighted Pair Group Method Algorithm (UPGMA). This method constructs a rooted tree and employs hierarchical clustering method that finds the structure present inside the similarity matrix. In UPGMA, at each step, the nearest two clusters are combined to a higher level cluster by averaging all pairwise sample distance. From this phylogenetic analysis, the adversary finds how each feature type evolves and computes the statistical frequency Sf and feasibility F of each feature types. Statistical frequency indicates the number of feature mutations of an API method. $Sf(i) = n$ if the mutation of the ith type feature appears for n times, and 0 otherwise. Feasibility indicates whether the feature value corresponding to a particular feature type has been mutated or not. $F(i) = 1$ if the mutation of the ith feature type exists and 0 otherwise. After computing the feasibility and statistical frequency, the adversary ranks different feature mutations. The ranking is given by:

$$R(i) = \alpha F(i) + (1 - \alpha)Sf(i)$$

where $\alpha = .1$ and i denotes mutation of the ith type feature. From this the adversary chooses highest ranked features for mutations and is fed to the mutation engine for generating mutants. In confusion attacks, the attacker mutates differentiating feature values to confusing feature values. The differentiating feature value represents features that are only present in the malware while confusing feature value represents feature values that are present both in malware and goodware. The idea is to induce feature values that exist both in malware and benign applications to the malware applications to confuse the malware detector. The authors experimented this attack in Genome (Zhou, Jiang, & Nazish, 2011), Contagio ("contagio mobile," n.d.), Virusshare("VirusShare.com," n.d.) and Drebin("The Drebin Dataset," n.d.) Android malware datasets. The features taken were RTLD (Resource, Temporal, Locale and Dependency) features. The attack was tested on Drebin(Arp et al., 2014), Appcontext (W. Yang et al., n.d.) and Virustotal ("VirusTotal," n.d.) malware detectors. The results show that the evasive variants generated by this method can successfully evade detection.

Obfuscations and Program Mutation Attacks

In addition to simple obfuscations, an adversary can use complex techniques like string encryption and java reflection techniques to manipulate the system call graphs to force misclassification. A java reflection mechanism can be used by the adversary to invoke the malicious APIs at runtime to force misclassification. Sen et al. (S. Chen et al., n.d.) demonstrated that adversarial attacks can be launched against malware detection classifiers like DroidAPIMiner (Aafer, Du, & Yin, 2013), Drebin and MaMadroid (Mariconti et al., 2016) by reflection techniques that loads malicious codes at runtime. Drebin uses support vector machines and takes many static features like intents permissions etc. for training the classifier. MaMadroid constructs markov chains from API calls to extract the features for classification. DroidAPIMiner on the other hand uses the frequency of API calls to detect the malware. This means that malware detection classifiers can be subjected to adversarial attacks, even if they use different classification algorithms.

Ambra et al.(Demontis et al., n.d.) discussed adversarial attacks in static Android malware detection by obfuscating applications with Dexguard, a commercially available tool used by the developers to protect their code. Adversary can adopt different techniques to generate variants of the same application to evade detection (C. Yang, Wu, Li, & Chen, 2017). These techniques embed a feature or code area from one app to another app. An adversary can adopt three different strategies for evading a malware detection classifier: Inter-method transplantation, inter component transplantation and inter app transplantation. Inter method transplantation involves migration of malicious resource features from one method to the other in the same app. Inter-component transplantation transplants malicious features from one component to another component of the same app. That is transplantation from the activity component to service component. In inter-app transplantation; a dependency feature of a malicious app is transferred to the host app. Here an adversary constructs a control-flow graph and then computes the sub-graph to find the behaviour of the controlling statements. The controlling statements involve values that trigger malicious behaviour. After that the attacker computes the dependencies of the malicious behaviour and then transfers the controlling statements and dependencies to the host app. The authors showed that the above feature manipulation technique can evade K- Nearest neighbour, decision tree and SVM classifiers.

Genetic Programming Based Attacks

Among the program mutation techniques employed in the literature, genetic programming is an efficient way to automatically generate malware variants that evade detection. Weilin et al.(Xu, Qi, & Evans, 2016b) used genetic programming to generate samples that evade PDF malware detection classifiers like PDFrate and Hidost. PDFrate uses a random forest classifier with object keywords as features. Hidost on the other hand employs an SVM classifier with RBF kernel that uses the logical structure of files with their contents as features for detection. Initially, a malicious seed (malware) is chosen. Then some mutations like object deletion, object addition and object replacement are carried out to generate variants that evade detection. An oracle which is a sandbox is used for testing whether the generated variants preserve the malicious functionality. At each step the method tries to generate a sample that is labeled as malicious by the oracle and legitimate by the classifier. If the generated variants do not evade the classifier, the sample is replaced by another variant. A fitness function is used to evaluate how well the generated variants can evade the detection. The oracle is modeled as a binary function where $oracle(x) = 1$ if the sample x exhibits malicious nature and $oracle(x) = 0$ otherwise. From the evasive variants, an adversary chooses variants with highest fitness function. A replacement mechanism in addition to the naïve selection process is chosen to avoid degeneration of the population. The corrupted variants that became non-malicious after mutation are replaced by either the original malicious file, or a best variant found in the previous generation.

TRANSFERABILITY OF ATTACKS

Papernot et al.(Papernot, McDaniel, Jha, et al., 2016) showed that adversarial attacks are transferable. This means that, the adversarial samples crafted to evade one machine learning model can also evade other machine learning models. Adversarial attacks get transferred even if the models use an entirely different training set or have different architectures. Papernot defined two types of transferability: intra-technique transferability and cross technique transferability. These two transferability properties were tested on support vector machines, deep neural networks, decision trees, logistic regression, K-nearest neighbours etc. Intra-technique transferability indicates the transferability of attacks among the models that use the same machine learning models but with different model parameters or with different datasets. They demonstrated that differentiable models like deep neural networks and logistic regression are more subjected to intra-technique transferability than non-differentiable models. Cross-technique transferability of adversarial attacks states that attacks can be transferred to the models that use an entirely different machine learning model. They experimented and found that decision trees are highly vulnerable to cross technique transferability across the other models while deep neural network is somewhat resilient to this type of attack. They also introduced a technique called reservoir sampling to reduce the number of queries against the oracle so that the attacker can remain being undetected. They carried out attacks against Amazon and Google yielding 96.19% and 88.94% misclassification rate by querying only with 800 number of queries. Transferability is a threat for designing secure ML that makes the model vulnerable to black box attacks. Unfortunately, adversarial training and defensive distillation cannot counter these attacks.

Florian et al. (Tramèr, Papernot, Goodfellow, Boneh, & McDaniel, 2017)analyzed the transferability of attacks on DREBIN Android malware detection classifiers and proved that if two models share the adversarial subspace, then it is more likely that the attack gets transferred from one model to the other. In addition to that, their analysis showed that decision boundary similarity enables transferability among models. In the case of Windows PDF malware detection classifiers, the evasive variants generated against Hidost PDF malware detection classifier can successfully evade PDFrate malware detection classifier. This is because of the different feature sets used by the classifiers. Hidost uses the structural properties of the files for malware detection. David et al.(Maiorca et al., n.d.) conducted experiments to evaluate the strength of classifiers like Random forest, SVM with linear and RBF kernel against adversarial attacks. Their experiments showed that Random forest was robust against evasion attacks than SVM with RBF kernels.

Usually, data randomization techniques are used to protect against adversarial attacks. However, this technique can also be used to generate robust adversarial samples that can exhibit transferability. Xie et al.(Dube, Bhattacharjee, & Petit-bois, n.d.) proposed a Diverse Input Iterative Fast Gradient Sign Method (DI2-FGSM) to generate adversarial samples that gets transferred to other models. They applied random and differentiable transformations to the input images to generate samples that can evade detection under white-box and black-box settings.

DEFENSIVE MECHANISMS

There are several defensive methods employed in the literature to protect the classifiers against adversarial attacks. Many of these techniques only apply for image processing applications and only a few mechanisms are developed to protect malware detection classifiers. The comparison of various defensive methods is given in Table 2.

Adversarial Re-Training

Goodfellow et al.(Goodfellow et al., 2014) introduced the concept of retraining to defend against adversarial attacks. The adversarial retraining method adds the adversarial samples to the original training set to enhance its robustness against adversarial attacks. Gross et al(Grosse et al., 2016)demonstrated that adversarial retraining on Android malwares is insufficient to protect against the attacks. The disadvantage of adversarial retraining method is that the adversarial samples crafted by the methods like Jacobian based or FGSM are outside the training distribution if we are using diverse datasets like malware. In addition to that, it lacks regularization ie the ability to detect new input instances.

Defensive Distillation

Papernot et al. (Papernot, McDaniel, Wu, Jha, & Swami, 2016)proposed a method called defensive distillation to reduce the input variations so as to make adversarial crafting process difficult. This method helps the DNN to generalize the samples outside the training set. The distillation method was invented to reduce the size of the DNN by transferring the knowledge from one architecture to another. Usually the softmax layer is used to normalize the final layer of DNN. The idea is to take the probability of the classes of the softmax output layer at temperature T of one neural network to train another neural network. The temperature is the parameter of the neural network including its weights, biases etc. ie instead of taking the labels of the DNN as the output; the method takes the probability vector of all the classes. From this probability vectors, a new training set is formed. Using this training set a new DNN with the same architecture is trained to detect adversarial samples. The defensive distillation training procedure is as follows:

1. Let X be the training sample and let $Y(X)$ be its associated label which is called the hard label.
2. Train a deep neural network F with a soft max output layer at temperature T. Let $F(X)$ be the probability vector of all the possible labels that can be assigned to X. Let θ_F be the model parameters of F for any label Y that can be assigned to X. Then $F(X) = p(Y \mid X, \theta_F)$ outputs the probability that the given label is Y.
3. Construct a new training set $(X, F(X))$. This means that instead of using the original class labels $Y(X)$, the method uses $F(X)$ ie. the probabilities of all class labels for training the second DNN. The second DNN which is called the distilled model has the same architecture as that of the original DNN with temperature T.

The experiments show that this method reduces the success rate of crafting adversarial samples from 95.89 to .45 when they are tested on CIFAR and MNIST datasets. Gross et al. (Grosse et al., 2016) evaluated the effectiveness of distillation in detecting adversarial attacks in Android malwares. Their results demonstrated that when distillation is used as a defense, then there is an increased resilience to adversarial perturbation than feature reduction techniques. However the misclassification rates are more than 40%. This means that simple distillation cannot act as a defense in malware detection.

Ensemble Based Detection

In ensemble based detection, multiple defense methods are combined together to increase the robustness of ML models against the attacks(Strauss, Hanselmann, Junginger, & Ulmer, 2017). Augmenting the training data with the perturbations crafted from other models is one such mechanism (Tramèr, Kurakin, Papernot, Boneh, & McDaniel, 2017). Among various defensive methods like distillation and weight decay, ensemble defense is more resilient to adversarial attacks against DNN based malware detection classifiers. They employed a majority voting scheme in which a sample is presented to many classifiers to evaluate whether it is malicious or not. The work also demonstrates that adding many layers will significantly increase the complexity of adversarial crafting mechanisms. However, the complexity increases, since to train multiple classifiers is a tedious process.

Data Sanitization

Data sanitization techniques are used to ensure the purity of the training data used in classification. The training phase is prone to attack when the classifier uses online data at periodic intervals to update the training instance. There are several data sanitization techniques employed in the literature. Nelson et al.(Nelson et al., 2009) evaluated the effectiveness of data sanitization methods in detecting adversarial attacks against spam filters like SpamBayes, MozillasThunderbird and SpamAssasin spam filter. The SpamBayes takes the tokens (words) and counts the occurrences of the tokens to detect the spam mails. When the user periodically re-trains the classifier, the attacker can inject malicious e-mail tokens that are obfuscated as legitimate. The attacker can also inject tokens in such a way that the legitimate e-mail is classified as spam. When the user notices that a legitimate e-mail is classified as spam, he may disable the spam filter, thus allowing all the spam emails into the inbox. As a countermeasure, the method uses RONI(Reject on Negative Impact)(Nelson et al., 2008)whereby instead of adding the incoming training instance to the training dataset, the method checks whether the accuracy of the classifier changes significantly from the initial value obtained without adding the training set. If there is a significant change between the two outputs, then the incoming training instance is examined for malicious content and is rejected if so. Sen et al.(S. Chen et al., 2018) showed that by using similarity measures like jaccard index, jaccard-weight similarity, and cosine similarity, to further check whether the malicious applications are camouflaged or not. Data sanitization method mostly applies for causative attacks and can be applied only for certain applications.

Differential Privacy

Many of the machine learning models use crowdsourcing from social networking sites and mobile apps to build the dataset for training the classifier. This causes sensitive information like personal information and other user data to be accessed by a third party. An adversary can make an analysis of the crowd sourced data available in public databases to understand the feature distributions. The differential privacy ensures the privacy of the data while collecting and analysing the data for various computational purposes. There are various methods employed in the literature to preserve the privacy of ML(Rubinstein, Bartlett, Huang, & Taft, 2009) . Ulfar (Erlingsson, Pihur, & Korolova, 2014)proposed a method to ensure strong privacy guarantees for each client by randomizing the user data. This prevents the server from learning the true representation of data, without losing sensitive information. Martin et al. (Abadi et al., 2016)proposed a method to ensure privacy in the deep neural network by controlling the training data in stochastic gradient descent computation. Even though privacy preserving mechanisms achieve better resiliency, complex security mechanisms like encryption increases the overhead of the classifier.

Game Theory

To improve the robustness of the classification model against adversarial attacks, game theories can be used for effective learning. Game-theoretic models secure classifiers by carrying out different evasion attacks by modifying the classification function with respect to each attack. Globerson et al. (Globerson & Roweis, 2006) used a minimax game in SVM to model a classifier that is resilient to feature deletion attack. The technique is modelled as a minimax game in which the adversaries goal is to delete the features of the dataset while the defenders role is to choose the robust classifier parameters. Samuel et al.(Bul, Biggio, & Pillai, n.d.) developed a randomized prediction game in which the attacker and the classifier make randomized strategy selections based on some probability distribution defined over a particular strategy set. This technique applied on spam detection and malware detection, show that competitive and secure SVM classifiers can be modeled using this approach even when the attacker may not play in accordance with the objective function hypothesized for the adversary. The randomized prediction game generally requires the attacker to make a reasonable number of manipulations to evade detection, regardless of the attack strategy chosen. They proposed that the proposed method exhibits robustness against adversarial attacks. Due to the dynamic defensive mechanism, game theory is an efficient method to protect against adversarial attacks. However to find the equilibrium is difficult in most of the cases.

Feature Selection Approaches

Chen et al.(L. Chen, Hou, & Ye, n.d.) developed a novel feature selection method to enhance the security of neural network malware detection classifiers. The authors demonstrated that an adversary chooses features with higher weights and lower costs. Weights indicate the features that are more relevant for discriminating a malware and a goodware while cost indicates the number of feature manipulations required by the attacker to evade detection. Their idea was to choose the features with low weights and high costs for modeling a secure classifier thus forcing the adversary to manipulate many features for carrying out an attack which is a tedious process. Fei et al.(Zhang et al., 2015) proposed an adversary aware feature selection approach against adversarial attacks against PDF malware detection classifiers. They proposed an adversary-aware feature selection method that can protect the classifiers against evasion attacks. Their feature selection approach called a wrapper based feature selection algorithm uses forward selection and backward elimination to select best features. This method iteratively adds or delete feature from the current candidate set. The features are selected in such a way that it maximizes the generalization capability and security against evasion attacks. Wang et al.(Wang et al., 2017) developed a random feature nullification method to enhance the resiliency against adversarial attacks. This technique introduces stochasticity to the input processing units of DNN by introducing an additional layer between the input and the first hidden layer. This layer is used to remove some of the input features to randomize it. The experiments were performed in Windows malwares. The jacobian matrix perturbation is used to craft adversarial samples.

THE OCCURRENCE OF ADVERSARIAL ATTACKS

Many researchers assume that adversarial attacks are noises that prompt misclassification. But these attacks are different and the studies show that a well-trained deep learning is robust to noise. Goodfellow et al(Goodfellow et al., 2014) demonstrated that the reason for adversarial attacks in DNN are not overfitting, instead the linearity of the neural network is the cause of adversarial samples. They showed that the change in the activation caused by the perturbation increases linearly as the dimension of the weight matrix increases. This means that for high dimensional problems, a small change to the input

Table 2. Comparison of various defensive methods

Defensive Techniques	Advantages	Disadvantages
Adversarial Training	(1) Applicable to a variety of classifiers. (2) Easy to implement.	(1) In certain cases, the adversarial samples are outside the training set. (2) Training overhead increases due to a large number of training instances.
Defensive Distillation	(1) Increases the generalization capability	(1) Cannot defend completely against the attack that targets malware detection classifiers. (2) Only applicable to models that have categorical probabilities.
Ensemble Methods	(1) Can integrate more than one defensive methods together.	(1) Not resilient to adversarial transferability phenomenon.
Differential Privacy	(1) Preserves the privacy of the training data.	(1) High overhead due to complex security mechanisms.
Data Sanitization	(1) Applicable to a variety of classifiers.	(1) Effective only for certain applications.
Game Theory	(1) Can effectively model the interaction between the defender and the adversary	(1) Finding the equilibrium is difficult in most of the cases.
Feature Selection Approaches	(1) Can effectively detect attacks since malware cannot perturb a feature that removes its malicious functionality.	(1) Does not take the dynamic nature of adversary unlike game theory models.

can cause a large change in the output value. They showed that non-linear models like RBF's are immune to adversarial attacks. However, the former hypothesis explaining the linearity of neural networks was rejected by Tany et al.(Tanay & Griffin, 2016)that proved that linear classifiers are not subjected to adversarial attacks all the time.

The robustness of the classifier has also been discussed in the perspective of the flexibility of the classifier. Ekin et al. (Cubuk, Zoph, Schoenholz, & Le, 2017)showed that the vulnerability of a neural network is because of the statistics of the logit differences of the model and is independent of the architecture. A logit can be defined as non-normalized input values that are given to the softmax function to generate a vector of normalized probabilities.

Rozsa et al.(Rozsa, Manuel, & Boult, 2018)showed that the attacks in DNN's are due to the evolutionary stalling of the training instances. The evolutionary stalling states that after training the classifier, the evolution of the decision boundary of the classifier stalls. As a result, the generalization capability of the classifier fails and the correctly classified instance get trapped close to the decision boundary. This in turn makes the samples susceptible to small perturbations that flip the label. In addition to that, they proposed a BANG algorithm to mitigate the adversarial attack. Till now, no theoretical proof has been found for the existence of adversarial samples in ML models. Defense against adversarial machine learning is an interesting area that needs to be explored more.

CHALLENGES AND RESEARCH DIRECTIONS

Many of the defensive mechanisms employed in the literature targets computer vision tasks and only a few mechanisms are developed for cyber security applications like malware detection. Hence there is an urgent requirement for developing defensive mechanisms against the attacks that target malware detection classifiers. It is very difficult to address the transferability of attacks that states that the attacks generated for one model can be transferred to other models. In addition to that, there are only a few works that explore how the features are perturbed by the adversary to evade the detection. Hence exploring the feature perturbation employed by an adversary is an interesting area that needs to be studied. Imposing huge security in machine learning classifier induces high overhead that deteriorates the performance of the classifier. Hence the defensive mechanisms should not lower the generalization performance of the classifier. There is no theoretical proof that explains the reason of adversarial attacks and it should be investigated. The defensive method should be dynamic in nature to defend a complex adversary. For this, the effectiveness of GAN's in defending the attack is to be explored more.

CONCLUSION

The existing defensive mechanism like simple retraining does not act as a defense in the case of malware detection. The disadvantage of adversarial retraining method is that the adversarial samples crafted by methods such as Jacobian based or FGSM are outside the training distribution in the case of malwares. Even though several defensive algorithms are employed in the literature, the effectiveness of these defensive algorithms is limited in the case of repeated attacks(Carlini & Wagner, 2016),(X. Chen, Li, & Vorobeychik, 2000). It is seen that, misclassification rate depends on the type of features used for classification. Certain features like API calls leads to higher perturbation than other features. However the features extracted from API call graphs is found to be less subjective to adversarial attacks but consumes high resources for constructing the graph. To detect adversarial attacks in malware detection classifiers, one should train the classifier with the features that is seen only on malwares. Hence an efficient feature selection technique that characterizes the behavior of malware should be developed. In addition to that, it has been demonstrated that an adversary can easily evade detection, if the classifier is using a reduced feature set for classification and prediction. Hence, large feature vectors that are effective to withstand against these attacks should be chosen along with the consideration of the performance of the classifier. Besides the above mentioned attack methods, there are several other attacks (Moosavi Dezfooli, Fawzi, & Frossard, 2016)etc. employed by the adversary. However these techniques for evading malware detection classifiers are yet to be explored. As machine learning is gaining popularity in IoT and Big Data, adversaries are employing sophisticated methods to evade machine learning based classification and prediction. Adversarial attacks on malware detection classifiers may damage IoT devices which is a serious threat nowadays.

ACKNOWLEDGMENT

This work is done as a part of Centre for Research and Innovation in Cyber Threat Resilience project (CRICTR 2018-19), which is funded by Kerala state planning board.

REFERENCES

Aafer, Y., Du, W., & Yin, H. (2013). Droidapiminer: Mining api-level features for robust malware detection in android. In *International conference on security and privacy in communication systems* (pp. 86–103). Academic Press. 10.1007/978-3-319-04283-1_6

Abadi, M., Chu, A., Goodfellow, I., McMahan, H. B., Mironov, I., Talwar, K., & Zhang, L. (2016). Deep learning with differential privacy. In *Proceedings of the 2016 ACM SIGSAC Conference on Computer and Communications Security* (pp. 308–318). ACM. 10.1145/2976749.2978318

Akter, R. (n.d.). *An Improved Genetic Algorithm for Document Clustering on the Cloud.* Retrieved from https://www.igi-global.com/article/an-improved-genetic-algorithm-for-document-clustering-on-the-cloud/213987

Anderson, H. S., Filar, B., & Roth, P. (2017). *Evading Machine Learning Malware Detection.* Academic Press.

Anderson, H. S., Kharkar, A., Filar, B., & Roth, P. (2017). *Evading machine learning malware detection.* Black Hat.

Antonakakis, M., Perdisci, R., Nadji, Y., Vasiloglou, N., Abu-Nimeh, S., Lee, W., & Dagon, D. (2012). From Throw-Away Traffic to Bots: Detecting the Rise of DGA-Based Malware. In *Security'12 Proceedings of the 21st USENIX conference on Security symposium* (p. 24). ACM.

Arp, D., Spreitzenbarth, M., Hubner, M., Gascon, H., Rieck, K., & Siemens, C. (2014). DREBIN: Effective and Explainable Detection of Android Malware in Your Pocket. In *Ndss* (Vol. 14, pp. 23–26). Academic Press.

Bhushan, K., & Gupta, B. B. (2017). Network flow analysis for detection and mitigation of Fraudulent Resource Consumption (FRC) attacks in multimedia cloud computing. *Multimedia Tools and Applications*. doi:10.100711042-017-5522-z

Bhushan, K., & Gupta, B. B. (2018). Distributed denial of service (DDoS) attack mitigation in software defined network (SDN)-based cloud computing environment. *Journal of Ambient Intelligence and Humanized Computing*. doi:10.100712652-018-0800-9

Biggio, B., Corona, I., Maiorca, D., Nelson, B., Šrndić, N., & Laskov, P. ... Roli, F. (2013). Evasion attacks against machine learning at test time. In *Joint European conference on machine learning and knowledge discovery in databases* (pp. 387–402). Academic Press.

Bul, S. R., Biggio, B., & Pillai, I. (n.d.). *Randomized Prediction Games for Adversarial Machine Learning. Academic Press.*

Calleja, A., Martín, A., Menéndez, H. D., Tapiador, J., & Clark, D. (2018). Picking on the family: Disrupting android malware triage by forcing misclassification. *Expert Systems with Applications*, 95, 113–126. doi:10.1016/j.eswa.2017.11.032

Carlini, N., & Wagner, D. (2016). *Defensive distillation is not robust to adversarial examples.* ArXiv Preprint ArXiv:1607.04311

Chen, L., Hou, S., & Ye, Y. (n.d.). *SecureDroid : Enhancing Security of Machine Learning-based Detection against Adversarial Android Malware Attacks*. Academic Press.

Chen, L., Ye, Y., & Bourlai, T. (2017). Adversarial Machine Learning in Malware Detection: Arms Race between Evasion Attack and Defense. In *Intelligence and Security Informatics Conference (EISIC), 2017 European* (pp. 99–106). Academic Press. 10.1109/EISIC.2017.21

Chen, S., Xue, M., Fan, L., Hao, S., Xu, L., Zhu, H., & Li, B. (2018). Automated poisoning attacks and defenses in malware detection systems: An adversarial machine learning approach. *Computers & Security, 73*, 326–344. doi:10.1016/j.cose.2017.11.007

Chen, S., Xue, M., Fan, L., Hao, S., Xu, L., Zhu, H., & Li, B. (n.d.). *Automated Poisoning Attacks and Defenses in Malware Detection Systems: An Adversarial Machine Learning Approach*. Academic Press.

Chen, X., Li, B., & Vorobeychik, Y. (2000). Evaluation of Defensive Methods for DNNS Against Multiple Adversarial Evasion Models. In ICLR 2017. doi:10.2507/daaam.scibook.2010.27

Chen, Y., Nadji, Y., Kountouras, A., Monrose, F., Perdisci, R., Antonakakis, M., & Vasiloglou, N. (2017). Practical attacks against graph-based clustering. In *Proceedings of the 2017 ACM SIGSAC Conference on Computer and Communications Security* (pp. 1125–1142). ACM. 10.1145/3133956.3134083

Contagio Mobile. (n.d.). Retrieved December 17, 2018, from http://contagiominidump.blogspot.com/

Cubuk, E. D., Zoph, B., Schoenholz, S. S., & Le, Q. V. (2017). *Intriguing Properties of Adversarial Examples*. ArXiv Preprint ArXiv:1711.02846

Demontis, A., Member, S., Melis, M., Member, S., Biggio, B., Maiorca, D., … Roli, F. (n.d.). *Yes, Machine Learning Can Be More Secure ! A Case Study on Android Malware Detection*. Academic Press.

Dube, P., Bhattacharjee, B., & Petit-bois, E. (n.d.). *Improving Transferability of Deep Neural Networks*. Academic Press.

Erlingsson, Ú., Pihur, V., & Korolova, A. (2014). Rappor: Randomized aggregatable privacy-preserving ordinal response. In *Proceedings of the 2014 ACM SIGSAC conference on computer and communications security* (pp. 1054–1067). ACM. 10.1145/2660267.2660348

Globerson, A., & Roweis, S. (2006). Nightmare at test time: robust learning by feature deletion. In *Proceedings of the 23rd international conference on Machine learning* (pp. 353–360). Academic Press. 10.1145/1143844.1143889

Goodfellow, I. J., Shlens, J., & Szegedy, C. (2014). *Explaining and harnessing adversarial examples*. ArXiv Preprint ArXiv:1412.6572

Grosse, K., Papernot, N., Manoharan, P., Backes, M., & McDaniel, P. (2016). *Adversarial perturbations against deep neural networks for malware classification*. ArXiv Preprint ArXiv:1606.04435

Gupta, B. (n.d.). *Assessment of Honeypots: Issues, Challenges and Future Directions*. Retrieved from https://www.igi-global.com/article/assessment-of-honeypots/196190

Hossain, M., Muhammad, G., & Abdul, W. (n.d.). *Cloud-assisted secure video transmission and sharing framework for smart cities.* Elsevier. Retrieved from https://www.sciencedirect.com/science/article/pii/S0167739X17305198

Hu, W., & Tan, Y. (2016). *Generating Adversarial Malware Examples for Black-Box Attacks Based on GAN.* Academic Press.

Huang, A., Hemberg, E., & Reilly, U. O. (n.d.). *Adversarial Deep Learning for Robust Detection of Binary Encoded Malware.* Academic Press.

Huang, L., Joseph, A. D., Nelson, B., Rubinstein, B. I. P., & Tygar, J. D. (2011). Adversarial machine learning. In *Proceedings of the 4th ACM workshop on Security and artificial intelligence* (pp. 43–58). ACM.

Kallivayalil, T. & Uddin, M. (2017). A Multifamily Android Malware Detection Using Deep Autoencoder Based Feature Extraction. In *Proceedings of 2017 IEEE Conference on Advanced Computing (ICoAC).* IEEE.

Kearns, M., & Li, M. (1993). Learning in the presence of malicious errors. *SIAM Journal on Computing, 22*(4), 807–837. doi:10.1137/0222052

Kurakin, A., Goodfellow, I., & Bengio, S. (2016). *Adversarial examples in the physical world.* ArXiv Preprint ArXiv:1607.02533

Maiorca, D., Biggio, B., Member, S., Chiappe, M. E., Giacinto, G., & Member, S. (n.d.). *Adversarial Detection of Flash Malware : Limitations and Open Issues.* Academic Press.

Mariconti, E., Onwuzurike, L., Andriotis, P., De Cristofaro, E., Ross, G., & Stringhini, G. (2016). *Mamadroid: Detecting android malware by building markov chains of behavioral models.* ArXiv Preprint ArXiv:1612.04433

Moosavi Dezfooli, S. M., Fawzi, A., & Frossard, P. (2016). Deepfool: a simple and accurate method to fool deep neural networks. In *Proceedings of 2016 IEEE Conference on Computer Vision and Pattern Recognition (CVPR).* IEEE. 10.1109/CVPR.2016.282

Nelson, B., Barreno, M., Chi, F. J., Joseph, A. D., Rubinstein, B. I. P., Saini, U., … Xia, K. (2009). Misleading learners: Co-opting your spam filter. In Machine learning in cyber trust (pp. 17–51). Springer.

Nelson, B., Barreno, M., Chi, F. J., Joseph, A. D., Rubinstein, B. I. P., Saini, U., ... Xia, K. (2008). Exploiting Machine Learning to Subvert Your Spam Filter. *LEET, 8,* 1–9.

Ouaguid, A. (2018). *A Novel Security Framework for Managing Android Permissions Using Blockchain Technology.* Academic Press. doi:10.4018/IJCAC.2018010103

Papernot, N., McDaniel, P., Goodfellow, I., Jha, S., Celik, Z. B., & Swami, A. (2017). Practical Black-Box Attacks against Machine Learning. In *Proceedings of the 2017 ACM on Asia Conference on Computer and Communications Security - ASIA CCS '17* (pp. 506–519). New York: ACM Press. 10.1145/3052973.3053009

Papernot, N., McDaniel, P., Jha, S., Fredrikson, M., Celik, Z. B., & Swami, A. (2016). The limitations of deep learning in adversarial settings. In *Security and Privacy (EuroS&P), 2016 IEEE European Symposium on* (pp. 372–387). IEEE. 10.1109/EuroSP.2016.36

Papernot, N., McDaniel, P., Wu, X., Jha, S., & Swami, A. (2016). Distillation as a defense to adversarial perturbations against deep neural networks. In *Security and Privacy (SP), 2016 IEEE Symposium on* (pp. 582–597). IEEE. 10.1109/SP.2016.41

Pham, H. N. A., & Triantaphyllou, E. (2008). The impact of overfitting and overgeneralization on the classification accuracy in data mining. In *Soft computing for knowledge discovery and data mining* (pp. 391–431). Springer. doi:10.1007/978-0-387-69935-6_16

Rozsa, A., Manuel, G., & Boult, T. E. (2018). *Towards Robust Deep Neural Networks with BANG.* Academic Press.

Rubinstein, B. I. P., Bartlett, P. L., Huang, L., & Taft, N. (2009). *Learning in a large function space: Privacy-preserving mechanisms for SVM learning.* ArXiv Preprint ArXiv:0911.5708

Stokes, J. W., Wang, D., Marinescu, M., Marino, M., & Bussone, B. (n.d.). Attack and Defense of Dynamic Analysis-Based. *Adversarial Neural Malware Classification Models.*

Strauss, T., Hanselmann, M., Junginger, A., & Ulmer, H. (2017). *Ensemble methods as a defense to adversarial perturbations against deep neural networks.* ArXiv Preprint ArXiv:1709.03423

Tanay, T., & Griffin, L. (2016). *A boundary tilting persepective on the phenomenon of adversarial examples.* ArXiv Preprint ArXiv:1608.07690

The Drebin Dataset. (n.d.). Retrieved December 17, 2018, from https://www.sec.cs.tu-bs.de/~danarp/drebin/

Tramèr, F., Kurakin, A., Papernot, N., Boneh, D., & McDaniel, P. (2017). *Ensemble adversarial training: Attacks and defenses.* ArXiv Preprint ArXiv:1705.07204

Tramèr, F., Papernot, N., Goodfellow, I., Boneh, D., & McDaniel, P. (2017). *The space of transferable adversarial examples.* ArXiv Preprint ArXiv:1704.03453

Valiant, L. G. (n.d.). *Learning Disjunction of Conjunctions. Academic Press.*

VirusShare.com. (n.d.). Retrieved December 17, 2018, from https://virusshare.com/

VirusTotal. (n.d.). Retrieved December 17, 2018, from https://www.virustotal.com/#/home/upload

Wang, Q., Guo, W., Zhang, K., Ororbia, A. G. II, Xing, X., Liu, X., & Giles, C. L. (2017). Adversary resistant deep neural networks with an application to malware detection. In *Proceedings of the 23rd ACM SIGKDD International Conference on Knowledge Discovery and Data Mining* (pp. 1145–1153). ACM. 10.1145/3097983.3098158

Xu, W., Qi, Y., & Evans, D. (2016a). Automatically Evading Classifiers: A Case Study on PDF Malware Classifiers. *NDSS.* Retrieved from https://www.semanticscholar.org/paper/Automatically-Evading-Classifiers%3A-A-Case-Study-on-Xu-Qi/5e4fa9397c18062b970910f8ee168d3297cf098f

Xu, W., Qi, Y., & Evans, D. (2016b). *Automatically evading classifiers*. Academic Press.

Yang, C., Wu, Q., Li, H., & Chen, Y. (2017). *Generative poisoning attack method against neural networks*. ArXiv Preprint ArXiv:1703.01340

Yang, W., Kong, D., Xie, T., & Gunter, C. A. (2017). Malware detection in adversarial settings: Exploiting feature evolutions and confusions in android apps. In *Proceedings of the 33rd Annual Computer Security Applications Conference* (pp. 288–302). Academic Press. 10.1145/3134600.3134642

Yang, W., Xiao, X., Andow, B., Li, S., Xie, T., & Enck, W. (n.d.). *AppContext: Differentiating Malicious and Benign Mobile App Behaviors Using Context*. Retrieved from http://taoxie.cs.illinois.edu/publications/icse15-appcontext.pdf

Yuan, X., He, P., Zhu, Q., Bhat, R. R., & Li, X. (2017). *Adversarial Examples: Attacks and Defenses for Deep Learning*. ArXiv Preprint ArXiv:1712.07107

Zantedeschi, V., Nicolae, M.-I., & Rawat, A. (2017). Efficient defenses against adversarial attacks. In *Proceedings of the 10th ACM Workshop on Artificial Intelligence and Security* (pp. 39–49). ACM.

Zhang, F., Member, S., Chan, P. P. K., Biggio, B., Yeung, D. S., & Roli, F. (2015). Article. *Evasion Attacks*, *46*(3), 1–12. doi:10.1109/TCYB.2015.2415032

Zhou, Y., Jiang, X., & Nazish, A. (2011). Dissecting Android Malware : Characterization and Evolution Summarized by : Nazish Asad. *Proceedings - IEEE Symposium on Security and Privacy*, (4), 95–109. 10.1109/SP.2012.16

Chapter 8

A Privacy–Preserving Feature Extraction Method for Big Data Analytics Based on Data–Independent Reusable Projection

Siddharth Ravindran
National Institute of Technology Puducherry, India

Aghila G.
National Institute of Technology Puducherry, India

ABSTRACT

Big data analytics is one of the key research areas ever since the advancement of internet technologies, social media, mobile networks, and internet of things (IoT). The volume of big data creates a major challenge to the data scientist while interpreting the information from raw data. The privacy of user data is an important issue faced by the users who utilize the computing resources from third party (i.e., cloud environment). This chapter proposed a data independent reusable projection (DIRP) technique for reducing the dimension of the original high dimensional data and also preserves the privacy of the data in analysis phase. The proposed method projects the high dimensional input data into the random low dimensional space. The data independent and distance preserving property helps the proposed method to reduce the computational complexity of the machine learning algorithm. The randomness of data masks the original input data which helps to solve the privacy issue during data analysis. The proposed algorithm has been tested with the MNIST hand written digit recognition dataset.

DOI: 10.4018/978-1-5225-8407-0.ch008

INTRODUCTION

In the era of ICE age (Information, Communication and Entertainment), the growth of the data is at an exponential rate. The statistics from IBM (Quick Facts and Stats on Big Data, n.d.) states that, there are approximately 294 billion of email sent and 230 million of tweets in a day and there are trillions of sensors populating the Internet of Things (IoT) with the real time data. The process of data generation has become a lot easier, thanks to the advancement in Smartphone, Internet and other sensor applications. In the current scenario, Data is not only a piece of information it is also an asset for the industries and organizations in order to reduce their operational cost and to improve the profit, apart from highly influencing working environment for betterment. The popular magazine forbes predicted that the revenue of the worldwide big data market for software and services are expected to increase from 42 Billion USD (2018) to 103 Billion USD (2027) with the compound annual growth rate of 10.48% (Columbus, L, 2018). The real problem of big data analytics arise if the system is not capable of addressing 5 V's (Volume, Velocity, Variety, Value and Veracity) to harvest the best yield from the huge amount of data (Tsai, C.et al., 2015). The sophisticated hardware is not only the solution to address the complexities in big data but also requires significant contributions from the software. This chapter highlights the research issues especially in software related data analysis and applications.

Issues in Big Data Analytics

Big data analytics needs significant research concern for solving the large, complex and unstructured data collected from various independent sources. The applications of big data analytics has been widely expanded to almost all the engineering and science domain (Ouf, S., & Nasr, M. (2015)). The main constraint for big data analytics is the various levels of information which could be obtained or inferred from the available large chunk of data. Among the 5 V's of big data, Volume is one of the key research areas since the voluminous of data frustrates the data scientist and programmers to take insights from the data. The more we collect the data, the more we get the information which is not always true in the case of big data analytics (Chen, C. P., & Zhang, C., 2014). All the collected data may not be useful for the data analysis because of the huge number of uninformative features in the data set. The humungous amount of data increases both the storage and computational complexity in big data analytics. This problem is commonly termed as Curse of Dimensionality (Xie et al., 2016). The traditional machine learning algorithm does not suit well for handling big data analytics due to the complex characteristics of big data like huge volume, different variety of data, etc. The dimension reduction techniques come into the scenario in order to reduce the complexity of existing machine learning algorithm. For example, consider a scenario where the data scientist wants to train a model to find the activity performed by the user using smart phone sensors using k- Nearest Neighbor (k-NN) classifier. k-NN is one of the most influential machine learning algorithm and it follows lazy leaning approach. If the user performs any activity, then the sensors transfer the test data to the k-NN for classification. k-NN computes distance between the test data with all the training data to find the k- nearest neighbors. The complex computation during testing makes the k-NN algorithm not suitable for big data analytics. Dimension reduction techniques reduce the complexity of machine learning algorithm either by projecting the data into lower dimensional space or by removing the unwanted features.

Dimension Reduction Techniques in Big Data

Dimension reduction (DR) is the prominent solution to address the Curse of Dimensionality issue. The DR methods help the machine learning algorithm to create the efficient model with only informative feature set for better analysis (Das, S., & Kalita, H. K. (2016)). Advantages of DR techniques are as follows:

1. Boosts the performance of the machine learning algorithm
2. Either removes or reduces the irrelevant or redundant features and offers a compact representation.
3. Preserves the structure of the data even without having all the features.
4. The memory requirement for performing machine learning algorithm largely reduces using the DR techniques.
5. The complexity of visualizing the data is reduced significantly.

Figure 1 represents the overview of DR techniques. Generally DR methods are broadly classified into

1. Feature selection
2. Feature extraction.

Feature selection chooses the subset of the original feature set to model the data mining problem. Many feature selection algorithm uses statistical approach to rank the features and select only informative features to perform data analysis (Aboudi, N. E., & Benhlima, L. (2017)). Domain knowledge is mandatory requirement for the users while using feature selection algorithms in order to select the features. The popular feature selection methods are filter method, wrapper method and embedded method. Unlike feature selection, *feature extraction* is an unsupervised approach where the domain knowledge is not required. Feature extraction transforms the original high dimensional input data into a new set of low dimensional feature set. The transformation can be either linear or non linear.

This chapter highlights the linear feature extraction due to the expensive computational requirement for the non-linear method (Hira, Z. M., & Gillies, D. F. (2015)). Some of the popular linear feature extraction techniques are PCA, SVD, LDA and random projection. Even though feature selection algorithm maintains the original features, it requires more computational power when compared to feature extraction techniques. The mandatory requirement of domain knowledge also adds additional constraint for the users (Li, J., & Liu, H., 2017). Hence, feature extraction is the viable option for most of the big data applications due to its unsupervised nature and less computational requirement. The original high dimensional input data (DS_{org}) is projected into low dimensional subspace by multiplying with the projection matrix R to get the reduced dimension (DS_{red}). This chapter introduces a new data independent reusable projection (DIRP) technique for feature extraction. The random projection is the core part of the DIRP method, where the projection of data is simple and straight forward (Benner, P.,2015). The data independent property indicates the generation of projection matrix R does not depend on the content of DS_{org}. In the DIRP method, the transformation of original features into a new subset of features adds an additional advantage to the users by preserving the privacy of the original data.

Figure 1. Overview of dimension reduction techniques

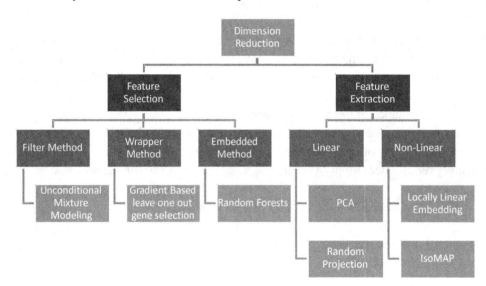

Data Privacy Issues in Big Data

Government and business agency are the main source of big data where most of the data deals with personal information (Priyadarshinee, P. (2018)). In these applications, the user's privacy is commonly at danger when the data is stores centrally in cloud environment. Particularly privacy preservation is one of the key issues while handling the big data in cloud infrastructure. Even though cloud computing makes the big data analytics much easier and distributed, it also induced the data privacy threat to the cloud users (Bhushan, K., & Gupta, B. (2017)). The big data life cycle is divided into three different phase 1. Data generation 2.Data storage and 3.Data analysis. The privacy issue arises in each phase of the big data life cycle (Jain, P. et al., 2016). In the data generation phase, the users either give the data explicitly to the third party or the data are generated by the user's online activity. Access restriction and falsifying the information is the commonly used methods to solve the privacy threat in data generation phase.

In data storage phase, the big data users most often go for cloud storage. If the storage system is compromised, then it is a critical issue as the personal information can be disclosed (Ramachandran et al., 2014). Application level encryption, file level and database level security schemes are the familiar solutions for protecting storage level privacy breach. For example, consider a user has large volume of his data stored in the data center and wants to perform some machine learning algorithm on the original data. The privacy issue arises when the cloud users are forced to give the data for analysis to the cloud service providers due to the lack of personal/own computing infrastructure available. In cloud computing, the users have less/no control over the data which leads to the privacy threat in the analysis phase (Bhushan, K., & Gupta, B. B. (2018, April 20)). De-identification and data anonymization are the widely used solutions for privacy threat in the analysis phase.

This chapter aims to introduce the DIRP technique for projecting the original high dimensional data into the low dimensional sub space for feature extraction and also anonymize the original data to prevent the privacy threat in the data analysis phase. Figure 2 shows the evolution of DIRP method. The distances in the high (original data) and low (anonymized data) dimensional space are nearly preserved with the

Figure 2. Evolution of DIRP

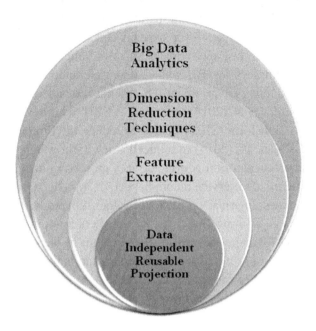

controlled amount of error (using the epsilon parameter). This property allows the technique to perform any machine learning algorithm in the low dimensional or anonymized data set. Figure 3 represents the data flow of the DIRP method while executing a machine learning algorithm. The data in the dotted rectangle box are outsourced to the third party for data analysis that needs privacy. The next section in this chapter provides a brief overview of the researches and studies related to the feature extraction and privacy preservation in big data analytics.

LITERATURE REVIEW

Feature extraction is the first step before doing data analysis. Principal Component Analysis (PCA) is one of the oldest and widely used feature extraction technique proposed by Pearson, K. (1901) which is basis for many feature extraction algorithms like Kernel PCA, Independent Component Analysis (ICA), Robust PCA, etc. Zhang, T., & Yang, B. (2018) proposed a modified version of PCA that suits for big data applications by scanning each row of data and applied the proposed PCA approach to minimize the storage complexity. Zhang, R., et al. (2018) proposed DRWPCA algorithm based on dimension reduction window scheme. Instead of mapping the data to another dimensional space, this method retains all most all the information by analyzing the correlation between the dimensions.

This method provides promising accuracy and also preserves the original information. The above two works based on PCA suffers with the high computational cost for scanning each row and finding the correlation between the dimensions. Kaur, D., et al. (2018) proposed a tensor based big data management scheme for dimension reduction in software define networking perspective. Random projection is a simple and computationally efficient feature extraction technique that preserves the information between the data in the high and low dimensional space (Bingham, E., & Mannila, H. (2001)). Thanei,

G., et al. (2017) discussed the application of random projection for large scale regression. The author also discussed the multiple random projections for parallel implementation.

The randomized dimensionality reduction for k-means clustering proposed by Boutsidis, C., et al. (2015) used random projection with fast approximate Singular Value Decomposition (SVD) factorization for efficient clustering. Damaševičius, R., et al. (2016) used random projection for human activity recognition in ambient assisted living environment. This method considered both activity identification and subject identification. Qin, Z., et al. (2014) proposed SecSIFT, a high performance privacy preserving Scalar Invariant Feature Transform (SIFT) system to reduce the limitation of encryption system. Rahulamathavan, Y., & Rajarajan, M. (2015) introduced a new light weight randomization scheme to avoid the complexity of encryption algorithm during privacy preservation. Qi, L., et al. (2017) proposed a novel privacy preserving distributed service recommendation approach DistSRLSH based on locality sensitive hashing. The randomness in privacy preservation algorithm reduces the computational requirement of traditional encryption algorithms. Due to the advantage of random projection in computational intensive task, the proposed DIRP technique utilizes the core part of random projection properties (i.e. data independent and distance preserving) to reduce the computational complexity by reusing the same projection matrix for different data of same size. The next section in this chapter introduces the DIRP technique which mainly intended to solve the curse of dimensionality and privacy issue.

DIRP TECHNIQUE

The DIRP technique works on the raw input data of the users who wants to perform any machine learning algorithm on the data. Based on the size of the original raw data, a new random projection matrix has been generated and populated with the independent and identically distributed values. Then the original raw data has been projected into the lower dimensional subspace using the random projection matrix. The new features in the lower dimensional space preserve the original information as much as possible with the controlled amount of error. Due to the randomness of the projection, the content of the new feature set is entirely different from the original feature set but interestingly maintaining the structure. This al-

Figure 3. Data flow of machine learning algorithm using DIRP

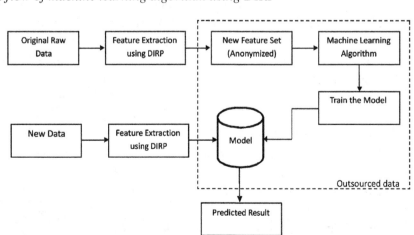

lows the users to mask the original feature set while doing data analysis in the compromised or multi user environment. Then the machine learning algorithm has been executed on the new low dimensional data. The experiment shows that the DIRP method reduces the running time of the algorithm and also preserves the privacy of the data with the negligible loss of accuracy. Random projection is the core operation of this DIRP technique. Figure 4 illustrates the flow chart of DIRP method.

Random Projection

Random projection maps the data from high dimensional space into low dimensional space and it also manages to approximately preserve individual lengths and pair-wise distances between the original and arbitrary data points, where data point refers the discrete unit of information/ any single fact (Bingham, E., & Mannila, H., 2001). In contrast with the other dimension reduction techniques like PCA, random projection does not rely on the input data at all (Haris, B. C., & Sinha, R., 2014). This property makes the direction of the projection to be independent and reduce the computational complexity. The projection technique of random projection is simple and straight forward. D represents the original high dimensional input data with M number of rows and N number of columns. R represents the random projection matrix filled with random numbers generated from statistical distributions with N number of rows and k number of columns, where k is the size of the low dimensional space. The original 'N' dimensional data is projected into reduced 'k' dimensional subspace. Matrix multiplication is the core

Figure 4. Flowchart of DIRP

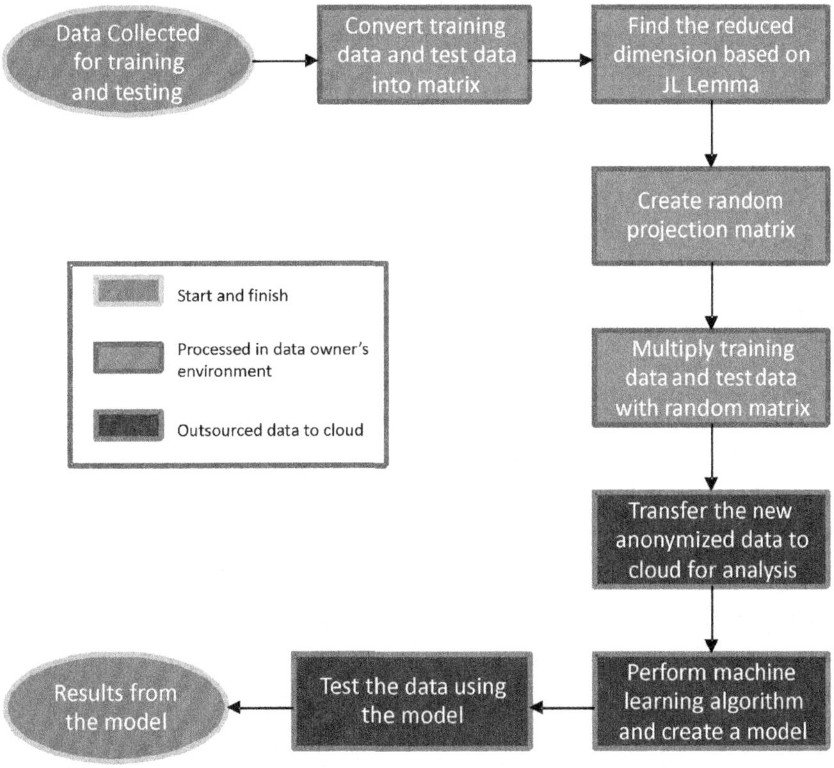

operation in random projection where D and R are multiplied to get the low dimensional projected data P with M number of rows and k number of columns.

$$P = D_{M*N} \cdot R_{N*k}$$

The matrix P hides the original features in the high dimensional space but it manages to approximately preserve the individual length and pair wise distance between the data points in the high and low dimensional space. The distance preserving property of this method helps the programmers to execute the machine learning task in the low dimensional space without revealing the original features.

There are two important operations in random projection. They are

1. Finding the value of 'k' and
2. Finding the suitable distribution to populate the random projection matrix R.

The Johnson- Lindenstrauss (JL) Lemma (Johnson, W. B., 1986) is the heart of the random projection which is used to determine the size of k. The next sub section describes the Johnson-Lindenstrauss lemma and its proof.

Johnson – Lindenstrauss Lemma

The lemma states that any *n* points in the high dimensional space can be embedded into a space of much lower *k* dimension, where k ≥ O(*log n /* $\in^2$) without distorting the Euclidean distance between any two data points more than a factor of *(1 ± ∈)*. The literature shows that the lemma has been successfully used in dimensionality reduction, compressed sensing, manifold learning and graph embedding. The lemma states that

Suppose X has 'n' data points, X = {$x_1,x_2,\ldots\ldots x_n$} in $\mathbb{R}^d$. Then for any set A of n points in $\mathbb{R}^d$ there exist a map f: $\mathbb{R}^d \rightarrow \mathbb{R}^k$ *such that for all u, v Є A*

$$\left(1-\epsilon\right)\left\|u-v\right\|^2 \leq \left\|f\left(u\right)-f\left(v\right)\right\|^2 \leq \left(1+\epsilon\right)\left\|u-v\right\|^2 \tag{1}$$

The $\in$ is the threshold parameter for distance preservation between any two points. For example, consider the situation where the user wants the deviation of the distance between the data points in the high dimensional and low dimensional space should not exceed 5%. Here 5 is the value of $\in$ and it should be in the range of 1 to 100%. The JL lemma also states that the number of dimension required to project the data in the lower dimension space is completely independent to the original number of dimension.

Proof of JL Lemma

Dasgupta, S., and Gupta, A. (2002) provides the elementary proof for the JL Lemma. The main result of the proof shows that

For any $0 < \in < 1$ and any integer n, let k be a positive integer such that

$$k \geq 4 \left(\frac{\in^2}{2} - \frac{\in^3}{3} \right)^{-1} \ln n \qquad (2)$$

The input dataset could be of any number of dimensions but the identification of k value for JL lemma requires only two parameters i) Number of dimension and ii) Threshold parameter $\in$. The higher value of $\in$ indicates that the higher distortion in the distances are accepted by user and which also points out that the less number of dimension in the low dimensional space leads to the faster computations. Here $\in$ is the trade-off parameter between faster computation and accuracy.

Properties of Random Projection

Random projection method has some unique properties that make it stand out from the crowd of many feature extraction algorithms. The step for finding PCA involves the computation of the covariance matrix for the input data. Then it decomposes the covariance matrix into singular value form and finally chooses the top n Eigenvectors from the decomposition. The computational complexity of PCA is O(MN²+N³), where M and N are rows and columns respectively. The computational complexity is largely reduced by the simple matrix multiplication computation. The computational complexity of random projection

Algorithm 1. To find Value of 'k'

```
Input              : Number of dimension 'N', ∈
Output        : Reduced Dimension 'k'
1. Begin
2. if N ≤ 0 then
3.         Goto Step 10
4. end
5. if (0 < ∈ < 1) then
6.         k =    4 log N
                 ─────────
                  ∈²   ∈³
                  ── − ──
                  2    3
7. else
8.     Goto Step 10
9. end
10. End
```

is O(kMN), where k is the reduced dimension value. Due to the complexity of the procedure outlined earlier, random projection is the viable option to perform feature extraction for big data applications.

The significant property of random projection is the data independent characteristics. In contrast to random projection, most of the other popular feature extraction techniques are data dependent. As mentioned in the earlier section, the projection of PCA depends on the content of the original data. In random projection, the projection matrix is being generated by random numbers where the matrix generation is no way related to the content of the data. Consider the IoT application, where the group of sensors sends the information to the server which requires feature extraction. For this application, PCA needs to wait until it received the last data and then compute the projection map. In the next time period, it is required to repeat the same step again. Where as in random projection, the projection matrix can be generated before the arrival of the data and also it could be reused for all the time slots unless and until there is a change in the number of features i.e. N. The reusable property further reduces the computational complexity of generating new projection matrix every time. The next important advantage of random projection is its distance preserving property. Random projection manages to approximately preserve the individual length and pair wise distance between the inter data points in the high and low dimensional space. This property helps the existing many machine learning algorithms that are working based on distances like k-nearest neighbor classification, k- means clustering algorithm, etc.

Even though the proposed scheme is random and independent to the data, the underlying structure has to be maintained using different statistical distributions. Figure 5 explains the distortion distribution of distance between original data points and projected data points. The 10,000 dimensions are projected into 692 dimensions with $\in$ value 0.1 (10%). The histogram shows that all the data are distorted by less than 10%. The next section lists the different projection distributions used to generate the random projection matrix R.

PROJECTION DISTRIBUTION

This section deals with the list of all distributions that are used to populate the random projection matrix R. The widely used distributions are 1. Gaussian 2. Probability 3. Achlioptas and 4.Li. The elements

Figure 5. Distortion distribution

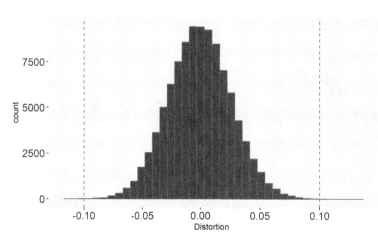

Gaussian Distribution

The elements in the random projection matrix R is filled with the elements chosen from gaussian distribution. In probability theory, the gaussian distribution is also called as normal distribution which is a continuous probability distribution used to represent real valued random variables whose distributions are unknown. The probability density function of normal distribution is given in Equation.3

$$f(x|\mu,\sigma) = \frac{1}{\sqrt{2\pi\sigma^2}} e^{-\frac{(x-\mu)^2}{2\sigma^2}} \tag{3}$$

where μ is the mean and σ is the standard deviation. The elements in the random matrix are drawn from normal distribution N(0,1/k), where 'k' value is calculated based on Algorithm 1.

Probability Distribution

In this distribution, the elements in the matrix R is filled with [+1, -1] with equal probability distribution.

$$R_{ij} = \begin{cases} +1 & p = \dfrac{1}{2} \\ -1 & p = \dfrac{1}{2} \end{cases} \tag{4}$$

Achlioptas Distribution

Achlioptas,D., et al. (2003) proposed a distribution which will be useful in a situation where the code for the gaussian distribution is not readily available. For example, In the case of database applications. The Achlioptas method generates sparse matrix in contrast to the dense matrix from gaussian distribution. The matrix was easy to generate and 2/3rd of the matrix elements were filled with zero to reduce the computation.

$$R_{ij} = \begin{cases} +1 & p = \dfrac{1}{6} \\ 0 & p = \dfrac{2}{3} \\ -1 & p = \dfrac{1}{6} \end{cases} \tag{5}$$

Algorithm 2. To generate matrix 'R'

```
Input                    : Row M, Column N, reduced dimension 'k'
Output           : Random matrix R N x k
1.        Begin
2.        if (M ≤ 0)  ∨ (N ≤ 0) then
3.             Goto Step 18.
4.        end
5.        if method =  Gaussian then
6.             Create R N x k using Equation 3.
7.             Goto Step 18
8.        else if  method =  Probability then
9.             Create R N x k using Equation 4.
10.            Goto Step 18
11.       else if  method =  Achlioptas then
12.            Create R N x k using Equation 5.
13.            Goto Step 18
14.       else if  method =  Li then
15.            Create R N x k using Equation 6.
16.            Goto Step 18
17.       end
18.       End
```

Li Distribution

Li, P. et al., (2006) proposed the generalized approach of Achlioptas distribution and generate very sparse random matrix. It improves the computational speed of random projection by $\sqrt{N}$ fold by giving s = $\sqrt{N}$, where N is the number of dimension in the original input data. The random matrix R is generated based on the Equation 6.

$$R_{ij} = +\sqrt{s} \begin{cases} +1 & p = \dfrac{1}{2s} \\ 0 & p = 1 - \dfrac{1}{2s} \\ -1 & p = \dfrac{1}{2s} \end{cases} \tag{6}$$

The above are the 4 widely used distributions to generate random projection matrix. The other distributions are Haar matrix, toeplitz matrix, hadamard matrix, etc. The random projection does not project the data into a complete arbitrary subspace rather it has an underlying structure which has a loose restriction within the structure. A careful selection of random projection matrix is mandatory based on the requirement in order to satisfy all the properties of the random projection. The following section highlights the experiments done in MNIST hand written digit recognition application and its result analysis to show the significance of DIRP method.

EXPERIMENTS

Image data is one of the most common and widely available data. Due to the popularity of social media applications, image became integral part of the communication and conversation. The DIRP method has been evaluated for the handwritten image dataset. The next subsection discusses the details of the dataset.

Dataset

The most commonly used dataset that are used to train the algorithms in computer vision and machine learning has been selected for testing. The Modified National Institute of Standards and Technology [MNIST] (Lecun, Y. et al., 1998) hand written digit dataset is the subset of popular handwritten dataset NIST. The dataset consist of 60,000 training set samples and 10,000 test set samples. All the sampled images were centered in 28 X 28 images with a total of 784 pixel information. There are ten class variables labeled from 0 to 9. Five sample images from each digit of the MNIST hand written digit dataset has been listed in Figure 6.

Hardware and Software Environment

The experiment has been carried out in the computing environment with Intel Xeon CPU E5-1607 with the primary memory of 4GB. The R version 3.3.1 installed in windows 7 operating system has been used for programming. k-Nearest Neighbor (k-NN) classifier which is one of the most popular machine learning algorithm has been used to train the classifier. k-NN classifier is famous for its lazy learning approach where the distance between the test data and training data is computed instantly without any explicit training step. The performance of the k-NN algorithm seriously suffers while testing with the high dimensional data due to its complex computational requirement at the testing phase. The proposed scheme perfectly fits the situation to handle the complexity of k-NN algorithm by reducing the dimension and reusing the same projection matrix. The evaluation metrics for the classifier has been listed in the next sub section.

Figure 6. Sample data from MNIST

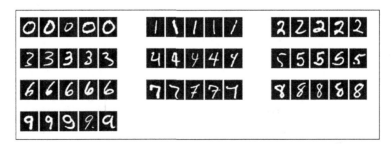

Evaluation Metrics

In order to analyze the performance of the classification algorithm, several performance metrics has been measured. The complete experiment has been iterated over 20 times and the average value has been presented in the result section. The evaluation metrics are listed below:

1. **Running Time**: The computation time has been calculated using proc.time() function available in the R language and the unit of measurement is seconds.
2. **Confusion Matrix**: A table in structure that shows the summary of prediction results of the classification algorithm. The default structure of confusion matrix is given below:

    The list of metrics derived from confusion matrix includes

1. Accuracy $= \dfrac{TP + TN}{TP + TN + FP + FN}$

2. Sensitivity $= \dfrac{TP}{TP + FN}$

3. Specificity $= \dfrac{TN}{TN + FP}$

4. Positive predictive value $= \dfrac{TP}{TP + FP}$

5. Negative predictive value $= \dfrac{TN}{TN + FN}$

6. **Kappa**: It is an important measurement for analyzing the performance of the classifier on imbalanced dataset. Sometimes it is also used to evaluate different classifier amongst them.

$$\text{Kappa} = \frac{OA - EA}{1 - EA},$$

where OA is Observed accuracy and EA is Expected Accuracy.

Results

This section shows the important observations collected from the application of DIRP technique on MNIST dataset. The entire dataset has been represented as a large matrix with each row is an image and each column is its corresponding pixel information. The data has been classified using k-Nearest

Table 1. Default structure of confusion matrix

	Predicted Class: Yes	Predicted Class: No
Actual Class: Yes	True Positive (TP)	False Negative(FN)
Actual Class: No	False Positive (FP)	True Negative (TN)

Neighbor algorithm and the classifier chooses the k-value based on the repeated cross validation. Table 1 shows the evaluation metrics of the k-NN classifier in the form of different performance metrics.

From Table 2, it is easily understood that the performance of the classifier is not distorted significantly and the running time of the classifier has been largely reduced.

The Table 3 provides the confusion matrix for the MNIST dataset. It represents the match between actual class and predicted class. This table is the source to calculate other evaluation metrics like accuracy, sensitivity, specificity, positive and negative predictive value. The highlighted portion in the Table 3 denotes the actual class that has been properly classified into the predicted class during testing phase. For example, consider the class 0 i.e. first row, 98.27% of the test data has been exactly classified as 0. The remaining 1.73% of data has not been predicted exactly. The sum of all the values in the each row is 100%.

The bar chart in Figure 7 represents the comparison of running time between different epsilon values with different distributions. The Epsilon ($\in$) value is inversely proportional to the running time of the algorithm. Whenever the $\in$ value is increased, the user is ready to accept higher amount of distortion

Table 2. Classifier evaluation metrics

S. No.	Evaluation Metrics	MNIST With DIR	MNIST Without DIRP
1.	Running Time	346.8 Seconds	10570.8 Seconds
2.	Accuracy	93.32%	94.03%
3.	Sensitivity	93.22%	94.04%
4.	Specificity	99.25%	99.33%
5.	Positive Predictive Value	93.47%	94.22%
6.	Negative Predictive Value	99.25%	99.33%
7.	Kappa	92.57%	93.36%

Table 3. Confusion matrix of MNIST DATASET

		Predicted Class									
		0	1	2	3	4	5	6	7	8	9
Actual Class	0	**98.27**	0.35	0	0	0	0.35	0.69	0	0	0.34
	1	0	**100**	0	0	0	0	0	0	0	0
	2	1.61	2.89	**84.56**	0.64	0	0.32	1.29	5.79	1.94	0.96
	3	0	0.68	0.34	**94.2**	0	2.4	0	1.02	1.36	0
	4	1	2	0	0	**91.97**	0.34	0.34	0.34	0.67	3.34
	5	0	1.58	0	2.77	0	**94.07**	0.79	0	0.79	0
	6	0.41	0.35	0	0	1.41	1.06	**95.07**	0.35	0	0.35
	7	0.71	1.06	1.06	0	0	0	0	**95.76**	0.35	1.06
	8	1	1	0.67	4.67	1.33	1	0.33	2.33	**82.33**	5.34
	9	0.34	0.67	0	0	1	0	0	0.67	0.34	**96.98**

in their output so obviously it requires less number of dimension to project the data. Thus the running time will get reduced.

The line graph in Figure 8 illustrates the comparison of accuracy of different epsilon value with four different distributions. Likewise running time, the accuracy is also inversely proportional to the value of Epsilon ($\in$). Figure 8 illustrates that the value of accuracy decreased approximately 1 to 2% when the $\in$ value changes from 25% to 50%. Then it was dropped 4 to 5% when the $\in$ value changes from 50% to 75%.

Figure 7. Running time comparison

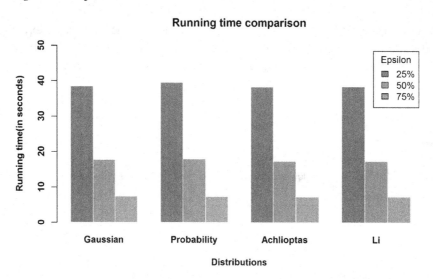

Figure 8. Accuracy comparison

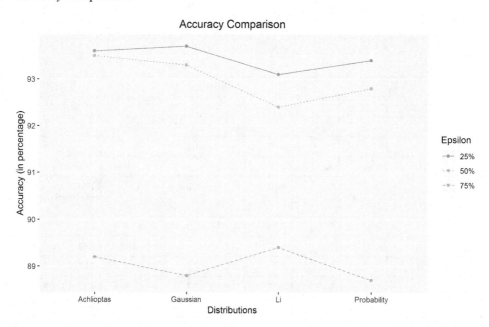

It is understood that choosing of epsilon value plays significant role in the entire process. The objective of DIRP method is to provide the solution for feature extraction with privacy preserving characteristics. As the classifier only work with the transformed low dimensional data, the privacy of the original data is maintained throughout the experiment.

CONCLUSION AND FUTURE SCOPE

This chapter identifies the two important issues in the big data analytics and also provides a solution in the form of new data independent reusable projection technique. The objective of the DIRP method is to reduce the computational complexity of the existing feature extraction dimension reduction method and also preserves the privacy of the data in the analysis phase. Leading to a data independent technique, all the properties of the DIRP method make the algorithm more suitable for dimension reduction in big data classification. The experiments conducted on MNIST dataset shows that the DIRP method has the capability to reduce the loss of distortion in the low dimensional space with the considerable reduction in the running time. The popular distributions to generate the random matrix are discussed. Due to the randomness of the data, the proposed technique may not be suitable for accuracy sensitive real time applications like medical image processing. The accuracy of the system will get hugely affected if the user provides inappropriate epsilon value. In future, the proposed system can be extended by providing additional function that guides the user to select the appropriate epsilon value based on application. This work can be extended to perform real time video processing applications.

REFERENCES

Aboudi, N. E., & Benhlima, L. (2017). Parallel and Distributed Population based Feature Selection Framework for Health Monitoring. *International Journal of Cloud Applications and Computing*, 7(1), 57–71. doi:10.4018/IJCAC.2017010104

Achlioptas, D. (2003). Database-friendly random projections: Johnson-Lindenstrauss with binary coins. *Journal of Computer and System Sciences*, 66(4), 671–687. doi:10.1016/S0022-0000(03)00025-4

Benner, P., Gugercin, S., & Willcox, K. (2015). A Survey of Projection-Based Model Reduction Methods for Parametric Dynamical Systems. *SIAM Review*, 57(4), 483–531. doi:10.1137/130932715

Bhushan, K., & Gupta, B. (2017). Security challenges in cloud computing: State-of-art. *International Journal of Big Data Intelligence*, 4(2), 81. doi:10.1504/IJBDI.2017.083116

Bhushan, K., & Gupta, B. B. (2018). Distributed denial of service (DDoS) attack mitigation in software defined network (SDN)-based cloud computing environment. *Journal of Ambient Intelligence and Humanized Computing*, 1–13. doi:10.100712652-018-0800-9

Bingham, E., & Mannila, H. (2001). Random projection in dimensionality reduction. *Proceedings of the Seventh ACM SIGKDD International Conference on Knowledge Discovery and Data Mining - KDD 01*. 10.1145/502512.502546

Boutsidis, C., Zouzias, A., Mahoney, M. W., & Drineas, P. (2015). Randomized Dimensionality Reduction for k -Means Clustering. *IEEE Transactions on Information Theory*, *61*(2), 1045–1062. doi:10.1109/TIT.2014.2375327

Chen, C. P., & Zhang, C. (2014). Data-intensive applications, challenges, techniques and technologies: A survey on Big Data. *Information Sciences*, *275*, 314–347. doi:10.1016/j.ins.2014.01.015

Columbus, L. (2018). *10 Charts That Will Change Your Perspective Of Big Data's Growth*. Retrieved from http://www.forbes.com/sites/louiscolumbus/2018/05/23/10-charts-that-will-change-your-perspective-of-big-datas-growth/#232420072926

Damaševičius, R., Vasiljevas, M., Šalkevičius, J., & Woźniak, M. (2016). Human Activity Recognition in AAL Environments Using Random Projections. *Computational and Mathematical Methods in Medicine*, *2016*, 1–17. doi:10.1155/2016/4073584 PMID:27413392

Das, S., & Kalita, H. K. (2016). Advanced Dimensionality Reduction Method for Big Data. *Big Data*, 2388–2400. doi:10.4018/978-1-4666-9840-6.ch108

Dasgupta, S., & Gupta, A. (2002). An elementary proof of a theorem of Johnson and Lindenstrauss. *Random Structures and Algorithms*, *22*(1), 60–65. doi:10.1002/rsa.10073

Haris, B. C., & Sinha, R. (2014). Exploring Data-Independent Dimensionality Reduction in Sparse Representation-Based Speaker Identification. *Circuits, Systems, and Signal Processing*, *33*(8), 2521–2538. doi:10.100700034-014-9757-x

Hira, Z. M., & Gillies, D. F. (2015). A Review of Feature Selection and Feature Extraction Methods Applied on Microarray Data. *Advances in Bioinformatics*, *2015*, 1–13. doi:10.1155/2015/198363 PMID:26170834

Jain, P., Gyanchandani, M., & Khare, N. (2016). Big data privacy: A technological perspective and review. *Journal of Big Data*, *3*(1), 25. doi:10.118640537-016-0059-y

Johnson, W. B., Lindenstrauss, J., & Schechtman, G. (1986). Extensions of lipschitz maps into Banach spaces. *Israel Journal of Mathematics*, *54*(2), 129–138. doi:10.1007/BF02764938

Kaur, D., Aujla, G. S., Kumar, N., Zomaya, A. Y., Perera, C., & Ranjan, R. (2018). Tensor-Based Big Data Management Scheme for Dimensionality Reduction Problem in Smart Grid Systems: SDN Perspective. *IEEE Transactions on Knowledge and Data Engineering*, *30*(10), 1985–1998. doi:10.1109/TKDE.2018.2809747

Lecun, Y., Bottou, L., Bengio, Y., & Haffner, P. (1998). Gradient-based learning applied to document recognition. *Proceedings of the IEEE*, *86*(11), 2278–2324. doi:10.1109/5.726791

Li, J., & Liu, H. (2017). Challenges of Feature Selection for Big Data Analytics. *IEEE Intelligent Systems*, *32*(2), 9–15. doi:10.1109/MIS.2017.38

Li, P., Hastie, T. J., & Church, K. W. (2006). Very sparse random projections. *Proceedings of the 12th ACM SIGKDD International Conference on Knowledge Discovery and Data Mining - KDD 06*. 10.1145/1150402.1150436

Ouf, S., & Nasr, M. (2015). Cloud Computing. *International Journal of Cloud Applications and Computing, 5*(2), 53–61. doi:10.4018/IJCAC.2015040104

Pearson, K. (1901). LIII. On lines and planes of closest fit to systems of points in space. *The London, Edinburgh and Dublin Philosophical Magazine and Journal of Science, 2*(11), 559–572. doi:10.1080/14786440109462720

Priyadarshinee, P. (2018). Cloud Computing Adoption. *International Journal of Cloud Applications and Computing, 8*(1), 97–116. doi:10.4018/IJCAC.2018010105

Qi, L., Xiang, H., Dou, W., Yang, C., Qin, Y., & Zhang, X. (2017). Privacy-Preserving Distributed Service Recommendation Based on Locality-Sensitive Hashing. *2017 IEEE International Conference on Web Services (ICWS)*. 10.1109/ICWS.2017.15

Qin, Z., Yan, J., Ren, K., Chen, C. W., & Wang, C. (2014). Towards Efficient Privacy-preserving Image Feature Extraction in Cloud Computing. *Proceedings of the ACM International Conference on Multimedia - MM 14*. 10.1145/2647868.2654941

Quick Facts and Stats on Big Data. (n.d.). Retrieved from http://www.ibmbigdatahub.com/gallery/quick-facts-and-stats-big-data

Rahulamathavan, Y., & Rajarajan, M. (2015). Efficient Privacy-Preserving Facial Expression Classification. *IEEE Transactions on Dependable and Secure Computing*, 1–1. doi:10.1109/TDSC.2015.2453963

Ramachandran, S., Chithan, S., & Ravindran, S. (2014). A cost-effective approach towards storage and Privacy preserving for Intermediate data sets in Cloud Environment. *2014 International Conference on Recent Trends in Information Technology*. 10.1109/ICRTIT.2014.6996145

Thanei, G., Heinze, C., & Meinshausen, N. (2017). Random Projections for Large-Scale Regression. *Contributions to Statistics Big and Complex Data Analysis*, 51-68. doi:10.1007/978-3-319-41573-4_3

Tsai, C., Lai, C., Chao, H., & Vasilakos, A. V. (2015). Big data analytics: A survey. *Journal of Big Data, 2*(1), 21. doi:10.118640537-015-0030-3 PMID:26191487

Xie, H., Li, J., Zhang, Q., & Wang, Y. (2016). Comparison among dimensionality reduction techniques based on Random Projection for cancer classification. *Computational Biology and Chemistry, 65*, 165–172. doi:10.1016/j.compbiolchem.2016.09.010 PMID:27687329

Zhang, R., Du, T., & Qu, S. (2018). A Principal Component Analysis Algorithm Based on Dimension Reduction Window. *IEEE Access: Practical Innovations, Open Solutions, 6*, 63737–63747. doi:10.1109/ACCESS.2018.2875270

Zhang, T., & Yang, B. (2018). Dimension reduction for big data. *Statistics and Its Interface, 11*(2), 295–306. doi:10.4310/SII.2018.v11.n2.a7

Chapter 9
An API for Development of User-Defined Scheduling Algorithms in Aneka PaaS Cloud Software:
User Defined Schedulers in Aneka PaaS Cloud Software

Rajinder Sandhu
Jaypee University of Information Technology (JUIT), India

Adel Nadjaran Toosi
Monash University, Australia

Rajkumar Buyya
University of Melbourne, Australia

ABSTRACT

Cloud computing provides resources using multitenant architecture where infrastructure is created from one or more distributed datacenters. Scheduling of applications in cloud infrastructures is one of the main research area in cloud computing. Researchers have developed many scheduling algorithms and evaluated them using simulators such as CloudSim. Their performance needs to be validated in real-time cloud environments to improve their usefulness. Aneka is one of the prominent PaaS software which allows users to develop cloud application using various programming models and underline infrastructure. This chapter presents a scheduling API developed for the Aneka software platform. Users can develop their own scheduling algorithms using this API and integrate it with Aneka to test their scheduling algorithms in real cloud environments. The proposed API provides all the required functionalities to integrate and schedule private, public, or hybrid cloud with the Aneka software.

DOI: 10.4018/978-1-5225-8407-0.ch009

1. INTRODUCTION

Cloud computing has proved to be the most revolutionary technology of the last decade which resulted in many organizations moving toward cloud-based infrastructure (Buyya, 2009). From mobile applications to large data intensive applications are using cloud-based infrastructure for fulfilling their IT resource requirement. With more data generation, the need for cloud computing is increasing day by day for many emerging IT technologies such as Internet of Things and Big Data (Gubbi et al, 2013). Cloud computing deployment models can be broadly classified into Public cloud, Private cloud and Hybrid cloud. Among all these models, hybrid cloud is gaining popularity with its features like infinite resources and cost benefits. Hybrid cloud utilizes public cloud resources if private cloud resources cannot complete the task with given Quality of Service (QoS) parameters. This makes hybrid cloud model a good candidate for many applications such as mobile devices, small industries, and other smart environments (Wang et al, 2013).

As cloud computing contains a colossal number of IT resources whether it is a private cloud or public cloud, it is difficult to test new algorithms for better and efficient scheduling. Many researchers use simulation tools to test and deploy different scheduling algorithms for different kind of applications in the cloud environment. A common used simulation tool is CloudSim (Calheiros et al, 2011) while other tools such as iFogSim and IoTSim (Gupta et al, 2017; Zeng et al, 2017) are also gaining popularity for testing IoT based applications on cloud computing environments. But, results from even the most efficient simulation software always differ from actual results because many other aspects such as network, bandwidth also play an important role. Infrastructure as a Service (IaaS) provider such as Amazon EC2, or Microsoft Azure (Zeng et al, 2017; "AWS", n.d.) give access to underlying IT resources to the user. But these IaaS providers do not give rights to the end user for making any change in the scheduling policies for the application. There are many options in the market for PaaS where the end user can create individual tasks and submit them to the PaaS provider. Many PaaS providers do not provide access to underlying IT infrastructure making it very difficult to change and test new scheduling policies (Shon et al, 2014). Due to these constraints, research in the development of new scheduling policies is taking a big hit for real cloud computing environments.

Aneka (Vecchiola et al, 2009) is a PaaS cloud provider developed in Microsoft .net for developing cloud computing infrastructure and applications using various programming models and available infrastructure. Aneka supports programming models such as Task, Thread and Map-Reduce while users can develop their own model. In Aneka, infrastructure can be developed using a cluster of multicore machines, private cloud and public cloud. Aneka contains inbuilt scheduling policies which are used to schedule jobs on private cloud created using multicore machines or using private cloud software such as OpenStack. Aneka provides dynamic provisioning feature which allows Aneka applications to use public cloud such as Amazon EC2 and Microsoft Azure when desired QoS cannot be achieved using the private cloud setup (Buyya et al, 2016). Aneka is one of its kind which gives the end user full freedom to develop applications in many languages and deploy it on any infrastructure available with them. It gives full access and right of underlying infrastructure to end user and well as full access to SDK for development of applications (Toosi et al, 2018). Aneka has many features but it is difficult for the end user to create their custom scheduling and provisioning policies.

In this chapter, we propose to develop an API for Aneka which allows end users to create and integrate their custom scheduling algorithms with Aneka. The user can develop their own applications in Aneka and then create a customized scheduling policy according to their application needs. Aneka also provides user with inbuilt sample applications such as Mandelbrot, Image Convolution or Blast to test their new scheduling algorithm. The proposed API bridges the gap between access to scheduling algorithms and using real cloud setup to test and create them.

The rest of the chapter has been organized as follows. Section 2 provides the introduction about the architecture of Aneka. Section 3 explains the proposed API with all classes. Section 4 provides sample codes and related discussion. Section 5 provides performance evaluation. Finally, Section 6 concludes the chapter and provides future directions.

Aneka

Aneka is a PaaS cloud software that facilities the development and deployment of applications with underline support of .net framework. Figure 1 shows an overview of the architecture of Aneka. It contains three layers which are infrastructure, middleware and application development which allows the end user to change underline infrastructure and middleware to support rapid and customized development of cloud applications. The infrastructure of Aneka can be multicore machine, grid environment, cluster of machines, private cloud and public cloud. Public cloud is only required when scheduler decides that desired QoS cannot be achieved from other available resources. Middleware provides the support for

Figure 1. Overview of Aneka Architecture
(Buyya et al, 2016)

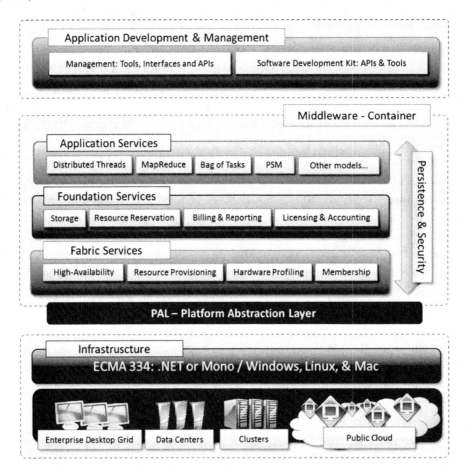

programming models such as thread, task and Map-Reduce. It also provides the billing, accounting, resource reservation, hardware profiling and other services. These service in Aneka can be plugged and unplugged as and when required from the Management console provided in the application development and management layer. Aneka also contains many components which are discussed below:

- **Aneka Master Container:** Aneka master is mainly responsible for the scheduling and monitoring of application tasks and resources in the Aneka. Aneka master also manages the billing and reporting services of all the worker nodes attached with an Aneka master. The end user's application sends the task to Aneka master which based on the availability of worker nodes further schedules these tasks. If any worker nodes fail without executing the task, master reschedules the task o another available worker node.

- **Aneka Worker Container:** Aneka worker is the component which basically deals with the execution of the tasks. It contains the executor for each type of programming models available with the Aneka. After completing any assigned task, it sends the result back to master for compiling and starts waiting for new tasks. Worker node is operating system independent, it can be run on Linux or Windows machines.

- **Aneka Daemon:** Aneka daemons are the basic services which need to be installed in all the machines before Aneka master and worker can be installed.

- **Management Studio:** Management studio is the interactive interface which end user uses to create and manage cloud environments created inside the Aneka cloud. The end user can easily add private and public cloud resources, manages all added resources, create bills, monitor added resources, add file repositories, and check current statistics of the Aneka cloud.

- **Aneka SDK:** Aneka also provides SDK for the development of applications which can be directly deployed on the Aneka cloud created using management studio. These SDKs contains programming language specific libraries and other tools.

Proposed API

Figure 2 shows the proposed API for Aneka cloud which acts as an independent interface which user can use to change the scheduling policies of Aneka. The user level scheduler is the new or proposed scheduler by the end user for its specific application or in general use. This user level scheduler is integrated with Aneka using the proposed scheduling API. This section explains different classes and interfaces used in the proposed API so that end user can easily write their own scheduling policies.

Aneka.Scheduling is the main project of proposed API which directly interacts with Aneka.Runtime project of Aneka to state which scheduling policy should be followed when any task arrives. Aneka. Runtime consults Aneka.Scheduling and based on the selected algorithm at the time of creation of Aneka master it schedules tasks on different worker nodes. Aneka.scheduling API contains six sub-projects out of which Aneka.Scheduling.Service and Aneka.Scheduling.Utils directly interacts with Aneka.Runtime project. These sub-projects are explained in details later in this chapter.

Aneka.Scheduling implements two interfaces which are ISchedulerContext and ISchedulerAlgorihtm as shown in Figure 4. Various events are associated with these interfaces which are triggered when there is a state change for the application or a task. Table 1 shows different event associated with Aneka. Scheduling.

Figure 2. Framework for scheduling API with Aneka PaaS Software

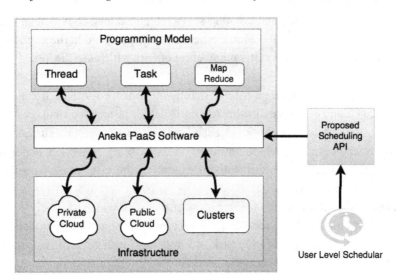

Figure 3. Code map of proposed Aneka.scheduling project in Aneka code

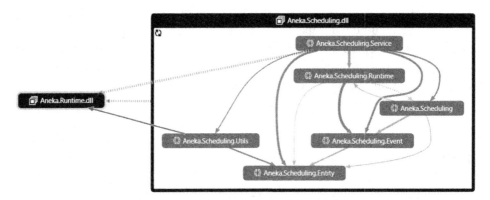

Figure 4. Interfaces implemented by Aneka.scheduling Project

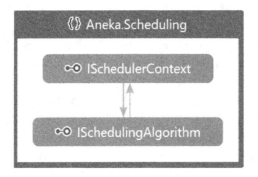

Table 1. Different events associated with Aneka.scheduling

S. No.	Event	Description
1.	SchedulerAlgorihtm	It selects the scheduling algorithm to use for scheduling tasks on worker nodes.
2.	ResourceDisconnected	Event when a resource is disconnected. For every task assigned to this Resource the TaskFailed event will also be fired.
3.	ResourceReconnected	Event when a resource is reconnected.
4.	ResourceProvisionProcessed	Event when a resource provisioning request is processed.
5.	ResourceProvisionRequested	Event when a resource provision request is triggered.
6.	ResourceReleaseRequested	Event when a resource release request is triggered.
7.	ResourcePoolsQueryRequested	This event is triggered when end user generates any resource pool related query. It is important event in case there are multiple pool in dynamic provisioning of Aneka cloud.
8.	TaskFinished	Event when a task is finished.
9.	TaskFailed	Event when a task is failed due the task failure. It is caused by something other than the resource disconnection
10.	TaskAborted	Event when a task is aborted due to the user action.
11.	TaskRequeued	Event when a task is requeued due the the user action

Aneka.Scheduling.Runtime

It contains two classes and one interface as shown in the code map in Figure 5. This is responsible for decision making during runtime of any scheduling algorithm such as timings, resources available, task completed etc. SchedulerContextBase class registers all context-based activity happening in the scheduler to their specific events. This class also generates the exception and records it in the logger file so that end user can analyse the errors generated.

Major activities performed by this class are

Figure 5. Classes and interface of Aneka.Scheduling.Runtime

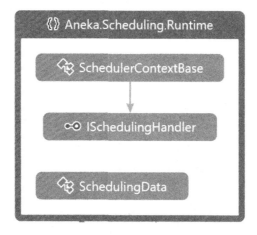

- Assign the value to the scheduling algorithm
- Register the event handler for the forwarded assign work unit event from the scheduling algorithm
- Hook the event handler for provision resources request
- Hook the event handler for release resources request
- Hook the event handler for a query for resource pools request
- Register the scheduler context to the scheduling algorithm

Class SchedulingData extends the Aneka reporting data class which can capture the information about the scheduling data (mostly timing) of the specific task allocation. Various data collected by Scheduling data class are:

- **Queue Time:** A value representing the total waiting time of the task in seconds. This time is computed since the task is moved from queued to scheduled state.
- **Execution Time:** A value representing the total execution time of the task in seconds as seen by the scheduler service.
- **Task Final State:** It provides the final state of the task submitted to the scheduler.

If the end user wants to add any new data point to the scheduling algorithm matrices, it can be easily added in this class. Interface ISchedulingHandler extends the IServiceNameAware interface of Aneka and provides a set of methods for the SchedulerService to specialize the activities of the scheduler. This interface allows separating all those management aspects that are common to several programming models, which reside in the SchedulerService class, from the specific aspects related to a given programming model, which reside in the component implementing this interface.

Aneka.Scheduling.Service

It contains two classes which are ScheulerService and IndependentSchedulingService as shown in code map in Figure 6. This is responsible for major scheduling responsibilities based on the selected algorithms.

Class SchedulerService specializes the ContextBase class of Aneka and implements the IService interface and IMembershipEventSink interface. It can be used as base application scheduler that needs to be further customized for handling the specific type of application according to the given programming model on which the application is based. The scheduled tasks directly performed by this scheduler are

Figure 6. Code map of Aneka.Scheduling.Service

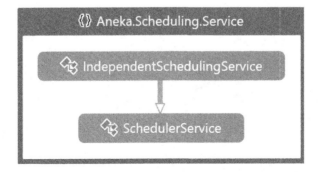

the interaction with the IApplicationStore interface to control the state of the application. It provides template methods that can be implemented by inherited classes to perform the WorkUnit level scheduled tasks. The activity of this service is supported by an implementation of ISchedulingHandler interface that deals directly with the programming model related scheduledTasks at a WorkUnit level.

Class IndependentSchedulingService defines a scheduling service for scheduling independent work units. Models featuring independent work units can use and specialize this scheduler policy in this class. Various parameters used in this class are:

- List of resources is maintained in this class on which scheduling can be done.
- Reservation list is present in this class.
- Starts and stops the scheduling service. Activates the scheduling algorithm and registers the resources with it.
- Fetches the list of WorkUnit instances that are in state Queued from the application store and delegates them back to the SchedulerAlgorithm.

Aneka.Scheduling.Algorithm

It contains different algorithm currently available with Aneka, all available scheduling algorithms extends AlgorihtmBase class for their proper execution as shown in Figure 7. This also contains one NewUserDefined which end user will use to code their own scheduling policy. End users can even extend or change already existing algorithms for more optimization. Class AlgorithmBase is the implementation class for the ISchedulingAlgorithm interface. This class can be used as a template for creating specialized algorithms because it provides the basic features for integrating scheduling algorithms into the Aneka scheduling service. Different variables used in this class are listed in Table 2 and methods available with AlgorithmBase class are listed in Table 3.

Let's take an example of FIFO strategy which is already implemented in the proposed API. It extends the AlgorithmBase class and provides an implementation of the First-In First-Out scheduling strategy. In this algorithm, the tasks are scheduled in their order of arrival. The Schedule function is changed in this implementation which checks that there is a task in the queue and a resource is also free. If both these conditions are true, then it schedules the first task in the queue to the first resource in the resource list. Similarly, other algorithms are proposed in the API and these algorithms are self-explained.

Aneka.Scheduling.Event

It provides all the events associated with the scheduling policies of Aneka. Proposed API provides the flexibility to end user to use already available events or create their own specific event. These events help scheduling policy designer to achieve desired performance and usability. These events are related to different components of Aneka which are listed in Table 4.

Selection of NewUserDefined from Management Studio

In this section step by step method to integrate the newly proposed scheduling policy is discussed. End user has to write new scheduling algorithm in NewUserDefined class of Aneka.Scheduling.Algorihtm. When Aneka master is being installed NewUserDefined should be chosen as shown in Figure 8. After

Figure 7. Code map of available scheduling algorithms

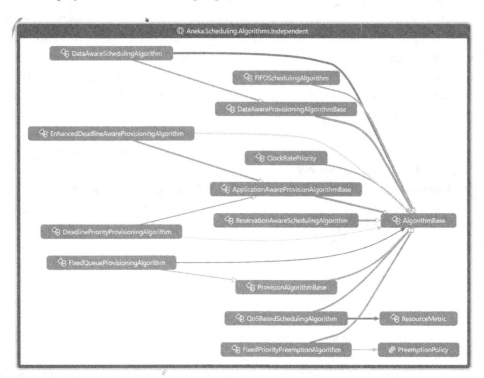

Table 2. Different variables/objects used in AlgorithmBase class

S. No.	Variable/Objects	Parent Class	Description
1.	rescheduledJobTimer	IDictionary	Dictionary mapping the each job reservationId to the timer used to reschedule them.
2.	bKeepRunning	N.A.	While this variable is true the scheduling loop will bKeep running.
3.	canSchedule	ManualResetEvent	Used to block the scheduling thread while there are no scheduledTasks or free resources.
4.	scheduler	ISchedulerContext	Holds a reference to the context that the scheduler is interacting with.
5.	SupportsProvisioning	N.A.	Whether the algorithm support dynamic provisioning or not
6.	canFireEvent	AutoResetEvent	Used to block the event thread while there are no events to fire.

this all the application running on Aneka if use dynamic provisioning will follow the scheduling policy desired in the proposed scheduling algorithm.

DEVELOPING NEW SCHEDULING ALGORITHMS

Scheduling algorithms in Aneka define the logic with which tasks are allocated to resources from Aneka runtime. Developing new scheduling involves writing the code for the new algorithm and plug it into the existing scheduling services with minimal knowledge of the internals of the Aneka runtime. As we stated

Table 3. Methods Available in AlgorithmBase Class

S. No.	Method Name	Description
1.	Start	Start the scheduling loop for assigned tasks.
2.	Stop	Stop the scheduling thread.
3.	Schedule	This method is called repeatedly by the AlgorithBase class for making scheduling decisions.
4.	AddTasks	Used to add new task to the scheduling queue.
5.	GetNextTask	Used to get next task to schedule from the queue.
6.	TaskFailed	Method is called when any task fails. Reschedule policy is checked in this method for the failed task.
7.	TaskAborted	Method is called when user abort the assigned task.
8.	TaskFinished	This is called when task is finished successfully and should be reported to the user its output values.
9.	TaskRequeued	This method requeued the task if it is failed or aborted.
10.	SetScheduler	This method hooks up the event handler for events fired with the desired scheduler.
11.	StartScheduleTask	Start the process to schedule a given task to a given resource.
12.	AddFreeResource	This method will be called when a resource has a task removed and it is not free.
13.	HaveFreeResources	Return the value if there are free resource available that can be used.
14.	RemoveFreeResource	Will be called when adding a task to the resource fills the slot of that resource. Can be called if resource get disconnected.
15.	ResourceReconnected	Hooks the event when resource get reconnected and also updates the list of available resources.
16.	ResourceDisconnected	Called when the resource get disconnected and updates the list of available resources.

Table 4. Different type of events created in Aneka.Scheduling.Event

S. No.	Event Type	Description
1.	Task Events	These events are related to tasks such as task finished, task aborted etc.
2.	Scheduling Events	These events are related to scheduling such as algorithm selected etc.
4.	Resource Pool Query Events	These events are related adding, selecting and deleting specific resource pools.
5.	Resource Events	These events are related to resource addition, deletion and selection.

earlier this can be done by implementing methods of two interfaces —— namely ISchedulerContext and ISchedulingAlgorithm —— that represent the interface with the Aneka runtime and the scheduling algorithm respectively. These interfaces and bases classes are part of the Aneka.Scheduling library.

Figure 9 shows the ISchedulingAlgorithm interface that each scheduling algorithm has to implement. The algorithm provides a feedback to the Aneka runtime about its scheduling decisions through the events exposed by the interface. SupportsProvisioning is a boolean value that is set to true if the algorithm supports dynamic provisioning. AssignTask is trigred whenever a task is allocated to a resource. and ReleaseResources are events which are triggered when the scheduling algorithm issues a request for additional resources and reguest release of a provisioned resource, respectively. Start and Stop methods are called when the scheduling begins and ends. To add new tasks and new resources AddTasks and AddResources methods are called respectively. The algorithm works with the Aneka runtime and inter-

Figure 8. Interface in Management Studio to Select NewUserDefined Scheduling Algorithm

Figure 9. ISchedulingAlgorithm interface

```
using Aneka.Provisioning;
using Aneka.Scheduling.Entity;
using Aneka.Scheduling.Event;

namespace Aneka.Scheduling
{
    public interface ISchedulerContext
    {
        bool SupportsProvisioning { get; }

        event EventHandler<SchedulingEventArgs> AssignTask;

        event EventHandler<ProvisionResourcesArgs> ProvisionResources;

        event EventHandler<ReleaseResourcesArgs> ReleaseResources;

        void Start();

        void Stop();

        void AddTasks(params Task[] tasks);

        void AddResources(params Resource[] resources);

        void SetScheduler(ISchedulerContext scheduler);
    }
}
```

faces by means of the ISchedulerContext interface which is set in the SetScheduler method. Figure 10 shows ISchedulerContext interface.

Only a subset of events and properties are of interest for the scheduling algorithm.

- ***ResourceDisconnected* and *ResourceReconnected*:** Notify the scheduling algorithm that a resource has disconnected or reconnected from a temporary disconnection.
- ***TaskAborted*, *TaskFinished*, *TaskFailed*, and *TaskRequeued*:** Notify the scheduling algorithm of the status of the tasks.
- ***ResourceProvisionProcessed*:** The only event from dynamic provisioning infrastructure that is of interest for the scheduling algorithm. This event provides information about the outcome of a resource provisioning request made earlier by the scheduling algorithm.

Example 1: FIFO Scheduling Algorithm

As stated earlier. *AlgorithmBase* implements the *ISchedulingAlgorithm* interface and can be used as a template for creating specialized algorithms. Figure 11 provides *FIFOSchedulingAlgorithm* Class body to show by simply overriding a few methods of the *AlgorithmBase* Class First-In First-Out scheduling strategy can be implemented where the tasks are scheduled in their order of arrival.

Figure 10. ISchedulingContext interface

```
using Aneka.Provisioning;
using Aneka.Scheduling.Entity;
using Aneka.Scheduling.Event;
using Aneka.Scheduling.Runtime;

namespace Aneka.Scheduling
{
    public interface ISchedulerContext
    {
        ISchedulingAlgorithm SchedulerAlgorithm { get; set; }

        ISchedulingHandler SchedulingHandler { get; set; }

        event EventHandler<ResourceEventArgs> ResourceDisconnected;

        event EventHandler<ResourceEventArgs> ResourceReConnected;

        event EventHandler<ProvisionEventArgs> ResourceProvisionProcessed;

        event EventHandler<ProvisionResourcesArgs> ResourceProvisionRequested;

        event EventHandler<ReleaseResourcesArgs> ResourceReleaseRequested;


        event EventHandler<TaskEventArgs> TaskFinished;

        event EventHandler<TaskEventArgs> TaskFailed;

        event EventHandler<TaskEventArgs> TaskAborted;

        event EventHandler<TaskEventArgs> TaskRequeued;
    }
}
```

Figure 11. FIFOSchedulingAlgorithm Class

```
using Aneka.Scheduling.Entity;
using Aneka.Scheduling.Event;
using Aneka;

namespace Aneka.Scheduling.Algorithms.Independent
{
public class FIFOSchedulingAlgorithm : AlgorithmBase
    {
        private List<Resource> _freeList = new List<Resource>();
        protected override bool HaveFreeResources()
        {
            return _freeList.Count > 0;
        }
        protected override void AddFreeResource(Resource r)
        {
            lock (this.synchLock)
            {
                int track = DebugUtil.EnterLock();
                if (r.IsConnected && r.FreeSlots > 0)
                {
                    _freeList.Remove(r);
                    _freeList.Add(r);
                }

                DebugUtil.ExitLock(track);
            }
        }
        protected override void RemoveFreeResource(Resource r)
        {
            lock (this.synchLock)
            {
                int track = DebugUtil.EnterLock();
                _freeList.Remove(r);

                DebugUtil.ExitLock(track);
            }
        }
        protected override void Schedule()
        {
            lock (this.synchLock)
            {
                int track = DebugUtil.EnterLock();

                if (_freeList.Count > 0 && TasksInQueue > 0)
                {
                    StartScheduleTask(_freeList.AsReadOnly(),GetNextTask());
                }
                else
                {
                    canSchedule.Reset();
                }

                DebugUtil.ExitLock(track);
            }
        }
    }
}
```

_freeList maintains the list of the currently available resources for scheduling tasks. *HaveFreeRe-sources()* method returns a Boolean value indicating whether there are free resources that can be used. *AddFreeResource* is called when a resource has a task removed. Since the recourse might be already on the free list, we remove it first and we add it again to avoid duplicates. *RemoveFreeResource* is called when adding a task to a resource fills all the slots or will be called for other reasons e.g., a disconnected resource. *Schedule()* starts the scheduling algorithm. If there is a task in the queue and a free resource in the *_freeList* it calls the *StartScheduleTask* method by passing *_freeList* and the next task in the queue. Otherwise, it resets the *canSchedule* to block the scheduling thread until the task can be scheduled again by any other resource.

Example 2: Deadline Priority Provisioning Algorithm

A new scheduling algorithm can be designed in a way that supports dynamic provisioning of virtual resources by leveraging the resource provisioning service. These are all defined in the namespace *Aneka. Scheduling.Algorithm.Independent*, which can be found in the Aneka library. *ProvisioningAlgorithmBase* is this class provides an abstract base class for all dynamic provisioning algorithms. The algorithm provides a basic management of the provisioning request that has been issued. *ApplicationAwareProvisioningAlgorithm* is specialized for the scheduling a collection of tasks as a whole in order to ensure that some specific QoS parameters that are defined for the application are met. Developers can design their new scheduling algorithms and new strategies for triggering resource provisioning by extending one of these two classes or specializing the previous two algorithms.

For example, Figure 12 shows *DeadlinePriorityProvisioningAlgorithm* that extends *ApplicationAwareProvisionAlgorithmBase* class and leverages dynamic provisioning in order to schedule the execution of the tasks within the expected deadline. If the local resources are not enough to execute all the tasks in time, a request for additional resources is issued. The class overrides two main methods of the base class called *ShrinkRequired* and *GrowRequired* to request release or adding of resources from the provisioner respectively. Both methods use the private method called ExceedResourceCapacity to set a Boolean indicator called required.

The *ExceedResourceCapacity* method checks whether the current allocation for the application is compliant with the requirements set for the corresponding application. A Boolean value *toGrow* indicates whether we need to check for additional resources to add when it is *true* or resources to release when it is *false*. *taskRemaining* keeps the total number of remaining tasks that must be executed. *taskResourceRatio* is then calculated based on the ratio of the number of remaining tasks to the number of current resources. Finally based on the indicative values of *AverageTaskExecutionTime* in the *requiredTime* is calculated and is compared to *timeRemaining* which indicates the time remaining to the deadline. *bRequired* value is then set accordingly to true when the required time is larger than the remaining time.

PERFORMANCE EVALUATION

For the sake of performance evaluation, we built a small-scale experimental testbed and tested our previously proposed resource provisioning and scheduling algorithm called Data-aware. We use our proposed API all to integrate Data-aware scheduling algorithm. For more details on the Data-aware algorithm and workload setup, please look at our paper in (Toosi et al, 2018). The testbed is a hybrid cloud environment constituting of two desktop machines (one master and one slave) residing at The University of Melbourne and dynamic resources provisioned from Microsoft Azure. Configurations of resources used in the experiment are shown in Table 5. Public cloud resources are dynamically provisioned from Microsoft Azure cloud when local resources are not able to meet application deadlines.

As an application, a Bag-of-Tasks for measuring a walkability index is used (Toosi et al, 2018). A walkability index is used to assess how walkable a given neighborhood is based on factors such as road

Figure 12. DeadlinePriorityProvisioningAlgorithm Class

```
using Aneka.Scheduling.Entity;
using Aneka.Scheduling.Event;
using Aneka;

namespace Aneka.Scheduling.Algorithms.Independent
{
public class FIFOSchedulingAlgorithm : AlgorithmBase
    {
        private List<Resource> _freeList = new List<Resource>();
        protected override bool HaveFreeResources()
        {
            return _freeList.Count > 0;
        }
        protected override void AddFreeResource(Resource r)
        {
            lock (this.synchLock)
            {
                int track = DebugUtil.EnterLock();
                if (r.IsConnected && r.FreeSlots > 0)
                {
                    _freeList.Remove(r);
                    _freeList.Add(r);
                }

                DebugUtil.ExitLock(track);
            }
        }
        protected override void RemoveFreeResource(Resource r)
        {
            lock (this.synchLock)
            {
                int track = DebugUtil.EnterLock();
                _freeList.Remove(r);

                DebugUtil.ExitLock(track);
            }
        }
        protected override void Schedule()
        {
            lock (this.synchLock)
            {
                int track = DebugUtil.EnterLock();

                if (_freeList.Count > 0 && TasksInQueue > 0)
                {
                    StartScheduleTask(_freeList.AsReadOnly(),GetNextTask());
                }
                else
                {
                    canSchedule.Reset();
                }

                DebugUtil.ExitLock(track);
            }
        }
    }
}
```

connectivity, gross dwelling density and the land use mix in the area. In our experiments, we use the walkability application to provide walkability indexes for 220 different neighborhoods in the city of Melbourne. The walkability application suits the purpose of our experiments since it is data-intensive and it can be broken into independent tasks, each computing a walkability index for a neighborhood. The test application contains 55 tasks, each calculating walkability indexes for four different neighborhoods of Melbourne city.

Figure 13. ExceedResourceCapacity method

```
private bool ExceedResourceCapacity(QoS qos, string applicationId, bool toGrow)
{
        bool bRequired = false;
        int currentResources = this.GetResourceCount(applicationId);
        if (currentResources > 0)
        {
            int taskRemaining = 0;
            if (toGrow == true)
            {
                taskRemaining = qos.TotalWork - qos.ScheduledTasks;
            }
            else
            {
                taskRemaining = qos.TotalWork - qos.WorkCompleted;
            }
            int taskResourceRatio = taskRemaining / currentResources;
            TimeSpan avgExecutionTimeForTask = qos.AverageTaskExecutionTime;
            TimeSpan timeRemaining = qos.TimeRemaining;
            double requiredTime = avgExecutionTimeForTask.TotalSeconds * taskResourceRatio;
            if (requiredTime > timeRemaining.TotalSeconds)
            {
                bRequired = true;
            }
        }
        else
        {
            bRequired = true;
        }
        return bRequired;
}
```

Table 5. Configuration of machines used in the experiments.

Machine	Type	CPU	Cores	Memory	OS
Master	Intel Core i7-4790	3.60 GHz	8	16GB	Windows 7
Worker	Intel Core i7-2600	3.40 GHz	8	8GB	Windows 7
Azure Instances	Standard DS1	2.4 GHz	1	3.5GB	Windows Server 2012

Experimental Results

We submit the walkability application to Aneka for execution with different deadlines, showing how the proposed algorithm behaves. All experiments are repeated for the other Aneka inbuilt scheduling algorithms, called *Default* and *Enhanced*. The Default scheduling algorithm makes an estimation of the expected completion time of the application with currently available resources, and if the expected completion time is later than the deadline defined in the Quality of Service parameters of the application, it requests extra resources from the public cloud to complete the application within given deadlines. The Enhanced algorithm is designed to utilize Amazon EC2 Spot Instance resources with an average higher deployment time but lower budget than the Default algorithm.

The execution time of the application without setting a deadline and only using private (local) resources takes 45.4 minutes. Figure 12 shows the results of the application execution under different deadlines. As shown by Figure 12, scheduling algorithms meet the deadline in all scenarios except in 3 cases, highlighted by "x" in the figure. Default and Enhanced algorithms violate the deadline constraint when the deadline is set to 35 minutes. The Default algorithm also misses the deadline when it is set to

40 minutes. The key reason is that these algorithms rely on only a single variable for measuring average runtime of tasks to allocate dynamic resources without considering data transfer time.

Experimental results demonstrate that the we can integrate new scheduling algorithm to Aneka Software using the proposed API. The results also show that the plugged-in scheduling algorithm works with qualitatively similar performance as the inbuilt scheduling algorithms and even outperforms them in some cases in terms of meeting deadline constraints.

CONCLUSION AND FUTURE WORK

Aneka is one of the prominent PaaS cloud software available in the market which allows you to change and manage the underline infrastructure as well as write applications in any programming model. Aneka has many features the research community well demands the customization of Aneka scheduling algorithm for dynamic provisioning. In this chapter, an API is proposed which provides all necessary libraries to develop new Aneka scheduling algorithm. The new algorithm created from this API can be easily integrated with Aneka interface using Management Studio. The proposed API will help cloud computing researchers to develop their application in a real cloud and test them with their custom scheduling algorithm.

As part of the future work, we will focus on the creation of graphical user interface for addition of new scheduling APIs. This interactive interface will feature the designing of scheduling algorithms for new paradigms such as Internet of Things (IoT) and Fog Computing. The future work will also consist of development of APIs which are compatible with creation of multi-level scheduling policies such as from IoT to Fog layer to Cloud computing layer. Using multi-layer scheduling policies users can design scheduling policies for latency sensitive applications running in Fog computing environments.

Figure 14. Execution time for Default, Enhanced, and Data-aware algorithms considering different application deadlines. The X symbol shows a violated deadline.

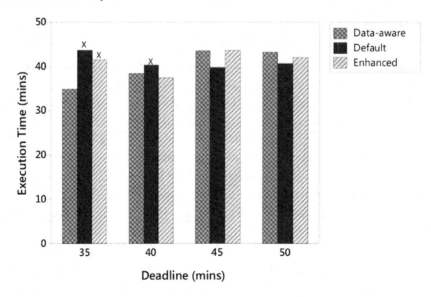

REFERENCES

AWS - Amazon EC2 Instance Types. (2014). Available: http://aws.amazon.com/ec2/instance-types/

Buyya, R. (2009). Market-oriented cloud computing: Vision, hype, and reality of delivering computing as the 5th utility. *2009 9th IEEE/ACM International Symposium on Cluster Computing and the Grid, CCGRID 2009.* 10.1109/CCGRID.2009.97

Buyya, R., & Barreto, D. (2016). Multi-cloud resource provisioning with Aneka: A unified and integrated utilisation of microsoft azure and amazon EC2 instances. *2015 International Conference on Computing and Network Communications, CoCoNet 2015.*

Calheiros, R. N., Ranjan, R., Beloglazov, A., De Rose, C. A. F., & Buyya, R. (2011, January). CloudSim: A toolkit for modeling and simulation of cloud computing environments and evaluation of resource provisioning algorithms. *Software, Practice & Experience, 41*(1), 23–50. doi:10.1002pe.995

Gubbi, J., Buyya, R., Marusic, S., & Palaniswami, M. (2013, September). Internet of Things (IoT): A vision, architectural elements, and future directions. *Future Generation Computer Systems, 29*(7), 1645–1660. doi:10.1016/j.future.2013.01.010

Gupta, H., Vahid Dastjerdi, A., Ghosh, S. K., & Buyya, R. (2017, September). iFogSim: A toolkit for modeling and simulation of resource management techniques in the Internet of Things, Edge and Fog computing environments. *Software, Practice & Experience, 47*(9), 1275–1296. doi:10.1002pe.2509

Microsoft Azure. (2016). *Microsoft Azure Pricing calculator.* Microsoft. Available: https://azure.micro-soft.com/en-us/pricing/calculator/

Nadjaran Toosi, Sinnott, & Buyya. (2018). Resource provisioning for data-intensive applications with deadline constraints on hybrid clouds using Aneka. *Futur. Gener. Comput. Syst.*

Shon, T., Cho, J., Han, K., & Choi, H. (2014, June). Toward advanced mobile cloud computing for the internet of things: Current issues and future direction. *Mobile Networks and Applications, 19*(3), 404–413. doi:10.100711036-014-0509-8

Vecchiola, C., Chu, X., & Buyya, R. (2009). *Aneka: a software platform for. NET-based cloud computing.* High Speed Large Scale Sci. Comput.

Wang, W. J., Chang, Y. S., Lo, W. T., & Lee, Y. K. (2013, February). Adaptive scheduling for parallel tasks with QoS satisfaction for hybrid cloud environments. *The Journal of Supercomputing, 66*(2), 783–811. doi:10.100711227-013-0890-2

Zeng, Garg, Strazdins, Jayaraman, Georgakopoulos, & Ranjan. (2017). IOTSim: A simulator for analysing IoT applications. *J. Syst. Archit.*

Chapter 10
A Cloud–Based Patient Health Monitoring System Using the Internet of Things

R. Murugan

https://orcid.org/0000-0002-9341-3810

National Institute of Technology Silchar, India

ABSTRACT

To conquer medical carelessness, a novel framework will be created on the grounds that daily medicinal services are essential. This framework conveys equipment, and Android application, the pulse, temperature of body, dampness rate are detected by the sensor in equipment. There is a Raspberry pi over which this detected information is transferred. The system dependent on internet of things (IOT) is utilized for remotely getting to information. With the end goal to get to the information universally, IOT used to keep all refreshed data on pages, a great opportunity to put information on mists. There is an Android-based application that can get to information from server through wi-fi to give us a chance to see the detected information. On the off chance that any of the anomalies are discovered, those must be settled, so it will send message to tolerant and individual specialists.

INTRODUCTION

Healthcare is the most imperative worry of numerous nations on the planet. Enhancing the lives of patients particularly in the weaker parts of the general public which incorporate the elderly, physically and rationally incapacitated and also the incessantly sick patients is the main consideration to be made strides. Clinics dependably require better administration (Petrakis et al, 2018). The database of all patients ought to be sufficiently helpful. Yet additionally, there ought to be information aversion. Additionally the patient information ought to be kept private on the off chance that. In existing framework, the information is recorded as printed material or on general stockpiling server. In any case, by and large that information is available to all the staff and specialists. In healing centers there are arrangements for nonstop observing of patients. Their pulses are constantly observed. There is no arrangement to check the parameters

DOI: 10.4018/978-1-5225-8407-0.ch010

when they come back to home. Furthermore, consequently quite possibly the infection may return once more. Patient's information (temperature, pulse, position) will be oftentimes estimated and sent to server. Time of sending (say each 3 min) can be set. Checking individual learns quiet particular edge. Say the customary body temperature of a patient is 37°c while one individual feels hot if his body temperature is 37°c. By utilizing an averaging system over a moderately prolonged stretch of time, Observer can take in these limits for patients. Utilizing Android Application in specialist's advanced mobile phone, specialist can see his patient's wellbeing status. At the point when any of the parameter goes past the edge esteem he will get a ready warning (Da Costa et al, 2018).

Utilizing Android Application in patient's or his guardian's advanced mobile phone the patient can see his wellbeing status. Early discovery and determination of conceivably lethal physiological conditions, for example, heart assault require persistent observing of patients wellbeing following exchange from healing facility to home. Studies have demonstrated that 30% of patients with a release determination of heart disappointment are readmitted in any event once inside 90 days with readmission rates going from 25 to 54% inside 3 – a half year. In light of these kinds of requirements, wellbeing checking frameworks are being proposed as a minimal effort arrangement. Such a framework comprises of physiological information

that stores, process and impart through a neighborhood way, for example, advanced mobile phones, PCs. Such frameworks ought to fulfill strict wellbeing, security, unwavering quality, and long haul constant activity necessities (Manogaran et al, 2018). In the proposed framework we present a wellbeing checking framework that uses the sensors for gathering information from patients, cleverly predicts patient's wellbeing status and gives input to specialists through their cell phones having android application. The patients will take an interest in the social insurance process by their cell phones and in this way can get to their wellbeing data from anyplace whenever. Today Internet has turned out to be one of the essential piece of our day by day life. It has changed how individuals live, work, play and learn. Web fills for some need trainings, back, Business, Industries, Entertainment, Social Networking, Shopping, E-Commerce and so forth. The following new super pattern of Internet will be Internet of Things (IOT).Visualizing a reality where a few items can detect, convey and share data over a Private Internet Protocol (IP) or Public Networks(PN). The interconnected questions gather the information at customary interims, break down and used to start required activity, giving a canny system to examining, arranging and basic leadership.

IoT is visual so it is a physical quantity. A wide network of various physical quantities such as sensors and electronic software are embedded together and they have ability to collect and share data around us and across Internet. IoT is very much beneficial in the fields such as healthcare, smart cities, smart environment, etc (Alavi et al, 2018). The IoT is for the most part considered as interfacing items to the Internet and utilizing that association for control of those articles or remote observing. Be that as it may, this definition was alluded just to part of IoT development considering the machine to machine showcase today. Yet, genuine meaning of IoT is making a splendid, undetectable system which can be detected, controlled and customized (Ray et al, 2018). The items created dependent on IoT incorporate implanted innovation which enables them to trade data, with one another or the Internet and it is evaluated that around 8 to 50 billion gadgets will be associated by 2020. Since these gadgets come on the web, they give better way of life, make more secure and more drew in networks and upset human services. The whole idea of IoT remains on sensors, portal and remote system which empower clients to convey and get to the application/data (Hassan et al, 2018).

Consequently another way of proposing a patient and specialists ready to impart through versatile application and web application. Our system deals with set of modules are which gives the facility of interacting the patient with the doctor through tele-monitoring. A set of medical sensors is used to sense the data from patient and this sensed data is relayed to raspberry pi anywhere in the world for the diagnosis of patient using internet. For easy of accessing the data it can store on cloud of medical history. The architecture of the proposed system design is to monitor patient from anywhere privately of home as well as in hospital. The system is very much suitable for a village's healthcare center where lack of medical facilities is available.

RELATED WORKS

The region of wellbeing as of late has been quickly incorporating innovation in the checking, analysis and treatment of patients remotely. Along these lines accomplishing to enhance the personal satisfaction of patients and more noteworthy traceability of data from them. Most investigations looked into point to a ceaseless infection checking specifically as in which are in charge of the main remote observing of fundamental signs and the second of a tele-restorative Electro Cardio Gram (ECG) arrangement of a patient (Kouicem et al, 2018).

Every one of these frameworks albeit very entire is your situation, incorporate individual issues with respect to the treatment of a few ailments that influence person in the monetary and social. Is an imperative method to build up a thorough arrangement where regardless of what sort of malady, the kind of check, the diverse units to be taken care of this can turn into a conceivable answer for successive observing of these patients. Different frameworks, for example, those proposed are settled in the IoT acquire favorable circumstances terms of recognition, transmission and utilization of data in the field points of view of wellbeing and restorative consideration. Empowering keen, an available and correspondence framework dependent on IoT facilitating portions, for example, therapeutic gear, data administration control drug of patients, telemedicine, versatile medicinal consideration, and individual wellbeing administration, among others (Banerjee et al, 2018).

Most proposed structures for remote wellbeing observing influence a three level design: a Wireless Body Area Network (WBAN) comprising of wearable sensors as the information securing unit, correspondence and organizing and the administration layer (Pantelopoulos et al, 2010). For example (Babu et al, 2013) proposes a framework that enlisted people wearable sensors to quantify different physiological parameters, for example, circulatory strain and body temperature. Sensors transmit the assembled data to a door server through a Bluetooth association. The entryway server transforms the information into an observation and measurement document and stores it on a remote server for later recovery by clinicians through the internet (Rahmani et al, 2018). Using a comparable cloud based restorative information stockpiling, a wellbeing observing framework is introduced in (Rolim et al, 2010) in which medicinal staff can get to the put away information online through substance benefit application. Focusing on a particular medicinal application, Wireless Any Network digital Assistant (WANDA) (Lan et al, 2012) a conclusion to end remote wellbeing observing and investigation framework is introduced for supervision of patients with high danger of heart disappointment.

Notwithstanding the innovation for information social occasion, stockpiling and access, therapeutic information investigation and perception are basic segments of remote wellbeing observing frameworks. Exact judgments and checking of patient's restorative condition depends on examination of therapeutic records containing different physiological qualities over an extensive stretch of time. Managing information of high dimensionality in both time and amount makes information examination errand very disappointing and mistake inclined for clinicians. In spite of the fact that the utilization of information mining and representation procedures had beforehand been tended to as an answer for the previously mentioned test (Wei et al, 2005; Mao et al, 2011) these techniques have as of late picked up consideration in remote wellbeing observing frameworks (Ukis et al, 2013; Rao, 2013).

While the appearance of electronic remote wellbeing observing frameworks has guaranteed to change the regular human services strategies, coordinating the IoT worldview into these frameworks can additionally build knowledge, adaptability and interoperability (Ray, 2014). A gadget using the IoT plot is interestingly tended to and identifiable at whenever and anyplace through the Internet. IoT based gadgets in remote wellbeing checking frameworks are fit for the regular detecting errands as well as trade data with one another, naturally interface with and trade data with wellbeing establishments through the Internet, essentially improving set up and organization undertakings. As exemplified in (Bui et al, 2011), such frameworks can give administrations, for example, programmed caution to the closest human services establishment in case of a basic mischance for a regulated patient.

In this work, we are observing different parameters of the patient utilizing IoT. In the patient checking framework dependent on IoT venture, the ongoing parameters of patient's wellbeing are sent to cloud utilizing internet network. These parameters are sent to a remote internet area with the goal that client can see these points of interest from anyplace on the planet.

There is a noteworthy contrast between Soft Message Service (SMS) based patient wellbeing observing and IoT based patient checking framework. In IoT based framework, points of interest of the patient wellbeing can be seen by numerous clients. The purpose for this is the information should be checked by visiting a website or Uniform Resource Locator (URL). Though, in Global System for Mobile Communication (GSM) based patient checking, the wellbeing parameters are sent utilizing GSM through SMS. This is one of the latest electronics project ideas identified with medical applications which building understudies can choose as their last year venture. One more advantage of utilizing IoT is that, this information can be seen utilizing a Personal Computer (PC). The PC, utilizing an Android cell phone comma utilizing a tab or Tablet. The client simply needs a working Internet association with view this information. There are different cloud specialist co-ops which can be utilized to see this information over Internet. Things speak, Sparkfun and IoT Geek are couple of well-known and simple to utilize specialist co-ops among these.

SYSTEM ARCHITECTURE

The patient health monitoring system is shown in figure 1, the major block and steps are described next. The Block diagram of the proposed system is shown in figure. The sensors temperature, humidity and heartbeat is connected to the Raspberry pi board. The values from the Raspberry pi is given to the web server using Wi-Fi Connectivity. The parameter values can be viewed by the android application installed in doctors and patient's smart phone.

This IoT patient monitoring has 3 sensors. First one is a temperature sensor, second is Heartbeat sensor and the third one is humidity sensor. This work is very useful since the doctor can monitor patient health parameters just by visiting website or URL and now a days many IoT apps are also being developed. Hence the doctor or family members can monitor or track the patient health through the android apps. To operate IoT based health monitoring system project, you need a Wi-Fi connection. The raspberry pi connects to the Wi-Fi network using a Wi-Fi module. This work will not work without a working Wi-Fi network. To create a Wi-Fi zone using a Wi-Fi module or to create a Wi-Fi zone using hotspot on your smartphone. The raspberry pi board continuously reads input from these 3 sensors. Then it sends this data to the cloud by sending this data to a particular URL/IP address. Then this action of sending data to IP is repeated after a particular interval of time. For example in this work the data has sent after every 30 seconds. The raspberry pi board continuously reads input from these 3 sensors. Then it sends this data to the cloud by sending this data to a particular URL/IP address. Then this action of sending data to IP is repeated after a particular interval of time.

Hardware and Software Description

Power Supply Unit

The Raspberry Pi 3 is powered by a +5.1V micro USB supply. The power supply for domestic applications is about 230 V AC. This 230 V AC supply is step down to the required 5 V using an IC7805 voltage regulator. The power supply setup consists of a transformer whose primary coils are connected to the mains supply. The secondary of the transformer is connected to the bridge rectifier and is step down to 12 V DC supply. The efficiency of bridge rectifier is high. But the output of the bridge rectifier is not exactly a DC signal and it contains ripples. A capacitor is connected to the diode so as to filter the ripples present in the output and a pure DC signal is obtained. The output can be further reduced to 5 V using 7805 voltage regulator.

The Raspberry Pi 3 Model B+

The Raspberry Pi 3 model B+ is the latest product in the Raspberry Pi 3 range, boasting a 64-bit quad core processor running at 1.4GHz, dual-band 2.4GHz and 5GHz Wireless Local Area Network(WLAN), Bluetooth 4.2/BLE, faster ethernet, and PoE capability via a separate PoE HAT The dual-band wireless LAN comes with modular compliance certification, allowing the board to be designed into end products with significantly reduced wireless LAN compliance testing, improving both cost and time to market. The Raspberry Pi 3 model B+ maintains the same mechanical footprint as both the Raspberry Pi 2 model B and the Raspberry Pi 3 model B.

Temperature Sensor

The LM35 series are precision integrated-circuit temperature devices with an output voltage linearly proportional to the Centigrade temperature. The output of this temperature sensor is calibrated in centigrade. It operates in the range of 4-30 V and suitable for low power consumption applications. It exhibits an accuracy of 0.5^0C at 25^0C and operates between -55^0C to 150^0C. The linear scale factor is about 10 mv/^{0}C4. The general equation used to convert output voltage to temperature is: Temperature (1^0C) = V (out) $*$ (100^0C/V) so if V (out) is 1V, then Temperature = 100^0C5.

Heartbeat Sensor

Heart beat sensor uses a pair of Light Emitting Diode (LED), Light Dependent Resistor (LDR) and microcontroller. Light is passed using LED from one side of the finger and intensity of light is measured

Figure 1. Components of a patient monitoring system that is based on an IoT-Cloud architecture.

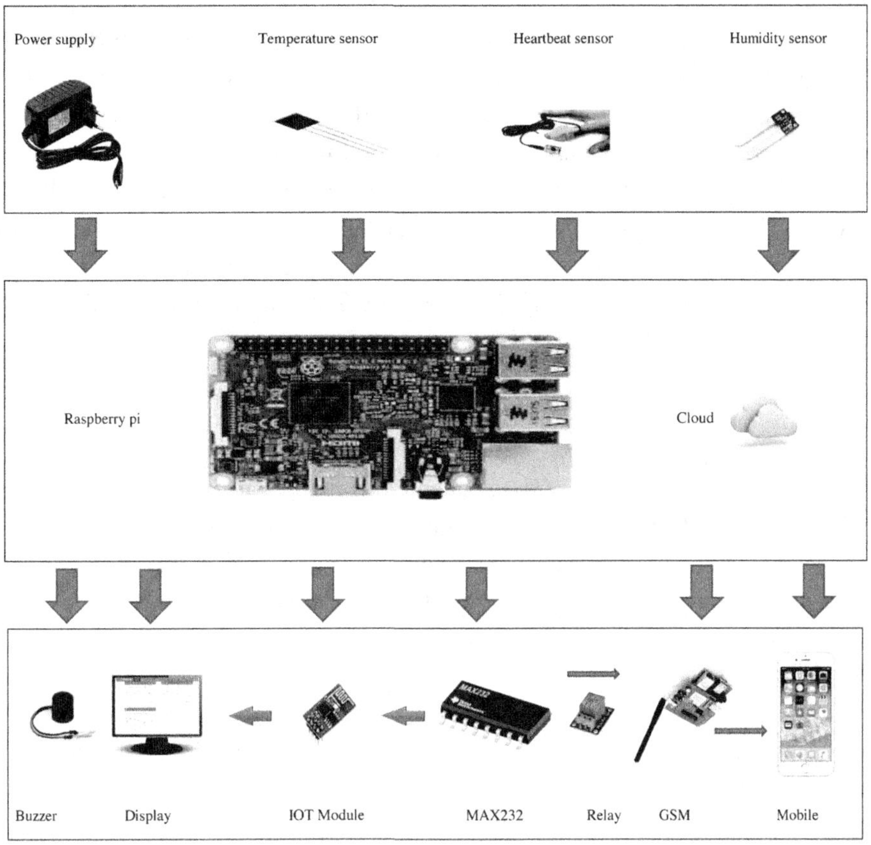

on the other side using an LDR. As the heart rate increases intensity decreases. As a result there will be a change in resistance value of LDR. The output voltage is amplified and detected using microcontroller.

Humidity Sensor

In medical applications, humidity control is required for respiratory equipment's, sterilizers, incubators, pharmaceutical processing, and biological products. The xcluma Dht11 digital humidity sensor used in raspberry pi. The humidity measuring range is 20 percent~90 percent, the accuracy is Â±50 percent, response time: <5s low power consumption and the size is 23 x 12 x 55 mm.

Max 232

MAX232 is an essential component in serial communication. It is used to convert the Complementary Metal Oxide Semiconductor (CMOS) logic levels to RS232 levels and vice versa. It acts as a bidirectional driver/receiver circuit. It reduces the noise and prevents from external short circuits. It operates at a speed of 120 kbits/s. It supplies a very low current of 8 mA.

GSM Module

A GSM module is a communication medium used for sending or receiving the data over the existing mobile architecture. It operates on a 5 V power supply. A sim card of any cellular operated should be inserted in it and the charges are levied on the user for availing the services provided by the cellular operator. It is operated on frequencies like 800/900/1800/1900 MHz. It can be interfaced with the computer or microcontroller through attention commands. The data can be transmitted as SMS or Multimedia Messaging Service (MMS) and voice messages. The access has avail with the help of GSM/General Packet Radio Service (GPRS) module. It supports various software features such as File Transfer Protocol (FTP), Hyper Text Transfer Protocol (HTTP), Secure Sockets Layer (SSL), Transmission Control Protocol (TCP), User Datagram Protocol (UDP) and jamming detection.

IoT Module

IoT module is useful for the transmission of data collected from the sensors to the internet by using Hyper Text Transfer Protocol (HTTP) through a GSM modem. The data is displayed over a webpage which can be viewed from anywhere all over the world. The data collected from this is stored on the cloud for continuous monitoring of patient health over a long period of time.

Liquid Crystal Display (LCD)

A 16X2 display module is employed to display 16 characters in 2 rows. LCD has two registers namely command and data. The command instruction stores the command instructions given to LCD. Data register stores data to be displayed on LCD. It has totally 16 pins. 8 Bi-directional data pins D7-D0.3 control lines RS, RW, EN.VCC-power supply, VEE-Contrast Adjustment, Ground, Backlight LED (0 V) and Backlight LED (5 V). The data that is being transmitted can be read from LCD module.

Relay

Anything connected to the 220 V mains supply can be switched on and off by using a relay enabled low voltage circuit. This work JQC-3FC (T73) DC12V relay is used. The typical usage of relay in this work is to switch the power supply between the IoT module and GSM module.

Buzzer

A piezoelectric buzzer is an electrical device which produces sound on the arrival of input voltage signal. This is used to alert the care taker in case of emergency condition.

Programming Using Embedded C

The embedded C program tool has used to develop software program for this work. The Code speed of embedded programs is governed by processing power and timing constraints. Code size of embedded programs is governed by program memory and use of programming languages. Processing power and memory is limited in embedded devices.

MPLAB IDE

Microprocessor Lab. Integrated Development Environment (MPLAB IDE) is a free, integrated toolset for the development of embedded applications employing microchips PIC microcontrollers. MPLAB IDE runs as a 32-bit application on Microsoft Windows, is easy to use and includes a host of free software components for fast application development and super-charged debugging. It supports various programming languages like embedded c and java. It has a graphical project manager.

INTERFACING

The raspberry pi is placed on a development board. Power supply system is connected to it and all the necessary code for accessing various features like Analog to Digital Conversion (ADC), Universal Synchronous/Asynchronous Receiver/Transmitter (USART), and LCD for accessing the sensors are written in embedded C language in MPLAB and is loaded into raspberry pi. All the required three sensors are connected to the general purpose input/output pins of raspberry pi. Each sensor is given a particular threshold value. The raspberry pi transmitter pin (RC6/TX) is connected to the IoT module receiver pin (RX). A sim card has to be inserted into the module so that it can access the mobile network of that particular network operator. The IoT module has a LEDs that glow on receiving the signal from the mobile network and indicates whether the strength of the signal is strong or weak. The raspberry pi is connected to this IoT module using max232 cable. The website address in which the results have to be displayed has to be linked to the IoT module. LCD and buzzer are connected to the GPIO pins of raspberry pi the relay driver is connected to the GPIO pins of the raspberry pi, IoT module and GSM modem. It switches the power supply between IoT module and GSM modem based on the delay time set in the raspberry pi. Because of this the results gets updated in the internet and the message is sent to the registered mobile number. The developed prototype is shown in figure 2.

WORKING

Data Acquisition

Data acquisition is carried out by the sensors that measure the various physiological data and carries these bioelectrical signals to the microcontroller.

Data Transmission

Typically the data collected by the raspberry pi is transmitted to the internet using IoT module and an SMS can be sent to the caretaker if any critical parameter is recorded. The mobile number of the caretaker is written in the program. Individual sensor's data can be accessed via computer or mobile connected to internet.

Figure 2. Developed prototype

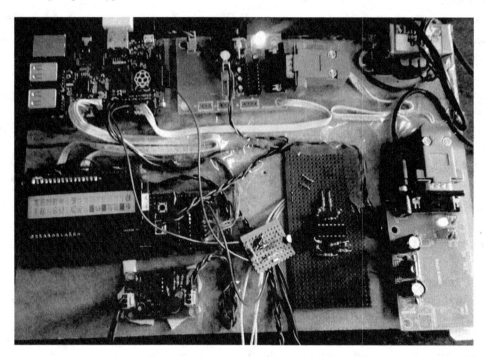

Cloud Processing

Diagnoses and prognosis of a number of health conditions and diseases can be done using the sensor data.

Long term storage of patient's health information can be done and the health information can be accessed using internet. In this work the results were display in the www.thinkspeak.com[20] website.

Visualization

ThingSpeak is an open source IoT application and API to store and retrieve data from things using the HTTP protocol over the Internet or via a Local Area Network. ThingSpeak enables the creation of sensor logging applications, location tracking applications, and a social network of things with status updates. ThingSpeak was originally launched by ioBridge in 2010 as a service in support of IoT applications. ThingSpeak is a free web service that lets you collect and store sensor data in the cloud and develop IoT applications. The ThingSpeak web service provides apps that let you analyze and visualize the data in MATLAB, and then act on the data. The Sensor data has sent to ThingSpeak from Raspberry Pi.

ThingSpeak is an IoT platform that uses channels to store data sent from apps or devices. With the settings described in Channel Configurations, to create a channel, and then send and retrieve data to and from the channel. To make your channels public to share data. Using the REST API calls such as GET, POST, PUT, and DELETE, you can create a channel and update its feed, update an existing channel, clear a channel feed, and delete a channel. To use the MQTT Publish method to update a channel feed and MQTT Subscribe to receive messages when a channel updates.

Table 1. Characteristics of temperature, heartbeat and humidity sensor

Sensor	Threshold Value	Characteristics
Temperature	Greater than 42⁰C	Temperature is High
	Less Than 42⁰C	Temperature is Normal
Heartbeat(BPM)	Greater Than 90	Abnormal
	Less than 90	Normal
Humidity (Grams of water vapour per cubic meter volume of air)	Greater than 45%	Abnormal
	Less than 45%	Normal

Figure 3. Values obtained from ThingSpeak website for tempeture sensor channel

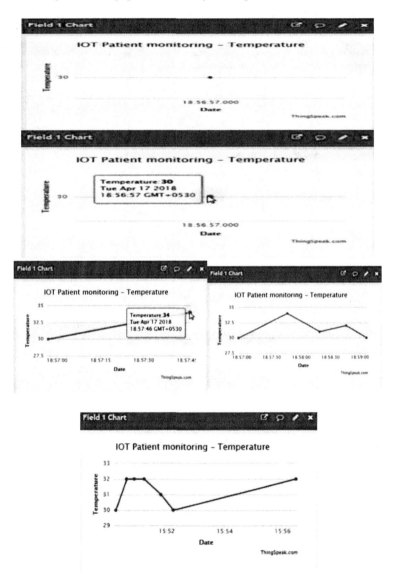

RESULTS

The proposed architecture was implemented in Embedded C with MPE IDE tools where runs needed on a desktop Intel(R) Core ™ i5-7500 CPU @ 3.40GHz, 8.00 GB RAM 64-bit OS,X64 based processor. The hardware modules are properly interfaced with personal computer and tested successful with software coding environment. The sensor value are fixed a particular threshold value and if there is any change in the reading it display the abnormality in the monitor, updates in the ThingSpeak is an IoT platform via internet and sends SMS to the care taker and sounds the buzzer. The following Tables 1 indicates the threshold values used for sensors and changes found during software the hardware prototype. The obtained channel results of three sensors values were displayed in figure 3,4 and 5 respectively.

Figure 4. Values obtained from ThingSpeak website for humidity sensor channel

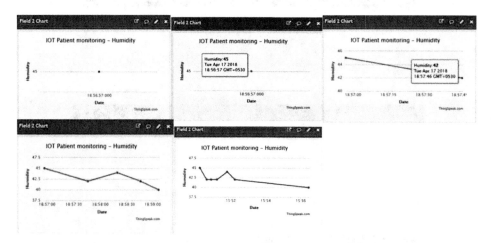

Figure 5. Values obtained from ThingSpeak website for heartbeat sensor channel

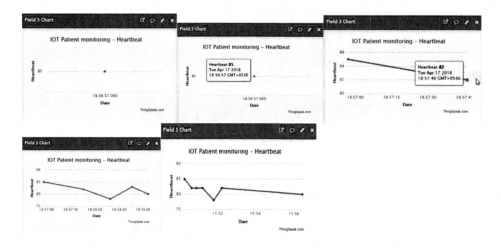

CONCLUSION AND FUTURE WORK

An IOT Healthcare is the most requesting field in the medicinal zone, in this paper, an IoT based health monitoring system was developed and implemented. The performance was analyzed using ThingSpeak an open source IoT application. In this proposed framework a portable physiological observing framework is exhibited, or, in other words ceaselessly screen the patient's heart beat, temperature and other basic parameters in the doctor's facility. The framework can do a long haul observing on patients condition and is outfitted with a crisis save instrument utilizing SMS.

In Future the GPS module will include in IoT persistent observing utilizing Arduino Uno and Wi-Fi module venture. This GPS module will discover the position or the area of the patient utilizing the longitude and scope got. At that point it will send this area to the cloud that is the IOT utilizing the Wi-Fi module. At that point specialists can discover the situation of the patient on the off chance that they need to make some preventive move.

REFERENCES

Alavi, A. H., Jiao, P., Buttlar, W. G., & Lajnef, N. (2018). Internet of Things-enabled smart cities: State-of-the-art and future trends. *Measurement*, *129*, 589–606. doi:10.1016/j.measurement.2018.07.067

Babu, S., Chandini, M., Lavanya, P., Ganapathy, K., & Vaidehi, V. (2013, July). Cloud-enabled remote health monitoring system. In *Proceedings of International Conference on Recent Trends in Information Technology (ICRTIT)* (pp. 702-707). IEEE.

Banerjee, M., Lee, J., & Choo, K. K. R. (2018). A block chain future for internet of things security: A position paper. *Digital Communications and Networks*, *4*(3), 149–160. doi:10.1016/j.dcan.2017.10.006

Bui, N., & Zorzi, M. (2011), Health care applications: A solution based on the internet of things. In *Proc. of the 4th Int. Symposium on Applied Sciences in Biomed. and Com. Tech., ser.* (pp.1–5). Academic Press. 10.1145/2093698.2093829

Da Costa, C. A., Pasluosta, C. F., Eskofier, B., da Silva, D. B., & da Rosa Righi, R. (2018). Internet of Health Things: Toward intelligent vital signs monitoring in hospital wards. *Artificial Intelligence in Medicine*, *89*, 61–69. doi:10.1016/j.artmed.2018.05.005 PMID:29871778

Hassan, M. K., El Desouky, A. I., Elghamrawy, S. M., & Sarhan, A. M. (2018). Intelligent hybrid remote patient-monitoring model with cloud-based framework for knowledge discovery. *Computers & Electrical Engineering*, *70*, 1034–1048. doi:10.1016/j.compeleceng.2018.02.032

Kouicem, D. E., Bouabdallah, A., & Lakhlef, H. (2018). Internet of things security: A top-down survey. *Computer Networks*, *141*, 199–221. doi:10.1016/j.comnet.2018.03.012

Lan, M., Samy, L., Alshurafa, N., Suh, M. K., Ghasemzadeh, H., Macabasco-O'Connell, A., & Sarrafzadeh, M. (2012). Wanda: An end-to-end remote health monitoring and analytics system for heart failure patients, In *Proc. of the Conf. on Wireless Health* (pp.1–9). Academic Press. 10.1145/2448096.2448105

Manogaran, G., Varatharajan, R., Lopez, D., Kumar, P. M., Sundarasekar, R., & Thota, C. (2018). A new architecture of Internet of Things and big data ecosystem for secured smart healthcare monitoring and alerting system. *Future Generation Computer Systems*, *82*, 375–387. doi:10.1016/j.future.2017.10.045

Mao, Y., Chen, Y., Hackmann, G., Chen, M., Lu, C., Kollef, M., & Bailey, T. C. (2011). Medical data mining for early deterioration warning in general hospital wards. In *IEEE 11th Int. Conf. on Data Mining Workshops*, (pp.1042–1049). Academic Press. 10.1109/ICDMW.2011.117

Pantelopoulos, A., & Bourbakis, N. G. (2010). A survey on wearable sensor-based systems for health monitoring and prognosis. *IEEE Transactions on Systems, Man, and Cybernetics*, *40*(1), 1–12. doi:10.1109/TSMCC.2009.2032660

Petrakis, E. G., Sotiriadis, S., Soultanopoulos, T., Renta, P. T., Buyya, R., & Bessis, N. (2018). Internet of Things as a Service (iTaaS): Challenges and Solutions for Management of Sensor Data on the Cloud and the Fog. *Internet of Things*, *3*(4), 156–174. doi:10.1016/j.iot.2018.09.009

Rahmani, A. M., Gia, T. N., Negash, B., Anzanpour, A., Azimi, I., Jiang, M., & Liljeberg, P. (2018). Exploiting smart e-Health gateways at the edge of healthcare Internet-of-Things: A fog computing approach. *Future Generation Computer Systems*, *78*, 641–658. doi:10.1016/j.future.2017.02.014

Rao, B. (2013). The role of medical data analytics in reducing health fraud and improving clinical and financial outcomes. *IEEE 26th International Symposium on Computer-Based Medical Systems,* 3–13. 10.1109/CBMS.2013.6627755

Ray, P. (2014). Home health hub internet of things (H3IoT): An architectural framework for monitoring health of elderly people. In *Proceedings of Int. Conf. on Science Eng. and Management Research*, (pp.1–3). Academic Press.

Ray, P.P. (2018). A survey on Internet of Things architectures. *Journal of King Saud University - Computer and Information Sciences, 30*(3), 291-319,

Rolim, C. O., Koch, F. L., Westphall, C. B., Werner, J., Fracalossi, A., & Salvador, G. S. (2010). A cloud computing solution for patient's data collection in health care institutions. In *Proceedings of International Conference on eHealth, Telemedicine, and Social Medicine*, (pp. 95-99). IEEE. 10.1109/eTELEMED.2010.19

Ukis, V., Rajamani, S. T., Balachandran, B., & Friese, T. (2013). Architecture of cloud-based advanced medical image visualization solution. In *IEEE Int. Conf. on Cloud Computing in Emerging Markets*, (pp.1–5). IEEE. 10.1109/CCEM.2013.6684428

Wei, L., Kumar, N., Lolla, V., Keogh, E., Lonardi, S., Ratanamahatana, C. A., & Van Herle, H. (2005). A practical tool for visualizing and data mining medical time series. In *Proc. 18th IEEE Symposium on Computer-Based Med. Sys.*, (pp.341–346). IEEE.

KEY TERMS AND DEFINITIONS

Complementary Metal Oxide Semiconductor (CMOS): It is a technology for constructing integrated circuits. CMOS technology is used in microprocessors, microcontrollers, static RAM, and other digital logic circuits.

General Packet Radio Service (GPRS): It is a packet oriented mobile data standard on the 2G and 3G cellular communication network's global system for mobile communications. GPRS was established by European Telecommunications Standards Institute in response to the earlier CDPD and i-mode packet-switched cellular technologies.

Global System for Mobile Communication (GSM): GSM is a standard developed by the European Telecommunications Standards Institute to describe the protocols for second-generation digital cellular networks used by mobile devices such as tablets.

Hypertext Transfer Protocol (HTTP): The hypertext transfer protocol is an application protocol for distributed, collaborative, hypermedia information systems.

Internet of Things (IoT): The internet of things is the network of devices, vehicles, and home appliances that contain electronics, software, actuators, and connectivity that allows these things to connect, interact, and exchange data.

IP Address: It is a numerical label assigned to each device connected to a computer network that uses the Internet Protocol for communication. An IP address serves two principal functions: host or network interface identification and location addressing.

Light-Dependent Resistor (LDR): An LDR is a component that has a (variable) resistance that changes with the light intensity that falls upon it. This allows them to be used in light sensing circuits.

Light-Emitting Diode (LED): The LED is a semiconductor device that emits visible light when an electric current passes through it.

Private Internet Protocol (PIP): PIP refers to connectivity into a private extranet network which by its design emulates the functioning of the internet.

Uniform Resource Locator (URL): An URL, colloquially termed a web address, is a reference to a web resource that specifies its location on a computer network and a mechanism for retrieving it. A URL is a specific type of Uniform Resource Identifier, although many people use the two terms interchangeably.

Wireless Any Network Digital Assistant (WANDA): The new concept design is powered by TI's OMAP(TM) processors, multiple TI wireless technologies, and Microsoft's Windows-Powered Pocket PC operating system (OS).

Chapter 11
Statistical Modelling and Analysis of the Computer-Simulated Datasets

M. Harshvardhan
https://orcid.org/0000-0001-8086-544X
Indian Institute of Management Indore, India

Pritam Ranjan
https://orcid.org/0000-0002-9917-6377
Indian Institute of Management Indore, India

ABSTRACT

Over the last two decades, the science has come a long way from relying on only physical experiments and observations to experimentation using computer simulators. This chapter focuses on the modelling and analysis of data arising from computer simulators. It turns out that traditional statistical metamodels are often not very useful for analyzing such datasets. For deterministic computer simulators, the realizations of Gaussian process (GP) models are commonly used for fitting a surrogate statistical metamodel of the simulator output. The chapter starts with a quick review of the standard GP-based statistical surrogate model. The chapter also emphasizes on the numerical instability due to near-singularity of the spatial correlation structure in the GP model fitting process. The authors also present a few generalizations of the GP model, reviews methods, and algorithms specifically developed for analyzing big data obtained from computer model runs, and reviews the popular analysis goals of such computer experiments. A few real-life computer simulators are also briefly outlined here.

DOI: 10.4018/978-1-5225-8407-0.ch011

INTRODUCTION

In early days, when the computers were not readily accessible to common people, statisticians and data analysts focussed on the development of innovative methodologies that were efficient for analyzing small datasets. Over the last two decades, we have come a long way from relying on only physical experiments and observations to experimentation using computer simulation models, commonly referred to as the computer simulators or computer models. These simulators are software implementation of the real-world processes, imitated based on the comprehensive understanding on the underlying phenomena. The applications range from simulating socioeconomic behaviour, impact due to a car crash, manufacturing a compound for drug discovery, climate and weather forecasting, population growth of certain pest species, cosmological phenomena like dark energy and universe expansion, emulation of tidal flow for harnessing renewable energy, the simulation of a nuclear reactions, and so on. Given the easier access to high performance computing power such as cloud computing and cluster grids, computer model data is now a reality in everyday life.

In this chapter, we focus on the modelling and analysis of data sets arising from such computer simulators. Similar to the physical experiments setup, the data obtained from the computer simulator runs have to be modelled and analysed for a deeper understanding of the underlying process. However, traditional statistical metamodels are often not very useful for analyzing such datasets. This is because, many a time, these computer models are deterministic in nature, that is, the repeated runs of such a computer simulator with a fixed input settings yield the same output / response. In other words, there is no replication error for the deterministic computer simulators. Recall that in the traditional statistical models, such as regression, the main driving force for model fitting and inference part of the methodology is the distribution of replication errors.

For deterministic computer simulators, the realizations of Gaussian Process (GP) models, trained by the observed simulator data, are commonly used for fitting a surrogate statistical metamodel of the simulator output. This is particularly crucial if the simulator is expensive to run, which is the case for many complex real-life phenomena. The notion of GP models gained popularity in late 1990 and early 2000 (e.g., Santner et al. (2003); Rasmussen and Williams (2006); Fang et al. (2005)), though it was first proposed in the seminal paper of Sacks et al. (1989). Section 2 of the chapter presents a quick review of the standard GP based statistical surrogate model. We will also briefly discuss the implementation procedure using both the maximum likelihood method and the Bayesian approach.

Almost all published research articles and books focus on the new methodologies and algorithms that can be used for analyzing the computer simulator data, and not on the small nuances related to the actual implementation which is extremely useful from a practitioners' standpoint. This chapter emphasizes on such computational issues. In particular, Section 3 of the chapter discusses the numerical instability due to near-singularity or ill-conditioning of the spatial correlation structure which is the key building block behind the flexibility of the GP-based surrogate model. In practice, the majority of researchers simply use a numerical fix to overcome this issue, but this inadvertently compromises with other aspects of the model assumptions. We present an empirical study to compare different current practices to address this ill-conditioning problem. We also discuss the best coding practices in the implementation of such model fitting exercise, for instance, which of the matrix decomposition method, LU / QR / SVD / Cholesky, is recommended from an accuracy and time efficiency perspective.

Given the revolution in the computing power, it is now easy to collect and process data sets that are spatio-temporal and functional in nature. Dynamic computer models, i.e. the simulator which returns time-series response (see Zhang et al. (2018b)), is a current hot topic of research in applied statistics and computer experiments. Section 4 of the chapter reviews several generalizations of the GP model that accounts for multiple sources of uncertainty in the simulation model, non-stationarity of the underlying processes, and dynamic nature of such computer simulator outputs.

With the advent of inexpensive high performance computing facilities on cloud servers and different grids, a plethora of big data is now available in the public domain. The standard methodologies and algorithms are typically not very efficient in analyzing such datasets. Section 5 of the chapter reviews methods and algorithms specifically developed for analyzing big data obtained from computer model runs. Some of the approaches are methodolgoical in nature, and use sparse matrix computation and localized model approximation based ideas to efficiently build the statistical surrogate, whereas others emphasize on the clever use of parallelization on CPUs and graphical processing units (GPUs) for handling the big data.

Section 6 of the chapter reviews the popular analysis goals of such computer experiments. For instance, Jones et al. (1998) proposed an innovative merit based criterion called the expected improvement for the process optimization; Linkletter et al. (2006) developed a variable screening approach for the identification of important inputs to the computer simulator and subsequently ignoring the non-important ones; Vernon et al. (2010), Pratola et al. (2013) and Ranjan et al. (2016) discussed the calibration of computer simulators to ensure the generation of realistic outputs. Finally, Section 7 presents brief outlines of a few real-life computer models.

Over the past decade or so, a few open source software (mostly in R) have been published which are becoming increasingly popular among the researchers and practitioners, for instance, GPfit (MacDonald et al., 2015), mlegp (Dancik and Dorman, 2008), TGP (Gramacy, 2007), DiceKriging (Roustant et al., 2012), laGP (Gramacy et al., 2016) and DynamicGP (Zhang et al., 2018a). In this chapter, we use several test function based computer simulators and real-life applications to illustrate the concepts and methodologies via these packages. We also provide code snippets of R to help understand how to apply use them in your research endeavours.

GAUSSIAN PROCESS MODEL

A stochastic process is a collection of random variables indexed by time or space. A Gaussian process is commonly used in statistical modelling because of its nice distributional properties and closed form expressions of moments and other summary statistics. In notation, $\{z(x), x \in [0,1]^d\}$, in short, $z(x) \sim GP\left(0, \sigma_z^2 R\right)$ with

$$E\left(z\left(x\right)\right) = 0, \ Var\left(z\left(x\right)\right) = \sigma_z^2, \text{ and } Cov\left(z\left(x_i\right), z\left(x_j\right)\right) = \sigma_z^2 R\left(x_i, x_j\right)$$

where R is a positive definite correlation function. Then, any finite subset of variables $\{z(x_1), z(x_2), ..., z(x_n)\}$, for $n \geq 1$, jointly follows multivariate normal distribution.

In conventional regression models, we set $y_i = f(x_i, \beta) + \varepsilon_i$, where ε_i is are *i.i.d.* $N(0, \sigma^2)$. Though the regression model can be very flexible if we choose the $f(x_i, \beta)$ carefully, this is not suitable for emulating the deterministic computer model outputs, as there is no replication error. In GP model (also sometimes referred to as the GP regression model), we aim to find a surrogate that is an interpolator of all the observed training data, that is, the fitted surface passes through all original $(x_i, y_i), i = 1, 2, ..., n$. In between the training points, the smoothness and curvature of the fitted surrogate is guided by the correlation structure $R(\cdot, \cdot)$. The GP model is formally presented in the next subsection.

Model Statement

Let the i-th d dimensional input and 1-dimensional output of the computer simulator be denoted by $x_i = (x_{i1}, x_{i2}, ..., x_{id})$ and $y_i = y(x_i)$, respectively. Suppose the set of all n training data are held together in the design $D = \{x_1, x_2, ..., x_n\}$ and the output vector $Y = (y_1, y_2, ..., y_n)'$. Then, the GP model is written as

$$y_i = \mu + z(x_i), i = 1, 2, ..., n, \tag{1}$$

where μ is the overall mean and $z(x) \sim GP(0, \sigma_z^2 R)$. Subsequently, Y follows multivariate normal distribution with mean $1_n \mu$ and variance-covariance matrix $\pounds = \sigma_z^2 R_n$, where 1_n is an $n \times 1$ vector of all 1's, and R_n is an $n \times n$ correlation matrix with (i, j)-th element given by $R(x_i, x_j)$ (see Sacks et al. (1989); Santner et al. (2003) for more details).

The most crucial component of this GP model is the correlation structure, which dictates the 'smoothness' of the interpolator that passes through the observations. In a multidimensional scenario, it tells us how wobbly and differentiable the fitted surrogate is. By definition, any positive definite correlation structure would suffice, but the most popular choice is the Gaussian correlation. In Machine Learning and Geostatistics literature, Gaussian correlation is also referred to as the radial basis function. Gaussian correlation is a special case (with $p_k = 2$) of the power-exponential correlation given by

$$R(x_i, x_j) = \prod_{k=1}^{d} \exp\{-\theta_k \mid x_{ik} - x_{jk} \mid^{p_k}\}, \tag{2}$$

where θ_k and p_k controls the wobbliness of the surrogate in the k-th coordinate.

The model described by (1) and (2) is typically fitted by either maximizing the likelihood or via Bayesian algorithms like Markov chain Monte Carlo (MCMC). As a result, the predicted response $\hat{y}(x_0)$ for an arbitrary input x_0 can be obtained as a conditional expectation from the following $(n + 1)$ dimensional multivariate normal distribution:

$$\begin{pmatrix} y(x_0) \\ Y \end{pmatrix} = N\left(\begin{pmatrix} \mu \\ \mu 1_n \end{pmatrix}, \begin{pmatrix} \sigma_z^2 & \sigma_z^2 r'(x_0) \\ \sigma_z^2 r(x_0) & \sigma_z^2 R_n \end{pmatrix} \right),$$ (3)

where $r(x_0) = \left[corr(x_1, x_0), \ldots, corr(x_n, x_0) \right]'$. The predicted response $\hat{y}(x_0)$, which is also the best linear unbiased predictor (BLUP), is the same as the conditional mean:

$$E\left(y(x_0) \mid Y \right) = \mu + r(x_0)' R_n^{-1} \left(Y - 1_n \mu \right),$$ (4)

and the associate prediction uncertainty estimate (denoted by $s^2(x_0)$) can be quantified by the conditional variance:

$$Var\left(y(x_0) \mid Y \right) = \sigma_z^2 \left(1 - r'(x_0) R_n^{-1} r(x_0) \right).$$ (5)

In practice, the parameters μ, σ and $\theta = \left(\theta_1, \ldots, \theta_d \right)$ are replaced by their estimates (maximum likelihood estimates or posterior means in MCMC) in (4) and (5).

Implementation Details

The key aspects of the implementation here is to efficiently maximize the likelihood and evaluate the predicted mean response and associated uncertainty measure. For this GP model, the likelihood is simply the joint probability density function of the multivariate normal distribution of Y, i.e.,

$$-2\log\left(L \right) \propto \log\left(\left| R_n \right| \right) + n\log\left(\sigma_z^2 \right) + \frac{\left(Y - 1_n \mu \right)' R_n^{-1} \left(Y - 1_n \mu \right)}{\sigma_z^2},$$ (6)

where $\left| R_n \right|$ is the determinant of the $n \times n$ correlation matrix R_n.

Minimizing $-2\log\left(L \right)$ gives closed form expressions for $\hat{\mu}$ and $\hat{\sigma}_z^2$ as

$$\hat{\mu} = (1_n' R_n^{-1} 1_n)^{-1} \left(1_n' R_n^{-1} Y \right),$$ (7)

and

$$\hat{\sigma}_z^2 = \frac{\left(Y - 1_n \hat{\mu} \right)' R_n^{-1} \left(Y - 1_n \hat{\mu} \right)}{n},$$ (8)

where R_n is a function of unknown $\theta = \left(\theta_1,...,\theta_d\right)$. Finding good estimates of the d-dimensional correlation hyperparameter vector θ is not easy. It is common to use numerical optimization techniques like multi-start Gauss-Newton type methods or evolutionary algorithms like particle swarm method and genetic algorithms to find $\hat{\theta}$.

For the convenience of researchers and practitioners in this area, several R packages have been developed that provide easy implementation of fitting this GP model, for example, TGP (Gramacy, 2007), mlegp (Dancik and Dorman, 2008), DiceKriging (Roustant et al., 2012) and GPfit (MacDonald et al., 2015).

In this section, we briefly illustrate the usage of GPfit (MacDonald et al., 2015) for fitting a GP model to a simulated data set. Suppose the simulator output is generated by a one-dimensional test function $f\left(x\right) = \log\left(x + 0.1\right) + \sin\left(5\pi x\right)$, and $X = \left\{x_1,...,x_{10}\right\}$ is a randomly generated training set as per the space-filling Latin hypercube design. Then the GP model can be fitted using the following code:

GPmodel = GPfit::GP_fit(X, Y, corr = list(type="exponential", power=2))

The GPfit object GPmodel contains the parameter estimates, which can be further passed on for generating the predictions along with uncertainty estimates at a test set. Figure 1 shows the fitted surrogate along with the true response.

In GPfit package, the estimate of θ is obtained by minimizing the deviance ($-2\log\left(L_p\right)$, where L_p is the profiled likelihood obtained after substituting $\hat{\mu}$ and $\hat{\sigma}_z^2$) using a multi-start gradient based search (L-BFGS-B) algorithm. As a side note, they use a slightly different parametrization, i.e., $\theta_k = 10^{\beta_k}$, and then find optimal $\beta = \left(\beta_1,...,\beta_d\right)$ (see Section 3.4 for more discussion on reparametrization of $R\left(x_i, x_j\right)$). The starting points of L-BFGS-B are selected using the k means clustering algorithm on a large space-filling design over the search space, after discarding β vectors with high deviance. The control param-

Figure 1. The blue dashed curve is the mean prediction obtained using GPfit ; the black solid curve is the true simulator response curve $f\left(x\right) = \log\left(x + 0.1\right) + \sin\left(5\pi x\right)$. The black solid dots are the training data points, and the shaded area represent the uncertainty quantification via $\hat{y}\left(x\right) \pm 2s\left(x\right)$.

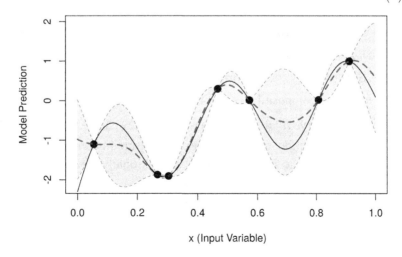

eter is a vector of three tunable parameters used in the deviance optimization algorithm. The default values correspond to choosing $2d$ clusters based on $80d$ best points (smallest deviance) from a $200d$ - point random space-filling design in β space. One can enhance the robustness of the optimal β estimates by increasing the arguments of control in GP_fit, however, this is a computationally expensive, with $O\left(n^3\right)$ complexity, where n is the size of the training data. Thus, one should balance between the computational cost and the robustness of likelihood optimization. For details see MacDonald et al. (2015).

COMPUTATIONAL ISSUES IN FITTING GP MODELS

Though fitting a GP model to the training data and prediction on a test set may seem like straightforward tasks, there are several issues like numerical instability, prediction accuracy, biases due to miss-specified model, and some concern due to the heavy computational cost, particularly when dealing with big data. In this section, we review a few such outstanding issues and popular approaches to address them.

Matrix Decomposition in Likelihood Evaluation

Different components of the GP model, including the likelihood (equivalently, the deviance expression), estimates of μ and σ_z^2, the predicted mean response and the uncertainty estimate (as shown in (4) - (8)), contain two computationally expensive terms, the determinant of R_n and the inverse of R_n. For finding optimal θ (or equivalently, β, as in GPfit), these expressions have to be evaluated hundreds to thousands of times for different realizations of θ. If the size of the training data, n, is small, numerous evaluations of $\left|R_n\right|$ and R_n^{-1} by any method is not a concern from computational cost standpoint, however, for large n, fast evaluations of $\left|R_n\right|$ and R_n^{-1} become crucial.

It is common to use matrix decomposition methods like LU, Cholesky, QR and SVD, for efficient computation of determinants and inverses of R_n, and terms like $R_n^{-1}w$, for some $n \times 1$ vector w. It turns out that these decomposition methods have different computational cost, and more importantly, exhibit different precision as well. In this section, we present a simulation study based comparison of these matrix decomposition methods for Gaussian correlation (2). The objective is to choose the right matrix decomposition method while implementing the GP model procedure.

The results are averaged over 1000 simulations. For each replication, we randomly generate $X = \left\{x_1, x_2, ..., x_n\right\}$ using a space-filling Latin hypercube design over $[0,1]^d$ and $\theta \in (0, \infty)^d$ and then evaluate R_n as in (2). Subsequently, we perform the decomposition and then obtain the reconstituted matrix. For instance, for LU decomposition, we obtain the triangular matrices L and U via $\mathrm{lu}\left(R_n\right)$, and then find $R_n^* = LU$. In theory, $R_n^* = R_n$, but in practice, they can be somewhat different. Both the empirical simulation study and the theoretical complexity measured in terms of big O, show that Cholesky and SVD have much greater accuracy and are computationally cheaper as compared to LU and QR.

Note that Cholesky decomposition method uses two sets of linear solves for computing $R_n^{-1}w$. That is, if $R_n = LL^T$, then $R_n^{-1}w = solve\left(L^T, solve\left(L, w\right)\right)$. Whereas, the SVD method finds R_n^{-1} by inverting the singular values as

$$R_n^{-1} = \sum_{i=1}^{n} u_i v_i^T / d_i,$$

where $R_n = UDV^T$ with $U = \left[u_1, ..., u_n\right], V = \left[v_1, ..., v_n\right]$ and $D = diag\left(d_1, ..., d_n\right)$. It turns out that for applications with large n and small input dimension d, both of these matrix decomposition methods suffer from numerical instability due to ill-conditioning of R_n. In this chapter, we only focus on Cholesky and SVD as the other decomposition methods are less efficient and inaccurate.

Near-Singularity of Correlation Matrix

Recall that an $n \times n$ matrix is said to be singular if at least one of its rows (or columns) is linearly dependent on the rest of rows (or columns), i.e., the matrix does not have full row (or column) rank, i.e., the determinant is zero. However in a near-singular matrix, the determinant is not exactly equal to zero but very small. One popular method of quantifying the near-singularity of R_n is via its condition number defined by, $\kappa\left(R_n\right) = \| R_n^{-1} \| \cdot \| R_n \| = \lambda_n / \lambda_1$ where $\| \cdot \|$ is the L_2 norm of the matrix, and λ_i is the i-th smallest eigen value of R_n. An $n \times n$ matrix R_n is said to be near-singular (or ill-conditioned) if $\kappa\left(R_n\right)$ is large. For Gaussian correlation, the near-singularity occurs when $\sum_{k=1}^{d} \theta_k \mid x_{ik} - x_{jk} \mid^2 \approx 0$, which implies either the two data points x_i and x_j are close to each other and/or θ_k's are close to zero. This further implies that the condition number is directly proportional to the sample size n and inversely proportional to d and θ. In other words, the larger the training data size, it is more likely to run into near-singularity, whereas if the input dimension and/or θ are large, it is less likely to run into near-singularity.

From an implementation standpoint, if the condition number is larger than say $1 / \varepsilon_M$, where ε_M is the machine precision (ε_M 2.220446e-16 for our desktop computer), the determinant of R_n would be too close to zero, and the linear solves using R_n become too sensitive and unreliable, if at all obtainable. If $\kappa\left(R_n\right) > 1 / \varepsilon_M$, Cholesky decomposition of R_n would crash, rendering the method infeasible. However, one can use SVD approach and approximates R_n^{-1} as

$$R_n^{-1} \approx \sum_{i=1}^{n} u_i v_i^T / d_i \cdot I(d_i > \eta),$$

where η is a pre-specified threshold that determines a cut-off for not using very small singular values in approximating the inverse of R_n. For details, see Jones et al. (1998) and Booker et al. (1999). It turns out that the SVD based approach is very sensitive with respect to the choice of η. That is, a large value of η would make the approximated R_n^{-1} too far from the true (unobservable) R_n^{-1}, whereas a small value of η would make approximated R_n^{-1} unreliable due to the inclusion of very large $1/d_i$.

A popular technique to resolve this numerical issue is to use a "nugget" (or also referred to as a "jitter") term δ in the model by replacing R_n^{-1} with $R_{n,\delta}^{-1}$, where $R_{n,\delta} = R_n + \delta I_n$ (Neal, 1997). This method works because $\kappa(R_{n,\delta}) = (\lambda_n + \delta)/(\lambda_1 + \delta)$ would be much smaller than $\kappa(R_n)$. Similar to the SVD based approximation, here also one needs to find δ, but interestingly, this nugget based approach is less sensitive to the choice to δ as compared to selecting appropriate η in the SVD method. Gramacy and Lee (2012) suggests estimating δ along with other model parameters in a Bayesian framework, however, the search space for δ has to be carefully chosen so that the lower limit is large enough to ensure well-conditioned $R_{n,\delta}$. To this effect, Ranjan et al. (2011) developed a lower-bound on δ which suffices well-behaved and accurate approximation of R_n.

If we choose $\eta, \delta > 0$, the resultant mean prediction function is not an interpolator. Thus, both the nugget and SVD based approaches lead to methodological consequences which may not be desirable for a deterministic simulator. Ranjan et al. (2011) proposed an iterative scheme that uses the lower bound of nugget to start with for well-behaved $R_{n,\delta}$ and then the iterative regularization makes the predictor converge to the interpolator. The following R code snippet illustrates the usage of GPfit package to specify the number of iteration (say, $M = 5$) in this iterative procedure:

```
GPprediction = GPfit::predict.GP(GPmodel, xnew, M=5)
```

Of course, one can argue on a philosophical ground that none of the realistic computer model is deterministic, and some sort of uncertainties and biases are always present. Thus, one must include a non-zero nugget term, and some amount of smoothing is a desirable feature for a predicted surrogate. Even in such a case, if the nugget parameter is estimated using the maximum likelihood method or a Bayesian approach (via MCMC), the lower limit of the search space for δ must be large enough to ensure well-conditioned $R_{n,\delta}$, for which the lower-bound of δ proposed by Ranjan et al. (2011) can be used.

Alternatively, one can consider approximating R_n^{-1} by $R_{n,\delta}^{*-1} = (R + \delta J)^{-1}$, where J is an $n \times n$ matrix of all 1's. A quick calculation reveals that the predicted surrogate similar to (4) - (5) will be an interpolator, unlike the scenario when we used $(R + \delta I)^{-1}$ as an approximation of R^{-1}. However, a thorough investigation is required to compare the model properties between $(R + \delta I)$ versus $(R + \delta J)$ approaches.

Reparameterisation of Correlation Functions

The estimation of the correlation hyperparameter $\theta = (\theta_1, ..., \theta_d)$ is the most crucial part of the GP model fitting procedure. Recall that the deviance function has to be minimized with respect to $\theta \in (0, \infty)$. For many applications, the deviance functions for such GP models are not easy to minimize. As an example, Figure 2 shows the deviance function with respect to θ for the 1-dimensional test function dis-

Figure 2. Deviance with respect to θ for the test function and data used in Figure 1. The left panel is the zoomed-in version of the right panel near zero.

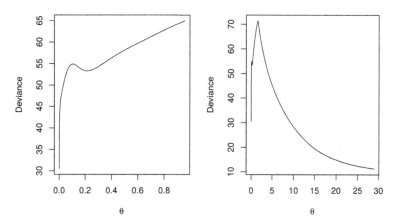

played in Figure 1. Since a large value of θ implies wigglier surrogate, we do not expect the estimated θ to be too big here. As a result, the deviance is a non-trivial function to minimize.

In the computer experiment literature, researchers have considered a variety of re-parametrizations of this Gaussian correlation. In this section, we briefly discuss these parametrizations and compare their suitability for easier optimization.

A popular alternative representation of the correlation function uses λ_k $(= 1 / \theta_k)$, and refers to it as a correlation length parameter (Santner et al., 2013). Thus, the correlation function becomes:

$$R\left(x_i, x_j\right) = \exp\left\{-\sum_{k=1}^{d} \mid x_{ik} - x_{jk} \mid^2 / \lambda_k\right\},$$

where $\lambda_k \in \left(0, \infty\right)$. Of course, this correlation length parameter has more intuitive interpretation, and λ_k close to zero indicates low spatial correlation and large λ_k implies high correlation between $y\left(x_i\right)$ and $y\left(x_j\right)$. However, as expected, this parameterization would not really ease of the optmization of likelihood with respect to λ_k.

Linkletter et al. (2006) replaced θ_k with $-4\log\left(\rho_k\right)$, i.e., the new correlation hyperparameter, $\rho_k \in \left(0, 1\right)$. This parametrization gives slightly better interpretability, as ρ_k close to 1-means smoother fit with highly correlated nearby responses, whereas ρ_k close to zero indicates spatially uncorrelated (i.e., very wiggly) surrogate fit. Unfortunately, this parametrization does not help much in the optimization of likelihood with respect to ρ_k. For the same 1-dimensional test function and data as used in Figure 2, the deviance surface with respect to ρ is equally difficult to optimize.

Recently, MacDonald et al. (2015) suggested another parametrization using β_k $(= \log_{10}\left(\theta_k\right))$. The main idea here is that the search for smooth fits correspond to negative β_k values, whereas, wigglier

Figure 3. Deviance with respect to ρ for the test function and data in Figure 1

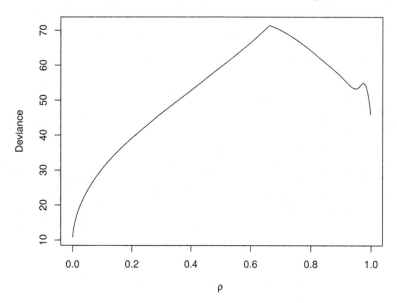

surrogates are represented by large positive β_k. Moreover, the search space is now linearized, so the optimization would be lot easier. Figure 4 presents the likelihood function with respect to β, and clearly this is a better function to minimize as compared to other parametrization presented above.

It is important to note that the practitioners have the liberty to choose an alternative correlation structure all together instead of Gaussian correlation. However, reparametrizations discussed above can also be applied to another correlation structure.

Figure 4. Deviance with respect to β for the test function and data in Figure 1

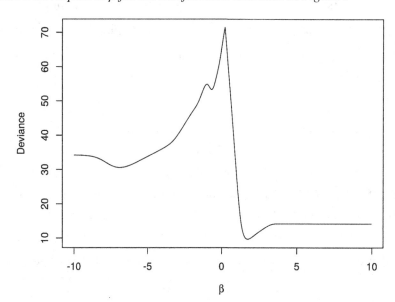

Choice of Correlation Function

Historically, Gaussian correlation function or kernel is the most popular choice for defining spatial correlation in many stochastic processes. The applications range from Geostatistics to Machine Learning and Artificial Intelligence. The commonly used related terminologies are kriging and radial basis kernel.

Recall that the Gaussian correlation is a special case of the power exponential correlation function presented in (2). For real-life applications the power parameters $p_k \in [1,2]$, which can also be estimated along with other model parameters. Assuming the other model parameters are fixed, p_k controls the smoothness (differentiability) of the predicted surrogate surface. See Figure 5 for an illustration of the GP model with different power exponential correlation for the same 1-dimensional test function as in in Figure 1.

Figure 5 shows that the predicted surrogate is spikier at the training points as p_k gets closer to 1, and much smoother as p_k is closer to 2. Theoretically, it can be shown that for $p_k \in [1,2)$ the correlation kernel is differentiable only once, whereas for $p_k = 2$, the kernel is infinitely differentiable. Thus, the Gaussian correlation may seems like the most desirable correlation kernel for GP modelling, however, as shown in Ranjan et al. (2011), the probability of a correlation matrix being ill-conditioned is substantially reduced if the power is reduced from $p_k = 2$ to even $p_k = 1.95$. Furthermore, from a practical standpoint, p_k close to 2-leads to reasonably smooth predictor (see $p_k = 1.9$ vs. $p_k = 2.0$ curves in Figure 5).

Another popular correlation kernel, originated from the kriging literature in Geostatistics, is called the Matern correlation. This correlation was originally obtained by letting the parameter in the Gaussian correlation follow Gamma distribution which yielded a positive and spherically symmetric density

Figure 5. Mean prediction as per the GP model fit with power exponential correlation with different p_k for the test function and data used in Figure 1. The solid curve represents the true underlying simulator output.

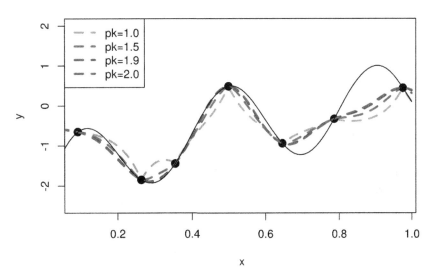

proportional to $R\left(x_i, x_j\right)$ and then finding that its Fourier transform was also a probability density (Guttorp and Gneiting, 2006). The Matern correlation kernel is given by:

$$R\left(x_i, x_j\right) = \prod_{k=1}^{d} \frac{1}{\Gamma\left(\nu\right) 2^{\nu-1}} \left(\sqrt{2\nu} \left|x_{ij} - x_{jk}\right| \theta_k\right)^{\nu} \kappa_{\nu}\left(\sqrt{2\nu} \left|x_{ij} - x_{jk}\right| \theta_k\right),$$ (9)

where κ_{ν} is modified Bessel function of order ν and $\Gamma\left(n\right)$ is Gamma function calculated at n. The sample paths are $\left\lfloor\nu\right\rfloor - 1 / 2$ times differentiable.

For large datasets in particular, Kaufman et al. (2011) used compactly supported correlation kernel to make the correlation matrices *sparse*, which leads to efficient evaluation and hence optimization of the likelihood using sparse matrix algorithms. Let $\tau = \left(\tau_1, ..., \tau_d\right)$ be the cutoff to determine the trimmed support of the design points, such that, $R_k\left(\left|x_{ik} - x_{jk}\right|; \tau_k\right) = 0$ whenever $\left|x_{ik} - x_{jk}\right| \geq \tau_k$, where $R_k\left(x_{ik}, x_{jk}\right)$ represents the correlation between x_i and x_j for the k-th coordinate. Assuming the product correlation form as earlier, let

$$R\left(x_i, x_j; \tau\right) = \prod_{k=1}^{d} R_k\left(\left|x_{ik} - x_{jk}\right|; \tau_k\right),$$

where Kaufman et al. (2011) used

$$R_k\left(h_k; \tau_k\right) = \left(1 - h_k / \tau_k\right) \cos\left(\pi h_k / \tau_k\right) + \sin\left(\pi h_k / \tau_k\right) / \pi .$$

This correlation kernel is twice differentiable and is mean square differentiable.

The range parameter, τ_k, plays an important role in this approach; very similar but greater than the role of θ in power exponential correlation. First, they control the degree of correlation in each dimension like correlation hyperparameter, θ. Second, unlike θ_k, τ_k controls the degree of sparsity in the matrix.

VARIATIONS OF GP MODELS

The GP model described thus far is the most basic version of the statistical surrogate developed by Sacks et al. (1989) for emulating the outputs of a scalar-valued deterministic computer model. Over the period of time, a host of variations and generalizations have been developed. In this section, we briefly review a few popular generalizations.

Non-Constant Mean Function

In the context of GP models with different mean functions, thus far, four different types of Kriging models have been developed: Ordinary Kriging, Simple Kriging, Universal Kriging and Blind Kriging. The GP model presented in Section 2 is referred to as the Ordinary Kriging model (i.e., the model with constant mean μ).

If we pre-specify $\mu = 0$ in the GP model of Section 2, it is referred to as the *Simple Kriging*. The closed form expressions for σ_z^2 and the mean prediction along with the uncertainty estimates are obtained by substituting $\mu = 0$ in the expressions for Ordinary Kriging:

$$E\left(y\left(x_0\right)\mid Y\right) = r\left(x_0\right)'R_n^{-1}Y, Var\left(y\left(x_0\right)\mid Y\right) = \sigma_z^2\left(1 - r\left(x_0\right)'R_n^{-1}r\left(x_0\right)\right),\,.$$

where $\hat{\sigma}_z^2 = Y'R_n^{-1}Y / n$ and the correlation hyperparameter θ (or another equivalent parameter) is estimated by maximizing the profiled likelihood.

Universal Kriging is a generalization of the Ordinary Kriging model, with the mean term μ being a linear function of the known basis, i.e., $\mu\left(x_0\right) = \sum_{j=0}^{m} f_j\left(x_0\right)\gamma_j$, where γ_0 is typically an intercept like term with $f_0\left(x_0\right) = 1$ for all x_0. The parameters and the mean prediction are obtained similarly as in the Ordinary Kriging, i.e.,

$$\hat{\gamma} = \left(F'R_n^{-1}F\right)^{-1}\left(F'R_n^{-1}Y\right), \hat{\sigma}_z^2 = \frac{\left(Y - F\gamma\right)'R_n^{-1}\left(Y - F\gamma\right)}{n},$$

and

$$E\left(y\left(x_0\right)\mid Y\right) = f\left(x_0\right)'\gamma + r\left(x_0\right)'^{R_n^{-1}}\left(Y - F\gamma\right), Var\left(y\left(x_0\right)\mid Y\right) = \sigma_z^2\left(1 - r'\left(x_0\right)R_n^{-1}r\left(x_0\right)\right).$$

Since it is impractical to assume that the basis functions in the mean term are known beforehand, Joseph et al. (2008) developed a new methodology to choose an appropriate set of basis functions from a class of feasible bases, for the problem at hand. They referred to this variation as the *Blind Kriging* model.

Noisy GP Model

As discussed earlier, realistic simulators of complex processes are sometimes non-deterministic, and hence the GP models presented thus far are not very appropriate to emulate such simulator behaviour. In the Machine Learning and Computer Experiment literature, the following version of the GP model has gained much popularity:

$$y_i = \mu + z\left(x_i\right) + \varepsilon_i, i = 1, 2, .., n,$$

where the additional error term ε_i's are iid $N\left(0, \sigma_\varepsilon^2\right)$ and independent of $\{z(x), x \in [0,1]^d\}$, the GP with mean zero, variance σ_z^2 and correlation kernel $R(\cdot, \cdot)$, as defined earlier (see Santner et al. (2003) for details). Of course, one can use different mean function instead of a constant mean μ as discussed in the previous section.

The inclusion of an additional error term does not introduce much deviation from the regular model fitting procedure, because the joint distribution of $Y = \left(y_1, y_2, \ldots, y_n\right)$, is multivariate normal with mean $\mu 1_n$ and variance-covariance matrix $\Sigma = \sigma_z^2 R_n + \sigma_\varepsilon^2 I_n$, where I_n is the $n \times n$ identity matrix. Note that rewriting $\Sigma = \sigma_z^2 \left(R_n + \delta I_n\right)$, where $\delta = \sigma_\varepsilon^2 / \sigma_z^2$ translates this model to the GP model with a nugget term as in Ranjan et al. (2011). Of course, here δ .will also have to be estimated along with other model parameters. As earlier, one must be cautious in defining the search space for δ as very small δ may lead to near-singular/ill-conditioned Σ. Moreover, there is no need to adopt t iterative regularization as the simulator is noisy and interpolation is not the objective.

Dynamic GP Model

Higdon et al. (2008) proposed an SVD-based GP model for the emulation of computer simulators with highly multivariate outputs, and recently, Zhang et al. (2018b) used it for simulators with time series responses. Consider a deterministic simulator with d dimensional input $x \in \mathbb{R}^q$, which returns a time series output $y(x) \in \mathbb{R}^L$ of length L.

Let $X = [x_1, \ldots, x_N]^T$ be the $N \times q$ input matrix and $Y = \left[y(x_1), \ldots, y(x_N)\right]$ be the $L \times N$ matrix of time series responses, then the SVD on Y gives $Y = UDV^T$, where $U = \left[u_1, \ldots, u_k\right]$ is an $L \times k$ column-orthogonal matrix of left singular vectors, with $k = min\{N, L\}$. $D = \mathrm{diag}\left(d_1, \ldots, d_k\right)$ is a $k \times k$ diagonal matrix of singular values sorted in decreasing order, and the matrix V is an $N \times k$ column-orthogonal matrix of right singular vectors. The SVD-based GP model for a deterministic simulator is given by,

$$y(x) = \sum_{i=1}^{p} c_i(x) b_i + \varepsilon, \tag{10}$$

where the orthogonal basis $b_i = d_i u_i \in \mathbb{R}^L$, for $i = 1, \ldots, p$, are the first p vectors of U scaled by the corresponding singular values. The coefficients c_i is in (10) are random functions assumed to be independent scalar response GP models, i.e., $c_i \sim GP\left(0, \sigma_i^2 R_i(\cdot, \cdot_i)\right)$ for $i = 1, \ldots, p$ (Rasmussen and Williams, 2006). The residual error ε in (10) is assumed to be independent Gaussian white noise, that is, $\varepsilon \sim \mathcal{N}\left(0, \sigma^2_L\right)$.

The built-in function called svdGP in the R package DynamicGP provides an easy implementation of this surrogate model (Zhang et al., 2018a). The arguments of svdGP can also be tuned to speed up the computation by parallelization.

Non-Stationary GP Model

Though we have not been very explicit yet, most of the discussion on GP models assumed that the underlying process / phenomena is stationary. The standard GP itself is defined to be covariance (i.e., weak) stationary. However, in reality, there are several phenomena that are non-stationary, which in a lay man terms is like a function with abrupt changes in the curvature or shape. For instance, Figure 6 shows two real-life applications. The left panel represents the output of a simplified simulator which generates the average maximum extractable power from the Minas Passage, Bay of Fundy, Nova Scotia, Canada, given that one turbine fence is already present in the Passage (Chipman et al., 2012). The right panel presents the simulated measurements of the acceleration of the head of a motorcycle rider as a function of time in the first moments after an impact (see mcycle data in the R library MASS for details). These are undoubtedly non-stationary processes, and standard GP models would not serve as adequate surrogate models (see the rightmost panel of Figure 7).

One naive way to capture the non-stationarity is to detrend the data via carefully chosen mean basis (as discussed in Section 4.1), and then use the standard GP model to emulate the residual stationary process. Over the last two decades, several innovative surrogates have also been developed to emulate the non-stationary computer model responses. For instance, Higdon et al. (1999) made some fundamental methodological contribution towards the non-stationary correlation structure, but the computer experiment literature itself was not mature enough until early - mid 2000's. Paciorek and Schervish (2004) further formalized this GP-based emulator. Gramacy (2007) combined the idea of regression trees with GP model and developed Treed GP model (TGP), which is simply fitting GP models instead of constants to the terminal nodes. Ba and Joseph (2012) suggested a sum of two GP model strategy to separately capture the local nuances and fluctuations versus the overall global trend. Chipman et al. (2012) further

Figure 6. Left panel: maximum extractable power from the Minas Passage (simplified computer model for turbine placement in the Bay of Fundy, Nova Scotia, Canada, see Chipman et al. (2012)). Right panel: acceleration of the head of a motorcycle rider as a function of time in the first moments after an impact (see mcycle in R library MASS for details).

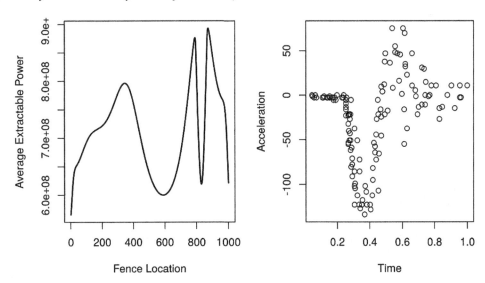

demonstrated that a Bayesian Additive Regression Tree (BART) can easily be used to emulate non-stationary computer simulator outputs and are perhaps more reliable than many other competitors for large datasets (see Figure 7 for an illustration on the motorcycle data). Recently, Volodina and Williamson (2018) used a mixture of GP based approach for this surrogate building exercise.

BIG DATA AND HIGH PERFORMANCE COMPUTING

The accelerated growth in the computing power of data processing and storage has led to a new area of science called the BIG data. Specifically, the data from computer simulators can easily get really large if the simulator is computationally fast. Over the last decade, the researchers have been investigating both aspects, the innovative methodologies for modelling and analysis, and efficient implementation techniques and algorithms for BIG data obtained from computer simulators.

Methodological Innovations

For Gaussian process models, exact calculations of R_N^{-1} requires $O\left(N^3\right)$ operations, which has to be done numerous times for likelihood optimization. Thus, efficient evaluation of the likelihood function is extremely crucial for GP modelling for a very large training dataset (of size N, say). Though there are several interesting methodological contributions, we briefly discuss a few very popular ones.

Stein et al. (2004) proposed an approach to break down the joint multivariate normal density into a product of conditional densities that significantly reduces the computational time. Furrer et al. (2006) and Kaufman et al. (2011) suggested using "tapering" in the correlation matrices via a compactly supported

Figure 7. Mean prediction for the Motor Cycle data (source: R library MASS) as per BART model (Chipman et al., 2012), TGP model (Gramacy, 2007) and standard GP model via GPfit (MacDonald et al., 2015) (in order, from left to right).

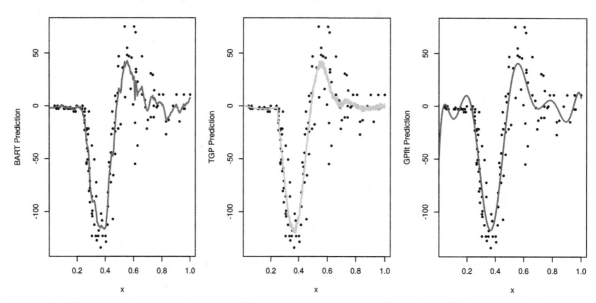

kernel (see Section 3.4), so that the sparse matrix algorithms can be better utilised for computational savings.

Another line of approach is to replace one big common GP model on a very large dataset (say N, with several local models based on small datasets of (say) size n ($\ll N$) each for approximating the predicted response at an arbitrary x_0 in the input space. Let X be the large training set of N points, and $X^{(n)}(x_0)$ or $X^{(n)}$ (in short) denote the desired subset of which defines the n point neighborhood of x_0 contained in X. We briefly discuss two methods of constructing this neighborhood set $X^{(n)}$. The first one, called as the *naive* approach, assumes the elements of the neighborhood set $X^{(n)}$ by finding n nearest neighbors of x_0 in X as per the Euclidean distance in the *k-nearest neighbor* method. The emulator obtained via fitting a GP model to this local set of points is referred to as k *nearest neighbor GP model* (in short, knnGP). Though, knnGP is computationally much cheaper than the *full GP model* (in short, fullGP) trained on N points, its prediction accuracy may not be satisfactory. Emery (2009) finds the neighborhood set $X^{(n)}(x_0)$ (for every x_0) using a greedy approach. Gramacy and Apley (2015) further improved the prediction accuracy by using a sequential greedy algorithm and an optimality criterion for finding a non-trivial local neighborhood set (see Figure 8 for an illustration). This method is also tailored for computation on modern day multi-processing, multi-threaded computers.

Figure 8. Local neighbourhood selection as per the k-nearest neighbour method (blue squares) and the greedy approach (red triangle) by Gramacy and Apley (2015) for prediction at the location marked by black plus

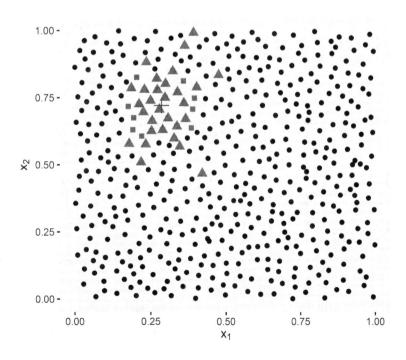

Computational Efficiency

In recent times, researchers have started focussing on the development of algorithms that are computationally efficient, can easily be parallelized, and in particular suitable for large data sets. Many of the software packages that are now being released, come with MPI, Open MP and CUDA code components, which have the option of running codes in parallel and/or use the built-in GPU components for faster processing.

Despite using sophisticated methodologies developed for handling big data, fitting GP models for big data can often be computationally expensive. Franey et al. (2012) demonstrate how Graphics Processing Units (GPU) give us more computing power than Central Processing Units (CPU) for standard GP models. For a quick reference, Table 1 presents a comparison of computation time for the standard CPU computing versus CPU+GPU implementation. Note that the results were obtained on a naive high performance computing (HPC) supported desktop (that a student could afford in 2011, the time of research), and now a much more significant improvement can be recoded on the latest HPC platform.

In summary, parallel-running GPUs when combined with CPUs are far more effective on per-dollar basis than most multi-core CPUs (alone). Gramacy et al. (2014) and Liu et al. (2018) investigated it further and developed more advanced methodologies and implementation algorithms particularly advantageous for large data sets. New R libraries like laGP (Gramacy, 2015) and DynamicGP (Zhang et al., 2018a) takes the advantage of multi-core processors and run specific tasks in parallel. One can also specify the number of threads to be assigned for a particular code in these packages.

HPC on Microsoft R has recently been gaining popularity as well. Microsoft R is an enhanced version of R which supports multithreading for calculations. The original R was designed to use single thread for computations and this modified version adds *Intel Math Kernel Library* (IMKL) which significantly

Table 1. Performance comparison of standard GP model fits. The outputs are generated via Hartman-6 function, and the inputs are random maximin Latin hypercube designs in [0,1]^6. The results are averaged over 10 simulations, except the last row of CPU implementation (denoted by *), which is based on only 1 simulation. See Franey et al. (2012) for details.

CPU Implementation					
	Time (s)				**SSPE**
64	32.32	125.94	0.1771	0.1403	77.4160
256	514.43	610.25	0.1105	0.1164	27.4311
1024	13325.86	2491.97	0.0609	0.0970	5.6504
4064	*161925.05	*8044.80	*0.0485	*0.0824	*0.5320
CPU Implementation					
	Time (s)			$\hat{\sigma}^2_z$	**SSPE**
64	9.45	103.70	0.1238	0.2989	91.7860
256	16.58	547.10	0.1397	0.1746	31.4641
1024	96.19	2665.58	0.1192	0.1390	4.3850
4064	1059.71	8698.28	0.0803	0.0700	0.5314

decreases computational expenses. Microsoft R functions exactly like R; so there is no change required in the code or library. Matrix operations in particular are immensely benefited by using multithreading approach. The benchmark reports can be accessed at https://mran.microsoft.com/documents/rro/multithread. To reproduce the results and better understanding, one can see GitHub repository: https://github.com/andrie/version.compare.

DATA ANALYSIS GOALS

There are several popular pre-specified objectives of running computer simulators and data analysis. For instance, (a) the overall understanding of the entire simulator response surface, (b) the estimation of a predetermined feature of interest, such as, the global minimum, a contour (also referred to as the inverse solution), a quantile, etc. (c) the calibration of the simulator itself, and (d) identification of important input variables.

A major portion of computer experiment literature emphasize on the "*design of computer experiments*", which refers to the technique of choosing a set of input combinations (x's) for running the computer simulator. For objective (a) listed above, several good designs have been developed. One of the most popular jargon in this section of the literature is Latin hypercube based designs with space-filling properties like maximin interpoint distance, minimum pairwise-coordinate correlation, and so on. Given that the goal is to explore the overall simulator response surface, the most common form of analysis is the "sensitivity analysis" - which sort of overlaps with objective (d).

Over the last two decades, many researchers in this area have focussed on developing innovative methods and algorithms for estimating process optimum. However, this was under the assumption that the computer simulator is computationally expensive to run, and subsequently, the training data is not large enough to be classified as BIG data. Though the size of the training data can sometimes be in thousands, the corresponding input dimension is too large (e.g., 20) to prevent thorough exploration of the input space using 1000 points. That is, the budget for the total number of simulator runs (say n) is pre-fixed and too small (with respect to the input dimension d) to use traditional optimization techniques, which led to the need for a new method for global optimization in computer experiments.

Jones et al. (1998) proposed an efficient sequential design scheme for finding the global minimum. The algorithm starts with choosing an initial design of size $n_0 (\ll n)$ and then selects the remaining $n - n_0$ follow-up points sequentially one-at-a-time by maximizing a merit-based criterion called the *expected improvement* (EI). In Jones et al. (1998), the EI criterion is simply the expectation of the improvement function,

$$I(x) = \max \left\{ f_{min}^{(k)} - y(x), 0 \right\},$$

with respect to the predictive distribution of $y(x)$ given the observed data on $n_0 + k$ points, where $f_{min}^{(k)}$ is the running estimate of the global minimum, and $y(x)$ is the unobserved response at the input x. This approach gained significant popularity because the EI criterion facilitated a tradeoff between the local exploitation and the global exploration, i.e., the algorithm made sure that the global minimum was found and did not get stuck in the local optimum. Since then a plethora of slightly different EI criteria have been proposed for the global minimum (see, for example, Schonlau et al. (1998) and Santner et al. (2003)).

Ranjan et al. (2008) extended the EI approach for estimating a pre-specified contour (also popularly referred to as the inverse solution) from an expensive to evaluate deterministic computer simulator. The notion of contour estimation was further adopted for quantile estimation and estimating the tail probability of failure (see Bingham et al. (2014) for a review). The complexity of the estimation of an inverse solution increased substantially when the computer simulator returns a time-series response instead of a scalar. Ranjan et al. (2016) tried to use a standard GP model based EI approach via scalarization technique for solving this inverse problem. Vernon et al. (2010b) proposed a history matching algorithm for this purpose, and recently, Zhang et al. (2018c) further extended the EI approach under the SVD-based GP models for dynamic simulator response.

REAL-LIFE COMPUTER MODELS

The applications of real-life computer models range over a wide spectrum of discipline, from behavioural models to the simulation of a nuclear reaction. In this section, we present brief descriptions of a few real-life simulators.

- **TDB Model:** The underlying objective is to gain a thorough understanding of the population growth of a pest called the European red mites (ERM) or Panonychus ulmi (Koch). ERM infest on apple leaves, resulting in poor yields, and hence a concern for apple farmers in the Annapolis Valley, NS, Canada. Franklin (2014) developed a mathematical-biological model based on predator-prey dynamics called the Two-Delay Blowfly (TDB) model, which consists of eleven parameters treated as the inputs to the model, and produces time-series outputs that characterize the ERM population growth. Ranjan et al. (2016) did some preliminary research on the calibration of this simulator. Recently, Zhang et al. (2018b) built a dynamic GP model for analyzing BIG data obtained from the TDB model. Zhang et al. (2018c) further extended the work to find the optimal set of inputs of the TDB model that gives a good approximation to a pre-specified target (e.g., the field data). The intent behind this inverse problem was to calibrate the TDB model to produce realistic outputs closer to the reality.

- **Tidal Power Model:** The Bay of Fundy, located between New Brunswick and Nova Scotia, Canada, is world famous for its high tides. Among others, Karsten et al. (2008) suggested harnessing this green / renewable tidal energy by installing a host of in-stream tidal turbines. However, the cost of building a turbine and installing it in the Bay of Fundy is extremely high (in millions of dollars). Thus, it is desirable to minimise the number of turbines to harness the maximum extractable total power. However, a physical experiment to find the optimal locations of these tidal turbines is infeasible due to the cost constraint. Karsten et al. (2008) developed a version of the finite volume community ocean model (Greenberg, 1979), for preliminary analysis and experimentation in the Minas Passage of the Bay of Fundy. Ranjan et al. (2011) used this computer model for finding the optimal location of one tidal turbine by maximising the power function. Chipman et al. (2012) used non-stationary surrogate model based optimization strategy for finding the optimal locations of several turbine fences for a case study by Karsten et al. (2008).

- **SWAT Model:** Soil and Water Assessment Tool (SWAT) model is an internationally recognised computer model which simulates runoff from watershed areas based on climate variables, soil types, elevation and land use data (Arnold et al, 1994). Bhattacharjee et al. (2017) used a modified history matching algorithm built upon the GP-based surrogate for calibrating this model with respect to the Middle Oconee River (Georgia, USA) data. The idea of history matching was popularised by Vernon et al. (2010, 2014) when calibrating a Galaxy formation simulator called GALFORM.

- **MRST Model:** Finding the optimal drilling locations for production and injection wells in an oil reservoir is of utmost importance (see Onwunalu and Durlofsky, 2010). Butler et al. (2014) used a Matlab Reservoir Simulator (MRST) (Lie et al., 2012) to generate the anticipated net present value (NPV) of the produced oil for a well to be drilled at a particular location. The goal here was to determine the configuration of wells that yields the best NPV.

CONCLUSION AND FUTURE DIRECTIONS

In this chapter, we have reviewed the Machine Learning and Statistics literature on design, analysis and modelling of data arising from computer simulation models. Recall that computer models are often used as cheaper alternatives for complex physical phenomena, however, simulators can also be computationally too expensive for thorough experimentation, and for which, statistical models are used to emulate the simulator output. For the last two decades, realisations of Gaussian process (GP) models are used for this emulation. Section 2 of this chapter presented a brief review of the most basic GP regression model. This non-linear semi-parametric regression model may appear to be straightforward, however, the numerical issues in fitting this model are somewhat involved. In Section 3, we have briefly reviewed the major computational concerns, i.e., the near-singularity of the correlation matrix, efficient matrix decomposition methods, choice of correlation kernels, and the reparametrization of the correlation length parameters. Section 4 summarized a variety of popular GP-based surrogates under the generalised setup such as non-stationarity, dynamic response model, and stochastic simulators. The treatment of BIG data obtained from computer models was briefly discussed in Section 5, and Section 6 reviewed a few popular analysis goals of such computer experiments. Finally, Section 7 presented a brief description of a few real-life computer models.

With respect to the future research directions, the relentless growth in the computing power demands for more advanced methodologies and efficient algorithms. Furthermore, not all methodologies developed thus far are full proof in every aspect. For instance, the nugget based approach had been developed only when the GP model was to be built for the overall good fit. If the objective is to estimate a pre-specified feature of interest like the global optimum, then the proposed lower bound of the nugget would not work, and is still an open research problem. On the other hand, the power-exponential correlation with $p_k < 2$ (say 1.95) substantially reduces the chances of near-singularity, however, does not completely resolves it. The development of new methodologies and analysis for dynamic GP models is still at the early stage, and much further work have to be done, e.g., the construction of optimal design for different analysis objectives. Under the umbrella of BIG data, most of the innovative work thus far focus on tweaking the existing methodologies, for example, via conditional likelihood or sparse computations. New innovative methodologies and algorithms (e.g., for building specific surrogate model and constructing optimal design) tailored towards BIG data are still open research problems.

ACKNOWLEDGMENT

The authors would like to thank the Editor and four anonymous referees for their thorough and helpful reviews. Ranjan's research was partially supported by the Extra Mural Research Fund (EMR/2016/003332/MS) from the Science and Engineering Research Board, Department of Science and Technology, Government of India.

REFERENCES

Arnold, J., Williams, J., Srinivasan, R., Kings, K., & Griggs, R. (1994). *SWAT: soil and water assessment tool*. Temple, TX: US Department of Agriculture, Agricultural Research Service, Grassland, Soil and Water Research Laboratory.

Ba, S., & Joseph, V. R. (2012). Composite Gaussian process models for emulating expensive functions. *The Annals of Applied Statistics*, *6*(4), 1838–1860. doi:10.1214/12-AOAS570

Bhattacharjee, N. V., Ranjan, P., Mandal, A., & Tollner, E. W. (2017). *Inverse mapping for rainfall-runoff models using history matching approach*. arXiv: 1709.02907

Bingham, D., Ranjan, P., & Welch, W. J. (2014). Sequential design of computer experiments for optimization, estimating contours, and related objectives. In *Statistics in Action: A Canadian Outlook* (pp. 109–124). Chapman & Hall/CRC. doi:10.1201/b16597-8

Booker, A. J., Dennis, J. E. Jr, Frank, P. D., Serafini, D. B., Torczon, V., & Trosset, M. W. (1999). A rigorous framework for optimization of expensive functions by surrogatess. *Structural and Multidisciplinary Optimization*, *17*(1), 1–13. doi:10.1007/BF01197708

Butler, A., Haynes, R. D., Humphries, T. D., & Ranjan, P. (2014). Efficient optimization of the likelihood function in Gaussian process modelling. *Computational Statistics & Data Analysis*, *73*, 40–52. doi:10.1016/j.csda.2013.11.017

Chipman, H., Ranjan, P., & Wang, W. (2012). Sequential design for computer experiments with a flexible bayesian additive model. *The Canadian Journal of Statistics*, *40*(4), 663–678. doi:10.1002/cjs.11156

Dancik, G. M., & Dorman, K. S. (2008). mlegp: Statistical analysis for computer models of biological systems using R. *Bioinformatics (Oxford, England)*, *24*(17), 1966–1967. doi:10.1093/bioinformatics/btn329 PMID:18635570

Emery, X. (2009). The kriging update equations and their application to the selection of neighboring data. *Computational Geosciences*, *13*(3), 269–280. doi:10.100710596-008-9116-8

Fang, K.-T., Li, R., & Sudjianto, A. (2005). *Design and modeling for computer experiments*. Chapman and Hall/CRC. doi:10.1201/9781420034899

Franey, M., Ranjan, P., & Chipman, H. (2012). *A short note on Gaussian process modeling for large datasets using graphics processing units*. arXiv:1203.1269

Franklin, J. (2014). *Modelling European red mite population using the inverse approach* (Master's thesis). Acadia University.

Furrer, R., Genton, M. G., & Nychka, D. (2006). Covariance tapering for interpolation of large spatial datasets. *Journal of Computational and Graphical Statistics*, *15*(3), 502–523. doi:10.1198/106186006X132178

Gramacy, R., Niemi, J., and Weiss, R. (2014). Massively parallel approximate Gaussian process regression. *SIAM/ASA Journal on Uncertainty Quantification*, *2*(1), 564–584.

Gramacy, R. B. (2007). tgp: An R package for Bayesian nonstationary, semiparametric nonlinear regression and design by treed Gaussian process models. *Journal of Statistical Software*, *19*(9), 1–46. doi:10.18637/jss.v019.i09 PMID:21494410

Gramacy, R. B. (2015). *laGP: Local approximate Gaussian process regression*. R package version 1.2-1.

Gramacy, R. B. (2016). lagp: Large-scale spatial modeling via local approximate gaussian processes in R. *Journal of Statistical Software*, *72*(1), 1–46. doi:10.18637/jss.v072.i01

Gramacy, R. B., & Apley, D. W. (2015). Local Gaussian process approximation for large computer experiments. *Journal of Computational and Graphical Statistics*, *24*(2), 561–578. doi:10.1080/10618600.2014.914442

Gramacy, R. B., & Lee, H. K. (2012). Cases for the nugget in modeling computer experiments. *Statistics and Computing*, *22*(3), 713–722. doi:10.100711222-010-9224-x

Greenberg, D. (1979). A numerical model investigation of tidal phenomena in the Bay of Fundy and Gulf of Maine. *Marine Geodesy*, *2*(2), 161–187. doi:10.1080/15210607909379345

Guttorp, P., & Gneiting, T. (2006). Studies in the history of probability and statistics xlix on the matrn correlation family. *Biometrika*, *93*(4), 989–995. doi:10.1093/biomet/93.4.989

Higdon, D., Gattiker, J., Williams, B., & Rightley, M. (2008). Computer model calibration using high-dimensional output. *Journal of the American Statistical Association*, *103*(482), 570–583. doi:10.1198/016214507000000888

Higdon, D., Swall, J., & J., K. (1999). Non-stationary spatial modeling. *Bayesian Statistics, 6*, 761–768.

Jones, D. R., Schonlau, M., & Welch, W. J. (1998). Efficient global optimization of expensive black-box functions. *Journal of Global Optimization*, *13*(4), 455–492. doi:10.1023/A:1008306431147

Joseph, V., Hung, Y., & Sudjianto, A. (2008). Blind kriging: A new method for developing metamodels. *ASME. Journal of Mechanical Design*, *130*(3), 031102, 031102–031108. doi:10.1115/1.2829873

Karsten, R., McMillan, J., Lickley, M., & Haynes, R. (2008). Assessment of tidal current energy for the Minas Passage, Bay of Fundy. *Proceedings of the Institution of Mechanical Engineers. Part A, Journal of Power and Energy, 222*(5), 493–507. doi:10.1243/09576509JPE555

Kaufman, C. G., Bingham, D., Habib, S., Heitmann, K., & Frieman, J. A. (2011). Efficient emulators of computer experiments using compactly supported correlation functions, with an application to cosmology. *The Annals of Applied Statistics, 5*(4), 2470–2492. doi:10.1214/11-AOAS489

Lie, K.-A., Krogstad, S., Ligaarden, I., Natvig, J., Nilsen, H., & Skaflestad, B. (2012). Open-source MATLAB implementation of consistent discretizations on complex grids. *Computational Geosciences, 16*(2), 297–322. doi:10.100710596-011-9244-4

Linkletter, C., Bingham, D., Hengartner, N., Higdon, D., & Ye, K. Q. (2006). Variable selection for gaussian process models in computer experiments. *Technometrics, 48*(4), 478–490. doi:10.1198/004017006000000228

Liu, H., Ong, Y.-S., Shen, X., & Cai, J. (2018). *When Gaussian process meets big data: A review of scalable GPs.* arXiv:1807.01065

MacDonald, B., Ranjan, P., & Chipman, H. (2015). GPfit: An R package for fitting a Gaussian process model to deterministic simulator outputs. *Journal of Statistical Software, 64*(12), 1–23. doi:10.18637/jss.v064.i12

Neal, R. (1997). *Monte Carlo implementation of Gaussian process models for Bayesian regression and classification. Technical Report, Deptartment of Statistics*, University of Toronto.

Onwunalu, J., & Durlofsky, L. (2010). Application of a particle swarm optimization algorithm for determining optimum well location and type. *Computational Geosciences, 14*(1), 183–198. doi:10.100710596-009-9142-1

Paciorek, C., & Schervish, M. J. (2004). Nonstationary covariance functions for Gaussian process regression. In *Advances in Neural Information Processing Systems 16* (pp. 273–280). Cambridge, MA: MIT Press.

Pratola, M. T., Sain, S. R., Bingham, D., Wiltberger, M., & Rigler, E. J. (2013). Fast sequential computer model calibration of large nonstationary spatial-temporal processes. *Technometrics, 55*(2), 232–242. doi:10.1080/00401706.2013.775897

Ranjan, P., Bingham, D., & Michailidis, G. (2008). Sequential experiment design for contour estimation from complex computer codes. *Technometrics, 50*(4), 527–541. doi:10.1198/004017008000000541

Ranjan, P., Haynes, R., & Karsten, R. (2011). A computationally stable approach to Gaussian process interpolation of deterministic computer simulation data. *Technometrics, 53*(4), 366–378. doi:10.1198/TECH.2011.09141

Ranjan, P., Thomas, M., Teismann, H., & Mukhoti, S. (2016). Inverse problem for a timeseries valued computer simulator via scalarization. *Open Journal of Statistics, 6*(3), 528–544. doi:10.4236/ojs.2016.63045

Rasmussen, C. E., & Williams, C. K. (2006). Gaussian processes for machine learning. 2006. The MIT Press.

Roustant, O., Ginsbourger, D., & Deville, Y. (2012). DiceKriging, DiceOptim: Two R packages for the analysis of computer experiments by kriging-based metamodeling and optimization. *Journal of Statistical Software*, *51*(1), 1–55. doi:10.18637/jss.v051.i01 PMID:23504300

Sacks, J., Welch, W. J., Mitchell, T. J., & Wynn, H. P. (1989). Design and analysis of computer experiments. *Statistical Science*, *4*(4), 409–423. doi:10.1214s/1177012413

Santner, T. J., Williams, B. J., & Notz, W. I. (2003). *The Design and Analysis of Computer Experiments*. New York: Springer-Verlag. doi:10.1007/978-1-4757-3799-8

Schonlau, M., Welch, W. J., & Jones, D. R. (1998). Global versus local search in constrained optimization of computer models. Institute of Mathematical Statistics, Hayward, CA, Lecture Notes-Monograph Series, 34, 11–25.

Stein, M. L., Chi, Z., & Welty, L. J. (2004). Approximating likelihoods for large spatial data sets. *Journal of the Royal Statistical Society. Series B, Statistical Methodology*, *66*(2), 275–296. doi:10.1046/j.1369-7412.2003.05512.x

Vernon, I., Goldstein, M., & Bower, R. G. (2010). Galaxy formation: A bayesian uncertainty analysis. *Bayesian Analysis*, *5*(4), 619–669. doi:10.1214/10-BA524

Vernon, I., Goldstein, M., & Bower, R. G. (2014). Bayesian history matching for the observable universe. *Statistical Science*, *29*(1), 81–90. doi:10.1214/12-STS412

Volodina, V., & Williamson, D. (2018). *Nonstationary Gaussian process emulators with kernel mixtures*. arXiv preprint 1803.04906

Zhang, R., Lin, C. D., & Ranjan, P. (2018a). *DynamicGP: Local Gaussian Process Model for Large-Scale Dynamic Computer Experiments*. R package.

Zhang, R., Lin, C. D., & Ranjan, P. (2018b). Local Gaussian process model for largescale dynamic computer experiments. *Journal of Computational and Graphical Statistics*, *27*(4), 798–807. doi:10.10 80/10618600.2018.1473778

Zhang, R., Lin, C. D., & Ranjan, P. (2018c). *A sequential design approach for calibrating a dynamic population growth model*. arXiv:1811.00153

ADDITIONAL READING

Chipman, H., Ranjan, P., & Wang, W. (2012). Sequential design for computer experiments with a flexible Bayesian additive model. *The Canadian Journal of Statistics*, *40*(4), 663–678. doi:10.1002/cjs.11156

Ranjan, P., Bingham, D., & Michailidis, G. (2008). Sequential experiment design for contour estimation from complex computer codes. *Technometrics*, *50*(4), 527–541. doi:10.1198/004017008000000541

Zhang, R., Lin, C. D., & Ranjan, P. (2018). Local Gaussian process model for large-scale dynamic computer experiments. *Journal of Computational and Graphical Statistics*, *27*(4), 798–807. doi:10.10 80/10618600.2018.1473778

KEY TERMS AND DEFINITIONS

Best Linear Unbiased Predictor (BLUP): An unbiased linear predictor with minimum variance among the class of all linear unbiased predictors is called the best linear unbiased predictor. In some sense it is the best linear unbiased estimator (BLUE) of the unobserved $y(x)$.

Condition Number: In most simple terms, the condition number of a matrix A gives the upper bound on the inaccuracy of solution x for the linear equation $Ax = b$ after approximation. More precisely, it's the maximum ratio of relative error in x to relative error in b, and the ratio of largest and the smallest singular value.

Correlation Length Parameter: It is the inverse of the correlation hyper-parameter, $1/\theta_k$, in the power-exponential correlation function, and used to quantify smoothness of the fitted surrogate.

Gaussian Process: A stochastic process $\left\{ z(x), x \in \chi \right\}$ is said to follow Gaussian Process (GP) if every finite subset of the random variables $\left\{ z(x_1), z(x_2) \ldots, z(x_n) \right\}$, for arbitrary $n \geq 2$, and $x_1, \ldots, x_n \in \chi$, follow multivariate normal distribution.

Near-Singular Matrix: A matrix which has its determinant *close* to zero, and whose inverse is unreliable, is called near-singular matrix or ill-conditioned matrix. The extent of ill-conditioning is defined by its condition number.

Nugget: (denoted by δ) It is a small positive constant added to the diagonal of the correlation matrix to evade ill-conditioning in the near-singular matrices.

Stationarity: (referred to weak-stationarity) In the context of response surfaces, a process is said to be non-stationary if the surface exhibit abrupt changes in the curvature and shape.

Chapter 12
Evaluation of Reliable Data Storage in Cloud Using an Efficient Encryption Technique

Saswati Sarkar
Computer Innovative Research Society, India

Anirban Kundu
Netaji Subhash Engineering College, India

Ayan Banerjee
Computer Innovative Research Society, India

ABSTRACT

Cloud-based reliable and protected data storage technique is proposed in this chapter. The proposed technique encrypts and protects data with less time consumption. Power consumption of storage is dependent upon capacity of storage and physical size of storage. Time analysis is presented graphically in this chapter. Reliable data storage is represented in cloud based proposed approach. Data is encrypted with minimum time complexity due to usage of proposed cloud-based reliable data storage. The competent ratio of time complexity is graphically observed in proposed data storage technique. Power consumption of storage has been typically dependent on the basis of capacity of storage and amount of storage. A ratio of power consumption and capacity of storage is presented in cloud-based approach. An efficient usage of energy is shown depending on current consumption and voltage in proposed reliable approach.

INTRODUCTION

Overview

Storage devices (as found in "http://smallbusiness.chron.com/difference-between-25-35-hard-drives-67453.html") consist of computer hardware that is used for storing data which can hold and store information temporarily and permanently. Computer data storage is known as storage or memory (as

DOI: 10.4018/978-1-5225-8407-0.ch012

found in "https://www.quora.com/How-do-hard-drives-of-the-same-physical-size-vary-in-capacity-of-storage"). Storage device is consisting of computer components used to retain digital data.

Storage devices are typcally utilized in internet based hardware and software reources, information technology paradigm shift, and cloud computing (Daniel J. A., 2009). There are different types of cloud computing services are available today such as Amazon EC2, Google Apps, Apple iCloud etc.. There are two factors such as advanced software applications and high-end networks of server-side computer systems are required for maintaining the reliability of services(Aboroujilah A., Amusa A.S.,2017). There are several components such as development of grid computing, parallel computing, distributed computing, big data analysis (Alsghaier H., Akour M., Shehabat I., Aldiabat S.,2017), and utility computing have been ncorporated in cloud computing(Agarwal H., Sharma A.2016). Cloud based services have been extended in distinct fields such as virtual IT, software and network storage (Kandukuri B. R., Paturi R. V., Rakshit A., 2009).

Reliability is a attribute, which has been measured depending on consistent performance of different computer related component such as network, software, hardware (Subashini S., Kavitha V., 2011) (Zhang X., Wuwong N., Li H., and Zhang X. J., 2010). Mean Time to Data Loss (MTTDL) matrix is required to calculate reliability. The amount of expected elapse time has been described by this matrix untill first data loss. There are two purposes such as encryption (IGI global,2017) of backed-up data, and decryption of backed-up data have been resolved by using two-way function called encryption. Encryption(IGI Global, 2016) has been incorporated as a characterstics of storage security (Das D., Misra R., 2011). There are two dfferent message formats such as plaintext and ciphertext have been required to perform encryption algorithm and decryption algorithm (Parsi K., Sudha S., 2012).

Power (as found in "http://www.tomshardware.com/reviews/geforce-radeon-power, 2122-7.html") is energy over time. The unit of power is watt. Power (Watts) is Joules per second.

Power (Watts) = E/T = Energy (Joules) / Time (Seconds).

Energy, E = P*T, where P = Power, and T = Time.

A watt hour is a unit of Energy, an alternative to Joules (Pinheiro E., Bianchini R., Dubnicki C., 2006). Voltage is known as electromotive force which is a quantitative expression of the potential difference in charge between two points in an electrical field.

P = IV (Power = Current * Voltage)

(http://www.tomshardware.com/reviews/desktop-hdd.15-st4000dm000-4tb,3494-6.html).

Related Works

Encryption (Kakkar A., Singh M. L., Bansal P. K., 2010) is a technique, which provides unreadable situation of scrambled data to unintended parties (Moghaddam F. F., Alrashdan M. T., and Karimi O, 2013). Triple data encryption algorithm (Triple DES (3 DES)), recognised as a symmetric algorithm in industry has used symmetric key block cipher and applied the DES cipher algorithm three times to each data block designed to replace the original Data Encryption Standard (DES) algorithm (Grabbe J., 2003) (Davis R., 2003). Triple DES uses three individual keys with 56 bits each. The total key length adds up to 168 bits. Triple DES manages to make a dependable hardware encryption solution for financial services and other industries.RSA is a public-key encryption (Kakkar A., Singh M. L., Bansal P. K., 2012) algorithm and the standard for encrypting data sent over the Internet. RSA (Diffiee W., Hellman M., 1976) is considered an asymmetric algorithm due to its use of a pair of keys. There are two types of keys are used in this algorithm, public key and private Key. Public key is used to encrypt the message, and a private key to decrypt data.Blowfish is an flexible encryption algorithm which has been utilied to split messages into blocks of 64 bits and encrypts them individually (Karthigai P.K., Baskaran K., 2010) (Gupta V., Singh G., Gupta R., 2012). In twofish algorithm, encryption keys have been recommended up to 256 bits in length and it follows a symmetric approach (Verma S., Choubey R., Soni R., 2012). Twofish is regarded as one of the fastest of its kind, and ideal for use in both hardware and software environments. Twofish is also freely available to anyone who wants to use it.

AES (Advanced Encryption Standard) is the algorithm (as found in https://sites.math.washington. edu/~morrow/336_09/papers/Yevgeny.pdf) in 128-bit form. AES also uses keys of 192 and 256 bits for heavy duty encryption purposes.AES is largely considered impervious to all attacks, with the exception of brute force, which attempts to decipher messages using all possible combinations in the 128, 192. The algorithm described by AES is a symmetric-key algorithm, meaning the same key is used for both encrypting and decrypting the data (Ahmadi M., Vali1 M., Moghaddam F.,Hakemi A., Madadipouya K, 2015).

Aim

Our aim is to achieve reliable storage by protecting data using encryption.The necessary focus of proposed approach is to perform data encryption for utilizing reliable storage with a proper KDD.The novelties of this chapter are as follows:

1.   Reliable and protected data storage is produced.
2.   New encryption technique is introduces to represend secured data storage.

Scope and Limitation

The scope of this paper is knowledge discovery in database (KDD) which consists of data encryption.

Motivation

The motivation of this research work is to evolve a reliable and protected storage using encryption.

Organization

Rest of the paper has been categorized as follows: In proposed work section, proposed architecture has been discussed along with proposed algorithm in the next section. Results of required experiments have been represented in the experimental discussions section. Finally, the conclusion section has been used to conclude our proposal.

PROPOSED WORK

Overview

Data has been encrypted and protected using efficient encryption algorithms (Verma S., Choubey R., Soni R., 2012) and is stored into a particular memory location of proposed cloud based system (Zhou T., Fang Y., Zhang Y., 2008). Proposed encryption technique is applied on the data storage to introduce reliability.

This technique is needed to make secured and protected data to achive reliable data storage(Xiao L.,Wei W., Yang W.,Shen Y., Wu X., 2017). New encryption algorithm is introduced in proposed work to protect data.

Proposed Framework

Consider an input matrix divided into two partitions. Each partition contains encrypted data for protection purpose using proposed encryption algorithm.

A matrix (M*N) of size (4*8) is shown in Table 1. Matrix of Table 1 is partitioned into two matrices, which are Partition 1 (P1) and Partition 2 (P2). Partition 1 (P1) is presented in Table 2. Partition 2 (P2) is presented in Table 3.

Parallel encryption is applied for Partition P1.

First, calculate number of rows=4

Rows are shifted depending upon the number of rows in input matrix.

Calculate number of column=4

Table 1. Input matrix

Matrix (M*N) where M = Number of Rows (4) and N = Number of Columns (8)		Number of Columns							
		0	1	2	3	4	5	6	7
Number of Rows	Row 0	1	5	9	13	1	2	3	4
	Row 1	2	6	10	14	5	6	7	8
	Row 2	3	7	11	15	9	10	11	12
	Row 3	4	8	12	16	13	14	15	16

Table 2. Partition 1 matrix

Matrix (P*Q) where P = Number of Rows (4) and Q = Number of Columns (4)		Number of Columns			
		0	1	2	3
Number of Rows	Row 0	1	5	9	13
	Row 1	2	6	10	14
	Row 2	3	7	11	15
	Row 3	4	8	12	16

Table 3. Partition 2 matrix

Matrix (R*S) where R = Number of Rows (4) and S = Number of Columns (4)		Number of Columns			
		4	5	6	7
Number of Rows	Row 0	1	2	3	4
	Row 1	5	6	7	8
	Row 2	9	10	11	12
	Row 3	13	14	15	16

Shift row0=1 position left shift

Shift row1=2 position left shift

Shift row2=3 position left shift

Shift row3 (last row) =no shift

After encryption, the Partition (P1) is as shown in Table 4.

Parallel encryption is applied for Partition P2.

First, calculate number of row=4

Then, calculate number of column=4

Rows are shifted depending upon the number of rows in input matrix.

Shift row0=1 position left shift

Shift row1=2 position left shift

Shift row2=3 position left shifts

Shift row3 (last row) =no shift

After encryption, the Partition (P2) is as shown in Table 5.

Then, Partition 1 (P1) and Partition 2 (P2) are merged.

Encrypted matrix is produced as shown in Table 6.

The matrix (refer Table 6) is reliable as data within matrix is protected using encryption technique.

Procedures

Algorithm 1 is used to partition particular location of memory space in cloud, and subsequently encrypt data of each memory partitions.Merge each encrypted partitions and get reliable encrypted matrix.

Algorithm 2 is used to encrypt data of each partition using proposed encryption algorithm in cloud.

Table 4. Encrypted matrix of Partition 1

Matrix (P*Q) where P = Number of Rows (4) and Q = Number of Columns (4)		Number of Columns			
		0	1	2	3
Number of Rows	Row 0	13	1	5	9
	Row 1	10	14	2	6
	Row 2	7	11	5	3
	Row 3	4	8	12	16

Table 5. Encrypted matrix of Partition 2

Matrix (R*S) where R = Number of Rows (4) and S = Number of Columns (4)		Number of Columns			
		4	5	6	7
Number of Rows	Row 0	4	1	2	3
	Row 1	7	8	5	6
	Row 2	10	11	12	9
	Row 3	13	14	15	16

Table 6. Proposed reliable encrypted matrix

Proposed reliable encrypted matrix (A*B) where A = Number of Rows (4) and B = Number of Columns (8)		Number of Columns							
		0	1	2	3	4	5	6	7
Number of Rows	Row 0	13	1	5	9	4	1	2	3
	Row 1	10	14	2	6	7	8	5	6
	Row 2	7	11	5	3	10	11	12	9
	Row 3	4	8	12	16	13	14	15	16

Algorithm 1. Partition_of_Memory_Location

```
Input: An input matrix
Output: Reliable encrypted matrix (To protect data using encryption algorithm,
reliable matrix is acheived)
Step 1: Partition(Total_Memory_Location) =Partition 1, Partition 2, …………, Par-
tition N
Step 2: Parallel_Encrypt(Partition 1, Partition 2, …………, Partition N)
Step 3: Merge(Partition 1, Partition 2, …………, Partition N)
Step 4: Encrypt(Total_Memory_Location)
Step 5: Stop
```

Explanation of Algorithm 1

In Algorithm 1, matrix based values are considered as inputs. In first step, total matrix is partitioned into N partitions. Then every partition is encrypted in parallel manner by applying proposed encryption algorithm. After parallel encryption merge partitions and get reliable encrypted matrix.

Explanation of Algorithm 2

In Algorithm 2, data of each partition of matrix (refer Figure 4 & Figure 5) have been encrypted in parallel manner to get abstract data in each particular memory location.

Algorithm 2. Encrypt(Total_Memory_Location)

```
Input: Partition 1, Partition 2, ............, Partition N (Each partition is consid-
ered as 4*4 matrix)
Output: Encrypt (Partition 1, Partition 2, ............, Partition N)
Step 1: Number of row =4      //Rows is shifted depending upon the number of
rows in input matrix.
Step 2: Number of column=4
Step 3: Shift row₀=1 position left shift
Step 4: Shift row₁=2 position left shift
Step 5: Shift row₂=3 position left shift
Step 6: Shift row₃ (last row) =no shift
Step 7: Stop
```

In this algorithm, first calculate number of rows and columns. Then data are shifted row-wise according to the proposed algorithm. First row is re-arrested as row_0, second row is represented as row_1, third row is represented as row_2, and last row is presented as row_3. In the next step, row_0 is shifted one position left, row_1 is shifted 2 position left, row_2 is shifted 3 position left, row_3 (last row) is not shifted. In this way, proposed algorithm is applied to encrypt each partition of reliable storage. To apply this algorithm the original data is to be protected. So that, the secured and reliable storage is introduced by applying this encryption algorithm.

Theoretical Development

Time complexities of existing approach and proposed approach are compared (refer Table 7) and have further proved that proposed approach presents better results than existing approach. In proposed approach, parallel concept is applied to encrypt data. When messge is divided into partitions, encryption is applied in parallel manner to achieve secured and protected data. Therefore, resultant time consumption is reduced, exhibiting better time complexity.

Motivation of Theorem 1

Time complexity is depending upon the message size containing data elements. If message size is divided into two partititons, and encryption algorithm is applied in a parallel manner in each partitions, then overall time complexity is reduced.

Theorem 1: Time complexity of proposed approach is better than existing approach.

Proof

Encryption and decryption are modular exponentiation of plain text or cipher text modulo 'n', with the respective exponents.

There are two cases in which Case 1 calculates the complexity of existing approach, and Case 2 calculates the complexity of proposed approach. We are going to proof that the complexity of proposed approach is less than the complexity of existing approach.

Case 1: Existing Approach

In square-and-multiply algorithm, encryption needs $O(1)$, decryption $O(n)$ multiplications and a similar number of modular reductions, each of n-bit which means about $O(n^2)$ elementary operations.

Therefore, time complexity of existing approach is $O(n^2)$.

Case 2: Proposed Approach

To establish reliable storage system, a new encrypted algorithm is presented in this paper.

Let, Message size = n

Put the message size into a mode of operation to encrypt longer messages. Then, the complexity would be $O(n)$; where n is the message size.

Divide message in two partitions, such as partition 1 and partition 2.

Parallel Encryption is applied for each partition.

Complexity encryption of partition $1 = O(n/2) \approx o(n)$

Complexity of encryption partition $2 = O(n/2) \approx o(n)$

Complexity after merging of partition 1 and partition $2 = O(nlogn)$

Total complexity of proposed approach $= O(n) + O(n) + O(nlogn) \approx O(nlogn)$

Therefore, $O(nlogn) < O(n^2)$ (Complexity of existing approach)

Hence, this is proved that time complexity of our proposed approach is better than existing approach. (End of Proof)

ANALYTICAL DISCUSSIONS

Time Analysis

In Figure 1, X axis is denoted by Primary axis (LHS Axis) and Y axis is denoted by secondary axis (RHS Axis). Primary axis is denoted by number of elements and Secondary axis is denoted by execution time. Figure 1 shows the pattern of inclination when execution time of existing approach is compared to the number of elements.

In Figure 2, X axis is denoted by Primary axis (LHS Axis) and Y axis is denoted by secondary axis (RHS Axis). Primary axis is denoted by number of elements and secondary axis is denoted by execution time. Above figure represents the execution time with respect to the number of elements of the proposed approach.

Benefits

Benefits of proposed approach are as follows:

Figure 1. Time analysis graph for existing approach

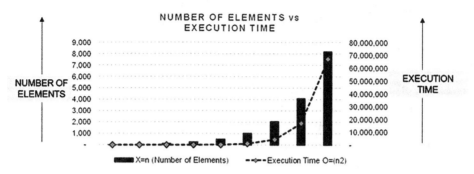

Figure 2. Time analysis graph for proposed approach

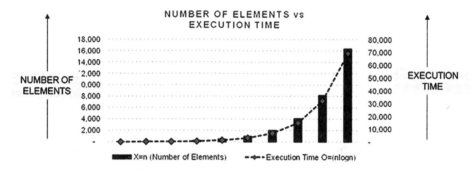

- Overall power consumption of proposed system framework is decreased due to applied encryption technique in each partitions. Power consumption is directly proportional to the capacity of storage.
- Power consumption also depends on physical size of storage. In this work, the encryption technique is applied in each partitions to achieve reliable storage. Therefore, physical size of storage is decreased.
- Time complexity is reduced in proposed approach.
- Reliable data storage is achieved to protect data using proposed encryption technique.

EXPERIMENTAL DISCUSSIONS

System Specifications

System specifications are as follows:

- Number of Servers: 50;
- Processor of each server: 2.70 GHz;
- RAM of each server: 2.00 GB;
- Drive Type: Hard Disk Drive
- Capacity: 750 GB

- System Type: 32 bit Operating System;
- Software used: VC++ Compiler

Relations between Encryption, Protection, and Reliability

Consider, protection of storage is presented by 'P';
Reliability of storage is presented by 'R';
Encryption of data within a particular storage is presented by E;
Then, P ∞ R; if and only if data is encrypted(E) properly.

Data encryption makes a storage secured and protected resulting in a reliable storage typically measured by decryption time. If time taken for decryption of existing data in storage is higher, then it is considered as more reliable system. Therefore, data is secured and protected resulting in a reliable storage.

Real Time Observations

In Figure 3, X axis is denoted by Primary axis (LHS Axis) and Y axis is denoted by secondary axis (RHS Axis). Primary axis is denoted by capacity of HDD in GB and Secondary axis is denoted by power consumption of HDD in Watt. Figure 3 represents the real time observations of power consumption of HDD with respect to the capacity of HDD. Figure 3 presents that capacity is directly proportional to power consumption.

In Figure 4, X axis is denoted by Primary axis (LHS Axis) and Y axis is denoted by secondary axis (RHS Axis). Primary axis is denoted by physical size of storage in inch and Secondary axis is denoted by power consumption of HDD in Watt. Figure 4 is the real-time observations of power consumption of HDD with respect to the physical size of HDD. Figure 4 depicts that power consumption is directly proportional to physical size of storage.

In Figure 5, X axis is denoted as primary axis (LHS axis) and Y axis is denoted as secondary axis (RHS axis). Primary axis is considered as number of elements and secondary axis is considered as decryption time.

Decryption time increases means storage elements are secured and protected. Hence, storage reliability is increased. In Table 6, protected data is generated after encryption. So, it takes more time when the elements of Table 6 are decrypted depending upon number of elements. Number of elements is increased along with the increased capacity of storage. Therefore, decryption time is also increased.

Figure 3. Real-time observation of power consumption with respect to capacity of HDD

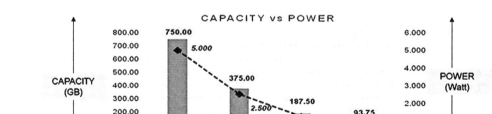

Figure 4. Real-time observation of power consumption with respect to physical size of storage

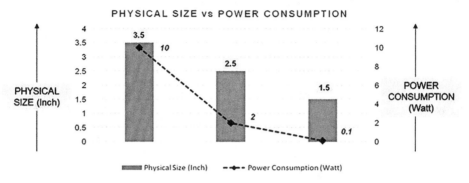

Figure 5. Real-time observation of decryption time

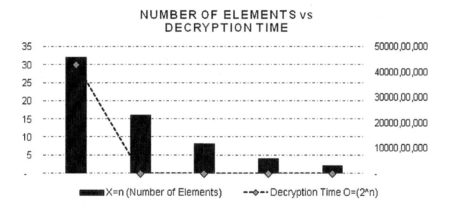

SYSTEM COMPARISONS

System Comparison Graph

In existing approach, total memory location is considered to calculate the power consumption with respect to capacity.

In proposed approach, total memory location is partitioned into two parts to calculate power consumption in each partition. We have observed that power consumption is decreased when capacity of memory decreases.

In Figure 6, X axis is denoted by Primary axis (LHS Axis) and Y axis is denoted by secondary axis (RHS Axis). Primary axis is denoted by power consumption in watt and Secondary axis is denoted by capacity of secondary memory in GB. Figure 6 shows the power consumption is directly proportional to the capacity of secondary memory. Proposed approach is better than existing approach that is shown in Figure 6.

Figure 6. System comparison graph

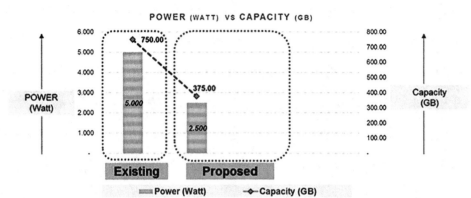

System Comparison Chart

In Table 7, time complexity and execution time of proposed approach show better results compared to existing approach. In proposed approach, power consumption with respect to capacity of storage and physical size of storage is less.

CONCLUSION

An encryption algorithm plays very important role in communication security and to achieve reliable data storage. Our research work surveyed about different existing encryption techniques like RSA, AES, TRIPLE DES, TWOFISH, and BLOWFISH. Proposed cloud based storage technique exhibits encryption and protection of data having less time consumption and less power consumption based on experimental results.

Table 7. Comparison values between existing approach and proposed approach

	Time Complexity	Physial Size (HDD)	Power Consumption (Watt)	Capacity (GB)	Power (Watt)	Number of Elements						
							32	64	128	256	512	1024
Existing Approach	$O(n^2)$ N=Number of elements	3.50	10.00	750	5.000	Execution Time	1,024	4,096	16,384	65,536	262,144	4,194,304
Proposed Approach	$O(n \log n)$ N=Number of elements	2.50	2.00	375	2.500	Execution Time	48	116	270	617	1387	3083
		1.50	0.10									

REFERENCES

Aboroujilah, A., & Amusa, A. S. (2017). *Cloud-Based DDoS HTTP Attack Detection Using Covariance Matrix Approach*. Journal Comp. Netw. and Communic. doi:10.1155/2017/7674594

Agarwal, H., & Sharma, A. (2016). A Comprehensive Survey of Fault Tolerance Techniques in Cloud Computing. In *International Conference on Computing and Network Communications (CoCoNet)*. IEEE.

Ahmadi, M., Vali, M., Moghaddam, F., Hakemi, A., & Madadipouya, K. (2015). A Reliable User Authentication and Data Protection Model in Cloud Computing Environments. *International Conference on Information, System and Convergence Applications*.

Alsghaier, H., Akour, M., Shehabat, I., & Aldiabat, S. (2017). The impact of big data analytics on business competitiveness. *Proceedings of the New Trends in Information Technology*.

Anderson, R., & Biham, E. (1996). Two Practical and Provably Secured Block Ciphers: BEAR and LION. In *Fast Software Encryption, Third International Workshop Proceedings*. Springer-Verlag.

Daniel, J. A. (2009). Data Management in the Cloud: Limitations and Opportunities. *A Quarterly Bulletin of the Computer Society of the IEEE Technical Committee on Data Engineering, 32*, 3–12.

Das, D., & Misra, R. (2011). Programmable Cellular Automata Based Efficient Parallel AES Encryption Algorithm. *International Journal of Network Security & Its Applications, 3*(6), 204. doi:10.5121/ijnsa.2011.3615

Davis, R. (2003). The data encryption standard in perspective. In *Communications Society Magazine* (pp. 5–9). IEEE.

Diffiee, W., & Hellman, M. (1976). New Directions in Cryptography. *IEEE Transactions on Information Theory, IT-22*(6), 644–654. doi:10.1109/TIT.1976.1055638

Grabbe, J. (2003). Data Encryption Standard: The Triple DES algorithm illustrated Laissez Faire city time. Academic Press.

Gupta, V., Singh, G., & Gupta, R. (2012). Advance cryptography algorithm for improving data security. *International Journal of Advanced Research in Computer Science and Software Engineering, 2*(1).

Kakkar A., Singh M. L., & Bansal P. K. (2010). Efficient Key Mechanisms in Multinode Network for Secured Data Transmission. *International Journal of Engineering Science and Technology, 2*(5), 787-795.

Kakkar, A., Singh, M. L., & Bansal, P. K. (2012). Comparison of Various Encryption Algorithms and Techniques for Secured Data Communication in Multi-node Network. *IACSIT International Journal of Engineering and Technology, 2*(1).

Kandukuri, B. R., Paturi, R. V., & Rakshit, A. (2009). Cloud Security Issues. *Proceedings of IEEE International Conference on Services Computing*, 517-520.

Karthigai, P.K., & Baskaran, K. (2010). An ASIC implementation of low power and high throughput blowfish crypto algo-rithm. *Microelectron. J., 41*(6), 347-355.

Moghaddam, F. F., Alrashdan, M. T., & Karimi, O. (2013). A Comparative Study of Applying Real-Time Encryption in Cloud Computing Environments. *Proc. of IEEE 2nd International Conference on Cloud Networking (CloudNet)*. 10.1109/CloudNet.2013.6710575

Parsi, K., & Sudha, S. (2012). Data Security in Cloud Computing using RSA Algorithm. *International Journal of Research in Computer and Communication Technology, 1*(4), 145.

Pinheiro, E., Bianchini, R., & Dubnicki, C. (2006). Exploiting redundancy to conserve energy in storage systems. *Performance Evaluation Review, 31*(1), 15–26. doi:10.1145/1140103.1140281

Subashini, S., & Kavitha, V. (2011). A survey on security issues in service delivery models of cloud computing. *Journal of Network and Computer Applications, 34*(1), 1–11.

Verma, S., Choubey, R., & Soni, R. (2012). An Efficient Developed New Symmetric Key Cryptography Algorithm for Information Security. *International Journal of Emerging Technology and Advanced Engineering*. Retrieved from www.ijetae.com

Xiao, L., Wei, W., Yang, W., Shen, Y., & Wu, X. (2017). A protocol-free detection against cloud oriented reflection DoS attacks. *Soft Computing, 21*(13), 3713–3721. doi:10.100700500-015-2025-6

Zhang, X., Wuwong, N., Li, H., & Zhang, X. J. (2010). Information Security Risk Management Framework for the Cloud Computing Environments. *Proceedings of 10th IEEE International Conference on Computer and Information Technology*, 1328-1334. 10.1109/CIT.2010.501

Zhou, T., Fang, Y., & Zhang, Y. (2008). Securing wireless sensor networks: A survey. *IEEE Communications Surveys and Tutorials, 10*(3), 6–28. doi:10.1109/COMST.2008.4625802

Chapter 13
Enabling Technologies for IoT:
Issues, Challenges, and Opportunities

Rajalakshmi Krishnamurthi
Jaypee Institute of Information Technology, India

Mukta Goyal
Jaypee Institute of Information Technology, India

ABSTRACT

The internet of things (IoT) is a fast-growing paradigm gaining position in the modern scenario of communication. It targets to provide interconnection among different objects at any time, and anywhere on the earth, under the leverage of internet. IoT has exhibited the promising enhancement in almost all dimensions of the everyday human life scenarios. The IoT applications are smart energy systems, manufacturing services, industrial automation, healthcare, education, smart city, transportation, and security and surveillance. However, there are several issues associated with IoT objectives such as data traffic, security and privacy, data analytics, device localization, and scalability. In addition to this, the IoT objects are resource constrained in terms of memory, computing power, energy, storage, and networking capability. Hence, IoT systems need enabling technologies to overcome these challenges by means of cloud computing, big data, cyber physical systems, and block chain. This chapter discusses how these enabling technologies can be integrated with IoT and its challenges.

INTRODUCTION

According to Gartner report, envisage that more than 26 billion of individual things will be connected by 2020 through Internet. It is prominent that by the concept of "Internet of Things", huge amount of data is generating from these things. In 2017, Capgemini Asia pacific Wealth Report predicts that particularly Asia pacific countries will contribute more towards the IoT growth. Compound Annual Growth Rate (CAGR) of around 33.3% is expected by 2020. IoT technology provides conglomeration of generic ICT technology with several other enabling technologies like cloud computing, big data, cyber-physical system, and block chain (Perera, et al. 2014). In addition, the IoT technology provides foundation for Leadership in Enabling & Industrial Technologies (LEIT). The IoT incorporates multiple stakeholders

DOI: 10.4018/978-1-5225-8407-0.ch013

like within its framework. The IoT ecosystem is dense with several key players rather than focusing on deployment of one specific technological solution. IoT systems exhibit multiple instances of applications and services in improving the quality of life of human beings. According to ITU and IERC-Internet of Things European Research Cluster, *"Internet of Things (IoT) is a dynamic global network infrastructure with self-configuring capabilities based on standard and interoperable communication protocols where physical and virtual "things" have identities, physical attributes, and virtual personalities and use intelligent interfaces and are seamlessly integrated into the information network"*.

Internet of Things is umbrella under which all the objects are connected through Internet. The IoT objects are needed to be uniquely recognized, their position of existence and status of liveability has to be monitored, and these objects should be accessible from anywhere through internet (Stankovic, 2014; Barbero, 2011). Further, (Violette, 2018) addressed the various IoT standards. In order to achieve these objectives, IoT architecture consists of three major components namely hardware, middleware, and services. The hardware components consist of sensors, computing devices, actuators, and embedded systems. The middleware component consists of functionalities that can gather the data from the hardware components through Internet, store these data and process the data for any specific applications as required. The services components consist of application services that met up the user specifications via effective user interfaces. According to (Palattell, et al. 2013; Atzori, et al. 2010)It is to be noted that, in recent years, IoT systems further enhanced through enabling technologies like Cloud computing, Big Data, Block Chain and Cyber physical Systems (CPS). The authors (Chin, 2017; Fitzgerald, 2018) discussed the need for convergence of different technologies in order to provide smart personalized services.

The cloud computing provides three major components as service namely Infrastructure as a Service (IaaS), Platform as a service (PaaS) and Software as a Service (SaaS). The objective of the cloud computing is to solve the problem of limited storage and computation capabilities of standalone network of systems. The cloud computing provides advanced features such as elasticity, scalability, and availability to any computing system connected to the Cloud resources. These resources from cloud are fetched through Internet connectivity to the IoT based end computing systems.

The cloud computing enables the IoT system through the features of infrastructure, platform, and services. The added features like "Sensing as a Service" are discussed by in literature that facilitates the storage of sensed data on to the cloud platform. The combination of IoT and Cloud Computing has been addressed widely as "Cloud of Things". This concept explores the process of gathering the sensor data through IoT and then stores the data in cloud for further data analysis.

The conventional techniques to store data are relational databases and sequential data processing. These techniques are efficient to handle and process limited data size. However, in today's scenario, there is very huge data been generated, through these conventional mechanisms, whereas fail to handle huge volumes of data. As a solution to this problem, Big Data mechanisms and tools are effective to handle these huge volumes of data sets. The Big Data concept has four major features embedded in it namely Volume, Variety, Velocity and Veracity.

The cyber physical system (CPS) provides standardized platform for combining the physical objects in the IoT system and the computational components of the IoT technology. In CPS different types of sensors are employed across the IoT systems for different purpose. Later, these sensors measure various metrics from the surrounding natural environment and disseminate these measurements in the form of data to the data management systems through networking technology available for IoT models. Also, in industrial applications, the CPS systems exhibit controlling mechanisms through enhanced monitoring equipment's and management systems. To mention few popular applications of ICS include smart grid system, healthcare systems, intelligent automotive systems, and distributed robotics system.

The objective of the IoT design is to provide decentralized and autonomous systems. In order to achieve this, privacy and security should be guarantee through technical designing of the IoT systems. The integration of block chain and the IoT systems promises to foster such objectives. The block chain mechanisms perform registration and authentication of all IoT devices and IoT system operations performed. Since, each IoT operations are monitored through block chain mechanism, the data abuse or tampering are detected and prevented. Any kind of suspicious data operations are prohibited. Hence, security and privacy of the IoT systems are enhanced through Block chain mechanism.

Key contributions of this chapter

1. To address the issues and challenges in existing IoT systems
2. To discuss how to enhance IoT systems through enabling technologies like cloud computing, big-data, cyber physical systems and block chain.
3. To study the existing real life examples for the enabled IoT technologies
4. To conduct comprehensive comparing for each of the enabling technologies towards IoT systems.

Section 1.2 discusses the various applications of IoT. Section 1.3 describes the architecture of IoT systems. Section 2, elaborates the necessity of enabling technologies for IoT based smart systems. Section 3, address the convergence of Cloud computing and IoT systems and also the challenges associated with such convergence. Section 4, discusses the Big Data based IoT systems and then the various challenges associated with the Big Data based IoT systems. Section 5, discusses the enabling of IoT systems along Cyber Physical Systems. Section 6, discusses the framework and challenges for Block Chain based IoT system. Section 7, presents smart parking system based on IoT framework. Finally, section 7 concludes the discussion on enabling technologies for IoT systems.

Applications of IoT

This section describes various applications of IoT in the real world scenarios. To mention few predominant applications namely traffic monitoring system, air quality monitoring system, noise monitoring system, energy monitoring system, waste management system, smart parking system and smart lighting systems and are discussed further.

*   **Traffic Monitoring System:** The IoT based traffic monitoring system is enabled by deploying camera for capturing videos of the traffic at various places across many cities throughout the world. Authors of (Pyyk¨onen, et al. 2013; Sezer, et al. 2015; Chapman, et al. 2014; Niyato, et al.2009) focused on IoT based traffic monitoring system in smart cities. The data traffic generated by cameras are processed for various level of services required for traffic management. The traffic services offered are beneficial for both city administrators and the citizens. For example, the city administrators can be offered with services like identifying traffic jam at particular road, traffic diverting, analysis for construction of flyovers at heavy traffic places, and identifying accident prone areas. For citizens, the IoT based traffic monitoring systems help to plan trips according to the current traffic situation across the city. Particularly, for the office goers or the people planning for road trip journey are benefitted by the traffic monitoring systems. The characteristics of IoT

camera based traffic monitoring systems are the video based data traffic generated through camera devices. Such data traffic is heavy in information. Further, the transmission of such heavy data through network requires huge data rate and widespread of communication bandwidth. In recent IoT based technologies, the traffic monitoring is enhanced through several efficient IoT protocol ecosystems Want, 2014; Zaneela, et al. 2014). The traffic information has the conglomeration of various sources of data such as GPS data, air quality system along the IoT enable roads of the smart city.

- **Air Quality Monitoring System:** According to (Stefan, et al. 2014; Marinov, 2016) the air quality monitoring system provides facility to monitor the level of chemical particles and other pollutants present in the atmosphere of the urban city. In case of urban city, the Carbon Monoxide (CO) level is very essential to be measured. The specialized sensors to measure the level of pollutants present are installed across the city. The measured levels are digitally recorded and monitored by the control centres. Based on these measurements the IoT based smart systems authorities can analyse the air quality status on real time. Also such air quality measurements are public available for the common people. These types of IoT based smart air quality monitoring systems are highly helpful for the better living of the people in the city. The authorities can alert, control and protect the pollutant causing factors and take authoritative actions against such by passers of law. Also, the citizens having health related issues can be warned and precaution by such air quality monitoring systems.

- **Noise Monitoring Systems:** Authors (Soufiene, et al. 2015) discusses about IoT based monitoring system for acoustic pollution through automated noise monitoring systems. The IoT based noise monitoring system measures the noise produced at any particular time and any particular location of the city. Further, the noise level can be measured using public microphones or sound detectors installed across the city. This measurement of noise can be mapped to space time frame to monitor abnormal activities like violence and accidents across IoT based smart city systems. Advanced sound processing algorithms and image processing methods can be used to identify the culprits within smart city. This sort of platform enhances the safety of public in greater extent.

- **Energy Monitoring Systems:** The IoT based smart energy monitoring system can provided up to date consumption of energy to the citizens of smart city. Authors of (Dai, et al., 2015) focused on the energy consumption monitoring across houses, building, and infrastructures of the city. The energy consumption could be like electricity, gas and water resources distributed to each citizens through pipelines. These pipelines can be monitored using sensors to measure the consumption of energy by individuals. Along with these services, other are like public lighting system traffic lights, public cameras, heating or cooling systems of buildings are also monitored through this energy monitoring system. Based on the IoT based energy monitoring systems the IoT based smart systems administration can plan their power production and distribution across the resource generating units.

- **Waste Management System:** The IoT based waste management system provides monitoring devices that are installed on the garbage bins across the streets of the smart city (Anagnostopoulos, 2017). This kind of IoT based smart waste management set up is significantly helpful for keeping the city clean, further economically and environmentally advantageous. The IoT based sensing devices installed on garbage bin monitors load of each bin, alert the garbage collector trucks, and also optimize the route of collecting such garbage bins. The overall cost of waste gathering is significantly reduced.

- **Smart Parking System:** As discussed in (Marinov, 2016;Want, 2014), the IoT based smart parking system monitors the available parking slots within the congested urban centre places. The Radio Frequency Identifier (RFID), Near Frequency Communication (NFC) is used for uniquely identifying the parking slots electronically. The advantages of IoT based smart parking system are reduced time of search vacant parking slot, reduction in CO levels, less traffic congestion and satisfied smart city people. The elderly or disabled persons driving their vehicles are also benefitted by this type of smart parking system.
- **Smart Lighting System:** IoT based facility for smart lighting system, consists of each public light pole is monitored for its status, operation during different weather conditions, and number of people around. Based on these factors the public lighting system are monitored and controlled by smart lighting systems administrative (Eduardo, et al. 2017).

Several other applications of the IoT based smart systems include building health monitoring systems, salubrity of public buildings etc.

Architecture of IoT Systems

The various components of IoT based smart system include end systems, link layer, network layer, transport layer and applications layer (Barbero, et al. 2011; Palatella, et. al., 2013) and is depicted in Figure 1.

- **IoT End Systems:** IoT end systems are the devices that are used to make the IoT based smart systems realizable, through communication among these devices. IoT end systems are classified based on their functionality and position of the devices in the IoT protocol stack namely ends nodes, gateways, backend servers.
- **IoT Nodes:** Nodes are the devices that are capable of generating data by monitoring natural environment, and then forward them to the data control systems. The devices are low cost and with limited computational resources. IoT nodes are classified based on number of parameters such as characteristics of the device, powering methods, networking capability, sensor/actuator and the data link layer mechanism used in these devices.
- **IoT Gateways:** Gateways interconnects the IoT end nodes and facilitates to communicate with the main processing infrastructure of the IoT system. The gateways provide the translation between conventional unconstrained Internet protocol stack with constrained IoT protocol stack. For example, the unconstrained protocol like IPv4, HTTP, and XML are mapped with functionalities of constrained protocols like 6LoWPAN, CoAP, EXI respectively. IoT gateways facilitate the interoperability of the IoT end systems and IoT controlling centers. Hence, the mapping of different protocols is performed across different gateway devices in the IoT network.
- **Backend Servers:** The functions of the backend servers are data gathering, storing and processing and then to perform value added services according to the user requirements. The back end servers are part of legacy infrastructure in IoT based smart systems. The back end servers facilitate accessing of open data and to process the huge pen data to provide variety of IoT based smart systems services. The various other functional systems that support backend servers are database management, web services, and enterprise resource planning (ERP). Database Management Systems provide mechanism to store the huge data gathered from IoT end systems and stored in a structural way or any other conventional methods. Websites Management Systems provides the

ease of accessibility by users through graphical user interface, interactive interoperable interfaces among various IoT stakeholders like consumers, service providers, authorities, public, and utility providers. Enterprise resource planning systems handles the information flow across business functional components of IoT based smart systems control and administration. The IoT database system and ERP system together enable the huge data gathering from IoT end systems and the efficient information flow through different functional components of any IoT services.

- **Link Layer:** The main objective of link layer is provide communication support to traffic flow from wide range of devices and aggregate the huge amount of data flow from extremely high number of IoT devices (Perera, et al. 2014). The link layer technologies for IoT based smart systems system are classified as unconstrained and constrained protocols. Unconstrained protocols include the conventional WAN, MAN, and LAN network types using communication protocols like Ethernet, WiFi, LTE/4G, Power Line Communication (PLC) and WiMax technologies. The characteristics of unconstrained protocols include high data rate, low delay, and the high reliability. However, the disadvantage of unconstrained protocols is that they are suitable for energy constrained network systems, due to the complex nature of the protocol functioning. On the other hand, the constrained protocol of the link layer technology includes the Bluetooth Low Energy, Zigbee Smart, Power Line Communication, Near Frequency Communication, and RFID. The characteristics of these link layer protocols are low data rates, limited power, and limited computing capabilities.

- **Network Layer:** The most popular unique IP addressing scheming using IPv4 exhausted, there is huge crunch to address devices uniquely (Stankovic, 2014). The IPv6 provides mechanism to address millions of devices to be uniquely allocation using 128 bit addressing scheme. Since, IoT network consists of billions of such devices and IP addresses associated with each device, the IPv6 is most suitable for resolving the IoT network addressing scheme. Although the IPv6 addressing scheme resolves the problem of unique IP address for devices, there is major constrained with devices to process the 128 bit address. It is noted that, these IoT devices are constrained in resources. These devices are limited by computing power, battery power. Hence, the IPv6 address is an overhead for these constrained devices. The low power networking protocol suited for IoT based constrained network is 6LoWPAN. This protocol resolves the problem of overhead due to

Figure 1. Basic architecture of IoT system

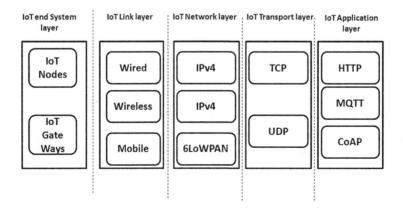

128 bit IPv6 address. The devices are mapped to its corresponding 6LoWPAN address with IPv6 address through border router. These routers perform the operation of translating the 6LoWPAN address with IPv6 addressing scheme for interacting with Internet.

- **Transport Layer:** The most commonly used application protocol is the HTTP to fetch the web pages from servers and also to utilize the web services across the network using Internet (Barbero, et al. 2011) However, the HTTP protocol has several factors due to which it is not suitable for implementing it directly on the resource constrained IoT devices. Moreover, the HTTP works upon the connection oriented TCP protocol. The objectives of TCP on LAN are reliability, flow control, guaranteed delivery of packets and network congestion control. These objectives are achieved with overhead of connection establishment through handshaking mechanism. The connection establishment and connection termination of TCP protocol has impact of huge overhead and definitely not suitable for resource crunched IoT end nodes. Also, the scalability is limited through TCP protocol, not suitable for small data transfer in highly lossy network environment of IoT. Hence to meet IoT transport layer objectives UDP protocol is used. The UDP protocol provides reliable data transfer only through retransmission techniques.
- **Application Layer:** The application protocol HTTP has several limitations like redundant and correlated data, highly verbose and strictly repeated content structuring method of HTTP tags. Hence HTTP application protocol causes heavy overhead for the small resource IoT devices. Constrained Application Protocol (CoAP) overcomes these disadvantages of HTTP. The ReST API methods such as GET, PUT, POST, and DELETE are supported by the CoAP. Similarly, the commonly used data representation namely eXtensibleMarkup Language (XML) is not suitable for IoT devices. Because parsing of XML data consumes heavy computing power, which is not favorable for the computing constrained IoT devices. Hence, Efficient XML Interchange (EXI) proposed by W3C solves the problem of XML data representation. EXI uses open data format for data representation and completely compatible with the XML data.

Challenges of IoT

The implementation and advancement in IoT need to overcome several challenges namely unification of standards, mobility handling, naming systems, transport layer issues, traffic characteristics, Quality of services for IoT applications, security and privacy of data. This section elaborates these challenges of IoT.

- **Unification of Standards:** Currently, in the IoT ecosystem, several standards do exist. However, there is no strong hold for integration of these diversified standards. Hence, it is a huge challenge to develop a comprehensive platform for the unification of standards.
- **Mobility:** Several research works has been done in area of object addressing in IoT systems. However, there exists insufficient research work related to the mobility of objects in IoT scenario. Hence, there is huge demand to solve critical problems like adaptability and scalability of the several heterogeneous technologies and millions of objects.
- **Naming System:** The domain naming system (DNS) for Internet protocol suite is a well stabilized and popularly followed mechanism for mapping the IP address with each computing devices within an IP network. However, there is need for mapping of object in IoT system with its associated identifier using description of each object connected with in the IoT network.

- **Transport Layer:** The transport layer of TCP/IP protocol suite is very well established with connection mechanism and reliability. However, it is to noted that, the end system in these TCP/IP scenarios are resource rich in terms of computing power, memory, energy, storage and networking. Whereas, this existing set up of transport layer is soon to be outdated. The overhead due to connection mechanism are real burden for the resource constrained IoT objects. Similarly, the existing mechanisms are unsuitable to handle the congestion due to the traffic generated by the IoT devices.

- **Traffic Characteristics:** The traffic patterns of the TCP/IP have been thoroughly studied in past research works. The traffic monitoring and controlling mechanism are also well stabilized for IP based networks. However, the traffic generated through IoT objects are yet to be studied. The dynamic nature of actual IoT traffic is not studied or experimented thoroughly so far. Also, the existing mechanism for traffic monitoring and controlling will not be sufficient to the dynamic and busty nature of IoT data traffic.

- **QoSsupport:** The Internet based services offered to the computer network are broadly classified as Integrated and differentiated services which are well established service with QoS mechanism. However, these services are mostly predefined with specifications and requirements. Users are allowed to fetch these static services as such whenever required. In the IoT scenario, the user has to choose among different services as per current user's requirements. And such services are mostly dynamic in nature and interdependent among different services. Hence, the QoS mechanism for interdependent heterogeneous services is still a major challenge in IoT systems.

- **Security and Privacy:** Security aspect of the IoT based smart systems involves the identification and prevention of illegitimate users to use the sensitive data offered by services. Hence, there is huge opportunity feasible to develop systems to handle security issues and avoid imposed security attacks both at real time as well on stored data. At present, techniques like light cryptography offers such security facility, however, needs further enhancement. Similarly, the privacy policies upon sensitive information of people such as health related data, localization issues, identify information have to handle appropriately. Hence, aIoT based smart system must provide platform to collect and process the user data in very effective without manipulating or malicious cause.

ENABLING TECHNOLOGIES

During the initial days of smart systems, the ICT based technologies are the key driving force (Eduardo, et al. 2017). However, the ICT has less impact over the expected high standard of quality of life for people. Challenges of ICT are approached as IT infrastructure based, Operational Cost based, Security and privacy based. Under IT infrastructure based challenges, their huge lack of integrating various administrative systems. Even the existing ICT based infrastructure lack clarity in level of integration. The non-functional components such as interoperability, elasticity, context awareness are not available under the ICT based Smart system frameworks. The compatibility between applications, underlying systems and software are weakly present. From the initial point of digitization, the current objective of smart systems is the sustainability. The enabling technologies for sustainable smart systems are Internet of Things, Cloud Computing, Cyber physical Systems, Big Data and Block Chain technology.

Internet of Things

According to (Want, 2014; Satyanarayanan, et al. 2001), Internet of Things is umbrella under which all the objects are connected through Internet. There are three main objectives of IoT. These objects are needed to be uniquely recognized, their position of existence and status of liveability has to be monitored, and these objects should be accessible from anywhere through internet. In order to achieve these objectives, IoT architecture consists of three major components namely hardware, middleware, and services. The hardware components consist of sensors, computing devices, actuators, and embedded systems. The middle component consists of functionalities that can gather the data from the hardware components through Internet, store these data and process the data for any specific applications as required. The services components consists of application services that will met the user specifications through effective user interfaces.

IoT enables the concept of the smart systems. In the way, the hardware components of IoT are the huge data collected through Internet from various devices across the world that are used in the service of smart systems. The middleware of the IoT enables the functionalities that process on the data gathered from the devices of Smart systems. Then the service component of IoT will serve the specific services of the smart systems. For example, air quality monitoring services of the Smart systems, posses the sensor to measure CO level of the atmosphere. The sensors at the hardware level of IoT, and data gather by sensing will be stored and processed at the middleware components of IoT. Finally, at the service level, the air quality will be analyzed using advanced functionalities of IoT to solve the specific requirement of air quality monitoring within the smart systems. There are several such potential applications of IoT for the Smart systems like waste management, noise level monitoring, water consumption, electricity usage. Table 1 depicts various other domains of IoT applications.

Cloud Computing

The cloud computing provides three major components as service namely Infrastructure as a Service (Iaas), Platform as a service (Pass) and Software as a Service (SaaS). The objective of the cloud computing is to solve the problem of limited storage and computation capabilities of standalone network of systems (Derhamy, et al. 2015; Kovatsch, et al., 2015; Garcia, et al. 2015). The cloud computing provides enhanced features such as elasticity, scalability, and availability to any computing system connected to the Cloud resources. These resources from cloud are fetched through Internet connectivity to the end computing systems.

Table 1. Various application domains of IoT and usage

IoT Application Domain	Usage
Transportation domain	Logistic driving, assisted driving, mobile ticketing, environmental monitoring, augmented maps
Healthcare	Tracking, Identification, authentication, data collection sensing
Smart environment	Comfortable homes, offices, industrial plants, smart museum and gym
Personal and social	Social networking, historical queries, losses and thefts
Futuristic	Robot taxi, City information model, Enhanced game room
Agriculture	Growing period of product, harvesting phase, packaging phase, transportation phase, delivery of product.

The cloud computing technology enables the smart systems by providing infrastructure, platform, and software as a service. The added features like "Sensing as a Service" are discussed by (Heydon, 2013) that facilitate the storage of sensed data on to the cloud platform. The combination of IoT and Cloud Computing has been discussed widely by (Kindberg, et al., 2002) as "Cloud of Things". This concept explores the process of gathering the sensor data through IoT and then stores the data in cloud for further data analysis. This idea largely favors the Smart systems, in which the sensors are part of the systems, and the sensor data are gathered by IoT enable technologies and then data and processed by the cloud computing platform. In addition, the highly dynamic nature of the sensors, resources, reconfiguration used in Smart systems are effectively handled by the Cloud Computing platform. According to (Salvatore, et al. 2012) together IoT and Cloud promise to serve several purposes of the requirements of Smart systems applications and provides City Application Software as a Service (CSaaS) and City Platform as Service (CPaaS).

Big Data

The conventional techniques to store data are relational databases and sequential data processing (Chin, et al. 2017). These techniques are efficient to handle and process limited data size. However, in today's scenario, there is very huge data been generated, in order these conventional mechanisms, and fail to handle huge volume of data. Big data mechanism and tools can handle the huge volume of data sets. The Big Data concept has four major features embedded in it namely Volume, Variety, Velocity and Veracity as depicted in Table 2.

- **Volume:** The Volume of the Big Data represents the amount of data generated and gathered from the real world. The scale of such data is huge and exponentially increasing day by day. Particularly, in IoT based smart systemconcepts, the amount of data generated are massive in quantity being gathered from different sources associated in city infrastructures and people.
- **Variety:** The variety of the Big Data represents the different type of data being gathered from different sources. For example, the different sources of data include data gathered from different sensors. In IoT based smart systemsfor environment monitoring, temperature recorded from temperature sensors, pressure recorded from pressure sensors, proximity measured by proximity sensors, radio communication data are few example. These data collected are different in their metrics as well data representation. Similar, the data are collected from different sources in IoT based smart systems like sources, actuators, medical equipments, smart phones, cameras, etc. Further, the data can have different representations like structured, semi structured and unstructured data formats.

Table 2. Characteristics of big data

	Characteristics			
	Volume	**Velocity**	**Variety**	**Veracity**
Components	Devices	Historical	Data Sources	Quality
	Scenario	Real Time	Data Vendors	Security
	People	Offline	Data Format	Privacy

Further, the data can be text, voice, images, audio, video represented in different formats provided by software vendors and applications developed.

- **Velocity:** The velocity of Big Data represents the rate at the gathered data are processed. In IoT based smart systems, the application services require real time processing of data and offline data processing. For example, in situations like traffic management, disaster management, and resource management systems, the data has to be monitored, gathered and processed instantaneously at real time. On the other hand, under IoT based smart systems concept, the authorities, governance and policymakers may monitor the infrastructural requirements, population growth and penetration, educational systems, and any other development requirements at offline for particular history of period.

- **Veracity:** The veracity of big Data includes the quality of the data, security, and privacy of the data. The quality of data represents the data gather from IoT based smart systems environment must be free from errors or loss. The security of data represents the mechanism to avoid tampering or misuse of the data by malicious intruders. The privacy includes mechanism to maintain trust, and originality of the data generated from IoT based smart systems environment.

Some of the Big Data platforms available for the IoT based smart systems concept are NoSQL databases like H-Base and MongoDB, Parallel data handling tools such as Apache Hadoop and Spark, real time data handling tools like Apace Storm.

Cyber Physical System

The cyber physical system (CPS) provides standardized platform for combining the physical objects in the IoT based smart systems and the computational components of the technology (Rajkumar, et al. 2010). Two categories of CPS are possible, namely Sensor Based Systems (SBS) and Intelligence Control Systems (ICS) (Li Da, et al. 2014) Under SBS model, different types of sensors are employed across the IoT based smart systems for different purpose. These sensors measure various metrics from the surrounding natural environment and disseminate these measurements in the form of data to the data management systems through networking technology available for IoT based smart systems model. In case of ICS, the systems exhibit controlling mechanisms through enhanced monitoring equipments and management systems. Examples of ICS include smart grid system, Healthcare systems, Intelligent Automotive systems, distributed robotics system. Across the world, there are several IoT based smart city projects that have already adapted to CPS model. Few examples are Live Singapore project, Digital China, Unified Operation center of Rio de Janeiro (Kusiak, 2014). Advantages of CPS to IoT based smart systems model are to provide enhanced IoT based smart systems services to the citizen, generate opportunities in addition to the existing value systems of the public infrastructures, modernization of resource management like Smart Grid systems. Further, CPS improves the accessibility and utilization of public resources and infrastructures like lighting systems, smart public furniture, smart surveillance, and smart kiosk systems. However, the challenges of CPS are interoperability and heterogeneity of components, devices, and data involved in the IoT based smart systems. Due to lack of steady and standardized financial aspects hold back the government of IoT based smart systems to acclimatize CPS for IoT based smart systems.

Block Chain

The integration of IoT and block chain plays a vital role in promoting the decentralized and autonomous mechanism for handling IoT generated data in secured and private mode (Antonopoulos, 2014). Especially for data sensitive as well as device sensitive IoT applications, the authentication and registration of legitimate users are essential. To achieve the security and privacy at the best, the block chain mechanism is very effective. The integrity, confidentiality, anonymity, adaptability are the issues handled by the block chain mechanism (Swanson, 2015). As the result of integrating, block chain and the IoT, the critical IoT application services are delivered excellent performance rate. Also, the large scale data generated through IoT network are stored and exchanged safely at different peer locations, while the authenticity and the privacy are guaranteed by the block chain.

CLOUD COMPUTING BASED IoT FRAMEWORK

The Cloud Computing based IoT architecture consists of three primary layers namely IoT infrastructure layer, Cloud layer and Application Layer as shown in Figure 2 given below.

- **IoT Infrastructure Layer:** The bottom most layer is the IoT infrastructure layer. This layer is further consists of end systems and the local cloud resources. The end system includes several devices such as sensors, smart phones, computing devices, actuators, offices, home, vehicles, road infrastructures, etc (Mayer, etal. 2015; Varga, 2015; Evans, 2011). It is to be noted that, these end systems are limited in resources, in the sense, the computing power, memory capacity, energy, networking are limited within these end systems. Further, these end systems are inter connected to one another through cloud based IoT systems. In the cloud based IoT systems, consists of two types cloud namely local cloud and global cloud. The end systems at the infrastructure layer will be controlled, monitored, and maintained by the local cloud systems. The local cloud environments are created adhoc as on when demand that are raised for the service requests by end devices. The objectives of local cloud systems are to provide resource and services with limited area and time. Local cloud consists of sufficient resources such as storage, computing power, energy and networking capacity to meet the requirements of customers within local geographical area. Further, these local cloud resources are time bounded, as per the services requested by the end users.
- **Cloud Layer:** The global cloud systems form the unlimited resource provider for large scope of demanding IoT systems. The objectives of global cloud systems are reliability, scalability, efficiency, ubiquity of providing services to the larger group of customers across the globe (Satyanarayanan, 2009; Alaya, et al. 2015). The global cloud systems are the traditional cloud systems with infinite elasticity of resources such as computing power, memory, energy, networking facility through virtualization. The global cloud systems are the backbone platform for the cloud service providers. The targets for global cloud systems are to expand the business opportunities through various services such as Platform as a service, Infrastructure as a service, and Software as a service at larger perspective. The objectives of global cloud systems are reliability, scalability, efficiency, ubiquity of providing services to the customers.

- **Application Layer:** The primary objective of the application layer in the Cloud based IoT systems is to handle the distributed sources, huge amount of data generated by the IoT end systems (Albano, et al. 2016; Pereira, et al. 2015; Jose et al. 2014). Further, the application layer has to provide the services as required by the IoT systems. Along with this, the application layer should posses the functionalities to handle the dynamic requirements of end users, real time handling of data processing. Hence, the application layer is sophisticated with context aware solutions that can handle dynamism effectively along with management and orchestration mechanism by the lower layer cloud systems.

Challenges of IoT and Cloud Convergence

1. **Interoperability:** Interoperability defines the ability hardware devices and system software that are belonging to IoT Cloud environment to exchange information and make utilization of information to user requirements. Generally, the interoperability has to be handled at the service level of the IoT - Cloud system. Hence, the interoperability needs to be achieved at different levels such application level, encoding techniques, compression levels and semantics of IoT stack. At application level, the different types of service oriented protocols exists namely CoAP, MQTT, REST, XMPP, uPnP, OPC-UA. At encoding level, there are several types of coding exist such as XML, CSV and JSON. Similarly, the compression techniques like EXI, DCT, and DWT. Also, the variety of semantics does exist such as SenML and SensML.

Hence, there is a need for common platform of service registry to meet interoperability at different levels of Cloud Computing based IoT systems. Next, is to make the interoperability through service discovery in form of semantics, compression and encoding mechanism. For this purpose, (Garcia, et al., 2015)

Figure 2. Cloud computing based IoT architecture

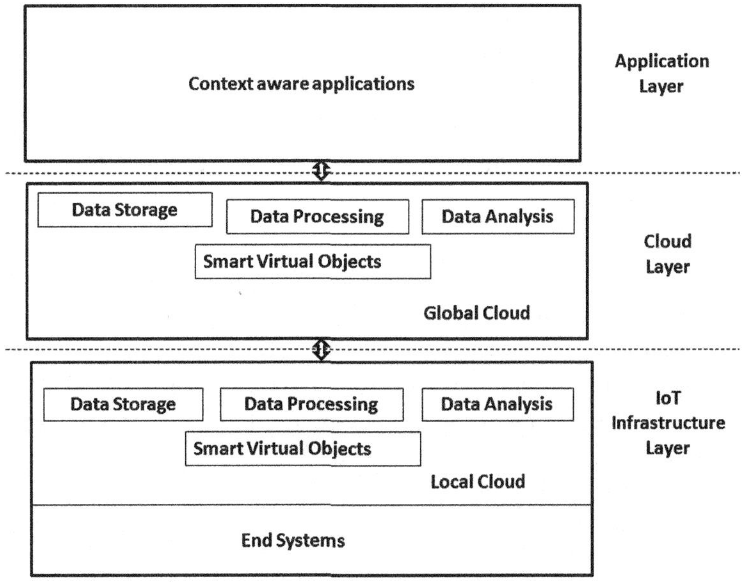

255

proposed DNS TXT based records for creating service metadata. Thus, the software developers can consume these publicly available meta data of services for developing the IoT –Cloud services.

The authors (Derhamy, et al. 2015) discusses about the device interoperability by means of protocol translation for services offered by different service protocols. It is to be noted that, such protocol translators require continuous monitoring for Quality of service offered at dynamic run time. Further (Pereira, 2015) discusses that the major trade-off in compression service is due t o the transmission delay and the computation efficiency of compression protocol.

2. **Scalability:** The scalability of Cloud based IoT system is possible by means cloud service transactions. These service transactions among local cloud solutions poses two important components namely service administration and service transaction on real time. The service administration is performed through, service discovery, service authorisation and service orchestration during transactions. The authors (Pereira, 2015)suggests the concepts of gateways for the inter cloud collaboration for various service transactions. Authors (Albano, et al. 2016) propose the broker concept like MQTT brokers handling the various transactions through publish/subscribe mechanism among MQTT clients through MQTT protocol.

3. **Stakeholders Diversity:** The Cloud based IoT involves different stakeholders like consumers, service providers, management, Government Authorities, legal service providers, governing bodies and etc. The primary requirement for diversified stakeholders are independent yet automated collaborative interactions among these stakeholders, dedicated commitment towards safety and security, and established mechanism for authentication of information transactions and also fool proof authorization of information handling across the systems.

4. **Security and Safety:** The security and safety concerns due to convergence of IoT and Cloud are sustainability of IoT cloud systems, trust of devices and software, authentication of service consumer as well as consumption and data integrity. The sustainability of the IoT based on cloud needs sheltered environment for the physical devices involved in the systems. The sustainability of Cloud based IoT system can be achieved through physical layers using firewall protection strategy. In recent research, DMZ technologies have exhibited sufficient level of sustainability. The sustainability towards dynamic of wireless channel communication, as discussed in (Varga et. al, 2015), can be achieved through incorporating standards such as IEEE 802.11.

Next, the trustability of devices and software involved in the cloud based IoT devices. The deployment of specialized modules is required for handling trust among services and devices. The dual interface for trust anchor (Martisch, et al., 2016) is proposed and extensively discussed for handling trust among devices and services.

Next, the authentication of service consumption and consumers needs to be addressed. The authentication can be provided through two mechanisms namely certificates and tickets. (Kapritsos, et al., 2012) discuss in detail about X.509 protocol for certification based authentication. Similarly ticket based authentication using Radius mechanisms is detailed in (Zhang, et al, 2015). The research outlines that the certificates for authentication involves heavy computation cost while the ticket is best suited for resource constrained devices of IoT systems.

Next, security concern is to provide data integrity for the information transmitted across the Cloud based IoT systems. The effective solution is to provide security at network layer of IoT stack through IPSec protocols. However, IPSec has the disadvantage of inefficient key distribution mechanism consuming high computational cost and energy.

BIG DATA BASED IoT FRAMEWORK

The Big Data based IoT framework consists of five layers namely data gathering layer, Validation layer, semantic layer, cognitive and Service layer (Sezer, et al. 2016; Saneja, et al. 2014; Hayes, et al., 2014;).

- **Data Gathering Layer:** The data gathering layer performs two basic functions namely data gathering and data transferring (Liu, 2016). The data gathering layer simply collects the data from different types of IoT based devices, sensors. These collected data constitutes huge data sets of specific IoT devices or sensors over the time. These large datasets, comprise of different features and values, are then transferred into the IoT framework. The data are in raw form without undergoing any validation or transformation.
- **Validation Layer:** The transformation layer performs three basic functions namely extraction, transformation and loading (Hachem, et al., 2011; Nambi, et al., 2014). During extraction phase, the data set is parsed for validation. In this, various issues like duplication of data, interpolation of missing data, merging of data, data type, data format and data precision are handled during validation. Then the each of these data are semantically annotated later to be used for rule based reasoning mechanism. Later, the transformation layer loads the semantically annotated data into semantic layer.
- **Semantic Layer:** The basic operation of semantic layer is to apply the rule based reasoning for inferring only the appropriate data as per the IoT service specifications and requirements (Wang, 2013). The semantic layer interacts with the domain specific rule base module to implement the reasoning upon data sets. In this, the semantically corrected relevant data are stored in the Resource Description Framework (RDF) format. This formatted RDF file is then transferred to the learning layer.
- **Cognitive Layer:** The cognitive layer performs three functions namely pre-processing, extracting and learning out the IoT sensed data. (Song, et al., 2010). During pre-processing, the data sets are analysed for correctness and error free, regression expression and grouped as per the requirements. Next, the relevant features or information are extracted from the source file on which the machine learning algorithms are implemented. Finally, the learning phase defines the machine learning process to obtain the most relevant information out of the large feature sets of data. In order to optimize the computation time and enhance performance, the machine learning algorithms are paralleled across distributed systems to handle the big data sets.
- **Service Layer:** The objective of service layer is to response to the query requested by user by evaluating the various results generated by the cognitive layer. The service layer may directed provide desired output as service or may recommend relevant possibility for the query request of IoT applications.

Challenges of Big Data and IoT

The challenges for convergence of Big Data and IoT are streaming of IoT data traffic, aggregators for Big Data, and classification component of big Data analysis (Nambi, et al. 2014).

- **Data Stream:** The data stream generated by IoT based devices are raw, unstructured in terms of size, abstraction, features etc. These data streams are contains issues such as enormous in quality, inconsistent, redundant, incorrect, anomalies. Hence there is need for role of Big Data to handle this huge IoT raw data stream.
- **Big Data Aggregators:** The aggregators basically perform data fusion of IoT data streams. The standardized format for data semantics are involved during data fusion operation. The standardized data semantic facilities to eliminate largely data anomalies present in the raw data stream. Further, data fusion ensures error free and quality enhancement of data.
- **Big Data Classifiers:** The main purpose of Big Data classifier is to decide the error free data into cluster based on parameters like domain, features, functionality of data stream. The advantage of such clustering mechanism is to ease accessibility, understand ability and usability of the data stream. According to the author (Perera, et al., 2013; Sezer, et al., 2016) IoT application involves different data related to maintenance information of IoT system, production information, status information, functional information during different life cycle stages of an IoT application.

In order to achieve scalability and efficient distributed hierarchical architecture is prepared to handle the large data base. The master node controls several storage nodes. The storage nodes maintain data in the form of tables based relational database schema. The table consists of row, columns, primary keys, elements within a table. The metadata of a storage node is maintained by the master node. Metadata contain all possible path links among each storage nodes.

CYBER PHYSICAL SYSTEMS

The cyber physical system architecture consists of four major layers namely sensing layer, communication layer, data computing layer and applications layer.

- **Sensing Layer:** The sensing layer consists of IoT sensor, computing objects, and actuators. Particularly, for CPS systems, the sensing layer basically performs operations on the real world through the amalgamation of connected actuators. It is obvious, that, the integration of IoT and CPS are basis for the many modern smart systems in the real world. Examples of sensing layer components are RFID, Infrared, Thermal, Acoustics, Biological sensors, Haptic Sensors, etc.
- **Communication Layer:** The sensing layer is supported by the communication layer in order to interface the sensing nodes with upper layer like data computing and system application layer. The communication layer supports both wired and wireless protocol. It is to be noted that, most of these communication protocols are already well established and standardized. Hence, the customization of communication protocols is not feasible. The Table 3 list the standard wireless protocols used for CPS/IoT communications.

Table 3. Range and frequency for various wireless standards

Wireless Standard	Range	Frequency
NFC	< 1m	13.56 MHz
RFID	< 100m	1GhZ
ZigBee	10-40m	2.4 GhZ
Bluetooth (LE)	100m	2.4 Ghz
802.11	35m	2.4 Ghz/ 5.8 Ghz
3GPP LTE	300m	1.9 Ghz
LoRa	~15km	0.9 Ghz
SigFox	~35km	0.9 Ghz

- **Data Computing Layer:** The data computing layer consists of several computation nodes that are capable of performing data analytics. The data gathered from the sensing layer are processed for further analysis and decision making by the data computing layer. In order to optimize and improve the efficiency of the CPS/ IOT systems, the data computation layer are enabled with cloud computing and Big Data Technologies. Based on physically sensed data, the cognitive decisions are made to provide wide range of IoT applications and its services.
- **Application Layer:** The objective of the application layers is to provide wide range of services to the CPS/IoT customers.The applications of such smart systems based on CPS/IoT are energy monitoring systems, healthcare, home security and automation systems, logistics and enterprise resource planning systems, autonomous vehicular systems, smart traffic and transportation systems, environment monitoring systems such as air quality, noise quality, smart lighting systems, natural resource (water, gas) monitoring systems. It is to be noted that the, integrated applications of CPS/ IoT with intelligent systems for handling the physical world has proved to have tremendous impact on economical uplift.

Challenges of CPS/IoT Systems

This section elaborates the major challenges of CPS/IoT systems such as communication protocols and security and privacy concerns.

- **Communication Protocols and Standards:** The physical layer, medium access layer and network layer of the IoT protocol suite has largely impacted by the communication protocols. These communication protocols are well established and standardized. However, the application layer of the CPS/ IoT systems are not capable of handling the wireless communications due to three major issues. First, the medium access layer of individual IoT device and router are different depending on the type of applications these IoT devices are intended. Second, the capacity and load handling mechanisms of the underlying communication links largely influence the performance of large scale IoT network. Third, the energy efficiency of the resource constrained IoT devices and the IoT network.

- **Security and Privacy:** The security and privacy of the CPS/IoT is needed to be researched further. Because there is huge gap between the security offered theoretically and practical application of security in the resource constrained IoT devices. The security mechanisms applied at physical layer are different from the cryptographic security solution at link, network and application layers. Hence, the challenges are to provide consistent mechanism of security at different layers of the IoT network. Further, there exists trade off between enhancing security mechanism and the overhead of security on performance of the CPS/IoT systems. Some of the security measures such as Physical sensitive device protection, access rights of users, data sharing and authentication are required. Next challenge is the emerging threats and attacks. Some well known types of attacks are Replay attack, Eavesdropping, Spoofing, GPS Spoofing, DDos, IP theft, Privilege overriding, Side channel attacks. These threats and attacks are performed across consumer, infrastructure and Industrial level. In addition, issues such as security policy designing, securing network devices and protocols, securing individual autonomous components, and auditing of such security systems are needed.

BLOCK CHAIN BASED IOT FRAMEWORK

This section elaborates the Block chain and IoT Architecture for IoT sensors Data Transaction. The processing of IoT sensor network for exchanging data usingbitcoin has been discussed by (Antonopoulos, 2014; Eris Industries, 2016) in elaborated manner. There are four main key players namely sensor web client, bitcoin network, requester client and sensor repository. The sensor web client performs two major functions, first to handle the request for data and then receive the respective bit coins for each data request. The requester client performs bitcoin sending depending on the nature of data it is needed from the IoT sensors. Upon successful transaction of bitcoins, the receiver client has to collect the data as obtained from the sensor repository. The Figure 3 below depicts the Bit coin based data transaction for the IoT system.

The bitcoin network performs four major functions (Douceur, 2012; Swanson, 2015; Kapristsos, et al. 2012). First receives the bitcoins with respect to each data request from the request client. Second, it forwards the received biotin payment notification to the respective sensor client. Third, transact with respective sensor for the data. Finally, bit coin network respond to requester client with data in corresponding to the bitcoin address.

The sensor repository performs registering of each sensor in order so that, the sensors data can be found in accordance with the requesters (Vukolic, 2015; Zhang, 2015). The sensor repository registry has the information such as bitcoin address for each data transaction, the data, the cost of each data transaction and addition information such as tags, energy, location, temporal details, and memory.

Apart from IoT sensor data, the block chain plays role in five different levels of IoT ecosystems. The Table 3below depicts the different IoT level and how block chain is used at each of these levels. At the IoT sensors level, the block chain is used for secured, public sharing of IoT sensor data (Herbet, 2015; Feld, 2014).

Figure 3. Bit coin based IoT sensor data transaction

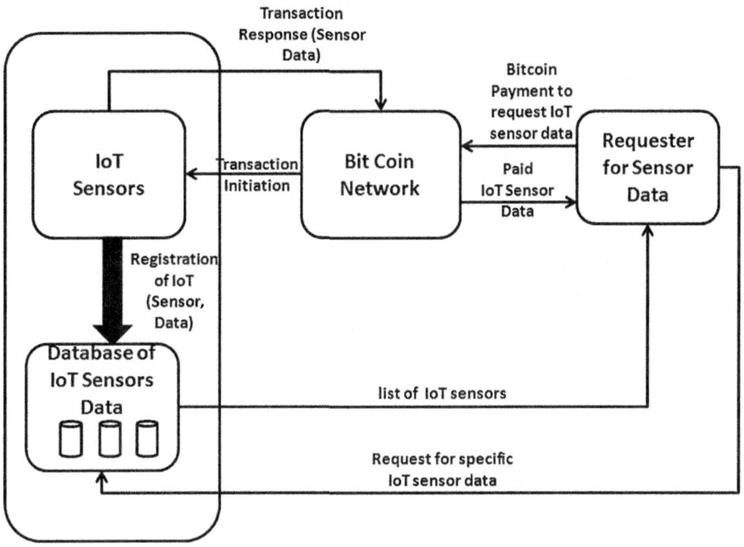

Table 4. Application of block chain at different level of IoT systems

IoT Levels	Application of Block Chain
IoT Storage Access Policies	Policies framework using Block Chain, Monitoring Policies Bylaws among IoT Consumers using public key cryptography
IoT data Storage & Management	Decentralized Storage, Private Standalone Database Management Systems
IoT Device Interaction	Block chain based transaction among IoT device through Public/Private Key
IoT device Authentication & Identification	Block Chain using Public Key based authentication and identification
IoT Sensors	Block chain for huge data collection of IoT Sensors and Devices

Challenges in Block Chain Based IoT Systems

The major challenges of block chain based IoT systems are Integrity, scalability, anonymity and Implementation.

- **Integrity:** The integrity of the block chain for IoT eco systems has challenges such as connectedness and vulnerable to attacks. It is to note that, the connectedness within the peer to peer network of block chain is not well established,as most of the peer to peer networks consist of independent autonomous systems. Hence, adding new blocks into the existing autonomous peer to peer block network become extensively difficult. Next, the block chain network is vulnerable to several attacks such as selfish mining attack, history-revision attack, and stubborn attack. In selfish mining attack, the attackers with limited computation capability and energy converse, exploits the computational capability of small mining nodes with means of deliberate forking. These selfish mining attackers will then create private mining nodes and intentionally generate several unwanted block chain forks. In history-revision attacks, the attacks with computation capability much higher than the legitimate mining nodes. Hence, the attacker overtakes others in terms of Proof of Work (PoW) difficulty, and change the history of existing block chain. In stubborn attacks, the attackers deliberately slow down the transaction among bit coin nodes.

- **Scalability:** The scalability of the bit coin network is limited due to enormous the number of transactions being carried out among block chain nodes and also hoarding of all the transaction on limited resource IoT device or sensors. Most of the time, these transaction involve heavy computation and thus limits the scalability. Similarly, block chain network involves verification of transactions at each block, thus creates problem scalability.

- **Anonymity:** The block chain based IoT network, suffers from linking the IoT devices with legitimate owners. The reason behind is the public nature of block chain network. In this public environment, it is very much possible to deanonymize the legitimate owner of any IoT device by simply monitoring the network traffic from the IoT device or from the transactions happening within the block chain.

- **Implementation:** The implementation of block chain can be carried out in both standardized and customized manner. In case of standard bit coin based block chain involves 80 bytes of reserved transaction using bit coin. Further, such standardized proof of work (PoW) involves highly complex computations. Usually, the standardized bit coin transactions involve high computation and may not be suitable for resource limited IoT devices. On the other hand, the customized transaction for block chain may be tuned according to capability of IoT devices. However, the customized way of mining techniques may lack security properties. Hence, there is need for less computation expensive solutions for PoW with respect to IoT network.

CASE STUDY: SMART PARKING SYSTEM

The objective of this IoT based Smart Parking System is to develop a mono-parking management architectural system which works on real-time basis. As the population increased in the metropolitan cities, the usage of vehicles got increased. It causes problem for parking which leads to traffic congestion, driver frustration, and air pollution. When people visit various public places like shopping malls, multiplex cinema hall & hotels during the festival time or weekends it creates more parking problem. Hence a proper mechanism is required to manage this type parking problem faced by the citizens and present a strong technical solution to this problem. To alleviate the aforementioned problems, the smart parking system has been developed. With the implementation of the smart parking system, patrons can easily locate and secure a vacant parking space at any car parking deemed convenient to them. The Figure 4 given below depicts the basic architecture of the smart parking system.

This smart parking system has IR sensor as its building block, IR sensors detect the obstacle in front of it by emitting IR rays and this principle is used. IR sensors fitted at the parking slots will detect whether a car is parked there or not. It is well know that IR sensor has a LED on it which glows when it detects any obstacle in front of it and if interfaced this voltage with Arduino, which will process this information.Then information can be transmitted in digital form that is 1 or 0. With the help of ESP8266, the Arduino processing board is connected to a Wi-Fi network and hence getting connected to a internet. After this the digital data is uploaded to an online server with the help of PHP programming language which will help in server side programming so as to make the data being readily available on the server directly from the Arduino without any interruption. The Transmission Control Protocol (TCP) is used for connecting to the internet so as to ensure the proper delivery of information to server and hence avoiding the data being lost. Using TCP, data communication is ensured that error checked delivery happens to the server and so that no distortion in data happens and hence proper information can be communicated to the patrons. To ensure that data being properly available from server for using it anywhere, an online database is incorporated, which will store this digital data and that data can be extracted from server for use anytime. All this will provide a proper storage platform for our data and also it is ensured that data stored on the server is private so that no unauthorized access to that information happens. For ensuring that data is properly distinguishable and readable SQL language is used. When required, the information can be retrieved from database and is used for android application.Further, this data is stored in distinguishable manner for various slots and hence will avoid the chance of information of different slots getting mingled up.

The final step in the development and working is an android application which can be accessed by the people to know about the parking space availability from anywhere anytime and hence take decision accordingly. Android studio is used for developing an android app. This app is extracting digital data about parking availability from the server and programmed this app in such a way so that if it receives 0 it will interpret that this parking slot is vacant and hence will show on screen that this space is available and hence anybody viewing this information on their smart phones can take decision accordingly similarly when 1 is received by the app it will be interpreted that this parking slot is occupied and hence this app will show blocked status under that slot. To ensure that this app is easily understandable by the user, the application is developed using a very simple user friendly user interface where a user can simply make his account by providing some important personal details and can login to view the information about parking on the mobile app as shown in Figure 5 and Figure 6 below. The information available on the app will continuously get updated at the gap of few seconds and hence providing real time accesses to app users.

Proposed system for the smart parking station has the power to simplify traffic and parking problems. As people are getting used to the easy use of smart phones and other devices which can access the internet can easily introduce it at a practical level. This proposed smart parking system is simple, economic and provides effective solution to reduce parking problems and traffic congestion in our country. It is a well designed system which is easy to understand and hence will provide our citizens some relief from the

Figure 4. Basic architecture of a smart parking system

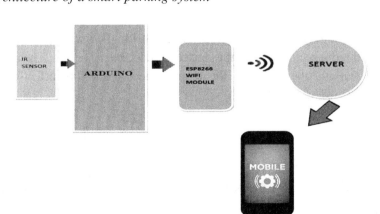

Figure 5. Mobile app for smart parking system

Figure 6. Output showing available parking slot

pain of searching for parking spaces whenever they visit outside. Due to this proportion of cars being parked on roadside will reduce and hence will reduce the unnecessary traffic. The above system is user friendly and provides real time monitoring to the people. The cost and time effective properties are the major plus points of this proposed system.

CONCLUSION

This chapter demonstrates the importance of integrating IoT with different enabling technologies such as cloud computing, big data, cyber physical systems and block chain. The sensor, actuator and computing devices of IoT ecosystem are the access points for gathering information from the dynamics of the physical world. When, these IoT devices are enabled further with other technologies, empower the human capability along with unique features, low cost and less time factors. It is observed that, the IoT network involves huge amount data generated and gathered from the physical world. Further, the sensors and device involved in the IoT ecosystem are resource constraint. In this chapter, it is addresses that, by integrating IOT systems with cloud computing, the resource constrained problems are resolves by the cloud computing services such as platform, infrastructure and software. Further, the chapter addresses that in order to offer the IoT consumers with efficient applications and services it is essential to handle the various IoT operations effectively and efficiently. The IoT operations involve data gathering, retrieval, management, processing, analysing, learning and decision making. Hence, integrating big data with IoT systems enhances the data management and knowledge discovering over the IoT data. Particularly, large scale IoT applications involving real time, dynamic analysis are highly enhanced by integration of the big data and IoT systems.

From the discussion of this chapter, it is evident that, the integration of block chain technology with IoT provides resilient, decentralized, trustable platform among wide range of IoT elements. The concept of smart contracts, Proof of work strengthens the security and privacy of the data and devices involved in IoT ecosystem. Further, with objective of IoT ecosystem to provide diverse variety of IoT applications, the integration of IoT and CPS has tremendous impact on the socio-economical dements. It is to be noted that, the integration of IoT and CPS provides affluent communication with real world and hence, the enhancement of the human life in all aspects. The chapter also discusses, the various challenges involved in integration of IoT with enabling technologies and are yet to be addressed in the future. The future scope of this chapter is to explore more efficient, reliable and cyber secure IoT frameworks. It is further essential to address various standards, practices and guidelines for handling the risk associated with IoT hardware and software. The various methodologies to handle and reduce the cyber risk associated with IoT enabling technologies are to be explored further.

REFERENCES

Alaya, M. B., Medjiah, S., Monteil, T., & Drira, K. (2015). Toward semantic interoperability in onem2m architecture. *IEEE Communications Magazine*, *53*(12), 35–41. doi:10.1109/MCOM.2015.7355582

Albano, M., Ferreira, L. L., & Delsing, J. (2016). Qos-as-a-service in the localcloud. *Proc IEEE ETFA, SOCNE Workshop*.

Anagnostopoulos, T., Zaslavsky, A., Kolomvatsos, K., Medvedev, A., Amirian, P., Morley, J., & Hadjieftymiades, S. (2017). Challenges and Opportunities of Waste Management in IoT-Enabled Smart Cities: A Survey. *IEEE Transactions on Sustainable Computing*, *2*(3), 275–289. doi:10.1109/TSUSC.2017.2691049

Antonopoulos, M. (2014). *Mastering Bitcoin: Unlocking Digital Cryptocurrencies* (1st ed.). Sebastopol, CA: O'Reilly Media, Inc.

Atzori, L., Iera, A., & Morabito, G. (2010). TheInternet of Things: A Survey. *Computer Networks*, *54*(15), 2787–2805. doi:10.1016/j.comnet.2010.05.010

Barbero, C., Zovo, P. D., & Gobbi, B. (2011). A Flexible ContextAware Reasoning Approach for IoT Applications. *IEEE 12th International Conference on Mobile Data Management*, 266–275.

Chapman, L., Young, D., Muller, C., Rose, P., Lucas, C., & Walden, J. (2014). Winter road maintenance and the internet of things. *Proceedings of the 17th International Road Weather Conference*, 18.

Chin, J., Callaghan, V., & Lam, I. (2017). Understanding and personalising smart city services using machine learning, the internet-of-things and big data. *Industrial Electronics (ISIE), 2017 IEEE 26th International Symposium on, IEEE*, 2050–2055. 10.1109/ISIE.2017.8001570

Chin, J., Callaghan, V., & Lam, I. (2017). Understanding and personalising smart city services using machine learning. *The Internet-of-Things and Big Data. IEEE 26th International Symposium on Industrial Electronics (ISIE)*, 2050-2055.

Dai, H., & Su, S. (2015). Method study on energy performance management of micro-grid under smart energy grid. *Smart Grid*, *3*(10), 895–900.

Derhamy, H., Eliasson, J., Delsing, J., & Priller, P. (2015). A survey of commercialframeworks for the internet of things. Emerging Technologies &Factory Automation (ETFA 2015), 1–8.

Distefano, S., Merlino, G., & Puliafito, A. (2012). Enabling the Cloud of Things. *Proceedings of the 2012 Sixth International Conference on Innovative Mobile and Internet Services in Ubiquitous Computing*, 858-863.

Djahel, S., Doolan, R., Muntean, G.-M., & Murphy, J. (2015). A communications-oriented perspective on traffic management systems for smart cities: Challenges and innovative approaches. *IEEE Communications Surveys and Tutorials*, *17*(1), 125–151. doi:10.1109/COMST.2014.2339817

Douceur, J. R. (2002). *The Sybil attack' in Peer-to-Peer Systems*. Berlin, Germany: Springer. doi:10.1007/3-540-45748-8_24

Eris Industries. (2016). *Documentation_Blockchains*. Available: https://docs.erisindustries.com/explainers/blockchains/

Evans, D. (2011). *The internet of things how the next evolution of the internet is changing everything*. Cisco, Tech. Report.

Feld, S., Sch¨onfeld, M., & Werner, M. (2014). Analyzing the Deployment ofBitcoin's P2P Network under an AS-level Perspective. *Procedia Computer Science*, *32*, 1121–1126. doi:10.1016/j.procs.2014.05.542

Fitzgerald, A. M. (2018). The Internet of disposable things: Throwaway paper and plastic sensors will connect everyday items. *IEEE Spectrum*, *55*(12), 30–35. doi:10.1109/MSPEC.2018.8544981

Foell, Kortuem, Rawassizadeh, Handte, Iqbal, & Marrón. (2014). Micro-navigation for urban bus passengers: Using the internet of things to improve the public transport experience. In *Proceedings of the 1st International Conference on IoT in Urban Space*. Institute for Computer Sciences, Social-Informatics and Telecommunications Engineering).

Galache, Yonezawa, Gurgen, Pavia, Grella, & Maeomichi. (2014). ClouT: Leveraging Cloud Computing Techniques for Improving Management of Massive IoT Data. *Proceedings of the 2014 IEEE 7th International Conference on Service-Oriented Computing and Applications*, 324-327.

Garcia Lopez, P., Montresor, A., Epema, D., Datta, A., Higashino, T., Iamnitchi, A., ... Riviere, E. (2015). Edge-centriccomputing: Vision and challenges. *Computer Communication Review, 45*(5), 37–42. doi:10.1145/2831347.2831354

Gartner Says 6.4 Billion Connected "Things" Will Be in Use in 2016, Up 30 Percent From 2015. (n.d.). Retrieved from http://www.gartner.com/newsroom/id/3165317

Hachem, S., Teixeira, T., & Issarny, V. (2011). Ontologies for the internet of things. In *Proceedings of the 8thMiddleware Doctoral Symposium on - MDS '11*. ACM Press.

Hayes, M. A., & Capretz, M. A. (2014). Contextual anomaly detection in big sensor data. *Big Data (BigDataCongress), 2014 IEEE International Congress on*, 64–71.

Herbert, J., & Litchfield, A. (2015). A Novel Method for Decentralised Peerto-Peer Software License Validation Using Cryptocurrency Blockchain Technology. ACSC, 159, 27–35.

Heydon, R. (2013). *Bluetooth Low Energy*. Prentice Hall.

IoT Centric Cloud: A catalyst for innovation in Europe. (2013). *Networking Session, ICT Event 2013*.

Kapritsos, M., Wang, Y., Quema, V., Clement, A., Alvisi, L., & Dahlin, M. (2012). All about eve: Execute-verify replication for multi-core servers. *Proceedings of 10th USENIX Symp. Oper. Syst. Design Implement. (OSDI)*, 237-250.

Kindberg, T. (2002). People Places and Things: Web Presence for the Real World. *ACM J. Mobile Networks and Applications, 7*(5), 365–376.

Kovatsch, M., Hassan, Y. N., & Mayer, S. (2015). Practical semantics for theinternet of things: Physical states, device mashups, and open questions. *Internet of Things (IOT), 2015 5th International Conference on the*, 54–61.

Kusiak, A., Zhang, Z., & Verma, A. (2013). Prediction, operations, and condition monitoring in wind energy. *Energy, 60*, 1–12. doi:10.1016/j.energy.2013.07.051

Li Da, X., Wu, H., & Shancang, L. (2014). Internet of Things in industries: A survey. *IEEE Transactions on Industrial Informatics, 10*(4), 2233–2243. doi:10.1109/TII.2014.2300753

Liu, L., Liu, D., Zhang, Y., & Peng, Y. (2016). Effective sensorselection and data anomaly detection for condition monitoring of aircraft engines. *Sensors, 16*(5), 623.

Marinov, M. B., Topalov, I., Gieva, E., & Nikolov, G. (2016). Air quality monitoring in urban environments. *39th International Spring Seminar on Electronics Technology (ISSE)*, 443-448.

Mayer, S., Wilde, E., & Michahelles, F. (2015). A connective fabric forbridging internet of things silos. *Internet of Things (IOT), 2015 5thInternational Conference on the*, 148–154.

Nakamoto, S. (2008). *Bitcoin: A Peer-to-Peer Electronic Cash System*. Available: https://bitcoin.org/bitcoin.pdf

Nambi, S. N. A. U., Sarkar, C., Prasad, R. V., & Rahim, A. (2014). A unified semantic knowledge base for IoT. *2014 IEEE World Forum on Internet of Things (WFIoT)*, 575–580. 10.1109/WF-IoT.2014.6803232

Niyato, D., Hossain, E. &Camorlinga, S. (2009). Remote Patient Monitoring Service Using Heterogeneous Wireless Access Networks: Architecture and Optimization. *IEEE Journal on Selected Area in Communications*, 412-423.

Palattell, M., Accettura, N., Vilajonasa, X., Watteyne,T., Grieco, L., Boggia, G. &Dolher M.(2013) Standardized Protocol Stack for the Internet of (Important) Things. *IEEE Communication Surveys & Tutorials*, 1389-1430.

Pereira, P. P., & Eliasson, J. (2015). An Authentication and Access Control Framework for CoAP-based Internet of Things. IEEE.

Perera, C., Liu, H. I. H., Jayawardena, S., & Chen, M. (2014). A Survey on Internet of Things from Industrial Market Perspective. *IEEE Access: Practical Innovations, Open Solutions*, 2, 1660–1679. doi:10.1109/ACCESS.2015.2389854

Perera, C., Zaslavsky, A., Compton, M., Christen, P., & Georgakopoulos, D. (2013). Semantic-Driven Configuration of Internet of Things Middleware. *9th International Conference on Semantics, Knowledge and Grids*, 66–73.

Pyyk¨onen, P., Laitinen, J., Viitanen, J., Eloranta, P., & Korhonen, T. (2013). IoT for intelligent traffic system. *Intelligent Computer Communication and Processing (ICCP), 2013 IEEE International Conference on*, 175–179. 10.1109/ICCP.2013.6646104

Rajkumar, R., Insup, L., Lui, S., & Stankovic, J. (2010). Cyber-physical systems: The next computing revolution. *Proc. 47th ACM/IEEE Des.Autom. Conf. (DAC)*, 731–736.

Saneja, B., & Rani, R. (2014). An efficient approach for outlierdetection in big sensor data of health care. *International Journal of Communication Systems*.

Santana, Chaves, Gerosa, Kon, & Milojicic. (2017). Software Platforms for Smart Cities: Concepts, Requirements, Challenges, and a Unified Reference Architecture. *ACM Computing Surveys*, 50, 6.

Satyanarayanan, M. (2001). Pervasive Computing: Vision and Challenges. *IEEE Personal Comm.*, 8(4),10–17.

Satyanarayanan, M., Bahl, P., Caceres, R., & Davies, N. (2009). The Case for VM-Based Cloudlets in MobileComputing. *IEEE Pervasive Computing*, 8(4), 14–23. doi:10.1109/MPRV.2009.82

Schlechtingen, M., & Santos, I. F. (2014). Wind turbine condition monitoring based on SCADA data using normal behavior models. Part 2: Application examples. *Applied Soft Computing*, 14(C), 447–460. doi:10.1016/j.asoc.2013.09.016

Sezer, O. B., Can, S. Z., & Dogdu, E. (2015). Developmentof a smart home ontology and the implementation of asemantic sensor network simulator: An internet of things approach. *Collaboration Technologies and Systems(CTS), 2015 International Conference on, IEEE*, 12–18.

Sezer, O. B., Dogdu, E., Ozbayoglu, M., & Onal, A. (2016). An extended iot framework with semantics, big data,and analytics. In Big Data (Big Data), 2016 IEEE International Conference on, 1849–1856.

Song, Z., Cardenas, A. A., & Masuoka, R. (2010). Semantic middleware for the Internet of Things. *Proceeding of 2010 Internet of Things (IOT)*, 1–8.

Stankovic, J. A. (2014). Research Directions for the Internet of Things. *IEEE Internet of Things Journal, 1*(1), 3-9.

Swanson, T. (2015). *Consensus-as-a-service: A brief report on the emergence of permissioned, distributed ledger systems*. Tech. Rep.

Varga, P., & Heged, C. (2015). Service interaction through gateways forinter-cloud collaboration within the arrowhead framework. *Proc GWS2015*.

Violette, M. (2018). IoT Standards. *IEEE Internet of Things Magazine, 1*(1), 6-7.

Vukoli¢, M. (2015). The quest for scalable blockchain fabric: Proof-of-work vs.BFT replication. *Proc. IFIP WG 11.4 Workshop Open Res. Prob-lemsNetw. Secur. (iNetSec)*, 112-125.

Wang, W., De, S., Cassar, G., & Moessner, K. (2013). Knowledge Representation in the Internet of Things: Semantic Modelling and its Applications. *Automatika Journal for Control, Measurement, Electronics, Computing and Communications, 54*(4).

Want, R. (2014). RFID: The Key to Automating Everything. *Scientific American*, 56–65.

Xianghui, C., Peng, C., Jiming, C., & Youxian, S. (2013). An online optimization approach for control and communication codesign in networked cyber-physical systems. *IEEE Transactions on Industrial Informatics, 9*(1), 439–450. doi:10.1109/TII.2012.2216537

Zanella, A., Bui, N., Castellani, A., Vangelista, L., & Zorzi, M. (2014). Internet of things for smart cities. *IEEE Internet of Things Journal, 1*(1), 22–32.

Zhang, Y., & Wen, J. (2015). An IoT electric business model based on the protocol of bitcoin. ICIN. IEEE, 184–191.

KEY TERMS AND DEFINITIONS

Big Data: The conventional techniques to store data are relational databases and sequential data processing. These techniques are efficient to handle and process limited data size. However, in today's scenario, there is very huge data been generated, through these conventional mechanisms, whereas fail to handle huge volumes of data. As a solution to this problem, big data mechanisms and tools are effective to handle these huge volumes of data sets.

Block Chain: The block chain mechanisms perform registration and authentication of all IoT devices and IoT system operations performed.

Cloud Computing: The cloud computing enables the IoT system through the features of infrastructure, platform, and services.

Cyber Physical Systems: The cyber physical system (CPS) provides standardized platform for combining the physical objects in the IoT system and the computational components of the IoT technology.

Chapter 14

A System for Natural Language Interaction With the Heterogeneous Information Network

Phuc Do
University of Information Technology, Vietnam

ABSTRACT

In this chapter, the authors present their system, which can use natural language query to interact with heterogeneous information networks (HIN). This chapter proposes a solution combining the GraphFrames, recurrent neural network (RNN) long short-term memory (LSTM), and dependency relation of question for generating, training, understanding the question-answer pairs and selecting the best match answer for this question. The RNN-LSTM is used to generate the answer from the facts of knowledge graph. The authors need to build a training data set of question-answer pairs from a very large knowledge graph by using GraphFrames for big graph processing. To improve the performance of GraphFrames, they repartition the GraphFrames. For complicated query, they use the Stanford dependency parser to analyze the question and build the motif pattern for searching GraphFrames. They also develop a chatbot that can interact with the knowledge graph by using the natural language query. They conduct their system with question-answer generated from DBLP to prove the performance of our proposed system.

INTRODUCTION

As the appearance of large knowledge graphs (KB) such as DBpedia, Freebase, Wikipedia, DBLP, many researchers are paying more attention to question answering over knowledge graph by using the natural language query. Using natural language based query is more convenient and user friendly. Natural language query is a question such as "who is the author of paper p0001?". The answer of this question will be generated from a triples such as <subject, predicate, object> in the knowledge graph. DBLP is a bibliographic information network which is a kind on HIN. We consider DBLP as a knowledge

DOI: 10.4018/978-1-5225-8407-0.ch014

graph. DBLP contains a large volume of knowledge triples which can support the researchers to find the knowledge in a specific research area.

Large graph is a research direction of big data processing. Large graph can be considered as a big linked data. In the context of big data there are several research works to use a distributed computing system to process big data. According to (Rodrigo Agerri, 2015) a solution was proposed to process huge amount of textual data in the Natural Language Processing (NLP) research area. A new approach for scalable distributed language processing with multiple computers was proposed. Apache Hadoop is a framework to perform large scale processing. Hadoop implements MapReduce, a programming model for developing parallel and distributed algorithms that process and generates large data sets and large graph. Moreover, Hadoop and MapReduce is not faster than Apache Spark which run mainly in the memory. Apache Spark can contain one master and several workers. The tasks in workers are processed concurrently. When all workers finish their tasks, the result will be sent back to the master machine of distributed system. Nowadays, the trend of big data processing is the distributed computing on the cloud computing environment.

According to (Paolo Nesi, 2015) a distributed computing system includes computer clusters and parallel computing paradigms have been used to process data-intensive contexts such as large volume of text. A system based on Hadoop with multiple nodes and MapReduce are used to process GATE application framework. Gate is a set of tools for natural language processing. The performance of NLP processing of this system for big data processing is improved significantly.

In our system, the Stanford Parser is used to classify the question. It analyses the question and detects the number of objects in the question and based on this number, the question will be classified simple or complicated question. The RNN-LSTM model is used to find the answer for the simple question and the motif search of GraphFrames Library is used for complicated question. The answer is built based on the facts (triples) in knowledge graph. This chapter will present how to generate the question-answer pairs of training data set for training the neural network by using GraphFramesF Library of Apache Spark. This chapter explains how to build the motif pattern of motif search of GraphFrames to access the triples of large scale knowledge graph. By combining GraphFrames Library and the RNN-LSTM model, our proposed system can improve the performance and the accuracy of query. In this research, knowledge graph is considered as a large HIN and the processing of large HIN is a difficult problem of big data analysis. In knowledge graph, each triple is expressed by two vertices and arc connecting subject vertex to object vertex. The predicate name is the label of arc connecting two vertices. There are millions of triples in a knowledge graph, so the knowledge graph is really a very large graph. Graph can be saved in Neo4j Graph Database and accessed by graph query language. In Neo4j graph database, Cypher is a graph query language to query a graph database. When user gives a query, the graph database will be accessed to provide the facts for the answer. Hadoop is a good platform for distributed computing with multiples computers. Since we work with a large scale knowledge graph, GraphFrames Library of Apache Spark for processing large scale graph on Hadoop distributed computing environment is used.

According to (Yongjun Zhu, Erjia Yan, Il-Yeol-Song, 2017), Neo4j graph database is used to store the knowledge graph. The natural language query is used to access the graph database. This natural language query is converted into graph representation. Then the dependency analysis is used to analyse the question and explore the bibliographic named entity of the query sentence. Bibliographic named entities are entities in the knowledge graph such as author, paper, venue.... In a question such as "who is the author of paper p0001?", the paper p0001 is a bibliographic named entity of DBLP knowledge graph. The dependency parser is used to find the bibliographic named entity and the dependency relations between words. Finally, the graph query is converted to Cypher graph query language and access the Neo4j Graph Database. One of the advantages of this approach is the system can process all the queries of DBLP with high accuracy. However, this approach has drawbacks. The query execution time of this approach is the time for formulation the graph query and the time for accessing the graph database. This query execution time depends on the length of the query sentences. The average time in 4.8 seconds for two named entity query.

This chapter studies this method for analyzing a question. Instead of using the Cypher graph query language, GraphFrames package is used to access triples of large scale knowledge graph. GraphFrames package is a library of Apache Spark on Hadoop distributed environment. GraphFrames Library can process large graph on the distributed computing environment with high performance.

(Abdalghani Abujabal, Mohamed Yahya, Kirek Riedewald, Gerhard Weikum., 2017) proposed a template for question answering over knowledge graph. Template is a mapping between natural language question and the triples of knowledge graph. Templates are learnt from question-answer pairs based on the results of dependency parsing.

(Weiguo Zheng, Jefferey Xu Yu, Leu Zou, Hong Cheng., 2018) proposed a method to understand natural language question by using the template. Templates are automatically generated. They used a knowledge graph and a text corpus. For each triple e=(v1,r,v2) of knowledge graph, they find all sentences of text corpus that are related to a specific triple. Finally they analyse the question and save patterns and triples into a dictionary. These templates will support to provide the facts for answering the questions. We learn this idea and develop a template based on the meta-path and meta-graph of HIN to generate the training data set from the triples of knowledge graph.

Recently, several studies about natural language query of knowledge bases based on neural network have been done. Sabin Kafle et al. (2017) presented a survey about the usage of neural network framework in the knowledge based question answering system. The question and answer are represented by the embedding vectors. The triples of knowledge graph have been converted to the training data of neural network.

In neural network approaches, a training data set must be generated for training neural question answering system. (Wanyun Cui et al., 2017) discussed question answer over a knowledge base by using a natural language query. They proposed a new kind of question representation over a billion scale knowledge base and a million QA corpora. This question answer corpus contains 41 million question answer pairs crawled form Yahoo Answer. (Zhiwen Xie, Zhao Zeng, Guangyou Zhou, Tingting He., 2016) proposed a topic entity extraction (TEEM) to extract the topic entities in questions and then search the knowledge triples in knowledge base to generate the answer. Topic entity is the main entity referring to the subject of the corresponding knowledge triple in knowledge base. Convolutional Neural Network (CNN) is used to develop TEEM model. They used data set released by NLPCC-ICCPOL 2016 KBQA task which contains 14,609 question-answer pairs and a knowledge base called nlpcc-iccpol-2016.kbqa. kb containing 43M knowledge triples.

(Iulian Vlad Serban, Alberto Garcıa-Dur, Caglar Gulcehre, Sungjin Ahn, Sarath Chandar, Aaron Courville, Yoshua Bengio., 2016) developed a method to generate the question-answer corpus by using RNN with the facts of knowledge bases. One of the drawbacks of this method is a large scale graph of the knowledge base. It takes too much time to generate the question-answer pairs from facts (triples) of the knowledge graph and the time for training the RNN with large training corpus.

(LIU, Kang; FENG, Yansong., 2018) presented the recent advances of using deep neural network in question answering over knowledge graph. The user will use natural language question and the system must understand the question and propose the correct answer for this question.

There are many datasets for training and testing neural network based question answering over knowledge graph such as:

Web Questions dataset contains 5,810 question-answer pairs which are crawled via Google Suggest service and annotated with Freebase answers through Amazon Mechanical Turk.

Simple Questions dataset is built by Bordes et al. (2015) containing 108,442 question-answer. They are built by manually annotating from triples of FreeBase.

BAbI: (Jason Weston, Antoine Bordes, Sumit Chopra, Alexander M. Rush, Bart van Merrienboer, Armand Joulin & Tomas Mikolov., 2015) is a machine comprehension data sets. It contains 20 subtasks where each subtask requires different answer skill.

This chapter studies the above methods and propose a system to solve the drawbacks of the existent systems. The generation of question-answer pairs based on the facts of knowledge graph plays an important role in using the neural network for accessing knowledge graph and the time for generating the training set is a significant issue in big data processing.

It is very expensive to collect a large data set of question-answer pairs from a big data sources. This is the reason why a solution to generate question-answer pairs from large scale knowledge graph by using GraphFrames motif search on distributed computing environment is proposed in this chapter.

This chapter has following contributions for solving the natural language interaction with bibliographic information network based knowledge graph as follows:

- The bibliographic information network is considered as HIN. The instances of meta-path and meta-graph of HIN are used as the templates for generating the question- answer pairs from the triples of knowledge graph organised as HIN.
- The dependency parser is used to classify the question. If the question is simple, the RNN-LSTM model is used to generate the answer. If the question is complicated, the dependency parsing result will be used to build the motif pattern, then the GraphFrames Library uses this motif pattern to access the triples of large HIN to generate the answer.
- To generate the training question-answer data set, GraphFrames Library of Apache Spark for graph processing on Hadoop distributed computing environment is used. GraphFrames Library can process efficiently a lot of triples of a large scale HIN graph. These triples are considered as path instances of meta-path or graph instances of meta-graph. They are used to generate the question-answer pairs for training the RNN-LSTM model.
- With the combining GraphFrames Library, RNN-LSTM and dependency parser, this solution can speed up the time for generating the training dataset from triples of DBLP, the time for accessing DBLP with simple question and the accuracy of answer for complicated question.

The paper is organized as follows 1) Introduction 2) Preliminaries 3) Using GraphFrames Library to generate the questions-answer pairs for training data set 4) The Recurrent Neural Network and Long Short Term Memory 5) Using the dependency relation to analyse questions 6) Experiment and discussion 7) Conclusions

PRELIMINARIES

Definition 1 - Knowledge Graph: A knowledge graph is a directed graph G=(V, E, L) where the entities and their relations are represented by nodes and arcs. Each arc is called a triple (v1, r, v2) where v1, v2 ∈ V and r is a predicate. L is a set of predicates. (Weiguo Zheng, Jefferey Xu Yu, Leu Zou, Hong Cheng., 2018)

Definition 2 - Information Network: An information network is defined as a directed graph G = (V, E) with an object type mapping function φ: V → A and a link type mapping function ψ: E → R, where each object v ∈ V belongs to one particular object type φ (v) ∈ A, and each link e ∈ E belongs to a particular relation ψ (e) ∈ R (Chuan Shi, Yitong Li, Jiawei Zhang, Yizhou Sun, and Philip S. Yu., 2017).

Example 1: DBLP is a typical HIN. To enhance the content of DBLP, we used LDA topic model (David M. Blei, Andrew Y. Ng, Michael, I. Jordan., 2003) (Thanh Ho, 2018) to discover the topic of documents in DBLP. So, our DBLP HIN has vertex types and link types. The vertex types are Author, Paper, Topic, Venue, Word. The link types are "write", "published_at", "mention", "contain", "cite". DBLP is used as a knowledge graph for developing the neural network based question answer system.

Definition 3 - Network Schema: The network schema is a meta template for a heterogeneous network G= (V, E) with the object type mapping φ: V → A and the link mapping ψ: E → R, which is a directed graph defined over object types A, with arc as relations from R, denoted as $T_G = (A, R)$.

Example 2 - Bibliographic Information Network Schema: For a bibliographic information network defined in Example 1, the network schema of this network is shown in Figure 1. Links exist between authors and papers denoting "write" or "written-by" relations, between venues and papers denoting the "publish" or "published-at" relations, between papers and topic denoting "mention" relation, and between papers, denoting "citing" or "cited" relations, between topic and words denoting topic "contain" relation. Figure 1 shows the bibliographic network of DBLP.

DBLP knowledge graph is stored in a Neo4j graph database and latter this DBLP will be read to graph of GraphFrames.

A system to manage and process the DBLP is implemented. DBLP is stored in Neo4j graph database. This system can find the path instances of meta-path such as A→P, P→V, P→T, A→P←A, A→P→V by using the Cypher graph query language. The system can generate and visualize the citing set which is the set of papers cited by a specific paper of a cited set which is the set of papers citing a specific paper.

Definition 4 - Meta-Path: A meta-path P is a path defined on the graph of network schema T_G= (A,R), and is denoted in the form of $A_1 \xrightarrow{R1} A_2 \xrightarrow{R2} .. \xrightarrow{Rl} A_{l+1}$, which defines a composite relation R = R ° R2° . . . ° Rl between type A_1 and A_{l+1}, where ° denotes the composition operator on relations.

Some meta-paths of DBLP are listed in Table 1.
Some path instances of meta-path A →P (Author− [Write] →Paper) are listed in Table 2.
Some path instances of meta-path P→V (Paper− [Published_At] →Venue) are listed in Table 3.
Some path instances of meta path A−P→V (Author−[Write] →Paper −[Published_At] →Venue) are listed in Table 4.

Figure 1. Network Schema of Bibliographic information network

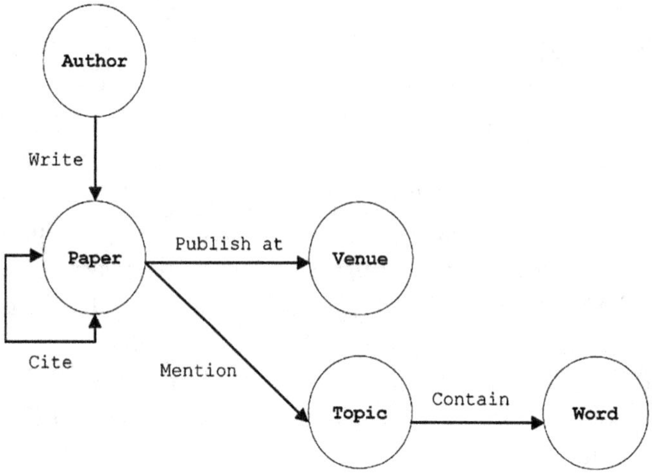

Table 1. Some meta-paths of DBLP

Meta-Path	Meaning
A→P	(Author−[Write] →Paper);
P→V	(Paper− [Published_At]-Venue),
P→T	(Paper−[Mention] →Topic),
T→W	(Topic− [Contain] →Word),
P→P	(Paper− [Cite] →Papers)
A→P→V	(Author-[Write]-Paper-[Published_At] →Venue)
P→P→V	(Paper− [Cite] →Paper)
P→P→T	(Paper− [Cite]-Paper-[Mention] →Topic)
P→T→W	(Paper− [Mention] →Topic− [Contain] →Word)
A→P→P	(Author− [Write] →Paper− [Cite] →Paper)
A→P→T→W	(Author− [Write] →Paper− [Mention]-Topics-[Contain] →Word)
A→P→P→T	(Author− [Write]-Paper→ [Cite] −Paper− [Mention]→Topic)

Table 2. Some path instances of meta-path A-P (Author- [Write]-Paper)

	Author	Paper
1	Li_Gong	Enriching_the_Expressive_Power_of_Security_Labels.
2	Xiaolei_Qian	Enriching_the_Expressive_Power_of_Security_Labels.
3	Dorothy_E._Denning	A_Lattice_Model_of_Secure_Information_Flow.
4	Rajiv_Mehrotra	Similar-Shape_Retrieval_in_Shape_Data_Management.
5	James_E._Gary	Similar-Shape_Retrieval_in_Shape_Data_Management.

Table 3. Some path instances of meta-path P →V

	Paper	Venue
1	Enriching_the_Expressive_Power_of_Security_Labels.	TKDE
2	A_Lattice_Model_of_Secure_Information_Flow.	CACM
3	A_Model-Based_Vision_System_for_Industrial_Parts.	COMPUTER
4	An_Intelligent_Image_Database_System.	TC
5	An_Intelligent_Image_Database_System.	TSE

Table 4. Some path instances of meta path A−P→V

	Author	Paper	Venue
1	Li_Gong	Enriching_the_Expressive_Power_of_Security_Labels.	TKDE
2	Xiaolei_Qian	Enriching_the_Expressive_Power_of_Security_Labels.	TKDE
3	Dorothy_E._Denning	A_Lattice_Model_of_Secure_Information_Flow.	CACM
4	Rajiv_Mehrotra	Similar-Shape_Retrieval_in_Shape_Data_Management.	COMPUTER
5	James_E._Gary	Similar-Shape_Retrieval_in_Shape_Data_Management.	COMPUTER

Definition 4. Meta-Graph: A meta-graph S is a directed acyclic graph (DAG) with a single source node n_s (i.e. with in-degree 0) and a single sink (target) node n_t (i.e., with out-degree= 0), defined on an HIN schema T_G = (L; R). Formally, S = (N; M; n_s; n_t), where N is a set of nodes and M is a set of edges.

Meta-path is a special case of meta-graph. We consider meta-graph as a meaningful combination of meta-path. The following meta-graph is the combination of meta-path A-P-T with meta-path A-P-T. (Zhipeng Huang, Yudian Zheng, Reynold Cheng, Yizhou Sun, Nikos Mamoulis, and Xiang Li., 2016).

This meta-graph can be changed to the question such as "who is the author of two different papers mentioning the same topic?" is in Figure 2.

USING GRAPHFRAMES LIBRARY TO GENERATE QUESTION - ANSWER PAIRS FOR TRAINING NEURAL NETWORK

Apache Spark and GraphX

According to (Yadav., Rishi, 2015), Apache Spark is a general purpose computer system to process big data on distributed computing environment. In (Paolo Nesi, 2015), a Hadoop based platform was developed for natural language processing. Map Reduce was developed on the Hadoop environment to process large text data set. Apache Spark is used to develop the proposed system, because Apache Spark is faster than Hadoop Map Reduce ((Yadav., Rishi, 2015). Apache Spark was developed by the AMPLab, University of Berkeley in 2009. Spark uses memory both to compute and stores objects in computing

Figure 2. A typical meta–graph

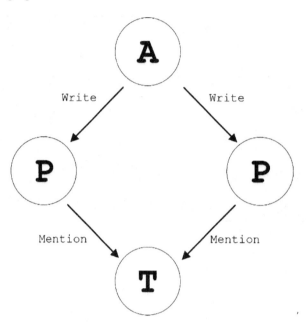

process. Apache Spark can work with Hadoop Distributed File System (HDFS). Apache Spark provides libraries for SparkSQL, Spark Stream, GraphX for graph processing, and MlLib for machine learning.

GraphX is a library of large scale graph processing system which was developed on the top of Apache Spark. Spark GraphX stores graph's edges in one file and graph's vertices in another file. Graph provides the graph processing algorithm such as: connected component, label propagation, page-rank, shortest path, strongly connected component, triangle count.

GraphFrames Library

GraphFrames Library was developed by Databricks in 2016 to process big data. GraphFrames Library is developed based on DataFrames. GraphFrames Library utilized the scalability and high performance of DataFrames on distributed computing environment. (Phuc Do, Phu Pham., 2018) used the capability of GraphFrames Library to process large scale graph on Hadoop distributed environment. In our proposed system, the motif finding of GraphFrames Library is used to search the structural patterns in a graph. DataFrames object is a dataset and organized as a table with many columns. DataFrames object looks like a table in a relational database. A DataFrames table is represented by a dataset of rows. A graph G(V,E) is represented by two DataFrames tables. One DataFrames table contains the vertices and the other contains arcs of the graph. When using GraphFrames Library, the Graph of knowledge graph is stored in two CSV files. They will be read into two DataFrames tables. These two DataFrames tables will be used to create the GraphFrames. With two DataFrames tables, we partition graph and store DataFrames in many partitions. By default, a partition is created for each Hadoop Distributed File System (HDFS) partition in block. Each block by default is 64MB. The functions of GraphFrames Library are listed as follows:

- **Breadth-First Search (BFS):** Graph traversal on bread first search
- **Motif Search:** Search for structural patterns in a graph
- **Label Propagation:** Find the community of vertices of graph
- **Triangle Count:** Count the number of triangles of graphs
- **Strong Connected Component:** Find the connected component of graph
- **Shortest Paths:** Find the shortest paths between nodes
- **PageRank:** Calculate the page-rank of all nodes in graph

These functions can be processed on distributed environment with Spark cluster. To import the DBLP which is stored in neo4j Graph Database to GraphFrames graph, we use 2 CSV files. These files are created from HIN DBLP in Neo4j graph Database. One file contains vertices and the other file contains arcs of graph.

The process of GraphFrames motif search can be described in Algorithm 1.

Example 3: We can list all the authors of DBLP who wrote two different papers with the same topic and they are published at the same venue (see Figure 3) by using the following motif search of GraphFrames Library:

```
MotifPattern = "(a)-[e1]->(p1);(a)-[e2]->(p2);
                    (p1)-[e3]->(v); (p2)-[e4]->(v);
                    (p1)-[e4]->(t); (p2)-[e5]->(t);"
filter_pattern= "a.vertextype='Author'
                    and p1.vertextype='Paper'  and  p2.vertextype='Paper'
and
                    and v.vertextype='Venue'  and  t.vertextype='Topic' "
FieldList="a.id,p1.id,p2.id,v.id,t.id"
ResultList= GraphFramesMotifSearch(MotifPattern, FilterPattern,FieldList)
```

Algorithm 1. Pseudo code for Motif Search of GraphFrames

```
Input:  MotifSearchPattern is the pattern which can be used Graph.Find() of
GraphFrames, FilterPattern is the pattern which can be used as a criteria for
filtering the result, FieldList is the pattern which can be used in select
phrase to choose the output .
Output: ResultList is the result of Motif Search of GraphFrames package
1: Function GraphFramesMotifSearch(var MotifPattern, var FilterPattern,var
FieldList):
2:  motifs = GRAPH.find(MotifPattern)
3:  Results =Motifs.Filter(FilterPattern)
4:  ResultList = Results.Select(FieldList).Collect();
5:  Return ResultList;
17: End Function
```

Figure 3. Meta-graph in example 3

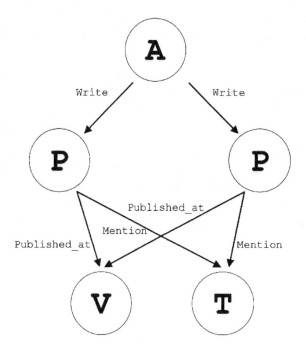

```
GraphFrames Library runs on Spark cluster with one Master and many worker
nodes.
```

The vertices DataFrames table and arcs DataFrames table of large HIN are divided into several partitions based on the number of workers. The task for accessing the knowledge graph will be executed on workers. Normally, the "join" operation is executed in each worker on a part of vertices DataFrames

Figure 4. The Spatk Cluster for GaphFrames Package

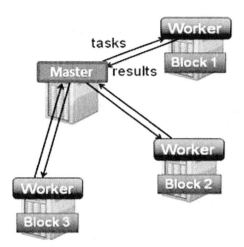

table and arc DataFrames table. When tasks finished, they will move the results back to the Master as shown in Figure 4.

Using Meta-Path as a Template for Generating Question-Answer Pairs

Generating Question - Answer Pairs From Path Instances of Meta-Path

In this session, we used the meta-path as a template to generate the question-answer pairs for training the neural network. We have the following meta-paths:

A→P (Author−[Write]→Paper)
P→V (Paper−[Published_At]→Venue),
P→T(Paper− [Mention]→Topic),
T→W (Topic− [Contain]→Word),

We may have question that is related to the first entity or second entity. The questions associate with the meta-paths are listed in Table 5.

With meta-path A→P (Author-[Write] →Paper), the question relating to the first entity is " Who are the authors of paper P?" and the question relating to the second entity is "What are the papers of author A?". The Who question is used with author entity and What question is used with the Paper entity.

With P→V (Paper− [Published_At] →Venue), the question relating to the first entity is " What are the papers of venue V? " and the question relates the second entity is "What are the venues of paper P?". What question is used with paper entity and venue entity.

With P→T(Paper− [Mention] →Topic), the question relating to the first entity is " What are the papers of topic T? " and the question relating to the second entity is "What are the topics of paper P?". The "What" question is used with paper entity and topic entity.

With meta-path T→W (Topic− [Contain] →Word), the question relating to the first entity is "What are the topic of word W?" and the question relating to the second entity is "What are the words of topic T?". The what question is used with topic entity and word entity.

For a particular answer, we may have several questions, for example. Two following questions will have same answers:

Who are the authors of paper P?

Who wrote paper P?

or

What is the venue of paper P?

Table 5. The associate questions of meta-paths

Meta-Paths	Question
A → P	Who are the authors of paper P?
P → V	What are the papers published at venue V?
P → T	What are the papers mentioning topic T?
T → W	What are the topics of word W?

Where is paper P published?

Algorithm for Generating Question-Answer Pair Based on Meta-Path

Algorithm 2 is used to generate question - answer pair from meta-path. This algorithm uses the Graph-Frames Motif Search to find the path instances of a meta-path. GraphFrames motif search can access efficiently path instances in Hadoop distributed environment.

Meta Path A→P (Author → Paper)

The following motif search to generate the question-answer pairs related to the path instances of meta-path A→P is used as follows.

```
MotifPattern=" (a) - [e] -> (p) "
FilterPattern="a.vertextype='Author' and p.vertextype='Paper' "
FieldList="a.id,p.id"
question="who is the author of paper"
answer="is the author of paper"
Relation="Write"
file =relation+".txt"
```

Algorithm 2. Pseudo code for generating question-answer pair from meta-path by using GraphFrames

```
Input: MotifSearchPattern is the pattern which can be used Graph.Find() of
GraphFrames, FilterPattern is the pattern which can be used as a criteria for
filtering the result, FieldList is the pattern which can be used in select
phrase to choose the output .
Output: ResultList is the result of Motif Search of GraphFrames package
1: Function CreateQuestionAnswerPairMetaPath(MotifPattern, FilterPattern,Field
List,relation, question,anwser,file)
2: ResultList = GraphFramesMotifSearch(MotifPattern, FilterPattern, FieldList)
3: i=1
4: For p in  ResultsList:
5: vertexAid=str(p[0])
6: vertexBid=str(p[1])
7: Temp1= vertexAid+"-[relation]->"+vertexBid
8: Temp2= str(i)+ vertexAid +answer+vertexBid
9: Temp3 = str(i+1)+question+vertexAid+ "?"+"\t"+vertexBid+"\t"+str(i)
10: WriteFile(Temp1,Temp2,Temp3,file)
11:  i=i+2
12: End for
13: Return
14: End Function
```

```
CreateQuestionAnswerPair(MotifPattern, FilterPattern,FieldList,relation,
          question,anwser,file)
```

The above statements will execute a motif search to scan the whole HIN and select the path instances of meta path A-[write]→P where A is the Author vertex, P is a Paper vertex.

With this motif pattern, a list of question-answer pairs are as follows

8925 a6047 is the author of paper p1287.
8926 who is the author of paper p1287? a6047 8925
8929 a6160 is the author of paper p1334.
8930 who is the author of paper p1334? a6160 8929
8933 a6159 is the author of paper p1334.
8934 who is the author of paper p1334? a6159 8933
"8925 a6047 is the author of paper p1287" expresses facts "a6047-[write]->p1287" of knowledge graph

where 8925 is the order number of sentence, a6047 is the authorId extracted from path instance, p1287 is the paperID extracted from path instance.

Meta Path P→V (Paper – [Published_At]→Venue)

For the meta path P-V with paper P and venue V, the following motif search is used to generate the question-answer pairs related to the path instances of meta path P-V.

```
MotifPattern="(p)-[e]→(v)"
FilterPattern="p.vertextype='Paper' and v.vertextype='Venue'"
FieldList=""p.id","v.id""
question=" what is the venue of paper "
answer=" is the venue of paper "
Relation="Published_At"
file =relation+".txt"
CreateQuestionAnswerPair(MotifPattern, FilterPattern,FieldList,relation,
                    question,anwser,file)
```

The above statements will execute a motif search to scan the whole HIN and select the path instances of meta path P-[published_at] →V where P is the paper vertex, V is a venue vertex. Based on these path instances, question-answer pairs are generated as follows:

409 v3826 is the venue of paper p354.
410 what is the venue of paper p354? v3826 409
411 p354 is published at v3826.
412 where is paper p354 published? v3826 411

Meta Path P→T (Paper –[Mention]->Topic)

For the meta path P→T with paper P and topic T, the following motif search is used to generate the question-answer pairs related to the path instances of meta path P→T.

```
MotifPattern=" (p)-[e] → (t)"
FilterPattern="p.vertextype='Paper' and v.vertextype='Topic'"
FieldList=""p.id","t.id""
question=" what is the topic of paper "
answer=" paper mentions topic "
Relation="Published_At"
file =relation+".txt"
CreateQuestionAnswerPair(MotifPattern, FilterPattern,FieldList,relation,
                    question,anwser,file)
```

The above statements will execute a motif search to scan the whole HIN and select the path instances of meta path P-[mention]→T where P is the paper vertex, T is a topic vertex. Based on these path instances, question-answer pairs are generated as follows:

48589 2316 paper mentions topic 162
48590 What is the topic of paper 2316? 162 48589
48591 2537 paper mentions topic 162
48592 What is the topic of paper 2537? 162 48591

Meta Path T→W (Topic –[Contain]→Word)

For the meta path T→W with topic T and word W, the following motif search is used to generate the question-answer pairs related to the path instances of meta path T-W.

```
MotifPattern=" (t)-[e]→(w)"
FilterPattern="p.vertextype='Topic' and v.vertextype='Word'"
FieldList=""t.id","w.id""
question=" what word is contained in topic "
answer=" topic contains word "
Relation="contain"
file =relation+".txt"
CreateQuestionAnswerPair(MotifPattern, FilterPattern,FieldList,relation,
          question,anwser,file)
```

The above statements will execute a motif search to scan the whole HIN and select the path instances of meta path T−[contain]→W where T is the "topic" vertex, W is a word vertex. Based on these path instances, question-answer pairs are generated as follows:

99 topic 254 contains word 274

100 What word is contained in topic 254? 274 99

101 254 topic contains word 262

102 What word is contained in topic 254? 262 101

Meta-Graph

Algorithm 3 is used to generate question - answer pair from meta-graph. In DBLP HIN, the meta-graph for author who writes 2 papers published at the same venue is shown in Figure 5.

Motif search can be used to generate the graph instances of the above meta-graph as follows:

```
MotifPattern = GRAPH.find("(a)-[e1]->(p1);(a)-[e2]->(p2); (p1)-[e3]->(v);(p2)-
[e4]->(v)")
FilterPattern = "a.vertextype='Author' and p1.vertextype='Paper' and
v.vertextype='Venue' and p2.vertextype='Paper' "
FieldList="a.id,p1.id,p2.id,v.id"
message1=" has paper "
message2=" and paper "
message3="  which are published at venue "
```

Algorithm 3. Pseudo code for generating question-answer pair from meta-path by using GraphFrames

```
Input:  MotifSearchPattern is the pattern which can be used Graph.Find() of
GraphFrames, FilterPattern is the pattern which can be used as a criteria for
filtering the result, FieldList is the pattern which can be used in select
phrase to choose the output .
Output: ResultList is the result of Motif Search of GraphFrames package
1: Function CreateQuestionAnswerPairMetaGraph(MotifPattern,
FilterPattern,FieldList, rmessage1,message2,message3,file)
2: ResultList = GraphFramesMotifSearch(MotifPattern, FilterPattern, FieldList)
3: i=1
4: For p in  ResultsList:
5: vertexAid=str(p[0])
6: vertexBid=str(p[1])
7: vertexCid=str(p[2])
8: vertexDid=str(p[3])
9: Temp1= str(i)+ vertexAid +message1+vertexBid  +message2+vertexCid + mes-
sage3+ vertexDid
10:  WriteFile(Temp1,file)
11:  i=i+1
12: End for
13: Return
14: End Function
```

```
relation="metagraph"
file = relation+".txt"
CreateQuestionAnswerPairMetaGraph(MotifPattern, FilterPattern,FieldList,
            rmessage1,message2,message3,file)
```

The graph instances are listed as follows:

a5617 has paper p1099 and paper p1199, which are published at venue v1099
a5618 has paper p1099 and paper p1199, which are published at venue v1099
a9086 has paper p2692 and paper p3692, which are published at venue v2692
a9087 has paper p2692 and paper p3692, which are published at venue v2692
a3791 has paper p338 and paper p4338, which are published at venue v338
a3789 has paper p338 and paper p4338, which are published at venue v338
a3790 has paper p338 and paper p4338, which are published at venue v338

RECURRENT NEURAL-NETWORK AND LONG SHORT TERM MEMORY

The Deep Neural Network (DNN) is a neural network model that can learn vector-to-vector mappings (Rafal Jozefowicz, Wojciech Zaremba, Ilya Sutskever., 2015). The Recurrent Neural Network (RNN) is a DNN that is adapted to sequence data, RNN can process sequential data modeling to identify and predict sequence. This structure allows the RNN to store, memorize and complex sequence processing over a long time. RNNs can map an input sequences to the output sequence step by step and predict the sequence in the next step. RNNs maintain a vector of activations for each time step, which makes the RNN extremely difficult to train. Many studies focus on solving the difficulty of training RNN.

Figure 5. Meta - graph for author who writes 2 papers published at the same venue

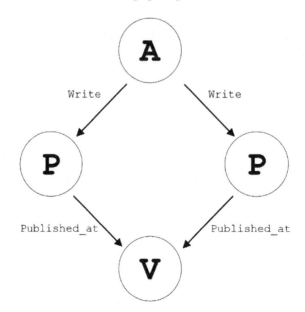

Figure 6. LSTM block

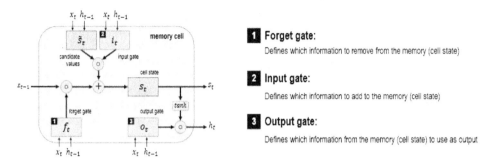

According to (Giancarlo Zaccone, Md. Rezaul Karim, Ahmed Menshawy., 2017), LSTM is a special RNN. LSTM was developed by Hochreiter and Schmidhuber in 1997. LSTM composes of LSTM blocks (cells). Each LSTM block contains three type of gates: input gate, output gate and forget gate. These gates allow LSTM block to remember information. In our proposed system, LSTM model is used as a sequence2sequence translator. It means that the proposed system will translate an input sequence into an output sequence. In our system, we want to translate the question to the answer. A LSTM layer will contain the weight matrices. LSTM model is trained by using the feed forward function and the training data set. The number of training loops is determined by training Epochs. The LSTM's output is typically taken to be h_t, and c_t is not exposed. The training process is the feed forward algorithm. It bases on the value of weighted matrices to calculate the output matrix of each LSTM block. LSTM composes of LSTM blocks (cells). Each LSTM block contains three type of gates: input gate, output gate and forget gate (see Figure 6). These gates allow LSTM block to remember information. We used LSTM model as a sequence2sequence translator. We want to translate the question to the answer.

Representing Words of Question

We use the Glove to represent words of question. We download Glove vectors from Glove's Website (https://nlp.stanford.edu/projects/glove/). This is a pre-trained model (Dennis Lukovnikov, Asja Fischer, Jens Lehmann, Soren Auer., 2017). Each word w_t of question is represented as a d-dimensional vector. This vector is accessed from the pre-training Glove model. With d =50, we have the word embeddings as follows:

football

[-1.8209 0.70094 -1.1403 0.34363 -0.42266 -0.92479 -1.3942 0.28512 -0.78416

-0.52579 0.89627 0.35899 -0.80087 -0.34636 1.0854 -0.087046 0.63411 1.1429

-1.6264 0.41326 -1.1283 -0.16645 0.17424 0.99585 -0.81838 -1.7724 0.078281

0.13382 -0.59779 -0.45068 2.5474 1.0693 -0.27017 -0.75646 0.24757 1.0261

0.11329 0.17668 -0.23257 -1.1561 -0.10665 -0.25377 -0.65102 0.32393 -0.58262

0.88137 -0.13465 0.96903 -0.076259 -0.59909]

to

[0.68047 -0.039263 0.30186 -0.17792 0.42962 0.032246 -0.41376 0.13228

-0.29847 -0.085253 0.17118 0.22419 -0.10046 -0.43653 0.33418 0.67846

0.057204 -0.34448 -0.42785 -0.43275 0.55963 0.10032 0.18677 -0.26854

0.037334 -2.0932 0.22171 -0.39868 0.20912 -0.55725 3.8826 0.47466

-0.95658 -0.37788 0.20869 -0.32752 0.12751 0.088359 0.16351 -0.21634

-0.094375 0.018324 0.21048 -0.03088 -0.19722 0.082279 -0.09434 -0.073297

-0.064699 -0.26044]

Glove covers 400,000 words, some words in question does not exist in Glove. For example with the question, "what is the author of paper p001?". In this question, word p0001 does not exist in the Globe. So, we will discard this word. We test the word in the Globe, if Globe contains word, we access the word embedding of this word in the glove.

Binary vector can be used to represent word. First the question-answer pairs are scanned to make the input vocabulary and output vocabulary. These question-answer pairs are used to calculate the input vocabulary, output vocabulary, the binary vector of word, question and answer.

1. Sun writes paper p123 .
2. who is the author of paper p123 ? -> sun 1
3. the genre of paper p345 is drama .
4. what is the genre of paper p345 ? -> drama 3
5. the language of paper p345 is English .
6. what is the language of paper p345 ? -> English 5
7. the release year of paper p345 is 1984 .
8. what is release year of paper p345 ? -> 1984 7
9. the star actor of movies m345 is john .
10. who is the star actor of movies m345 ? -> john 9

The input vocabulary of these above sentences is listed as shown in Box 1.

This input vocabulary can be used as a vector space to encode the word. Each word will be represented by a binary vector with the value 1 for the jth- component where j is the index of this word in input vocabulary. The binary vector word "Author" is as shown in Box 2.

When using the binary vector for word representation, we scan the question-answer pairs and store all the words in question-answer pair in input vocabulary.

Box 1.

0		6	Drama	12	M345	18	Phuc	24	Writes
1	.	7	English	13	movies	19	Release	25	year
2	1984	8	Genre	14	Of	20	Star		
3	?	9	Is	15	P123	21	The		
4	Actor	10	John	16	P345	22	What		
5	Author	11	Language	17	Paper	23	Who		

Box 2.

	0	1	2	3	4	5	6	7	8	9	10	11	12	13	14	15	16	17	18	19	20	21	22	23	24	25
Author	0	0	0	0	0	1	0	0	0	0	0	0	0	0	0	0	0	0	0	0	0	0	0	0	0	0

We discover that the number of words to be encoded in binary vector is greater than number of Glove encoded words. Therefore, the binary encoding mechanism is more flexible than Glove embedding. However the dimension of binary vector will be long if there are many different words in question-answer pairs of data set.

Representing Questions

Each word wt of question is represented as a d-dimensional vector. This vector is accessed from the pre-word2Vec model as Glove. A question is an ordered sequence of word such as sentence s= w1 w2 w3... wk. The question "Where is John?" will be encoded by embedding vectors as follows:

where

[6.9237e-01 4.4971e-01 -2.0293e-01 -1.6783e-01 3.0503e-01 -4.8760e-01 -6.9028e-01

1.8163e-01 -1.6295e-01 -4.7477e-01 -3.3044e-03 -6.5208e-01 -1.0148e-01 -5.7510e-01

3.0189e-01 3.5639e-01 2.8629e-01 4.7367e-01 -7.1456e-01 -1.8865e-02 1.7096e-01

2.7097e-01 1.9071e-01 7.6326e-01 -1.7586e-01 -1.7981e+00 -3.3722e-01 2.7325e-01

5.4095e-02 -5.2350e-01 3.4908e+00 -2.7619e-02 -2.3949e-01 -8.6976e-01 2.6612e-01

8.7956e-02 -1.9885e-01 1.8534e-01 4.3250e-01 4.1208e-01 -3.9190e-01 2.2857e-01

7.3443e-02 1.0901e-01 -2.3495e-01 1.6082e-01 -1.6364e-02 -1.0347e+00 -2.4160e-01

-4.8680e-01]

is

[6.1850e-01 6.4254e-01 -4.6552e-01 3.7570e-01 7.4838e-01 5.3739e-01 2.2239e-03

-6.0577e-01 2.6408e-01 1.1703e-01 4.3722e-01 2.0092e-01 -5.7859e-02 -3.4589e-01

2.1664e-01 5.8573e-01 5.3919e-01 6.9490e-01 -1.5618e-01 5.5830e-02 -6.0515e-01

-2.8997e-01 -2.5594e-02 5.5593e-01 2.5356e-01 -1.9612e+00 -5.1381e-01 6.9096e-01

6.6246e-02 -5.4224e-02 3.7871e+00 -7.7403e-01 -1.2689e-01 -5.1465e-01 6.6705e-02

-3.2933e-01 1.3483e-01 1.9049e-01 1.3812e-01 -2.1503e-01 -1.6573e-02 3.1200e-01

-3.3189e-01 -2.6001e-02 -3.8203e-01 1.9403e-01 -1.2466e-01 -2.7557e-01 3.0899e-01

4.8497e-01]

john

[-6.1106e-02 9.2698e-01 -2.4740e-02 -8.2404e-01 3.5838e-01 5.1235e-01 -1.7368e+00

-7.7074e-02 -5.2803e-01 -9.1106e-01 -8.9816e-01 1.3488e+00 -5.2135e-01 -6.8333e-01

-6.1652e-05 -2.2163e-01 3.4219e-02 -8.0921e-01 -1.0316e+00 -3.3231e-01 -2.6263e-01

2.1177e-01 -1.6616e-01 -6.3857e-01 5.6367e-02 -1.8269e+00 -1.9825e-01 -9.0269e-01

-7.0902e-01 5.5313e-01 1.7004e+00 -7.5809e-01 5.5337e-03 -6.1740e-01 5.4148e-01

-4.1653e-01 2.9324e-01 -2.4988e-01 2.9099e-01 -4.1196e-01 5.5186e-01 1.1609e+00

-1.0677e+00 -2.3122e-01 2.8835e-01 7.2285e-01 -5.9046e-01 -9.2790e-01 -8.2795e-01

1.0663e+00]

?

[-1.4578e-01 5.0459e-01 4.7525e-02 -4.6463e-01 4.4249e-01 -1.6772e-01 -4.0334e-01

-3.9223e-01 -4.1543e-01 2.7637e-01 -6.3027e-01 6.9033e-01 -4.5441e-01 1.5845e-03

1.3120e+00 5.2413e-01 3.7380e-01 2.8156e-01 -4.0563e-03 -5.2664e-01 -5.7061e-01

3.6561e-01 5.9174e-01 3.4713e-01 4.5009e-01 -2.1454e+00 -1.3795e+00 3.0700e-01

1.4876e+00 -9.6313e-01 2.8403e+00 5.0247e-01 -8.6752e-01 6.4130e-02 -3.6376e-01

-1.4019e-01 1.1975e-01 -4.5442e-02 7.2682e-01 -4.4447e-01 -2.7226e-01 1.5030e-01

1.1489e-01 7.1237e-01 1.1341e-01 2.2835e-01 -4.0801e-02 -4.1468e-01 1.1054e-01

1.1681e+00]

With the binary vector, the sentence representation is as shown in Box 3.

Representing Answer of Question-Answer Pairs

The keywords of answers are listed as shown in Box 4.

The answer is coded as a binary vector with the value 1 of the jth-component where j is the index on answer. With the question-answer:

1.   1 Sun writes paper p123 .
2.   2 who is the author of paper p123 ? -> sun 1

The binary vector for the answer will be <0,0,0,1>
If we use the embedding model, the keyword of answers is bedroom and the answer is coded as follows: bedroom

[1.0657 0.72647 0.25544 -0.74902 1.0527 0.14292 -0.66961 -0.20144 -0.53611

Box 3.

	0	1	2	3	4	5	6	7	8	9	10	11	12	13	14	15	16	17	18	19	20	21	22	23	24	25
Sun	0	0	0	0	0	0	0	0	0	0	0	0	0	0	0	0	0	0	1	0	0	0	0	0	0	0
writes	0	0	0	0	0	0	0	0	0	0	0	0	0	0	0	0	0	0	0	0	0	0	0	0	1	0
Paper	0	0	0	0	0	0	0	0	0	0	0	0	0	0	0	0	0	1	0	0	0	0	0	0	0	0
P123	0	0	0	0	0	0	0	0	0	0	0	0	0	0	0	1	0	0	0	0	0	0	0	0	0	0
.	0	1	0	0	0	0	0	0	0	0	0	0	0	0	0	0	0	0	0	0	0	0	0	0	0	0
who	0	0	0	0	0	0	0	0	0	0	0	0	0	0	0	0	0	0	0	0	0	0	0	1	0	0
Is	0	0	0	0	0	0	0	0	0	1	0	0	0	0	0	0	0	0	0	0	0	0	0	0	0	0
The	0	0	0	0	0	0	0	0	0	0	0	0	0	0	0	0	0	0	0	0	1	0	0	0	0	0
Author	0	0	0	0	0	1	0	0	0	0	0	0	0	0	0	0	0	0	0	0	0	0	0	0	0	0
Of	0	0	0	0	0	0	0	0	0	0	0	0	0	1	0	0	0	0	0	0	0	0	0	0	0	0
Paper	0	0	0	0	0	0	0	0	0	0	0	0	0	0	0	0	0	1	0	0	0	0	0	0	0	0
P123	0	0	0	0	0	0	0	0	0	0	0	0	0	0	0	1	0	0	0	0	0	0	0	0	0	0
?	0	0	0	1	0	0	0	0	0	0	0	0	0	0	0	0	0	0	0	0	0	0	0	0	0	0

Box 4.

0	1	2	3	4
1984	Drama	English	John	Sun

-0.061052 -1.1714 -0.68148 0.15074 0.5099 0.6523 0.54193 -0.65898 0.25774

0.61302 -0.41448 0.77832 1.5309 -1.1495 0.45295 -0.55471 -0.29468 -0.28287

0.88688 0.69938 -0.4333 1.5905 -0.31955 0.32229 0.35761 0.80771 1.1232

0.48697 0.12981 1.0354 -0.7582 0.13029 0.34778 0.022731 0.78253 -0.33915

-0.23697 0.27324 -2.2262 0.05615 -0.19115]

USING THE DEPENDENCY GRAPH TO ANALYZE THE QUESTIONS

There are some complicated questions such as the question generated with motif-graph will have the wrong answer. In this case, we use the GraphFrames Package to access the large HIN. To classify a question is simple or complicate, a Stanford parser is used to classify a question is simple or complicated. If the question contains only one object, the question will be fed to RNN-LSTM model, otherwise a motif pattern will be generated based on the result of dependency parsing, then the GraphFrames motif search will be executed to scan large HIN to generate the facts for the answer.

The Stanford typed dependencies graph represents all sentence relationships uniformly as typed dependency relations. That is, as triples of a relation between pairs of words. The dependency parsing is to analyze syntactic dependency structure of an input sentence (Yongjun Zhu et al. 2017) The problem of find the dependency graph of a sentence can be stated as: Given a sentence $x = w_0\ w_1, \ldots, w_n$ where w_0 is a root node. Create a dependency graph $G = (V, A)$ for sentence x where $V = \{0, 1, \ldots, n\}$ is the vertex set, A is the set of arcs, i.e., $(i, j, k) \in A$ represents a dependency relation from word w_i to word w_j with label l_k of label set L.

There are 37 universal grammatical relations. They have three types of structures such as nominal, clauses, modifier words and function words. Some of them are listed in Table 6.

Example 4: With the query question "Who is the author of paper p0001?", the dependency graph of this question is in shown in Figure 7 and Table 7.

There are two kinds of nodes. They are author (nsubject) and paper (nobject). From the dictionary, relationship between them is Write relation, and the triple <subject,predicate,object> is discovered with edge=6:paper->7:p0001 with nn, the constraint of paper is paper="p0001". The number of objects in this question is one, we call this question is a simple question. The question will be encoded by Word2vec

Table 6. Some dependency relations of dependency parser

#	Abbreviation	Meanings
1	Nsubj (nominal subject).	A nominal subject is a noun phrase which is the syntactic subject of a clause
2	iobj (indirect object).	The indirect object of a VP is the noun phrase which is the (dative) object of the verb
3	csubj (clausal subject)	A clausal subject is a clausal syntactic subject of a clause, i.e., the subject is itself a clause.
4	Ccomp (clausal complement).	A clausal complement of a verb or adjective is a dependent clause with an internal subject which functions like an object of the verb, or adjective.
5	Nsubjpass (passive nominal subject)	A noun compound modifier of an NP is any noun that serves to modify the head noun.
6	Nn (noun compound modifier).	A noun compound modifier of an NP is any noun that serves to modify the head noun.
7	Det (determiner)	A determiner is the relation between the head of an NP and its determiner.
8	Advmod (adverb modifier).	An adverb modifier of a word is a (non-clausal) adverb or adverb-headed phrase that serves to modify the meaning of the word.
9	Pobj (object of a preposition).	The object of a preposition is the head of a noun phrase following the preposition, or the adverbs "here" and "there". (The preposition in turn may be modifying a noun, verb, etc.)

Table 7. Vertices and arcs of dependency graph of the simple question

Vertices	Arcs
1:Who WP _ 2 attr	arc =1:who→2:be with attr
2: is VBZ _ 0 null	arc =3:the→4:author with det
3:the DT _ 4 det	arc =4:author→2:be with nsubj
4:author NN _ 2 nsubj	arc =5:of→4:author with prep
5: of IN _ 4 prep	arc =6:paper→7:p0001 with nn
6: paper NN _ 7 nn	arc =7:x→5:of with pobj
7: p0001 NN _ 5 pobj	arc =8:? →2:be with punct
8: ? . _ 2 punct	

model and it is fed to RNN-LSTM to generate the answer. Figure 7 is the dependency graph of question Who is the author of paper p0001?. Table 7 contains the vertices and arcs of this dependency graph.

Example 5: With the query question "Who wrote paper p0001 which is published at v0001 ?". The dependency graph of this question is in Figure 8. The vertices and arcs of this dependency graph is shown in Table 8.

The number of objects in this question is two (greater than one), this question is called a complicated question. The question will be encoded by GraphFrames motif search as follows:

Figure 7. Dependency Parsing result of the simple question

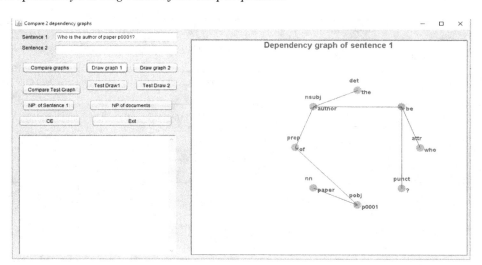

Table 8. Vertices and arcs of dependency graph for complicated question

Vertices	Arcs
1:Who WP _ 2 nsubj	arc=1:who→2:write with nsubj
2:wrote VBD _ 0 null	arc =3:paper→4:p0001 with nn
3:paper NN _ 4 nn	arc =4:p0001→2:write with dobj
4:p0001 NN _ 2 dobj	arc =5:which→7:publish with nsubjpass
5:which WDT _ 7 nsubjpass	arc =6:be→7:publish with auxpass
6:is VBZ _ 7 auxpass	arc =7:publish→4:p0001 with rcmod
7:published VBN _ 4 rcmod	arc =8:at→7:publish with prep
8:at IN _ 7 prep	arc =9:venue→10:v0001 with nn
9:venue NN _ 10 nn	arc =10:v0001→8:at with pobj
10:v0001 NN _ 8 pobj	arc =11:? →2:write with punct
11:? . _ 2 punct	

```
motifs = GRAPH.find("(a)-[e]->(p); (p)-[e2]->(v)")
filter_pattern= "a.vertextype='Author' and p.vertextype='Paper' and
v.vertextype='v0001' "
results=motifs.filter(filter_pattern)
resultsList=results.select("a.id","p.id","v.id")
```

This motif search will access the large HIN to collect facts for gnerating the answer of the queston.

We hold that the symbol to identify the simple and the complicated question is the number of objects in question. If this number of objects is greater or equal to 2, the question is complicated, otherwise it is a simple question.

Figure 8. Dependency Parsing result for complicated question

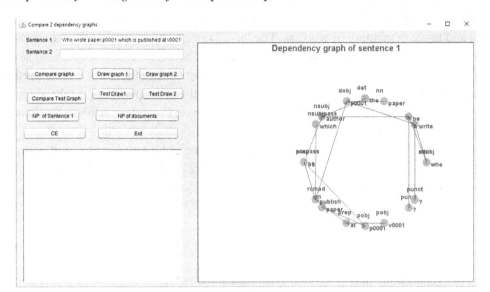

EXPERIMENT AND DISCUSSION

To evaluate our proposed method which use GraphFrames Library on Hadoop distributed environment to generate the training data set for RNN-LSTM based natural question-answer system.

Dataset

A portion of DBLP-Citation-network V3: 117,210 vertices and 529,968 citation relationships (2010-10-22) is used for testing. This DBLP was downloaded from Aminer website (https://aminer.org/citation) and store DBLP in Neo4j graph database.

The Distributed Environment for Running GraphFrames Library

The GraphFrames Library is used to generate question-answer pairs. The GraphFrames Library runs on Hadoop Spark cluster with one master and 3 worker nodes. The task for accessing the knowledge graph will be executed on workers. Normally, they are join operations. Because most of arcs of the same source vertices are in the same partition, the "join: operation can be executed without moving the arcs among partitions. When tasks finished, they will move the results back to the Master.

Improving the Performance of GraphFrames Motif Search by Repartition

In this session, we divide the graph into several partitions for distributed processing. As mentioned above, each graph in GraphFrames graph is represented by two DataFrames tables. One DataFrames table is used to store arcs of the graph. To execute "(a)-[e]->(p); (p)-[e2]->(v)"), The first arc is (a)-[e]->(p) is joined with the second arc is (p)-[e2]->(v).

In distributed computing environment of Spark. Graph is created from two DataFrames tables for vertices and arcs. Based on the number of partitions, these DataFrames table will be partition into several small tables and move to memory of workers. The "join" operation is executed at each worker with the small part of DataFrames which is moved to the memory of worker. A loop is executed several times until the "join" operation is finished and the result will be sent back to the master. If we partition graph so that the arc (a)-[e]->(p) and arc (p)-[e2]->(v) are not in the same partition, it take significant time to move them to the same partition before joining. If they are in the same partition, the joining will be executed intermediately and the result will be returned.

In GraphFrames Library, a repartition is done by sorting the DataFrames tables containing arcs. This DataFrames table will be sorted on source vertex of arcs. After sorting, the DataFrames table containing arcs will be divided into 5 partitions by using the following Python statements:

```
EDGE_RP= EDGE.repartition(5,"src")
GFrame = GraphFrames(VERTICES,EDGE_RP)
```

Based on this repartition, most of arcs with the same source vertex will be stored in the same partition and the execution time for joining will be improved. An experiment is conducted to generate question-answer from facts of DBLP which is stored in GraphFrames tables with two scenarios.

Scenario #1, we use the default partition with 4 partitions of GraphFrames.

Scenario #2, we make repartition to 5 partitions by sorting the source vertex of arc before creating GraphFrames. A portion of 5 partitions are in Table 9.

GraphFrames Library runs on Hadoop distributed environment to generate question-answer pairs and evaluate the execution time for each meta-path as shown in Table 10. Figure 9 shows the execution time of GraphFrames motif search. The experiment proves the performance of GraphFrames with repartition based on sorting the source vertex of edges. The time for accessing GraphFrames graph with reparation is faster than the time with the default partition.

Comparing with the access time of Cypher Query language which run on a unique computer, GraphFrames can run more faster than Cypher because GraphFrames Library works on a distributed environment with one computer as master and several computers as workers.

Table 9. A portion of 5 partitions after repartition

Partition 1	Partition 2	Partition 3	Partition 4	Partition 5
52,6	96,97	133,134	194,195	1,2
52,53	96,6	133,135	194,196	1,3
52,54	96,98	133,136	194,103	1,4
52,55	96,99	133,6	194,934	1,5
52,56	96,100	133,137	194,197	1,6
52,57	96,101	133,138	194,12	1,7
52,58	96,102	133,139	194,17	1,8
52,59	96,103	133,103	194,198	1,9

Table 10. Comparison of default partition scenario and repartition scenario

Motif	Default Partition Scenario (Seconds)	Repartition Scenario (Seconds)
A → P	125.65	106.96
P → V	139.35	117.80
P → T	145.88	123.51
T → W	63.75	45.580
A → P→ V	217.02	203.731
A → P← A	264.44	231.882

Figure 9. Chart of time execution comparison of default and repartition

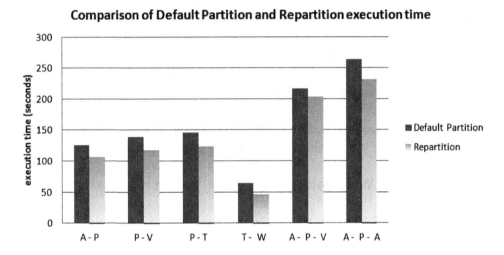

Training and Testing LSTM

Question-answer pairs are generated by using GraphFrames Library and use this data set to train the RNN-LSTM recurrent neural network. Based on the above meta-path and meta-graph, we generate the path instances and graph instances. These question – answer pairs are used to train RNN-LSTM. A sample of training data set for RNN-LSTM is as follows:

1.   v8360 is the venue of paper p2349.
2.   what is the venue of paper p2349? v8360 1
3.   p2349 is published at v8360.
4.   where is paper p2349 published? v8360 3
5.   v7539 is the venue of paper p1968.
6.   what is the venue of paper p1968? v7539 5
7.   p1968 is published at v7539.
8.   where is paper p1968 published? v7539 7
9.   v9954 is the venue of paper p3057.

10. what is the venue of paper p3057? v9954 9
11. p3057 is published at v9954.
12. where is paper p3057 published? v9954 11
13. v10755 is the venue of paper p3370.
14. what is the venue of paper p3370? v10755 13
15. p3370 is published at v10755.

In our approach, LSTM embedding matrices are used. The value of hyper-parameters of LSTM model are shown in Table 11.

We train LSTM model on the computer with core i-5, 16GB RAM with 1,000 question-answer pairs by the implementation of RNN-LSTM by using the TensorFlow with Python. With two data sets, one date set contains 1,000 question-answer pairs for training and the other data set contains 1,000 question-answer pairs for testing. Training consumed 1036.74 seconds. Time for testing 1000 questions is 12 milliseconds

To demonstrate the performance of our proposal method, we compare with the solution proposed by Yongjun Zhu (2017). In this approach, they use Neo4j Graph database to store the knowledge graph. They use dependency parser to analyze the question and after recognize the object, they generate the Graph Query then they use Cypher to access the Graph Database. The average time for seeking a matched answer is 4 milliseconds. Comparing with, our proposal method, the time for accessing answer is 0.012 millisecond.

The accuracy is the ratio between the number of questions with correct answers and the number of question with incorrect answer. We test our system and received the accuracy as 75% average accuracy.

Chatbot for Interacting With Natural Language Based Knowledge Graph

A Chatbot is developed which help user to interact with the natural language based knowledge graph as shown in Figure 10.

When user types a natural language based question, the question will be parsed using the dependency parser. If the question is simple, the question is converted to embedding vector or binary vector as mentioned above. Then the vector of question will be fed into LSTM trained model to receive the facts of the answer. The question will be changed to the answer by using predefined rules. For example, when

Table 11. Value of hyper-parameters of LSTM

Hyper-Parameters	Value	Meaning
recurrent_cell_size	128	number of dimensions used to store data passed between recurrent layers in the network
Embedding_size	50	number of words (vector dimensions)
learning_rate	0.005	Learning rate
batch_size	128	Number of questions we train on at a time
ff_hidden_size	256	Feed Forward layer sizes
training-iteration	40,000	Number of training iteration

the user types question "What is the venue of paper p3371?". The LSTM model will provide "v10758" as a fact for answering this question. The word "what" of the question will be replaced by this fact. At last, the following answer for this question is built: v10758 is the venue of paper p3371. If the question is complicated, the Motif Search of GraphFrames will be built and run. The extracted triples will be used to generate the answer. for this question.

The question and answer will be displayed in the dialog box of the Chatbot as shown in Figure 10.

CONCLUSION

In this chapter, we develop a system for natural language question answer system. Neo4j Graph database is used to store HIN as a knowledge graph. The question is analyzed by dependency parser. If the question is simple, the RNN-LSTM will be used. If the question is complicated, the Graph Database model will be used. We use GraphFrames Library to generate the question-answer pairs data set. This data set is used to train the RNN-LSTM. The repartition strategy is used to do repartition the arcs of graph. This repartition can help process motif search efficiently because the arcs needed for joining will be contained in the same partition. We conduct the experiment. With the RNN-LSTM model, the time for answering a question is very fast, comparing with the time for doing a GraphFrames motif search. However, the time for generating training data set and training RNN-LSTM is very long. We propose a solution to use GraphFrames Library with a smart repartition to speed up the time for generating the

Figure 10. Using the Chatbot to interact the knowledge graph by using the natural language query

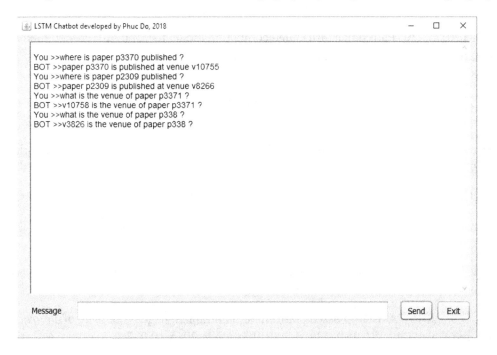

training dataset. The average accuracy of RNN-LSTM for simple question is high (more than 90%), but the average accuracy for complicated question is low (75%). With the GraphFrames Library and Dependency model, the time for accessing the graph database is low, but the accuracy of answering the question is high (more than 90%). These experiments prove the performance of our hybrid model. Finally, we also develop a Chatbot which can interact the knowledge graph by using the natural language query based on the hybrid model.

ACKNOWLEDGMENT

This research is funded by Vietnam National University Ho Chi Minh City (VNU-HCMC) under the grant number B2017-26-02.

REFERENCES

Abujabal, Yahya, Riedewald, & Weikum. (2017). Automated Template Generation for Question Answering over knowledge graph. *IW3C2*.

Blei, D. M., Ng, A. Y., & Michael, I. J. (2003). Latent Dirichlet Allocation. *Journal of Machine Learning Research*.

Cui, W., Xiao, Y., Wang, H., Song, Y., Hwang, S., & Wang, W. (2017). KBQA: Learning question answering over QA Corpora and Knowledge bases. *Proceedings of the VLDB Endowment International Conference on Very Large Data Bases*, *10*(5), 565–576. doi:10.14778/3055540.3055549

Do & Pham. (2018). DW-PathSim: a distributed computing model for topic-driven weighted meta-path-based similarity measure in a large-scale content-based heterogeneous information network. *Journal of Information and Telecommunication*, 1-20.

Huang, Z., Zheng, Y., Cheng, R., Sun, Y., Mamoulis, N., & Li, X. (2016). *Meta structure: Computing relevance in large heterogeneous information networks*. ACM. doi:10.1145/2939672.2939815

Jozefowicz, Zaremba, & Sutskever. (2015). An Empirical Exploration of Recurrent Network Architectures. *JMLR: W&CP, 37*.

Kafle, S. (2017). *Neural Question Answering: the role of knowledge bases*. Academic Press.

Liu & Feng. (2018). Deep Learning in Question Answering. In Deep Learning in Natural Language Processing. Springer.

Lukovnikov, D., Fischer, A., Lehmann, J., & Auer, S. (2017). *Neural Network based Question Answering over knowledge Graphs on Word and Character*. ACM.

Paolo Nesi, G. P. (2015). A hadoop based platform for natural language processing of. *Journal of Visual Languages and Computing*, *31*, 130–138. doi:10.1016/j.jvlc.2015.10.017

Rodrigo Agerri, X. A. (2015). Big data for Natural Language Processing: A streaming approach. *Knowledge-Based Systems*, *79*, 36–42. doi:10.1016/j.knosys.2014.11.007

Serban, I. V., Garcıa-Dur, A., Gulcehre, C., Ahn, S., Chandar, S., Courville, A., & Bengio, Y. (2016). Generating Factoid Questions With Recurrent Neural Networks: The 30M Factoid Question-Answer Corpus. *Proceedings of the 54th Annual Meeting of the Association for Computational Linguistics*, 588–598. 10.18653/v1/P16-1056

Shi, C., Li, Y., Zhang, J., Sun, Y., & Philip, S. Yu. (2017). A Survey of Heterogeneous Information Network Analysis. *IEEE Transactions on Knowledge and Data Engineering*, 29(1), 17–37. doi:10.1109/TKDE.2016.2598561

Thanh Ho, P. D. (2018). Social Network Analysis Based on Topic Model with Temporal Factor. *International Journal of Knowledge and Systems Science*, 9(1).

Weston, Bordes, Chopra, Rush, van Merrienboer, Joulin, & Mikolov. (2015). *Towards AI-complete Question Answering: A set of perquisite toy tasks*. Academic Press.

Xie, Zeng, Zhou, & He. (2016). Knowledge Base Questions Answering based on Deep Learning Models. *Natural Language Understanding and Intelligent Applications: ICCPOL 2016*, 300-311.

Yadav, R. (2015). *Spark Cookbook*. Packt Publishing.

Zaccone, Karim, & Menshawy. (2017). Deep Learning with TensorFlow. Packt Publishing.

Zheng, W., Yu, J. X., Zou, L., & Cheng, H. (2018). *Question Answering over knowledge graphs: Question Understanding Via Template Decomposition*. VLDB Endowment. doi:10.14778/3236187.3236192

Zhu, Y., Yan, E., & Song, I.-Y. (2017). The use of a graph-based system to improve bibliographic information retrieval: System design, implementation, and evaluation. *Journal of the Association for Information Science and Technology*, 68(2), 480–490. doi:10.1002/asi.23677

Chapter 15
Fog Computing:
Concepts, Applications, and Countermeasures Against Security Attacks

Bhumika Paharia
National Institute of Technology Kurukshetra, India

Kriti Bhushan
National Institute of Technology Kurukshetra, India

ABSTRACT

Fog computing is an extension to cloud computing that inhibits its limitations and enhances its amenities. Being similar to cloud computing, it has some more fascinating features that escalate the overall performance of the system. It faces many new disputes besides those already inherited from cloud computing. Fog computing is actually a paradigm that provides services at the network's edge as it serves the end-users with data, applications, storing, and computing capabilities. Fog computing is a new breed in services and applications to the end-users by enabling the above features, hence making its security and privacy aspects much more challenging then the cloud computing. Further, in this chapter, the basic concepts of fog computing are discussed with its applications as a high lighting feature. In addition, discussion about the attacks that could setback the advantages of fog computing and some defense mechanisms to overcome the effects of these attack have been discussed, giving a comprehensive study of fog computing.

INTRODUCTION

This section basically enlightens the concepts of fog computing with its characteristics enhancing and properties. Then the need of fog computing and how it can affect the overall performance of the network are discussed. Then, the history discussing the origin, background, and working of Fog computing are discussed. The next two sections provide the comparison of fog computing with cloud and edge computing respectively. Further some examples, advantages and disadvantages of fog computing are discussed in next sub-sections.

DOI: 10.4018/978-1-5225-8407-0.ch015

Fog Computing

Cloud computing is used to store large data files on a platform so that no space is occupied on smart devices (phones, desktops etc.); however, can access the data when needed (Xiao et al, 2013). Cloud computing being a traditional concept needs some advancements to handle the growing needs of technology hence fog computing came into picture.

Fog computing extends cloud computing and provides services to the network's edge. It reduces cloud's workload as well as services. It is a distributed platform for services like estimate, store, and network resources (Stojenovic et al, 2014). Fog computing, also referred as edge computing, is a mechanism which instead of performing centralized computing conducts computing st network's edge making it distributed computing (Banafa, 2014).

In figure 1, shows the fog layer residing in between cloud and end devices. Fog layer (intermediate servers) reside between the network's edge (smart devices) and the cloud layer (global servers). The concentration on fog computing is done in a way that data processing should be local on smart devices instead of sending them to the cloud (Stojmenovic et al, 2014)

Rather than authenticating channels for storage and utilization on cloud, it probably can be understood as some resources and processes placed at network's edge. It comprises of many fog nodes which inhibits some processing and storage abilities (Choo et al, 2018; Osanaiye et al, 2017). It can be helpful for deployment of Cloud of Things (CoT), IoT and support applications which have real-time demand and lower latency (Roopaei et al, 2017). Seldom difference between the two terms fog computing and edge computing is they rely on the infrastructure and "things" in the network respectively (Shi et al, 2016).

According to (Xiao et al, 2016), in hypothetical data transmission, users upload their data directly to the cloud server. In traditional cloud storage, as a result of separate management and ownership of data, the Cloud Server Provider (CSP) replaces user from managing data. This user is no longer able access the physical storage of its data. It overcomes the limitations of cloud either because of its infrastructure or technical faults, by extending it towards network's edge (Banafa et al, 2014).

Figure 1. Intermediate fog layer

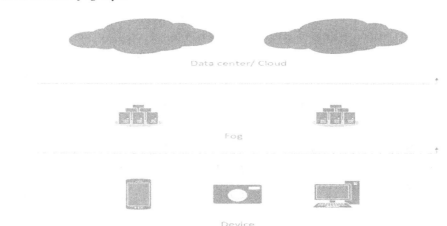

Need of Fog Computing

Cloud computing is already discussed as pay-as-you-go computing model with the increase in the popular demands of IoT's devices and their techniques. Cloud computing standard are capable of fulfilling the need to support mobility, also should be aware of location as well as latency should be low (Stojmenovic et al, 2014). It is generally used as an approach for IoT's emerging concept. Being an application to distributed environment, it aggregates every bit of information at certain access points instead of overburdening cloud with it. This helps in overcoming the major limitations of cloud by lessening the usage of bandwidth (Banafa et al, 2014).

Fog computing model plays an important role in advertising, entertainment, computing and various applications, properly kept for distributed and analytical data collection points (Abdelskour et al, 2015). It basically works on lowered latency and improved QoS. It can be useful in hosting access points and set-up boxes like end services. The principal aim of fog computing is to put information at network's edge near to user.

Origin

On November 19, 2015, Cisco Systems, ARM Holdings, Dell, Intel, Microsoft, and Princeton University, founded the OpenFog Consortium, to promote interests and development in fog computing. Cisco Sr. Managing-Director Helder Antunes became the consortium's first chairman and Intel's Chief IoT Strategist Jeff Faders became its first president (Stojmenovic et al, 201). The OpenFog consortium's mission was to advance the open reference architecture and sends the business value.

Metaphorically, fog is a meteorological term which can be seen as a part of cloud being close to ground, in computing located at network's edge. The word was coined by Ginny Nicholas, Cisco's product line manager.

Working of Fog Computing

Fog nodes needs developers either to write IoT applications or port the edge of the network. The data/information from IoT devices is absorbed by the closest fog nodes to the network's edge. This data is stored temporary with a response time of about milliseconds to subsecond covering geographical area of about one city block. Considering telemedicine and training applications as the examples here. They work upon the most time-sensitive data. The figure 2 shows the working of all three layers.

Difference Between Cloud and Fog Computing

This section discusses about the differences between cloud and fog computing in general and in terms of resource requirements (Deepali et al, 2017; Deepali et al, 2017B; Chaudhary et al, 2018). These are presented in table and table 2 respectively.

Figure 2. Working of each layer of fog computing

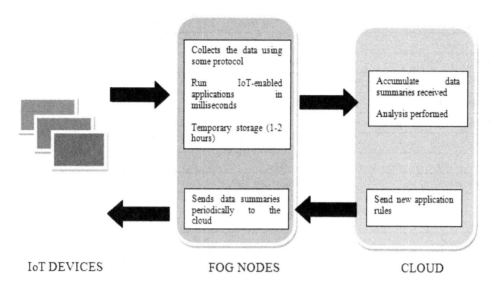

Table 1. Cloud vs. Fog computing

Cloud Computing	Fog Computing
Requires more time for large data sets and applications to be processed	Requires less time as it operates on network's edge
Consumes more bandwidth as there is a need to transfer every bit of data or information to the clouds	Consumes less bandwidth instead of sending to cloud, data is aggregated at definite access points
Problem like scalability and response time being slow arise due to dependent server at remote places	Due to location of servers in the visible spectrum of user i.e. network's edge, the scalability and response time problem can be easily avoided.
Response time takes minutes to days to weeks	It responds within few seconds to some minutes
Data stored here for months or years	Short duration data storage perhaps hours, days to weeks
Applications like graphical dashboards, data analytics, etc.	Simple analytics, virtualization etc. are some applications used here

SIMILARITIES AND DIFFERENCES BETWEEN FOG AND EDGE COMPUTING

Similarities

Both are system and network architectures which endeavour collection, analysis and processing data which results to be more efficient than traditional cloud computing particularly in applications like manufacturing and automations. Some identical objectives of these are (Abdelshkour et al, 2015).

1. Data sent to cloud in reduced amount
2. Latency either network or internet is lowered
3. Response time of the system is improved

Table 2. Difference between cloud and fog in terms of requirements

Requirements	Cloud	Fog
Latency	High	Low
Service location	In the internet	At network's edge
Awareness of location	No	Yes
Geographical Distribution	Centralized	Distributed
Mobility support	Limited	Supported
Client-to-server distance	Multiple hops	One hope
Jitter delays	High	Very low
Data enroute vulnerability	High probability	Very low probability
Security	Undefined	Defined
Type of last mile connectivity	Leased line	Wireless
Real-time interactions	Supported	Supported

The architecture of both suggests same source for data generation like motors, relays, pumps, sensors etc. physical resources. These are called the "Things" in IoT. Real-time applications like sensing, switching circuits, pumping water etc. works for both.

Differences

Differences between fog and edge computing are given in Table 3.

EXAMPLES OF FOG COMPUTING

Fog operations are as distinctive as variation in IoTs but also, they both have monitoring and analysing capabilities for real-time data from a network of connected entities triggering with an action. This action

Table 3. Fog vs. Edge computing

Fog Computing	Edge Computing
Intelligence is placed at LAN (local area network)	Intelligence, communication and processing power are located directly into the devices like programmable automation controllers
Transmission from endpoints to gateway then to source	Edge device supporters promotes the reduction of failure points
Its Supporters promotes it is more scalable	Each device works independently
Multiple data points	Reduces the potential failure of communication link and also simplifies the channel
Data processing done at fog node or IoT gateway	Time efficient and cost effective
Associate multiple layers of conversed data and complexity	Reduces networks' architecture as well as its complexity
Each and every communication link can be a potential failure in a channel	

can be a human-machine interaction (HMI) or machine – to - machine communications (M2M). Shutting a door, employing brakes in a train, alteration in settings of equipments, a video camera's zooming function, according to the readings of pressure the valve is open or close, or designing a bar-chart etc. concludes the examples of fog computing. There exist infinite possibilities in this scenario. There is an accelerated expansion in the fields of oil and gas, transportation, mining, manufacturing, public sector and utilities.

Merits and Limitations of Fog Computing

Merits and limitations of Fog computing are given in table 4.

ARCHITECTURE

Being an extension to cloud computing, fog computing has emerged as a new model for computing. It is the current area of interest for many researchers which was firstly proposed by Bonomi in 2011. Bonomi explained fog to be an identical computing of cloud. Being close to edge of the network, fog computing can be seen as a mid-computing to help cloud communicate with edge devices. With the growing demand for edge technologies, fog computing is gaining much of attention with different perspectives of different researchers.

The fog computing architecture is a three-layer architecture in (Laun et al, 2018) as Mobile-Fog-Cloud hierarchy. The most important concerns in today's realm from cloud storage perspective are capacity of storage, quality of service (QoS) and data security. Due to many enhancements in cloud storage field, such as IBM Cloud Object Storage. They have an ascendable capacity to store any amount of data, from all petabyte to certain exabyte, so storage capacity is at less concern. The second important concern QoS comprises of availability, reliability, and recovery from disaster which completely depends on QoS of Cloud Service Provider (CSP).

The most concerned part here is assuring the security of data. As traditional architecture supports storage of data on cloud server and if anything happens on cloud server, the data stored is at threat. There is a need for assurance of security of private data stored on cloud server. A solution to this problem fog computing came into picture. A fog-based scheme was proposed by (Wang et al, 2018), which enhance the cloud storage and equip users with secure high-quality services.

Table 4. Merits and limitations of fog

Merits	Limitations
Data sent to cloud is reduced	Physical location benefit of cloud cannot be kept
Network bandwidth is conserved	MiTM, IP address spoofing, DDoS attacks arise
Response time of system is improved	Issues related to privacy, security
As data kept at network's edge which gives better security	Not cost effective
Mobility is supported	Trust, authentication and availability concerns
Network and/or internet latency is lowered	Concerned for security of wireless network

Figure 3 shows the architecture where fog nodes exist as some intermediary nodes between IoT devices and sensors at terminal layer and the cloud layer. Fog layer collect and analyse the data or information that requires less response time or immediate response. Other than this fog simply transfers it to cloud where further processing is done.

The scheme depicted in figure 4, there is no direct data transfer to cloud, instead fog layer is used in-between to do so in the following ways:

1. User's data is segregated into blocks
2. According to the reputation values of CSPs, users selects them.
3. Once the CSPs confirmed, separate upload of user data in appropriate proportion to cloud and fog servers. Here fog devices work as an intermediary function which collects and transfers data. In addition to data processing and storing, it also locally highlights the most evident difference between cloud and fog computing (Wang et al, 2018).
4. Allocation of user's data in appropriate amount in various CSPs.
5. A proportion of users' data, giving major part i.e. 80-90% to cloud server and rest i.e. 20-10% to fog server is done.

Advantage of scheme presented in (Wang et al, 2018).

1. Decreased transmission delay
2. As the distance between cloud and end-user is large as compared to fog and end-users, hence requires less transfer rate when transmission is occurring between latter entities (Wang et al, 2015).
3. Better data security

Figure 3. Three-layer architecture

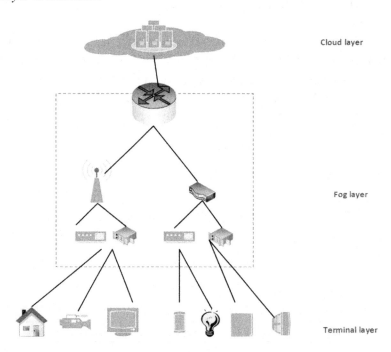

Figure 4. The architecture of fog-based cloud storage system

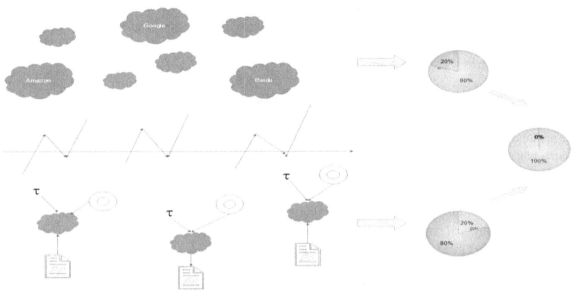

4. As all the information of data is not stored at one place only like done in cloud server, so attacker cannot retrieve data from any part of the network. In interim, almost all cyber threats aggravate users' data.

APPLICATIONS

Things done with fog computing have six motivating scenarios: a) Connected vehicles and Smart traffic lights; b) Wireless sensor and actuator networks; c) Smart grid; d) IoT and Cyber-physical systems(CPSs); e) Software defined networks (SDN); f) Decentralized smart building control (Stojmenovic et al, 2014). Explained briefly as:

Connected Vehicles (CV) and Smart Traffic Lights Systems (SMTS)

In (Stojmenovic et al, 2014) with the help of some examples such as, an approaching ambulance, by its flashing light, can be sensed by the video camera, installed at the intersections of the roads. They can convert the blocked traffic light to open, so that the ambulance passes away without any delay. In addition, smart traffic light also measures the distance and speed of any approaching vehicles by interacting with the sensors installed locally after it encounter any presence of bikers, other vehicles or the pedestrians.

A splendid composition of connectedness and cooperation is demonstrated in three possible way (Abdelshkour et al, 2015).

1. Vehicle to vehicle
2. Vehicle to access points (SMT, 3G, WI-FI)
3. Access points to access points

The figure 5 suggests a smart traffic light system (Bonomi et al, 2014) in which intelligent lights are installed. These lights turn on after sensing any movement and turns off as the traffic passes. These smart lights turn out to be the neighboring fog nodes harmonizing to devise green traffic signals and also sends warning signals to imminent vehicles (Bonomi et al, 2012). Smart traffic lights, 3G, road side units, Wi-Fi like wireless access points are set up on the roads.

Wireless Sensor and Actuator Networks (WSAN)

The genuine Wireless Sensor Networks (WSNs) devised to conduct at low power particularly. In order that the battery life can be extended or energy production can be made achievable. Predominantly all of these WSNs engage lesser amount of bandwidth, energy, no petty memory nodes, operates as source of sink (collector), power of processing is lowered, unidirectional (Abdelskhour et al, 2015). The conventional wireless sensor networks narrow down the applications that outstrips sensing and tracking. But when applying physical tasks like employing open, import and close for sensors, they need actuators (Bonomi et al, 2012). Particularly in this scenario, fog nodes acting as actuators does take control of measurement process, the oscillatory behaviors and stability achieved by a closed-loop system set up.

It can be understood with the example of self-maintaining trains, which have sensor monitors to detect the heat level inside the train. If it goes beyond the permissible heat level then these sensor monitors generate automatic alert signal to the operator of the train. In result of that the train can be halt at the next nearest station and emergency maintenance can be done such as heat level can be checked and brought back to normal. No impairment done. Also, in life-saving scenario inside mines, the air vent system's sensors keep a check on the air conditions which are flowing in and out of mines. If mines inside became hazardous for miners there is an automatic change in air-flow conditions (Stojmenovic et al, 2014).

Figure 5. Connected vehicles and smart traffic light system

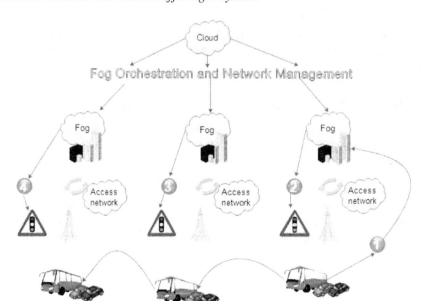

Smart Grid

The applications of load balancing for energy may get executed at terminal devices of network for e.g. micro-grids (Wei et al, 2014) and smart meters. Establishing the criteria of availability, low cost and demand, these devices get swapped to substitutes of energy like solar and wind.

As shown in the figure 6, fog devices located at edge process the data and also release the control commands to actuators. This data is generated by the grid sensors and devices (Bonomi et al, 2012). Here data filtration occurs locally, and the rest is distributed among the high-level tier such as transactional analytic, generates reports based on real-time and visualization. Fog computing supports the architecture by providing lower transient storage and higher semi-permanent storage. By accommodating cloud with business intelligence analytics, global coverage can be achieved (Stojmenovic et al, 2014).

IoT and Cyber-Physical Systems (CPSs)

Fog computing-based systems becomes a significant class. To interrelate local physical objects and identified addressing needs an IoT network. On the other hand, physical aspects and computation of system together makes a combination for CPSs piece. It organizes data centric engineered and physical systems and also incorporates computer (Abdelshkour et al, 2015).

IoT network can associate physical objects with the identified addresses with the help of Internet and telecommunication like traditional networks (Atzori et al, 2010). They both together keep the potential to reconstruct real world into new links between natural real world, computer-based communication and control systems, and engineered systems. Just like embedded systems here fog computing is built where software and programs installed into devices. Some e.g. for this maybe medical devices and machinery and entertainment article like toys, cars etc.

Figure 6. Implementing smart grids

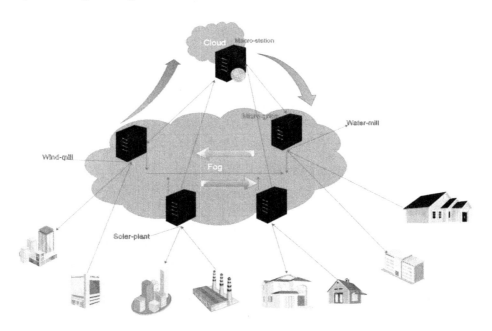

The aim consolidates the accuracy and abstractions of software and networks with the physical environment having properties such as dynamics, noise and uncertainty (Stojmenovic et al, 2014). A combination CPSs with emerging methods, principles and knowledge are capable to expand the future generations of intelligent devices such as in medicals, buildings, robotics, highways etc.

Software Defined Networks (SDN)

It helps in resolving many issues like vehicular networks, capricious connectivity, higher loss of packets and collisions, unified control and augmenting vehicle to vehicle and vehicle to infrastructure communications arising in fog computing (Abdelshkour et al, 2015; Bhushan et al, 2018; Paharia et al, 2018).

The architectural model of SDN given in figure 7 illustrates the residing three layers which are described as follows:

1. Application layer consisting of business applications such OpenStack and SDN orchestration tools.
2. Control layer subsist a controller responsible for transferring network devices to business applications through programmable APIs.
3. Infrastructure layer resides all the network devices.

The figure 8, suggest the network module of SDN consisting various devices and protocols.

The figure 9 shows the fog computing scheme that can be enforced to achieve the SDN approach for vehicular networks. It is an emerging technology for computing as well as networking (Kirkpatrick et al, 2013). It splits the control and data communication into two layers. Control is accomplished at server which is centralized and decides communication path for nodes to adhere. Here, the server sometimes may need an implementation which requires distributed environment. SDN approach can be considered in wireless sensor networks, mesh networks, and WLAN but does not support multi-hop routing and wireless communications. Further, they do not provide communication between peers particularly in this scheme. First proposal for SDN approach in Vehicular network given by (Liu et al, 2014).

Figure 7. Architecture diagram of SDN

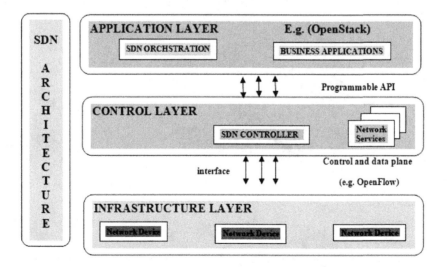

Figure 8. SDN network

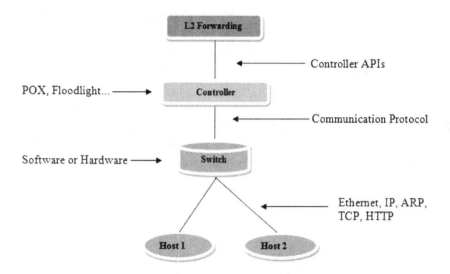

Figure 9. SDN in vehicular network

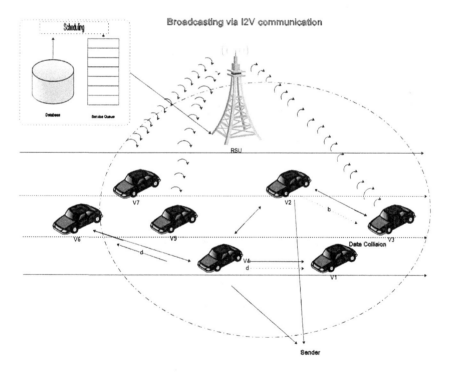

Decentralized Smart Building Control

It is enabled via wireless sensors applications located to compute humidity, temperature or gas levels of different types allowed in the atmosphere of the building. In order to form some failure proof methods, exchange and analysis of information among all nodes is necessary (Abdelshkour et al, 2015).

Here, (Stojmenovic et al, 2014) information must be exchanged between all the sensors on the floor. In order to form a reliable measurement, all the readings taken from the floor should be combined. The sensors at fog devices uses activation and distributed decision making to counter data. The other components of the system help in lowering the temperature and do some immediate actions like opening the windows or injecting some fresh air. Air conditioners can be helpful in either removing moisture or to increase the humidity inside the building.

It is very well-known fact that sensors sense the movement and react accordingly e.g. switching light on or off (Stojmenovic et al, 2014). The fog devices can be authorized at each floor and then cooperate with higher level of actuations. Smart building can be entrusted to emphasize the internal and external environments so that they can conserve resources like water, energy, etc.

ATTACKS ON FOG COMPUTING

Classification of attacks on Fog computing is shown in figure 10(a).

The connotations of the attacks make the point of understanding clearer about attacks (as shown in figure 10(b)).

Specifically, enlightening two most vulnerable attacks on fog computing below:

Figure 10. a) Categorization of attacks, b) Connotations of attacks

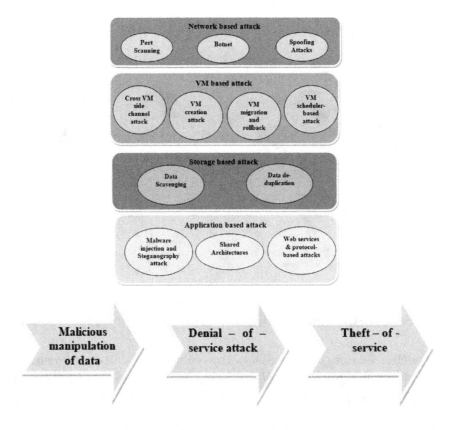

Man -in- the- Middle Attack (MiTM)

This attack has a great potential to effect fog computing. In this attack scenario, basically the fog devices serving as gateways are either compromised or replaced with forged ones. This attack is smooth to launch but hard to recognise. It goes unnoticeable when used with traditional anomaly detection scheme. As a result, no measures are taken after the attack is performed. Also, even the communication channel among fog and mobile user are at risk even after applying some encryption and decryption methods which are not effective and also consume a lot of battery of mobile devices.

The difficulty in protecting gateways from being altered rise because of the setup of fog devices in sectarian control normally. For e.g. legitimate customers of KFC or Star Bar connected to the access points, which are either compromised or injected with malicious entity. These produce deceitful service set identifier work as publicly demonstrated legit users. Even the confidential communications of legit users are hijacked as soon as the gateways are under the control of attackers (Stojmenovic et al, 2104).

Distributed Denial of Service (DDoS)

DDoS attack is a service threat attack in which the availability of service is altered. Services such as resources existing in the network and legitimate user requests for data are made unavailable when network is flooded by IP spoofing. IP spoofing following the DDoS attack make it easier for the malicious request to look different. The source of flooding is also hidden but if the source of flooding is kept same it can be blocked. In this attacking scenario, several machines in the network are compromised functioning as bot targeting the same network synchronously (Ankita et al, 2015; Bhushan et al, 2018; Bhushan et al, 2018 B; Bhushan et al, 2017). A classification of DDoS attacks on resource is given in figure 11.

Figure 11. Classification of DDoS attack on resources
(Ankita et al, 2015)

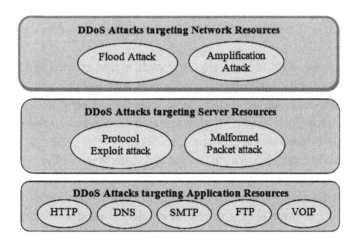

EXISTING COUNTERMEASURES

Assurance of security and privacy in fog nodes is essential like the other technologies required for users (Ruilong et al, 2016). The research work in this domain is seldom notably for design and implementation for security and privacy concern in fog computing. Some of the privacy preserving and security solutions given by (Quratulain et al, 2017; Siani et al, 2011; Wang et al, 2016) for cloud computing cannot be extended to network's edge. Hence does not gratifies for fog computing environment. Briefly there arise some threats which is attainable in a well-managed cloud computing environment (Choo et al, 2018). Taxonomical representation of DDoS attack detection, mitigation, and prevention is shown in figure 12.

Fog computing needs to have some paradigms for increasing the security and privacy aspects for better performance from the overall network by devoting attention towards emerging and already existing challenges. This scrutiny has been achieved by (Rodrigo et al, 2018) in his special issue paper of review and examining the challenges arising in security and privacy.

Cryptography is very crucial approach when talked about assuring the confidentiality and preserving privacy of data/information when there is a third party say, fog node or cloud service provider (Beiter et al, 2014; Xun et al, 2016). To ensure a secure communication in a naturally unsecured public channel, a key establishment protocol can be deployed like in (Kim-Kwang et al, 2014) called as key agreement protocol. A vPAKE (Password Authentication Key exchange) protocol (Peng et al, 2018; Yuexin et al, 2018), where the fog nodes extract some short secrets which are used at higher layer of physical layer to establish a secret key by users, instead of relying on assumption of password sharing.

An anonymous secure aggregation scheme and model proposed by (Huagun et al, 2018) for public cloud computing which is fog-based with proofs of performance. Some of the attribute-based encryption (ABE) like ciphertext-policy ABE for a novel threat i.e. key-delegation abuse scheme (Yinhao et al, 2018) and chosen ciphertext attack-secure ABE scheme with outsourced decryption (Cong et al, 2018). Some data duplication scheme has been proposed for cloud computing environment (Xue et al, 2017). For reduction of overheads due to storage and communication must be deployed for fog computing environment. (Dongyoung et al, 2018) discusses a scheme which preserves fog nodes privacy of location with help of position-based cryptography. A fine-grained access control mechanism using key at user-level and updation in (Dongyong et al, 2018), proposed a secure duplication scheme in management of fog-storage.

More schemes of access control in fog computing such as fine-grained leakage-resilient (Zouxia et al, 2018) as well as attribute update and support for outsourcing capabilities in (Peng et al, 2018; Yuexin et al, 2018). In order to expedite sharing of data, some schemes (Ximeng et al, Yannan et al, 2018) over the data outsourced, to scrupulous sharing of both verification and search privileges, the users receive a single aggregate key distributed by data owners.

Other than confidentiality, data integrity is also at stake, there is an efficient need for some mechanism such as (Yannan et al, 2018; Yannan et al, 2017) just instantiated their recommended technique with auditing scheme of Shacham-Waters, in addition gave a key-updating and authenticator-evolving technique for data auditing at cloud having stored files' zero knowledge privacy.

In (Wang et al, 2018), they combine fog computing with traditional cloud computing. They proposed a model where segregation of the users' data storing major into cloud and rest to fog servers. Their scheme ensured CIA (Confidentiality, Integrity and Availability) triads.

Figure 12. Taxonomical representation of DDoS attack detection, mitigation, and prevention

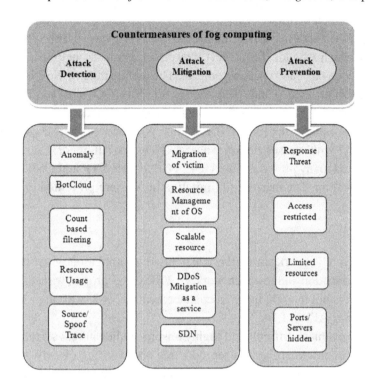

In fog computing, security issues are discussed which elaborate PKI (Public Key Infrastructure), smart meters encrypt the data and send it to the fog device, such as a home-area network(HAN) gateway. Then an example i.e., MITM (man-in-the-middle) attack. Here, hijacked communication is shown between the phone and the PC. A 3G user do video call to a WLAN user. The key in this attack is to compromise the gateway who is serving as fog device since MITM attack needs to control the interactions between the phone and PC. Then results of stealth test is discussed and privacy issues (Stojmenovic et al, 2013).

In (Luan et al, 2016), they have suggested intrusion detection techniques which are beneficial in detecting various kinds of attacks such as insider attack, port scanning, Virtual machine (VM) and hypervisor attacks; and flooding attack (DoS). This system monitors and analyses policies of access control, user logging information and a log file to detect any intrusion behaviour. In order to detect some malicious activities e.g. port scanning, DoS at the network's side.

EXISTING TOOLS

This section enlightens the tools which can be helpful in implementing Fog layer architecture. Those are briefly explained as:

NS2

It is basically an object-oriented network simulator of discrete-event driven type. NS-2 is a version 2 of network simulator which extends Tcl (OTcl) interpreter. With the help of C++ for implementing frequently executable code basically creating objects. The architecture of NS2 is shown in figure 13.

There is an increase in efficiency and speed; and OTcl (Tcl+ OO) works as front-end structured for simulator, objects configuration and event scheduling which gives system configuration and easy usage.

It can be implemented platforms like UNIX, Linux Windows etc. NS-2 consist of Tcl/TK, OTcl (Object Tcl), TclCL (Tcl with classes library), nam-1 (Network Animator), xgraph for graph plotting and more. It is used to aid many protocols like UDP, TCP, HTTP, FTP and DSR This can be simulated on wired or wireless medium. The merits and limitation of NS2 are presented in table 5

NS-3

This also is a discrete-event network simulator, which provide simulation of network to be open and extensible, idealized for education and research work. In 2006, Ns-3 project was established to develop an open-source Ns-3. Ns-3 is not thought to be an enhancement of Ns-2. Although Ns-3 like Ns-2 employ C++ but does not support API's of Ns-2.

Use of ns-3 helps to evaluate difficult and highly absurd studies in real systems such as highly controlled behavior based, environment that is reproducible and working of networks. Currently Ns-3 is restricted to working based on network and Internet protocols but can be extended to non-Internet based in future ("Ns-3 tutorial", n.d.). The architecture of NS3 is shown in figure 15(a).

Figure 13. NS2 architecture

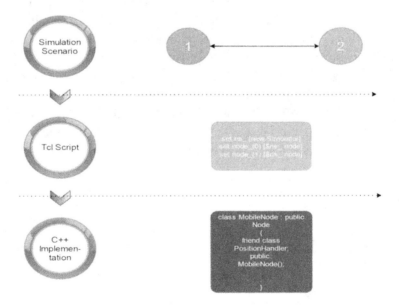

Figure 14. a) NS2 Simulation, b) Simulation Tools

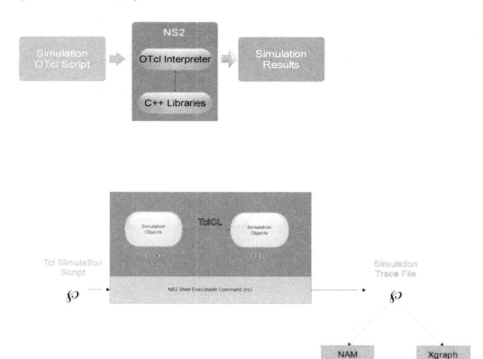

Table 5. NS2 merits and limitations

Merits	Limitations
It is freely available	It is unreliable
Most of components of network can be implemented over it.	It doesn't provide any technical aid.
Day by day increase in interest of researchers.	It gives difficulty in troubleshooting.
Addition of any new functions and modification are easily done.	It consists of bugs.
	They provide unrealistic abstraction model.

Some distinctive characteristics are: firstly, they are designed to create a combination of set of libraries consolidated together and also externally defined other software libraries. Rather than other platforms for simulation environment where all assignment carried out only support the users for single, integrated GUIs (Graphical user interface), a modular approach used by Ns-3. Additional features such as tools for data analysis and visualization and external animators used and CLI (Command line interface) worked with software development tools in Python/C++.

Secondly, it is used mainly on Linux platform such as FreeBSD, windows such as Cygwin and still developing for supporting Windows Visual Studio. Lastly, it is not an official product for software supported by any company, in fact on the basis of mailing lists of Ns-3, best effort is searched ("Ns-3 Tutorial", n.d.). NS3 implementation mechanism is depicted in figure 15(b). The relationship of NS3 with NS2 is given in table 6.

Figure 15. a) Ns-3 architecture, b) Ns-3 implementation

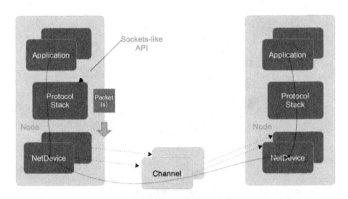

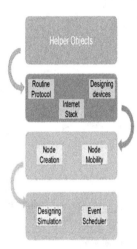

Table 6. Relationship of NS3 with Ns-2

Similarity	Difference
Implemented in core C++ software.	OTcl used by Ns-2 is being replaced by either C++ programs or python scripts.
Have license for GNU GPL version 2.	Almost all of the core is rewritten.
Having Ns-2 models portability such as models for error, calendar queue scheduler, OLSR and random variables.	Working changes due to new tools for configuration or animators.
	Instead of Ns-3, Ns-2 is not supported or maintained actively.

Mininet

This is a network emulator specifically called network emulation orchestration system. It operates on single Linux kernel with all together routers, switches, links and end-users. For a single system uses lightweight virtualization which makes it look alike to complete network runs same code on same kernel or system. It can be seen that host Mininet exactly works like real machines. For e.g. one could start by doing ssh and bridging its network to the host; and executing arbitrary programs i.e. everything stored on Linux system.

Often the programs executing, transmits packets to resemble to Ethernet interface having link speed and delay. The transmitted packets processed with some definite amount of queueing via router, middle-box and a real ethernet switch. Whenever communicating via Mininet, there is a need to compute the performance of two innate mechanisms, when using iperf client and server like programs.

Particularly about Mininet's switches, virtual hosts, controllers and links are real things in the networking environment. Instead of using software for creation of these constituents of Mininet they use hardware. Almost similar to discrete hardware elements in terms of behavior. These Mininet network mostly make resemblance to hardware networks or vice versa. It is done so that both platform can execute binary code and applications without any interruptions. The architecture of Mininet is given in figure 16. Moreover, the benefits and limitations are discussed in table 7.

IFogSim

It is being developed as the identification of fog computing infrastructure having similar characteristics as of cloud computing infrastructure located just close to network's edge. Rather than assisting communication being peer – to – peer, it works on hierarchy of fog nodes as suggested by fog environment.

The placement of application is only allowed in north – south direction, and currently it is bit challenging to offload modules placed same level of hierarchy for another device. For e.g. the scheme where offloading between smartphones to smartphones is needed, cannot be applied in current version. And also, two devices on same level of hierarchy can not directly communicate due to the current organization of hierarchy. Advancements are in process according to the current requirements. Table 8 illustrarte various benefits and challenges in IFogSim.

Figure 16. Mininet architecture

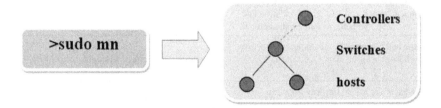

Table 7. Mininet benefits and limitations

Mininet Benefits	Mininet Limitations
Fast: It takes few seconds to start a simple network which gives less time - consuming run - edit - debug events.	Limited resource: It foist limited resource usage, for e.g., a server with 3GHz of CPU which switch simulated traffic of nearly 10Gbps, exhibits need of a balance among the switches and the virtual hosts.
Customized topologies: It can create topologies according to the requirement of the system such as a single – switch, the Stanford backbone, larger scale topologies like Internet, data center and/or anything else.	Use single Linux kernel for all virtual host: For all virtual hosts, Mininet uses a single Linux kernel so no software's depending on other operating system kernel like Windows, BSD etc.
Executable real programs: It enables executing very flexible as long as it is available on Linux such as web servers, TCP window monitoring tools, Wireshark and some more executable.	Create own OpenFlow controller: If there is a need for custom switching and routing behavior, need to develop controller as per requirements.
Customized build up for forwarding of packets: The constituents of Mininet like switches with the use of OpenFlow protocol are easily programmable. Particular influencing line-rate packet forwarding scheme, Mininet executing customized SDN (Software Defined Network) designs can be transformed into hardware OpenFlow switches.	Isolated: Although Mininet network being isolated from Internet and LAN is beneficial but sometimes there is a need for connecting to the Internet which can be done individually either by using NAT (Network Address Translation) object or --nat option and also by attaching hardware interface real or virtual.
Machine-independent: Mininet is executable over any machine such as laptops, VMs (Virtual Machine), server, Linux box already included in Ubuntu 12.10+! and in Amazon EC2 cloud and many more.	Shared files: Mininet by default shares the host file system and PID space which needs security from running malicious files and preference of legit files among all.
Sharable and replicative results: The results produced are accessible to other users once packages are formed.	Time inefficient: It depends on real time as it does not have any strong notion for virtual time which makes it harder to emulate it.
Easy to use: By using simple or complex Python scripts creation and execution of Mininet programs can be achieved.	
Open source projects: It is an open source projects helps to examine its source code, do any modification to fix bugs, issues in files, featuring requests and finally submitting patches or pull requests. Addition can also be done in case of giving clarifications or any other additional information in the source code.	
Continuous development: It is under active development so more and more enhancements done with the growing demands.	

Table 8. IFogSim benefits and limitations

Benefits	Limitations
It is scalable in the context of IoT.	Mobility supported
It will activate the speedy development for IoT and especially fog computing environment having end – to- end simulation and modelling suggesting creative policies for resource management.	Resource management policy for power - aware
It approves to investigate and compare the techniques of resource management fundamentally depending upon QoS criteria e.g. latency.	Resource management strategies for priority – aware
Used to simulate IoT, edge or fog computing environment.	Modelling fog devices to avoid failure
	Resource scheduling
	Virtualization technique
	Application modelling schedules

FUTURE DIRECTIONS

Challenges/ Issues Arising

In the prospect of fog computing there exist some issues which needs to be studied and are discussed in table 9.

Emerging Technologies

In addition to these there is a definite need to modify the existing countermeasure techniques to compete with the emerging technologies and also two-layer architecture of cloud-fog model (Lu et al, 2011; Wang et al, 2013). The work done in (Egwutuha et al, 2014) can be extended by reconstructing its mobility workload as fog devices are capable to carry-out computational-intensive tasks. Others emerging applications are smart grids, STLS

The figure below shows fog computing embodied with the emerging technologies such as (Luan et al, 2016):

1. **SDN:** As gaining more and more attention in the growing world, fog being an extension of cloud, needs to support and update data frequently synchronized with the cloud. Cloud with a global view of network manage it by using SDN. Most of the attention will be received by vehicular networks possessing fog-based SDN network.
2. **Device Hardware:** Consist of SoC-SIP Microbatteries.

Table 9. Challenges in Fog computing

Challenges	Brief
Security issue	The authentication, access control, anomaly-based and misbehaviour-based detection raises the security concerns. New challenges came into light when running the droplet applications need some secure sandboxes.
Privacy issue	For e.g. here hiding details, privacy preserving and demand response (Bonomi et al, 2014) raises the issues.
Trust issue	Bidirectional trust between communicating parties in sandboxing and isolating mechanism.
Error correction (Egwutuoha et al, 2014)	The fault tolerance capability needs to be improved in order to protect data loss.
Allurements (Wang et al, 2014)	These are the motivation, reasons or the things which entice the data protection.
Customized applications (Ottenwalkder et al, 2013)	According to the demand, fog-based server must have customized applications used by network operator at a specific location which in turn is not feasible.
Scalability and placement (Luan et al, 2016)	According to the demand of fog server, network operator needs to prepare and expand resources and the supply should be sufficient. An association of multiple fog server to provide some services to the mobile user may improve the overall performance but with multiple locations and various user demands its employment is a challenging task to perform.
Standardization (Vaquero et al, 2014)	There are no existing standard mechanisms for each entity of the network to indicate its availability to other in the same network for further executing their software.

3. **Network Function Virtualization (NFV):** It is the nodes software whose objective is to enable virtualized network functions in the interior of nodes present in the network such as routers, switches etc. Fog computing targets the virtualized location-based applications at the edge to be enabled and supply beneficial services to mobile users locally.
4. BluetoothLE, ANT + ZigBee and RFE4CE
5. **5G/ WAN/LAN/MAN:** Fog computing targets to serve customized location-based applications to mobile edge users. Some of the existing network access technology are Wi-Fi, 5G with an architecture which is virtualized.
6. Network Edge protocol like for mesh – MANET/ WMN/ P2P and for IoT – MQTT/CoAP, DDW

CONCLUSION

This chapter presents the vision of fog computing and gives a detailed description of its key concepts, architecture and applications. It is conjectured as a platform dispatching new modules of services and applications at the network's edge. The prediction has been made about fog computing that it will provide solutions to emerging problems of today's and future technologies. It gives a hierarchical and distributed platform to deliver services such as compute, store and process network resources. It is being shown that how fog counterpart and broaden the concept of cloud computing.

The chapter demonstrate that fog computing is devoted to serve mobile users particularly for location-based applications. Fog computing consumes the exhaustive mobile traffic utilizing fast-rate connections locally. Moreover, it assist the back and forth long transmission of data amid cloud and mobile edge devices via setting up restricted communication and computing resources closest to the edge. This in result, not only promote the QoS (Quality of Service) recognized by the users at the edge also, reduces the consumptions of bandwidth, cost, and energy in the backbone of Internet. Moreover, in order to solve the problems residing in cloud-based Internet and mobile computing, fog computing appears to be an efficient, scalable and viable paradigm.

The outcome for fog fiercely varies with the current discipline which employs most of layer in IT stack for e.g. network traffic management, accounting, network/service provision, apps development and collaboration mechanisms etc.

REFERENCES

Abdelshkour, M. (2015, March 27). *IoT, from Cloud to Fog Computing*. Retrieved from https://blogs.cisco.com/perspectives/iot-from-cloud-to-fog-computing

Ankita & Khatiwala. (2015). Survey on DDoS Attack Detection and Prevention in Cloud. *International Journal of Engineering Technology, Management and Applied Sciences, 3*(2).

Atzori, L., Iera, A., & Morabito, G. (2010, October). The internet of things: A survey. *Computer Networks*, *54*(15), 2787–2805. doi:10.1016/j.comnet.2010.05.010

Banafa, A. (2014, August 31). *What is fog computing?* Retrieved from https://ahmedbanafa.blogspot.com/2014/08/what-is-fog-computing.html

Bhushan, K., & Gupta, B. B. (2017). Security challenges in cloud computing: State-of-art. *International Journal of Big Data Intelligence*, *4*(2), 81–107. doi:10.1504/IJBDI.2017.083116

Bhushan, K., & Gupta, B. B. (2018). Distributed denial of service (DDoS) attack mitigation in software defined network (SDN)-based cloud computing environment. *Journal of Ambient Intelligence and Humanized Computing*, 1–13.

Bhushan, K., & Gupta, B. B. (2018, February). Detecting DDoS Attack using Software Defined Network (SDN) in Cloud Computing Environment. In *2018 5th International Conference on Signal Processing and Integrated Networks (SPIN)* (pp. 872-877). IEEE.

Bhushan, K., & Gupta, B. B. (2018). A novel approach to defend multimedia flash crowd in cloud environment. *Multimedia Tools and Applications*, *77*(4), 4609–4639. doi:10.100711042-017-4742-6

Bonomi, F. (2014). *Fog Computing: A Platform for Internet of Things and Analytics. In Big Data and Internet of Things: A Roadmap for Smart Environments* (Vol. 546, pp. 169–186). SCI.

Bonomi, F., Milito, R., Zhu, J., & Addepalli, S. (2012). Fog computing and its role in the internet of things. *Proceedings of the First Edition of the MCC Workshop on Mobile Cloud Computing*, 13–16.

Chaudhary, D., Bhushan, K., & Gupta, B. B. (2018). Survey on DDoS Attacks and Defense Mechanisms in Cloud and Fog Computing. *International Journal of E-Services and Mobile Applications*, *10*(3), 61–83. doi:10.4018/IJESMA.2018070104

Choi, N., Vu, H., Burchfield, R., & Yazd, S. A. (2012). *Introduction to NS-2*. Retrieved from https://www.utdallas.edu/~venky/acn/Handouts/ns2-sara.pdf

Choo, K.-K. R., Lu, R., Chen, L., & Yi, X. (2018). A foggy research future: Advances and future opportunities in fog computing research. *Future Generation Computer Systems*, *78*(2), 677–697. doi:10.1016/j.future.2017.09.014

Cong, Z., Jun, S., Wei, G., Xie, M., & Min, J. (2018). CCA-secure ABE with outsourced decryption for fog computing. *Future Generation Computer Systems*, *78*(2), 730–738.

Deepali, Bhushan. K. (2017, May). DDoS attack defense framework for cloud using fog computing. In *Recent Trends in Electronics, Information & Communication Technology (RTEICT), 2017 2nd IEEE International Conference on* (pp. 534-538). IEEE.

Deepali, Bhushan., K. (2017, August). DDoS attack mitigation and resource provisioning in cloud using fog computing. In *Smart Technologies For Smart Nation (SmartTechCon), 2017 International Conference On* (pp. 308-313). IEEE.

Deng, R., Lu, R., Lai, C., Luan Tom, H., & Hao, L. (2016). Optimal workload allocation in fog-cloud computing toward balanced delay and power consumption. *IEEE Internet of Things J.*, *3*(6), 1171–1181.

Dongyoung, K., & Junbeom, H. (2018). Privacy-preserving deduplication of encrypted data with dynamic ownership management in fog computing. *Future Generation Computer Systems*, *78*(2), 739–752.

Egwutuoha, I. P., Chen, S., Levy, D., Selic, B., & Calvo, R. (2014). Cost-oriented proactive fault tolerance approach to high performance computing (HPC) in the cloud. *International Journal of Parallel, Emergent and Distributed Systems*, *29*(4), 363–378. doi:10.1080/17445760.2013.803686

Gupta, H., Dastjerdi, A. V., Ghoshy, S. K., & Buyya, R. (2017). iFogSim: A Toolkit for Modeling and Simulation of Resource Management Techniques in Internet of Things, Edge and Fog Computing Environments. *Special Issue: Cloud and Fog Computing*, *47*(9), 1275–1296.

Hua, W., & Xun, Y. (2016). Protecting outsourced data in cloud computing through access management. *Concurrency. Pract. Exp.*, *28*(3), 600–615. doi:10.1002/cpe.3286

Introduction to Mininet~miniet/mininet Wiki~Github. (n.d.). Retrieved from https://github.com/mininet/mininet/wiki/Introduction-to-Mininet

Jian, L., Li, J., Lei, Z., Dai, F., Zhang, Y., Meng, X., & Jian, S. (2018). Secure intelligent traffic light control using fog computing. *Future Generation Computer Systems*, *78*(2), 817–824.

Jiang, Y., Willy, S., Yi, M., & Guo, F. (2018). Ciphertext-policy attribute-based encryption against key-delegation abuse in fog computing. *Future Generation Computer Systems*, *78*(2), 720–729. doi:10.1016/j.future.2017.01.026

Kirkpatrick, K. (2013, September). Software-defined networking. *Communications of the ACM*, *56*(9), 16–19. doi:10.1145/2500468.2500473

Li, D., Aung, Z., Williams, J. R., & Sanchez, A. (2014). No peeking: Privacy preserving demand response system in smart grids. *International Journal of Parallel, Emergent and Distributed Systems*, *29*(3), 290–315. doi:10.1080/17445760.2013.851677

Li, Y., Yong, Y., Bo, Y., Min, G., & Huai, W. (2018). Privacy preserving cloud data auditing with efficient key update. *Future Generation Computer Systems*, *78*(2), 789–798. doi:10.1016/j.future.2016.09.003

Li, Y., Yong, Y., & Min, G. (2017). Fuzzy identity-based data integrity auditing for reliable cloud storage systems. IEEE Trans. Dependable Secure Comput., 1-12.

Liu, Ng, Lee, Son, & Stojmenovic. (2014). *Cooperative data dissemination in hybrid vehicular networks: Vanet as a software defined network*. Submitted for publication.

Liu, X., & Deng Robert, H. (2018). Hybrid privacy-preserving clinical decision support system in fog–cloud computing. *Future Generation Computer Systems*, *78*(2), 825–837. doi:10.1016/j.future.2017.03.018

Liu, Z., Tong, L., Ping, L., Jia, C., & Jin, L. (2018). Verifiable searchable encryption with aggregate keys for data sharing system. *Future Generation Computer Systems*, *78*(2), 778–788. doi:10.1016/j.future.2017.02.024

Lu, R., Li, X., Liang, X., Shen, X., & Lin, X. (2011). GRS: The green, reliability, and security of emerging machine to machine communications. *IEEE Communications Magazine*, *49*(4), 28–35. doi:10.1109/MCOM.2011.5741143

Luan, T. H., Gao, L., Li, Z., Xiang, Y., Wei, G., & Sun, L. (2015). Fog computing: focusing on mobile users at the edge. *Comput. Sci.*

Mehdi, R., Paul, R., & Raymond, C. K.-K. (2017). Cloud of things in smart agriculture: Intelligent irrigation monitoring by thermal imaging. *IEEE Cloud Comput.*, *4*(1), 10–15. doi:10.1109/MCC.2017.5

Michael, B., Casassa, M. M., Chen, L., & Siani, P. (2014). End-to-end policy-based encryption techniques for multi-party data management. *Computer Standards & Interfaces*, *36*(4), 689–703. doi:10.1016/j. csi.2013.12.004

Ns-3 tutorial, Release ns-3-dev. (2018). Retrieved from https://www.nsnam.org/docs/tutorial/ns-3-tutorial.pdf

Osanaiye, O., Chen, S., Yan, Z., Lu, R., Choo, K., & Dlodlo, M. (2017). From cloud to fog computing: A review and a conceptual live VM migration framework. *IEEE Access: Practical Innovations, Open Solutions*, *5*(99), 8284–8300. doi:10.1109/ACCESS.2017.2692960

Ottenwälder, B., Koldehofe, B., Rothermel, K., & Ramachandran, U. (2013). MigCEP: operator migration for mobility driven distributed complex event processing. *7th ACM Int. Conf. Distributed Event-based Systems*, 183-194. 10.1145/2488222.2488265

Paharia, B., & Bhushan, K. (2018, July). DDoS Detection and Mitigation in Cloud Via FogFiter: A Defence Mechanism. In *2018 9th International Conference on Computing, Communication and Networking Technologies (ICCCNT)* (pp. 1-7). IEEE. 10.1109/ICCCNT.2018.8493704

Peng, Z., Chen, Z., Liu Joseph, K., Liang, K., & Liu, H. (2018). An efficient access control scheme with outsourcing capability and attribute update for fog computing. *Future Generation Computer Systems*, *78*(2), 753–762.

Quratulain, A., Malik, S. U. R., Adnan, A., Raymond, C. K.-K., Saher, T., & Masoom, A. (2017). A cross tenant access control (CTAC) model for cloud computing: Formal specification and verification. *IEEE Transactions on Information Forensics and Security*, *12*(6), 1259–1268. doi:10.1109/TIFS.2016.2646639

Raymond, C. K.-K., Junghyun, N., & Dongho, W. (2014). A mechanical approach to derive identity-based protocols from Diffie-Hellman-based protocols. *Inf. Sci.*, *281*, 182–200. doi:10.1016/j.ins.2014.05.041

Rodrigo, R. (2018). *Mobile edge computing, Fog et al.: A survey and analysis of security threats and challenges* (Vol. 78). Future Gener. Comput. Syst.

Shi, W., Cao, J., Zhang, Q., Li, Y., & Xu, L. (2016). Edge computing: Vision and challenges. *IEEE Internet Things J.*, *3*(5), 637–646. doi:10.1109/JIOT.2016.2579198

Siani, P. (2011). *End-to-end policy-based encryption and management of data in the cloud*. CloudCom.

Stojmenovic, I. (2014). Fog computing: A cloud to the ground support for smart things and machine-to-machine networks. *IEEE Australasian Telecommunication Networks and Applications Conference (ATNAC)*, 117-122. 10.1109/ATNAC.2014.7020884

Stojmenovic, I., & Wen, S. (2014). The fog computing paradigm: Scenarios and Security Issues. *Proceedings of the 2014 Federated Conference on Computer Science and Information Systems*, 2, 1–8. 10.15439/2014F503

Vaquero & Rodero-Merino. (2014). *Finding your Way in the Fog: Towards a comprehensive Definition of Fog Computing*. HP Laboratories.

Wang, H., Wang, Z., & Josep, D.-F. (2018). Anonymous and secure aggregation scheme in fog-based public cloud computing. *Future Generation Computer Systems*, *78*(2), 712–719. doi:10.1016/j.future.2017.02.032

Wang, J. (2004). *ns-2 Tutorial (1)*. Multimedia Networking Group, The Department of Computer Science, UVA. Retrieved from http://www.cs.virginia.edu/~cs757/slidespdf/cs757-ns2-tutorial1.pdf

Wang, T., Cai, Y., Jia, W., Wen, S., Wang, G., Tian, H., ... Zhong, B. (2015). Maximizing real-time streaming services based on a multi-servers networking framework. *Computer Networks*, *93*(1), 199–212.

Wang, T., Zhou, J., Huang, M., Zakirul Alam Bhuiyan, M. D., Liu, A., Xu, W., & Xie, M. (2018, June). Fog-based storage technology to fight with cyber threat. *Future Generation Computer Systems*, *83*, 208–218. doi:10.1016/j.future.2017.12.036

Wang, W., & Lu, Z. (2013). Cyber security in the Smart Grid: Survey and challenges. *Computer Networks*, *57*(5), 1344–1371. doi:10.1016/j.comnet.2012.12.017

Wang, X., Cai, Y., & Li, Z. (2014). A novel hybrid incentive mechanism for node cooperation in mobile cyber-physical systems. *International Journal of Parallel, Emergent and Distributed Systems*, *29*(3), 316–336. doi:10.1080/17445760.2013.852194

Wei, C., Fadlullah, Z., Kato, N., & Stojmenovic, I. (2014, July). On optimally reducing power loss in micro-grids with power storage devices. *IEEE Journal on Selected Areas in Communications*, *32*(7), 1361–1370. doi:10.1109/JSAC.2014.2332077

Xiao, L., Li, Q., & Liu, J. (2016). Survey on secure cloud storage. *J. Data Acquis. Process.*, *31*(3), 64–472.

Xiao, Z., & Xiao, Y. (2013). Security and privacy in cloud computing. *IEEE Communications Surveys and Tutorials*, *15*(2), 843–859. doi:10.1109/SURV.2012.060912.00182

Xue, Y., & Lu, R. (2017). Achieving efficient and privacy-preserving cross-domain big data deduplication in cloud. IEEE Trans. Big Data, 1-12.

Xun, Y., Athman, B., Dimitrios, G., Andy, S., & Jan, W. (2016). Privacy protection for wireless medical sensor data. *IEEE Transactions on Dependable and Secure Computing*, *13*(3), 369–380. doi:10.1109/TDSC.2015.2406699

Yang, R., Xu, Q., Ho, A. M., Yu, Z., Hao, W., & Lu, Z. (2018). Position based cryptography with location privacy: A step for Fog Computing. *Future Generation Computer Systems*, *78*(2), 799–806. doi:10.1016/j.future.2017.05.035

Yu, Z., Ho, A. M., Xu, Q., Yang, R., & Han, J. (2018). Towards leakage-resilient fine-grained access control in fog computing. *Future Generation Computer Systems*, *78*(2), 763–777. doi:10.1016/j.future.2017.01.025

Zhang, Y., Yang, X., Wei, W., & Abdulhameed, A. (2018). A variant of password authenticated key exchange protocol. *Future Generation Computer Systems*, *78*(2), 699–711. doi:10.1016/j.future.2017.02.016

Chapter 16
Survey on Industrial Internet of Things (IoT) Threats and Security

Andrea Chiappetta
https://orcid.org/0000-0001-7135-7777
Marconi International University, USA

ABSTRACT

Analyzing the evolution of new generation peripherals can affirm that the next decade will be characterized by the exponential increase in the number of "objects" interconnected to the internet that will be more able to communicate with each other independently and will lead to the affirmation of the paradigm internet of things (IoT), which will revolutionize everyday life on a global level. This evolution will concern not only the business realities, interested in the development of applications and systems necessary to emerge and be competitive on the market but also the ordinary citizens who will be surrounded by interconnected objects able to facilitate their everyday life. This aspect implies particular attention to the implementation of solutions oriented to cyber security necessary to guarantee an efficient and effective level of protection against the threats coming from the "world" internet, known by the term cyber space.

SURVEY OF INDUSTRIAL IOT THREATS

Industrial IoT threats are the dangers of likely attack against devices and machines connected through IoT in various industries like power generation, transportation, construction as well as healthcare. Considering the fact that the industrial IoT has a high potential, the risks involved are also relatively high.

Analyzing the evolution of new generation peripherals we can affirm that the next decade will be characterized by the exponential increase in the number of "objects" interconnected to the Internet which will be more and more able to communicate with each other independently and will lead to the affirmation of the paradigm " Internet of Things (IoT) "or" Internet of Things "which will revolutionize everyday life on a global level. This evolution will concern not only the business realities, interested in the development of applications and systems necessary to emerge and be competitive on the market

DOI: 10.4018/978-1-5225-8407-0.ch016

but also the ordinary citizens who will be surrounded by interconnected objects able to facilitate their everyday life.

The IoT paradigm is relatively new but has an essential evolutionary potential due to the rapid evolution of transmission technologies characterized by ever-increasing speeds and used today for access to the Internet to fly the interconnection of "objects" which will be increasingly independent in the control and exchange of information useful for infrastructure management.

The technologies related to the IoT paradigm will have to evolve according to the basic rules of cybersecurity to guarantee the protection of data Privacy and Critical Infrastructures, where present, in compliance with the Critical Infrastructure Protection Directive (2008/114/EC) new European Data Protection Regulation (GDPR 679/2016) which was implemented on 25 May 2018 and the European Network and Information Security Directive (NIS 1148/2016) performed on 9 May 2018.

As for the private sector also for the industry, the Internet of Things (IoT) is seen as a valuable tool to offer opportunities, but often they do not appropriately evaluate the risks to which they might exhibit. This aspect, on the one hand, provides excellent opportunities deriving from having a great variety of apparat/systems always connected, on the other, it exposes to security breaches as the equipment is not always designed taking this aspect into account.

It is precisely this tremendous concrete opportunity for IoT technological growth that is the fundamental pillar for the development of the so-called "Fourth Industrial Revolution" known by the term Industry 4.0 (Figure 1).

Comparisons Between Industrial IoT and Other IoT Applications

The Industrial IoT is quite different from the other IoT applications because its main focus entails connecting devices and machines in various industries like gas and oil, construction and transport, healthcare and power utilities among others. IoT entails devices at the consumer level like bands of fitness or smart appliances and other applications which do not typically form situations of emergency if some aspects

Figure 1. The fourth industrial revolution: "Industry 4.0"

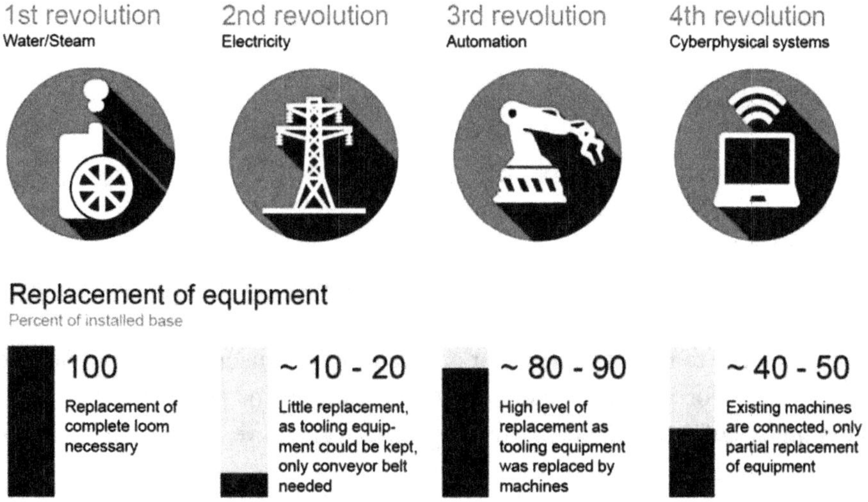

do not go as expected. That is to say, the deployment of industrial IoT has more at stake whereby failures in the system and downtime can lead to situations that are of high risk or life-threatening. Industrial IoT brings together computers from IT to operational technology, creating more possibilities to enhance instrumentation, which in turn leads to major productivity and efficiency gains for any operations in the industry.

The uniqueness of Industrial IoT comes in different ways. However, it is important to note that it works using the same principals to any other form of IoT technology instrumentation that is automated and reporting being used to do stuffing that never had the abilities before. With that in mind, its scale is quite different than just a normal system that lets one mess with the thermostat on a phone.

Industrial IoT has quite a number of unique challenges. This is because industrial IoT devices have long lives of service than the gadgetry of consumers. Even past the longevity and raw scale involved in the Industrial IoT, the process of implementation can be very complex, allowing for loopholes likely to affect the security of the Industrial IoT. Ensuring security in the Industrial IoT applications needs a strategy dedicated to collect the data from endpoints, having the data stored in a format that can be easily accessed (whether in the cloud or a data center) and feed it to the engine of analysis and converting the insights into vital information that can be used to enhance security.

Need for Industrial IOT

Industrial IoT is very important because organizations have information that they want to protect and they have invested a lot of funds in that. Thus, with the unique features of industrial IoT, various industries will be connected to one another and communication will be easy. At the same time, the security of data shared among the select industries is enhanced because of the way industrial IO is configured and applied.

Network Architectures and Technologies of IoT Systems

The network architecture typically used by IoT systems has 3 distinct levels:

- Interface with the physical world;
- Mediation;
- Control Center.

At the first level belong all the "objects" that can:

- Interact with the surrounding environment;
- Provide your identification code (id);
- Acquire specific information;
- Execute certain commands.

The systems belonging to this network layer can be passive sensors, which do not require a power supply, or active sensors for which an energy source is needed for power supply. These sensors are characterized by limited information processing capabilities and have apparent hardware limitations on data storage.

To allow communication with the second level units, they are provided with specific network interfaces for wired (wired) connections or radio (wireless) connections.

At the second level belong all the "objects" that can:

- Read the identification codes (ID);
- To convey network traffic.

The systems belonging to this network layer are mainly RFID readers and gateways. The role of these "objects" is critical as they have to deal with the collection of information coming from the nodes belonging to the first level and propagate them to the systems belonging to the third level or the Control Centers.

Finally, the systems able to:

- Receive information from second-level units;
- Memorize the information received;
- Process the information collected;
- Make the processed data available.

Central purchasing systems and operations centers perform the tasks listed above. They require superior hardware and software technical features as they play a decisive role in the elaboration of the information acquired by the nodes belonging to the network sub-levels.

The current limit of the different IoT devices on the market is that they are produced with characteristics that frequently are not able to share the communication standard (e.g., proprietary network protocol) and the application protocol in contravention of the technological paradigm of " Internet of Things "or:

"Communicate and cooperate directly in an automated way." The previous is referred to in the technical jargon of Machine to Machine (M2M) communication, which differs from the Machine to Human (M2H) communication which indicates, instead, the exchange of information between the device and the real mode surrounding it (people).

According to the analysts of the IoT Observatory of the Politecnico di Milano[1], a possible solution to allow a new approach to the design of network architectures for IoT systems is to move from a vertical path interested in ad-hoc design of software, hardware and communication protocols, a more horizontal approach oriented to the design of applications able to exploit sensor networks that are interoperable with each other at the apparatus level.

The technologies involved by the IoT are many and concern the most different devices in everyday and industrial use, among which:

- Cameras;
- Environmental sensors;
- Thermostats;
- Detectors;
- wearable items, such as watches and bracelets;
- Electric meters;
- Medical devices;
- Advertising signs;
- Variable message panels.

FUTURE EVOLUTION OF THE IOT

A.T. Kearney recently conducted unique, in-depth research and analysis of IoT to more thoroughly understand the value it offers the EU28 and the ways that member countries can best address the hurdles that will keep them from realizing its fullest benefits. There overarching finding: Within the next ten years the market for IoT solutions will be worth €80 billion, and its potential value for the EU28 economy could reach nearly €1 trillion (see Figure 2).

There are many areas of interest related to the future development of innovative IoT solutions, all of which are interested in improving sectors such as industrial production, agricultural cultivation, energy saving, physical, road, and IT security. For this reason, companies will be directly involved in economic growth combined with the competitiveness that will encourage operators in the sector to emerge and position themselves among the pretenders to commercial success.

The expected result will be a sufficient change in the way people work and face everyday life, which will be increasingly combined in the IoT ecosystem. An important consideration regards the growth trend of "online" devices.

A total of 2.9 billion People—40% of the world's population—are online today. It has been predicted that by 2020, over 40 billion more devices will be made "smart" through embedded processors and intelligence. The Internet of Things (IoT) has already grown beyond niche industrial and medical applications and has entered every market and industry. Observers expect its growth to be exponential. So transformative are its expected ramifications that some have labeled it "Industry 4.0." The transformation will, in any case, result from an understanding of how digitization is modifying existing relationships

Figure 2. The market IoT
Source: A.T. Kearney analysis[2]

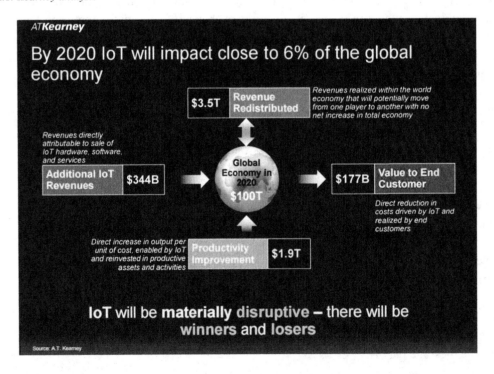

and balance of power and responsibilities among the different actors along the value chain: suppliers, buyers, competitors, and substitutes. The following shifts in relationships and strategies are expected from digitization:

- The growing integration of the value chain, full life-cycle management supported by a continuous data-thread.
- Shift from the transport of goods to the transmission of data, enabling distributed production, predictive maintenance, and optimization.
- Enhanced customization / collaborative design, trend back to customer proximity, shift from a consumer to a "prosumer" model.
- The emergence of new factory types: smart automated plants, customer-centric plants, e-plants.
- Development of new business models.

The IoT indicates a context consisting of billions of devices connected to the Internet during their normal operation and have the ability to communicate, perceive and have intelligence. These devices also have a physical/virtual identity, multi-modal attributes, and interfaces (Haller et al, 2008, Wann and Ranjan, 2015). It is expected that in the next future developments will be based on systems that contain semi-automated IoT applications. If we refer to the graph (figure 1), it is easy to see how these data created or used by IoT devices represent a real challenge. The IoT industry assumes that you can trust your data, but this usually does not respond to the truth because each placement could potentially be easily hacked (Paolicchi, 2018).

IoT in Compliance With the GDPR and the NIS

Communications carried out through the many modern smart systems contain specific indications concerning the personal data of users. Also, the devices can communicate the position of individuals through geolocation and track the various activities they perform during regular use. The resulting risk is the possibility of storing this information, making it available and available to third parties interested in the value of the data itself which, if combined and aggregated, becomes a potential source of business.

Figure 3. Unites of IoT installed by category from 2014 to 2020[3]

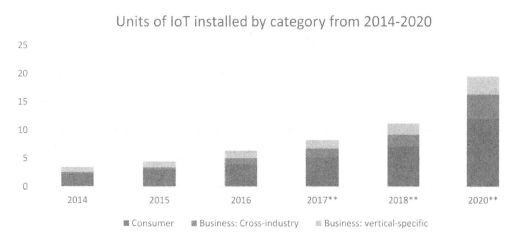

As is understandable it is necessary to pursue the achievement of a balance between the need to apply security rules and at the same time protect the privacy of the individual.

From May 25th, 2018, the European Data Protection Regulation (679/2016), known by the acronym GDPR (General Data Protection Regulation), was implemented by all EU Member States. The introduction of this regulation is aimed at the protection of individuals with particular attention to the processing of personal data and the free circulation of the same and regards both the public sector and the private sector.

The legislation will be applied and also extended to companies that reside outside the European Union and process data coming from the European territory. The regulation has become necessary in the face of technological development that has involved in an overwhelming way advanced technical solutions capable of endangering the protection and security of personal data.

The GDPR Regulation has two primary objectives:

- Adaptation of Data Protection (data protection);
- Elimination of the application fragmentation of the legislation.

In the first point, the regulation aims to adapt data protection to the continuous and exponential technological progress that increasingly involves the transmission of personal data through the Internet connection which has simplified the transit of data between the Member States of the Union European and extra-European.

In the second point, the fundamental objective is to group under a single shared law all the European States, effectively eliminating the problem due to the presence of different standards applied in the European Union.

Consequently, to all this, the Internet of Things systems will have to be developed according to criteria compatible with the objectives established by the European GDPR Regulation and the European NIS Directive. This is because they are devices that, due to their technical characteristics, turn out to be potential targets for direct or indirect cyberattacks. In the second case, the IoT systems could be used to carry cyber-attacks distributed to specific targets, substantially increasing the effectiveness of the damage caused.

GDPR is meant to perform the following duties:

1. Harmonization of the laws of data privacy across the European continent
2. Protecting and empowering all citizens within the EU and ensure their data has enough privacy and is well protected.
3. Reshape the approach taken by companies throughout Europe in dealing with the privacy of their data.

NIS deals with the security of information and network systems as well as the digital data within the network and information systems. Whereas GDPR deals with the security of personal data, NIS deals with the security of systems. Nevertheless, the two overlap in quite a number of issues because of the provisions by GDPR on security and the possibility that many companies covered by NIS could also turn out to be data controllers.

IoT Threats

In most cases, the cyber-threats which target the IoT infrastructure are aimed at destroying or harming some of their aspects like integrity, consistency, availability, integrity, privacy, and trust. Some of the most harmful cyber-threats aimed towards IoT include Botnets, malware, leakage of information, Denial of Service, Ransomware and physical manipulation.

Malware is malicious software which works through hijacking the functions of sensors and then spread them in the IoT infrastructure to gather operational intelligence. The botnet, on the other hand, entails a network of devices that are infected and spread through the world and controlled remotely from a single master, using a client-server architecture. On the other hand, ransomware attack by targeting facilities of data storage and then blocks the access to the data collected through encryption (Distefano, Merlino and Puliafito 2012).

The use of 6LoWPAN, which is made up of IPv6 and IEEE 802.15.4 weaknesses and brings in many other threats from both sides, therefore, aiming for different IoT network architecture layers. That starts from the network's application layer, all the way through to the physical layers. The most usual threats against the network's most vulnerable three layers include availability attacks or DoS attacks and unauthorized data access according to Ferdous et al., (2016)

Threats on the Perception Layer

The layer entails the physical place where highly-distributed, resource constrained and heterogeneous IoT devices operate (Distefano, Merlino and Puliafito 2012). Considering the constrained type of the devices used and also given that objects are not resistant to tampering and the lack of sufficient security mechanisms in place, different attackers can easily gain access to the physical layer of devices with a motive of reprogramming their functionalities or damage them. Some of the technologies that can be applied to tamper with the systems include LTE, Wi-Fi, RFID as well as WiMax. Some of the most common attacks have been discussed below:

Brute Force Attacks

The attacks are cryptanalytic in nature and can be applied in attempts to do data decryption on any form of data that has been encrypted for security purposes. In many cases, several smart home devices are quite susceptible to such types of attacks. That leaves home internet users connected with IoT very susceptible to attacks. Some of the most common attacks include:

1. Side-channel attacks
2. Masquerading attacks

Side-Channel Attacks

According to the Cloud Security Alliance (2013), the attacks are any forms of attacks done on the basis of the information obtained from physically implementing a certain cryptosystem. The attacks entail issues on evaluating leaked data and information that comes from physically implementing to recuperate the password or pin being used by the gadget under attack. That can be done by tracing power or timing the operations of the device's inner operations, or even defective outputs that the device produces. Considering IoT's openness, there are many types of side-channel attacks that can be initialized including fault induction attacks and timing attacks (Gope, and Hwang, 2015).

Masquerading Attacks

In this regard, the hacker hardens and attempts to utilize the identity of the node that has been authorized by the device in the given network. In most cases, such attacks are triggered and initiated at the network layer. Different other attacks, in this case, can include physical and tampering attacks, jamming attacks, collision attacks, eavesdropping and corrupting data (Gope, and Hwang, 2015).

Network Layer Threats

In networks, the network layer contains the most intermediate layer applied in transmitting and aggregating any form of sensed data moving from the perception layer in a network, to the application layer in the same network. The movement of data is done through the use of existing wireless and wired networks of communication like Wi-Fi and LAN. Ferdous et al., (2016) state that the network layer is IoT's "backbone" of them. The network layer is a Wireless Sensor Network and it is a very popular IoT network I term of the capability to cover different huge areas of things and still be able to maintain enough energy for consumption. At the same, the IoT features need to be pinpointed in all networks of 6LoWPAN, the layer is made up of two other smaller layers that make the 6LoWPAN quite susceptible to any form of routing attack. Different forms of attacks that target the two smaller layers within the layer are quite well-known (Gope, and Hwang, 2015).

Attacks on the Adaptation Layer

The main function of the adaptation layer is the translation of the packets between the internet and 6LoWPAN network. Thus, the layer is susceptible to various attacks related to 6LoWPAN including:

1. Authentication attacks
2. Fragmentation attacks
3. Confidentiality attacks

Authentication Attacks

The major weakness of 6LoWPAN is that's it has no mechanism that can be used in authenticating its nodes before they are allowed to join and be part of the network. Thus, it is quite clear that any harmful nodes can easily enter into the network and activate other attacks from within the network, which is a very dangerous thing to any IoT applications. There have been proposals for several protocols of authentication but only in theory and literature and have not seen their implementation taken seriously. Despite all the proposed protocols, there is still very high danger looming through threats and attacks to IoT applications and devices (Gope, and Hwang, 2015).

Fragmentation Attacks

In many cases, the border router is a node wired and is well-protected through very strong security mechanisms. Nevertheless, the progress of reassembling and packet fragmentation will still be susceptible to some extent. In such attacks, the hacker can reconstruct or change the fields of fragmentation of the packet such as the datagram offset. Such attacks are dangerous and can lead to considerable damages to a certain node, like the overflow of reassembling buffer due to re-sequencing of packets, exhaustion of resources or even shutting down and restarting of the device or application. At the same time, there is no existing technique to authenticate and at the receiver end to check if the fragment received is not duplicated or spoofed as the attacker could insert his personal fragments in the chain of fragmentation (Liu, Xiao, and Chen, 2012).

Confidentiality Attacks

In a well-secured network, it is expected that only the authorized nodes can gain access to, overview and control data within the network. Offering sufficient confidentiality in 6LoWPAN can assist in abating different attacks like eavesdropping, spoofing attacks and MITM. When it comes to authentication. Managing identities forms part of a very aspect to make sure that there is sufficient confidentiality. All the same, cryptography is taken as one of the major techniques used in dealing with authentication and confidentiality problems. It is also important to note that IPSec offers layer security on the network on the basis of end-to-end through enabling the encryption and authentication of interchanged packets of IP (Liu, Xiao, and Chen, 2012).

IoT Security

The issue of computer security has evolved over the last decade in a predominant IT (Information Technology) focusing first on the protection of computers, then on the protection of smartphones and tablets to currently focus on the protection of all Internet objects of Things (Figure 4) including vehicles, appliances, environmental sensors, technical and health equipment, wearable products such as bracelets, watches and many other devices connected via the Internet.

The growing number of interconnected and pervasive IoT devices present in the most varied daily activities draws attention to a very critical issue called cybersecurity (Cyber Security) which, compared to the classical concept of computer security, focuses more on "objects" interconnected the latest generation belonging to the Internet of Things ecosystem. Each of these smart devices can potentially be exposed to security problems ranging from the typical cyber-attack to the most subtle and veiled espionage.

Intruders can target many connected devices of daily use with consequent risk for privacy and physical security of people. Critical vulnerabilities have been highlighted by specific studies concerning not only the IoT devices connected but also the related management applications and not least the cloud services increasingly used by companies and users. Verizon has recently conducted a study that has made it possible to determine that most vulnerabilities have been identified by security researchers. These vulnerabilities allowed and still allow to take control of multiple devices among which we can highlight:

Figure 4. Representation of the internet of things ecosystem

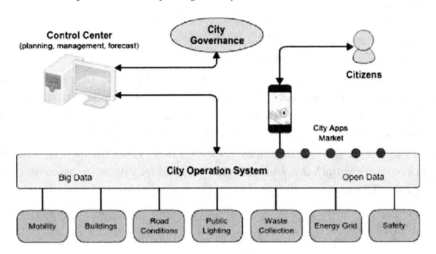

- Supply systems of a building;
- Water heating systems;
- Road traffic management systems;
- Devices for the administration of wind power plants;
- Systems for the management of automatic car washings.

There are also areas even more critical than those indicated above because they intervene in specific environments and public utility:

- Systems and devices used in healthcare;
- Transport networks, monitoring, and energy control;
- Devices used in industrial production;
- Application systems in the military field.

The analysis carried out by Gartner highlights the great innovation introduced by the IoT[4]: "The ability to change the state of the environment around connected objects and even their state." This implies the possibility that an IoT system, compromised by an attacker, modifies its "behavior" by altering the actions that had been configured initially. The system could dangerously change the management of the plant to which it refers, for example, could modify the surrounding environmental values to damage and danger of public health in a controlled environment as could be a chemical laboratory, a nuclear power plant, a refinery oil. Not only that, the device could irreparably change the trajectory of an aircraft or the course of a boat with potential risks to safety.

The enormous diffusion and density of vulnerable IoT devices provide cybercriminals with numerous opportunities to break the system and exposes the inexperienced to the real risk of becoming unknowingly infectious. These episodes are evidence of the fact that companies and consumers often ignore the basic principles of security applied to peripheral devices or networks, with consequences that may prove disastrous.

A very critical event occurred in October 2016 when the most massive DDoS attack[5] (Distributed Denial of Service) was distributed to a significant service provider called Dyn using an IoT botnet (IoT device network). Remotely controlled by a hacker and composed of devices infected with specialized malware). The result of the cyber-attack through the Mirai malware was the extended interruption of the Internet service that hit and damaged significant entities such as Twitter, Guardian, Netflix, and CNN. The spread of malware was possible because each infected system continuously searched the Internet for vulnerable IoT devices using predefined utilities and passwords to access and propagate the infection.

General Threats

All IT infrastructures and device face some general threats that expose them to attacks from malicious people.

The table contains the general threats that could affect an IT infrastructure like railways, airports and smart buildings. These threats can be divided into 5 groups, the first is related to the malicious actions and methods like:

- **Denial of Service:** In most cases, IoT devices communicate through radio access technologies in the physical layer. The wireless link is very susceptible to the Denial of Service (DoS) attacks, which may take their form in signal distortion or jamming. DoS attacks may compromise system availability. While spread spectrum techniques can be used against wireless jamming,
- **Exploitation of Software Vulnerabilities:** Just like Malware, software vulnerabilities have very adverse implications in security. There are so many dices connected through IoT than in the previous years. That is a great advantage to the hackers since they make sure that they utilize machines like cameras and printers that were never created with protection from strong attacks. That has led to several organizations restructuring their plans to deal with the latest vulnerabilities. The attackers use the vulnerabilities found in such software and penetrate to the firm networks, affecting all the IoT connected devices. The vendors of software know that such vulnerabilities exist, thus the reason why they frequently release updates on their software to counter them (Atzori et al., 2010).

Figure 5. General threats that could affect an IT infrastructure

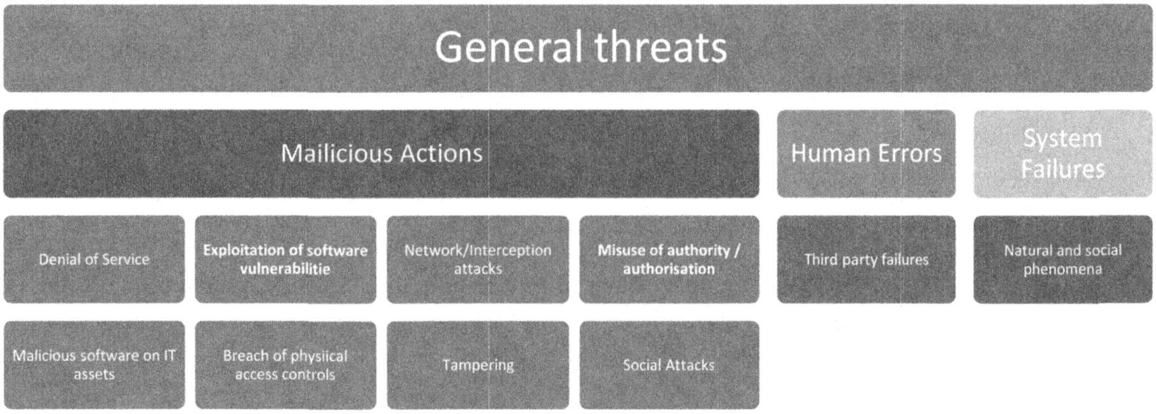

- **Misuse of Authority/Authorization:** The increased interconnection between devices in IoT has led to a great demand for strong responses insecurity, including storing sensitive information about some companies and individuals, data on financial transactions, marketing, and product development. That has prompted companies to ensure that they restrict the number of people with access to such information. The misuse of authority delegated to individuals leads to access and sharing and even wrong use of information for individual gains instead of the company's interest (La Diega and Walden, 2016).

- **Network/Interception Attacks:** The IoT networking layer suffers all sorts of security threats that are known within the computer networks community. Although there are specialized attacks for Wireless Sensor Networks (WSN), the aggregation network (often referred to as Gateway or Link layer), and the transport network between aggregation points and the cloud and its applications (A.T Kearney, n.d).

- **Tampering:** Tampering is an action when an attacker performs physical modifications on the device or on the communication link. This physical layer provides a great attack surface. Hardware elements can be accessed, identity stolen or replaced, which can violate confidentiality, availability and Integrity objectives. One way to avoid this is to use tamper-resistant packaging [15]. However, this may be too expensive considering cheap low-power sensors or consumer devices which are the main drivers of IoT. Tampering the communication link can be in the form of disconnecting or changing the physical link which is a case of Denial-of-Service attack or altering the transmitted data which is a case of a Man-in-the-Middle attack (Wu, 2012).

- **Breach of Physical Access Controls:** The breach of physical access controls in a system or organization comes from the people within the company. Even though there are strong measures in place at a data center, the greatest security risk emanates from inside the organization. Despite some individuals accessing systems with malicious plans, some of the security breaches are accidental making up for 9-18% of all breaches. Many standalone traditional systems can only be breached through physical access, and interconnected devices are affected after such attacks. Thus, the breach of physical access controls is a great concern that should be dealt with through ensuring physical security like lock-ups to servers and rooms with delicate information access (Khan & Khan, 2012).

After understanding the different general threats, it is also vital to briefly introduce and understand the threats that face our SPS (Security, Privacy and Safety). With regard to security, it can be grouped in terms of the CIA triad:

1. Confidentiality
2. Availability
3. Integrity.

According to Sicari et al. (2015), threats to safety can be taken as being similar to those of privacy and security. The threats to safety come from flaws in aspects like maintenance, production, design, or even deployment of various IoT projects.

Additionally, data could be utilized to accomplish different purposes and tasks than the initial intention when the data collection was being done (normally referred to as a function creep) (Sundarkumar et al., 2015). Encrypting data is not a permanent solution to the above issues since encrypted data can in many cases be decrypted through a combination of various sets of data.

The SPS threats have to be taken into consideration at the time of the entire IoT system lifecycle (pre during and post-deployment). In the pre-deployment stage, the threats to SPS need to be applied while making IoT system designs. That is normally called Safety design, privacy and security. When applied to gather and store personal data, the devices of IoT should be changed to be SPS-friendly, for example, through the addition of features like a button to offer "Delete" option and also an option to leave the system when one needs. At the time of deployment and after post-deployment, there should efforts to ensure that the devices of IoT are accountable and transparent enough (Sadeghi, Wachsmann, and Waidner, 2015).

The framework proposes the deployment of SPS by design to minimize SPS threats, and identifies four obstacles in realizing this: 1) IoT complexity, 2) lack of awareness, 3) lack of incentives, and 4) lack of monitoring and enforcement. The framework also shows how these obstacles, and solution directions to overcome them, are related to each other in that addressing one impacts the other one(s) and vice versa. The conclusion that can be drawn from this work is that there is no one-size-fits-all measure to address SPS threats. Instead, a variety of measures is needed to create an SPS-friendly IoT

Hardware and Software Limits of IoT Objects

The main problem associated with IoT devices is the level of security which is very low because they are interconnected objects through insecure channels and transmission protocols. This flaw makes the systems belonging to the Internet of Things ecosystem a reasonably straightforward target for cybercriminals.

IoT devices are mainly divided into embedded systems, sensors and actuators. For this reason, the hardware of which they are composed turns out to be very variable and limited. IoT systems are typically small in size, equipped with operating systems associated with processors (CPUs) and memories with essential performance and features.

An illustrative example is the list of hardware features typical of the simplest IoT devices:

- **Flash Memory:** 196 kB;
- **SRAM:** 24 Kb;
- **Clock Speed:** 32 MHz

From the information above, it can be understood how a simple IoT device, used in a specific field such as temperature or pressure monitoring, is characterized by minimum components that are not able to guarantee the necessary predisposition to the development of safety. Analyzing the chapter on IoT security written by Verizon, we can deduce that the increase in each bit of memory and the increase in processing capacity on devices considerably increases production costs. The economic burden also doubles for the development of software which must be able to support the functionality necessary for system security (Wu, 2012).

The Weak Link of IoT Devices: "The Firmware"

The firmware, an expression consisting of the terms firm (stable) and ware (component), is a program present within each electronic component and performs a critical task. Its fundamental role is to start the functioning of the same component allowing it to communicate with further integrals or cards present in the device in which they are installed. How much shared allows us to determine the importance it has to release firmware updates otherwise it may happen that an IoT device, updated and therefore safe at the time of purchase, becomes dangerous for the consumer when cybercriminals discover a vulnerability of the system. In today's context, smart devices using the Internet of Things ecosystem are increasingly being used. However, the technology companies producing these evolved systems tend to underestimate the potential risks to which they are exposed since the latter are connected continuously to the Internet. The greatest danger is caused by superficial behavior conducted by the manufacturers themselves who are oriented to release the firmware updates with an excessively low frequency and sometimes, fortunately only in extreme cases, and the updates are not indeed released. This superficial behavior allows hackers to take advantage of a huge amount of potentially vulnerable devices.

Not always the failure to update the software is attributable to the choices of the manufacturer; also the end user plays an active and harmful role in this sense. Often, due to personal inexperience or lack of knowledge of the technological product used, the consumer does not check for updates and does not install the firmware versions released and recommended by the manufacturer. To overcome this specific situation and reduce as much as possible the risks related to the security of software platforms, the most advanced devices, including computers, are programmed to perform updates automatically without the need for customer intervention the final. Unfortunately, protecting and updating the security features of the systems belonging to the Internet of Things world is not, and for this reason, it will not be trivial to implement solutions oriented to this purpose.

In this regard, the company ARM Holdings[6], a company specializing in the technological development and known on the market to be the manufacturer of processors based on the ARM architecture, is engaged in the launch of the process that will lead to the approval of a standard for the Internet of Things. The company ARM Holdings has already released a formal document called "IoT Firmware Update Architecture"[7] demonstrating the commitment placed in the firmware security field. The paper presents a set of rules that all smart system manufacturers should follow during the implementation steps of the firmware update mechanism of the implemented devices.

The problem of security is even more evident if we consider that IoT devices are already on the market already vulnerable and become useful targets for cybercriminals from the first connection to the Internet. As highlighted in an editorial called "Cyber Security News" published by the General Department of the General Staff of the Air Force[8], it is clear that:

- IoT devices are often sold with default credentials or known security holes.
- Millions of unsafe devices are already connected, and millions of new ones are added every day.
- IoT devices are connected to the Internet 24 hours a day, so they are available for an attack at any time.
- IoT devices are often connected to high-speed Internet connections allowing the spread of extended attacks.
- IoT devices are extremely useful to use as anonymous proxies.

- The technology and knowledge to detect, violate and use IoT devices, and then use them in cyber-attacks, have been made public and are currently used in various services.

Critical Infrastructure Protection

At the Global level, all nations defined a list of Critical Infrastructure (and related services) that must be considered strategic and need to respect determinates rules (Anderson et al., 2012). The US level issued the first approach during the Clinton Administration in the 90s, then followed by Canada (in February 2001, Canada initiated OCIPEP (Office of Critical Infrastructure Protection and Emergency Preparedness) within the National Defense organizational structure Department and Europe (the European Commission adopted a Green Paper on a European program for Critical Infrastructure Protection, and in 2008, the European Council issued the Directive 2008/114/EC) (Fuchs et al., 2016).

The main characteristics essential for evaluating Critical Infrastructure are resilience, absorbability, adaptability, robustness, structural robustness, precautionary robustness, susceptibility, preparedness, recoverability, responsiveness, reparability, redundancy, overload capacity, safety, and security. These characteristics apply to each type of Critical Infrastructure (e.g., transport) and for any level of detail selected for the Critical Infrastructure analysis (system, subsystem, component).

The Critical Infrastructure characteristic's tree shows the relationship between the Critical infrastructure characteristics by the logic gates AND. Resilience is a series of processes form an umbrella attribute which is formed by partial features9. Resilience so can be divided down to the basic indivisible features. These essential characteristics can be evaluated through one or several parameters. Furthermore, the components at the higher level can be assessed through appropriate settings. Based on the Critical Infrastructure characteristic tree we can identify two types of interrelations among the Critical Infrastructure: additive and non - additive. The additive interrelation is valid for the Critical Infrastructure characteristics.

Another important aspect is related to the Critical Infrastructures interdependencies that usually fall into four principal classes:

- **Physical:** Operating one infrastructure is dependent on the other one's real output.

Figure 6. Critical infrastructure characteristic tree

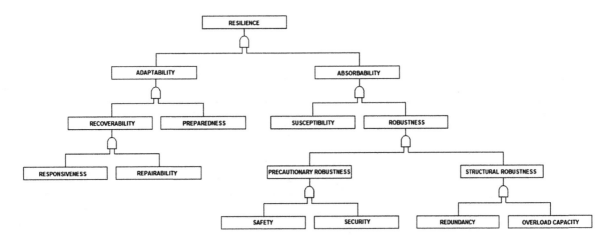

- **Cyber:** The level at which the information transmitted via the infrastructure can be depended upon.
- **Geographic:** The level of depending on the local environmental effects which instantaneously impacts several infrastructures.
- **Logical:** Any dependency not grouped as geographic, cyber or physical. A comprehensive analysis of all types of interdependencies is challenging and requires extensive modeling efforts to provide a better understanding of CI systems.

Table 1 provides an overview of the legal framework adopted at EU and US level that identify the management and role of critical infrastructure and the generally accepted standards.

Concerning the ENISA report on past incidents of cyber-attacks and ENISA's role in cyber-security, it is evident that cyber threats are a growing menace, spreading to all industry sectors that are relying on ICT systems10. Such incidents could be prevented by policies that neutralize the various market failures acting as a barrier to optimize private investment in cyber-security from public and private institutions, where an efficient cooperation and coordination in the real world experiences highlight the economic need for coordinated cyber defense (Brynjolfsson and Oh, 2012) to lower expenses on security for all partners involved (Flater et al., 2016).

The EU is working towards eliminating the cybersecurity threats. Although the issues of cyber-security are on the rise, the EU MS have all the policies and tools needed to deal with the issue of Cyber-security. All member states in the EU should come together and work towards achieving the common goal. Among the solutions proposed by NIS include all the members of the EU to bring in and implement independent national strategies on the security of information systems and networks. ENISA has the responsibility of implementing the directive provided by NIS (ENISA, 2017).

Standards

There is a lot of guidance created by the NIST (National Institute of Standards and Technology) and any organization can easily use such guidance. For instance, the SP (Special Publication) for NIST was created for different information systems and it is very efficient in the creation of a plan for security in any firm (Quashie & Tweneboah-Koduah, 2016). The IEC (International Electrotechnical Commission)

Table 1. Regulations overview

EU Regulations	US Regulations
Security: Large data volumes of data transfer are considered vulnerable to security breaches.	**Security:** There should be protection from harm to consumers from misuse and unauthorized access to personal information.
A privacy impact assessment should always be carried out before a device is released.	On data security, it is recommended that the device manufacturers use a privacy-by-design method.
Raw data should be deleted from the device immediately it has been extracted.	While endorsing the importance of limit retention and collection of data from users, there should be a flexible approach applied.
All principles of privacy-by-design-by-default should be followed.	The notice and choice are recognized to play a vital role and should always be applied.
All users should be informed once data has been collected and allow them to access the data, review it and do editing before transferring it.	

along with ISA (International Society of Automation) have created several standards of ISA/IEC-62443 which help in defining the procedures used to implement secure systems of control and the directions are applicable to system integrators, end-users, manufacturers of control systems and also the personnel dealing with system security issues (GAO, Government Accountability Office, 2015).

One of the major ways to close down on the gap existing between the standards for information security for railways and general systems has been offered by the European Commission regulation (Roman, Zhou & Lopez, 2013). That can be found in regulation number 402/2013 which deals with the most common methods of safety. The regulations point out three major techniques to help show that there is sufficient safety in railway systems:

1. Through following the available standards and rules (applying the codes of practice).
2. Through analyzing in a similar way, by displaying that the selected railway system can equally serve as a used and proven one.
3. Through explicitly analyzing risks, whereby the risks are clearly assessed and demonstrated as being acceptable.

It is assumed that from the process perspective, security can be regarded just as safety is, thus indicating that the threats might be treated as specific threats. That is done through the use of an approach under mutual criteria or in the case of railway systems, there can be the use of ISA99/IEC62443 (Boyes, 2013).

Considering the fact that IEC 62443 is coming up as a center for the group of standards for the railway system was also indicated by different other speakers at the workshop, with some reiterating that IEC 62443 is a standard for cybersecurity to approach the use of IoT in railway systems (Quashie & Tweneboah-Koduah, 2016).

The main notion of IEC 62443 is that it needs a group of synchronized steps to be taken, a technique that is mainly considered as defense-in-depth. The common adoption of IEC 62443 is can be seen in the DIN VDE V 0831-104; VDE V 0831-104:2015-10: Electric signaling systems for railways – Part 104: IT Security Guideline based on IEC 62443 (62443-3-3:2013) (a Germany standard).

From SCADA to Cloud Computing and IoT in the Supply Chains

SCADA means supervisory control and data acquisition; the first use is started in the 1960s to monitor and control remote gear grew that is part of the Control Systems family, that includes ICS (Industrial control system), DCS (Distributed control systems), PCS (process control system), etc. Early systems were built from mainframe computers and required human oversight to operate. With the technological development became automated reducing the involvement of human control. These systems are used to monitor and control a plant in industries in many different sectors like energy, transport, waste control, etc. In recent years, Cloud Computing and Internet of Things (IoT) have been rapidly advancing as the two fundamental technologies of the "Future Internet" concept (Gubbi et al., 2013).

Since the IoT ecosystem can often have critical infrastructure components, it will inevitably be a target for attack and espionage, as well as vulnerable to denial-of-service and many other types of cyber-attacks. (Chiappetta, 2017)[11] The heterogeneous functional and operational nature of interconnected and cooperating IoT systems of systems will evolve to a point where the security threat canvas is of a size and scale that will be difficult (if not impossible) to accurately represent in formalized security threat models, implying a need for compensatory techniques to help guarantee security imperatives are met.

The ENISA report on ICS and SCADA [12]identifies a series of the evolution of these systems that impact how cyber-security has to be implemented for those systems.

Cybersecurity in a Transportation Sector and Smart Buildings

Intelligent systems are everywhere - controlling road and rail infrastructure, improving vehicle performance and enhancing the passenger and driver experience. The proliferation of ECUs etc. inside vehicles, interfacing with external data sources including entertainment, GPS, and diagnostics, creates new vulnerabilities and opportunities for cyber-intrusion. A fundamentally fresh and holistic design approach, building security into vehicles and transportation from the ground up, is required.

Analyzing the transport section of the Cisco 2017 Cyber Security Report[13], based also on the evaluation of feedback received from its customers, the following exposures can be determined:

- **Top Transportation Threats Are Advanced Persistent Threats (APTs) and the Increased Use of Mobile Devices:** More than a third of transportation security professionals said that APTs and the proliferation of BYOD and smart devices were high-security risks to their organizations.
- **Security Talent Shortage:** More than half of transportation security teams reported having fewer than 30 employees dedicated to security. And, 29 percent said the lack of trained personnel is a major obstacle to adopting advanced technologies and processes (Alomari et al., 2012).
- **Breaches Are Frequent; Processes Are Flawed:** Nearly half of transportation security professionals have already dealt with public scrutiny due to a data breach. In fact, 35 percent said they see thousands of daily threat alerts, of which only 44 percent are investigated.
- **Outsourcing Is on the Rise:** Connected transportation teams are learning from past mistakes and finding new ways to better secure their networks.

Transportation across all modes is a vital service in all smart cities. Traditionally cities' transportation infrastructure has been built on closed, proprietary systems, today smart cities are increasingly moving toward more digitalized, connected transportation infrastructure. They're doing this because of the many benefits connected transportation provides citizens, such as improved safety, faster response times for emergency responders, timelier infrastructure repairs, and improved traffic flow and even reduce CO_2 emissions.

Table 2. Historical cyber-attacks until 2018

Transport	Worcester Airport (1997)	Port oh Houston DoS (2001)	CSX, Washington (2003)	Railcorp, Sydney (2004)	L.A. Traffic engineers' Strike (2007)	Lodz Trams (2008) Polland	Port Of Antwerp (2011 and 2013)	Tesla Hijacking competition (2014)	Maersk (2017) JNPT (2017)
Transport	Danish State Rail Operator (2018) DDoS Attack	Deutsche Bahn (2017) Ransomware	UK Rail (2016) – according to the cyber observatory at least 4 attacks were carried out	Pacific Northwest (2011), USA	Tram Hack (2008) Poland	CSX US Railway (2003) East Rail	Uber (2016) Port of Rotterdam (2016)	San Francisco Public Transport (2015) Sweden Airports (2015) Port of LA (2015)	

Rail Sector

The purpose of this section is to analyze the aspects of computer security applied to the railway transport sector with the aim of analyzing exposures deriving from the use of IoT systems.

The dynamism of our times, the need to provide information in real time and competition with other forms of transport, today also requires the use of IoT devices in this sector.

Take for example what happened in 2016 in the United Kingdom, where the railway network suffered four cyber-attacks[14].

Although these attacks have been more than exploratory and non-destructive, the introduction of digital rail transport plans such as digital signaling as part of the European Railway Traffic Management System (ERTMS) and other modernization initiatives will increase the likelihood of network infiltration. Both in number and extent of the impact. Such infiltrations could be used for data collection, perturbations or, in extreme cases, for potential derailments.

In March 2016, the South Korean National Intelligence Service said it had halted the attempt to hack the railway workers and close their e-mail accounts[15].

Switzerland is already using the ERTMS digital system on some of the busiest railway lines, while in March of this year hackers violated the websites of the Swiss Federal Railways exposing the vulnerability of the portals to online attacks[16].

Also in India in 2016, Al-Qaida hacked a microsite of the Railnet page of the Indian railway[17]: the hacked page of the Bhusawal division of the central railway personnel department and part of a large intranet created for the administrative needs of the department was replaced by Al-Qaida who left a distinctive message.

The main areas of exposure that will be analyzed are shown in Table 3.

Combining highly responsive, intelligent and autonomous vehicles helps in enabling communication amongst the vehicles, helped with the intelligent infrastructure, making sure that there are reliable and safe operations. That is done while ensuring that there is a combined running as well as contribution to drastically decrease the costs of the life cycle. That is achieved upon successfully deploying the next generation of management systems used in traffic like the ERTMS (European Railway Traffic Management System) and mass transit CBTC.

European Integrated Radio Enhanced Network (EIRENE) and European Rail Traffic Management System (ERTMS)

While introducing the EIRENE project, the European nations realized that they needed to introduce and enhance interoperability through their networks. On that realization, they came up with different prototypes and new radio system to help them meet the international and global standards of such networks, consequently, the railways required a complete comprehension of the issues connected to the installation and operation of the different digital cellular networks, enabling verification along with investigation of the actual costs related to implementing a future radio in European Railways.

Considering the current systems, the project has been modified and created to support standard applications of managing European Railways and an extension will be provided to the multimedia services provided to passengers. That includes extending the GSM standard system, so as to be a the bar with the following requirements of safety and operation:

Table 3. Cybersecurity and Privacy Technologies with respective Cybersecurity and Privacy Engineering Process

Cybersecurity and Privacy Technologies	Cybersecurity and Privacy Engineering Process
Cybersecurity of sensors and cyber-physical systems	Cybersecurity engineering process
Design of resilient architectures and applications	Privacy by design
Privacy and data protection issues in transportation systems	Security throughout the system life-cycle
Hardware security and secure hardware modules	Vehicle-related information sharing and vulnerability coordination
Security of vehicular communications (onboard, between vehicles, and between vehicles and infrastructure)	Software assurance and formal methods
Security of application platforms	Security standardization
Intrusion and anomaly detection systems with a specific activity of Forensics and analytics	Supply chain integrity and traceability
Security of legally mandated applications (e.g., event data recorders, flight data recorders, tachographs, etc.)	Communication of cybersecurity risks
Security of cloud-based infrastructure	Cybersecurity assurance testing
Security of road pricing, restricted area access, and vehicle monitoring	Information and processes to drive organizational awareness
Security of road pricing, restricted area access, and vehicle monitoring	Incident response
Security of vehicle theft deterrent, immobilization, and theft response solutions	Collaboration and engagement of stakeholders
Security of vehicular rights control and audit (e.g., feature activation)	Reverse engineering and penetration testing
Security of emerging technologies (e.g., automated driving, unmanned aerial vehicles, and electric vehicles)	
Anti-reverse engineering	

1. **Railway Operations:** MMI (Man Machine Interfaces) numbering and addressing schemes.
2. **Railway Telecommunications:** Group and broadcast calls.
3. European Rail Traffic Management System (ERTMS).

On the other hand, digitizing the railway sector and the step taken towards going from the electromagnetic operations to operations that are IP-enabled has been supported by the European Union, coming in the form of ERTMS.

The ERTMS can be described as a standard system used in managing and interoperating the signaling for different railway systems, with its application going beyond Europe into some Asian, American and African countries.

IACS (Industrial Automated Control Systems) no longer appear or operate alone from the outside, with the interconnection of railway systems continuing through the use of ATO (Automatic Train Operations) and as a form of intelligent transport mechanisms. However, cyber-attacks on different commercial and industrial systems of control hiked by over 600% between the year 2012 and 2014. Such attacks have led to intense safety and financial concerns.

IEC TC 9 is known to be part of the advisory committee for IEC on data and information security (ACSEC). To support the ACSEC activity, they created an ad hoc section (TC 9/AHG 20) to help researchers more and understand ACSEC Guide 120 while considering the effects of the TC 9 work.

The IEC TC 9, CENELEC mirror committee has directed its efforts towards the CENELEC electro-technical standardization, while providing CLC/TC 9X/WG 26 dealing with railway systems cyber-security.

Railway Sector Cybersecurity Threats

The modern railway systems are reliant on a wide variety of digital tools. That exposes them to greater risk levels as hackers have a lot of avenues through which they can attack. Train stations and waysides depend on digital systems for CBI (computer-based interlocking), centralized control of traffic, protecting level crossing and automation of yard switching (Kovacs, 2015).

Airports Sector

The security devices at the airports are applied in different configurations, on grounds of various security dimensions, stakeholder requirements, the flow of passengers, the space of operation and different other requirements of cybersecurity and infrastructure (Atzori et al., 2010).

To respond to the latest escalating cyber-security threats, ENISA has provided a report which will work as a guide to the decision-makers to help them in implementing the existing policies and practices, ensuring passenger security as well as the security of their operations (ENISA, 2016). There are a number of recommendations provided to enhance a resilient and secure operating environment for European airports and they include:

1. Setting cyber-security as a top priority for safety.
2. Creating clear cyber-security policies in airports and ensuring enough allocation of resources to cybersecurity experts.
3. Continuously revising the existing policies of cyber-security on the basis of good monitoring practices.
4. Implementation of threat management, holistic risk, and network-based processes and policies for cyber-security at airports.

According to (ENISA, 2016), the integration of IoT on the available infrastructure in airports will help bring new challenges to security. To make sure that there is sufficient security, the operators have to include cyber-security in all phases of the lifecycle of security.

Smart airports ensure that they integrate components of IoT to bring services that are value-added. Through the integration of smart components, there is exposure of airports to new attack vectors and a larger attack surface (SESAR, 2017). Thus, the airports have to guarantee daily improved cyber-security levels because of the possible effect that the cyber disruptions and attacks can hold on operator and passenger safety. Enhanced awareness of the risks of cyber-security and enhancing the resilience and security of the whole airport lifecycle at the airport is a top priority[18].

After the terrorist attack of 11 September 2001, there have been profound changes regarding the approach to airport security, "Cyber" issue is identified as a new risk for aviation security.

At the global level, the governing body is ICAO19 that described in Annex 17 to the Convention on International Civil Aviation, introduced in 1974 as the first release and amended, improved etc (Aven, 2006). 15 times, the 10th edition became applicable in 201720, describe the Security – Safeguarding International Civil against acts of unlawful interference introducing the universal security audit programme[21].

Specifically, 3 main areas were taken into consideration and required particular attention:

The research is also focused on the Airport side, providing an overview of the main threats that could interest the landside, Airside and Terminal.

1. Landside representing the nearby airport structure, such as roads and connecting tracks, bus stops, nearby hotels, etc.
2. Airside, which is the operational part of the flight such as Air Strip, Air Parking, Taxation Areas, Service Areas, Supply Areas, etc.
3. Terminal where passengers are registered and redirected to their doors.

Each of these parts are managed by connected devices both in the Landside layer passengers are allowed by default and there is no restriction and in Airside part, passenger is not allowed but is a staff only area in which only authorized personnel can access, Terminal Layer is a middle layer in which some passenger are gathering more authorization after strict control in order to access to flight gate, the

Table 4. The costs of a cyber-security breach can

€1m/hour cost to the economy of disruption at a major European airport
The €2m+ direct cost of a serious cyber-compromise
€250m in lost European airport revenue alone for a six-day closure
170 days is the average time to detect a malicious or criminal attack
90% of large organizations reported suffering a security breach
75% of board directors are not involved in the review of cyber-security risks

Figure 7. The framework of the three major areas of concern

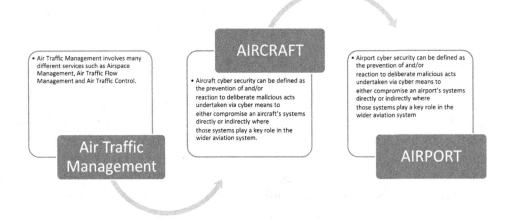

closest point to the Airside, all these areas are generally controlled by security IP cameras, connected by hardliners or LAN to the main network center (Darklord, 2008).

Analyzing the result of numerous studies conducted to evaluate the effectiveness of the security measures taken at airports, a useful contribution is contained in the Securing Smart Airports study carried out by ENISA[22] (Elias, 2008).

With respect to what is shared we can determine the main elements to consider in order to guarantee an appropriate cybernetic resilience:

- Ensuring that an airport is secure by design
- Establishing strong cybersecurity leadership and effective governance
- Adopting a lifecycle approach to cybersecurity
- Aligning cyber, physical and personnel security
- Establishing a security monitoring and incident response capability
- Ensuring cybersecurity stakeholders are identified and managed
- Underpinned by the establishment of a strong cybersecurity culture

The assets considered here are derived from the ENISA Smart Airports Functions and Assets document (Anon., 2016). Assets can be classified according to the impact of a determined disruption time. An asset can be considered vital if its disruption cannot last more than 2 hours because too many flights would be immediately delayed and then canceled[23]. An asset is critical if its disruption cannot last more than 24 hours because too many flights would be delayed. Otherwise, an asset is useful or not applicable (N/A).

Current optimization trends indicate the relevance of integration strategies and real-time communication in the management of existing systems, overcoming system isolation (i.e. SCADA3 systems) and therefore improving performances. Modern hubs are hyper-connected environments where information flow connects all systems. For instance, Passenger Name Record (PNR) system and Network Operation Plan (NOP) will be connected to the Airport Operation Plan (AOP).

Assessment methodologies are a significant aspect of mitigation strategies. They include:

Figure 8. Airport High-Level Representation

Table 5. Functions and Assets

Functions	Assets
Airline/Airside operations	Airport Operation Plan AOP
IT and Comms Airline/Airside operations	Local Area Network Systems (LAN) De-icing systems
	Network Operation Plan (NOP)
IT and Comms	Global Positioning System
	IT Equipment Hardware and Software
	Common Communications Networks
	Wide Area Networks (WAN)
Landside Operations	A-SMGCS
Safety and Security	Authentication Systems
	Customs and Immigration Smart Surveillance Systems

- Penetration testing;
- Compliance Requirements;
- Network Traffic Review;
- System Configuration Review;
- Network Discovery: Airport and Protocol Identification;
- Vulnerability Scanner;

Security assessment in aviation sector refers to CANSO Cyber Security and Risk Assessment Guide.

Increased Technology Usage

Airports continue to invest in new and innovative Operational technologies to increase speed and reliability at common bottlenecks. Examples of this include the use of electronic tags for baggage handling and tracking, remote check-in, smart boarding gates, faster and more reliable security screening technologies, and biometric immigration controls, which drive major efficiency benefits at airports.

Communication between the air traffic control tower and aircraft is increasingly shifting away from traditional radio voice communications towards data-link technologies. This is facilitated by the use of electronic flight strip systems in tower environments, which support the automatic generation of clearance messages. The use of data-link in this way provides clear benefits to both controllers and pilots, in terms of efficiency and the removal of human error and ambiguity in voice messages.

Hyper-Connectivity

Aiming to make the best of the available information, airports have moved towards centralized architectures. These connect different systems through middleware platforms, integrating all the information in central operational data repositories, often called airport operational databases.

These centralized systems take account of the different information requirements of the users involved in the operations, allowing for real-time and two-way data sharing across diverse systems and networks of the different internal and external airport stakeholders (e.g. ground handlers, airlines, etc.).

At the same time, travelers' expectations for connectivity are ever increasing, and they demand access to high bandwidth networks wherever they go. Even at airports, passengers want easy and high-speed internet and multimedia options. They're also increasingly looking for real-time information, and to interact with the airports and related stakeholders directly and on the go. This brings a larger attack surface for cybercriminals to exploit and the possibility that they could affect multiple stakeholders.

Data-Sharing Obligations

Air navigation service providers (ANSPs) are increasingly under pressure to reduce charges and to integrate and harmonize national airspace and air navigation services. System Wide Information Management (SWIM) has evolved into a global concept that has been adopted by the International Civil Aviation Organization to facilitate greater sharing of air traffic management (ATM) system information.

The SWIM programme is an integral part of this transformation. It will connect air traffic control systems and will also enable interaction with other decision-makers, including other government agencies, airports, and airspace users. SWIM is now part of development projects in both the United States (Next Generation Air Transportation System, or NextGen) and the European Union (SESAR programme).

Customer Centricity

Following in the steps of airlines, airports are now increasingly seeking to engage with passengers through airport-related apps, providing consistent messaging to develop brand recognition and sharing notifications of flight delays and services.

To achieve this, operators need to be able to track passengers throughout the airport in order to gather and link information to understand the preferences and behavior of individual customers. They then need to customize and adapt the services provided to them. As a result, airports will hold more personally identifiable information and have to deal with related security issues.

IT/OT Towers

Some airports generate significant income from non-aviation sources, such as retail concessions. Traditionally, IT systems have been isolated from OT systems. However, the integration of the two can bring significant efficiencies, allowing real-time data gathering, processing, and decision-making.

This integration is becoming easier with the growing use of commercial off-the-shelf products, and typically IT-related protocols (eg the Internet Protocol) found in most modern OT systems. The record amount of information on ICS and OT online, including user and operation manuals, can potentially facilitate cyber-attacks.

Remote Towers

ANSPs, airport owners and operators, and related stakeholders face growing pressure to reduce their operating costs while maintaining safety and efficiency. In this context, the interest in digital remote towers as a replacement for the primary control tower, or even as a contingency, has grown significantly in the last few years.

Ornskoldsvik Airport in Sweden was the first in the world to get this system approved as the primary provider of air traffic control. And since 2015, flights have been controlled by a remote tower 110 miles away. Today, there are several test sites around the world (Leesburg International Airport, the United States; Værøy heliport, Norway; Alice Springs airport, Australia), and many major airports across the world, that are considering adopting this approach.

Unlike physical control towers, these critical systems become highly dependent on the data links that transmit the information from one place to another. So a cyber-attack (denial of service, network flooding) or physical attack (cable cutting, damaging network equipment) could disrupt operations. That would make it impossible to manage airport traffic.

Airports as Mega Hubs

In their ambition to grow their business, airports have become hubs, providing services for particular airlines or regions, and bringing a significant increase in operational volume and the need for greater integration. As the airports become larger, collaborative decision-making technologies and processes are commonly implemented to share greater data flows between the different stakeholders involved in airport operational processes. They also utilize more integrated systems.

Larger infrastructure and greater operational complexity are also needed to achieve more passenger throughput, which results in the installation of more efficiency-oriented technology and greater automation of the IT and OT systems.

These airports are then more exposed to attacks, and their iconic status makes them more appealing for attackers.

The main threats that could involve airports, according to the SESAR projects results are shown in Table 6.

The vulnerabilities identified that can allow the attacks are contained in Table 7.

SMART BUILDING

The BAS (Building automation systems) and BOS (Building Operating Systems) have greatly improved and changed from the physical aspects to IT-enabled smart operations. At the same time, there is currently a new generation of intelligent and new buildings that are IoT powered. The increased entry of several vendors in technology packages indicates a totally transformational stage in the trajectory of smart buildings.

The modern smart buildings are increasingly being connected with IoT and made to operate well through the increased convergence of Information technology and Operational Technology systems in the buildings. Many new components like remote access, the cloud, data analytics and sharing as well as shared and connected networks have basically changed the way different environments are being operated and used. At the same time, such components have utilized a closed-loop architecture in buildings and changed them into components that necessitate the open control and access of several service providers and operators (Aazam et al., 2014).

Table 6. Treats that could involve airports.

Scenario 1: Distributed Denial of Service Attack on the Airport's Internet Connection	Scenario 2: Deep and Slow Infiltration to Steal Data	Scenario 3: Major Integrity Loss	Scenario 4: Blended Attack	Scenario 5: A Low-Level Attack on APOC ICS/SCADA Infrastructure
A group of attackers wants to blackmail large companies into paying a ransom by threatening them with a volumetric distributed denial of service attack (DDoS). The attackers have identified that an airport operating company could be a great target since it relies on its Internet connection and controls significant financial resources.	A group of highly motivated and skilled cyber-criminals wants to infiltrate an airport network to steal data. The final part of their attack is to clean their tracks by destroying some of the airports' IT systems.	A highly motivated group wants to disrupt operations at the airport and, if possible, operations at other European airports. In order to do this, they send incorrect flight information to the targeted airport using a messaging service deployed around the world and used by airlines, airports, handlers and other businesses related to aviation. It is, therefore, relatively easy for an attacker to gain physical or digital access to a connection by compromising one of these legitimate businesses.	A group of hackers wants to disturb an airport but without being noticed too quickly. They could achieve this by modifying flight information using the method described in Scenario 3 however this type of attack is too obvious. Instead, to reach the goals they use a blended attack that consists of several attacks with one being obvious, intended to divert attention, and the main attack intended to be conducted in such a way as to remain undetected.	Programmable Logic Controllers (PLCs) are simple devices that can be used to control physical processes. They run bespoke firmware and do not use conventional operating systems. No logging or forensic capability typically exists for these devices nor do they have any intrusion detection facility. PLCs are an integral part of Supervisory Control And Data Acquisition (SCADA) devices. There are hundreds of thousands of them at every airport, but they are often 'invisible' because they are stand-alone components controlling everything from power distribution through air-conditioning and baggage handling. APOCs increase the integration of these devices through IP interfaces that enable stakeholders to monitor their behavior.

A functional management plan for intelligent buildings is vital as it helps in mitigating the risks likely to be faced throughout the phases of design, installation, and operation in the lifecycle of a system. Several firms emphasize more on the creation of secure designs and taking fewer steps toward the maintenance of security as they progress over time. Such a method is analogous to creating a protective wall securing a castle and deciding not to use guards watching over, which will allow people to intrude easily. Creating a plan like that needs coordination from all parties involved in the system all the time as it is in its lifecycle. Some of the parties include the network administrators, system integrators as well as facility personnel. Everyone contributing should have an idea of the unique challenges of ensuring security in an intelligent building management system.

INTEGRATED BUILDING NETWORKS

A smart building's integrated network is one whereby the actual benefits of a converged and smart infrastructure are obtained by the building operators and owners. Nevertheless, this is also the stage that a building is exposed to extreme threats. Moving from the conventional standalone systems to smart buildings, the industry of smart buildings has greatly moved towards a flexible environment characterized by open protocols and systems governing their aspects of the operation.

Table 7. The vulnerabilities identified that can allow the attacks

Types	Vulnerabilities	Scenario 1	Scenario 2	Scenario 3	Scenario 4	Scenario 5
Hardware	Lack of periodic replacement schemes.		✓			
Hardware	Lack of efficient configuration change control.					✓
Software	Well-known flaws in the software.		✓			
Software	Lack of an audit trail.					✓
Software	Poor password management		✓			
Software	Uncontrolled use and downloading of software,					✓
Network	Unprotected lines of communication.		✓			
Network	Single point of failure.	✓		✓	✓	
Network	Lack of authentication and identification of receiver and sender.			✓	✓	
Network	Transfer of passwords in clear.					✓
Network	Inadequate network management (Resilience of routing)	✓			✓	
Personnel	Insufficient security training		✓			
Personnel	Lack of security awareness.		✓		✓	
Personnel	Lack of monitoring mechanisms.			✓	✓	
Organization	Lack of formal process of registering and deregistering users.		✓			
Organization	Lack of formal process for access right review (supervision)		✓			
Organization	Lack of Fault reports recorded in administrator and operator logs.			✓		
Organization	Lack of records in administrator and operator logs.			✓		

Figure 9. The landscape of smart building service providers.

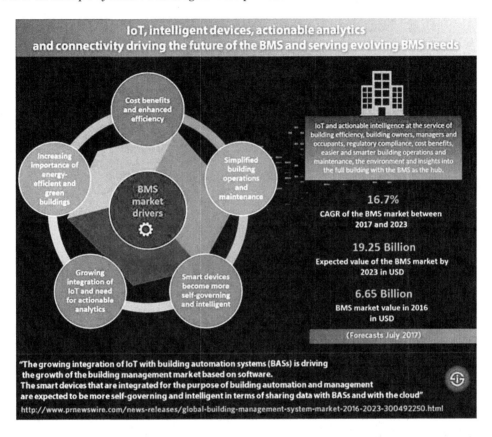

The old norm where there was protection through obscurity used in standalone systems is not an option in the interconnected and intelligent systems that run on open protocols with remotely each physical system integrated into the building under the control of some supervisors. For example, a BAS enabled with a network can practically control each physical system, starting from ventilation, heating, lighting, air conditioning, physical security and much more. In this case, if attackers manage to infiltrate the BAS, they will also be able to infiltrate and interfere with the whole firm (Aazam et al., 2014).

Cyber-Threats to Smart Buildings

With the help of converged and complex IoT systems, the hackers can take advantage of the weak points in smart buildings to make their way into areas with better protection. For instance, Stuxnet only used a USB drive to enter into and affect nuclear centrifuges, whereas Havex utilized an infected website as their vector for attack (Aazam et al., 2014).

Figure 10. A smart Building overview

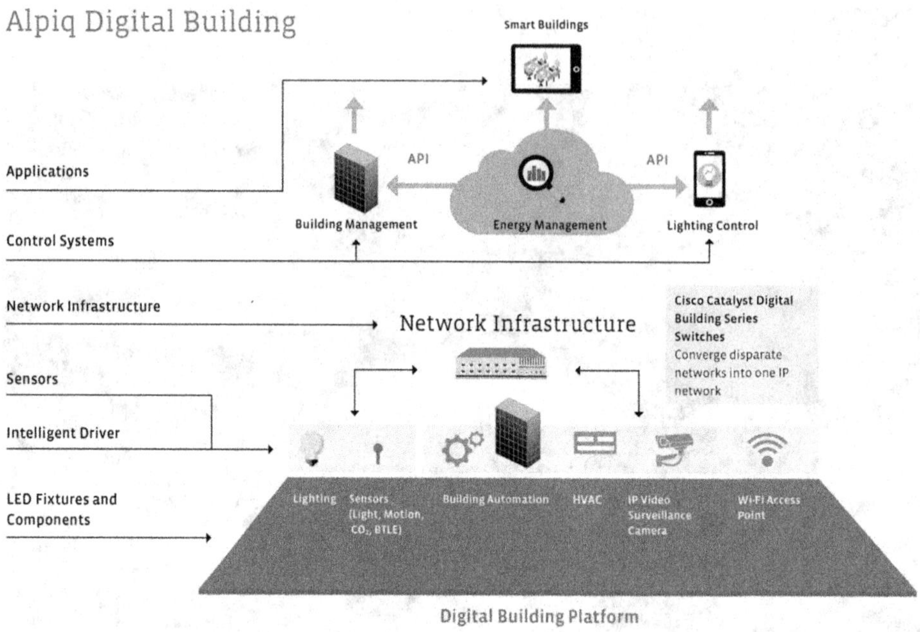

Communication Threats

Attackers on smart buildings use channels of communication between various IoT connected devices to launch their attacks. Some of the threats include availability threats, spoofing, eavesdropping, replay attacks, and MITM (Man-in-the-middle) attacks.

Spoofing

This type of attack enables the attacking individual to impersonate another user within the system over the same channel of communication, soliciting very important information that can be used against the company. The most common spoofing attacks in smart buildings include Address Resolution Packet (ARP) spoofing and IP spoofing (Alomari et al., 2012).

Man-in-the-Middle Attack

In this form of attack, the attacker unsuspectedly becomes an intermediary between the sender and receiver of important information. Through that, he or she can easily intercept data packets being transferred and gain important information. At the same time, the attacker can intercept the data and replace it with malicious data, which will be used when it reaches the destination (Aazam et al., 2014).

Physical Cyber Threats to Smart Buildings

These threats are actualized if the attacker can be able to compromise the physical devices operating on IoT belonging to this category. The main threats include node damaging and device capture (Aazam et al., 2014).

Node Damaging

In this attack, the attackers with physical and access to the physical address of IoT devices can damage them physically to an extent that they cannot be used in data transfer. If by any chance the attacker is able to damage them in large numbers, a possible DoS situation will occur and paralyze normal operations in such smart buildings (Alohali, Merabti & Kifayat, 2014).

CONCLUSION

The latest trends in technology come with different challenges as the society embraces new techniques like IoT and cloud computing. Cloud computing offers a new model for processing which in turn improves efficiency, provides on-demand access to the pool of resources being shared. Consequently, IoT offers a platform through which people and devices interconnect, enabling them to seamlessly interact and communicate. A combination of the two paradigms of technology to enable the processing and storage of unlimited amounts of data created by various IoT devices is the next assignment that innovators are considering.

With the new trends in technology, several privacy and security issues have emerged in different sections like airports, railways and smart buildings. Many of the cyber threats come because of the intrinsic nature of IoT, as different IoT devices create data which involves human beings. Based on the device generating the data, the type of personal data created can be very sensitive to be exposed. Data of that type can be simultaneously collected in an automatic way with the victims being unaware of the process behind the collection of their data. That, in turn, makes it very hard for anyone to offer a clear consent at the time of collecting data. At the same time, data is normally collected in various environments and managed by different signatories.

Even though there have been several attempts to have IoT secured from both internal and external threats, the success of having it fully deployed is strongly dependent on standardization and depth elaboration of various security protocols. Taking into consideration the heterogeneity and diversity of various IoT devices, applications, and systems, many open security issues stand in different sectors like cryptographic and authentication network protocols, identity and data management, trusted architectures and self-assessment. At the same time, there does not exist any single mechanism of defense which can be used effectively for each area of application and can totally overcome all the threats to security. Nevertheless, even though the IoT applications are different, some of them might share common measures of security and mechanisms of defense against cyber threats.

Of the many ways existing in ensuring privacy and security in IoT systems, one of the major ways is developing and designing a privacy-friendly and secure IoT system. However, a challenge stands on how experts will formulate strategies to mitigate the security threats. The strategies will, in turn, be applied to creating various privacy and security requirements. Ensuring that the requirements are fulfilled will make sure that such threats are abated. Nevertheless, the greatest challenge is designing a system capable of fulfilling all the requirements. With such challenges in mind, there are great chances of research opening up and can be taken up for future projects and scholars interested in the area.

The main concerns that could be summarized from this survey are that today it seems important to take into account the inadequate security culture. Many companies and individuals tend to undermine the issue of cybersecurity. That leaves their employees unaware of the impending danger that they face. However, if the culture of security is implemented in companies, it is very easy to deal with the majority of the threats. Lack of security skills and lack of knowledge present a significant vulnerability which may be exploited by malicious third parties. The security behavior of the managers and employees of authorities and businesses is vital to achieving an adequate level of protection.

An increasing number of devices are connected via the Internet. This provides new opportunities but also increases vulnerability to attacks due to the potential for more rapid spread of security incidents. The ready availability of hacking tools on the Internet means that anyone who wishes to hack a system can do so relatively easily and cheaply

There is also a high dependency on digital infrastructure. Vital digital infrastructure is a precondition for carrying out activities in the public and private sectors. Lack of accessibility, integrity, and confidentiality in digital infrastructure can have significant repercussions for society.

One of the best ways to prevent such attacks is taking extra measures and precautions while performing sensitive operations. That can be attained by applying software inventory tools and whitelisting. Ensuring strong scanning and documentation channels also help prevent cyber threats by a greater deal.

REFERENCES

Aazam, M., Khan, I., Alsaffar, A. A., & Huh, E. N. (2014). The cloud of Things: Integrating the g Internet of Things and cloud computing and the issues involved. In *Applied Sciences and Technology (IBCAST), 2014 11th International Bhurban Conference on* (pp. 414-419). IEEE.

Alohali, B., Merabti, M., & Kifayat, K. (2014). *A Secure Scheme for a Smart House Based on Cloud of Things (CoT)*. Academic Press.

Alomari, E., Manickam, S., Gupta, B. B., Karuppayah, S., & Alfaris, R. (2012). *Botnet-based distributed denial of service (DDoS) attacks on web servers: classification and art.* arXiv preprint arXiv:1208.0403

Atzori, L., Iera, A., & Morabito, G. (2010). The internet of things: A survey. *Computer Networks*, *54*(15), 2787–2805. doi:10.1016/j.comnet.2010.05.010

Aven, T. (2006). A unified framework for risk and vulnerability analysis covering both safety and security. *Journal of Reliability Engineering and System Safety, 92*(6), 745–754.

Bou-Harb, E. (2017). On the Impact of Empirical Attack Models Targeting Marine Transportation. *5th IEEE International Conference on Models and Technologies for Intelligent Transportation Systems.* DOI: 10.1109/MTITS.2017.8005665

Boyes, H. A. (2013). Cyber Security of Intelligent Buildings: A Review. *8th IET International System Safety Conference incorporating the Cyber Security.* 10.1049/cp.2013.1698

Brunner, E. M., & Suter, M. (2008). *International CIIP Handbook 2008/2009*. Center for Security Studies, ETH Zurich. Retrieved from http://www.css.ethz.ch/content/dam/ethz/special-interest/gess/cis/center-for-securities-studies/pdfs/CIIP-HB-08-09.pdf

Chiappetta, A. (2017). Critical Infrastructure Protection: Beyond the Hybrid Port and Airport Firmware; Security; Cyber-security applications on transport. *5th IEEE International Conference on Models and Technologies for Intelligent Transportation Systems*. DOI: 10.1109/MTITS.2017.8005666

Chiappetta, A. (2017). Hybrid ports: The role of IoT and Cyber Security in the next decade. *Journal of Sustainable Development of Transport and Logistics*, 2(2), 47–56. doi:10.14254/jsdtl.2017.2-2.4

Cloud Security Alliance. (2013, February). The Notorious Nine. Cloud Computing Top Threats in 2013. *Security*, 1–14.

Covington, M. J., & Carskadden, R. (2013). Threat implications of the Internet of Things. *IEEE 5th International Conference on Cyber Conflict (Cycon)*, 1-12.

Cy, V. O. D. (2017). a novel trinity multimedia social network scheme. *Multimedia Tools and Applications*, 76(18), 18513–18529. doi:10.100711042-016-4162-z

Darklord. (2008). *Little progress in U.S. airport security. Fly away simulation*. Retrieved Mar. 3, 2008: http://flyawaysimulation.com/article2330.html

Directive (EU) 2016/1148 of the European Parliament and of the Council of 6 July 2016 concerning measures for a high common level of security of network and information systems across the Union ["NIS Directive"], Brussels, July 2016.

Distefano, S., Merlino, G., & Puliafito, A. (2012). Enabling the cloud of things. In *Innovative Mobile and Internet Services in Ubiquitous Computing (IMIS), 2012 Sixth International Conference on* (pp. 858-863). IEEE. 10.1109/IMIS.2012.61

Elias, B. (2008). *National Aviation Security Policy, Strategy, and Mode-Specific Plans: Background and Consideration for Congress*. CRS Reports for Congress, Congressional Research Services, Order Code RL34302.

ENISA. (2016). *Smart Airports: How to protect airport passengers from cyber disruptions*. Retrieved from https://www.enisa.europa.eu/news/enisa-news/smart-airports-how-to-protect-airport-passengers-from-cyber-disruptions

ENISA. (2017). *EU strategies to secure the EU cyberspace and critical infrastructure against hackers. Speech by ENISA's Executive Director, Prof*. Dr. Udo Helmbrecht - AECA Round-Table Conference-Luncheon.

Ferdous, M. S., Hussein, R., Alassafi, M., Alharthi, A., Walters, R., & Wills, G. (2016). Threat taxonomy for Cloud of Things. *Internet of Things and Big Data Analysis: Recent Trends and Challenges*, 1, 149–191.

GAO, Government Accountability Office. (2015). Cybersecurity: Actions Needed to Address Challenges Facing Federal Systems. GAO-15-573T. Washington, DC: GAO.

Gope, P., & Hwang, T. (2015). Untraceable Sensor Movement in Distributed IoT Infrastructure. *IEEE Sensors Journal*, *15*(9), 5340–5348. doi:10.1109/JSEN.2015.2441113

Gubbi, J., Buyya, R., Marusic, S., & Palaniswami, M. (2013). Internet of Things (IoT): A vision, architectural elements, and future directions. *Future Generation Computer Systems*, *29*(7), 1645–1660. doi:10.1016/j.future.2013.01.010

Kearney, A. T. (n.d.). *The Internet of Things: A New Path to European Prosperity*. Retrieved from https://www.atkearney.com/documents/10192/7125406/The+Internet+of+ThingsA+New+Path+to+European+Prosperity.pdf/e5ad6a65-84e5-4c92-b468-200fa4e0b7bc

Khan, R., & Khan, S. (2012). Future Internet: The Internet of Things Architecture, Possible Applications, and Key Challenges. *Proceedings of 10th International Conference on Frontiers of Information Technology*.

Kim, S. H., & Kim, D. (2015). Enabling Multi-tenancy via Middleware-level Virtualization with Organization Management in the Cloud of Things. Services Computing. *IEEE Transactions on*, *8*(6), 971–984.

Kovacs Eduard. (2015). *Trains Vulnerable to Hacker Attacks: Researchers*. Retrieved from https://www.securityweek.com/trains-vulnerable-hacker-attacks-researchers

La Diega, G. N., & Walden, I. (2016). *Contracting for the 'Internet of Things': Looking into the Nest*. Queen Mary School of Law Legal Studies Research Paper No. 219/2016.

Levanti, N. (n.d.). UK railways had four major cyber-attacks in one year. *Infrastructure Intelligence*. Retrieved from http://www.infrastructure-intelligence.com/article/jul-2016/uk-railways-had-4-major-cyberattacks-one-year

Liu, J., Xiao, Y., & Chen, C. L. P. (2012). Authentication and Access Control in the Internet of Things. *2012 32nd International Conference on Distributed Computing Systems Workshops*, 588–592. 10.1109/ICDCSW.2012.23

Mahalle, P., & Anggorojati, B. (2012). *Identity establishment and capability-based access control (IECAC)*. Retrieved from http://ieeexplore.ieee.org/xpls/abs_all.jsp?arnumber=6398758

Paolicchi, F. (2018). *Benefits for companies which adopt Internet of Things (IoT)*. Retrieved from https://iotlab.tertiumcloud.com/2018/03/21/why-should-enterprises-embrace-internet-of-things/

Quashie Azasoo, J., & Tweneboah-Koduah, S. (2016). *Cybersecurity architecture in smart metering systems. In Smart living and privacy*. Unpublished paper. CMI Annual Conference, Copenhagen, Denmark.

Ravikumar, D. (n.d.). *Role of PSUs for Smart City Ecosystem*. Retrieved from http://smartcity.eletsonline.com/wp-content/uploads/2018/01/Bharat-Electronics-Ravikumar-D.pdf

Rocque, M. (2017). The cybersecurity threat to transportation. *SmartCitiesWorld*. Retrieved from https://www.smartcitiesworld.net/special-reports/special-reports/the-cyber-security-threat-to-transportation

Roman, R., Zhou, J., & Lopez, J. (2013). On the features and challenges of security and privacy the n distributed internet of things. *Computer Networks*, *57*(10), 2266–2279.

Ronald, V. L., & John, P. (2018). *What You Don't Know About the Internet of Things - CloudTweaks*. Retrieved from https://cloudtweaks.com/2016/04/dont-know-internet-things/

Sadeghi, A.-R., Wachsmann, C., & Waidner, M. (2015). Security and privacy challenge in the n industrial internet of things. *Proceedings of the 52nd Annual Design Automation Conference*, 54. doi:10.1016/j.comnet.2012.12.018

SESAR. (2017). *Addressing airport cyber-security*. Executive summary report.

Sicari, A. S., Rizzardi, L. A., Grieco, L. A., & Coen-Porisini, A. (2015). Security, privacy and trust the n internet of things: The road ahead. *Computer Networks*, *76*, 146–164. doi:10.1016/j.comnet.2014.11.008

Sundarkumar, G. G., Ravi, V., Nwogu, I., & Govindaraju, V. (2015). Malware detection via API calls, topic models and machine learning. *2015 IEEE International Conference on Automation Science and Engineering (CASE)*, 1212–1217. 10.1109/CoASE.2015.7294263

United States Government Accountability Office. (n.d.). *GAO-16-116T, Maritime Critical Infrastructure Protection*. Retrieved from https://www.gao.gov/assets/680/672973.pdf

Wu, M. (2012). Research on the architecture of the Internet of things. *Proceedings of 3rd International Conference on Advanced Computer Theory and Engineering*, 20-22.

Wu, W.-C., & Hung, S.-H. (2014). Droiddolphin: a dynamic android malware detection framework using big data and machine learning. *Proceedings of the 2014 Conference on Research in Adaptive and Convergent Systems*, 247–252. 10.1145/2663761.2664223

ENDNOTES

[1]   https://www.osservatori.net/it_it/osservatori/internet-of-things
[2]   Source: ATKearney - The Internet of Things: A New Path to European Prosperity
[3]   Source: HIS – Market, as reported in Forbes - https://www.forbes.com/consent/?toURL=https://www.forbes.com/sites/louiscolumbus/2017/12/10/2017-roundup-of-internet-of-things-forecasts/
[4]   https://www.gartner.com/imagesrv/books/iot/iotEbook_digital.pdf
[5]   https://dyn.com/blog/dyn-analysis-summary-of-friday-october-21-attack/
[6]   https://www.arm.com/
[7]   https://tools.ietf.org/id/draft-moran-suit-architecture-01.html
[8]   https://www.af.mil/
[9]   https://prod.sandia.gov/techlib-noauth/access-control.cgi/2006/066399.pdf
[10] Sectors relying on ICT are the most vulnerable to attacks.
[11] Hybrid ports: the role of IoT and Cyber Security in the next decade. Journal of Sustainable Development of Transport and Logistics,2(2),47-56.doi:10.14254/jsdtl.2017.2-2.4. http://www.jsdtl.sciview.net/plugins/generic/pdfJsViewer/pdf.js/web/viewer.html?file=http%3A%2F%2Fwww.jsdtl.sciview.net%2Findex.php%2Fjsdtl%2Farticle%2Fdownload%2F29%2F19%2F
[12] https://www.enisa.europa.eu/publications/ics-scada-dependencies
[13] https://www.cisco.com/c/m/en_au/products/security/offers/annual-cybersecurity-report-2017.html
[14] https://news.sky.com/story/four-cyber-attacks-on-uk-railways-in-a-year-10498558

15   https://www.reuters.com/article/us-northkorea-southkorea-cyber-idUSKCN0WA0B6

16   https://www.ibtimes.co.uk/hackers-breach-swiss-political-party-federal-railways-websites-exposing-vulnerabilities-1550907

17   https://www.indiatoday.in/technology/news/story/al-qaida-allegedely-hacked-indian-railways-website-311375-2016-03-02

18   https://www.enisa.europa.eu/news/enisa-news/smart-airports-how-to-protect-airport-passengers-from-cyber-disruptions

19   https://www.icao.int/

20   https://www.icao.int/Security/SFP/Pages/SecurityManual.aspx

21   http://www.aviationchief.com/uploads/9/2/0/9/92098238/icao_doc_9985_-_atm_security_manual_-_restricted_and_unedited_-_not_published_1.pdf

22   Securing Smart Airports – December 2016 - ENISA

23   https://www.paconsulting.com/insights/2018/cyber-security-in-airports/

Chapter 17
Chaos Theory and Systems in Cloud Content Security

Kanksha Zaveri
Dwarkadas J. Sanghvi College of Engineering, India

Niti Shah
Dwarkadas J. Sanghvi College of Engineering, India

Ramchandra S. Mangrulkar
Dwarkadas J. Sanghvi College of Engineering, India

ABSTRACT

Cloud computing involves storing data using a third party that ensures that confidential data cannot be accessed even by the cloud itself. Thus, security is one major issue in cloud computing. Recent advancements in exploiting chaotic systems' sensitivity to initial conditions, and their ability to extract strings of random numbers for confusion and diffusion have helped enhance security. They can provide resistance from statistical attack and protection against reconstruction dynamics. However, the concept of chaos for security is still in its emerging stages. This chapter presents how chaos theory can be used for random number generation to further secure data in the cloud. The authors have discussed and compared some popular methods for authentication and encryption of data, images, and videos. The overview of chaos engineering discusses the discipline of experimenting on multi-server systems to ensure its ability to tackle glitches.

INTRODUCTION

Chaos theory is the study of complex nonlinear dynamic systems. These systems follow deterministic laws themselves, yet the behavior of these systems appears to be random and unpredictable. Chaotic systems are known for their sensitivity to initial conditions. The creation of minuscule changes in the initial state of a copy of the same system will exhibit large differences in both of them. Systems becoming so disparate due to small amounts of change is why it only makes sense to predict these systems within a certain time period. Beyond that time period, the predictions become highly inaccurate. Dependence

DOI: 10.4018/978-1-5225-8407-0.ch017

on initial conditions is illustrated in the "butterfly effect" where a tornado in Texas could be traced back to something as minor as a butterfly flapping its wings in Africa.

Chaos is found in all sorts of places from planetary motion, to chemical systems, population growth, electrical circuits, and encryption schemes. Its ability to generate seemingly random numbers and extreme sensitivity towards the initial state is what makes it exciting in security.

Cloud Content Security refers to the protection of the data and the processing in the cloud from external attacks. Cloud is a third party application used to provide storage, servers and the processing at the network, and ease the user of the load of handling those locally.

The objective of the chapter is to understand the ways in which chaotic systems can be used in cloud content security. The rest of this chapter is organized as follows: a background of chaotic systems is given in Section 2. Section 3 introduces cloud content security. Section 4 contains the link between chaos and cryptography, and a review of current schemes using chaos for security in the cloud. In Section 6, security analysis of such schemes is discussed. Section 7 is a case study on Chaos Engineering, and Section 7 contains the conclusion.

BACKGROUND

Chaos Theory

Chaotic systems are complicated, nonlinear, and dynamic. Dynamic means that they depend on time and implies the constantly changing nature of the system. Nonlinearity implies recursiveness - every state depends on the previous state, which further depends on the previous state, and so on. Thus chaos theory can be thought of as the study of non-constant systems based on recursion.

Imagine the trajectory of the ball in a game of squash between two people lasting forever (the ball never bounces on the floor twice). It depends on where the person begins, and a slight change in the force or angle of the service would change where it bounces back from changing the entire game. Eventually, the ball would have covered the entire court's 3D space, and since the game does not end and every shot is different, it is irregular and lasts forever. Think of the players as two parameters controlling the ball that the trajectory depends on. Individually each player (parameter) knows what the next move would be if the ball arrives in a certain manner which makes the system deterministic, but a lack of clarity in the initial condition of how the game will begin generates the randomness. Thus, chaotic systems can be defined to have the following characteristics. (Walker, J., n.d.).

1. **Sensitive Dependence on Initial Conditions:** Small changes in the initial state of a system can result in a completely different final state. This sensitivity is the reason why the system is pseudo-random.
2. **Topological Mixing:** It refers to how the trajectories of equations visit all parts of the phase space from its initial conditions. In other words, when an open set intersects other open sets in the phase set, it can be said that topological mixing has taken place. Chaotic systems explore a large variety of the phase space.
3. **Aperiodic Behavior:** This implies that the trajectories have period infinity orbits i.e. they are irregular and do not converge to a point.

These properties make chaotic systems - both real, and pseudo-random - an asset for cryptographic schemes. Various random numbers are produced by different maps/attractors from their orbits based on the initial conditions, in completely random ways, or a mix of both. From those random numbers, sometimes a key is selected for encryption. Based on the key that controls the encryption algorithm, a binary sequence is generated and further processing is done. Apart from generating keys, chaotic systems are used to modify values sequentially by the sequences they generate, generate noisy signals, and as (pixel) shufflers. It can be summarized that chaotic systems are used for Confusion, Diffusion, Key Generation, Authentication, S-Box creation at different stages. Before taking a look at how chaos is used in cryptography, the following is an overview of random number generators that lie at the center of it.

Random Number Generators

The security of cryptographic schemes depends on the algorithms and the keys. Most cryptographic schemes either require keys that are to be used once and discarded, or regeneratable random numbers to encrypt and decrypt data. Chaos helps create these random numbers.

Totally Random Number Generators

Totally random number generators are completely random. They help in generating a one-time pad or key which is used only once. Without any patterns or logic behind generating the sequence, it becomes unbreakable. An attacker is unable to predetermine the bit sequence even with unbounded memory and time resources. Consequently, the use of an unconditionally secure system only remains information-theoretic secure if its indeterministic functions are founded on unpredictable random values. (Rohe, 2018).

Computers themselves are quite awful at coming up with completely random numbers. Originally the computer's internals was used, like network data or the seek time of disks. They later shifted to phenomena occurring outside the device like mouse clicks or the timing of users pressing keys on the keyboard. One firm that uses chaos for generating totally random numbers is CloudFlare. CloudFlare is a cloud network and security firm and currently generates totally random numbers using radioactive decay, the motion of fluids, atmospheric noise, or other chaos.

Pseudo-Random Number Generators

Pseudo-random number generators are deterministic. They tend to follow recurrence relations of some sort in which new states depend on their previous states. One of the most popular (uniformly distributed between zero and one) random number generator scheme is the linear congruential method. It requires to choose a modulus, multiplier, increment, and an initial value to be plugged into $X_{n+1} = \left(aX_n + c\right) mod\, m$. There are several modifications of this method including the multiplicative and quadratic congruential method. But another method to obtain a sequence between zero and one is using different chaotic maps for different chaotic systems.

Linear systems have sink, source, or spiral kind of behavior. The orbit - trajectory of a system in the phase space - either converges to or diverges away from fixed points. For instance, on swinging a pendulum it eventually comes to rest at the center. Its motion creates a zig-zag reaching the point of rest. This point of rest is known as an attractor. This specifically can be called a point attractor. (Crystal, n.d.)

But every attractor is not just a point. In case of nonlinear dynamic systems, the orbit converges to a 'set-of-points'. This orbit is known as the limit cycle of the system. Repeated motion along the same orbit can be thought of as some sort of attraction towards that form of motion. It is periodic, going over the same set of points repeatedly. The number of iterations it takes (passing through the Poincare plane) to come back to the beginning point is known as its period. Thus the orbit could be a loop (period one limit cycle), double loop (period two limit cycle), or even a hundred-loop (period hundred limit cycle). In fact, it could even be an infinite loop (period infinity limit cycle) which are actually fractals. And these are the attractors/maps where chaotic behavior is observed. (Indian Institute of Technology, Kharagpur., 2009, December 31).

One such map is the Logistic Map. This was used to understand population growth and is represented by the equation $x_{n+1} = rx_n \left(1 - x_n\right)$. The idea is to pick some value of r and see how the behavior of the map changes as r .does. One dimensional maps help visualize the motion of a single variable over discrete steps in time. If a system $x_{n+1} = f\left(x_n\right)$ is considered where x_n is the current state of the system, and x_{n+1} the next state, while it is known that the system is fixed wherever $x_{n+1} = x_n$ drawing Cobweb Diagrams is a simple way to determine its fixed points.

Assume $r \in \left(0, 4\right)$. Refer to Figure 1.

When r is lesser than 1, x_{n+1} eventually tends to zero. When r is between 1 and 2, x_{n+1} for all except 0 and 1 will converges to $\dfrac{r}{1-r}$. This is because $\dfrac{r}{1-r}$ is the fixed point attracting everything else.

When r crosses 2 it can be seen that the value switches between alternate sides of the fixed point while converging instead of a single side.

The graph becomes even more strange when r is greater than 3. The flip-flop behaviour is still evident, but instead of converging, the value is seen diverging away from the point $\dfrac{r}{1-r}$ that is its fixed point. (Lipa, n.d.).

This is how chaotic maps help generate pseudo-random numbers. The infinite period cycle combined with topological mixing implies that the trajectory is all over the place and seems random. And the sensitivity to initial conditions ensures that unless the attacker has access to the exact initial value and level of precision the calculations are being done with, the attacker will not be able to acquire the string of seemingly random numbers.

To illustrate this clearly, using the logistic map with $r = 3.9$ and taking $x_o = 0.4$ and an extremely close value $x_o = 0.40001$, the results are compared in Table 1. Figure 1 has the plot of both values and chaotic nature is observed.

There are multiple chaotic maps - the Arnold Cat map, Lorenz Attractor, Rossler Attractor, Henon Map, Tent Map, Baker's 2D Map, and the Piecewise Linear Chaotic Map to name a few - and each of these maps has its own constraints under which it becomes chaotic. They can all be used as pseudo-random number generators.

Figure 1.

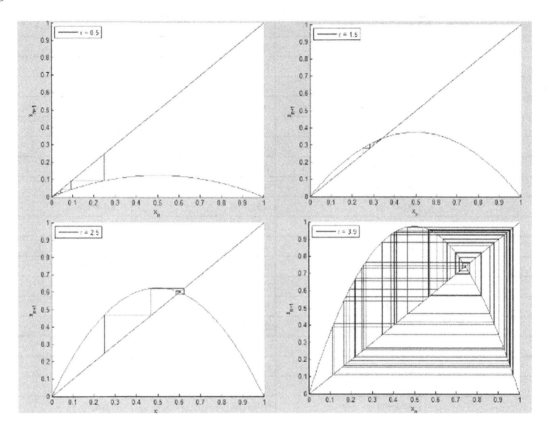

Hybrid Random Number Generators

Hybrid random number generators are created by coupling totally random number generators to provide seeds for pseudo-random number generators. When a totally random number is generated and used as a seed to generate pseudo-random numbers, then it can be said that a hybrid random number generator is being used. These number generators are useful because they keep the initial condition unpredictable, yet are not vulnerable to consistencies possible in totally random number generators. They provide benefits of both pseudo-random and totally random numbers.

Theoretical and Computational Problems of Using Chaotic Systems

1. Stability is hard to achieve. (Blackledge & Ptitsyn, 2011). It is difficult to maintain the same cycle length and a stable system over time. For the same initial conditions, the same Lyapunov exponent should be present. There is no way to ensure that the same bitstream will be produced for any specific initial condition. Such conditions are difficult to maintain. Additionally, tests must be performed and calculations for each iteration have to be done to verify them.
2. Asymmetric systems using chaos are yet unknown. A one-way system or an asymmetric system which uses chaos is difficult to decrypt using the exact reverse flow. Unlike the RSA algorithm that relies on a trapdoor function (based on prime number properties) which cannot be computed in

Table 1. Display of sensitivity to initial conditions

Iteration			Differences
0.0	0.4	0.40001	-1.0E-5
1.0	0.936	0.936008	-8.0E-6
2.0	0.233626	0.233599	2.7E-5
3.0	0.698274	0.698219	5.5E-5
4.0	0.821681	0.821766	-8.5E-5
5.0	0.571434	0.57122	2.14E-4
6.0	0.955099	0.955218	-1.19E-4
7.0	0.167252	0.166829	4.22E-4
8.0	0.543186	0.542089	0.001097
9.0	0.967726	0.968091	-3.65E-4
10.0	0.121805	0.120474	0.001332
21.0	0.379625	0.454169	-0.074544
22.0	0.918488	0.966808	-0.04832
23.0	0.291983	0.125152	0.166831
24.0	0.806243	0.427008	0.379235
25.0	0.60924	0.954221	-0.344981
26.0	0.92846	0.170364	0.758096
27.0	0.259046	0.551226	-0.29218
28.0	0.748571	0.964766	-0.216195
29.0	0.734029	0.132571	0.601458
30.0	0.761398	0.448484	0.312914

the opposite direction without certain information, there is no such equivalent function in chaotic cryptography.

3.   Using floating point arithmetic is time-consuming. This is because the number streams are converted to bit streams. They require high precision which can be achieved using large cycles but most of the algorithms used currently have relatively low cycles.

4.   Unpredictability is not completely predicted. Currently, there is no method to calculate or guarantee whether the chaotic system is completely unpredictable or not. Also, chaotic maps display chaotic behavior but they have their own set of constraints. For example, the logistic map displays chaotic behavior only when the values of r are between 3.57 and 4. The value of x is restricted between 0 and 1.

Cloud Content Security

Cloud computing can be described as a method to run applications in a seamless manner without having the load of running the servers locally, or storing all the data or having access to the required hardware to run it. It provides a number of benefits such as optimizing cost, providing scalability and helping users execute programs without much maintenance.

Security can be defined as protection against any kind of attack be it software or hardware or any computing service. The three main components of security are Confidentiality (data should be hidden), Integrity (data should not be modified or tampered) and Availability (data should be accessible). A threat is anything that has the potential to do harm to one's system. Thus, when one needs to secure their system, they would draft a policy to declare what is allowed and what is not. Implementing the policy in the right way would be a mechanism. When two or more policies are conflicting, they lead to security vulnerabilities.

Hence, cloud computing security or cloud content security focuses on protecting the data in the cloud from misuse or attacks. Since data is stored, processed and transmitted at the cloud. (The cloud is managed by a third party agent known as the cloud service provider (CSP)) the user should be convinced that neither the CSP nor other unauthenticated users have access to their data. Another issue with cloud computing is that the same cloud can be accessed by multiple users. Hence, the infrastructure shared is the same. Making the user not feel like he has complete control is a serious issue.

Cloud security is important to tell the user that data in the cloud is protected and secure. It a sub-area of computer security, network security, and information security. Since cloud is based on a network, the network security model is discussed further. It consists of the six steps described in the next paragraph. (Indian Institute of Technology, Kharagpur., 2017, June 8).

First, one needs to establish an entire description of the model such that the policies reflect the network design. This is followed by the installation and configuration of security measures. Next, one needs to learn everything about the network. One should then try to use different types of scanners to look for vulnerabilities or exploit them. Penetration testing should be done next wherein safe attacks are conducted to remove the detected vulnerabilities. A final case study is done to review the attack pattern and its implications.

An important thing to note in the concept of cloud security is the notion of fairness between the two parties involved. Li, Gupta, and Metere (2018) talk about how fairness and cooperation can be ensured using the concept of social conformity. Fairness implies that in a two-way communication, both parties receive the services exchanged or both do not. The concept of game theory is applied here. If both the participants are rational in their behavior, and their strategies are to balance with the majority, then the parties can achieve fairness in their exchange. This combined with social conformity (a kind of reinforcement learning), can lead to fairness and cooperation.

Data is stored, processed, and transmitted. Ideally, at each time it should be in an encrypted state. But the cloud has to do processing even when the data is encrypted. This led to the origin of homomorphic encryption.

Craig Gentry, an American computer scientist, proposed a Fully Homomorphic Encryption (FHE) to perform this functionality. The term 'homomorphic' talks about how operations can be performed on ciphertext without performing the decryption. Basically, by Gentry's scheme, it is now possible to perform operations on the ciphertext in the cloud without access to the private key. Two types - Partially Homomorphic Encryption (PHE) and Fully Homomorphic Encryption (FHE). (Chumbley, Williams, & Duna, n.d.).

Following is an example of FHE. Suppose a restaurant has a signature dish whose ingredients are secret and the head chef does not even want the junior chefs to know which ingredients are used. Then he will put all the ingredients in the box ('encrypt' them) and give it to them. All they can do is put their hands inside the box and make the food but cannot see what is inside. Thus, the dish will be prepared without the chefs themselves knowing what was used. This is a parallel to how homomorphic encryption actually works. It can be safely predicted that cloud content security will soon be heavily dependent on FHE. It was also observed that, when the algorithm was run over simple functions, much faster results were obtained.

This method was initially taking up an overhead up to 10 trillion compared to the time taken for using non-homomorphic encrypted data. Later, when Gentry tried another solution along with Nigel Smart, they could get the time reduced to an overhead of 1 billion. This itself is a huge number and thus, in some time, one can safely predict that cloud content security would be heavily dependent on FHE. It was also observed that, when the algorithm was run over simple functions, the results were obtained in a much faster time.

Currently, a general data security model is composed of three phases in which each module performs its own task independently. The first phase is responsible for authentication between the cloud provider and the user. The second phase involves encryption and hashing of the data using an appropriate algorithm. The third phase involves the recovery of data by the cloud server. (Meslhy, Abd elkader, & El-etriby, 2013).

Besides Cloud Computing, Internet of Things (IoT) is an emerging concept in the technological sector. IoT can be described as the exchange of data among a network of devices, vehicles, and appliances connected through sensors and electronics. Stergiou, Psannis, Kim, and Gupta, 2018 talk about how the two concepts of IoT and Cloud Computing can be integrated together to form a new framework of connectivity for real and virtual devices. Mobile Cloud Computing is a key concept here. It is the integration of mobile devices with Cloud Computing. The integration of IoT and Cloud Computing can provide many benefits. Cloud Computing can solve the issue of storage in IoT while IoT can resolve the limited scope of Cloud Computing. Their integration involves a few downsides too such as multi-tenancy and constraints in computation. Moreover, studies predict that their performance and reliability could get affected too. Using the AES algorithm, however, could overcome some of these disadvantages. Thus the integration of IoT and Cloud Computing could prove to be beneficial in the future if the security issues are kept in mind and resolved appropriately.

There are three layers present in the cloud architecture, each of which represents a cloud service model: Software as a Service (SaaS), Platform as a Service (PaaS), and Infrastructure as a Service (IaaS). Table 2 summarises the security issues in various service delivery models of cloud and whether chaotic systems can be used to tackle them. (Bhushan & Gupta, 2017).

CHAOS FOR CLOUD CONTENT SECURITY

Chaos to Encrypt Videos and Still Allow Foreground Extraction

Videos captured by surveillance cameras are often stored and analyzed in the cloud server. This could be for various tasks such as matching suspects or looking for license plate numbers. Due to the increase in cameras put up, it cannot be determined how private the footage actually is. The content of footage in cloud is vulnerable to attacks.

The Chu et al. method for real-time privacy preserving moving object detection in the cloud has major drawbacks. The contours of foreground objects are evident to the server decreasing the security of data stored. Additionally, decryption with a key close enough can provide information making the method

Table 2. Security issues in service delivery models of cloud and whether chaotic systems can be used to tackle them

Service Delivery Model	Key Security Elements	Possibility of the use of chaos
Infrastructure-as-a-service (IaaS)	Physical security	No
	Availability of services	No
	Data confidentiality in storage	Yes
	Data integrity in storage	Yes
	Virtual cloud protection	No
	Network security	No
	Data breaches during transmission through network	Yes
Platform-as-a-service (PaaS)	Access control	Yes
	Application security	Yes
	Application data security	Yes
	Availability	No
Software-as-a-service (SaaS)	Access control	Yes
	Software security	Yes
	Availability of services	No
	Data confidentiality	Yes
	Data integrity	Yes
	Data privacy	Yes
	Data and application backup	No
	Authentication and authorization	Yes

more susceptible to a brute force attack. The use of chaos in encrypting videos for foreground extraction helps increase security by avoiding the leak of contours and resisting brute force attacks.

The method proposed by Jin, et al., 2016 uses the logistic map for random inverse, frame confusion, and frame diffusion.

- **Random Inverse:** Pick μ and x to generate a sequence of random numbers from the logistic map the size of MxN where M and N are the length and height of the video frame. Select the eighth digit from sixteen digits after the decimal point to obtain the final sequence. If the value of the pixel is less than or equal to 5, it is kept as it is. Otherwise, it is inversed.
- **Confusion:** Another pair of μ and x is selected and the sequence is sorted in ascending order. The sequence is indexed and a confusion matrix is generated from it to shuffle the pixels.
- **Diffusion:** Logistic chaotic mapping is used to change the value of each pixel randomly. Q confusion matrices are generated. The frames from each matrix are added which gets further divided by a coefficient to ensure that each pixel is still in the range of [0, 255].

The Gaussian model is used to perform foreground extraction as it displays homomorphic properties. This is why it is important to make sure that the Gaussian of pixels does not change. The inverse operation changes the mean of the Gaussian distribution. Since confusion does not change any pixel individually but only shuffles them, and every pixel has its own Gaussian Distribution, there is no effect on the Gaussian Distribution. The inverse, confusion, and diffusion matrices used are common for every frame, so every pixel continues to follow a Gaussian distribution. Lastly adding up Gaussian variables also gives a Gaussian. This is how the three operations only shift the Gaussian distribution.

Improvements on Incorporating Chaos

Experimental results display that the correctness rate of this method has slightly improved, the server cannot infer anything from the encrypted video, and that the method is secure enough from brute force and statistical attacks. Chaos plays a role for the same.

Contours are not visible after encryption. Only a mix of white and black can be seen with nothing recognizable. The key space is large enough and includes a range of parameters for random inverse, confusion, and diffusion. Decrypting a frame with a wrong key with a difference of even 0.000000000000001 also gives indistinguishable output. Thus the sensitivity of the secret key makes it better to resist a brute force attack. Lastly, the histogram of encrypted images is flat lines which make statistical attacks impossible.

On the other hand, work done by Hossain, Muhammad, Abdul, Song, and Gupta (2018) propose a watermarking scheme for secure video sharing for smart cities. On capturing a video, a genetic algorithm is applied to detect key frames of the video. A certain number of key frames are detected. The next step is to generate the watermark. The digital signature which is a two-dimensional matrix is first protected with BCH codes. Level 3 subbands contain the watermark of the protected signature. After generating the protected signature, it is inserted into all the key frames detected by the genetic algorithm. For this, a discrete wavelength transform is applied to all of those frames. Level 3 details in all directions are extracted and wavelet coefficients are sorted at decomposition level 1 for the blue, green, and red components in ascending order. The wavelet coefficients are quantized. Finally, the watermark is inserted randomly in locations specified by a chaotic key in blue, green, and red components of the decomposed key frame. The logistic map is used for key generation.

For extraction of the watermark, a secret sharing algorithm is used to transmit the key generated by the logistic map to specify locations of the inserted watermark. This method enables the sharing of the signature to different clouds in a space optimum and secure way.

Chaos to Generate Secret Keys or Passwords

The flowchart in Figure 2 shows that the state of a chaotic system is first digitised to obtain a binary string. Another binary string is obtained after a cryptographic hash. This second binary string is sent as a seed into a pseudo-random number generator. These generated random numbers are used as secret passwords or keys.

Different Chaotic Systems and How to Digitise Them

Atmospheric Noise

Atmospheric noise can be taken from the office, or a frequency at which the radio does not operate and sampled. Sampling outputs stream of bits. These undergo a skew correction algorithm so that there is a balance between the zeroes and ones. There are multiple skew correction algorithms. The Von Neumann strategy involves discarding the '00' and '11' when bits are read two at a time.

Figure 2.

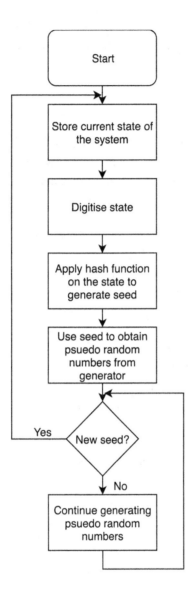

Motion (of Clouds, the Sea, and Fluids)

To use the chaotic system to generate a random number, there are some means of converting the state of the system into a sequence of bits (i.e., a binary number). Multiple sources can be used to generate chaos. These include the output of a noisy diode, sound of radio static, output of a Geiger counter, or even the motion of clouds. There are standard techniques to convert the chaotic systems to binary strings. For instance, a pseudo-random binary string can be generated from the digital recording of static noise via a digital microphone. Another way to implement this is to sample a noisy diode at a suitable frequency and convert it to a digital signal. It can also happen by capturing parts of the sky and scanning and digitizing the image. These resulting binary strings that are generated over time are generally random in nature. (Noll, Mende, & Sisodiya, 1996). Lava lamps are a good choice because every lava lamp forms different patterns. They are a mix of two different colored fluids with different properties that interact in unpredictable ways. With lava lamps, images of them are taken and the color or their intensity help create binary strings of the pixels. These binary strings from individual pixels are concatenated together.

Radioactive Decay

The Heisenberg Uncertainty principle limits what can simultaneously be known about the momentum and position of a particle. A similar uncertainty principle also applies to the energy and time period. If the energy of the particle is known with increasing certainty, the time period of how long it possesses that energy becomes unclear. And if the time period of a certain state is known, how much energy it possesses in that state is not. Generating random numbers from radioactive decay exploits the unknown time period for random values.

One way that particles can reduce their energy is through beta decay. Beta decay occurs when one particle's neutron converts to a proton and releases an electron in that process. If a large sample of particles is present, it can be predicted that about fifty percent of them will decay in their half-life. For example, the Ca-137 nucleus has a half-life of 30.17 years. While it can be said that half of the Ca-137 nuclei will decay in 30.17 years from a large sample, when exactly they will decay, or which nuclei will decay is unknown. The decay is only inferred by detecting the ejecta. This randomness in decay and the unpredictable time interval between two decays is tracked to generate random bit sequences. There are multiple methods to do so. One method proposed involves comparing the delay between two consecutive decays. (Alvarez & Li, 2006). If the time between one decay is T1 and the other decay is T2, then if T1 is greater than T2, one bit is emitted, if it is lesser than T2, a zero bit. If both are the same, they are discarded and the next pair is considered. This method provides one bit from two decay bits. Additionally, two registers are required and there is a possibility of an overflow. Another method that provides a random bit for every decay is modulo 2 over every time interval.

Need of Using a Cryptographic Hash Function

Sometimes chaotic systems are not entirely random. They are predictable either completely or partially. This could be because they depend on certain outside sources, and the attacker could reasonably guess localities in the system to identify a small space or eliminate a large key space. This results in the reduction of a key's possibilities.

Pseudo-random number generators help eliminate the time required to transform the state of a chaotic system into a number. Cryptographic hash functions make it harder to identify the chaotic system. Moreover, slight changes in the state of a chaotic system will lead to very different hashed outputs allowing localities to exist and yet keeping the system secure. It is also extremely hard to find an alternate state that will generate the same hashed output.

Thus it can be said that cryptographic hash functions help strengthen the security of using a chaotic system. On feeding the hashed binary string into a pseudo-random number generator, a deterministic function is repeatedly applied to it to generate new random states until a pattern emerges.

Chaos to Generate OTP for One-to-Cloud Operations

On using an OTP, a key distribution problem is created. Every person who wants access to the data will require to possess the key. That is why this method is specifically targeted towards One-To-Cloud applications where there is only one client who has the OTP key. One concern might be that the OTP is as long as the plaintext and would hence require high storage space, but with storage space becoming cheaper and the application target that of high security, this would not be a problem.

Here, first states in totally chaotic systems (noise) are converted to streams of binary numbers. Two unrelated data streams different from each other from the Lorenz and Chua chaos sources are mixed with each other to obtain alternate bit independence in an OTP binary string. (Blackledge, McKeever, L. Tobin, & P. Tobin, 2018).

Once the OTP is generated, it is XOR'ed with data to be stored. The OTP is saved on a storage device not connected to the internet. This device is plugged in when data needs to be decrypted and reverse mapping is done to obtain the plaintext.

When data is encrypted before being placed on Cloud using an OTP, the only thing keeping it secure is the key. If someone gets access to the secret key or initial condition of the chaos sources, the entire system may be at risk. An idea to mitigate such a risk is to replace the problem of keeping track of keys with devising a method to generate multiple encryption algorithms based on chaos theory - multialgorithmicity.

In the following approach by Blackledge and Ptitsyn (2011) encryption is done using user-specific portable USB flash memory units. Each unit has a unique set of algorithms. These algorithms are combined to increase the security where one map's output is used as a seed to another map. The last floating point number of a current block cipher is used to seed the next block cipher. The initial conditions, parameters, and algorithm all get decided on the basis of properties of the file to be encrypted.

The reason chaotic maps are used is that chaos opens up the possibility of developing limitless algorithms for multi-algorithmic solutions. As mentioned, m different maps are initialized using a secret key. These maps are connected to each other by using the output of one system for the next. Each map contributes some amount of output on a pre-decided iteration. These m bytes are put together using XOR. This process is repeated until a one time pad is created that can finally be XORed with the plaintext.

Another way in which chaos can be used to generate OTP on a One-To-Cloud basis is through a strong key management system and a client end cryptosystem. (Mosola et al., 2017).

Methods generally used for encryption processes have weak key management systems making it easy to attack and break them. The data stored on the cloud too would be encrypted on the Cloud Service Provider (CSP) end, thus the third party would have to be trusted for every single piece of data.

Working on the concept of the client end cryptosystem, using the neural network, a personalized algorithm can be developed. Chaos is used here for totally random number generation using atmospheric noise as input and using the Eureka system to create a number of fitness functions. From these functions, one time pads are generated.

The noise generated is passed as input to the Eureqa system from where one gets a fitness function. Using this function, one generates random numbers which are converted to binary streams to generate the key. Then the plaintext (PT) is encrypted along with which the key pair is fed into the neural network. The neural network trains on these patterns to output the final ciphertext for storage on cloud. The system also discards the encryption key immediately after the encryption is done. The encryption algorithms used are like DES, 3DES, AES etc. They have also implemented their own algorithm - Cryptor which has its own cryptographic techniques. A counterproductive neural network is used to train the network. It is a hybrid of supervised and unsupervised learning. The two layers used are Kohonen (unsupervised) and Grossberg (supervised). During decryption, the same neural network is used and the output of the neural network is compared with the target value set. If they are the same, only then is the same encryption key generated. The overall performance of all these algorithms proves that the encryption scheme is effective and at the same time low on memory consumption.

Such systems have to ensure that firstly the Cloud Service Provider has no access to the algorithms or the keys generated during the process. Also, the system must be able to ensure that it uses minimal resources so that it can be operated on multiple devices. Once encryption is complete, the key is discarded so that there is no chance of attacks.

Hence, chaos can be used to generate one time pads which can be further used to encrypt data using fitness functions.

Chaos for 'Chaotic Neurons' for One-to-Cloud Operations

Chaos can also be applied to generate hybrid random numbers which can be further used as values for initializing neurons. Since the values have been generated using chaotic parameters, they may be called chaotic neurons. These neurons, when applied to complex neural networks, generate complex sequences which can be used for encryption of data in a one-to-cloud fashion. (Blackledge, Bezobrazov, & Tobin, 2015).

The various methods implemented for encryption of data on cloud are discussed first. One could implement synchronized neural networks. where two identical neural networks are used. The inputs are kept the same, weights are adjusted till they become equal at both sides. The common identical weights are then used as a key in encryption. Another method uses the concept of chaotic neurons. The input value for each neuron is calculated using the value from a chaotic map which makes neurons chaotic. Another approach can be using a chaotic Hopfield neural network with time varying delay, which is used for generating binary sequences. A permuted sequence is used for masking the plaintext. For an image, a triple key chaotic neural network can be used. The term 'Triple Key' implies three parameters used to control the various operations on the image. Lastly, another solution discusses multilayer neural networks in cryptography where a general regression neural network can be used. Keys are created. The message to be sent is broken down into a number of parts which are equal to the number of keys. These parts are sent as input to the neural network one block at a time. Such a process has given better results than previous traditional approaches.

The approach describing this usage of chaos uses evolutionary computing. Evolutionary computing is mainly used to be able to perform biological mechanisms to generate the best population.

Chaos here is mainly used to generate seed using random noise. Noise source (maybe atmospheric noise or radioactive decay) having a high entropy input is applied to an evolutionary algorithm. A function is obtained. Post-processing of this nonlinear function yields a low entropy output. Finally, a check for cryptographic strength of generated output is carried out. Specifically, the neural network used is the Radial Basis Function network (RBF). The RBF network has 3 layers - the input layer with a few linear neurons, the hidden layer and the output linear layer which gives a weighted sum of the radial basis function.

A noise source is taken as input and the system is 'forced' to generate an output which is an approximation to the outside noise. This 'forcing' produces the Pseudo-Randomness required. An equation to generate this nonlinear output is defined in the paper. Two tools have been tried along with chaos to check encryption. The first one - using the Eureqa tool - which uses evolutionary computations. The second approach was to use an ANN Both the methods have given good results, however, the one with the ANN provides a time advantage.

The main improvement in the model by addition of chaos is that it guarantees that such a large database of PRNG is available that personalized encryption algorithms for one-to-one communications with the Cloud can be implemented.

There are a few challenges that this model faces. This equation, however, does not guarantee if the system is structurally stable. For instance, if the constant is generated by a hash function from a low bit private key and then there is a possibility of lack of structural stability. Secondly, the author of this paper has not considered the effect of the algorithmic complexity of their model. This could lead to a major problem while using chaos in cryptography.

Chaos to Encrypt Images

A hyperchaotic system can be used to generate pseudo-random numbers and encrypt them on the cloud. Such a system is one which uses four parameters at least to define its system wherein two of them should be specifically positive Lyapunov exponents along with a negative and a null exponent. One application using chaos for image encryption is by using visual cryptography for encrypting data before putting it on the cloud. It uses the Visual Cryptography Scheme (VCS) for the authentication process using an Image Captcha. (Ayyub & Kaushik, 2015)

In visual cryptography, an image is split into a number of parts in such a way that it can be decrypted only when the person has at least a fixed number of parts available. There are different threshold VCS schemes defined. Any (k, n) Threshold VCS will divide the image into n parts such that only when k parts are present together, can the secret image be decrypted.

The given Figure 5 shows an example of a (2,2) VCS scheme. The overall process can be described as follows. The image owner will upload the original image in an encrypted form on the cloud. He will further create a key matrix of the key and ID used for encryption and send it to cloud in an encrypted form. Now, a cloud user who wants access to the image will first have to prove his authenticity. If authentic, he will get access to the key matrix from where he will extract the index of the original picture. He will send this index to the cloud server. The cloud performs the operation and returns the result in an encrypted form to the user who will then decrypt to get the final image.

User authentication can be carried out using a two-step approach. The first step involves registration between the cloud user and the cloud owner. Here, the cloud user first sends a string to the owner. After which, the owner will enter a string from his side. Both these strings are concatenated to generate an image captcha. A logistic map is then used to encrypt the image. The image is divided into MxN blocks. Using the current value of the logistic map, one can multiply it with a large number (say about 10^{14}) and take modulus over MxN to generate a new value and replace the original image value with that. This value is kept iterating till one gets all distinct values between 0 and MxN-1. The modified image is thus produced. Upon this image, a (2,2) VCS scheme is applied. (Hence n =2, k = 2). Since n=2, two shares of this image will be created. The first one is kept with the cloud user and the second one with

Figure 3. (2,2r the encryption process, the original image is XORed with an image from Flicker (a social media account), then hashing is done. After applying a hyperchaotic mask, shuffling of the pixels is done.

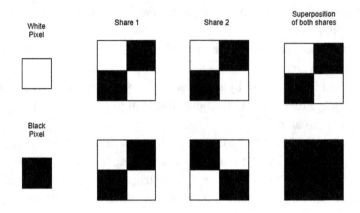

the original image captcha is with the owner. The second step involves verification. When the cloud user wants to retrieve the image, he is asked to enter his share while the owner enters his share. Both of these two images are combined to generate the original image and are verified with the original copy. If verified, the user is authenticated.

Importance of chaos can be highlighted by the following reasons. Chaos helps in increasing the security of the algorithm by generating numbers which are deterministic and that are sensitive to initial conditions. Thus, they are better suited to use in the authentication part. A performance analysis using histogram and a correlation coefficient check proved that using chaos the encrypted image gave better results compared to other conventional methods.

Chaos to Generate S-Boxes

Another scheme which provides both confidentiality and integrity and which is optimal too uses the concept of chaotic S-maps. S-boxes are substitution boxes in cryptography used for confusion generally. A chaotic S-box is basically a substitution box whose values are based on a chaotic map. (Zheng, et al., 2018).

The reason chaos is not used yet is that the computational cost can sometimes get very high. There is a possibility of the occurrence of dynamic degradation too. Chaos can sometimes lead to periodic behavior too if the values are not initialized properly. This scheme overcomes some of the given weaknesses by using cloud and cryptography using a chaotic coupled lattice map. A coupled lattice map is a dynamical multidimensional system of many elements wherein each element is based on a chaotic map. The S-box coupled map lattice (SCML) used here is composed of N identical objects. Each object will take a state from 0 to 255 which is updated according to a predefined function. A static chaotic map helps to reduce hardware costs as the floating point module is removed. The Lyapunov exponent and a correlation coefficient test should be performed to check the strength of the SCML.

The process involves generation of keystream with SCML and is used later for encryption and decryption. The internal states of the SCML are updated and iterated 17 times. For the main encryption and authentication, first initialization is done using the Initialization Vector (IV). Then the data is split into a number of blocks. Next, the encryption is done by masking the generated keystream with the data.

Each step depends on the term from the previous step. After encryption, a tag should be generated for the process of authentication. After decryption, another tag is generated for verification. Only if both the tag are equal, that the original message can be accessed. A hardware implementation of the same can be done through VHDL (for both the SCML and the encryption system part). One should also ensure that each key generated is random, each (key, IV) pair is unique and on verification failure, there should not be any data related message given.

After the 17 rounds in the SCML, the final values obtained should be completely different from the original ones. Tests for statistical analysis such as randomness tests or testing for the avalanche effect should be done i.e. the sensitivity of IV, key and message should be checked. A large key space should be used to avoid a brute force attack. Key sensitivity should be tested using a change of minimal differential in the key and verifying the results. Analysis to check differential and linear characteristics should also be performed. For the authentication tag, it should be ensured that the key is unique and cannot be recovered easily. Also one should check for internal state collision. The authentication tag should also be checked for sensitivity. The throughput of the hardware implementation should also be checked. This proposed system was found to work with better efficiency than other conventional cryptosystems.

Chaos to Hash Keywords for Searchable Encryption Techniques on Cloud

To search or index such encrypted data is very difficult and hence a new application for chaos is to use it to perform searchable encryption (SE) techniques. (Awad, Matthews, Qiao, & Lee, 2018).

SE will permit one to search keywords and extract the particular data files even when they are in encrypted form. The proposed methodology combines chaotic fuzzy transformations and a ranking scheme to index queries and gets effective results.

The problem with traditional search encryption methods was that they either gave a boolean result for the presence or absence without any detail or they gave a result for an exact match of a keyword which would make them impractical to use. Thus, using a fuzzy keyword search can enable one to get closest possible matches. A fuzzy keyword search method generally uses hashing methods such as the locality sensitive hashing (LSH) to enable the fuzziness. The different LSH methods that can be applied are minhash, OmegaFlip and an amplified minhash which performs AND-OR over normal minhash.

Chaos can be advantageous here as it can be used for encoding a word where a new minhash algorithm can be used based on the Piece Wise Linear Chaotic Map (PWLCM). It is a simple chaotic system which constitutes multiple linear functions depending on the condition of the positive control parameter.

The proposed encryption method consists of two parts. The first one being uploading data on the cloud. When a file is to be uploaded, a user first encrypts this file. This file is then sent to cloud. Each file has a unique id and the location of the file depends on this id. This id is also added to a posting list (an index list containing the mapping from words to the location of files) to the corresponding keyword by the user. The values are hashed using the PWLCM and added to the cloud. For the ranking, an order preserving encryption is used so that even the ranking order is not given away to a potential attacker. The next part of the process is to query a requested keyword and get the correct file from the cloud. The client first applies a fuzzy transformation on the keyword and sends it to the cloud. The cloud uses this fuzzy keyword to get the encrypted mapping from the posting list. The cloud then returns the requested number of files in encrypted form to the user. The user then decrypts it at the client end to get back the original file.

Different LSH methods can be tried and tested for results to analyze the proposed method. It was observed amplified chaotic kuzu minhash algorithm gave the best results. Effect of indexing files should be checked to understand the most optimal time. Next, the effect of the number of files stored can be analyzed. And finally, changing the chaotic parameter and checking the overall results. Security analysis can be performed too to check the strength of the encryption algorithm.

Chaos for Simultaneous Encryption and Compression

Data compression refers to the decrease in the size of the message to reduce the amount of data stored or transmitted. Data is encrypted with the aim that only users who have access to the key (information required to decrypt data) can understand it. It is possible to sequentially compress and encrypt data. But this method requires piping the output of the first operation to another. Piping of output is an expensive operation, hence methods to simultaneously encrypt and compress data are being investigated.

Arithmetic coding is one such approach. It encodes variable length messages with variable length symbols of the alphabet. This is done with prior knowledge of the probabilities of the alphabet symbols. A range is divided according to the probabilities into as many intervals as the symbols. The selected symbol of the message is subdivided again according to the probabilities. This happens for every symbol in the message until an end is reached. Each messages' encoding is the binary of the range it lies between. This is how the message is encrypted and compressed at the same time.

Chaos can be used with arithmetic encoding for simultaneous encryption and compression for an improved method. (Usama & Zakaria, 2017). A chaotic map like the piecewise linear Markov map (PWLM) could be used. The plaintext is generally divided into a certain number of blocks (say N), where each block is encoded using a forward interval function. An example of this could be found <insert here>. The initial range must be large enough to allow subdivision of it such that the subdivisions remain non-zero.

A Tent Map and a Logistic map is used. There is one secret key for each map. The first secret key generates a stream of bits from which N cyclic keys are generated. The functions corresponding to the intervals are cyclically shifted depending on the value of the cyclic key.

Once the compressed and encrypted data is generated, the second key and map generate another stream of bits. Chaotic masking is done and the encrypted data and header (which consists of probabilities, number of blocks, and distinct symbols in the alphabet) are XOR'ed with the stream of bits.

This is how chaos is used to control the PWLM mode and perform a masking operation on the compressed file to increase randomness and also encode the header.

Decryption is the same process in the opposite direction. First unmasking is done. The header data can be identified. A stream of bits from the first key is generated once again, cyclic shift keys are generated from it, and binary data codewords are decoded and decompressed.

Another method for simultaneous encryption and compression prior to outsourcing work to the cloud is to use the concept of compressive sensing. Ashwini and Amutha (2018) have designed a new measurement matrix/sensing matrix for compressive sensing. The measurement matrix is responsible for the sparse representation of data for compression without losing important information. Thus it largely affects the reconstruction of data. Appropriate measurement matrix that satisfies the Restricted Isometry Property (RIP) must be used. (Candès, 2008)

Many deterministic and non-deterministic matrices have been proposed previously. Most prior work uses linear programming to solve the problem of outsourcing reconstruction on the cloud, but this is time-consuming and very complex. In the work done by Ashwini and Amutha (2018) to design a quick outsourcing of data using compressive sensing, data is encrypted before compressive sensing. For this, they have proposed a new chaotic map given by

$$z_{n+1} = mod\left(\left(\left(\mu cos\left(\pi z_n\right) + \left(1 - 4z_n\right)\right), 1\right)\right.$$

where $\mu \in [0, 500]$ is the control parameter, $\in [0, 1]$ is the nth chaotic number and n denotes the number of iterations. The proposed map is chaotic in the entire parameter range of $\mu \in [0, 500] \in [0, 1]$ is the nth chaotic number and n denotes the number of iterations. The proposed map is chaotic in the entire parameter range of $\mu \in [0, 500]$ while the logistic map is chaotic only for $\mu \in [3.57, 4]$. Also, the generated chaotic sequence is different for different μ values. The chaotic map satisfies the RIP property and generated random numbers help create the sensing matrix. An algorithm involving substitution and shuffling is performed for encryption. The data is then sent to the cloud which carries out the reconstruction process while it is encrypted. Following this, the data is decrypted at the user end.

Table 3 summarises different approaches of using chaos for cloud content security to make the similarities and differences clearer.

CHAOS ENGINEERING: AN OVERVIEW

Even though it was originally developed by Netflix, the concept of Chaos Engineering is not restricted solely to the company. It can be applied to various other technology giants such as Google, Amazon, Microsoft, and others. (Rosenthal C., Hochstein L., Blohowiak A., Jones N., & Basiri A., 2017).

Chaos Engineering refers to testing for faults in a large scale distributed system on the cloud by shutting down one or more servers and checking if that weakens the system or results in a domino effect. This is usually carried out during production time, to identify glitches in the system through experimentation to eventually build more robust systems. Some kinds of faults which are checked are a sudden increase in traffic, a disk failure, or a server going down. Chaos Engineering is named so because of its random and uncertain behavior.

The practice of Chaos Engineering was applied at Netflix mainly when Chaos Monkey was introduced and later Chaos Kong. Chaos Monkey was used to select a running instance using pseudo-random numbers. The chosen instance was then turned off during working hours to mainly check if the other instances disappear or further come up with a solution to tackle such a failure. Such an approach helps the system become more resilient by already solving the major faults and fallbacks that can occur during the production stage itself. Due to the strength of the Chaos Monkey tool, Netflix has experienced only one experience of an instance failing and causing disruption. Thus, such a tool is beneficial not only to understand the flaws of the system but to help the engineers better build up a robust software. The Chaos Kong tool was used to pseudo-randomly select an entire AWS (Amazon Web Services) and turn it off. This kind of attack forced the engineers to come up with a stable transitioning system in case of region failure such as this one. Performing such an activity on a regular basis strengthened the overall system to a great extent.

Chaos Engineering is not exactly the same as though it relies on fault injection too. But is mainly used to check the increase in traffic, the nodes generating faulty behavior and their effect on the system using experimentation. This approach is completely different from that of normal testing methods as

Table 3. Comparison of different applications of chaos in cloud content security

Paper Name	For	Generator	Mapping used	Confusion	Diffusion	Key Generation	Others
Private Video foreground extraction through chaotic mapping based encryption in the cloud (2016)	Videos	Pseudo Random	Logistic Map	Yes	Yes	No	Random Inverse of video footage
Method for seeding a pseudo-random number generator with a cryptographic hash of a digitisation of a chaotic system (1998 patent)	Ensuring security of a system from unauthorized access	Totally random chaos coupled with any chaotic map	Lava Lamp recording and Blum, Blum, Shub			Yes	generating a secret password or cryptographic key
Securing images in cloud using Hyper Chaos with user authentication (2015)	images on cloud and user authentication	Pseudo random	Logistic map	No	Yes	No	Visual Cryptography scheme for user authentication using Image Captcha
Cryptography using Artificial intelligence	one to cloud operations in neural networks	total + pseudo random number generation	atmospheric noise, nonlinear function	Yes	No	Yes	
Chaos based encryption keys and neural keystore for cloud hosted data confidentiality	one to cloud operations for generating strong keys	totally random number generation	atmospheric noise			Yes	A personalized secure encryption algorithm is generated at the client end. Hence, security is high here.
A lightweight authenticated encryption scheme based on chaotic scml for railway cloud service	s boxes using chaos	Pseudo random	s box lattice	yes	yes	yes	
Chaotic Searchable encryption for mobile cloud storage	chaos to use searchable encryption techniques	Pseudo random	Piecewise linear chaotic map	No	Yes	No	chaotic fuzzy transformations and ranking based system used
Secrecy and Randomness: Encoding Cloud data Locally using a One-Time Pad	Data	Totally random seeding pseudo random	Electronic noise to initialize maps, Chua map, Lorenz map for pseudo random	No		Yes	XOR the OTP with plaintext
On the Applications of Deterministic Chaos for Encrypting Data on the Cloud	Data	Pseudo random	Any number and combination of mappings	No	No	No	XOR the OTP generated from multiple algorithms with plaintext
Chaos-Based Simultaneous Compression and Encryption for Hadoop	Data	Pseudo random	piecewise linear Markov map, A Tent Map and Logistic map		Yes		The bitstream generated is used to cyclically shift the PWLM

they are used to test one condition while Chaos Engineering is used to provide new areas to explore and analyze. Some of the different ways to implement chaos experiments are making system clocks out of synchronization or causing exceptions to occur, increasing the latency between services or purposely leading to failure of a particular server or an entire region on the cloud.

Any complex system will have several modules being worked upon simultaneously. Chaos Engineering helps one the most by increasing the speed of efficiency of individual modules and helping in increasing the strength of the system. An issue which is commonly faced by complex systems is the integration period. Even though the individual modules work smoothly, one might see unpredictable system behavior during integration. This behavior can be detected through Chaos Engineering and thus it is a useful measure.

As one comes up with chaos experiments for their systems, there are some basic principles of chaos which need to be kept in mind. (Principles of Chaos Engineering., 2018, May). They are broadly defined as follows:

- An expected outcome around a fixed metric should be developed. Basically one needs to decide on a metric which is measurable in terms of system's output or the user satisfaction of the product being developed. A metric which has steady and quantifiable values and whose range can be determined easily. Finally, design or build an expected outcome around this metric and its behavior.
- List down the probable events that can occur according to their frequency and potential of the impact such as disk failure or surge in traffic and compare it with the cost and complexity of the system.
- Induce these events to analyze them. Try to run these list of possible events during production environment to test the overall behavior of the system. Such an execution helps one analyze the strength of their system to external vulnerabilities and attacks.
- Automate all chaos experiments designed till now. Reduce manual work and increase efficiency and analysis by automating the whole procedure.
- Minimize impact by doing accurate analysis at each step. A small glitch can lead to a cascading effect affecting the system at a large scale. To prevent this from happening, a proper risk analysis should be performed to ensure that the entire process of Chaos is innocuous.

Thus, implementing these principles can help one achieve Chaos Engineering in their software with improved security in distributed systems.

CONCLUSION

The heart of cloud computing lies in using computer services, software, or infrastructure present at another location which gets delivered over the Internet to terminals. Since access to the data stored does not solely lie with the owner but is distributed on clusters somewhere in the world, security is a major concern.

This chapter highlights how data can be kept secure by using chaos theory. Chaotic systems help generate strings of totally random or pseudo-random numbers. Random numbers generated have multiple use cases. Some common ones are using them as a one-time pad, for chaotic masking, or shuffling of data. They are also useful for simultaneous encryption and compression. Additionally, chaos can be used for chaotic neurons in one-to-cloud operations, to encrypt images, and videos as well.

FUTURE SCOPE

A lot of promising work has already been done, but there are issues that can be addressed. There is no way to guarantee the randomness of strings. Work can be done to identify the range of parameters where systems are chaotic and make a log to keep track of that. New chaotic systems with an increased randomness can also be proposed. Proofs against reconstruction would help instill confidence about the lack of possibility of recreation of generated random strings.

Asymmetric systems use one-way trapdoor functions in cryptography. RSA is such an example where with a known secret value, it is possible to calculate the inverse. However, there is no equivalent of a trapdoor in chaotic systems. This could also be an area of research.

While working on these problems would be helpful, exploiting more homomorphic properties of chaos has a lot of research potential. To keep data secure on the cloud, homomorphic encryption is essential. We have discussed how chaos can be used to encrypt videos and still allow foreground extraction. Similar applications can be searched for. Overcoming issues in performance and security to enable safe integration of cloud computing and IoT is also a research area.

REFERENCES

Alvarez, G., & Li, S. (2006). Some Basic Cryptographic Requirements For Chaos-Based Cryptosystems. *International Journal of Bifurcation and Chaos in Applied Sciences and Engineering, 16*(08), 2129–2151. doi:10.1142/S0218127406015970

Ashwini, K., & Amutha, R. (2018). Fast and secured cloud assisted recovery scheme for compressively sensed signals using new chaotic system. *Multimedia Tools and Applications, 77*(24), 31581–31606. doi:10.100711042-018-6112-4

Awad, A., Matthews, A., Qiao, Y., & Lee, B. (2018). Chaotic Searchable Encryption for Mobile Cloud Storage. *IEEE Transactions on Cloud Computing, 6*(2), 440–452. doi:10.1109/TCC.2015.2511747

Ayyub, S., & Kaushik, P. (2015). Securing Images in Cloud using Hyper Chaos with User Authentication. *International Journal of Computers and Applications, 121*(17), 18–23. doi:10.5120/21632-4951

Bhushan, K., & Gupta, B. (2017). Security challenges in cloud computing: State-of-art. *International Journal of Big Data Intelligence, 4*(2), 81. doi:10.1504/IJBDI.2017.083116

Blackledge, J., Bezobrazov, S., & Tobin, P. (2015). Cryptography using artificial intelligence. *2015 International Joint Conference on Neural Networks (IJCNN)*. 10.1109/IJCNN.2015.7280536

Blackledge, J., McKeever, M., Tobin, L., & Tobin, P. (2018). Secrecy and Randomness: Encoding Cloud data Locally using a One-Time Pad. *International Journal on Advances in Security, 10*(3 & 4), 2017.

Blackledge, J., & Ptitsyn, N. (2011). On the Applications of Deterministic Chaos for Encrypting Data on the Cloud. *Third International Conference on Evolving Internet INTERNET*.

Candès, E. J. (2008). The restricted isometry property and its implications for compressed sensing. *Comptes Rendus Mathematique, 346*(9-10), 589–592. doi:10.1016/j.crma.2008.03.014

Chumbley, A., Williams, C., & Duna, A. (n.d.). *Homomorphic Encryption*. Retrieved from https://brilliant.org/wiki/homomorphic-encryption/

CrystalE. (n.d.). Retrieved from http://www.crystalinks.com/chaos.html

Hossain, M. S., Muhammad, G., Abdul, W., Song, B., & Gupta, B. (2018). Cloud-assisted secure video transmission and sharing framework for smart cities. *Future Generation Computer Systems*, *83*, 596–606. doi:10.1016/j.future.2017.03.029

Indian Institute of Technology Kharagpur. (2009, December 31). *NPTEL: Electrical Engineering - Chaos, Fractals & Dynamic Systems*. Retrieved from https://nptel.ac.in/courses/108105054/6

Indian Institute of Technology Kharagpur. (2017, June 8). *NPTEL: Computer Science and Engineering - NOC:Cloud computing*. Retrieved from https://nptel.ac.in/courses/106105167/26

Jin, X., Guo, K., Song, C., Li, X., Zhao, G., Luo, J., . . . Wang, H. (2016). Private Video Foreground Extraction Through Chaotic Mapping Based Encryption in the Cloud. MultiMedia Modeling Lecture Notes in Computer Science, 562-573. doi:10.1007/978-3-319-27671-7_47

Li, T., Gupta, B. B., & Metere, R. (2018). Socially-conforming cooperative computation in cloud networks. *Journal of Parallel and Distributed Computing*, *117*, 274–280. doi:10.1016/j.jpdc.2017.06.006

Lipa, C. (n.d.). *Introduction to the Logistic Map*. Retrieved from http://pi.math.cornell.edu/~lipa/mec/lesson3.html

Meslhy, Abd elkader, & El-etriby. (2013). *Data Security Model for Cloud Computing*. doi:10.13140/2.1.2064.4489

Mosola, N. N. (2017). Chaos-based Encryption Keys and Neural Key-store for Cloud-hosted Data Confidentiality. In *Southern Africa Telecommunication Networks and Applications Conference (SATNAC, 2017)*. Royal Caribbean International.

Noll, L. C., Mende, R. G., & Sisodiya, S. (1996). *U.S. Patent No. US5732138*. Washington, DC: U.S. Patent and Trademark Office.

Principles of Chaos Engineering. (2018, May). Retrieved from http://principlesofchaos.org/

Rohe, M. (2018). *RANDy -A True-Random Generator Based On Radioactive Decay*. Academic Press.

Rosenthal, C., Hochstein, L., Blohowiak, A., Jones, N., & Basiri, A. (2017). *Chaos Engineering*. O'Reilly Media, Inc.

Rukhin. (2010). *A statistical test suite for the validation of random number generators and pseudo-random number generators for cryptographic applications*. NIST Special Revised Publication 800-22.

Stergiou, C., Psannis, K. E., Kim, B., & Gupta, B. (2018). Secure integration of IoT and Cloud Computing. *Future Generation Computer Systems*, *78*, 964–975. doi:10.1016/j.future.2016.11.031

Usama, M., & Zakaria, N. (2017). Chaos-Based Simultaneous Compression and Encryption for Hadoop. *PLoS One*, *12*(1), e0168207. doi:10.1371/journal.pone.0168207 PMID:28072850

Walker, J. (n.d.). *How HotBits Works*. Retrieved from https://www.fourmilab.ch/hotbits/how3.html

Zheng, Q., Wang, X., Khan, M. K., Zhang, W., Gupta, B. B., & Guo, W. (2018). A Lightweight Authenticated Encryption Scheme Based on Chaotic SCML for Railway Cloud Service. *IEEE Access: Practical Innovations, Open Solutions*, 6, 711–722. doi:10.1109/ACCESS.2017.2775038

ADDITIONAL READING

Awad, A., & Lee, B. (2016). A Metaphone based Chaotic Searchable Encryption Algorithm for Border Management. *Proceedings of the 13th International Joint Conference on E-Business and Telecommunications*. 10.5220/0005953503970402

Bremnavas, I. (2015). Secured Medical Information Transmission Using Chaos Through Cloud Computing. *Middle East Journal of Scientific Research*, 23(10), 2552–255. doi:10.5829/idosi.mejsr.2015.23.10.22764

Chatterjee, S., Roy, S., Das, A. K., Chattopadhyay, S., Kumar, N., & Vasilakos, A. V. (2018). Secure Biometric-Based Authentication Scheme Using Chebyshev Chaotic Map for Multi-Server Environment. *IEEE Transactions on Dependable and Secure Computing*, 15(5), 824–839. doi:10.1109/TDSC.2016.2616876

Chen, Y., & Liao, X. (2005). Cryptanalysis on a modified Baptista-type cryptosystem with chaotic masking algorithm. *Physics Letters. [Part A]*, 342(5-6), 389–396. doi:10.1016/j.physleta.2005.05.048

Ibtihal, M., Driss, E. O., & Hassan, N. (2017). Homomorphic Encryption as a Service for Outsourced Images in Mobile Cloud Computing Environment. *International Journal of Cloud Applications and Computing*, 7(2), 27–40. doi:10.4018/IJCAC.2017040103

Nakouri, I., Hamdi, M., & Kim, T. (2017). A new biometric-based security framework for cloud storage. 2017 *13th International Wireless Communications and Mobile Computing Conference (IWCMC)*. doi:10.1109/iwcmc.2017.7986318

Pandey, D., & Rawat, U. S. (2016). Chaotic Map for Securing Digital Content. *International Journal of Rough Sets and Data Analysis*, 3(1), 20–35. doi:10.4018/IJRSDA.2016010102

Roy, S., Chatterjee, S., Das, A. K., Chattopadhyay, S., Kumari, S., & Jo, M. (2018). Chaotic Map-Based Anonymous User Authentication Scheme With User Biometrics and Fuzzy Extractor for Crowdsourcing Internet of Things. *IEEE Internet of Things Journal*, 5(4), 2884–2895. doi:10.1109/JIOT.2017.2714179

Stalin, S., Maheshwary, P., Shukla, P. K., Tiwari, A., & Khare, A. (n.d.). Fast Chaotic Encryption Using Circuits for Mobile and Cloud Computing. *Advances in Computer and Electrical Engineering Soft-Computing-Based Nonlinear Control Systems Design*, 252-277. doi:10.4018/978-1-5225-3531-7.ch012

Yeang, A., Zaaba, Z. F., & Samsudin, N. F. (2016). Reviews on Security Issues and Challenges in Cloud Computing. *IOP Conference Series: Materials Science and Engineering*. doi:10.1088/1757-899X/160/1/012106

Yu, C., Li, J., Li, X., Ren, X., & Gupta, B. B. (2017). Four-image encryption scheme based on quaternion Fresnel transform, chaos and computer generated hologram. *Multimedia Tools and Applications*, 77(4), 4585–4608. doi:10.100711042-017-4637-6

Chapter 18
A Study on Recent Trends in Cloud-Based Data Processing for IoT Era

John Shiny J.
Thiagarajar College of Engineering, India

Karthikeyan P.
Thiagarajar College of Engineering, India

ABSTRACT

Cloud computing has become one of the most important technologies in our day-to-day lives. The computing resources are delivered to the customers based on subscription basis via internet. Big data storage and processing are main application of cloud. Furthermore, the development of internet of things provides the platform for interconnecting devices over internet. This includes everything from mobile phones, washing machines, lamps, headphones, wearable devices, and everything else we never think of. This enables machine-to-machine communication, also applies to the components of the machine. The main objective of this chapter is to give an overview of cloud computing, big data, and internet of things and the advance research topics.

INTRODUCTION

In modern world, cloud has become an important technology for many IT operations and many IT industries adopt this technology to deliver their services to the customer. The standard definition of cloud is defined by American national Institute of Standards and Technology as "Cloud computing is a model for enabling ubiquitous, convenient, on-demand network access to a shared pool of configurable computing resources (e.g., networks, servers, storage, applications, and services) that can be rapidly provisioned and released with minimal management effort or service provider interaction". It covers the entire stack from underlying hardware to software services and applications. This categorize cloud service model into IaaS, PaaS and SaaS. Also introduce the concept of everything as a service called as XaaS by Buyya (2013). Hence, cloud provides the platform for manipulating large volumes of data.

DOI: 10.4018/978-1-5225-8407-0.ch018

Big data is a term used to refer the study and applications of data sets that are very big and complex structure. The traditional data processing application software are not able to process such a huge data set. There are more challenges associated with big data includes data storage, processing, analysis, sharing, querying, updating, security and privacy. There are five Vs associated with big data that is Volume, velocity and Variety by Reichman (2011). Other concepts like Veracity and Value is later attributed with big data.

The term Internet of Things became very popular in recent years, it is the interconnection of computing devices connected via internet. According to Riggins (2015), there are various definitions of Internet of Things exist but it is generally defined RFID group as "the worldwide network of interconnected objects uniquely addressable based on standard communications protocols". Initially, it was defined by uniquely identifiable, interoperable devices connected via RFID. Later on, Internet of Things is related with more technologies such as sensors, actuators, RFID tags, mobile devices, GPS devices, wearable devices etc.

With a rapid growth in academic and industrial communities, the IOT consists of thousands of connected devices for information gathering, analyzing, managing, decision making and finally collect the information generated by physical devices with respect to real time environment. According to S. P. Mohanty (2016), Yinbiao (2017), Continuum (2017), to achieve the above said factors, there are several technical challenges are involved including big data processing and cloud computing. The sensor devices in the IoT can generate high volume, variety, and volume and velocity data sets. M. Armbrust (2010) said that, the cloud with massive computing power, storage, and scalability handle the challenges brought by IoT big data. The big data processing applications that require cloud for their management includes healthcare, weather forecasting, social media analysis, business analysis etc. When the convergence of cloud, IoT and big data become trending now, how to use the massive computational power and cloud computing platforms for processing big data generated by IoT applications and offering response action to IoT motivates new research directions.

RELATED WORK

Cloud computing is a technology to offer computing resources through subscription or rental basis and it follows pay-per use strategy. Since cloud has elastic infrastructure it needs to be used to process big data applications. Zaslavsky (2013) stated that, the cloud needs to bind to the Internet of Things. Very large Internet of Things based sensor networks use cloud to manage process and store the computational data.

According to Riggins (2015), big data comes from variety of sources in large amount and often have real time data. This can be driven by mobile devices, intelligent sensors, social media tools, health care applications, weather forecasting applications; Internet of Things enabled devices etc. As Riggins (2015) found, Big data classification comprises of data sources, content formats, data stores, data staging, and data processing. Although hadoop has become the platform for big data analytics, hide the complex execution environment. Some of big data handling approaches are data warehouses, batch processing, real time processing and edge computing.

Wang (2015) suggested that, Internet of Things forms a communication network of a large amount of devices include mobile phones, RFID tags, sensors and actuators etc .The data generated from Internet of Things devices has the features such as Heterogeneity, large scale data, strong time and space correlation, small portion of big data in effective data sets. Suciu (2015) said, the fundamental technology of big data is RFID. In addition Identification and tracking technologies like sensors, bar code, QR code, communication technologies and networks also is a part of Internet of Things.

Andreas P. Plageras (2018) investigated new system for collecting and managing smart building data which operates in IoT environment. The proposed system includes sensors which measures the temperature, moisture, light for better management of building and also make the building smart and efficient. Moreover cloud server is deployed to store the information from sensors and building's management. B.B Gupta (2018) focused on, major challenges in the areas such as Radio Frequency Identification (RFID) and Wireless Sensor Networks (WSN). This work also focuses on classifying in the major challenges in IoT as follows: architecture based, entity based, technology based, feature based. Figure 1 shows the estimate of devices connected to the internet from 2003 to 2020.

Stergiou (2018) listed, the security challenges of Iot and cloud computing and also investigate the common features in order to gain the benefits of their integration. Additionally, security model for both the architecture is also contributed in that work. Bhatt C(2018) illustrate the overview of Iot in healthcare, big data in health care, health informatics. The major requirements for Iot based healthcare applications are Wireless Sensor Networks, Ubiquitous Sensor Networks. Knowledge plays a vital role in healthcare applications. The various types of knowledge discussed in this work is as follows: Patient knowledge, Organizational knowledge.

Figure 1. Estimate of connected devices over internet from 2003 to 2010 B.B Gupta et al (B.B.Gupta, 2018)

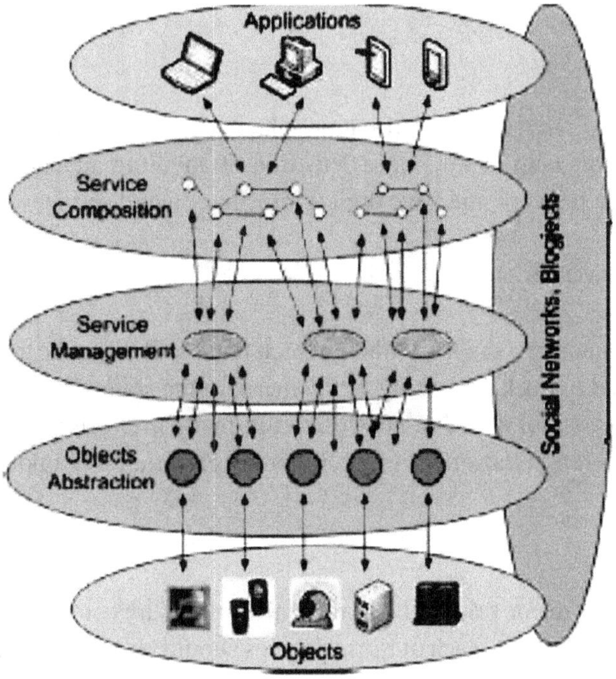

OVERVIEW OF CLOUD COMPUTING, IOT AND BIG DATA

Internet of Things

Internet of Things is a new paradigm has a worldwide network of interconnected objects uniquely addressable based on standard communication protocols whose point of convergence is the internet. The basic idea behind this encompasses all the people of things, can measure, monitor, understand and even change the entire environment. IoT comprises recent advances of variety of devices and communication technologies, things included in IoT are not only mobile devices but also the everyday objects like food, transport, landmarks, furniture, cloths, paper etc. With these objects, sensors and actuators are able to interact each other to attain a goal.

IoT plays a vital role in everyday life of users. IoT enable drastic changes in home and work places, where it can play a leading role in near future in e-health care, smart home, transportation etc. Consequently, it can also adopted for business applications in terms of finance, industrial automation, security, privacy etc. As per the survey done by NIC (2008) states that, IoT has been reported by US National Intelligence Council as one of the six technologies which offer potential impact on US interests towards 2025. According to Dobre (2014), In 2012, the number of interconnected devices was estimates as 9 billion, and it was expected to reach 24 billion in 2020. This statistic implies that IoT become one of the important origin of Big data.

Some of the Important Aspects of IoT

RFID

RFID is referred as Radio Frequency IDentification, plays a key role in IoTera. RFID consists of one or more readers and tags. This help in automatic detection of anything attached to, assign unique digital identifiers, connected to a network and have digital information and services associated with it.

Wireless Sensor Networks

This is one of the important aspects in IoT without which there will be not be any communication among the devices. They are used to track something or the measure the state of something and the like. Those networks provide various useful data and are utilized in many areas like healthcare, government and environmental services defense, hazardous environment exploration, seismic sensing, etc.

Addressing

Both IPv4 and IPv6 play a major role in the communicating address modes. Since a large number of devices come into play in an IoT era, each of those devices should be given a unique, persistent addresses to identify them uniquely.

Middleware

Middleware solve the interoperability issues by abstracting the functionalities and capabilities of different devices. Figure 2 represents the middleware architecture of IoT paradigm. According to A.K. Evangelos (2011), the Middleware can be divided into various layers: object abstraction, service management, service composition and application

Cloud Computing

According to S. Patidar (2012), Cloud computing is a technology which enables on demand access to computing resources based on subscription or rental basis. This enables the availability of virtually unlimited storage and processing capabilities at low cost, in which virtual resources are dynamically provisioned and leased on demand basis. Furthermore, it offers computing facilities as utilities like water, electricity, gas etc. Large companies like Google, Facebook and Amazon adopted this technology for their economic and technical benefits.

The cloud architecture is split into four different layers: data center, Infrastructure layer, Platform layer (Middleware), Application layer. Each layer can be seen as a service layer above and consumer for the layer below. Cloud service model comprise of Infrastructure as a Service, Platform as a Service, Software as a Service. Everything as a Service model or anything as a Service (XaaS) is trending now and provide facilities for the users to customize their computing environment.

Figure 2. IoT paradigm overview by A.K. Evangelos (2011)

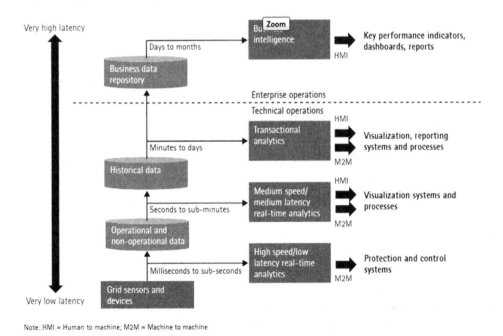

Note: HMI = Human to machine; M2M = Machine to machine

Cloud can be deployed in different ways such as Private cloud, public cloud, hybrid cloud and community cloud. Private cloud is owned by an organization and computing resources are controlled within the premises of an organization. Public cloud is provisioned and used by public users. Hybrid cloud is the combination two or more clouds (private, public, community). Community cloud is provisioned exclusively for the certain community of users.

The major benefits of cloud are energy efficiency, optimization, elasticity, scalability, effective resource utilization, isolation of runtime environment.

Integration of Cloud and IoT

In general, IoT can extract benefits from the unlimited capabilities and resources of Cloud to adjust its technological constraints (e.g., storage, processing, and communication). For example, Alam (2010) found, Cloud can deliver an effective solution for IoT service management and composition for implementing applications and services. They exploit the things or the data produced by them. On the other hand, Cloud technologies can benefit from IoT in a more distribute and dynamic manner and also for delivering new services in a large number of real life scenarios.

In this section we discuss about cloud IoT that is the integration of cloud and IoT. There are three important categories that drive cloud with IoT. They are communication, storage and computation. IoT is defined by a heterogeneous set of devices, technologies, and protocols and it lacks the important properties such as interoperability, scalability, efficiency, availability, security. Cloud has provided the above said characteristics. Cloud also offers reduced cost and ease of use. The new areas explored by cloud IoT is Sensing as a service, Sensing and Actuation as a service, Sensing Event as a service, Sensor as a service, Database as a service, Data as a service, Identity and policy management as a service, Video Surveillance as a service. Let us see in detail about each of the service paradigms.

Sensing as a Service (SaaS)

Gartner defines cloud computing as a style of computing in which massively scalable IT-related capabilities are provided as a service using internet technologies to multiple external customers. Sensor is a device to detect, measure or manage the physical phenomenon. According to Perera (2014), an object can be connected with one or more sensors to detect the real time events. Further, the sensed data is send to the cloud. A sensor owner has the ownership of a specific sensor at a given time. This ownership may vary over time. The sensors are classified into personal or household, private organization places, public organization places and commercial sensors

Sensing and Actuation as a Service (SAaaS)

According to Satpathy (2018), Sensing and Actuation as a service is an advanced paradigm used for various on demand applications. The main objective is to use the physical sensors and actuators for gathering data and transmit to cloud computing framework for further processing in order to satisfy their demands. Here, the physical sensors and actuation devices are managed by various cloud approaches. This paradigm receives on demand services and executes them to satisfy the Quality of Service requirements.

Sensor Event as a Service (SEaaS)

According to Satpathy (2018), time window technique is mostly used in sensor event detection. This enables the dispatching of services when sensor event is triggered. However, in the context of smart home, sensor data is generated discrete manner, where fixed time window technique is not feasible

Sensor as a Service (SenaaS)

According to Alam (2010), SenaaS increase the utilization of sensor operations. This enables ubiquitous management of remote sensors by using web services Ali (2017). Further, it exposes only the functional aspects of sensors and hides the technical details from customer. This method is useful for specifying, discovering, creating, managing sensor capabilities and functionalities. Sensor world is facing lot of challenges in terms sensor modeling, sensor orchestration and security. These challenges are overcome by SenaaS.

Database as a Service (DBaaS)

According to Köhler (2015), DBaaS model efficiently allocating computing resources to its consumers. An effective assignment reduces the number of physical server and satisfies the customer expectations in terms of priceTaft (2016). DBaaS use various techniques typically it enforces Confidentiality Preserving Indexing approaches.

Data as a Service (DaaS)

Since data has been increased exponentially due to development of internet and use of social networks and cloud computing. Thus make the challenge in storing, processing, managing, monitoring and securing data. Park (2015) found, the conventional techniques do not process such huge volumes of data, so that the big data paradigm begun to emerge. It is certain that big data help users to develop analysis of services effectively.

Video Surveillance as a Service (VSaaS

According to Limna (2016), VSaaS support the video recorders and surveillance image processors, and online video storage. The main benefit of using VSaaS is that users can less concern about system hardware and software maintenance can only focus on providing Internet protocol cameras. Additionally, users can choose new image processing solutions instead of system reinstallation. Also reduce cost and offer best quality image processing functionalities. Recent VSaaS provide motion detection, storage space and alert system.

Identity and Policy Management as a Service (IPMaaS)

According to Singh (2016), IPMaaS provide access to policy and identity management. Thus, focuses on authentication, authorization and administration of identities. Identity management always allows single sign on across cloud service and application providers. Policy management ensures the privacy of data among its datasets, where the data is centralized and aggregated that may be distributed over the network. This centralization of data access ensures that such policy mainly for accounting data combination concerns.

Communication

Data and application are the two major cloud IoT layers that fall under communication category. Cloud IoT offer ubiquitous access to applications and that can be delivered through IoT. Cloud offers a solution to connect, track and manage anything from anywhere through its built-in apps. Although, cloud IoT infers major benefits, it can represent bottleneck in some scenarios: the data storage density and processing power increased over the past 20 years as 10^{18} and 10^{15} respectively, where the bandwidth capacity is increased only $10^{4.}$ In addition to that practical implementation problems arise while transferring huge volumes of data from the edge of the internet to cloud.

Storage

IoT devices produce large volumes of unstructured and semi-structured data. These data has the typical three characteristics of big data such as volume, variety and velocity. Such large volumes of data require a storage that is possible in cloud, provide virtually unlimited, low cost and on demand storage capacity. Cloud is the cost effective and convenient solution to deal with the data generated by IoT devices like sensors and actuators.

Computation

IoT devices have limited processing and energy resources that do not allow complex and on-demand data processing. The collected data is move to more powerful nodes and aggregation and processing is performed but scalability is not achieved here. Cloud offers virtually unlimited resource access and processing capabilities for sensor-centric applications and perform task offloading for energy saving.

Big Data Processing

Big data processing is not new concept or topic. Earlier concepts of big data were limited to few organizations like Google, Microsoft, and Yahoo etc. However, the recent advancement in technologies such as sensors, computer hardware and cloud reduces the cost for processing and storing data as well as rapidly reduce processing power. Due to inexpensive storage and processing facilities the sources like humans, applications and sensors start generating data and store them for a long duration. Once the big data is stored, a number of challenges arise in terms of processing and analyzing. Thus big data become a latest trend in industry.

There is no clear definition for big data. It is defined based on the characteristics like volume, variety and velocity. Some researchers also consider veracity and value of data.

- **Volume:** Volume specifies the data size in terabytes(TB), petabytes (PB), zettabytes (ZB)
- **Variety:** Variety relates the types of data. Different sources will produce different forms of data such as sensors, devices, social networks, web applications and mobile phone data etc. The data

could be structured data such as web logs, sensor readings and unstructured data such as social networking data, audio and video streaming data.

- **Velocity:** Velocity means how frequently the data is generated. For example, seconds, milliseconds, minutes, hour, day, week, month and year. This can vary from the user requirements. Some data need to be processed continuously in real time and some can be processed when required. There are three major categories in processing data occasional, frequent and real time.
- **Value:** This means that somewhere within data, there is some valuable information
- **Veracity:** This implies the uncertain or imprecise data.

EMC has defined by Florissi (2012) as, big data as any attribute that challenges constraints of a system capability or business need. For example EMC has considered 40MB is the typical size of PowerPoint presentation and if it is exceeds that will be considered as a big data. Furthermore, in the earlier days of computing 1MB storage cost around 1 $. Nowadays due to developments in infrastructure and computing it is not at all a thing of concern. Further, the data we consider big may not be considered big by tomorrow.

Zikopoulos (2012), D.L. Jones (2012) found, some of the major areas that produce big data are meteorology, environmental science, simulations, medical, physics etc. Further some of the typical areas of big data analytics are log analysis, manufacturing, power plants, weather broadcasting, traffic control, search engines, security, fraud and risk and trade analysis

The big data can be explained by the following statistics of social network by Gutierrez (2017). For context as of April 2018, worldwide total population is 7.6 billion and there are 3.03 billion active social media accounts. For example Facebook stores 240 billion user photos, additionally 350 million new photos are added every single day. To store these photos, Facebook deploys a datacenter of 7 petabytes of storage.

The Barcelona city Cramer (2011) in Spain offers smart parking meters that manage on city wide wi-fi, by giving real time updates through their phone. Further, smart bus stops provides passengers with real time updates via touch-screen panels and city wide sensor provide the details of temperature, air quality, noise level, and traffic to the residents. All these technology innovations are built a big data system on Microsoft Azure to process and analyze such huge data.

Big data and IoT are making tremendous growth in agriculture. One of the leading manufacturer John Deere developed the John Deere field connect system. It monitors moisture levels and send data through wireless connection for farmers. Also measure air, soil temperature, wind speed, humidity, rainfall and leave wetness.

Disney world's proprietary magicband is a the fantastic example of Big data and IoT working together. It took $1 billion to get off the ground. The magic band is a wearable, sensor laden, wristband the visitors used this to check in the hotel room, get their food and go through the turnstiles at the amusement parks. Disney collects data on visitor movement via RFID.

Boeing Jet Cramer (2011) generates 10 terabytes (TB) of data per engine every 30 minutes. A single six hour flight would generate 240 terabyte (TB) of data. In addition, there are about 28537 commercial flights in the sky in United States on any given day. These statistics make us to realize and understand the scale of sensor data generated. However, all these collected data may not be processed all time. Typically, the information is analyzed during airplane crashes.

According to Gutierrez (2012), the diverse challenges in big data analytics include:

- What happens when you have too much data?

- How are these data is being converted into beneficial insights?
- How do you make sense of it when the data volume is on a continued upward trajectory?
- How can you keep up with the volume of data?

A Cloud-Based IoT Data Gathering and Processing Platform

The authors have used Openstack platform with Linux. The underlying virtualization platform is KVM. The use case used was to have sensors and actuators connected to the data processing platform tank are used. The sensors were used to find out the water levels in the tank. Once the tank level falls below the threshold level, there is a trigger to process the data related to water level and make the actuator to fill the tank once again. Their work was based on the below architecture:

On the Use of IoT and Big Data Technologies for Real-Time Monitoring and Data Processing

Hardware sensors like pulse oximetry and temperature sensors were used. The experiment was conducted to find out a building occupant's health when there is limited ventilation in the room. Arduino boards were used as micro controllers. They contain the sensors and actuators. MQTT (Message Queue Telemetry Transport) protocol was used to transfer the read data from sensors and data is passed to cluster based infrastructure. It has six nodes to process the data related to a person's health.

Big Data Analytics in IoT

Big data are generated by an infrastructure using IoT applications. These IoT applications using cameras, sensors and actuators which emit bulk data that must be managed, monitored and analyzed in real time to obtain the relevant insights. In case of manufacturing industry applications, IoT devices continuously generate huge data to improve the productivity of industry operations. Big data techniques are adopted to analyze such huge data in terms of testing and designing new products, identifying defects and increase profits. Big data in the IoT platform primarily used for storage management of sensor data, perform data analytics, perform forecasts and generate alters in case of any abnormal events are detected.

Big data and analytics comprise of five major components. They are data acquisition, data retention, data transport, data processing and data leverage. Big Data acquisition involves gathering, filtering and cleaning data before the data is transferred into the data warehouse. This component is monitored by 5Vs of big data. Big Data retention policy requires the management to meet the archival requirements. This big data retention policies concern about the privacy of data, archival rules, retention period, encryption methods and data formats. Big data must be transported to different locations to guarantee integrity, replication and continuity. Big data used for complex and large datasets will not be processed by traditional software. Big data leveraging involves ensuring how much benefit we can get from the data to increase their revenue.

The big data enabling technologies in the context of IoT are ubiquitous wireless technologies, real time analytics, machine learning, sensors and embedded systems.

The ubiquitous wireless communication technologies that are used for transporting big data generated by IoT devices are IEEE 802.15.4, IEEE 802.11, IEEE 802.15.1, IEEE 802.16. Real time analytics make the big data to be useful when they enter into the system. Machine learning techniques are used to extract the hidden data with minimal human intervention. Big data in IoT are collected using several sensors and actuators. These sensors collect the sensed data and transport to edge devices for further processing.

Big data analytics in the IoT paradigm has four key elements. They are input; rules or policy engine, edge computing devices and output data. The raw input data is collected from different sources and given to policy engine. The policy engine applies rules to the data to get more insights. The processed data is given to edge devices to reduce the latency, minimal bandwidth consumption, integrity, security Ahmed (2017).

Data analytics is classified into three categories predictive analytics, descriptive analytics, perspective analytics. Descriptive analytics is about what is happened and what is happening. Predictive analytics is about what will happen and why it will happen. Perspective analytics is about what should I do and why should I do. Decision supporting systems collect and investigate the various choices and provide suggestions to decision makers.

SECURITY AND PRIVACY CONCERN ON CLOUD BASED DATA PROCESSING FOR IOT APPLICATIONS

Security

Since the use of cloud based data processing for things, there are strong concerns regarding service qualities in terms of data security and data privacy. In recent years there are more research is going in this area. Especially, data security has been considered as a big concern in using cloud. In cloud the consumer data sets are fully outsourced from the cloud service provider, which means they are no longer stored in their physical local infrastructure. As cloud service providers seem to be not fully trusted, this brings several new issues. The foremost thing is when utilizing cloud environment, most of the traditional security mechanisms may not be effective while handling big data. Second thing is not only the cloud service provider needs to deploy the security mechanisms, but also the users should follow the data verification mechanisms to ensure the integrity of data.

Internet of Things is currently emerging platform that is integrated into our daily life. Recently, IoT related research is still its early stage there is no standard architecture for its design and implementation. Since IoT deals with real time applications, IoT datasets can be very large when data is generated for significant amount of time. IoT data must be put to cloud for data processing. Further, the IoT data must be protected as they are personal, such as health care and location data. Therefore security in cloud is very essential.

Data security has many dimensions. The three major dimensions are confidentiality, integrity and availability. Data confidentiality refers the mechanisms to protect data from unauthorized disclosure. This can be achieved through encryption of data. Data integrity Liu (2015) means that data is needed to be maintained intact. Data Integrity is checked by the traditional mechanisms such as Message Authentication Code (MAC), hash functions, digital signatures, and checksums and so on. Availability refers that data is accessible to authorized users. This mechanisms guard against various DoS attacks. In cloud environment, data loss may occur due to natural disasters, attacks, data center failures. In such cases, cloud service provider use backup and recovery mechanisms to ensure the availability of data. The backup of data center is dispersed and maintained in different geographical locations to withstand such failures.

Privacy

Privacy concern arise when user outsource cloud for their storage. This concern has become a serious effect with a introduction of big data analytics and data mining, which require personal information to produce correct results, through the access to location and personalized information from third party data stores. Thus the personal information is exposed results the rise of concerns on profiling, stealing data, data loss.

The acquisition and analysis of data in the IoT applications has many objectives. For example user centric sentimental analysis, performed to improve recommendations for better experience. Additionally, smart cities, government extract the knowledge to place new traffic light, building of new roads and bridges etc. However, the data collected by IoT devices (sensors, actuators) may contain sensitive information with respective to type of application and datasets. So such data must be managed carefully to avoid any privacy violations. Next section will discuss various privacy preserving techniques for the data stored in the cloud in detail said by Abaker (2015).

Currently, data privacy is ensured through various encryption techniques. Most of the encryption algorithms are written in the form $Y = E_k(X)$ where X represents plain text, k represents secret key and Y represents cipher text. In Z.Xuyun (2013) discussed the problem of preserving privacy in the datasets stored in the cloud service provider's data center. The author argued that neither encryption techniques are computationally effective or cost effective because of the time consumed to perform encryption and decryption of datasets. The recent research is going on to reduce the cost of encryption by investigating immediate datasets. A new variant of symmetric predicate encryption mechanism is proposed to preserve privacy of cloud storage. Multi-keyword query scheme (MKQE) that reduce the maintenance overhead of keyword expansion. This would significantly reduce the data leakage and data indexing problem. Three tier data protection mechanism provide multi-level data privacy to cloud users. A new encryption technique is adopted with differential entropy levels to measure the privacy of cloud datasets.

APPLICATIONS

Cloud Iot is adopted by various set of smart devices and applications and most of the applications make use of machine to machine communications. This section describes various set of applications using cloud Iot for significantly improve performance. The applications we considered here are smart cities, smart home, health care, video surveillance, smart energy and smart grid, agriculture. In figure 3 author B. B. Gupta et.al (Gupta 2018) shows the estimate of IoT application areas by 2025.

Smart Cities

Iot with cloud enables the creation of services that interact with surrounding environment. Sustainable development in urban areas is a key challenge and require a new, user and eco friendly services and technology further development. Cloud IoT can provide a common middleware for the development of smart cities by collecting information from different heterogeneous environment, accessing all kinds of geo-location and IoT technologies. The common challenges considered for this kind of applications are impossibility of using any camera connection due to the limited tools and technologies and high heterogeneity due to the lack of service standards and service schemes cloud project (2014).

Figure 3. Growth of IoT applications by 2025 by B. B. Gupta (2018)

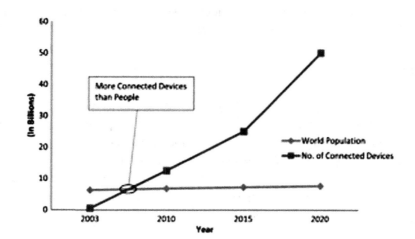

Smart Home

Home networks are identified as the environment where the user mainly uses. Home environments adopted heterogeneous set of embedded devices and the Cloud enables the automation of common in-house activities. Thus merging of computing with physical things requires the access to internet and can represent the services through web services. Most of the smart home applications adopted wireless sensor networks and they are connected to the internet in order to monitor their behavior. Say for example remotely monitoring lighting and air conditioning etc. Specifically, smart lighting recently attracted the research community. These smart lighting systems save the energy up to 45%L. said by Martirano (2011). Cloud offers the necessary infrastructure for building flexible applications and performing home automation task.

Cloud can enable direct interaction of the users to sensors or actuators, remote control, automation and internal network connection. Also enables ubiquitous solutions where any device can be individually accessed.

The major challenges occur in such kind of application implementation are lack of reliability and standards. Moreover, the home devices must be web enabled and their interaction should be uniform.

Healthcare

The use of cloud IoT in the healthcare field can significantly improve the healthcare services and can bring more opportunities to medical IT. It simplifies the healthcare processes and increases the quality of medical services. According to Bhatt (2018), the common features/uses of the IoT health monitoring are as follows:

- It gathers data from sensors using wireless sensor networks (WSNs)
- It supports user displays and interfaces
- It allows network connectivity to access infrastructure services
- It provides robustness, accuracy, reliability and durability.

In this healthcare field the sensors will collect the patient details, store the patient's medical records in cloud storage, process and manage the data provided by sensors, ensure ubiquitous access and sharing medical data as Electronic Healthcare Records (EHR).

Security and Emergencies

The cloud based IoT applications have their presence in security fields too. Perimeter access control is one of the main applications of cloud-IoT as it detects and control people movements in restricted areas. In such applications sensors are deployed and they track the trespassers and intimate the concerned persons or systems so that appropriate actions world is taken. Moreover in case of emergencies that prevail in nuclear, atomic power stations where gases would leak at times and they have to be detected when they cross their threshold limits. In such instances too IoT enabled sensors would analyze the levels of those gases continuously with the help of cloud servers.

Smart Agriculture

IoT devices are used in agriculture too in this era. These devices sense the need in the fields such as the level of chemical needed to grow certain varieties of crops at appropriate seasons. Analytics are nowadays very essential in agriculture because with the help of big data gathered over a period of time using IoT devices, large clustered parallel servers are used in getting some predictions over the type of crops that could be cultivated at certain time intervals. They are used in green houses to control micro climatic conditions for enhanced production of crops and optimized cultivation. Cloud based IoT devices are helpful selective irrigation method particularly in dry areas. Meteorological networks are used to sense and forecast climatic conditions, rain, drought areas.

Domestic and Home Automation

Most of the modern apartments that were built nowadays use IoT enable sensors for many purposes. Such devices can be used as intrusion detection systems in which the devices would sense the movements of trespassers in the home and its surroundings. Energy and water conservation is one of the important applications of IoT under home automation. Because of many such meters that help in cutting down electrical and energy expenses, IoT has gained a great momentum thus leading to a better lifestyle. They are also used in arts and goods preservation. This is done with the help of cloud computing by continuously monitoring museums and the arts present in it.

Industrial Control

In large industries, there will be machine to machine communications. Moreover it is used inside chemical plants to maintain air quality so that it would help the workers to work in a healthy environment. Auto diagnosis of conditions of machines is again one of the recent usage of IoT enabled devices. In this use case, sensors are configured in the vehicles that would help in monitoring the conditions of spare parts for ensuring proper working of the vehicle as a whole. Temperature monitoring is also a very major concern of many type of industries. But now it has been overcome by the introduction of IoT sensors.

BENEFITS OF MERGING CLOUD WITH IOT

Affordable

Customers do not have to invest their money for building infrastructure or equipment. Thus cloud enhances the economy of scale of customer after a long run. Moreover, payment is based on pay as you go basis that depends on the demand of the resources. This will avoid the unnecessary investments and extra payments of resource

Safe and Secure Data Access

Assume that the data is stored in portable devices like mobile phone, laptop. If the device is lost entire data is lost but in case of cloud customer doesn't bother about the data. In addition we can access the data anywhere else all over the world. However, the data stored in the datacenter is lost due to some technical failure or due to natural disasters cloud has backup and recovery management technique to ensure the availability of data.

Elasticity and Scalability

The important characteristic of cloud is elasticity that is if the resource required by the customer is not available in the provider side; outsource the resource from other cloud service provider. Thus make the cloud market have all the resources in one place. In case of scalability, if the consumer acquired certain set of resources from the provider and in the run-time the consumer demands for additional resources. Cloud environment has the capability to provide such extra resources are known as scale-up and the reverse process is known as scale-down.

Reduce Downtime and Delay

Cloud is a network of connected servers. Therefore if one server fails, that can be overcome by another secondary backup server. So the data processing or storage on the cloud never incur any downtime and additional delay.

Energy Efficiency

Cloud computing has adopted virtualization technology for effective utilization of resources. Therefore the energy consumption is getting reduced significantly. In addition, the live migration and load balancing approaches avoid overloading servers and switch off the servers which are not in use.

Pricing

Pricing scheme in Cloud model is flexible than traditional models. Cloud provider has its own pricing schemes. Pricing is based on the time of job submission (peak/off-peak), nature of resource (reserved/on demand), and demand of the resource. In cloud model users are charged for their actual use of resources.

Customer no need to give the capital cost of the resource. Thus offer additional benefit for the customer to utilize the cloud platform for their individual and business needs.

CHALLENGES IN EXISTING IOT CLOUD AREAS

Standardization:

At present many cloud platforms Ray (2016) do not confirm to common standards in data processing and in communication. Standards in data processing, security, communication, identification have to be evolved so that the real essence IoT could be felt. The interoperability and compatibility issues also have to be taken care of.

Heterogeneity

IoT clouds are very heterogeneous in nature. Because of this increases the complexity in the communication medium and the protocols used in it. This may lead to even fraudulent activities in the communication channels leading to major loss to concerned parties involved. A lot of middleware technologies are used for interaction between heterogeneous modules of IoT-clouds. So this adds too much of the complexity. Therefore the IoT cloud should be reassessed to make a common standard for seamless operations.

Context Awareness

A lot of devices are connected together and they keep on sensing. But which data to process is a very big question of concern. Always all data is not needed for any kind of computation or analysis or prediction.

So only data, which is of relevant for some context is needed for a particular calculation. So identification of context aware data by cloud enabled IoT sensors is very essential for a accurate and speed computation.

Middleware

Most of the clouds are created and enabled for particular applications alone. So this makes interoperability very complicated. Therefore middleware evolved as a third layer to make a sound communication between products of different vendors. It paves way for horizontal information flow of data among different vendor's devices, protocols and applications. Because of such connections, a centralized control is made so that queries can be processed easily.

IoT Device Identification

Since there would be lot of nodes to be connected in a cloud enabled IoT era, uniquely identifying each of them is vital. Moreover because of the depleting nature of IPv4 address, IPv6 is gaining momentum recent years. This is because of the length of bytes used as IP addresses. The future is in the hands of IPv6 protocol. So this leads to IoT devices and cloud servers to cope up with IPv6 address features. Also there should be a proper backward compatibility with IPv4 too because all the IPv4 addresses cannot be replaced by IPv6 address space at the end of a day.

Energy Management

This one of the most important issue in IoT enables cloud systems. Because of many IoT devices involved in solving real world problems energy consumption plays a vital role in maintaining the economy of scale of the vendor community. The sensors should be turned off when not in use and should use minimum power to operate on its own.

Fault Tolerance

To make IoT enable cloud systems to be flawless proper fault tolerant measures should be in place. Since many hardware devices are involved in IoT enabled systems, there is high risk of devices being damaged or running out of power. Moreover sometimes the devices may read faulty values or readings which may also lead to faulty results. In battery outages, one of the alternative solutions is to use solar power. This is currently used by many countries and even government subsidies are provided to encourage usage of solar power operated devices. So vendors should switch their devices to alternative power sources which will not get depleted.

RESEARCH TRENDS IN CLOUD COMPUTING, BIG DATA AND INTERNET OF THINGS:

Cloud Computing

Cloud computing has three major service model such as IaaS, SaaS and PaasS. Other than these three service models Ebin Deni Raj et al (Ebin Deni Raj, 2014) stated that there are numerous other special services such as Communication as a Service, High end computation as a Service, Network as a Service, Database as a service, Security as a service etc. Here are the few new areas in cloud computing era

- Fog and Mobile edge computing
- Green Cloud Computing
- Internet of Everything(IoE)
- Cloud Security and privacy
- Serverless computing
- AI bots in the cloud
- Graphics-as-a service
- Cloud-as-a service
- Cloud Composition, Federation, Bridging, and Bursting
- Hybrid Cloud Integration
- Compliance Management in Cloud
- Cloud DevOps
- Smart cloud automation

- Cloud Configuration and Capacity Management
- Service management automation
- Scientific Computing and Data Management
- Storage, Data, and Analytics Clouds
- Autonomic Business Process and Workflow Management in Clouds

Big Data

José Moura et al (José Moura, 2015) Big data can be used in computing and networking infrastructures .It addresses three main aspects such as extraction of knowledge from heterogeneous and unstructured large data sources, enhancing the performance and efficiently manage infrastructure for large amounts of data. Here are the few new areas in Big data era

- The need for flexible architecture in analytics tools
- Convergence of Internet of Things, cloud and big data
- Automated data discovery
- Meeting the Dark Data
- AI and machine learning
- Economic Analysis
- Business Performance Management
- Business Model Innovations and Analytics
- Enterprise Management Models and Practices
- Government Management Models and Practices
- Smart Planet
- Natural Language Processing techniques on Big Data

Internet of Things

IoT referring to the world of smarties such as Smart Energy, Smart Parking, Smart Homes, Smart Grid, Smart Lighting, Smart Cars, Smart Tags, Smart Health, Smart City. Here are the few new areas in IoT era:

- Green Internet of Things
- Context-aware Internet of Things solutions:
- Sensing-as-a service:
- Smart objects or Intelligent Things
- Internet of Things security
- Social Internet of Things
- Energy management
- Internet of Things Semantics
- Communication in Internet of Things

FUTURE RESEARCH DIRECTIONS

Fog Computing and IoT

According to Bonomi (2014), Fog computing is a new paradigm that IoT adds to big data analytics: a substantially distributed data sources at edge.

The pay as you go cloud model is an alternative to managing and owning data centers for data processing and batch processing of customer applications. Several factors that enhance the economy of scale of data centers such as higher predictability data acquisition, effective resource utilization via virtualized set of resources improve the performance, less cost, reduce the power consumption.

Cloud computing becomes a problem for latency-sensitive applications which require nodes at the edge to satisfy their delay requirements. An emerging trend IoT requires geo-distribution, mobility support, location awareness and low latency. This requirements need a platform so as called as fog computing.

Fog computing extend the concept of cloud computing at the edge of the network. Both fog and cloud computing use the same resources such as network, compute, storage and use the same mechanisms virtualization, service oriented computing, multi-tenancy. The fog computing has some fundamental differences in processing data when compared to cloud computing. The vision fog is to address applications and services that do not fit well in cloud paradigm. They are

- Applications that require low and predictable latency
- Geo-distributed applications
- Fast mobile applications
- Large scale distributed control systems
- What make unsetting with IoT applications

Recent survey says that the number of edge devices, for example smart phones, tablets, laptops is around three to four billions. This number is expected to grow in trillion in a few years later. This exponential growth leads to major scalability problem in near future in terms of architecture and communication model. Some scalability will be addressed, but the issue is to rethink the changes in existing IoT paradigm.

The first changes deal with the nature of endpoints. Today scenario we have wide variety of end points. For example the smart vehicle has many sensors and actuators that communicate among them, with the other vehicles, with the road side units, with the traffic signals and with the internet. The same case is applicable for smart cities, smart enterprises, smart grids, Industrial automation etc. This makes the conclusion that IoT force us to adapt the system view rather than the individual view. This conclusion is applicable for the below scenarios.

- A community of individual developer, working with the android platform or the apple platform, contributes today with android applications
- A various number of IoT use cases like smart cities, smart grid, connected rail require geographically dispersed locations
- Low latency and predictable automation are the important attributes in IoT use cases and industrial automation.

Key Attributes of Fog Computing

There are many use cases like smart traffic light system, wind farm, smart cities, smart grid can differentiate the fog computing platform from cloud computing platform. The key attributes of fog computing platform are mobility, multi-agent orchestration, heterogeneity. However, both cloud and fog support multi-tenancy i.e. the support of a multiple client organization without interference. There are delicate differences, though, in the nature of cloud and fog platforms

The typical users of cloud comprises of individual and enterprises. Most of the enterprises off load their IT into the cloud to satisfy the peak demand. The pay-as-you go and job-oriented model dominates in cloud. Fog computing platform also supports job-oriented compute and storage requests but the dominant mode is making the difference. Both platforms run the jobs 24 x 7 manners depends on the demand. In case of IoT brings novel set of interactions among the owner of the infrastructure, the industry or agencies run the service, the users of the service. Thus makes the difference with cloud computing platform.

Figure 4 shows the timescale of cloud computing and fog computing ranges from milliseconds to months. The machine to machine interactions at the millisecond-sub second level include the high speed/low latency analytics. The second level seconds to stub minutes includes machine to machine and human to machine interactions at medium speed/medium latency real time analytics. The next third level minutes to days includes the same in second level for transactional analytics. For instance, the business intelligence level that operates on data collected over months, may cover the different geographical locations, possibly a whole country or beyond.

Power and Energy Efficiency

The IoT based applications mainly depend on continuous and frequent data to the cloud servers. This happens almost mainly from Smartphone which are actually battery operated. Such devices would soon get drained out of battery power thus leading to some data leaks. This may lead to main data points being missed in transmission ultimately leading to false and misleading results. Therefore energy efficiency is important for both data processing and transmission. Many literature studies are carried out mainly in the areas of data compression before transmission, data caching mechanisms which don't send data as continuous streams rather they send in blocks after some time of caching.

Figure 4. Timescale from cloud to fog by Haak (2010)

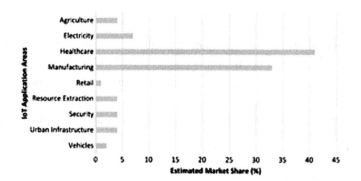

Big Data

Nowadays data gathered is very huge in size and also they don't follow strict structure thus forming what is called big data. Big data needs a good communication network to get the data being transmitted from the sensors to the cloud servers for necessary processing. Big data processing is carried out in cloud servers that are large configuration machines and they may be parallel in nature to support faster processing. In IoT world even for a single application multiple sensors will be needed for getting data from different aspects of an application. In such cases different events will trigger different types of data. There should also be proper synchronization among the data transfers so that there will be a proper flow in the data transmission. Once the data flow is proper, there should be semantic correlation so that data pertaining to the context is captured and necessary information is derived.

Security and Privacy

In recent years there is a large threat from hacking community to hack the sensitive data thus leading to loss of precious data. This is happening due to the leakage in data transmission mainly. Since IoT cloud applications deal with data being transmitted in a continuous basis data has to be secured. Recent news also tells that malware are being injected into sensors so that they read tampered values. This may prove to be very dangerous in case of critical applications. Applications like healthcare, banking industries have large amount of data to be processed in a very critical and secured way. Healthcare industry uses many sensors fitted to the hospital wards to monitor patient's health conditions for various ailments. In those cases, security and privacy play a very vital role.

In Kriti Bhushan (2018) author discussed the integration of Software Defined Network (SDN)in cloud platform. In SDN based cloud platform the limited flow table size is vulnerability which results Distributed Denial of Service attack. Thus this work focus on increasing the resistance of cloud system with minimal DDoS attack. Kriti Bhushan (2017) proposed a new approach based on network flow analysis in order to reduce Fraudulent Resource Consumption (FRC) attack on cloud environment. Kriti Bhushan (2017) investigated, the security issues in cloud, DDoS attacks and DDoS defense mechanisms in cloud environment.

Intelligence

Since data originates from different sources and they are processed centrally, proper compatibility measures have to be in place for ensuring correct results. The data analytics techniques are used to properly coordinate the data emanating from various heterogeneous sources. Since they originate from different sources of different vendors they may not follow standards. So proper intelligence measures must be in place to ensure correct results.

Integration Methodology

Many of the cloud Iot applications are built for specific applications which may have different requirements altogether. To integrate all of them, the common requirements of those applications have to be identified and then integration should take place. A generic platform would solve the purpose.

Pricing and Billing

Various entities involved in cloud-IoT-big data systems are under different administrators thus having different set of customer preferences and different service management policies. To compete in the market businesses are trying to reduce the cost for the customers. However this kind of integrated applications should evolve specific set of rules and regulations for engaging customers with respect to pricing and billing so that they could capture a marketplace for their business.

Network Communications

New solutions are needed to enhance the network for cloud-IoT applications. Since these applications will transfer data in a stream basis the bandwidth becomes the need of the hour. But recent research reveals that current bandwidth will not be adequate for future transmissions and optimization of network will become a very hot research topic in the near future. The cloud-IoT applications will require a reliable method of data transfer and also security should be there in the communication network. Machine to machine communication is of paramount importance in the recent days. This is because all the devices nowadays are able to transmit their captured data to some cloud servers for processing. But in this aspect, different vendors have different protocols to be used thus leading to disintegration.

Scalability and Flexibility

Cloud-IoT applications should be scalable in nature to handling the growing nature of the applications and the data they capture. Moreover flexible subscriptions should be available for the customers for good consumer service management.

Detecting Environment Changes

Context based cloud-IoT solutions are the need of the hour. They deploy many sensors that have to detect changes in the environment in which they are deployed. This is a very important research topic that attracts many of the researchers. This may lead to optimized algorithms for perfecting and continuously detecting changes in the context in which they are placed.

Multi-Networking

Connection handover is very much needed when there is a communication among different devices in the cloud-IoT era. Roaming is necessary for good network reliability for those applications. Maintaining QoS measures, tolerating faults are very much essential for such applications. In those cases multiple networks are used for transmission. For example consider a healthcare application where sensors are connected to patients' body. They read temperature and pulse related data from the body and transmit the data to remote cloud servers through those sensors. In such cases remote hospitals servers will be connected to those sensors networks. In reality there will be different types of network protocols and they all should coordinate together so that those different data could be processed in sync and deriving proper information will become easier.

Increasing Volume

The ever increasing volume, variety, and speed of data produced by the IoT will make to explode the data in an unpredictable manner in the near future. A survey tells that estimates ranging from 16 to 50 billion Internet connected devices by 2020,the most tough challenge for data intensive applications, context-aware applications is to look into ever growing data streams that begin from day-to-day devices. Then there will be a procedure to extract hidden but relevant and useful information. By doing so, it will be easy to detect behavioral patterns that may reap out of it. To extract the full benefits, successful solution should be able to build context-aware data-intensive applications and services. Also it must be able to make this valuable information transparent. Moreover this information should be available at a much higher frequency. If it is so then there would be a substantial improvement in decision making and prediction capabilities of such data intensive and processing oriented applications and services.

Self Healing Devices

This is one of the major research focuses. Since the majority of devices are battery operated they will run out of power or drain after transmission of a particular amount of data. But IoT-cloud applications will need continuous data transmission. For this to become true there should be self healing devices which are in other words fault tolerance in nature. This can be done with the help of redundant networks and devices that act as a backup whenever there are failures in either data transmission or processing.

Distributed Nature

Most of the IoT cloud applications are distributed in nature. This means that sensors would be in a place, servers in different places. They may not only be single set of servers for processing, but also multiple set of servers in different geographic locations for data processing. In such cases different vendor's products are used in different aspects of single applications. So there should be some centralized mechanism for controlling the distributed nature of the application. In such instances, middleware come into play. There are software components that are designed to act as adaptors for interconnecting different mechanism and protocols. Even in olden days component based object models were famous in dealing with distributed applications. So researchers will not find it hard to build better middleware for proper connectivity among distributed devices of same application.

CONCLUSION

Big data analytics is a rapidly growing research area covers the field of computer science, information management to solve complex problems in different disciplines. The use of big data is found largely in the field of Internet of Things. Cloud computing provide the platform for storing and processing such huge volumes of data set.

Integration of cloud and IoT represents tremendous growth in the future internet. The applications emerging from this new integration open up new directions in business and research fields.

In this chapter we have given the overview of various aspects of cloud computing, big data, analytics and IoT and their integration. Thus, this paradigm adopted several new applications. We analyzed the benefits and challenges involved in the integration paradigm in order to identify the future research directions in this era. Finally, we enlist the recent trends in the above said platforms.

REFERENCES

Ahmed, M. H., & Rehmani, M. H. (2017). Rehmani, Mobile edge computing: Opportunities, solutions, and challenges. *Future Generation Computer Systems*, *70*, 59–63. doi:10.1016/j.future.2016.09.015

Alam, S., Chowdhury, M. M. R., & Noll, J. (2010). SenaaS: An event-driven sensor virtualization approach for Internet of Things cloud. *2010 IEEE International Conference on Networked Embedded Systems for Enterprise Applications*. 10.1109/NESEA.2010.5678060

Armbrust, M., Fox, A., Griffith, R., Joseph, A. D., Katz, R., Konwinski, A., ... Zaharia, M. (2010). A view of cloud computing. *Communications of the ACM*, *53*(4), 50–58. doi:10.1145/1721654.1721672

Bhatt, C., Dey, N., & Ashour, A. S. (Eds.). (2017). Internet of things and big data technologies for next generation healthcare. Academic Press. doi:10.1007/978-3-319-49736-5

Bhushan & Gupta. (2017). Distributed denial of service (DDoS) attack mitigation in software defined network (SDN)-based cloud computing environment. *Journal of Ambient Intelligence and Humanized Computing*, 1-13. . doi:10.100712652-018-0800-9

Bhushan & Gupta. (2018). Network flow analysis for detection and mitigation of Fraudulent Resource Consumption (FRC) attacks in multimedia cloud computing. *Multimedia Tools and Applications*, 1-32. . doi:10.100711042-017-5522-z

Bonomi, Milito, Natarajan, & Zhu. (2014). *Fog Computing: A Platform for Internet of Things and Analytics*. Springer.

Buyya. (2013). *Mastering cloud computing*. Morgan Kaufman.

Cloud Project. (2014). Retrieved from http://clout-project.eu/

Cramer, Rost, Bentley, & AymanShamma. (2011). *2nd workshop on research in the large. using app stores, wide distribution channels and big data in ubicomp research*. Retrieved from http://doi.acm.org/10.1145/2030112.2030244

Dobre, F., & Xhafa, F. (2014). Xhafa, Intelligent services for big data science. *Future Generation Computer Systems*, *37*, 267–281. doi:10.1016/j.future.2013.07.014

Ebin Deni Raj, L. D. (2014). *Forecasting the Trends in Cloud Computing and its Impact on Future IT Business*. IGI Global.

Evangelos, A. K., Nikolaos, D. T., & Anthony, C. B. (2011). *Integrating RFIDs and smartobjects into a UnifiedInternet of Things architecture*. Advances in Internet of Things.

Florissi, P. (2012, February). *Emc And Big Data - A Fun Explanation*. Retrieved from http://www.youtube.com/watch?v=eEpxN0htRKI

Gupta, B. B., & Quamara, M. (2018). An overview of Internet of Things (IoT): Architectural aspects, challenges, and protocols. In *Concurrency and Computation: Practice and Experience*. Wiley. doi:10.1002/cpe.4946

Gutierrez. (2017). *InsideBIGDATA Guide to Data Analytics in Government*. DELL EMC, Intel.

Haak, D. (2010). *Achieving high performance in smart grid data management*. White paper from Accenture.

Hashem. (2015). The rise of big data on cloud computing: Review and open research issues. *Information Systems*, *47*, 98–115.

Hashem, I. A. T., Yaqoob, I., Anuar, N. B., Mokhtar, S., Gani, A., & Khan, S. U. (2015). The rise of "big data" on cloudcomputing: Review and open research issues. *Information Systems*, *47*, 98–115. doi:10.1016/j.is.2014.07.006

Intelligence, C. B. (2008). Disruptive civil technologies. Six Technologies with Potential Impacts on US Interests Out to 2025.

Köhler, Jünemann, & Hartenstein. (2015). Confidential database-as-a-service approaches: taxonomy and survey. Journal of Cloud Computing: Advances, *Systems and Applications*, *4*, 1. doi:10.118613677-014-0025-1

Limna & Tandayya. (2016). A flexible and scalable component-based system architecture for video surveillance as a service, runningon infrastructure as a service. In *Multimed Tools Applications*. Springer. doi doi:10.100711042-014-2373-8

Liu, Yang, Zhang, & Chen. (2015). External integrity verification for outsourced big data in cloud and IoT: A big picture. *Future Generation Computer Systems, 49*, 58–67.

Martirano, L. (2011). A smart lighting control to save energy. *Intelligent Data Acquisition and Advanced Computing Systems (IDAACS), 2011 IEEE 6th International Conference on*, 132–138. 10.1109/IDAACS.2011.6072726

Mohanty, S. P., Choppali, U., & Kougianos, E. (2016, July). Everything You wanted to Know about Smart Cities. *IEEE Consumer Electronics Magazine*, *6*(3), 60–70. doi:10.1109/MCE.2016.2556879

Moura, J. (2015). *Intelligent Management and Efficient Operation of Big Data*. IGI Global.

Park, K., Nguyen, M. C., & Won, H. (2015). Web-based Collaborative Big Data Analytics on Big Data as a Service Platform. *ICACT, 17th international conference*.

Perera, Zaslavsky, Christen, & Georgakopoulos. (2014). Sensing as a Service Model for Smart Cities Supported by Internet of Things. *Transactions on Emerging Telecommunications Technologies*, 1-12. doi:10.1002/ett

Plageras, A. P., Psannis, K. E., Stergiou, C., Wang, H., & Gupta, B. B. (2018). Efficient IoT-based sensor BIG Data collection–processing and analysis in smart buildings. *Future Generation Computer Systems*, *82*, 349–357. doi:10.1016/j.future.2017.09.082

Radenkovic, B. (2017). *From Ubiquitous Computing to the Internet of Things.* IGI Global.

Ray. (2016, December). A survey of IoT cloud platforms. *Future Computing and Informatics Journal-Volume*, *1*(1–2), 35–46.

Reichman, O. J., Jones, M. B., & Schildhauer, M. P. (2011). Challenges and Opportunities of Open Data in Ecology. *Science*, *331*(6018), 703–705. doi:10.1126cience.1197962 PMID:21311007

Riggins, F. J., & Wamba, S. F. (2015). Research directions on the adoption, usage, and impact of the internet ofthings through the use of big data analytics. In *48th Hawaii International Conference* (pp. 1531–1540). HICSS.

Satpathy, Sahoo, & Turuk. (2018). Sensing and Actuation as a Service Delivery Model in Cloud Edge centric Internet of Things. *Future Generation Computer Systems, 86*, 281–296.

Shu, Y. (n.d.). *IEC White Paper for "Internet of Things: Wireless Sensor Networks."* Retrieved from http://www.iec.ch/whitepaper/pdf/iecWP-internetofthings-LR-en.pdf

Singh, Pasquier, Bacon, Ko, & Eyers. (2016). Twenty Security Considerations for Cloud-Supported Internet of Things. *IEEE Internet of Things Journal, 3*(3), 269–284. doi:10.1109/jiot.2015.2460333

Stergiou, C., Psannis, K. E., Kim, B. G., & Gupta, B. (2018). Secure integration of IoT and cloud computing. *Future Generation Computer Systems*, *78*, 964–975. doi:10.1016/j.future.2016.11.031

Suciu, G., Suciu, V., Martian, A., Craciunescu, R., Vulpe, A., Marcu, I., ... Fratu, O. (2015). Big Data, Internet of Thingsand Cloud convergence–an architecture for secure e-healthapplications. *Journal of Medical Systems*, *39*(11), 1–8. doi:10.100710916-015-0327-y PMID:26345453

Taft, Lang, & Duggan. (2016). *STeP: Scalable Tenant Placement for Managing Database-as-a-Service Deployments.* SoCC '16, Santa Clara, CA

The Continuum: Big Data, Cloud & Internet of Things. (n.d.). Retrieved from https://www.ibm.com/blogs/internet-of-things/big-data-cloud-iot/

Wan, J., O'Grady, M. J., & O'Hare, G. M. P. (2015). Dynamic sensor event segmentation for real-time activity recognition in a smart home context. *PersUbiquitComput*, *19*, 287–301.

Wang, H., Osen, O. L., Li, G., Li, W., Dai, H. N., & Zeng, W. (2015). Big data and industrial internet of thingsfor the aritime industry in northwestern Norway. TENCON, IEEE Region 10 Conference, 1-5.

Xuyun, Chang, Nepal, Pandey, & Jinjun. (2013). A Privacy Leakage Upper Bound Constraint-Based Approach for Cost-Effective Privacy Preserving of Intermediate Data Sets in Cloud. *Parallel and Distributed Systems, IEEE Transactions on, 24*, 1192–1202.

Zainab Hassan Ali. (2017). *A New Proposed the Internet of Things (IoT) Virtualization Framework Based on Sensor-as-a-Service Concept*. Wireless PersCommunication. doi:10.100711277-017-4580-x

Zaslavsky, A., Perera, C., & Georgakopoulos, D. (2013). Sensing as a service and big data. *Proceedings of the International Conference on Advances in Cloud Computing (ACC)*.

Zikopoulos, P. (2012, March). *IBM Big Data: What is Big Data Part 1 and 2*. Retrieved from http://www.youtube.com/watch?v=B27SpLOOhWw

Chapter 19

A Perspective on Using Blockchain for Ensuring Security in Smart Card Systems

Ankur Lohachab

(iD) https://orcid.org/0000-0002-5291-7860

Kurukshetra University, India

ABSTRACT

Due to the momentous growth in the field of Internet of Things (IoT), various commercial and government organizations are exploring possibilities of mass issuance of smart cards in different applications. Widespread deployment of smart card-based systems in heterogeneous environment would facilitate card holders to participate in these applications in a personalized manner. Despite the security features, valuable data and access to decisive services make these systems prime target for attackers. These systems can be subjected to a range of security attacks – from hardware exploitation to exploitation of software bugs, from unauthorized data access to social engineering, and so forth. In the future, where many sectors will be trying to adopt the concept of Blockchain, it will create new opportunities for benefiting citizens with enhanced security over their data. In this chapter, the author performs in-depth analysis over the role of Blockchain in securing the smart card ecosystem.

INTRODUCTION

Introduction of the concept of smartness in technology is bringing more promising solutions to the modern digital world. Wireless Sensor Networks (WSNs) are taking the form of Internet of Things (IoT), chip cards are getting transformed into smart cards, and so forth. By addressing the issues of advanced underlying technologies like WSN, IoT further extends the idea of inter-connected networks by embedding networking features into physical world objects. In a similar fashion, smart cards also extend the concept of chips cards by making them more resourceful. Although magnetic-stripe enabled cards remained popular for around 30 years, industries over time have realized the need of storing more static data over the card itself. However, due to certain limitations as given in Table 1, magnetic-stripe cards are not considered as a reliable choice.

DOI: 10.4018/978-1-5225-8407-0.ch019

Table 1. Magnetic-stripe cards and limitations

Parameter	Description
Security	These cards provide minimal level of security because it is easy to read and write data from these cards very easily. Hence, information can be easily stolen and the card can be easily duplicated.
Storage	These cards have limited amount of storage and thus can store only limited amount of information.
Functionality	Magnetic stripe cards support restricted functionality and thus, are not suitable for many real-time applications.
Biometric information storage and matching	These cards cannot store biometric templates of users as well as do not support on-card biometric matching.
Data diversity	These cards are not capable of storing diverse types of data.
Digital signature storage	These cards cannot store digital signature for enabling efficient auditing process.
Two-factor authentication	These cards do not support two-factor authentication.

Upon realizing these limitations, researchers are continuously putting efforts on the same-sized cards in order to make them more convenient. These cards are referred as "smart cards" as unlike chip or magnetic-stripe cards, they not only have a unique identifier, but can also participate in automated transactions in a secure manner (Jiang, Ma, & Wei, 2018). Advent of technologies like Micro-Electro-Mechanical-Systems (MEMS) makes it possible to embed more features and functionalities on the card. For instance, Radio Frequency Identification (RFID) enabled cards work in a contactless fashion that have certain level of benefits as compared to contact cards. Other points that distinguish smart cards from magnetic chip cards include difficulty of duplication, more durability, more security, more cost, and so forth. Microprocessor chips used in the smart cards are not very different from those of a modern personal computer, but they have very limited functionality. For instance, Trusted Computing Base (TCB) (the amount of code trusted by the CPU for enabling secure operations) is very limited in the smart card chips. Despite the fact that these chips are only 9 mm² less as compared to processors, they contain sufficient amount of memory (Rankl & Effing, 2004). However, as this memory is not suitable for executing complex algorithms, the operations are generally performed over it considering the resource constraints.

Since the applications of smart cards range from diverse payment based applications to healthcare and citizenship cards, the security features must be robust enough for ensuring the safe-keeping of end user's data. Various public and private organizations have successfully implemented or are trying to implement standards, such as Europay, MasterCard and Visa (EMV) in payment based smart cards (Mayes & Markantonakis, Smart Cards, Tokens, Security and Applications, 2008); (Degabriele, Lehmann, Paterson, Smart, & Strefler, 2012); (Ward, 2006). These smart card issuing organizations claim that their cards encompass unique features that may be advantageous to the users as shown in Figure 1 (Thornton, 2017). However, same security standards may not be able to satisfy the security requirements of heterogeneous applications. Smart card security problems can be associated with hardware and software aspects, where hardware include smart card chip and reader, and software include application programs, operating system and user interface, and all are required to be secured (Guyot, 2010). Service providers are endeavouring to protect the data which is considered as treasure in the smart world. However, attackers are somehow becoming capable of stealing the sensitive information. Although, many encryption algorithms are present in the literature, now-a-days, researchers are implementing light-weight encryption schemes on these devices due to resource constraints. Data Encryption Standard (DES) has been implemented in the smart cards for financial applications. However, it has been replaced by Advanced Encryption Standard (AES) which is a symmetric encryption standard and is used over DES because of its different key lengths that provide specified security levels for heterogeneous applications.

Apart from the cards, smart card system consists of readers and background support system. These components also require adequate security as of smart cards. Many sensitive applications of smart cards require verification of signature and storage of certificates. These attributes require public key algorithms to be implemented in the smart card system. Public key crypto-systems like RSA and Elliptic Curve Cryptography (ECC) require arithmetic units on the card chips for the implementation of modulo and exponential operations (Jiang, Ma, & Wei, 2018). Traditionally, smart card chips required dedicated co-processors as they had 8-bit architecture for performing large number of calculations. These public key crypto-systems have been very popular for implementing the authentication protocols, despite the fact that they require more powerful smart cards with enhanced size. Another perspective for providing the authentication and increasing level of security is Random Number Generators (RNG). These RNGs generate random numbers that are widely used for key generation and to authenticate the identity of involved entities. For the purpose of enhanced security and to avoid replay attacks, random numbers used in the smart cards are true random numbers that are produced by hardware based random generators, rather than software produced pseudo-random numbers. Various measures are required to be taken during random number generation, as these values can be fluctuated by the external parameters including high or low temperature (Tunstall, 2017). By adding more parameters for ensuring security, complexity of the system also increases unintentionally which in turn becomes enemy of reliability. Increasing complexity in the smart card systems requires more resources which also increases the cost of production up-to a certain extent. In many financial applications, there is no mechanism to implement One-Time Passwords (OTPs). For instance, when a transaction is done from another country, OTP is not required. In some cases, biometrics cannot be implemented as it would increase the threat of cloning the sensitive credentials. Instead of integrating lots of parameters like biometrics, OTPs, and so forth, there should be a single technology for ensuring security.

The smart cards that we use today may not be considered as smart in future as we are dealing with the Internet of Transactions in the near future. Need of digitalization is like a wind of change which is delving into the technology and trying to find new possibilities. Similarly, researchers are trying to find new solutions that are capable of securing smart card applications. Accordingly, the security solutions should be precise and should be able to deal with this new paradigm. By looking at this problem from a different perspective, the lens of immutability of decentralization may give the desired solution by enabling peer-to-peer transactions of digital things. Blockchain, which is a next generation decentralized infrastructure is not limited to Bitcoins, although this concept has been recognized by the arrival of Bitcoins. This novel infrastructure enables validation, verification, consensus and immutable recording that give this concept ability to be used in wide range of applications. Electronic wallets, crypto-currency and various applications facilitate customers with reliable ways of doing transactions (Kim & Lee, 2018). For instance, there are various applications where multiple cards can be stored in devices like smartphones, and customers will have the option to select the card of their choice. Near Field Communication (NFC) has revolutionized the concept of electronic wallets in the last few years by standardizing various close range communication technologies and bringing them together under one realm (Zorzi, Gluhak, Lange, & Bassi, 2010). However, in some cases, devices like mobile phones are rooted with untrusted third party applications which will certainly increase the threat of stealing the user information. Considering this, researchers still believe that dedicated smart cards are more preferable over these mobile phone devices.

Figure 1. Smart card features and benefits

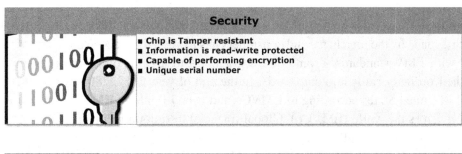

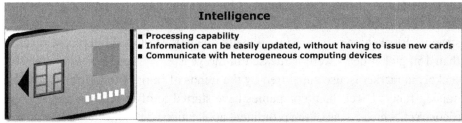

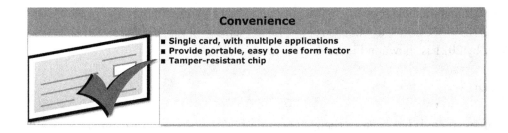

EVOLUTION, STATISTICS AND MOTIVATION

In this section, evolutionary aspects of smart cards and Blockchain including the work done in these areas for their improvement, related statistics and motivation of using Blockchain technology in smart card security are summarized.

Historical Background

Smart cards and technologies that depend upon Blockchain, are popular and expeditious network trends in the new generation. Although the concept of smart cards is not new, they are very popular today due to their wide range of applications. On the other hand, Blockchain which is popular due to crypto-currencies, is expanding its utilization towards other applications. By looking into the past events, it is more complacent for understanding their current state of importance. Table 2 summarizes the major events associated with the evolution of these two technologies.

Statistical Assessment

Electronic chips in smart cards having EMV standards have been adopted adequately after 2015. Combinedly efforts made by the merchants and consumers has increased the acceptance rate of the new chip technology with EMV standards. From college graduates to high-income persons, almost everyone is turning their ordinary cards into chip cards. In the end of year 2017, 780 million EMV chip cards were issued in United States according to EMVCo and over 7.0 billion EMV based smart cards were in circulation across the world (EMVCo). Global financial institution members of the Visa, Discover, American Express, JCB, UnionPay and MasterCard, reported statistics of the adoption rate and number of EMV cards in the global market. Latest statistics for the same taken from these institutions are shown in Figure 2 and 3 (EMVCo).

Market space of Blockchain is increasing globally due to the colossal interest of investors. Startups with more than 150 global deals were witnessed in the year 2017 (Iansiti & Lakhani, 2017). Growth of global Blockchain market is also supported by the trends of Initial Coin Offering (ICOs), as for the purpose of raising funds, Blockchain companies have started to offer ICOs as the sale of tokens and coins. Smart contract, which is one of the prominent application of Blockchain, plays an important role in the growth of the Blockchain market value as smart contracts assist individuals and organizations in the transactions on their property, electricity and shares by eliminating the need of the middlemen (gemalto, 2018). According to Statista report, huge increase in the global market share of Blockchain technology by 2021 is shown in Figure 4.

Motivation

Security of smart cards has been a crucial concern for a long time and researchers are trying to handle this this issue by developing admirable mechanisms. In many research papers on smart card security, researchers focus on developing authentication schemes. However, along with the authentication, there are several other issues that require the same attention as authentication mechanisms. By effective utilization of Blockchain in various applications of smart cards, any individual or organization can provide security to its infrastructure. The broader concept of using Blockchain is to establish trust among unknown entities while they are sharing their valuable resources. Electronics-enabled transactions are already showing results of the benefits of using Blockchain. For instance, now-a-days, digital currency is the most popular and trending currency among users due to its tamper-proof and secure features. Although crypto-currencies are showing satisfactory security results, but with the help of complex mathematics and software rules, real world attackers are able to penetrate the best designed Blockchain systems. Hence, for understanding the security of these technologies in detail, there is a need to explore how these technologies can collaborate with each other, what are the possible advantages that can contribute to their integration, and the possible challenges. Collaboration of smart cards and Blockchain seems to be a near future. Hence, smart card system vendors and Blockchain service providers are actively involving today.

The main contributions of this chapter are threefold:

- Discussion over the working of the smart card systems and Blockchain mechanism.
- Discussion over the security challenges faced by Blockchain and smart card systems.
- Discussion over how Blockchain will provide security features in smart card based applications.

Table 2. Unfolding progress in the field of smart cards and concept of blockchain

Year	Events
1970	First patent on the concept of smart card filed by Dr. Kunitaka Arimura of Japan.
1974	Integrated Circuit (IC) card patient was filed by Roland Moreno of France that was later dubbed as "smart card".
1979	In the French banking sector, Motorola developed the first claimed single secure chip microcontroller.
1984	Successfully field trials of Automated Teller Machine (ATM) bank cards having chips.
1987	Besides financial sectors, smart cards were implemented as Peanut Marketing Card in the United States and driver license in Turkey.
1994	80 million health smart cards were issued in Germany; Joint specifications for global microchip-based bank cards (smart cards) were published by Europay, MasterCard and Visa (EMV).
1998	Windows operating system compatible with smart cards was announced by Microsoft; Multiple applications using single smart card were implemented by United States Navy Joint forces; France introduced a pilot project of smart health cards for its 50 million citizens.
2006	Infrastructure for contactless payment in the United States came into existence.
2008	The concept of Blockchain came forefront with the introduction of Bitcoin in white paper by Satoshi Nakamoto.
2009	Transaction of first Bitcoin in the form of "Genesis Block" between Hal Finney and Satoshi Nakamoto and thereafter, market of Bitcoin was established.
2010	For the first time, Bitcoin was used to purchase items in the form of two pizzas worth 10,000 Bitcoins.
2011	Exchange value of Bitcoin reached parity with the United States dollar.
2013	Market capitalization of Bitcoin reached 1 billion dollar; In a white paper, concept of Blockchain was enhanced by Etherum and Smart Contracts.
2014	With the introduction of EMV cards in the United States, 3.4 billion EMV cards were circulated worldwide; First Smart Contract was launched in the form of Ethereum via crowdfunding.
2015	The Hyperledger Project established by the Linux Foundation; First trial of Blockchain began by NASDAQ.
2016	Official recognition of Virtual currencies by Japan; Number of circulated Bitcoins reached 16.5 million.
2018	More recently, Switzerland started accepting taxes in the form of Bitcoins.

SMART CARD SYSTEM AND BLOCKCHAIN: AN OVERVIEW

In this section, basic concepts and working of smart cards and Blockchain technology are discussed.

Concept of Smart Card System

The term smart card can be understood as a "pocket-sized computer" as it contains one or more integrated chips and these chips facilitate smart cards with memory, microprocessor and input/output interface (Odelu, Das, & Goswami, 2015). Although there has always been a debate over the characteristics and capabilities of a device that can be considered as a smart card. Smart cards have broader application areas ranging from healthcare to mobile communication, but people still believe that smart cards are only for the financial transactions. No definition or standards have been developed for the label "smart card" by the International Standard Organization (ISO) (Lin, Wen, & Du, 2015). However, standards have been developed for Integrated Circuit Cards (ICC). There were some major developments in smart card capabilities during the year 1989 to 2009 that are shown in Figure 5 (Dabosville). Table 3 summarized smart card standards with their respective sizes and their applications.

Figure 2. Global adoption rate of EMV chip cards

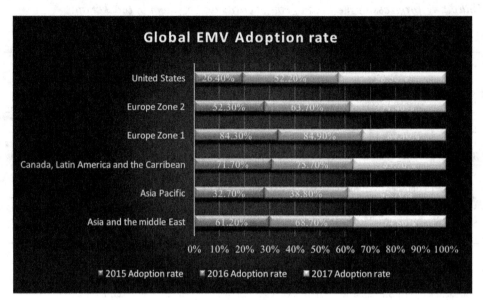

Figure 3. Global deployment of EMV chip cards

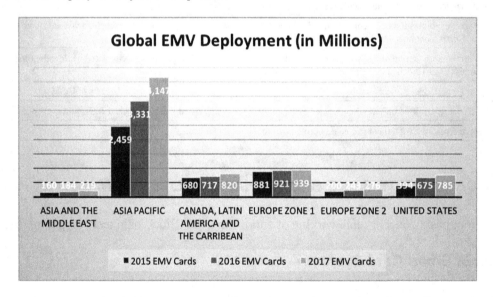

Based on the hardware architecture, capabilities, security services, configuration and applications, smart cards can be broadly classified into two types.

Magnetic Stripe Card

Similar to the stripes used in cassette recorders, magnetic stripe cards use a piece of plastic or durable paper for the carriage of the stripe. Low cost and easy read/write features make these cards popular for the use of credit and debit cards in financial applications. However, they are being utilized in various

Figure 4. Global market size of blockchain technology

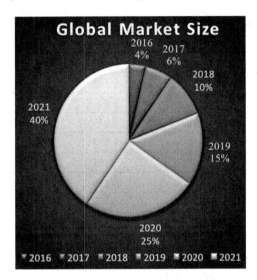

heterogeneous sectors including access control systems, tickets and entitlement cards. Magnetic stripe cards contain strong magnetic field which is capable of controlling the alignment of the dipoles into numerous orientations along the length (Biro & Bartczak, 2013). Generally, multiple horizontal stacked tracks that occupy a portion of the stripe are able to store various types and amount of data.

Reader decodes the information for transaction when the card is swiped through it. Despite the fact that these cards are convenient to use, they have a major drawback in terms of security, as they are easy to clone and forgery can be done. Among various attacks, two kinds of attacks are popular in magnetic stripe frauds. First is skimming, in which the useful information from the valid card is copied and with the help of this copied information, another card is developed with the intention of carrying fraud trans-action. Another is counterfeiting, in which humans are directly involved and attacker copies the carrier of the card rather than stripes, for the purpose of making fool of the people instead of performing any automated transaction. Due to these drawbacks, organizations do not recommend these cards for any type of secure services.

Figure 5. Developments in smart card processing capabilities

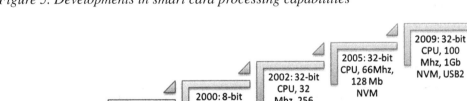

Table 3. Smart card size and general applications

Type of Card	Standard	Height (mm)	Width (mm)	Area (mm)	Usage
Plug-In	1989	15	25	375	Finance
Micro-SIM	2004	12	15	180	Communication
Nano-SIM	2012	8.80	12.3	108	
MFF2	2009	5	6	30	
ID-000	ISO/IEC 7810	15	25	375	SIM cards
ID-1		53.98	85.6	4621	Banking and ID
ID-2		74	105	7770	Visas
ID-3		88	125	11000	Passports

Chip Card

By embedding an electronic chip, plastic cards or conventional chip cards can be easily identified by the color characteristics of the contact which is generally golden or silver. Chip cards have overall 8 pins and earlier manufacturers use only 6 pins with two lower pins as Reserved for Future Use (RFU). However, in some cases manufacturers use two pins for USB interface, and VCC pin is replaced by Single Wire Protocol (SWP) for enabling **NFC (Mayes, An Introduction to Smart Cards, 2017). Transformation diagram of pin based architecture is shown in Figure 6. When a conventional chip comes in contact** with the reader, the contact provides the power via VCC/GND pins, and VPP pin is used for re-programming the EE-PROM. Half-duplex communication with two-level protocols can be used for exchanging information, i.e. T=0 is preferred by the mobile communication industry and T=1 is preferred by the financial institutions. Conventional chip cards are not very dissimilar from magnetic cards in terms of security. Memory chip cards provide storage facility for the users, but information can be copied easily. Hence, these cards also fail to provide better security features. Although few organizations use these memory features in the chip cards to provide security and hence, referred as secure memory chip cards (e.g. MIFARE DESFire EV1). Due to limited functionality of these conventional chip cards, they are sometimes referred as microcontroller rather than microprocessor.

Another category which falls under the category of chip cards are microprocessor chip cards and in a general perspective, these cards are referred as smart cards. This category of chip cards is not only able to store information, but is also capable of processing the information locally and implement security protocols in a much efficient manner.

Figure 6. Pin diagram of chip card

VCC		GND		VCC		GND
RST	2008	VPP	➡	RST	2016	SWP
CLK		I/O		CLK		I/O
RFU		RFU		USB+		USB-

Smart Card Construction

Regardless of their type, a smart card or chip card is generally a plastic card in which a computer chip is installed along with a layered architecture which is able to provide specific functionality by integrating the layers in an appropriate manner (Finn, Lotya, & Molloy, Smart card constructions, 2018). For the purpose of durability, material used in the cards can be polycarbonate or Polyvinyl Chloride (PVC). Various steps involved in the construction of a smart cards are shown in the Figure 7 (Agarwal).

1. **Designing:** The first step towards the construction of a smart card is the process of designing a smart card according to the needs of the customers. Features that are considered during the designing include size, functionality, clock speed, memory size, operating system, application software, security protocols, and so forth.
2. **Chip Fabrication:** Chip fabrication is an extended step of designing, where by using a die solution silicon chip can be mounted on an epoxy glass substrate along with gold plated connectors. Wire bonding technique can be used for bonding the silicon chip to the connectors through wires. Thereafter, sealing of the chip is done by using epoxy resin and then it is pasted with the card substrate.
3. **Code Loading:** This step is important from the security and functionality point of view as in this step, smart card memory is loaded with the specific code using the special commands. Sometimes, a small bug in the code can exploit the smart card, and implementation of the security protocols is also dependent on the effectiveness of this step.
4. **Data Loading:** This step involves loading the information related to the smart card holders into PROM. Identity and other information are being stored carefully so that only the legitimate users are able to access their respective cards.

During the process of construction of smart cards, manufacturers carry out the production process according to various features. However, now-a-days, customer's needs are considered on the basis of connection of the smart card with the reader on the basis of which, smart cards can be categorized into following ways –

*   **Contact Cards:** As the name suggests, these cards are able to communicate with their respective readers on the basis of the physical contacts. Usually, the gold-plated contacts (i.e. chip or magnetic stripe) are embedded into the plastic card and when these contacts are inserted or swiped, then with the help of contacts, the card is able to connect to the reader (Liu, Dong, GUAN, Zou,

Figure 7. Steps in the construction of a smart card

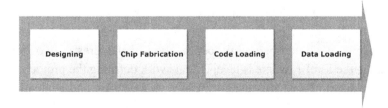

& WANG, 2017). After the successful establishment of connection, further processing of data, instructions and status is done. As these cards are not battery-powered, they are totally dependent on the connection with the reader. Contact cards have wide range of applications ranging from finance sectors to mobile communication industry.

- **Contactless Cards:** In the era of IoT, people prefer smart cards that are able to connect with the reader without any physical connection. Especially during the financial transactions, RFID-enabled communication motivates for using short range wireless communication. NFC based financial transactions have revolutionized the way of doing business in the last decade throughout the globe and have brought a great comfort in the life of millions of people. Contactless smart-cards are able to establish the communication with the help of RFID or through electromagnetic radiations. Sometimes, people think that smart cards, and RFID or NFC enabled cards are same (Prodanoff, Jones, Chi, Elfayoumy, & Cummings, 2016). But this is not the case as smart cards are more sophisticated version of RFID or NFC cards due to the implementation of the security protocols and also incorporate other measures. Generally, these cards are also not battery powered, so they have to generate the power from the reader when come in specified range. For instance, proximity cards generate the power from electromagnetic field after coming in proximity of the reader. Although they have limited amount of memory, they are generally used for the identification purposes, whereas vicinity cards can be used in other applications. Contactless smart cards can be either microprocessor or memory cards that are totally dependent on the application, but contactless smart cards come under the category of chip cards (Lee, Kim, Ha, Kim, & Kim, 2015).
- **Dual Interface Cards:** Now-a-days, smartcard industry is realizing the needs of the users and preference of contactless mechanism. However, shifting from contact based cards to contactless cards is going to take a certain amount of time. Considering this, smartcards including both features (i.e. contact and contactless) with dual interface are being developed (Sutera, 2014). A single chip is able to support multiple applications by embedding contact and contactless based mechanisms. These cards are beneficial from different perspectives. For instance, customers are able to communicate with contact-enabled mechanism during financial transactions and during access control, they are able to utilize the contactless feature.
- **Hybrid Cards:** These cards have same applications as of dual interface cards, but they have a separate mechanism for working. These cards contain separate chip for contact and contactless mechanism instead of using multiple interfaces on the same chip. Hence, these chips work on their own interface and during the process like up-dation, they cannot be simultaneously updated (Finn & Ummenhofer, Coupling in and to RFID smart cards, 2015). These cards can be considered as multi-level cards from the perspective of security as they can be able to support different security features on their chips. Accordingly, manufacturers are able to include the required features.

No matter which mode of connection establishment is adopted, the only important thing is that some sort of standard is to be followed for better and secure communication. In case of financial transactions, institutions are trying to adopt the EMV standards, as these standards define the requirements during the adoption of bank cards. For the purpose of ensuring the standards for smart card enabled payments, EMV is an open standard set of interoperability specifications that addresses two levels in which electromagnetic is defined on the level 1, whereas level 2 deals with defining the protocols and data elements. A layered and standardized approach is used by EMV certification and evaluation scheme which is followed in a step-wise manner starting from IC, then operating system and thereafter, application, as shown in the Table 4 (Alliance, 2011).

Concept of Blockchain

Without the need of any intermediaries, Blockchain enables peer-to-peer transfer of digital assets. It is a technology originally created to support the famous crypto-currency, Bitcoins. The Blockchain has permeated a broad range of applications across many industries including finance, healthcare, government, manufacturing and distribution (Pass, Seeman, & Shelat, 2017). The Blockchain is poised to innovate and transform a wide range of applications including goods transfer (for example, supply chain), digital media transfer (for example, sale of art), remote services delivery (for example, travel and tourism), platform for decentralized business logic (for example, moving computing to data sources), and distributed intelligence (for example, education credentialing). Additional applications of Blockchain include distributed resources (for example, power generation and distribution), crowd funding (for example, start-up fund raising), crowd operations (for example, electronic voting), identity management (for example, one ID for all your life's functions), and government public records and open governing. Moreover, Blockchain can enable an inclusive economy. It can enable a person in the remote corner of the world to partake in a democratic process. Opportunities for innovative applications are endless. There is a dire need for critical thinkers, designers and developers who can envision and create newer application models on Blockchain to benefit the world (Ramamurthy).

Two major contributions of crypto-currency Bitcoin are – a continuously working digital currency system, and a model for autonomous decentralized application technology called the Blockchain. In the

Table 4. Certifications of EMV based chip software

EMV Chip Architecture	Certifications and Evaluations
Data Level • Cardholder data • Personalization data • Parameters of risk management • Cryptographic certificates and keys	Financial institutions validate the card personalization before issuance
Application Level • American Express AEIPS, ExpressPay • Visa VSDC, payWave qVSDC / MSD • JCB J Smart • MasterCard Mchip, PayPass Mchip / Magstripe • Discover D-PAS	Financial institutions certify the applications
Operating System Level • Native • MULTOS • GlobalPlatform Java Card	• MUTOS or EMVCo certifies the open source operating systems • Certifies native OS EMV implementations
Hardware Level • ROM • Logic of memory protection • EEPROM • Cryptographic engine (PKI)	

year 2008 and 2009, when the institutions and markets we trusted went crumbling down and everybody was running away from the Wall Street, a mysterious person, called Satoshi Nakamoto, introduced a new digital currency, a crypto-currency called Bitcoin. Bitcoin enabled an innovative platform for peer-to-peer transfer of value without any central authority (Eyal & Sirer, 2018). By implementing software programs for validation, verification, consensus in a novel infrastructure called the Blockchain (Yermack, 2015); (Bonneau, Miller, Clark, Narayanan, Kroll, & Felten, 2015); (Garay, Kiayias, & Leonardos, 2015). Later on in about 2012 and 2013, computation elements were added to the Blockchain infrastructure that opened up a whole world of possibilities beyond simple currency transfer. Blockchain is about enabling peer-to-peer transactions in a decentralized network, establishing trust among unknown peers, and recording the transaction in an immutable distributed ledger. Let us understand centralized versus decentralized network as follows. Consider a scenario where customer wants to buy an item using his/her credit card. Let us enumerate the intermediaries involved in accomplishing this task. We have a credit card agency, a customer bank, a credit card bank, an exchange, the merchant's bank and finally, the merchant. This is an example of a centralized system that we are used to. Now compare this with a system where peers can transact directly with each other irrespective of where they are located. Functions of the intermediaries are shifted in the periphery to the peer participant in the Blockchain infrastructure. Peers are not necessarily known to each other. This is a decentralized system. How do we establish trust among the peers in such a decentralized system? By having a process in place to validate, verify, and confirm transactions. Record the transaction in a distributed ledger of blocks, create a tamper-proof record of blocks (chain of blocks), and implement a consensus protocol for agreement on the block to be added to the chain. So, validation, verification, consensus and immutable recording lead to trust and security of the Blockchain.

Blockchain Structure

Structure of the Blockchain is quite different in different applications. Considering the example of Bitcoin and Ethereum, the basic structure and operations involved in the Blockchain are discussed in this section.

Transaction is the basic element of the Bitcoin Blockchain. These are validated and broadcast. Many transactions form a block, and many blocks form a chain through a digital data link. Blocks go through a consensus process for the selection of the next block which will be added to the chain. Chosen block is verified and added to the current chain. Validation and consensus processes are carried out by special peer nodes called miners. These are powerful computers executing software defined by the Blockchain protocol. For more clarity of this structure, single transaction in a Bitcoin is discussed below. A fundamental concept of a Bitcoin network is an Unspent Transaction Output, also known as UTXO. The set of all UTXOs in a Bitcoin network collectively define the state of the Bitcoin Blockchain. UTXOs are referenced as inputs in a transaction. UTXOs are also outputs generated by a transaction. All the UTXOs that are in a system are stored by the participant nodes in a database. The transaction uses the amount specified by one or more UTXOs and transmits it to one or more newly created output UTXOs according to the request initiated by the sender. The structure of a given UTXO is very simple. It includes a unique identifier of the transaction which created this UTXO, an index or the position of the UTXO in the transaction output list, a value or the amount it is good for, and an optional script (the condition under which the output can be spent). The transaction itself includes a reference number of the current transaction, references to one no more input UTXOs, references to one or more output UTXOs newly generated by the current transaction, and the total input amount and output amount. Participants can validate the transaction contents (Croman, et al., 2016).

During the initial years of Blockchain, it was utilized in the form of Bitcoins. Although now-a-days, the concept of Blockchain is extended as Bitcoin Blockchain which is open-source and the entire code is available on the GitHub. During the initial years beginning roughly in 2009, this open-source code was extended to release different crypto-currencies and about 300 plus crypto-currencies were introduced. Bitcoin supports an optional and special feature called scripts for conditional transfer of values. Around 2013, a framework for code execution was introduced by Ethereum founders. Ethereum Blockchain extended the scripting feature into a full-blown code execution framework called smart contract. Comparison of the stacks of Bitcoin and Ethereum Blockchain is shown in Figure 8. On the left is the Bitcoin Blockchain and a wallet application for initiating transactions. On the right is Ethereum that took a significant step towards transforming the Blockchain into a computational framework that opened up a whole new world of opportunities in the decentralized realm. Ethereum supports smart contracts and machine on which smart contracts execute. Smart contracts in turn enable decentralized application which accomplish more than a transfer of value (Corbet, Lucey, & Yarovaya, 2018). A smart contract is a piece of code deployed in the Blockchain node and provides powerful capability of code execution for embedding business logic on the Blockchain. Execution of a smart contract is initiated by a message embedded in the transaction. Digital currency transfers request for simple addition and subtraction.

Ethereum enables transaction which may carry out more sophisticated operations. For example, a transaction could require a conditional transfer, it may require some evaluation, it may need more than one signature for transfer of assets, or it may involve waiting for a specific time or date. Structurally, a smart contract resembles a class definition in an object-oriented design. It has data, functions or methods with modifiers public or private, along with getter and set of functions (Delmolino, Arnett, Kosba, Miller, & Shi, 2016).

Figure 8. Stacks of Bitcoin and Ethereum

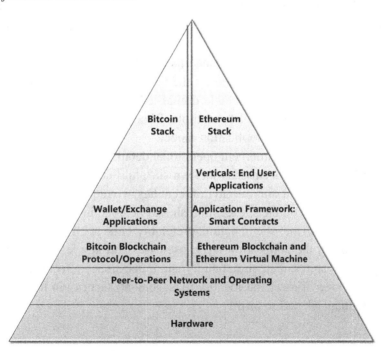

Specific programming languages have been designed for coding smart contracts. Solidity is one such language. Every node in Ethereum network should be able to execute the code irrespective of the type of underlying hardware or operating system. Ethereum Virtual Machine (EVM) provides a run anywhere obstruction layer for the contract code. A smart contract written in high level programming language is translated into EVM byte code, and then deployed on the EVM (Hirai, 2017). Every node will host the same smart contract codes on the EVM. Currently, there are many applications based on the Blockchain architecture, and most of them are based on common Blockchain architecture that consists of a network layer, a data layer, a consensus layer, an execution layer, and an application layer as shown in Figure 9 (Mosakheil, 2018).

- **Network Layer:** This layer in the Blockchain includes transaction transfer and block propagation discovery with the inter-node communication, for instance in Ethereum Blockchain (DEVp2p library). This layer uses P2P protocols as they are able to distribute data to the parties with same capabilities in a decentralized manner. Despite the fact that centralized model reduces replication of data and network traffic, Blockchain uses decentralized protocols as decentralization is the core concept of Blockchain for assuring more independency to the peer nodes. For finding the peer nodes in ethereum, DEVp2p nodes use the RLPx discovery protocol suite which is a cryptographic P2P protocol. On the other hand, Bitcoin uses an unencrypted persistent TCP connection in their peer-to-peer based network structure.
- **Consensus Layer:** Primary role of the consensus layer is that all the participating nodes in the system are agreed upon the Blockchain content and this layer integrates its works with the data model layer. So if a new node wants to add a block, the other nodes must also append and approve the same copy of the block. This layer contains protocols for verification and appending the block, and it also utilizes a spectrum of Byzantine fault-tolerant protocols. Various consensus algorithms like Proof-of-Work (PoW), Proof-of-Authority (PoA), Ripple, Steller, Practical Byzantine Fault Tolerance (PBFT), Proof-of-Burn (PoB), are broadly used for consensus mechanism. Proof-of-Work is the most popular and widely used in existing Blockchain based applications and it is also effective against the popular Sybil attack.
- **Data Model Layer:** Data model layer concerns about structure, operation, and content of the block. In this layer, blocks are identified by the hash of their content and these cryptographic hashes link together to form an immutable digital ledger. Generally, the data models contain a block, transaction and block header. For example, Bitcoin uses the Input-Output transaction data model, while ethereum uses state replication model.
- **Execution Layer:** Runtime environment operational details are contained by the execution layer, as every Blockchain based systems has its own scripting and programming language. For example, contracts executed in a runtime environment has two requirements: First, as blocks contain multiple transactions and contracts, execution should be done in a speedy manner and secondly. These executions are deterministic in nature, preferably same at all nodes.
- **Application Layer:** In the application layer, use-cases and key features of the Blockchain are used. Among these features, data immutability and transparency affect the market in the form of applications in the area of asset and identity management, security in IoT and Cloud infrastructure, healthcare, financial, and so forth.

Figure 9. Architecture of blockchain abstraction layers

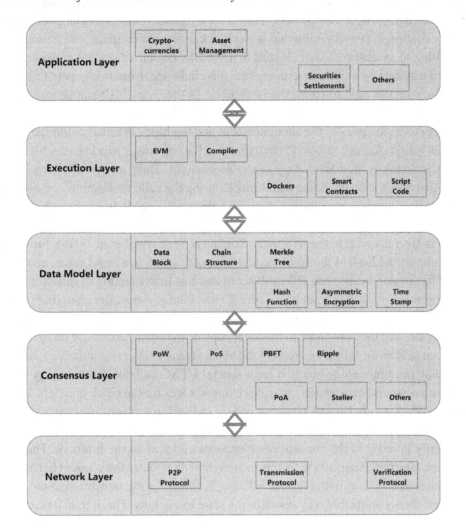

Operations in the decentralized network are the responsibility of the peer participants and their respective computational nodes (e.g. laptop, desktop and server racks). These operations include validation transactions, gathering the transactions for a block, broadcasting the ballot transactions in the block, consensus on the next block creation, and chaining the blocks to form an immutable record. The participants involved during the operations have two major roles. Participants that initiate transfer of value by creating a transaction, and additional participants called miners, who pick on added work or computation to verify transactions, broadcast transaction, compete to claim the right to create a block, work on reaching consensus by validating the block, broadcasting the newly created block, and confirming transactions. For doing an additional work, the miners are incentivised with Bitcoins for the efforts in managing the Blockchain. Transaction validation is carried out independently by all miners. The process involves validation of more than 20 criteria including size, syntax etc. Some of these criteria are – Referenced Input Unspent Transaction Output, UTXOs are valid, recall, reference output UTXOs are correct, reference input amount and output amount matched sufficiently, invalid transactions are rejected and will not be broadcast. All the valid transactions are added to a pool of transactions (Kiayias, Russell, David, & Oliynykov, 2018). Miners select a set of transactions from this pool to create a block which creates a challenge. If every miner adds the block to the chain, there will be many branches to the chain, resulting in inconsistent state. Recall that the Blockchain is a single consistent linked chain of flux. We need a system or a solution to overcome this challenge. Miners compete to solving a puzzle to determine who earn the right to create the next block. In the case of Bitcoin Blockchain, this parcel is a computation of parcel and the Central Processing Unit (CPU) intensive.

Once a miner solves the puzzle, the announcement and the block is broadcast to the network. Then, other participant verifies the new block. Participants reach a consensus to add a new block to the chain. This new block is added to their local copy of the Blockchain. Thus, a new set of transactions are recorded and confirmed. Process of adding a new block during the valid transaction is shown in Figure 10.

The algorithm for consensus is called proof-of-work protocol, since it involves work on computational power to solve the puzzle and to claim the right to form the next block. Proof-of-work (PoW) uses hashing, and is used in Bitcoin and Ethereum (Sankar, Sindhu, & Sethumadhavan, 2017). From miner's point of view, first compute the hash of the block header elements which is a fixed value, and a nonce which is a variable. If hash value is less than 2^{128} for Bitcoin and less than function of difficulty for Ethereum, the puzzle has been solved. If it has not been solved, repeat the process after changing the nonce value. If the puzzle has been solved, broadcast the winning block which will be verified by other miners. Non-winning miner nodes add the new block to the local copy of the chain, and move on to work on the next block. The winner gets an incentive for creating the block. Transaction zero, index zero of the confirmed block is created by the miner of the block. It has a special UTXO and does not have any input UTXO. It is called the coinbase transaction which generates a minor's fees for the block creation. This is how new coin is maintained in Bitcoin. Bitcoin blocking state is defined in terms of unspent transaction outputs UTXOs and a reference implementation of the Wallet application which holds the account reference. Ethereum formally introduced the concept of an account as a part of the protocol. The account is the originator and the target of a transaction. A transaction directly updates the account balances as opposed to maintaining the state, such as in the bitcoin UTXOs. It allows for the transmission of value, messages and data between the accounts that may result in the state transitions. These transfers are implemented using transactions. There are two types of accounts – Externally Owned Accounts (EOAs) and Contract Accounts (CAs). EOAs are controlled by private keys. CAs are controlled by the code and can be activated only by an EOA. An externally owned account is needed to participate in the Ethereum network. It interacts with the Blockchain using transactions. CA represents a smart contract. Every account has a coin balance. The participant node can send transaction for Ether transfer or it can send transaction to invoke a smart contract code or both. Both types of transactions require fees. An account must have sufficient balance to meet the fees needed for the activated transactions activated. Fees are paid in Wei which is a lower denomination of Ether. One Ether is equivalent to 10 to the power of 18 Weis. A transaction in Ethereum includes the recipient of the message, digital signature of the sender authorizing the transfer, amount of Wei to transfer, an optional data field or payload that contains a message to a contract, and STARTGAS which is a value representing the maximum number of computational steps the transaction is allowed. Gas price is a value representing the fee sender is willing to pay for the computations. Of course the smart contract execution incurs fees and the amount available is specified by the various gas fields. Ethereum block structure has a header, transaction, and runner-up block headers.

Figure 10. Process of adding a new block during the valid transaction

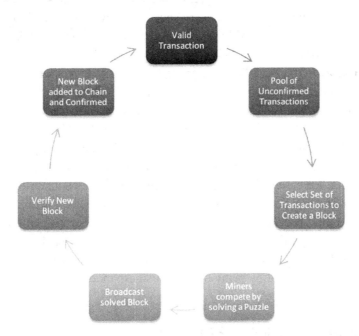

Based on the capabilities, three major types of Blockchains emerged from Bitcoin foundation. Type one deals with the coins in crypto-currency currency chain, e.g. Bitcoin. Type two deals with crypto-currency and a business logic layer supported by code execution, e.g. Ethereum. Type three involves no currency and supports software execution for business logic, e.g. The Linux Foundation's Hyperledger. With the addition of code execution, comes serious consideration about public access to the Blockchain. Hence, based on access limits, Blockchain can be classified into three categories – public, private, and permissioned, as shown in Figure 11. These are described as follows –

- **Public Blockchain:** We have been watching Bitcoin Blockchain continuously in operation since its inception because it is open to all and is characterized by its public participants. Thus, Bitcoin is a fantastic example of a public Blockchain class. Anybody can join and leave the system as per

Figure 11. Types of blockchain based on their access control rights

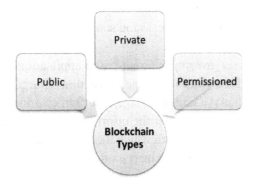

the wish (Zheng, Xie, Dai, Chen, & Wang, 2017). Transaction blocks and the Blockchain are publicly observable, even though participants are anonymous which makes it open-source. New coin digital currency can also be created by modifying the Bitcoin code. Wallet applications provide the basic interface to transfer value through the Bitcoin Blockchain.

- **Private Blockchain:** In a private Blockchain, access to the Blockchain is limited to selected participants. For example, participants within an organization. This restriction helps in simplifying the normal operations, such as block creation and contingence model (Sharples & Domingue, 2016).
- **Permissioned Blockchain:** The third classification of Blockchain is permissioned Blockchain, also called consortium Blockchain. It is meant for a consortium of collaborating parties to transact on a Blockchain for ease of governance, provenance and accountability. For example, a consortium of all automobile companies or healthcare organizations. Permissioned Blockchain has the benefits of a public Blockchain with allowing users with permission only to collaborate and transact. In summary, significant innovations, such as smart contracts have opened up broader applications for Blockchain technology. Private and permissioned Blockchain allow for controlled access to the Blockchain enabling many diverse business models (Vukolić, 3-7).

BLOCKCHAIN IN SMART CARD SECURITY

Capabilities and features of Blockchain technology can be used to secure smart card based systems and applications in following ways [summarized in Table 5]:

- **Cryptography and Trust:** Cryptographic protocols have been a crucial aspect in the security of smart card based applications from the beginning. For instance, in e-banking, ATM security, and so forth. In order to support communication among non-trusting entities, a central trusted party is required. Modern cryptographic techniques secure point-to-point communications. However, Blockchain technology emphasizes on replacing the idea of trusted third party among the underlying communicating entities with its technological aspects. It brings into picture new trust models, where it utilizes cryptographic technologies for anonymity, privacy and integrity (Cachin, 2017).
- **Data Integrity:** To ensure that the past transactions made using smart cards are maintained as such (cannot be erased or manipulated), Blockchain manages a database of such transactions which is shared among a set of participating entities. These participants verify the transactions and the data once entered into the system, cannot be erased or manipulated by unauthorized entities. This feature is particularly useful in healthcare applications where patient's records are kept intact and e-Health cards can be utilized to access the same (Zikratov, Kuzmin, Akimenko, Niculichev, & Yalansky, 2017).
- **Identity Management:** Ever growing Internet based applications and proliferating use of smart cards in such applications is responsible for the generation of large number of corresponding identities. However, in conventional identity management frameworks like Single-Sign-On (SSO), users are not provided with full control over the information they provide to the centralized systems and have no idea of the other entities with which their information can be shared. They rely on the trusted parties when accessing a remote smart card based application. Blockchain technology ensures transparency of information usage by enabling card holders to become a part of the identity

management framework, and to validate and verify the records and transactions. This fasten-up the pace of the claiming process and ensures required control for the end-users (Baars).

- **Single-Points-of-Failure (SPF):** Public-Key Infrastructure (PKI) is an important aspect of smart card based applications as it enables managing the transmission of keys through which entities communicate with each other over insecure communication channels. However, PKI is susceptible to a serious issue of single-points-of-failure. In this scenario, Blockchain plays a major role by addressing the requirements of PKI requirements and constructs distributed PKI based on Blockchain to eliminate SPF which involves publishing of the PKI events among honest Blockchain contributors. Distributing content across multiple parties in such a manner assists in limiting the damage by easy attack detection and denying access, thereby preventing any affect on the accuracy of the records (Axon & Goldsmith, 2017).

- **Privacy:** Since smart cards can be used for multiple purposes, there is a high possibility that attackers may exploit the aspect of repeated use of public keys for performing transactions at multiple places. It is important to prevent back-tracing of the underlying entities performing transactions in such applications. To ensure privacy requirements, Blockchain technology supports privacy-aware PKI which involves disclosure of the user's identity and public keys used in the previous transactions by the user only or by the consensus of the majority of network participants. It avoids public linking of the user's public key with its identity or short term public keys used in the past that are posted on the Blockchain. In addition, key updates can be kept anonymous (Axon & Goldsmith, 2017).

- **Prevention Against Linking Attacks:** The information corresponding to the smart card holders and device specific data is stored by the miner using unique public keys. Thus, using unique keys in each transaction prevents linking attacks by avoiding disclosure of previous transaction's key details. An attacker thus, is not able to establish link between multiple transactions to identify the nature of device or identity of the user (Dorri, Kanhere, Jurdak, & Gauravaram, Blockchain for IoT security and privacy: The case study of a smart home, 2017).

- **Prevention Against Distributed Denial of Service (DDoS) Attacks:** Blockchain technology establishes an extra layer of security by enabling transaction validation and verification by miner. It ensures that an attacker cannot install malware directly into the smart card based systems and the DDoS attack traffic is blocked by the miner (Dorri, Kanhere, Jurdak, & Gauravaram, Blockchain for IoT security and privacy: The case study of a smart home, 2017).

- **Spoofing Attacks:** Blockchain technology provides security against spoofing attacks in smart card based applications because approved Blockchain cannot be altered and fake users cannot establish connection with the network by injecting fake information in the record (Kshetri, 2017).

- **Authentication:** Since all the traffic coming from the client side is controlled by miner, it prevents direct access to the Internet. Miner analyzes the traffic which when not adhering to the policies defined by the core system, drops the data (Dorri, Kanhere, & Jurdak, Towards an Optimized BlockChain for IoT, 2017).

- **Prevention From Hacking:** With the use of Blockchain technology, hacking in smart card based applications is practically not possible because attacker requires to modify and falsify 51% of all the peer's ledgers due to limitation of resources (Park & Park, 2017).

- **Data Verification and Validation:** Decentralized nature of Blockchain technology allows entities to cross-check the signatures over all the ledgers across the network and to verify whether they have not been changed.

- **Malicious Software Detection:** Blockchain technology also enables detection of malware or malicious software. Gu et al. (Gu, Sun, Du, Wang, Zhuang, & Wang, 2018) presented a framework developed using consortium-based Blockchain which is capable of extracting the malware evidence in android based operating systems and also detect corresponding malicious codes in malware. They carried out feature modelling by using the statistical analysis method for extracting malware family features including function call, software package, permission and application feature. Multi-feature detection method is developed using Blockchain for enhancing the detection capability of malware variants and to decrease false-positive rate.

Case Study: Financial Payments

Use of Blockchain in smart cards security can be understood by taking an example of financial payments. Contactless smart cards along with Blockchain concept can be utilized for decentralized peer-to-peer exchange of the money. For example, a tap and pay mobile application Plutus was developed to convert the Bitcoin currency into contactless Near Field Communication (NFC) payments without using any centralized exchange (Alliance S. T., 2017). It utilizes smart contracts running on Ethereum Blockchain for handling the trading of the digital currency.

Blockchain technology makes it possible to record digital transactions in a transparent and secure way. These transactions are auditable and are resistant to outages (Banafa).

Table 5. Role of blockchain features in smart card security

Security Aspect	Blockchain Feature
Cryptography and Trust	Decentralized Framework
Data Integrity	Immutability, Traceability
Non-Repudiation	Digital Signatures and Timestamps
Identity Management	Card Holders as Member of Blockchain
Single-Points-of-Failure (SPF)	Distributed PK
Privacy	Privacy-aware PKI
Prevention against Linking Attacks	Unique Public Keys
Prevention against DDoS Attacks	Traffic Validation and Verification by Miner
Prevention of Spoofing Attacks	Alteration not possible
Authentication	Traffic Analysis by Miner
Authentication without Human Intervention	SSL Certificates
Prevention from Hacking	51% Rule
Data Verification and Validation	Decentralized Framework and Signature Cross-Checking

SMART CARD WITH BLOCKCHAIN: REAL TIME APPLICATIONS

Billions of dollars have already been invested in the implementation of Blockchain based applications. In-fact now-a-days, this technology is growing more rapidly. Blockchain provides a solution to the security problems related to transaction handling, identity management, user anonymity, and so forth. Besides crypto-currencies, several other use cases of Blockchain are also emerging including IoT, asset registry, inter-bank fund transfer, and anti-counterfeiting. Many application areas of smart card based applications are also using Blockchain technology for better security management. Some of them are discussed as follows –

1. **SETL:** SETL company provides financial services based on Blockchain technology. For ensuring consumer's safety, SETL's FCA Sandbox participation developed a project for creating a "safe space" which provides a live environment in which companies are able to test products and their delivery mechanism. SETL also provides contactless smart card which uses Blockchain for payment (Finextra, 2016).

2. **Deloitte:** Deloitte Touche Tohmatsu Limited is a company which is known for its accounting and financial services, and it is among the top accounting organizations. In this company, Blockchain based technology is used for the purpose of identity management. The developers found Blockchain based ID solution much reliable and secure for their organization, and they referred this project as "smart identity" project (Finextra, 2016).

3. **Metrobank:** This bank is one of the largest banks in Philippines, and popularly known for its financial and insurance services. Craig Donaldson who is the CEO in Metrobank believes that only few players dominate the retail payment sector, and potential of Blockchain offers more flexible and efficient services to the end users. Metrobank utilizes the Blockchain technology in the form of connected client accounts, i.e. they connect the accounts of the clients using Blockchain (Finextra, 2016).

4. **Net1 Technologies (UEPS):** Smart cards, especially debit cards are based on the Blockchain technology patented by the Net1 Technologies (UEPS) which is financial technology company. This debit card is EMV compatible and it works in both offline and online environments by using distributed ledger. This company claimed that this Blockchain based debit card is first of its kind and is used by around 3 million people for free cash flow generation (Teed, 2018).

5. **TAXTOKEN:** It is software company which utilizes Blockchain technology for the enhancement of the present personal accounting methods. The company enhanced the multi-facet of accounting by saving the client's time and money. They provide facility to the users to download the application and then synchronise it with smart card. During everyday use of smart cards, transactions are recorded on the Blockchain and artificial intelligence based software sorts the transactions according to their tax deductions. Lastly, when the tax due date comes, this application shoes the recommended tax and based on user's suggestion files the tax with the Internal revenue service (TAXTOKEN).

6. **BANKEX:** For bringing the financial transparency in charity drinking water program, this organisation implements Blockchain on NFC based smart cards. These cards do not contain money. Instead, these cards contain unique identity along with the available water. This card is governed by the Ethereum smart-contract which is based on the ERC-20 token standard (BANKEX).

OPEN CHALLENGES AND FUTURE RESEARCH DIRECTIONS

Several types of security attacks and their associated risks are prevented by Blockchain. However, in some cases, most prominent and promising use-cases of Blockchain show vulnerability in the core structure. Features of Blockchain technology for providing security may open opportunities for the attackers. Possible security threats and attacks on Blockchain based systems are summarized in Table 6 (Mosakheil, 2018). Blockchain based applications are required to provide features including integrity of a transaction, robustness, securing unique account addresses, standard approach to uniquely identify the participants in the decentralized network, authorization of transaction by the sender through digital signature, and verification of the content that the transaction is not modified. For this, Blockchain uses a combination of hashing and public key cryptography. For instance, addresses of accounts are generated using public and private key pair. First, 256-bit random number is generated and designated as the private key which is kept secure and locked using a passphrase. Then, ECC algorithm is applied to the private key to get a unique public key which makes the private-public key pair (Seo, 2017). After that, a hashing function is applied to the public key to obtain account address. The address is shorter in size – only 20 bytes or 160 bits.

These cryptographic and hashing based solutions contain vulnerabilities in their mechanisms (Gupta & Quamara, An overview of Internet of Things (IoT): Architectural aspects, challenges, and protocols, 2018); (Lohachab & Karambir, Critical Analysis of DDoS—An Emerging Security Threat over IoT Networks, 2018); (Tewari & Gupta, 2016) . Attackers take the advantage of these vulnerabilities and perform attacks on the basis of their security weaknesses. Researchers are trying to develop mechanisms and solutions to the existing security attacks. Few solutions of the discussed attacks are shown in Table 7 (Liu, et al., 2017); (Bae, Jaewon, & Lim, 2018); (Boireau, 2018); (Dogru, Mody, & Leonardi, 2018); (Zhang, White, C, Lenz, & Rosenbloom, 2018); (Uchibeke, Kassani, Schneider, & Deters, 2018).

Based on the above discussed challenges, research efforts are needed in this area. For example, most popular consensus algorithm requires an improvement as PoW wastes many computing resources. Integrating Blockchain with smart cards is itself a challenging task, as Blockchain works in a distributed manner and in the current scenario, smart cards require a central authority. Hence, there are major research opportunities in this direction for the convenience of the end-user.

CONCLUSION AND FUTURE SCOPE

In this chapter, in-depth analysis is done over the role of Blockchain for securing smart card based systems and applications. Starting with historical background and statistical assessment of the two technologies, the author investigated how smart card based applications are exploited by the use of weak security techniques, and the motivation of using Blockchain technology for smart card security. Afterwards, various types of smart cards along with their specifications and different applications have been discussed. Subsequently, the author discussed the concept of Blockchain technology along with its layered architecture and features. By looking into the possibilities of Blockchain over the current security methods, the limitations and challenges in the area are also discussed. The chapter also explores the on-going research efforts in this area. Finally, it is concluded by highlighting the possibilities of using Blockchain in the area of smart card system security in future.

Table 6. Security threats and attacks associated with blockchain technology

Security Threats	Attack Vectors	Cause	Affected Layer
Double-Spending Threats	Race Attack	Transaction Verification Mechanism	Consensus
	Finney Attack		
	Vector 76 Attack		
	Alternative History Attack		
	51% Attack	Consensus Mechanism	Network, Consensus, Data Model
Mining/Pool Threats	Selfish Mining/Block-Discard Attack		Network, Consensus
	Block-Withholding Attack		
	Fork-After-Withhold Attack		
	Bribery Attack		
	Pool Hopping Attack		
Wallet Threats	Vulnerable Signature	ECDSA Flaws - Poor Randomness	Data Model
	Lack of Control in Address Creation	Public Nature of the Blockchain	
	Collision and Pre-Image Attack	Flaws in ECDSA, SHA256 and RIPEMD 160	
	Flawed Key Generation	Flaws in Implementing ECDSA	
	Bugs and Malware	Client Design Flaws	
Network Threats	DDoS Attack	External Resources, Contracts Under-priced Operations	Network, Consensus
	Transaction Malleability Attack	Flaws in Blockchain Protocols – Transaction ID	Consensus, Data Model
	Time-jacking Attack	Flaws in Blockchain protocols – Timestamp Handling	Network, Consensus, Data Model
	Partition Routing Attack	Flaws in Internet Routing - Routing Manipulations	
	Delay Routing Attack		
	Sybil Attack	Structured P2P Network Limitation – Forged Identities	Network
	Eclipse Attack	Flaws in Blockchain Protocols – Outgoing Connections	
	Refund Attack	Flaws in BIP70 Payment Protocol – Bitcoin Refund Policy	Application – Bitcoin
	Balance Attack	Consensus Mechanism	Network, Consensus
	Punitive and Feather forking Attack		Network, Consensus, Data Model
Smart Contracts Threats	Vulnerabilities in Contracts Source Code	Program Design Flaws	Execution
	Vulnerabilities in EVM Byte code	EVM Design Flaws	Execution
	Vulnerabilities in Blockchain	Program Design Flaws	Network, Consensus
	Eclipse Attack on Smart Contract Blockchain	EVM Design Flaws	
	Low-level Attacks	Under-priced Operations	Consensus, Data Model
Threats associated with NFC	Cost	Equipment production and maintenance cost	Compromise of overall system due to lack of risk investment
	Security	Unauthorized access to physical devices and information	Compromise overall system

Table 7. Preventive measures for malicious attacks

Malicious Attack	Preventive Measures
Double Spending [59]	The complexity of the mining process
Record Hacking [60]	Distributed consensus
51% Attack [61]	Detection techniques; Wide adoption of Blockchain technology
Identity Theft [62]	Identify and Reputation Blockchain
Illegal Activities [63]	Detection techniques, Laws and regulations
System Hacking [64]	Robust systems and advanced intrusion detection methods

As of future work, we plan to extend the work by adding discussion on how Blockchain technology can protect the edge computing using smart card based applications. This will not only include strengthening the authentication process, but also enhancing the data attribution and flow of data among various system and network entities. Moreover, it can be discussed that how Blockchain will ensure the security of the cryptographic keys stored on the smart cards to improve the Public Key Infrastructure (PKI).

REFERENCES

Agarwal, T. (n.d.). *How does the Smart Card Works?* Retrieved October 8, 2018, from ElProCus – Electronic Projects for Engineering Students: https://www.elprocus.com/working-of-smart-card/

Alliance, S. C. (2011). *Card Payments Roadmap in the United States: How Will EMV Impact the Future Payments Infrastructure?* Smart Card Alliance. Retrieved from www.smartcardalliance.org

Alliance, S. T. (2017). *Blockchain and Smart Card Technology*. Secure Technology Alliance. Secure Technology Alliance.

Axon, L., & Goldsmith, M. (2017). *PB-PKI: a privacy-aware blockchain-based PKI. SCITEPRESS*. SCITEPRESS.

Baars, D. S. (n.d.). *Towards self-sovereign identity using blockchain technology*. University of Twente.

Bae, J., & Lim, H. (2018). Random Mining Group Selection to Prevent 51% Attacks on Bitcoin. In *2018 48th Annual IEEE/IFIP International Conference on Dependable Systems and Networks Workshops (DSN-W)* (pp. 81-82). Luxembourg: IEEE.

Banafa, A. (n.d.). *How to Secure the Internet of Things (IoT) with Blockchain*. Retrieved December 3, 2018, from DATAFLOQ.COM: https://datafloq.com/read/securing-internet-of-things-iot-with-blockchain/2228

BANKEX. (n.d.). *The First NFC-solution on Blockchain*. Retrieved October 20, 2018, from blog.bankex.org: https://blog.bankex.org/the-first-nfc-decision-on-blockchain-d49692e26ee7

Biro, A., & Bartczak, J. K. (2013). Patent No. US9165235B2. United States Patent Office.

Boireau, O. (2018). Securing the blockchain against hackers. *Network Security*, *2018*(1), 8–11. doi:10.1016/S1353-4858(18)30006-0

Bonneau, J., Miller, A., Clark, J., Narayanan, A., Kroll, A. J., & Felten, W. E. (2015). SoK: Research Perspectives and Challenges for Bitcoin and Cryptocurrencies. In *IEEE Symposium on Security and Privacy* (pp. 104-121). San Jose, CA: IEEE. 10.1109/SP.2015.14

Cachin, C. (2017). *Blockchain, cryptography, and consensus*. IBM Research. doi:10.4204/EPTCS.261.1

Corbet, S., Lucey, B., & Yarovaya, L. (2018). Datestamping the Bitcoin and Ethereum bubbles. *Finance Research Letters*, *26*, 81–88. doi:10.1016/j.frl.2017.12.006

Croman, K., Decker, C., Eyal, I., Gencer, E. A., Juels, A., Kosba, A., & ... . (2016). On Scaling Decentralized Blockchains. In *International Conference on Financial Cryptography and Data Security* (pp. 106-125). Sliema, Malta: Springer. 10.1007/978-3-662-53357-4_8

Dabosville, G. (n.d.). *Past & Future Issues in Smartcard Industry*. Retrieved October 5, 2018, from Oberthur Technologies: https://www.cosic.esat.kuleuven.be/ecrypt/courses/albena11/slides/guillaume_dabosville_smartcards.pdf

Degabriele, P. J., Lehmann, A., Paterson, G. K., Smart, P. N., & Strefler, M. (2012). *On the Joint Security of Encryption and Signature in EMV*. Berlin: Springer. doi:10.1007/978-3-642-27954-6_8

Delmolino, K., Arnett, M., Kosba, A., Miller, A., & Shi, E. (2016). Step by Step Towards Creating a Safe Smart Contract: Lessons and Insights from a Cryptocurrency Lab. In *International Conference on Financial Cryptography and Data Security* (pp. 77-94). Sliema, Malta: Springer. 10.1007/978-3-662-53357-4_6

Dogru, T., Mody, M., & Leonardi, C. (2018). *Blockchain Technology & its Implications for the Hospitality Industry*. Boston University.

Dorri, A., Kanhere, S. S., & Jurdak, R. (2017). Towards an Optimized BlockChain for IoT. In *Proceedings of the Second International Conference on Internet-of-Things Design and Implementation* (pp. 173-178). ACM.

Dorri, A., Kanhere, S. S., Jurdak, R., & Gauravaram, P. (2017). Blockchain for IoT security and privacy: The case study of a smart home. In *2017 IEEE International Conference on Pervasive Computing and Communications Workshops (PerCom Workshops)* (pp. 618-623). Kona, HI: IEEE. 10.1109/PERCOMW.2017.7917634

EMVCo. (n.d.). *Worldwide EMV® Deployment Statistics*. Retrieved October 10, 2018, from emvco.com: https://www.emvco.com/about/deployment-statistics/

Eyal, I., & Sirer, G. E. (2018). Majority is not enough: Bitcoin mining is vulnerable. *Communications of the ACM*, *61*(7), 95–102. doi:10.1145/3212998

Finextra. (2016, November 15). *Metro Bank tests smartcard payments on the blockchain*. Retrieved October 20, 2018, from finextra.com: https://www.finextra.com/newsarticle/29764/metro-bank-tests-smartcard-payments-on-the-blockchain

Finn, D., Lotya, M., & Molloy, D. (2018). Patent No. US9960476B2. United States Patent Office.

Finn, D., & Ummenhofer, K. (2015). Patent No. US8991712B2. United States Patent Office.

Garay, J., Kiayias, A., & Leonardos, N. (2015). The Bitcoin Backbone Protocol: Analysis and Applications. In *Annual International Conference on the Theory and Applications of Cryptographic Techniques* (pp. 281-310). Berlin: Springer. 10.1007/978-3-662-46803-6_10

gemalto. (2018). *Smart card basics – A short guide (2018)*. Retrieved October 1, 2018, from gemalto security to be free: https://www.gemalto.com/companyinfo/smart-cards-basics

Gu, J., Sun, B., Du, X., Wang, J., Zhuang, Y., & Wang, Z. (2018). Consortium Blockchain-Based Malware Detection in Mobile Devices. *IEEE Access: Practical Innovations, Open Solutions*, 6, 12118–12128. doi:10.1109/ACCESS.2018.2805783

Gupta, B. B., & Quamara, M. (2018, September 16). An overview of Internet of Things (IoT): Architectural aspects, challenges, and protocols. *Concurrency and Computation*, 4946. doi:10.1002/cpe.4946

Guyot, V. (2010). Smart Card Security. In G. Pujolle & G. Pujolle (Eds.), *Management, Control and Evolution of IP Networks*. Wiley Online Library.

Hirai, Y. (2017). Defining the Ethereum Virtual Machine for Interactive Theorem Provers. In *International Conference on Financial Cryptography and Data Security* (pp. 520-535). Sliema, Malta: Springer. 10.1007/978-3-319-70278-0_33

Iansiti, M., & Lakhani, R. K. (2017). The Truth About Blockchain. *Harvard Business Review*, 95(1), 118–127.

Jiang, Q., Ma, J., & Wei, F. (2018). On the Security of a Privacy-Aware Authentication Scheme for Distributed Mobile Cloud Computing Services. *IEEE Systems Journal*, 12(2), 2039–2042. doi:10.1109/JSYST.2016.2574719

Kiayias, A., Russell, A., David, B., & Oliynykov, R. (2018). Ouroboros: A Provably Secure Proof-of-Stake Blockchain Protocol. In *Annual International Cryptology Conference* (pp. 357-388). Santa Barbara, CA: Springer.

Kim, Y. C., & Lee, K. (2018). Risk Management to Cryptocurrency Exchange and Investors Guidelines to Prevent Potential Threats. In *2018 International Conference on Platform Technology and Service (PlatCon)* (pp. 1-6). Jeju, South Korea: IEEE. 10.1109/PlatCon.2018.8472760

Kshetri, N. (2017). Can Blockchain Strengthen the Internet of Things? *IT Professional*, 19(4), 68–72. doi:10.1109/MITP.2017.3051335

Lee, H., Kim, J., Ha, D., Kim, T., & Kim, S. (2015). Differentiating ASK Demodulator for Contactless Smart Cards Supporting VHBR. *IEEE Transactions on Circuits and Wystems. II, Express Briefs*, 62(7), 641–645. doi:10.1109/TCSII.2015.2415653

Lin, H., Wen, F., & Du, C. (2015). An Improved Anonymous Multi-Server Authenticated Key Agreement Scheme Using Smart Cards and Biometrics. *Wireless Personal Communications*, 84(4), 2351–2362. doi:10.100711277-015-2708-4

Liu, S., & Dong, R. (2017). Patent No. US9665866B2. United States Patent Office.

Liu, Z., Zhao, H., Chen, W., Cao, X., Peng, H., & Yang, J. (2017). Communications in Computer and Information Science. In *National Conference of Theoretical Computer Science* (pp. 133-143). Wuhan, China: Springer. 10.1007/978-981-10-6893-5_10

Lohachab, A., & Karambir, B. (2018). Critical Analysis of DDoS—An Emerging Security Threat over IoT Networks. *Journal of Communications and Information Networks*, *3*(3), 57–78. doi:10.100741650-018-0022-5

Mayes, K. (2017). An Introduction to Smart Cards. In *Smart Cards, Tokens, Security and Applications* (Vol. 1). Cham: Springer. doi:10.1007/978-3-319-50500-8_1

Mayes, K., & Markantonakis, K. (2008). *Smart Cards, Tokens, Security and Applications* (Vol. 1). New York: Springer Cham. doi:10.1007/978-0-387-72198-9

Mosakheil, J. H. (2018). *Security Threats Classification in Blockchains*. Herberger School of Business, Information Assurance and Information Systems. St. Cloud State University.

Odelu, V., Das, K. A., & Goswami, A. (2015). A Secure Biometrics-Based Multi-Server Authentication Protocol Using Smart Cards. *IEEE Transactions on Information Forensics and Security*, *10*(5), 1953–1966. doi:10.1109/TIFS.2015.2439964

Park, H. J., & Park, H. J. (2017). Blockchain Security in Cloud Computing: Use Cases, Challenges, and Solutions. *Advanced in Artificial Intelligence and Cloud Computing*, *9*(8), 164.

Pass, R., Seeman, L., & Shelat, A. (2017). Analysis of the Blockchain Protocol in Asynchronous Networks. In *Annual International Conference on the Theory and Applications of Cryptographic Techniques* (pp. 643-673). Paris, France: Springer. 10.1007/978-3-319-56614-6_22

Prodanoff, G. Z., Jones, L. E., Chi, H., Elfayoumy, S., & Cummings, C. (2016). Survey of Security Challenges in NFC and RFID for E-Health Applications. *International Journal of E-Health and Medical Communications*, *7*(2), 1–13. doi:10.4018/IJEHMC.2016040101

Ramamurthy, B. (n.d.). *Blockchain Basics*. Retrieved September 30, 2018, from coursera.org: https://www.coursera.org/learn/blockchain-basics

Rankl, W., & Effing, W. (2004). *Smart Card Handbook* (K. Cox, Trans.). Munich, Germany: John Wiley & Sons.

Sankar, S. L., Sindhu, M., & Sethumadhavan, M. (2017). Survey of consensus protocols on blockchain applications. In *2017 4th International Conference on Advanced Computing and Communication Systems (ICACCS)* (pp. 1-5). Coimbatore, India: IEEE.

Seo, Y. (2017). Practical Implementations of ECC in the Blockchain. *Journal of Analysis of Applied Mathematics*, 43.

Sharples, M., & Domingue, J. (2016). The Blockchain and Kudos: A Distributed System for Educational Record, Reputation and Reward. In *European Conference on Technology Enhanced Learning* (pp. 490-496). Lyon, France: Springer. 10.1007/978-3-319-45153-4_48

Sutera, M. C. (2014). Patent No. US8640965B2. United States Patent Office.

TAXTOKEN. (n.d.). *Blockchain accounting solutions.* Retrieved October 20, 2018, from taxtoken.io: https://taxtoken.io/wp-content/uploads/2017/12/TaxToken-OnePager-AccountingSolutions-Website.pdf

Teed, D. (2018, June 21). *The First Blockchain Debit Card.* Retrieved October 20, 2018, from Seeking Alpha: https://seekingalpha.com/article/4183096-first-blockchain-debit-card

Tewari, A., & Gupta, B. B. (2016). Cryptanalysis of a novel ultra-lightweight mutual authentication protocol for IoT devices using RFID tags. *The Journal of Supercomputing, 73*(3), 1085–1102. doi:10.100711227-016-1849-x

Thornton, G. (2017). *The blockchain timeline From inception to maturity.* Retrieved October 10, 2018, from granthornton.global: https://www.grantthornton.global/globalassets/1.-member-firms/global/insights/blockchain-hub/blockchain-timeline_final.pdf

Tunstall, M. (2017). Smart Card Security. In *Smart Cards, Tokens, Security and Applications* (pp. 217–251). Cham: Springer. doi:10.1007/978-3-319-50500-8_9

Uchibeke, U. U., Kassani, H. S., Schneider, A. K., & Deters, R. (2018). Blockchain access control Ecosystem for Big Data security. *Computer Science - Cryptography and Security.* arXiv preprint arXiv:1810.04607

Vukolić, M. (2017). Rethinking Permissioned Blockchains. In *Proceedings of the ACM Workshop on Blockchain, Cryptocurrencies and Contracts.* Abu Dhabi, UAE: ACM. 10.1145/3055518.3055526

Ward, M. (2006). EMV card payments – An update. *Information Security Technical Report, 11*(2), 89–92. doi:10.1016/j.istr.2006.03.001

Yermack, D. (2015). Is Bitcoin a Real Currency? An Economic Appraisal. In D. Lee, & K. Chuen (Eds.), Handbook of Digital Currency Bitcoin, Innovation, Financial Instruments, and Big Data (pp. 31-43). Elsevier. doi:10.1016/B978-0-12-802117-0.00002-3

Zhang, P., White, J. C. D., Lenz, G. S., & Rosenbloom, T. S. (2018). FHIRChain: Applying Blockchain to Securely and Scalably Share Clinical Data. *Computational and Structural Biotechnology Journal, 16,* 267–278. doi:10.1016/j.csbj.2018.07.004 PMID:30108685

Zheng, Z., Xie, S., Dai, H., Chen, X., & Wang, H. (2017). An Overview of Blockchain Technology: Architecture, Consensus, and Future Trends. In *2017 IEEE International Congress on Big Data (BigData Congress)* (pp. 557-564). Honolulu, HI: IEEE. 10.1109/BigDataCongress.2017.85

Zikratov, I., Kuzmin, A., Akimenko, V., Niculichev, V., & Yalansky, L. (2017). *Ensuring data integrity using Blockchain technology. In Proceeding of the 20th Conference of Fruct Association* (pp. 534–539). IEEE.

Zorzi, M., Gluhak, A., Lange, S., & Bassi, A. (2010). From today's INTRAnet of things to a future IN-TERnet of things: A wireless- and mobility-related view. *IEEE Wireless Communications, 17*(6), 44–51. doi:10.1109/MWC.2010.5675777

ADDITIONAL READING

Pilkington, M. (2016). 11 Blockchain technology: principles and applications. *Research handbook on digital transformations*, 225.

Preneel, B. (2007). A survey of recent developments in cryptographic algorithms for smart cards. *Computer Networks*, *51*(9), 2223–2233. doi:10.1016/j.comnet.2007.01.008

Sullivan, C., & Burger, E. (2017). E-residency and blockchain. *Computer Law & Security Review*, *33*(4), 470–481. doi:10.1016/j.clsr.2017.03.016

KEY TERMS AND DEFINITIONS

Blockchain: Blockchain may be defined as a digital ledger that records the transactions associated with bitcoin or any other crypto-currency in chronological order and publicly.

Double-Spending: Double-spending is a flaw in which a digital currency or single digital token is spent twice.

Ethereum: It is a public or open source blockchain-based decentralized computing platform that features smart contract functionality.

Internet of Things (IoT): IoT can be defined as an idea of interconnecting everyday life objects through Internet, which gives them the capability to transmit data and information.

Radio Frequency Identification (RFID): RFID technology utilized electromagnetic waves for identifying and tracking the tags attached to the objects.

Smart Cards: Smart cards are pocket-sized computers that contain one or more integrated chips that facilitate these cards with storage, processing, and input/output interface.

Wireless Sensor Networks (WSNs): WSNs are defined as collection of sensors that are spatially distributed and are dedicated to perform certain functions including monitoring the environmental conditions through wireless links.

Chapter 20
Delay Tolerant Networks:
Architecture, Routing, Congestion, and Security Issues

Vandana Kushwaha
Banaras Hindu University, India

Ratneshwer Gupta
Jawaharlal Nehru University, India

ABSTRACT

Opportunistic networks are one of the emerging evolutions of the network system. In opportunistic networks, nodes are able to communicate with each other even if the route between source to destination does not already exist. Opportunistic networks have to be delay tolerant in nature (i.e., able to tolerate larger delays). Delay tolerant network (DTNs) uses the concept of "store-carry-forward" of data packets. DTNs are able to transfer data or establish communication in remote area or crisis environment where there is no network established. DTNs have many applications like to provide low-cost internet provision in remote areas, in vehicular networks, noise monitoring, extreme terrestrial environments, etc. It is therefore very promising to identify aspects for integration and inculcation of opportunistic network methodologies and technologies into delay tolerant networking. In this chapter, the authors emphasize delay tolerant networks by considering its architectural, routing, congestion, and security issues.

INTRODUCTION

Delay Tolerant Networking (DTNs) is a new way of communication that facilitates the data transfer between source and destination even if a fully connected path may not exist between two end nodes. The Delay Tolerant Network (DTN)(Cerf et al., 2007) is an emerging area that has attracted keen research efforts from both academia and industry. DTNs consider an extreme network condition that is different from the traditional communication networks. There may not exist a complete end-to-end path between the data source and destination, and thus network is subject to dynamic node connections and unstable topologies. The communication in DTN is done by exploiting the characteristic of nodes i.e. mobility,

DOI: 10.4018/978-1-5225-8407-0.ch020

available connections, and provided buffer space etc. DTNs find broad applications in the situations where legacy networks cannot work effectively, such as data communications in rural areas where stable communications infrastructure is not available or is costly. DTN is useful for extreme environments like battlefields, volcanic regions, deep oceans, deep space, developing regions etc., where they suffer challenging conditions as military wars and conflicts, terrorist attacks, earthquakes, volcanic eruptions, floods, storms, hurricanes, severe electromagnetic interferences, congested usage, etc. These challenging conditions result in excessive delays, severe bandwidth restrictions, remarkable node mobility, frequent power outages and recurring communication obstructions (Khabbaz et al., 2011). Vehicular networking is a wide and growing field of DTNs, where many applications are being explored (Benamar et al., 2014). One of these applications is to provide Internet access to vehicles by connecting to roadside wireless base stations (Ott and Kutscher, 2004). Non-commercial applications include monitoring and tracking wildlife animals (Juang et al., 2002), and environmental monitoring, such as lake water quality monitoring and roadside noise monitoring. DTNs can be applied in a variety of other fields ranging from healthcare to education to economic efficiency (Abdelkader et al., 2016).

The idea of Delay Tolerant Network (DTN) (Warthman, 2012) was taken from Inter Planetary Networks (IPN) (Burleigh et al., 2003), this was started in 1970s. The IPN was invented to communicate between earth and mars. The DTN is a type of wireless ad-hoc network which tolerates the intermittent connectivity. The intermittent connectivity can be defined as the sudden change of state (up/down) of any communication link between the nodes. The DTN can also be defined as intermittently connected wireless ad-hoc network ("Mobile Ad-Hoc and", n. d.) that can tolerate longer delays, intermittent connectivity and prevent data from being lost by using store-carry-forward approach. The Store-carry-forward approach enables the nodes to take the message, store it in the buffer provided at each node and forward the same whenever new node comes in its communication range. DTN technology has become a new research focus in many fields including deep space communications, military tactical communications, and disaster rescue and internet access in remote areas. Internet Research Task Force (IRTF) has organized Delay-Tolerant Research Group (DTNRG) to research OTN technology, and as an important research theme, DTN technology has been accepted by the guidelines in MobiCom 2008 and Milcom 2009(Lu et al., 2010).

With the advent of the Internet of Things (IoT) a number of new devices will become part of our day today life. Constrained Application Protocol (CoAP), and its extensions, are specially designed to address the integration of these constrained devices in IoT environment. However, due to their limited resources, they are often unable to be fully connected and instead form intermittently connected and sparse networks in which Delay Tolerant Networking (DTN) is more appropriate, in particular through the Bundle Protocol (BP).

The chapter is organized as follows. In next section, the characteristics of DTNs, types of DTNs and applications of DTNs are mentioned in different sub-sections. The architectural structure of DTNs is described in further section. Then Routing and buffer management of DTNs are explained. Security aspects of DTNs are mentioned further. Some case studies of DTNs are given in last section.

Characteristics of Delay Tolerant Networks

A DTN have the following basic characteristics (Fall et al., 2008):

Intermittent Connection

As the node's mobility and energy are limited, DTN frequently disconnects, thus resulting in continue change in DTN topology. That is to say, the network keeps the status of intermittent connection and partial connection so that there is no guarantee to achieve end-to-end route.

High Delay, Low Efficiency, and High Queue Delay

End-to-end delay specifies the sum of the total delay of each hop on the specified route. The end-to-end delay involves queuing time, waiting time and transmission time (Cerf et al., 2007). Each hop delay might be very high due to the fact that DTN intermittent connection keeps unreachable in a very long time and thus further leading to a lower data rate and showing the asymmetric features in up-down link data rate. In addition, queuing delay plays a main role in end-to-end delay and frequent fragmentations in DTN make queuing delay increasing.

Limited Resource

Node's computing and processing ability, communication ability and storage space is weaker than the function of an ordinary computer due to the constraints of price, volume and power. In addition, the limited storage space resulted in higher packet loss rate.

Limited Life Time of Node

In some special circumstances of the restricted network, the node is common to use the battery power on the state of hostile environment or in harsh conditions, which will cut the life time of node. When the power is off, then the node cannot guarantee normal work. That is to say, it is very possible the power is off when the message is being transmitted.

Dynamic Topology

Note that the DTN topology is dynamic changing for some reasons such as environmental changes, energy depletion or other failures, which results in dropping out of network. The requirements of entering DTN also make topology change.

Poor Security

Due to the lack of specialized services and maintenance in real world DTN is vulnerable to threats like eavesdropping, message modification, routing spoofing and Denial of Service (DoS) etc.

Heterogeneous Interconnection

The architecture of DTN is based on asynchronous message forward and operates as an overlay above the transport layer. DTN can run on different heterogeneous network protocol stacks and DTN gateway ensures the reliable transmission of interconnection message.

The above mentioned characteristics make DTNs different from traditional wired networks and mobile ad-hoc networks.

Types of DTNs

According to the application domains, DTNs can be categorized as follow:

DTN for Satellite Communications

Space communication can be generally characterized by long link delay and frequent link disruptions. Despite of these characteristics of space communication DTN has been developed to enable automated network communications. DTN was originated from a generalization of requirements identified for interplanetary networking (IPN). Ordinary TCP/IP architectures fail to provide satisfactory performance because of the presence of one or more of the following impairments: long delays, disruptions, intermittent links, network partitioning etc. Satellite network is one among the challenged network. It is the network that includes one or more satellite links. LEO (low earth orbit) satellite networks were immediately recognized as a perfect candidate for DTN applications, because of the satellite link intermittency (Cerf et al., 2007). In deep space and LEO satellite networks the communication opportunities or contacts are known in advance i.e. are fully deterministic as they are related to the orbital characteristics of planets and space assets. This kind of connectivity is addressed by specific DTN solutions such as "scheduled contacts" where transport protocol connections start and stop at the beginning and at the end of contacts. In such networks routing must be designed to cope with scheduled contacts and not with opportunistic connectivity as in other challenged networks, therefore specific routing algorithms as contact graph routing designed by NASA. On the other hand GEO satellite networks are not pure challenged networks because they can offer a continuous connectivity at least for fixed terminals. However they are classified as challenged networks because of its long propagation delay of order 600 ms.

DTN for Deep Space Communications

Delay/disruption tolerant networking (DTN) technology offers a novel way to significantly stressed communications in space environments, especially those with long link delay and frequent link disruptions in deep space missions (Burleigh et al., 2003, Fall, 2003). DTN was considered as the most suitable technology to be employed in space internetworking by NASA and hopes to fly with it on space missions soon ("Recommendations on a", 2008). There are numerous research work has been done related with DTN for space communications in the past several years. The Space Internetworking Strategy Group (SISG), which is composed of technical experts appointed by the Inter-agency Operations Advisory Group (IOAG) agencies, considers DTN to be the only mature candidate protocol available to handle long propagation delays, frequent and lengthy network disruption inherent in space missions involving multiple spacecraft ("Recommendations on a", 2008).

Vehicular DTN (VDTN)

Vehicular Delay-Tolerant Networks (VDTNs) are DTNs where vehicles communicate with each other and with fixed nodes placed along the roads in order to disseminate messages. Some of the potential applications for these networks are the following: notification of traffic conditions (unexpected jams),road accident warnings, weather reports (ice, snow, fog, and wind),advertisements (free parking spots, nearby fuel prices, etc.),cooperative vehicle collision avoidance, web or email access, or even the gathering of information collected by vehicles such as road pavement defects. Vehicular networks have also been proposed to implement transient networks to benefit developing communities and disaster recovery networks (Isento et al., 2013).

DTN for Underwater Communications

Underwater networks (UWNs) have the potential to find applications in a wide range of aquatic activities, such as oceanographic data collection, pollution monitoring, offshore exploration, seismic monitoring, assisted navigation and tactical surveillance. In most cases, these networks will operate in harsh and constrained environments where communication disruption (and, hence, delay) is frequent. In this respect, an underwater network can be viewed as a delay/disruption-tolerant network (DTN) requiring specialized communication protocols.

DTN for Emergency Communications

Delay-tolerant networks can be used to improve situational awareness during the response to a large-scale disaster. Delay/Disruption Tolerant Networks (DTNs) can be used in man-made or natural disaster stricken areas with communication infrastructure breakdown or power outages. DTN has been developed as a solution to wireless networks experiencing frequent disruptions. DTNs can provide communication support in disaster relief and rescue operations. An evaluation carried out by (Trono et al., 2015) using DTN MapEx a disaster map generator that operates over a DTN with responders and volunteers, carrying mobile devices shows that DTN can improve information availability in disaster stricken areas.

Applications of DTNs

Some of the major applications of DTNs are summarized below:

Deep Space Exploration

In the next few decades, NASA and other agencies will plan a series of projects of lunar exploration, Mars exploration and others. In September, 2003, Cisco router (CL EO) was launched by satellite to monitor disaster in UK. Till to December 2008, CL EO has done a lot of routing tests in space environment including using Saratoga protocol of bundle layer instead of pervious protocol making full use of the link source to overcome serious asymmetry link conditions. The experiment shows it is feasible to use Bundle Protocol (Wood et al. 2008) in space.

Studies of Wild Zebra

The Zebranet project (Zhang et al., 2004) has installed a global positioning system (GPS) in a zebra collar to study the habits of zebra activities, which is one of the early DTN projects and was started in 2004. Collars start every few minutes to record GPS location information, and every 2 h open radio function, when two collars' distance is in communication range they would exchange information (adopted Epidemic routing algorithms). After a period of time, every horse collar stores the position information of others activities. In this experiment, the researcher can know the exact location of zebra only with little information. The further experiment of this project is to resolve the issues of equipment energy, adaptability and data compression.

Rural Communication

There are many rural communication projects in remote villages to provide the access to Internet. Some of which is try to reduce the cost of communications using the way of asynchronous information transmission. For example, Wizzy digital courier service provides Internet access for some village schools in South Africa. This project adopted a simple one-hop delay network, letting couriers drive a motorcycle with USB storage device to come and go between rural schools and cities with permanent Internet connection (such a round-trip may take several hours of time), so as to realize the connection between the school and the Internet.

Lake Quality Monitoring

European Union advises state and local government to launch protect water quality activities (Farrell and Cahill, 2006), in this project, the researchers didn't choose end-to-end communication mode, but using special node (data mule) in the lake to cruise, realizing DTN storage and forwarding mechanism. When the ship (data mule) back to dock, mule can exchange information with the gathering nodes accessing Internet. In this project, using data mules--besides low overhead--still can be independent with infrastructures and set flexibly in various carries. Other one such as Ad hoc being used for collecting battlefield information or collecting data in depopulated area is actually one application of DTN. That's to say, DTN has come into people's lives. Notice that with further development of DTN research, its range of applications will be larger, and more fields will be benefited.

Military Applications

Military communication network is a multi-hop wireless network, and is an ad hoc network. As a result of the impact of the battlefield special circumstances, such as, mobile nodes, enemy interference, geographical environment, etc, the connection between network nodes is intermittent, uncertainties and non-periodic. Therefore military communication network is a typical DTN network. DTN technology can be fully applied in military communication networks.

Public Transportation System

There are several promising applications of DTN in public transport.

Data Dissemination Application

For high volume and non-urgent data, it is not wise to use expensive network transmission techniques. Instead, DTN technique could be used as a low cost data dissemination method in Fog computing, particular for data dissemination among Fog servers and mobile devices (Gao et al., 2017.). DakNet (Pentland et al., 2004) is a DTN technique based application and developed by researchers from the MIT Media Lab. It has been deployed in remote parts of Cambodia and India at a cost two orders of magnitude less compared to traditional landlines networks.

DTN ARCHITECTURE

The existing TCP/IP-based internet, while fabulously successful in many environments, does not suit all environments. The ability of the "TCP/IP suite" to provide service depends on a number of important assumptions: (i) existence of end-to-end path between source and destination during communication session; (ii) (for reliable communication) that the maximum round-trip time over that path is not excessive and not highly variable from packet to packet; and (iii) that the end-to-end loss is relatively small. Delay Tolerant Networks may not satisfy some of the assumptions due to their different characteristics such as long or variable delays, frequent partitioning, data rate asymmetry and interoperating among differently-challenged networks. The DTN architecture should provide the means for dissimilar networks to interoperate (Cerf et al., 2002).The network architecture used for the conventional networks may not be used as it is for DTNs.

The DTN architecture provides a common solution for interconnecting heterogeneous gateways or proxies that employ store-and-forward message routing to overcome communication disruptions (Cerf et al., 2007). At its inception, the concepts behind the DTN architecture were primarily targeted at tolerating long delays and predictably-interrupted communications over long distances (i.e., in deep space). At this point in time, the work was architecture for the Interplanetary Internet (IPN). By March 2003, when the first draft of the eventual RFC 4838 was published, one of the authors had coined the term Delay Tolerant Networking suggesting the intention to extend the IPN concept to other types of networks, specifically including terrestrial wireless networks. Terrestrial wireless networks also suffer disruptions and delay, and the DTN architectural emphasis grew from scheduled connectivity in the IPN case to include other types of networks and patterns of connectivity (e.g., opportunistic mobile ad-hoc networks with nodes that remain off for significant periods of time) (Fall et al., 2008).

The DTN architecture creates a "network of Internets" by providing an end-to-end layer above the transport layer. We call this the "bundle layer." (Cerf et al., 2002). The name "bundle" derives from considering protocols that attempt to minimize the number of round-trip exchanges required to complete a protocol transaction, and dates back to the original IPN work. By "bundling" together all information required completing a transaction (e.g., protocol options and authentication data), the number of exchanges can be reduced, which is of considerable interest if the round trip time is hours, days or weeks (Fall et al., 2008). Bundles comprise a collection of typed blocks. Each block contains meta-data; some also contain application data. (Fall et al., 2008). The first or primary block of each bundle, illustrated in Figure 1, contains the DTN equivalents of the data typically found in an IP header on the Internet: version, source and destination EIDs, length, processing flags, and (optional) fragmentation information. It also contains some additional fields, more specific to the bundle protocol: report-to EID, current custodian EID, creation timestamp and sequence number, lifetime and a dictionary. Most fields are variable in length, and use a relatively compact notation called self-delimiting numerical values (SDNVs). Early designs for the primary bundle block used more fixed-length fields, but the relative merit of choosing a fixed-length field for simplicity was ultimately found to be less compelling than the flexibility offered

Figure 1. The structure of the primary block of a bundle (Scott and Burleigh, 2007)

Version(1 byte)	Bundle Processing Control Flags (SDNV)
Block Length (SDNV)	
Destination Scheme Offset (SDNV)	Destination SSP Offset (SDNV)
Source Scheme Offset (SDNV)	Source SSP Offset (SDNV)
Report-to Scheme Offset (SDNV)	Report-to SSP Offset (SDNV)
Custodian Scheme Offset (SDNV)	Custodian SSP Offset (SDNV)
Creation Timestamp (SDNV)	
Creation Timestamp Sequence Number (SDNV)	
Lifetime (SDNV)	
Dictionary Length (SDNV)	
Dictionary (byte array)	
Fragment Offset (SDNV, optional)	
Application data unit length (SDNV, optional)	

by SDNVs. By setting various bits in the bundle processing control flags, the sender can request a report for any of the following events: receipt at destination node, custody acceptance at a node, bundle forwarded/deleted/delivered route, and receipt by destination application. (Scott and Burleigh, 2007).

The DTN architecture uses store-and-forward message switching technique by overlaying a new transmission protocol, called the bundle protocol on top of the lower-layer protocols such as Internet protocols. The bundle protocol ties together the lower-layer protocols so that application programs can communicate across the same or different sets of lower-layer protocols under conditions that involve long network delays or disruptions. The bundle-protocol agent stores and forwards entire bundles (or bundle fragments) between nodes. A single bundle protocol is used throughout a DTN. On the other hand, the lower-lower protocols below the bundle protocol are chosen depending on the characteristics of each communication environment. The figure below (top) illustrates the bundle-protocol overlay and (bottom) compares the Internet protocol stack (left) with a DTN protocol stack (right).

Some important characteristics of DTN architectures are as follows.

Store-and-Forward Message Switching (Warthman, 2012)

DTNs use store-and forward message switching technique to resolve the problems associated with intermittent connectivity, long or variable delay, asymmetric data rates, and high error rates. A DTN-enabled application sends messages of arbitrary length, also called Application Data Units or ADUs. Whole messages (ADUs) or pieces (fragments) of such messages are forwarded from a storage place on one node (switch intersection) to a storage place on another node, along a path that eventually reaches the destination.

Figure 2. Bundle-protocol overlay with DTN protocol stack (Warthman, 2012)

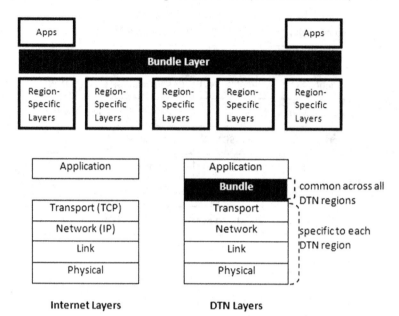

Figure 3. Store-And-Forward Message Switching (Warthman, 2012)

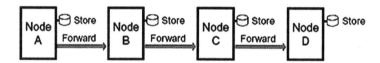

Store-and-forwarding methods are also used here are not node-to-node relays (as shown above) but rather star relays where both the source and destination independently contact a central storage device at the centre of the links.

DTN routers need persistent storage for their queues for one or more of the following reasons:

- A communication link to the next hop may not be available for a long time.
- One node in a communicating pair may send or receive data much faster or more reliably than the other node.
- A message, once transmitted, may need to be retransmitted if an error occurs at an upstream (toward the destination) node, or if an upstream node declines acceptance of a forwarded message.

By moving whole messages (or fragments thereof) in a single transfer, the message-switching technique provides network nodes with immediate knowledge of the size of messages, and therefore the requirements for intermediate storage space and retransmission bandwidth.

Nodes and Endpoints (Warthman, 2012)

A *node* is an entity with a bundle-protocol agent overlaid on lower-layer communication protocols in DTN. At any moment, a given node may act as a source, destination, or forwarder of bundles:

Source or Destination Function

As a source or destination, a node sends or receives bundles to or from another node, but it does not forward bundles received from other nodes. If the node operates over long-delay links, its bundle protocol requires persistent storage in which to queue bundles until outbound links are available. The node may optionally support custody transfers.

Forwarding Function

A DTN node can forward bundles between two or more other nodes in one of two situations:

Routing-Equivalent Forwarding.

The node forwards bundles between two or more other nodes, each of which implement the same lower-layer protocols as the forwarding node. If a forwarding node operates over long-delay links, its bundle protocol requires persistent storage in which to queue bundles until outbound links are available. The node may optionally support custody transfers.

Gateway-Equivalent Forwarding:

The node forwards bundles between two or more other nodes, each of which implement different lower-layer protocols while the forwarding node implements all such protocols. The node must have persistent storage; support for custody transfers is optional but typically advisable.

A bundle endpoint is a set of zero or more nodes that all identify themselves by the same endpoint ID. The common case in which only one node has a given endpoint ID is called a singleton endpoint. Every node is uniquely identified by at least one singleton endpoint. Source nodes are always singleton endpoints or null (anonymous source) endpoints, and destination nodes may or may not be singleton endpoints. Endpoints may also be multicast (multiple destination nodes with the same endpoint ID) or null (no nodes). Endpoints may contain multiple nodes, and nodes may be members of multiple endpoints.

Priority Classes (Cerf et al., 2002)

The DTN architecture offers relative measures of priority (low, medium, high) for delivering ADUs. These priorities differentiate traffic based upon an application's desire to affect the delivery urgency for ADUs, and are carried in bundle blocks generated by the bundle layer based on information specified by the application.

Three relative priority classes are defined to date. These priority classes typically imply some relative scheduling prioritization among bundles in queue at a sender:

Bulk

Bulk bundles are shipped on a "least effort" basis. No bundles of this class will be shipped until all bundles of other classes bound for the same destination and originating from the same source have been shipped.

Normal

Normal-class bundles are shipped prior to any bulk-class bundles and are otherwise the same as bulk bundles.

Expedited

Expedited bundles, in general, are shipped prior to bundles of other classes and are otherwise the same.

Applications specify their requested priority class and data life time for each ADU they send. This information, coupled with policy applied at DTN nodes that select how messages are forwarded and which routing algorithms are in use, affects the overall likelihood and timeliness of ADU delivery. The priority class of a bundle is only required to relate to other bundles from the same source. This means that a high priority bundle from one source may not be delivered faster (or with some other superior quality of service) than a medium priority bundle from a different source. It does mean that a high priority bundle from one source will be handled preferentially to a lower priority bundle sent from the same source.

Congestion Control

The Delay Tolerant Networking architecture (DTN) (Fall, 2003) supports a custody transfer concept implemented by an acknowledged transfer of data to persistent, reliable storage. A node "taking custody" of a message makes a commitment to deliver the message to its destination or another custodian node, effectively migrating one or both of the ends described in the end-to-end argument (Saltzer and Clark, 1984) to new locations. The goal of custody transfer is to use hop-by-hop (custodian-to-custodian) reliability to improve end-to-end reliability and to free retransmission buffers at a sender as soon as possible. To implement this facility, the node taking custody ("custodian") must generally reserve storage for messages it takes custody of, resulting in a reduced amount of storage remaining for either taking custody of subsequent messages or for merely doing its ordinary task of switching messages. When faced with persistent demand, a custodian unable to release or otherwise transfer custody of its messages will ultimately exhaust its storage resources– a form of DTN congestion. This type of congestion can easily result in head-of-line blocking, preventing further traffic from flowing even when some outgoing connections are available (Fall et al., 2003). Easing congestion at a custodian is a nontrivial task. The options include discarding messages, moving them toward their ultimate destination (typically the most desirable case), or moving them to some other place. The potential of long delays and interruptions of custody transfer operations between custodians makes the management of message migration to combat congestion especially difficult (Seligman et al., 2006).

ROUTING AND BUFFER MANAGEMENT IN DTN

DTN uses store-carry-and-forward protocols: there, a node may store a message in its buffer and carry it along for long periods of time, until an appropriate forwarding opportunity arises. Additionally, multiple message replicas are often propagated to increase delivery probability. This combination of long-term storage and replication imposes a high storage overhead on unbounded nodes (e.g. handhelds). Thus, efficient buffer management policies are necessary to decide which messages should be discarded, when node buffers are operated close to their capacity ("Recommendations on a", 2008). This section highlights the issues and challenges in buffer management in DTN. This section will also cover some efficient approaches for buffer management in DTN.

Delay Tolerant Networks are wireless networks where disconnections may occur frequently due to propagation phenomena, node mobility, and power outages. Propagation delays may also be long due to the operational environment (e.g. deep space, underwater). In order to achieve data delivery in such challenging networking environments, researchers have proposed the use of store-carry-and-forward protocols: there, a node may store a message in its buffer and carry it along for long periods of time, until an appropriate forwarding opportunity arises. Additionally, multiple message replicas are often propagated to increase delivery probability. This combination of long-term storage and replication imposes a high storage overhead on untethered nodes (e.g. handhelds). Thus, efficient buffer management policies are necessary to decide which messages should be discarded, when node buffers are operated close to their capacity.

In DTN, the "store-carry-forward" mechanism is used for message transmission. These messages are delivered to their final destinations in a hop-by-hop manner. As a result, many problems arise such as how to drop and how to schedule the messages, in the buffer due to the impulsive nature of the nodes. Many changeable situations may occur like limited storage node capacity, short contact duration between the two nodes, and so on (Ahmed et al., 2016). Buffer Management technology is a fundamental approach that manages the various resources among different situations as per the technique used. An efficient buffer management technique decides at each step which of the messages is to be dropped first, when the buffer is full as well as which messages are to be transmitted, when bandwidth is limited (Fathima and Wahidabanu, 2011).

The nodes in the DTN require proper buffer management approach to get low delay and high data delivery. The buffer management, in this case, refers to the proper use of scheduling and dropping policies used by the nodes at the time of the buffer overflow and congestion (Mansuri, 2013).

Buffer Management Policies

The popular dropping policies techniques for buffer management used in DTNs are described.

Drop Least Recently Received (DLR)

In the DLR buffer management technique, as the name implies, the packet which is stays for a long time in the buffer will be dropped first. This is due to the fact that it has less probability of being conceded to the other nodes (Mansuri, 2013)

Drop Oldest (DOA)

In the DOA technique, the message with the shortest remaining life time (TTL) is dropped first. The idea behind dropping such messages is that of the messages whose TTL is small, then these are in the network from a long period of time and, thus, have the high probability of having already been delivered (Rashid et al., 2011).

Drop Front (DF)

This technique drops the messages on the basis of the order in which they enter into the buffer. For example, the first message that enters the queue will be the first to be dropped (Grundy, 2012).

Drop Largest (DLA)

In the Drop Largest (DLA) buffer management technique, the message with a large size will be selected in order to be dropped (Rashid et al., 2011).

Evict Most Forwarded First (MOFO)

MOFO attempts to maximize the propagation of the messages through the network by dropping those messages that have been forwarded the maximum number of times. As such, the messages with a lower hop count are able to travel further within the network (Grundy, 2012).

Drop Last (DL)

Drop the newly received message, irrespective of whether it is new or old, that is why responsible for maximize drop ratio.

Evict Most Favourably Forwarded First (MOPR)

MOPR maintains the value of each message in its queue. Thus, each time when a message is replicated the value in the message is increased based on the predictability of the message being delivered. Therefore, the message with the highest value is dropped first (Grundy, 2012).

Evict Shortest Life Time First (SHLI)

This technique uses the timeout value of the message, which indicates when it is no longer useful. This means that a message with the shortest remaining life time is dropped first (Grundy, 2012).

Evict Least Probable First (LEPR)

This technique works by a node ranking the messages within its buffer based on the predicted probability of delivery. The message with the lowest probability is dropped first (Grundy, 2012).Basically buffer management policies can be divided into three types (Jain and Chawla, 2014):

- Global buffer management policy which utilize network-wide information regarding all messages.
- Local buffer management policy which use partial network knowledge like number of copies of message in the network, instead of all network-wide information correlated with messages and additional message properties like remaining TTL, size etc.
- Traditional buffer management policies like drop head, drop tail, drop random.

Routing in DTN

The traditional routing protocols which consider an essential platform for most traditional mobile networks do not work well in DTN since these protocols assume an existing of the continuous route between the source node and destination (Fall, 2003). Since the DTN are intermittently connected networks where a continuous end-to-end path may not exist, the main objective of routing in DTN is to maximize message delivery to the destination while minimizing end-to-end delay. The routing protocols in DTN can be differentiated based on queue management, the amount of information available when making the forwarding decisions and the number of destinations a message can have (Warthman, 2012).

Routing in DTN is the main issues and challenging because of frequent and long duration periods of disconnectivity (Dopico et al., 2011). The properties of DTN certainly raise a number of interesting issues in routing (Mehta and Shah, 2014) which are summarized as follow:

Routing Objectives

The main and most important routing objectives in DTN are to minimize resource consumption such as network bandwidth, battery energy, and network bandwidth as well as maximize message delivery probability.

Buffer Space

Since DTN are intermittently connected networks, messages in these networks must be buffered for long periods of time. This means that the intermediate nodes require enough buffer space to store all messages until that intermediate nodes meet the specific destination nodes. The process of storing messages requires sufficient buffer space to store all pending messages as required.

Energy

Nodes in these networks normally have a low level of energy because of the mobility of nodes and the difficulties of connection to the power station. Much of energy is consumed during messages routing, as well as energy consumed for sending, receiving, storing, and computation of messages.

Reliability

Routing protocols in DTN should have some acknowledge for reliable delivery of data, which guarantee successful and stable delivery of information. Where some acknowledgment messages should be sent back when messages correctly reach to the final destination.

Security

Security has always been a significant problem for both traditional and DTN networks. The messages may go along arbitrary path through intermediate nodes before reaching their final destination. Therefore, based on the requirements of security of applications, users may require securing guarantees about the authenticity of a message. The cryptographic mechanisms may be useful to secure intermediate routing. To overcome the problem of intermittent connectivity and partitions in the networks, routing in DTN utilizes nodes mobility and messages buffering which makes it possible for a node to carry a message and bridge partitions in the networks.

Routing in DTN can be classified into different categories based on their characteristics as deterministic and stochastic. In deterministic scheme the network topology and/or its characteristics are assumed to be known. Contrarily, for stochastic case no exact knowledge of topology is assumed.

Processing Power

Processing Power is one of the goals of delay-tolerant networking is to connect devices that are not performed by traditional networks. These devices may be very small having small processing capability, in terms of CPU and memory. These nodes will not be capable of running complex routing protocols. The routing strategies presented here could still be used on more powerful gateway nodes, in order to connect the sensor network to a general purpose delay-tolerant network.

Classification of Routing Protocols

The existing routing protocols in DTNs are classified with respect to their strategies for controlling message copies and making the forwarding decision (Cao and Sun, 2012) shown in Figure 4.

Number of Destination

According to the number of destination nodes of a message, routing protocols can be classified into three categories: unicast routing, multicast routing, and broadcast routing.

- **Unicast Routing:** Single destination for each message.
- **Multicast Routing:** Group of destination nodes for each message.
- **Broadcast Routing:** All the nodes in the network are destination nodes for each message.

Number of Copy

Depending on the number of message copies utilized in the routing process, protocols can be classified into two categories (Spyropoulos et al., 2008a, Spyropoulos et al., 2008b): single-copy and multiple-copy.

- **Single-Copy Routing Protocols:** Only a single copy for each message exists in the network at any time.

- **Multiple-Copy Routing Protocols:** Multiple copies of same message can be generated and distributed into the network. Moreover, multiple copy routing protocols can be further divided into flooding-based and quota based.
- **Flooding-Based Routing Protocol:** Dissemination copies of each message to as many nodes as possible.
- **Quota-Based Routing Protocol:** Intentionally limit the number of message copies.

Available Network Knowledge

In addition, according to whether the forwarding decision is based on the knowledge derived from the nodes' encounters or not, protocols can as well be classified into two categories: Deterministic and Non-deterministic (Opportunistic) (Bulut et al., 2009).

- **Deterministic Routing Protocol:** Complete knowledge of node trajectories, encounter probability of nodes and node meeting times and period to make the forwarding decision.
- **Non-Deterministic Routing Protocols:** Zero knowledge of predetermined path between source and destination. These algorithms either forward the messages randomly or prediction based (Probabilistic based).

DTN Routing Protocols

The routing protocols used in DTN are listed below:

Epidemic Protocol (EP)

In this protocol all nodes can become the carrier, and it is ensured that messages can be delivered with a high probability. However, the network re-sources are consumed heavily ("Recommendations on a",

Figure 4. Classification of DTN Routing Protocols (Bulut et al., 2009)

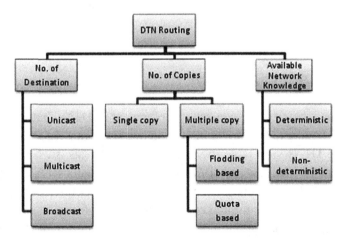

2008). In other words, to deliver messages to the final destination, EP provides a redundant number of random messages exchange. This leads to guaranteeing the destination node receiving the messages in anyway.

Spray and Wait (SnW)

The SnW (Isento et al., 2013) algorithm is the advanced version of the epidemic routing protocol. In this algorithm the nodes are not distributing the message to each and every node but an optimal number of nodes (L) are selected to which the source node will relay the message. This algorithm consists of two phases spray phase and wait phase. In the spray phase, the source node replicates the message to the L-nodes and these L- nodes will further relay the message to L relay nodes. The relay nodes will store the message and perform direct transmission if the destination is not found in spray phase.

PROPHET

PROPHET is proposed in (Lindgren and Doria, 2012). The protocol estimates a node metric called delivery predictability, $P(a, b)$, at each node a for each destination b. When two nodes meet, they update their delivery predictability toward each other. Then, the two nodes exchange their delivery predictability list toward other nodes update their delivery predictability.

MaxProp

MaxProp (Spyropoulos et al., 2005) is a flooding-based routing protocol designed for vehicle-based delay tolerant networks. The buffer of this protocol is divided into two phases. First, messages are stored from low to high based on hop count information. Secondly, messages are arranged by cost from high to low. The first phase uses the front end of the buffer, while the second phase uses the back end of the buffer.

Routing in DTN is a big challenge because of frequency and length of the disconnection time between nodes in the network. However, the main role of routing in DTN is to find an opportunity to connect nodes and to transmit data between them when the nodes meet each other if possible. In general, DTN routing protocols are designed to be as efficient as possible in cases of highly sparse networks and intermittent connectivity. Furthermore, an efficient routing protocol should be simple, scalable and capable of working at both low and high message load. Moreover, it should have optimal delivery probability, low delay and low overhead ratio.

SECURITY FOR DTN APPLICATIONS

Security is one of the main barriers to wide-scale deployment of DTNs, but has gained little attention so far. On the one hand, similar to traditional mobile ad hoc networks, the open channel and multi-hop transmission have made DTNs vulnerable to various security threats, such as message modification/ injection attack or unauthorized access and utilization of DTN resources. On the other hand, the unique security characteristics of DTNs including: long round-trip delay, frequent disconnectivity, fragmentation, opportunistic routing as well as limited computational and storage capability, make the existing security protocols designed for the conventional ad hoc networks unsuitable for DTNs. Different from conventional ad hoc networks, DTNs represent a new network concept and therefore introduce new unique security characteristics and challenges. These unique characteristics including long round-trip delay, frequent disconnectivity, fragmentation as well as opportunistic routing, make the existing security protocols designed for the conventional ad hoc networks unsuitable for DTNs (Zhu, 2009). DTNs are vulnerable to many security threats and also introduce a number of new security challenges. In particular, the use of open networks to transmit data offers unprecedented opportunities for security attacks, and allows attackers to compromise information integrity, authenticity, user privacy and system performance. For example, in DTNs, malicious routers can arbitrarily insert false information into the messages. If innocent routers further propagate these forged messages, the attacks may generate large amounts of unwanted traffic to the network. Due to resource-scarcity characteristic of DTNs, the extra traffic may pose a serious threat on the operation of DTNs (Farrell and Cahill, 2016).

DTN Security Threats (Farrell et al., 2008a)

The possible security threats regarding to DTNs can be summarized as follows:

Messages (or Bundles) Modification Attack

In DTNs, bundles may traverse underlying heterogeneous networks. Therefore, the first security threat in DTNs is the modification of messages (or bundles) in transit for malicious purposes, e.g. for masquerading attacks.

Unauthorized Access

Due to the resource-scarcity characteristics of DTNs, unauthorized access and use of DTN resources can be a serious concern. For example, if an unauthorized application were able to control some DTN infrastructure (e.g. by attacking a routing control protocol), the resource consumption could be catastrophic for the networks.

Bundle Injection Attack

Attackers can try to inject fake bundles to consume precious DTN resources. Further, DTN nodes can unwittingly be used to assist or amplify resource consumption behavior (e.g. not detecting unplanned replays or other misbehavior).

Passive Threats

Due to the broadcast nature of satellites, passive threats such as eavesdropping and traffic analysis are major concerns.

Active Threats

Active threats (or attacks) are more difficult to implement successfully, but must also be addressed. Examples of active attacks are masquerading, message modification, and denial-of-service (DoS) attacks.

Security Requirements (Farrell et al., 2006)

This section lists some of the security requirements which were agreed as priorities during the development of the DTN security mechanisms.

End-to-End-ish-Ness

Traditionally, protocols tend to provide security services which are used either (or both) on a hop-by-hop or end-to-end basis. For DTN security though, we require that these services be usable also between nodes which are not endpoints, but which can be in the middle of a route. In order to define services which can be used in these ways we distinguish between the sender of a bundle and the security-sender for an application of one of these services. Similarly, we can distinguish between the bundle recipient and the security-recipient (or security-destination) for a given application of a security service. Basically, the security-sender is the DTN node that applied the security service, and the security-recipient (or security destination) is the DTN node which is the target for the security service - say the node expected to decrypt or do integrity checking.

There is one more example of the ways in which DTN security services seem to differ from more "normal" network security services, that is worth mentioning here. When a message is authenticated using a digital signature, then in principle any network element on the path can do some checking of that signature. If the message contains sufficient information (the supposed signer's public key or a resolvable reference thereto) than any node can at least check the cryptographic correctness of the signature.

Confidentiality and Integrity

DTN protocols should provide a way to encrypt protocol elements so that messages in transit cannot practically be read. The extent to which a confidentiality service should be able to be applied to any or all protocol elements is a somewhat open issue. Similarly, DTN protocols should provide a way to apply an integrity check to a message so that the identity of the security-sender can be established and so that changes in sensitive parts of the message can be detected. Again, this implies a need for key management which is not, so far, really met. Clearly a protocol should allow for fairly flexible combinations of applications of the confidentiality and integrity services, though hopefully disallowing insecure combinations e.g. a plaintext signature which is out of scope of a confidentiality service allows plaintext guesses to be verified. However these services are provided they should allow for sensible combinations of a range of standard cryptographic algorithms to be used and should also allow for changes to the set of acceptable algorithms to be made over time.

Policy Based Routing

Since the DTN, as a piece of infrastructure, may be quite fragile, we require protocols to be cautious in how they consume network resources. Protocols and implementations support mechanisms for policy-based routing, in other words each DTN protocol specification should state the security-relevant policy variables based upon which it is reasonable to expect an implementation should be able to make routing and forwarding decisions. In particular, since forwarding even a single bundle will consume some network resources, every single DTN node must implicitly incorporate some element of policy-based routing.

In fact, a DTN node can be programmed to forward all bundles received in a deterministic manner, say flooding the bundle to all peers other than then one from which it was received. Even such a simple minded node is however, implicitly implementing a policy - in this case a simple flooding policy. So, though we require all nodes to implement some policy, that policy can be very simple.

It must be noted that policy based routing, if not deployed appropriately, may inadvertently create bundle sinkholes. Consider the case in which a bundle is fragmented, and if one fragment of the bundle reaches a router who's policy requires it to see the entire bundle, then all fragments of that bundle must also pass through that same router. If they do not, then eventually the fragment at our paranoid router will expire and ultimately the entire bundle never arrives at the intended destination. This is clearly a case to avoid - doing so, may however be difficult to arrange without good control over routes.

Issues in DTN Security

DTN mechanism represents a new network concept and therefore introduces new unique security challenges. Some issues in DTN security are discussed as follows.

Key Management

The major open issue in DTN security is the lack of a delay-tolerant method for key management. We are at the stage where we only really know how to use existing schemes, which ultimately require an on-line status checking service or key distribution service which is not practical in a high delay or highly disrupted environment. The only generally applicable schemes we currently have are basically equivalent to shared secrets or else irrevocable public key (or certificate based) schemes. Clearly, this is an area where more research work could produce interesting results.

Lack of End-to-End Connectivity

As a major characteristic of DTNs, lack of end-to-end connectivity not only brings challenge to routing but also makes the existing security solutions, which have been well studied in conventional networks, not applicable in DTNs. For example, end-to-end confidentiality using traditional encryption mechanisms requires the multiple-round key agreement between the sender and the receiver in advance. However, in DTNs, such key agreement may not be feasible since there may be no network connectivity at the time of sending message (Asokan et al., 2007). Therefore, one way, non-interactive key distribution is more suitable in DTNs. The same is true for authentication. Due to the highly time-constrained opportunistic links, non-interactive authentication scheme is more suitable for DTNs, where interactive communication suffers from long round-trip delays and frequent disconnection (Kate et al., 2007). Lack of end-to-end connectivity is also a challenge to public key certificate revocation. In a traditional Public Key Infrastructure (PKI), the most commonly adopted certificate revocation scheme is through Certificate Revocation List (CRL), which is a list of revoked certificates stored in central repositories prepared by the Certificate Authorities (CAs). However, in DTNs, the nodes may suffer from delayed or frequent loss of connectivity to CRL servers. Therefore, distributed CRL distribution or periodical public key updating is preferred in DTNs (Farrell et al., 2008b).

Fragmentation

In DTNs, due to high mobility, each network link becomes available only for a short period of time. Therefore, when a message is large, it may not be possible to send the entire message at once. One possible solution is to split the message into smaller pieces and let each become its own bundle, or "fragment bundle", and send some pieces of a large message through the current link and rest of the message through another link later to make the best use of limited resources. Due to fragmentation, traditional authentication scheme, e.g., the sender generates the signature over an entire message, may not work well since the intermediate receiver cannot authenticate any of the received fragments if it has not yet received the entire message. To address this problem, one approach called "toilet paper" was proposed in ("DTNRG", 2005). The main idea is to make each fragment self-authenticating by attaching a signature to the end of each fragment separately. However, this approach may lead to a more serious performance issue since the intermediate nodes have to spend more computational efforts on verifying a growing number of signatures.

Resource-Scarcity

Resource-scarcity is another major concern in DTN security design. In DTNs, due to limited contact time, DTN nodes need to receive, check and forward a large number of bundles in a limited time. Therefore, bandwidth restriction and computational consumption are critical issues in DTN security design. On one hand, security operations such as authentication are regarded as a necessity to protect precious DTN resources from unauthorized access and use. On the other hand, security mechanisms will themselves inevitably introduce extra computation and transmission overheads. In some cases, the resource consumption to support security can introduce denial of service (DoS) opportunities for attackers (Zhu, 2009).

Bundle Accumulation

Due to the store-carry-and-forward propagation feature, the bundles may be accumulated at some intermediate nodes. Therefore, bundle accumulation can be regarded as an intrinsic characteristic of DTNs. From the security perspective, the accumulation of bundles can be translated into the accumulation of computational, storage and transmission costs. For example, an intermediate bundle forwarder may contemporarily receive, store and authenticate multiple bundles from different senders before these bundles are forwarded to the next hop. Since authentication operation normally involves computational expensive operations such as signature verification, the accumulated authentication related security operations may introduce large computational overhead, which makes the conventional security solutions unsuitable in DTNs (Zhu, 2009).

Resilience to Denial of Service Attacks

DoS attacks can be imposed at any layer of the protocol stack and at any network or security service (Samuel et al., 2010.), (Loukas and Oke et al., 2010.). Since most DTN nodes are resource constrained in some sense, an attacker can usually find some kind of DoS that may damage any given DTN, e.g., the attacker could simply send many large bundles from a well-connected node, through some kind of gateway node into an area with low bandwidth or storage capacity. Compared to a host on the Internet, DoS recovery for a DTN node can be far more problematic, in particular, for remote nodes. DoS mitigation techniques can often be directly applied in DTN; for example, the LTP protocol (a BP convergence layer) includes a cookie mechanism (Farrell et al., 2008c) which, when applied, should limit DoS attempts to on-path attacks. Similar schemes have also been proposed for the BP (Ansa et al., 2010).

Access Control

Access control protects the network and its resources from unauthorized access. The relative resource scarcity of DTNs makes access control arguably more important than in the Internet. For example, in space communications link capacities and storage resources are definitively constrained. Standard access control mechanisms may be unworkable in DTN networks. In a seminal DTN paper (Fall et al., 2003) Fall proposed a public key-certificate-based approach where each participating entity is issued public/private key pairs. This approach uses access control lists though it is claimed to be partially susceptible to node compromise. In traditional Internet, the AAA architecture (Laat et al., 2012) is used for access control. It tends to be relatively centralized (Hu et al., 2006.), and can impose single points of failure in DTNs, if not carefully deployed. Distributed and hierarchical architectures may suit multiregional DTNs with region-specific policies. Thus, a workable access control solution for DTN should be simple and scalable, support offline processing, not impose too many communication overheads, and combine key and broader policy management. In (Johnson et al., 2010), a hierarchical architecture is proposed.

Security and Privacy for Cloud-Based IoT

Due to the unique characteristics of resource constraints, self-organization, and short range communication in IoT, it always resorts to the cloud for outsourced storage and computation, which has brought about a series of new challenging security and privacy threats. Zhou et al. (Zhou et al., 2017) have proposed the architecture and unique security and privacy requirements for the next generation mobile technologies on cloud-based IoT. They identified the inappropriateness of most existing work, and addressed the challenging issues of secure packet forwarding and efficient privacy preserving authentication by proposing new efficient privacy preserving data aggregation without public key homomorphic encryption.

The Bundle Security Protocols (Kate et al., 2007)

The Bundle Security Protocol (BSP) provides data integrity, authentication, and confidentiality. Only security-aware (SA) nodes with the capacity to originate and process BSP security blocks provide these services. Processing may require some action on a bundle—which may include discarding it—to conform to that node's security policy.

The BSP defines four types of security blocks:

Bundle Authentication Block (BAB)

Ensures bundle authenticity and integrity along the path from forwarding SA node to the next receiving SA node. If a BAB is used, its header must be the last header applied to a bundle.

Payload Integrity Block (PIB)

Ensures integrity of payload by verifying the signer.

Payload Confidentiality Block (PCB)

Encrypts bundle payload.

Extension Security Block (ESB)

Provides security for non-payload blocks.

The default security policy for SA nodes requires a BAB. If an SA node has no security policy, only a BAB is required. By default, a BAB policy violation at an SA receiving node requires deletion of the bundle. This default BAB requirement is intended to protect the DTN from DDoS attacks by ensuring the maintenance of trusted relationships between adjacent SA nodes.

DTN FOR IoT AND CLOUD ENVIRONMENT

In the current era of mobile and Internet, a number of new devices will become part of our everyday life due to emergence of the Internet of Things (IoT). From household things such as refrigerators, air-condition, TV and wrist bands to industrial things such as smart-grid meters in smart-grid communication systems, everything is being connected to the Internet. To extend connectivity over disrupted environments, the latest research (Auzias et al., 2015), (Raveneau et al., 2015), (Amendola et al., 2014.)on Internet of Things (IoTs)is focused on enabling IoTs to be connected to Internet with the help networks such as Delay-Tolerant Networks (DTNs).For instance, to enable a delay tolerant IoT, the authors in (Auzias et al., 2015) propose and implement DTN Bundle Protocol (BP)binding for IoT's Constrained Application Protocol (CoAP).This implementation (Auzias et al., 2015) embeds DTN stack into the device, and the IoT application interacts with the integrated-DTN through a custom developed API, thereby creating a paradigm of IoT-over-DTN architecture. The authors in (Raveneau et al., 2015) consider a light-weight DTN BP protocol custom tailored for hardware constrained IoT devices. The authors in (Nuevo et al., 2015) extend AllJoyn, a D2D-based communications framework with custom opportunistic communications. Constrained Application Protocol (CoAP), and its extensions, are specifically designed to address the integration of these constrained devices. However, due to their limited resources, they are often unable to be fully connected and instead form intermittently connected and sparse networks in which Delay Tolerant Networking (DTN) is more appropriate, in particular through the Bundle Protocol (BP) (Auzias et al., 2015).

Xu et al. (Xu et al., 2016.) have identified that for preserving the semantics of IoT, and also seamlessly utilizing the DTN-based communications an 'IoT-cum-DTN' based framework is essential. They proposed a novel Internet of Hybrid Opportunistic Things framework based on the aforementioned 'IoT-cum-DTN' paradigm. Al Noor et al.(Al Noor et al., 2016) have found that ggathering information and providing remote assistant is a common trend as it saves time and cost associated with visiting the actual location in person. They also observed that the widely available mobile sensors are used in collecting information during a task processing. However, gathering information from a remote place, or an area of disaster, is not trivial, given the unavailability of appropriate infrastructure. They found that existing delay tolerant networking approaches address this issue but suffer from unsatisfactory performance due to the lack of sufficient user participation. They proposed the Delay-tolerant Cloud Computing framework (D-CLOC), a cloud framework utilizing the contextual information of a mobile client. Their proposed architecture combines crowd sourcing and the cellular network and forms a temporal delay tolerant cloud. D-CLOC uses a bidding incentive model to ensure and promote user participation in the cloud.

IoT interconnects sensor augmented physical objects anywhere anytime for many application domains (industry, military, smart home, etc.). Enabling delay tolerant communication in IoT will allow smart objects to better communicate even with the presence of disruption in their connectivity. For example, in case of road traffic control applications with limited connectivity, vehicles recording important information on road status may need to store/carry data until they find an opportunity to forward. However, existing DTN schemes have to be tailored to IoT applications to fit their specific requirements, such as: heterogeneity, huge amount of exchanged message, information-centric based protocol, intermittent connection (ICN), etc. Although, many interesting surveys on DTN solutions can be found in the literature, just a few of them address the utilization of DTN schemes in IoT applications regarding their specific requirements. The objective of this work is to study the opportunities and challenges in using DTN strategies for IoT. In the past few years, significant research efforts have been made on IoT to widen its application domains and overcome its constraints. One of the most challenging constraints in IoT is prolonging network lifetime considering resource limitation, and maintaining connectivity in order to deliver data all over the network to the final destination. For these two reasons, DTN schemes seem to be a perfect solution to handle intermittent connectivity, overcome resource constraints and network disconnection. To better understand the benefit of DTN for IoT, we explain with the following examples: suppose a sensor network where sensors are not powerful enough to send data to a collecting station all the time or scheduled to be wake/sleep periodically to save their battery consumption. Similarly, a military network where nodes (e.g., tanks, airplanes, soldiers) may move randomly and are subject to being destroyed. Both networks may face difficulties to deliver data to final destination. Hence, researchers have identified DTN schemes as potential enablers for the IoT.

CASE STUDIES

In this section, we have given some case studies of DTN.

Delay Tolerant Networking Over the Metropolitan Public Transportation

Solutions leveraging on human mobility have been extensively studied; however, the unpredictability of human movements poses severe challenges to network management. Instead, opportunistic solution deployed on top of a Public Transportation System (PTS) has proven more viable than its human counterpart. In this context, buses move along predetermined paths and follow an a priori known schedule, offering a quasi-deterministic encounter model (Acer et al., 2012). Routing algorithms can thus be devised on reasonable assumptions and probabilistic predictions of encounters (Demmer and Fall, 2007, Palazzi and Bujari, 2012). Despite these positive features, even this carrier-based approach has an important, and still unresolved, technical challenge: network scalability when considering a metropolitan-wide area with a growing number of lines and a potentially huge offered load. Since the PTS topology and size are tied to human and organizational factors, network delivery delay may ramp up with the covered area due to the increasing number of hops that each packet must traverse.

Bujari et al. (Palazzi and Bujari, 2012) have analyzed the performance of Mobile Delay/Disruption Tolerant Network (MDTN): a delay tolerant application platform built on top of a PTS and able to provide opportunistic service connectivity. In essence, the PTS is used as a communication backbone. However, different from other approaches relying on a backbone of vehicles to support connectivity, data forwarding is achieved by implementing a delay tolerant, store-carry-and-forward, communication model where a mobile user can delegate a request for service involving Internet access to a carrier entity (e.g., an access point on a bus). The request also contains the information regarding the bus line where the user is expecting the response to be available. Depending on the model of the accessed service (pull or push), the user is later on provided with the requested content or a simple notification of request satisfiability. Once a request has been issued, it is opportunistically forwarded by the carrier toward Internet Gateways (IGs) located at bus terminals and, finally, the response has to reach the bus line where it will be collected. This process involves multi-hop opportunistic routing of both request and response, from carriers toward one of the IGs and from the IG toward the bus line hosting the destination, respectively. Along its trip, the request can be served by an IG at any traversed line end. From there on, the message will be considered a response and forwarded toward the destination line. If, during forwarding, the request ends up on the destination line, it will be up to the destination line to satisfy the request using its terminal IG.

They proposed concrete deployment architecture and an applicative scenario exploiting the PTS as a service delivery platform. To this end, they have modeled two realistic deployment scenarios where carriers are public buses with routes corresponding to actual PTS lines in Milan (Italy) and Chicago (IL, USA) while users are mobile entities owning handheld devices issuing data requests for data available elsewhere. They study the performance trend of their Mobile Delay Tolerant Network (MDTN) in a metropolitan-wide deployment under different routing strategies and data distribution schemes. Nevertheless, performance indexes of the considered routing policies have shown that there is no golden rule for routing. Infrastructure aided delivery will actually make a difference in the service provisioning. On the other hand, MaxProp and multi-copy routing approaches have to be preferred in loosely connected environments.

DT-WBAN: Disruption Tolerant Wireless Body Area Networks in Healthcare Applications (Büsching et al., 2013)

Delay or disruption tolerant protocols can be used in several application areas. In the area of Ambient Assisted Living (AAL) or healthcare, these protocols are well suited to provide a seamless handover between online and offline monitoring of vital parameters or activity data; this also implies a synchronization of offline gathered data. In many wireless monitoring scenarios – e.g. a patient equipped with a Body Area Network (BAN) for vital parameter monitoring – data is transmitted wirelessly to a sink. Compared to interplanetary communication, these Wireless Sensor Network (WSN) or WBAN scenarios have similar or even more sophisticated challenges to cope. Even in human activity monitoring scenarios, no continuous end-to-end connection between the data capturing BAN and the sink can be assumed.

While the movement of satellites and probes is clearly computable, the movement of humans is not predictable in most cases. First – due to shadowing, packet collisions, and other physical influences – even in (more or less) steady wireless connections, the data rate of the wireless channel can change. Second, when the monitored person leaves the communication range of the sink, the data transmission completely collapses. In the first case, the quality of data would suffer; in the second case, data will be lost. That again may jeopardize a whole field study, as important data of certain times of the day of are missing, because the monitored person has left the building. All that could be handled by an appropriate dimensioned communication protocol.

In countless field studies and surveys, BANs or WBANs are used to record vital parameters, activity data and other information. These data are either processed offline or online, but, sooner or later, the data are transferred to a sink where the further processing is performed. This transfer is either accomplished physically, e.g. by the exchange of an SD card, or wirelessly by a radio connection, whereas there seems to be a trend towards wireless transmission.

Here, a disruption tolerant communication protocol comes into play. If the same data of the same sensors are used, a unified data transmission would be the next step. The basic idea is to immediately transmit data, if in communication range of the sink, and to store the data locally on the node, if not. Applications that rely on immediately transmitted data would still function as always – as long as the device is within the communication range of the sink. Additionally, these applications could benefit from an improved fault tolerance, as short disruptions due to fading or a briefly disturbed radio channel would also be handled by such a protocol. Applications that need constantly recorded data also work as always, with the additional benefit that this data are automatically transferred to a base station if in range. Thus, an inconvenient exchange of SD cards will have to be performed no longer, as an implicit synchronization is performed by the DTN protocol. A DTN protocol therefore is supposed be transparent to the user and handle all processes automatically. Connection setup, transmission, storing and caching of data, routing, etc. is performed by the DTN layer. The user or software developer just sends the desired data to the DTN layer which is responsible for all the rest.

They have presented two typical use cases for patient monitoring and activity detection that could take advantage of disruption tolerant protocols for data transmission. In fact, they claim that in many use cases in the area of AAL and healthcare, the overhead of DTN protocols would be exceeded by its benefits by far. Pure data collecting use cases can profit from the implicit synchronization. Online monitoring scenarios can benefit from the DTNs capability to also handle short disruptions or interference on the radio link; thus, in such scenarios the loss of data is avoided by the DTN protocol.

Delay Tolerant Network for Developing Countries (Rahman et al., 2013)

Originally DTN was developed to be used in inter planetary network. Later on researchers found it suitable for developing system to deliver public services to the people living in the remote part of the developing countries. On the other hand developing countries are largely incapable to consider the investment from a futuristic vision. In this situation to reach the people living in the last mile it is better to consider some communication architecture, which can absorb the limitations of the existing communication infrastructure and deliver the service in acceptable performance. In the last decade DTN was used in some similar situation with acceptable performance.

DTN supports interoperability of regional networks by accommodating long delay between and within regional networks. It also translates the varying characteristics of different regional networks. If we consider an isolated remote village as a network in a planet then the whole Bangladesh can be considered as a galaxy. Connecting those nodes may form an IPN. To reduce the cost of transportation from one planate (village) to another planate (village) we can use bus having a DTN box installed inside. The DTN box will have a WiFi router and look for presence of any nearby WiFi network opportunistically. If the detected network is a member of the same DTN, it establishes a connection. The DTN box maintains a routing table and identifies which bundles to be transferred in which DTN node or gateway. Immediately it sends the data relevant to this DTN box and receives any data sent from the node. After the bus moves out of the range of the WiFi signal the connection terminates and it starts sorting the data to create stack of bundles for the nodes on the way.

The villages in Bangladesh possess very few resource and infrastructural support. Although many people are capable to use computers but infrastructural challenges discourage them. In this context we consider a Village Information Center (VIC) in all villages of Bangladesh. VICs are public facilities owned by local government institutions, which delivers different ICT based services to the villagers in an affordable price. These VICs can be made self-sustained by increasing the number of essential services delivered through those.

IoB-DTN: A Lightweight DTN Protocol for Mobile IoT Applications to Smart Bike Sharing Systems (Zguira et al., 2018)

Public bicycle systems, also known as bicycle-sharing systems have been introduced as part of the urban transportation systems in several cities. They have been introduced in European cities in the mid-2000's and have spread worldwide. Such systems are today operating in more than 1,000 cities around the globe, with more than one million bicycles (Midgley, 2009). Here in this case study Zguira et al. (Zguira et al., 2018) have focused on the use of IoT in connected bicycles. More specifically, they considered a "smart" bike sharing system as follows:

- The bikes have embedded sensors and a 802.11p communication device (Zhao et al., 2014).
- Each bike periodically reads its sensors, generates a packet and stores it in its buffer.
- Each bike sharing station is equipped with a base station that is connected to the Internet. It has a 802.11p interface and acts as a fixed sink.
- All sinks are equivalent. The IoB-DTN protocol relays the packets until they reach one of the sink.

Delay Tolerant Networking (DTN) is an alternative paradigm. However, usual DTN protocols are not suitable to be applied out-of-the-box for the context of IoT because of their need for higher computing power or memory storage. Several DTN protocols for IoT have been studied, in particular by specializing each protocol to a given application. "IoB-DTN", a DTN-like protocol dedicated to the following characteristics of a connected bike scenario:

- Converge cast traffic: the data sensed by the bikes have to be collected on "the Internet" through a given set of sinks. There is no point-to-point traffic.
- Time bounded disconnection: at worst, each bike is getting back to a sharing station. All stations are sinks.
- Urban mobility: our mobility patterns are human generated, hence unpredictable and without known random properties to exploit.
- Energy and computing power constrained.

In particular, IoB-DTN can be seen as a "lightweight" version of several n-copy DTN protocols, since many features of these protocols are useless and removed, thus decreasing the memory required. No complex computations are performed either (e.g. statistics on the history of neighborhood).

CONCLUSION

While this new form of communication has created great interest in the research community, it is still in its infancy in terms of emerging communications architectures, algorithms, protocols, tools, modeling, and standards. It is therefore very promising to identify aspects for developing standards for DTNs. This would require to judiciously considering the various activities in a DTN for this purpose. Such an effort would finally aim at re-modeling of Delay Tolerant Networks in context of opportunistic networks.

REFERENCES

Abdelkader, T., Naik, K., Nayak, A., Goel, N., & Srivastava, V. (2016). Goe,l N., Srivastava, V. (2016).A performance comparison of delay-tolerant network routing protocols. *IEEE Network*, *30*(2), 46–53. doi:10.1109/MNET.2016.7437024

Acer, U., Giaccone, P., Hay, D., Neglia, G., & Tarapiah, S. (2012). Timely data delivery in a realistic bus network. *IEEE Transactions on Vehicular Technology*, *61*(3), 1251–1265. doi:10.1109/TVT.2011.2179072

Ahmed, K., Omar, M. H., & Hassan, S. (2016). Routing Strategies and Buffer Management in Delay Tolerant Networks, *Journal of Telecommunication. Electronic and Computer Engineering*, *8*(10), 139–143.

Al Noor, S., & Hasan, R. (2015). D-cloc: A delay tolerant cloud formation using context-aware mobile crowdsourcing. In *Cloud Computing Technology and Science (CloudCom), 2015 IEEE 7th International Conference on* (pp. 147-154). IEEE.

Amendola, D., Rango, F. D., Massri, K., & Vitaletti, A. (2014). Efficient neighbor discovery in RFID based devices over resource-constrained DTN networks. *ICC 14: Proceedings of the IEEE International Conference on Communications*, 3842–3847. 10.1109/ICC.2014.6883920

Ansa, G., Johnson, E., Cruickshank, H., & Sun, Z. (2010). Mitigating denial of service attacks in delay- and disruption-tolerant networks. *Proc. Int. Conf. Personal Satellite Services*, 221–234. 10.1007/978-3-642-13618-4_16

Asokan, N., Kostiainen, K., & Ginzboorg, P. (2007). Applicability of identity-based cryptography for disruption tolerant networking. *Proc. Of Mobi Opp*, 52-56.

Auzias, M., Mahéo, Y., & Raimbault, F. (2015). CoAP over BP for a delay tolerant internet of things. *FiCloud 15: Proceedings of the International Conference on Future Internet of Things and Cloud*, 118–123. 10.1109/FiCloud.2015.33

Benamar, N., Singh, K. D., Benamar, M., Ouadghiri, D. E., & Bonnin, J. M. (2014). Routing Protocols in Vehicular Delay Tolerant Networks: A Comprehensive Survey. *Computer Communications*, *48*, 141–158. doi:10.1016/j.comcom.2014.03.024

Broch, J., Maltz, D. A., Johnson, D. B., Hu, Y.,Jetcheva, J. (1998). A Performance Comparison of Multi-Hop Wireless Ad Hoc Network Routing Protocols. *ACM Mobicom.*

Bulut, E., Wang, Z., & Szymanski, B. K. (2009). Impact of social networks on delay tolerant routing. IEEE GLOBECOM '09. doi:10.1109/GLOCOM.2009.5425860

Burleigh, S., Hooke, A., Torgerson, L., Fall, K., Cerf, V., Durst, B., ... Weiss, H. (2003). Delay-tolerant networking: An approach to interplanetary internet. *Communications Magazine, IEEE, 41*(6), 128–136. doi:10.1109/MCOM.2003.1204759

Büsching, F., Bottazzi, M., Pöttner, W., & Wolf, L. (2013). *DTWBAN: Disruption Tolerant Wireless Body Area Networks in Healthcare Applications,*. In The International Workshop on e-Health Pervasive Wireless Applications and Services (eHPWAS'13), Lyon, France.

Cao, Y., & Sun, Z. (2012). Routing in delay/disruption tolerant networks: Taxonomy, Survey and Challenges. *IEEE Communications Surveys and Tutorials*, 1–24.

Cerf, V., Burleigh, S., Hooke, A., Torgerson, L., Durst, R., Scott, K., Fall, K., & Weiss, H. (2002). *Delay-Tolerant Network Architecture: The Evolving Interplanetary Internet.* draft-irtf-ipnrg-arch-01.txt.

Cerf, V., Burleigh, S., Hooke, A., Torgerson, L., Durst, R., Scott, K., Fall, K., & Weiss, H. (2007). *Delay Tolerant Networking Architecture.* Internet RFC 4838.

Demmer, M., & Fall, K. (2007). DTLSR: delay tolerant routing for developing regions. *Proceedings of the 1st ACM SIGCOMM Workshop on Networked Systems for Developing Regions*, 1–6. 10.1145/1326571.1326579

Dopico, N., Gutiérrez, A., & Zazo, S. (2011). Performance analysis of a delay tolerant application for herd localization. *Computer Networks, 55*(8), 1770–1783. doi:10.1016/j.comnet.2011.01.007

DTNRG. (2005). *Delay tolerant networking research group: dtn-interest mailing list archive.* Available from http:// mailman.dtnrg.org/pipermail/dtn-interest/2005-April/

Fall, K. (2003). A Delay-Tolerant Network Architecture for Challenged Internets. In *Proc. ACM SIGCOMM '03.* New York: ACM Press. 10.1145/863955.863960

Fall, K., & Farrell, S. (2008). DTN: An architectural retrospective. *J. IEEE Journal on Selected Areas in Communications, 26*(5), 828–836. doi:10.1109/JSAC.2008.080609

Fall, K., Hong, W., & Madden, S. (2003). *Custody Transfer for Reliable Delivery in Delay Tolerant Networks.* Technical Report IRB-TR-03-030, Intel Research Berkeley.

Farrell, S., & Cahill, V. (2006). *Delay-and disruption-tolerant networking.* Norwood, MA: Artech House.

Farrell, S., & Cahill, V. (2016). Security considerations in space and delay tolerant network*s. Proc. of SMC-IT'06.*

Farrell, S., Ramadas, M., & Burleigh, S. (2008c). *Transmission ProtocolSecurity Extensions.* Internet RFC 5327. Available: http://www.rfc-editor. org/rfc/rfc5327.txt

Farrell, S., Symington, S., & Weiss, H. (2006). *Delay-Tolerant Networking Security Overview.* draft-irtf-dtnrg-sec-overview-01.txt.

Farrell, S., Symington, S., Weiss, H., & Lovell, P. (2008a). *Delay- Tolerant Networking Security Overview.* draft-irtf-dtnrg-sec-overview-04.txt.

Farrell, S., Symington, S., Weiss, H., & Lovell, P. (2008b). *Bundle Security Protocol Specification.* draft-irtf-dtnrg-sec-overview-04.txt.

Fathima, G., & Wahidabanu, R. (2011). Integrating Buffer Management with Epidemic Routing, in in Delay Tolerant Networks. *Journal of Computational Science, 7*(7), 1038–1045. doi:10.3844/jc-ssp.2011.1038.1045

Gao, L., Luan, T. H., Yu, S., Zhou, W., & Liu, B. (2017). FogRoute: DTN-based data dissemination model in fog computing. IEEE Internet Things J., 4(1), 225–235.

Grundy, A. (2012). *Congestion control framework for delay-tolerant communications.* University of Nottingham.

Hu, V. C., Ferraiolo, D. F., & Kuhn, D. R. (2006). *Assessment of access control systems.* U.S. Nat. Inst. Standards Technol., Interagency Rep. 7316.

Isento, J., Rodrigues, J., Dias, J., Paula, M. C. J., & Vinel, A. (2013). Vehicular delay-tolerant networks - A novel solution for vehicular communications. *IEEE Intelligent Transportation Systems Magazine, 5*(4), 10–19. doi:10.1109/MITS.2013.2267625

Jain, S., & Chawla, M. (2014). Survey of buffer management policies for delay tolerant networks. *Journal of Engineering, 7,* 1–7.

Jain, S., Fall, K., & Patra, R. (2004). Routing in a delay tolerant network. *Computer Communication Review, 34*(4), 145–158. doi:10.1145/1030194.1015484

Johnson, E., Ansa, G., Cruickshank, H., & Sun, Z. (2010). Access control framework for delay/disruption tolerant networks. *Proc. Int. Conf. Personal Satellite Services,* 249–264. 10.1007/978-3-642-13618-4_18

Juang, P., Oki, H., Wang, Y., Martonosi, M., Peh, L., & Rubenstein, D. (2002). Energy-Efficient Computing for Wildlife Tracking: Design Trade-Offs and Early Experiences with Zebranet. *SIGARCH Comp. Architure News, 30*(Oct), 96–107. doi:10.1145/635506.605408

Kate, A., Zaverucha, G. M., & Hengartner, U. (2007). Anonymity and security in delay tolerant networks. *Proc. of SecureComm'07.* 10.1109/SECCOM.2007.4550373

Khabbaz, M., Assi, C., & Fawaz, W. (2011). Disruption-tolerant networking: A comprehensive survey on recent developments and persisting challenges. *IEEE Commun. Surveys Tuts.,* 1–34.

Laat, C., Gross, G., Gommans, L., Vollbrecht, J., & Spence, D. (2012). *Generic AAA architecture.* Internet RFC 2903. Available: http://www.rfc-editor. org/rfc/rfc2903.txt

Lindgren, A., & Doria, A. (2012). *Probabilistic Routing in Intermittently Connected Networks.* Internet-Draft, draft-irtf-dtnrg-prophet.

Loukas, G., & Oke, G. (2010). Protection against denial of service attacks: A survey. *The Computer Journal, 53*(7), 1020–1037. doi:10.1093/comjnl/bxp078

Mansuri, S. (2013). *Performance Analysis of Epidemic Routing Protocol for Buffer Management Policies in DTNs using ONE.* Int. J. Eng. Assoc.

Mehta, N., & Shah, M. (2014). Performance of Efficient Routing Protocol in Delay Tolerant Network: A Comparative Survey. *International Journal of Future Generation Communication and Networking, 7*(1), 151–158. doi:10.14257/ijfgcn.2014.7.1.15

Midgley, P. (2009). The role of smart bike-sharing systems in urban mobility. *Journeys, 2*(1), 23–31.

Mobile Ad-Hoc and DTN Networks at IPCAS Lab. (n.d.). Available: http://www.ece.gatech.edu/research/labs/WCCL/DTN2.html

Nuevo, L., Valles, D. R., & Pallares, R. M. (2015). OIoT: A platform to manage opportunistic IoT communities. *Proceedings of the International Conference on Intelligent Environments*, 104–111. 10.1109/IE.2015.22

Ott, J., & Kutscher, D. (2004). Drive-Thru Internet: IEEE 802.11b for Automobile Users. *Proceedings - IEEE INFOCOM.*

Palazzi, C. E., & Bujari, A. (2012). Social-aware delay tolerant networking for mobile-to-mobile files sharing. *International Journal of Communication Systems, 25*(10), 1281–1299. doi:10.1002/dac.1324

Pentland, A., Fletcher, R., & Hasson, A. (2004). DakNet: Rethinking connectivity in developing nations. *Computer, 37*(1), 78–83. doi:10.1109/MC.2004.1260729

Rahman, A., Nakanishi, T., & Fukuda, A. (2013). Delay tolerant network for developing countries. *International Conference on Informatics, Electronics and Vision (ICIEV).* 10.1109/ICIEV.2013.6572625

Rashid, S., Ayub, Q., Zahid, M., & Abdullah, A. (2011). E-drop: An effective drop buffer management policy for DTN routing protocols. *Int. J. Computer Applications*, 118-121.

Raveneau, P., & Rivano, H. (2015). *Tests Scenario on DTN for IOT III Urbanet collaboration.* Inria - Research Centre Grenoble – Rhone-Alpes; INRIA, Technical Report RT-0465.

Recommendations on a strategy for space internetworking. (2008). Report of the Interagency Operations Advisory Group, The Space Internetworking Strategy Group (SISG). Retrieved from: https://cwe.ccsds.org/ioag/Final%20Products/SISG%20Report%20v1.4%20FINAL.pdf

Saltzer, J., & Clark, D. (1984). End-to-end Arguments in System Design. *ACM Transactions on Computer Systems, 2*(4), 277-288.

Samuel, H., & Zhaung, W. (2010). Preventing unauthorized messages and achieving end-to-end security in delay tolerant heterogeneous wireless networks. *Journal of Communication, 5*(2), 152–163.

Scott, K., & Burleigh, S. (2007). *Bundle Protocol Specification.* Internet RFC5050.

Seligman, M., Fall, K., & Mundur, P. (2006). Alternative custodians for congestion control in delay tolerant networks. In *Proc. ACM SIGCOMM Workshop on Challenged Networks*. New York, NY: ACM Press. 10.1145/1162654.1162660

Spyropoulos, T., Psounis, K., & Raghavendra, C. S. (2005). Spray-and-Wait: Efficient routing scheme for intermittently connected mobile networks. *ACM SIGCOMM Workshop on Delay Tolerant Network (WDTN)*. 10.1145/1080139.1080143

Spyropoulos, T., Psounis, K., & Raghavendra, C. S. (2008a). Efficient routing in intermittently connected mobile networks: The single-copy case. *IEEE/ACM Transactions on Networking, 16*(1), 63–76. doi:10.1109/TNET.2007.897962

Spyropoulos, T., Psounis, K., & Raghavendra, C. S. (2008b). Efficient routing in intermittently connected mobile networks: The multiple-copy case. *IEEE/ACM Transactions on Networking, 16*(1), 77–90. doi:10.1109/TNET.2007.897964

Trono, E., Arakava, Y., Tamai, M., & Yasumoto, H. (2015). DTN MapEx: Disaster area mapping through distributed computing over a Delay Tolerant Network. *Eighth International Conference on Mobile Computing and Ubiquitous Networking (ICMU)*, 179–184. 10.1109/ICMU.2015.7061063

Warthman, F. (2012). *Delay-and Disruption-Tolerant Networks (DTNs) Version 2.0*. Warthman Associates.

Wood, L., Ivancic, W., Eddy, W., Stewart, D., Northam, J., & Jackson, C. (2008). Investigating operation of the Internet in orbit: Five years of collaboration around CL EO. *IEEE Communications Society Satellite and Space Communications Technical Committee Newsletter, 18*(2), 10-11.

Xu, Y., Mahendran, V., & Radhakrishnan, S. (2016). *Internet of hybrid opportunistic things: a novel framework for interconnecting IoTs and DTNs*. IEEE Conference on Computer Communications Workshops (INFOCOM WKSHPS), San Francisco, CA.

Zguira, Y., Rivano, H., & Meddeb, A. (2018). *IoB-DTN: a lightweight DTN protocol for mobile IoT Applications to smart bike sharing systems. WD2018, 10th IFIP Wireless Days, April 2018*, Dubai, UAE.

Zhang, P., Sadler, C. M., Lyon, S. A., & Martonosi, M. (2004). *Hardware design experiences in ZebraNet. In Proc of the 2nd IntConf on Embedded Networked Sensor Systems* (pp. 227–238). New York: ACM.

Zhao, Z., & Cheng, X. (2014). *IEEE 802.11 p for vehicle-to-vehicle (v2v) communications*. IEEE.

Zhou, J., Cao, Z., Dong, X., & Vasilakos, A. V. (2017). Security and privacy for cloud-based IoT: Challenges. *IEEE Communications Magazine, 55*(1), 26–33. doi:10.1109/MCOM.2017.1600363CM

Zhu, H. (2009). *Security in Delay Tolerant Networks* (PhD Thesis). University of Waterloo.

KEY TERMS AND DEFINITIONS

Buffer Management: The buffers available in routers are valuable resources. A router uses them for storing incoming packets to forward them later. Due to the large number of packets that arrive in a router and limited buffer size, not all packets can be saved at the router. The quality of buffer management can define the quality of service provided to the customers. The buffer management module takes care of managing buffers shared by a number of modules and interfaces within the network layer. The default "best-effort" packet-forwarding service of IP is typically implemented in routers by a single, fixed-size, FIFO queue shared by all incoming packets.

Delay-Tolerant Networks: Delay-tolerant networking (DTN) is an approach to computer network architecture that seeks to address the technical issues in heterogeneous networks that may lack continuous network connectivity. DTN is the key internet engineering technology needed for interplanetary networking. DTN is actually a suite of experimental protocols developed by members of the Delay & Disruption Tolerant Networking Research Group. Examples of such networks are those operating in mobile or extreme terrestrial environments, or planned networks in space.

DTN Architecture: The DTN architecture provides a common method for interconnecting heterogeneous gateways or proxies that employ store- and-forward message routing to overcome communication disruptions. It provides services similar to electronic mail, but with enhanced naming, routing, and security capabilities. The architecture embraces the concepts of occasionally-connected networks that may suffer from frequent partitions and that may be comprised of more than one divergent set of protocols or protocol families. The basis for this architecture lies with that of the interplanetary internet, which focused primarily on the issue of deep space communication in high-delay environments.

Opportunistic Networks: An opportunistic network is a network of wirelessly connected nodes. Communication range between two connected nodes is not further than walking distance. Nodes are connected only temporarily, and the network topology may change due to node mobility or node activation and node deactivation respectively. The network provides at least the following functionalities: Node discovery. A network node is able to discover other network nodes in direct communication range. One-hop message exchange. A node is able to send and receive arbitrary data to or from any other node in direct communication range.

Security: Network security is the security provided to a network from unauthorized access and risks. It is the duty of network administrators to adopt preventive measures to protect their networks from potential security threats. Computer networks that are involved in regular transactions and communication within the government, individuals, or business require security. The most common and simple way of protecting a network resource is by assigning it a unique name and a corresponding password.

Chapter 21
The Impact of Internet of Things Self–Security on Daily Business and Business Continuity

Hasan Emre Yılmaz
BTCTurk.com, Turkey

Altan Sirel
BTCTurk.com, Turkey

M. Fevzi Esen
Istanbul Medeniyet University, Turkey

ABSTRACT

The number of devices operating on IoTs has exceeded billions globally. This chapter aims to examine the cyber security risks of such systems with widespread use and investigate some IoT vulnerabilities. It examines the effects of these vulnerabilities on business life and personal life, and the precautions to be taken to eliminate them. In addition, the regulations and measures to be applied at the state level is discussed. The safe use of IoT systems cannot be achieved solely by individual awareness. An awareness and sense of responsibility in the manufacturing layer is also a must. This chapter investigates the reasons behind the lack of security precautions taken in the manufacturing phase of IoT devices and suggests solutions. It also discusses the details of malwares such as Mirai, whose targets are mainly IoT vulnerabilities.

DOI: 10.4018/978-1-5225-8407-0.ch021

INTRODUCTION

With the growth of Internet bandwidth, many new technologies have emerged which have profound effects on daily life. These new technologies, which facilitate not only our business life but also our social life, are based on high speed internet. Evolution of 3G and 4G mobile internet speeds have already exceeded terrestrial line speeds. Hence, the geographical / physical conditions in which terrestrial lines have difficulties are also overcome. It turned out that the Internet is not just a server/client specific requirement, and that other 'things' can also easily communicate over the Internet. Thus, the concept of 'Internet of Things' (IoT) has emerged.

According to Gartner (2017), it is estimated that up to 8.4 billion IoT devices are connected to the Internet in 2017, since the day a remote controlled coke machine was converted to IoT. Security of IoT devices are often ignored by both manufacturers and end users as a result of their price and their intended purpose of use. The significance of IoT security was realized more heavily after Mirai malware which is a malicious software that creates botnet networks using IoT weaknesses (known as the IoT Hunter), started to create extremely large botnets to carry out the biggest DDoS (Distributed Denial of Service) attacks recorded in history. Mirai showed how dangerous an IoT device, which is configured in the manufacturing phase and has a selling price of $10, can be.

Mirai has performed the largest DDoS attacks ever recorded using IoT devices in its botnet, devices it already confiscated. In 2016, scale of DDoS attack, realized using 175,000 IoT devices, was measured at 620 Gbps. Developers of Mirai released the source code of the malware around the same date, making Mirai a framework that can be used and developed by everyone. Another large attack targeted DNS service provider Dyn. Thus, Twitter, Netflix and other large organizations that use Dyn, were also victims of Mirai (Woolf, 2016).

Purdy & Davarzani (2015) claims that the IoT triggers the emerge of new market segments and business models. IoT can accelerate productivity, design, security and efficiency through innovation in circural economies. These smart systems cause changes in the way of business by exceeding the standard limits business models for firms (Schuh et al., 2014). With highly flexible and centrally controlled smart devices, product – service – material and information will be adapted to the real time processes by vertical integration between or inside the coorporations. The organizational structure of companies and interaction types of smart devices, sensors and machines classified the tasks and goals of autonomous systems by implementing security and privacy protocols (Khan et al., 2018).

Securing IoT connected networks is as important as ensuring IoT's own security (IoT's-Communication Security). For the security of individually used IoT's (camera, TV, baby radio, fitness t-shirt, smart Jacuzzi, smart home systems etc.), it may be advisable to connect the IoT to the internet only when it is used, or even to activate it only when necessary. An IoT that is 'on' even though it is not in use, is always a target for the exploiters. Timed on and off features of some IoTs can be helpful in this context (Pan et al., 2016). Furthermore, network structures of IoTs used in a large network (companies, factories, public spaces) should be physically isolated completely from the corporate network, if possible. Separating networks with VLANs in some implementations is also an acceptable security measure under certain circumstances.

The vulnerabilities of internal software are as important as the security of the networks where IoTs are located. It is rarely possible to have a firewall or a packet filtering software inside these devices since they're limited in terms of processor, storage and RAM in order to reduce costs. The urge of the producer to release its product -which has a high market demand- without any further research, surpasses the urge to spend more time on its security in the manufacturing phase. Not only the products, but also the product lines such as SCADA systems should be considered as IoTs; thus, they contain the same risks. Security patches of a software that controls a plastic injection machine are often ignored. Even if we assume that operating system updates have been made, vulnerabilities need to be regularly monitored, reported and patched so that the software provided by the manufacturer (or from third party providers) is not affected by current cyber security risks and attacks. In cases like IP cameras and smart watches -which targets end users and have low prices- and in industrial IoT devices, the focus of the manufacturer is mainly on the well-functioning of the device. It is a fact that the security of the software provided externally by the manufacturer and network-connected objects is often neglected and leads to the birth of hunters like Mirai.

This chapter is organized as follows: Section 1 discusses the expectations both on user side and manufacturing side of IoT business. Furthermore it introduces several recent and popular attacks realized either on IoT devices or by using them. Section 2 explains the vulnerabilities of IoT devices that cause these kinds of attacks whereas Section 3 brings up the solutions to IoT's security that are being discussed in the literature.

IOT'S SELF SECURITY

The most difficult and important layer of IoT security precautions is IoT's self-security. In the case of IoT's own security, the first topic that comes to mind is the operating system and the applications running on the OS in order to ensure the proper functioning of the IoT. Both should be monitored and updated regularly by the manufacturer. Regular updates on these applications and the OS itself are often ignored; thus, leaving the user alone with potential risks. Even if we assume that IoT safety at this point is a problem that must be solved by the manufacturer, the preferences of the end users should also influence the producers to make this issue more serious.

Mirai seizes IoT systems with dictionary attack as one of the oldest attack method. A simple work flow of Mirai is shown in Figure 1. Changing the default password with a strong one, which is configured by the manufacturer, can be considered sufficient enough to avoid IoT hunters like Mirai. Manufacturers, who set simple username/password combinations to ease the configuration process (almost all manufacturers choose this method), can aid their customers simply by encouraging them to change the password during/after the first configuration. These simple or complex measures are necessary for IoT's Self Security and must be provided by the manufacturer.

Choosing to buy IoT products of major manufacturers is a safe zone for end-users. Major manufacturers pay more attention to possible security vulnerabilities that will tarnish their brands as they carry commercial interest as well as reputation concerns. Hence, they invest more in this issue to avoid risks. Many major IoT producers also suffer from vulnerabilities and face exploits related to these vulnerabilities. When it comes to cyber security, it is not possible to achieve 100% security, but it is very important that, in the face of a cyber security incident, manufacturers are quick to take precautions, publish patches and update the software. O'Donnell (2018) discusses the success of Swann -an USA based security firm- to quickly react to a vulnerability in their cameras patched the device to fix the problem, which allows attackers to monitor remotely through the camera. Bauer et al. (2017) are others who believe that cost is a main issue which differs major manufacturers from mid-level manufacturers when it comes to employ security measurements in IoTs. Bauer et al. (2017) claim that the customers of mid-level IoT producers

Figure 1. Functioning of Mirai (Figure is formed by authors)

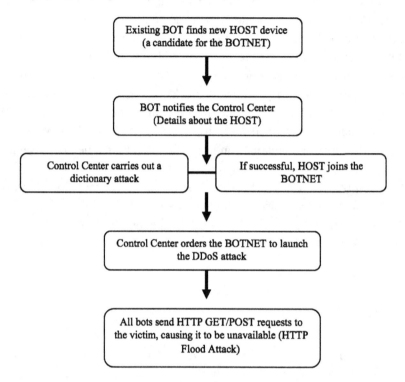

are unwilling to pay for device security even though they demand employment of security measurements. Thus, the manufacturer is asked to implement a mechanism that he is forced not to expect any profits.

Most of the IOTs are delivered to the end-user with a preload that can be configured very easily; so that the users can start using the device without any technical support required. Users should not only be choosing the right manufacturer, but they should have some kind of awareness about the IoT device when configuring and using it. It is inevitable to know and implement very basic security measures such as not using easily predictable passwords or making sure that IoTs management panel is not open to Internet.

Not only end-user awareness, but the precautions that must be taken by the manufacturer for IoT safety are also important in many respects. There are many examples where a malware that targets IoT devices has caused serious damage to country economies. Stuxnet is a good instance for these malwares. Stuxnet, which US and Israeli aggressors have developed to disrupt Iran's nuclear power plant operations, has been unveiled in June 2010. It is one of the largest and most popular IoT/SCADA malwares in history, scanning the Siemens Step7 software in the infected PLC control circuits and manipulating the system by injecting malicious code in the case of its existence. On the other hand, another feature that makes Stuxnet so interesting is that unlike traditional malwares, it targets computers that are not connected to the Internet. Shakarian et al. (2013) discuss that before the emergence of Stuxnet, many believed that cyber-war against an industrial control system was out of the question. In addition, they acknowledge that infecting a specific control system (Control System of Iranian Nuclear Facility) was the sole purpose of the virus and this may be one of the reasons it wasn't caught or noticed until after it succeeded. Stuxnet developers, who knew SCADA systems are used in closed networks that are not connected to the Internet, have designed Stuxnet to spread via USB flash drives and not via email or network. This feature of Stuxnet reaffirms the importance of IoT's self-security. Fildes (2010) states that Stuxnet virus targets the systems that are traditionally not connected to the internet for security reasons. In addition, the loss of business continuity and financial losses resulting from the DDoS attacks, using hacked IoTs, are very high.

Following the DDoS attack on his own blog site, which was realized with 24.000 IoT devices that belongs to a Mirai Botnet and which exceeded 620Gbps; Brian Krebs (2018) defines the reason why IoT manufacturers do not take security precautions that cause their devices to be used in such attacks, by the term externality and demonstrates "environmental pollution" as a similar example. Krebs (2018) also indicates that victims on such Botnet attacks have caused six or seven zero figures losses and that the costs for the perpetrators (for organizing the attack) are between $0- $100, while owners of IoT devices used in the attack have only a few dollars of losses due to bandwidth usage and energy loss. While the total cost of energy and bandwidth usage in the attack against is $ 323,973.95, the cost per device is $13.50 when it is divided the total cost by 24.000 -which is the number of Botnet member IoT devices used in the attack. According to Mims (2017) the hosts, whose IoT devices are part of the Botnet are secondary targets, used to attack the primary target, the real victim. Mims (2017) also claims that these Botnets generate an amount of data much greater than a single machine would be able to. Krebs (2018) supports his reasoning with the arguments of the researchers (Fong et al., 2018). According to Fong et al. (2018) explain misguided incentives of the IoT security problem on both sides as follows:

- Manufacturers often run the devices on simple open source based operating systems and take minimum safety precautions. Some methods applied in order to facilitate configuration and repair process' cause security vulnerabilities (e.g. default username/password).
- Consumers who expect IoT devices to be user-friendly, often do not have the technical knowledge to protect or update the device, even if they are competent to use it. Users who cannot distinguish the difference in safety quality naturally prefer to buy cheaper products.

Given the fact that users of the IoT devices that are used in a DDoS attack are not affected by the attack (if we ignore small cost caused by the bandwidth usage and the energy loss) and considering Fong et al (2018) arguments above, it can be better understood why the manufacturers try to keep the safety on the backplane and pull the cost down as much as possible. Chadd (2018) discusses a new IoT Botnet called Satori and claims that even low-level cyber criminals can launch an attack through it without having any struggle. But, Fong and et al. (2018) also approaches this issue from a different perspective. They assume that monthly fixed bandwidth charges may increase in the near future, while assuming that costs incurred due to unauthorized use are difficult to be recognized by IoT users as long as the monthly usage quota is not exceeded. The rationale behind this thinking is that unauthorized use consumes the bandwidth of Internet Service Providers, even if they don't cause the individual quota to fill up; and as a result, IPS firms will be forced to increase their fixed charges in order to balance their economy. As this will directly affect the IoT users (or all Internet users) manufacturers may want to spend more time and money on IoT's security measurements for minimizing the amount of unauthorized usage.

Costigan & Lindstrom (2016) state that the use of IoT will become more and more widespread. They claim that developments in other fields will affect the development of IoT and discuss the deficiencies in IoT security and the security layers that are likely to be developed in the future.

According to Costigan & Lindstrom (2016), there are three main reasons why industry-oriented experts need to be closely involved in the development of IoT: First is the fact that IoTs are a great contributor to economic development. According to McKinsey (2018), in 2025 the annual contribution of the IoT to the economy is expected to be around $ 2.7- $ 6.2 trillion. The second reason is IoT addresses many other fields and contributes to interdisciplinary development. IoT technology has a growing use especially in healthcare, infrastructure and public sector; and people will encounter concepts such as smart cities or personalized health-care services in the near future as a result of developments both in IoT and these other sectors. The third reason is, IoT has a wide range of use that cannot be ignored. If not given importance, such a widely used technology can cause unintended/unexpected consequences in fields such as public service or infrastructure. After discussing the importance of IoT with their reasoning, Costigan & Lindstrom (2016) states that the possible future of the industry by explaining what trends the IOT world expects.

In the near future of IOT, there are three important trends: First is the expansion rate that cannot be avoided. According to same study of Costigan & Lindstrom (2016), this rate will continue to increase as the number of IoT use increased by 30% in 2015 compared to the previous year. A research published by Gartner (2014) underlines that, between 2015 and 2020, the use of IOT is expected to increase by around 500% globally (Table 1). According to another report from Gartner (2017) may have slightly lowered estimates of total IOT use in 2020, but if we look from the first report's publication date to today, we can say that their estimates are still accurate and expect the IoT usage to increase widely. If these estimates are even a little closer to reality, there will be significant changes in the society's habit of collecting, displaying and processing information. Weber (2015) claims that the spreading rate of IOT will be affected by two separate developments:

- Developments in the fields such as communication protocols, energy stock, microelectromechanical systems (MEMS) and processor power.
- Developments that will occur in areas such as nanotechnology, artificial intelligence, or data intelligence that will affect the applicability of IOT.

The second IOT trend is the widely emerging machine communications (M2M). The steady increase in the instantaneous communication while monitoring or processing, causes the relationship between the devices to be multidimensional, complex, stochastic and random. Given this situation, the control and security of specific relationships between devices can become complex and unpredictable. In fact, it is now widely recognized that the MQTT protocol, which is the most common use for IOT communications, has security vulnerabilities. Regarding MQTT -which is a publish/service protocol that runs

Table 1. IoT devices per sector in billions by years (Gartner, 2014)

Category	2015	2020	Percentage Increase
Automotive	372	3.511	944%
Consumer	2.875	13.173	458%
Generic Business	624	5.159	827%
Vertical Business	1.009	3.164	314%
Total	**4.880**	**25.007**	**512%**

on top of TCP/IP- Olzak (2017) underscores that the protocol cannot provide security if it is deployed with basic standards, so it must be supported by TLS or similar mechanisms during its implementation. This is a responsibility that has to be met by the manufacturer, who is responsible for making the risk analysis and proper configuration.

The third issue is the increase in the number of machine-generated data, which will arise due to the widespread use of IOT and M2M; and consequently, the changes to be made in the procedures for obtaining, processing, storing and sharing the data. According to a study published by IDC Digital Universe (2012), 15-times increase in the number of machine-generated data is expected by 2020. The survey also underlines that, if this estimate becomes a fact, 40% of all data on the earth will be machine-generated when we come to 2020.

While billions of IoT devices are in use, the security of the devices has a quite minimal importance, especially on the manufacturer side. The lack of motivation of manufacturers - caused by the need to meet the increasing demand while keeping the cost low- to give sufficient importance to the security of the devices and the balance between personal rights and security measures are two possible security problems that can spawn as a result of the IoT revolution. The developments in the areas such as healthcare, nanotechnology will also increase the use and dissemination of IOT.

THE VULNERABILITIES OF IOT'S SELF-SECURITY

Firmware

Akatyew & James (2017) discuss that IoT networks are facing the same vulnerabilities as traditional computer networks However since they are often in interaction with the physical world, they are also distressed against physical threats. Hence, one can consider different vulnerability vectors and exploitation points in many different IoT types. However, the most common weakness of IoT's self-security is strictly the usage of default usernames and passwords. The Mirai malware, mentioned through this article, is a good example to understand the details of the default username and password vulnerability and to understand IoT's self-security concept. Mirai's primary goal is to find and capture vulnerable IoT devices (as in all IoT malwares). It uses the "Dictionary Attack" model, one of the earliest attack methods, to infiltrate IoT devices, and infiltrates the IoT system by trying out the usernames and passwords shown in Table 2.

Despite the simple method it uses, Mirai is a harmful software worth considering and examining. After finding the IoT devices it can infect and exploit, it first stops the entire remote management services to prevent the user of the product from accessing the device:

killer_kill_by_port(htons(23)) // Kill telnet service
killer_kill_by_port(htons(22)) // Kill SSH service
killer_kill_by_port(htons(80)) // Kill HTTP service

After the services are killed (disabled) the user won't be able to access to device to disrupt Mirai's agenda. Mirai then performs a much more interesting act. It checks whether or not the IoT device is infected by "Anime", which is also an IoT malware that can be deemed as an opponent to Mirai. If the IoT is infected by "Anime", Mirai goes on and destroys it. Thus, gets rid of the competition. With just

Table 2. Username/password combinations used in Mirai's dictionary attack (Cluley, 2016)

Username	Password	Username	Password	Username	Password
root	xc3511	support	support	admin	smcadmin
root	vizxv	root	(none)	admin	1111
root	admin	admin	password	root	666666
admin	admin	root	root	root	password
root	888888	root	12345	root	1234
root	xmhdipc	user	user	root	klv123
root	default	admin	(none)	Administr	ator admin
root	juantech	root	pass	service	service
root	123456	admin	admin1234	supervisor	supervisor
root	54321	root	1111	guest	guest
guest	12345	root	anko	admin	1234
guest	12345	root	zlxx.	admin	12345
admin1	password	root	7ujMko0vizxv	admin	54321
tech	tech	admin	meinsm	admin	123456
admin	7ujMko0admin	root	jvbzd	admin	1111111

a simple traditional dictionary attack, malicious software that can take control of the entire device can use it in any way they want. This is how large botnets, such as the ones caused the biggest DDoS attacks in history (as mentioned before), are created.

Ammar et al. (2018) claim that the better part of IoT frameworks haven't still handled some of the common security vulnerabilities. To prove their point, they address commercial of the shelf microprocessors that are deployed on almost every existing IoT device. Ammar et al. (2018) state that these devices (microprocessors) are deployed without any hardware security support and state of the art IoT frameworks are not taking these device into consideration when they're implementing security measurements. They also point out the fact that these microprocessors are enduring and that they may outlive the lifetime of current encryption algorithms. Furthermore, Ammar et al. (2018) acknowledge that IoTs using cloud services may face indirect security challenges, especially if they have no backup plan. Although this may not be a vulnerability of the IoT device, a successful denial of service (DoS) attack on the cloud service in use can cause the availability of the IoT to be corrupted.

Omitola & Wills (2018) are others who are concerned with IoT security and they suggest four vulnerability points concerning IoTs:

- Manufacturers prefer low energy consumption in order to obtain long battery life. Thus, IoTs that are using cryptography are forced to use encryptions algorithms that are computationally simple.
- Most IoTs are designed to have low cost and this causes deficiency in processing, memory and operating system.
- IoTs are often intended to have a long lifetime which would lead them to outlive the security mechanisms from the time when the device is designed, if not updated regularly. According to

Omitola & Wills (2018), long lifetime could also be a risk if a vulnerability discovered can't be patched within a given IoT endpoint.

- Vast majority of IoT devices are physically reachable to the attackers which leaves all hardware components and interfaces at risk.

Sha et al. (2018) point out the fact that in order to achieve low cost, typical IoT devices run an 8-bit or 16-bit system. They claim that current security solutions are not designed to work on low capable devices. Manufacturers use cloud services to provide storage to IoTs, when needed. Cloud services are relatively more economical and efficient solutions. For example, instead of putting a 2GB of storage in a smart clock, a smart watch manufacturer would prefer to provide 2GB of storage space on self-developed or rented cloud services. This strategy will not only reduce the cost of the product due to lowering the hardware costs, but it will also provide the advantage of not suffering data loss in unexpected events (stolen, broken, etc.) - which can be used as a market strategy. The Apple Icloud leakage in August 2014 is not exactly an example of this, but it points out that cloud security is another issue to be taken seriously when considering IoT's self-security.

Apple, the world's first company to reach a total value of $1 Trillion (Davies, 2018), leaked a number of obscene photos of several famous people in 2014, because of the lack of a simple captcha protection. The quality and security of Cloud services should also be considered as one of the factors affecting IoT security, and the Cloud service of an IoT product should be carefully examined before buying it. End users must choose IoT products that are using reliable cloud services. Another common potential vulnerability of IoTs is the data communication methods. IoT's data transfer methods are usually done with clear-text protocols, instead of more secure method. Hence, not only IoT authentication/authorization information, but also very sensitive information that varies according to the work done by IoT are likely to be leaked. For instance, when a smart wristwatch holding health information transfers its data to the cloud, this sensitive information can easily be passed down to unwanted third parties, if the protocol it uses for data transfer is not secure.

The management and configuration interfaces of these devices are usually presented to the end user in the form of a web interface. There exist several known vulnerabilities in these web interfaces. Due to the potential vulnerabilities in IoT's management panel (Cross Site Scripting, SQL Injection, etc.), IoTs become targets of both botnets and individual attackers. The fact that these management interfaces are open to Internet, leads to the possibility of infiltration of malwares like Mirai.

Operating System

One of the most basic security needs of any computer that runs on an operating system, whether it be a personal computer, an IoT or a large server; is the need of updating. The need for updating is an essential requirement for any device that has a network connection, not just devices that store sensitive data. Some manufacturers believe that they don't face any risk because their devices don't require any internet or network connection. Thus, they think that all the requirements for the software are fulfilled when they obtain high functionality. However, as we can recall from the Stuxnet example, IOTs (and, of course, all devices that host an operating system) do not need to be connected to the Internet in order to be affected by a malicious software. If we assume that IoT devices that are not connected to the Internet / network are no longer targeted, we can list the reasons why IoTs with Internet/network connections need to be updated:

- **For the operating system (OS) not to be affected by new attack vectors:** Every smart device has an operating system. These operating systems are mostly open source, Linux variants unless the devices have very specific purposes, and the attack vectors that apply to these operating systems also apply to IoT devices. Recent vulnerabilities in openSSL and openSSH, the most popular open source applications have shown how critical this issue can get. With the emergence of heartbleed vulnerability on the openSSL application, all devices that use the corresponding version of this application (IoT devices, servers, security devices) have become exploitable, and the instant RAM information of every vulnerable device and all the passwords and sensitive data contained therein can be read.
- In order to prevent the application running on the OS from being affected by new attack vectors.

Open Source Applications Embedded to the Device

Whether IoT or not, every device that serves a purpose has an operating system and an application developed for that purpose. For instance, a storage device on an IP camera is provided with an operating system for opening and managing the system, and a software to retrieve the image from the lens, process it properly and save it over the network. This may be a software developed by the manufacturer, or an open source software commonly used by the manufacturers. When buying an IP camera, one does not pay attention to the details of the software the manufacturer employs. While products below a certain price range prefer software co-used by each manufacturer, slightly larger manufacturers and well-known brands offer devices that has their own software running on them. At this point two different risk categories arise:

- Security updates required for co-used software are at the initiative of the developer. As these software are offered to the manufacturers with very low prices (or even free), no software updates are offered in most cases.
- Major manufacturers and well-known brands only conduct security checks and updates of their own software. This is, once again, the initiative of the company.

IoT's operating system and software updates are entirely at the manufacturer/developer initiative in both cases. One of the most interesting IoT types that developed lately is perhaps the wearable IoTs. Of course, this is one of the IoT types that suffer the most from data privacy breaches as a result its usage area. Like every IoT, wearable IoTs are also produced in a rush, and has the potential vulnerabilities available in every IoT. Three essential vulnerabilities of wearable IoTs are described below. These vulnerabilities may also apply to other IoT types as well. Figure 2 explains these vulnerabilities:

- **Unencrypted Storage and Communication (Figure 2 - Issue A):** In order to lower the cost; IoT devices such as smart bracelets, smart watches etc. store the data they will later send to phones or cloud services in an unencrypted state. It is highly probable that the data stored here will be confiscated by third parties in case of an intended/unintended attack. For example, if these products are stolen/lost, the sensitive data such as health-care information, can easily be passed to third parties intentionally or accidentally. In addition, due to the ability of these devices to record audio and video, not only health information but also any stored or synced data (address book, notes etc.) are in the same risk class.

Open Source Libraries Used on Applications on the Device

- **3rd Party Applications (Figure 2 - Issue B):** IoT manufacturers can share sensitive personal data they collect via their hardware with a cloud service, or send it to mobile phones and store it in an application. These applications, which are used to store and process sensitive data, are 'generic' mobile applications commonly used by manufacturers selling cheaper IOT devices. Evidently, most of these applications are not subjected to a regulation on how to store and where to store the data they collect. In addition to the storage and transfer standards of data held in these applications, it is also a serious question whether or not they share these data with 3rd parties. The manufacturers have no control over how these applications use the data once they've collected it.

- **Cloud Services (Figure 2 - Issue C):** The data that wearable IoTs do not want to store for a long time due to different reasons are stored in the cloud services, which reduces the cost and saves time for the processes that require processing power such as analysis and reporting. However, ensuring the security of these cloud services and the software running on these services, keeping them under constant updating and to regularly monitoring, is a kind of activity which IoT producers do not want to spend time and money. Besides the risks that the data stored in Cloud services face, the transportation model of the data transferred to these services is highly crucial in terms of the privacy of the stored data.

ENSURING IOT'S SELF-SECURITY

In this section, possible solutions to security problems aforementioned is discussed. It is certain that IoT device users should have some kind of awareness about the security of their device; but as noted in many places in the text, the biggest task at this point is belongs to the manufacturer.

Figure 2. IoT and cloud services communication (Figure is formed by authors)

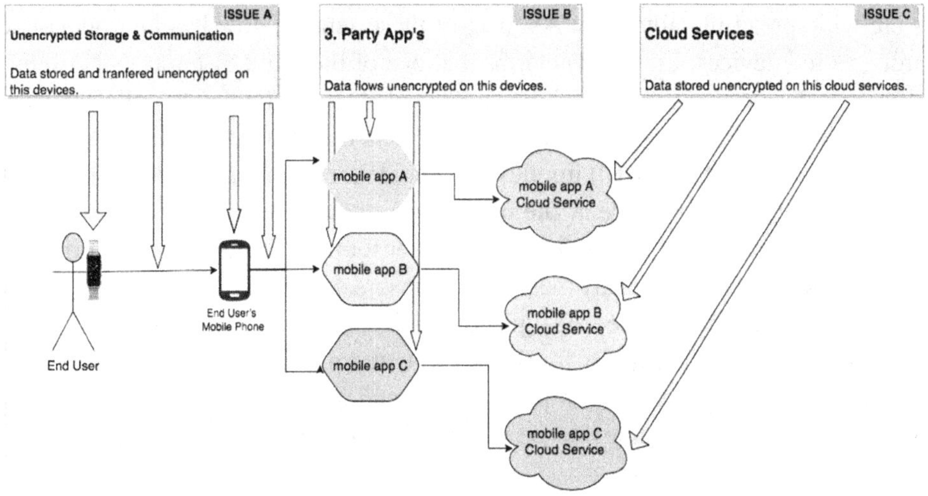

IoT devices exist in many different areas of our life. The different utilization areas cause the operation of the devices to differ from one and other. As Costigan & Lindstrom (2016) argued, it is becoming more and more difficult to anticipate any interruptions that may arise, especially when IoT devices communicate with each other. Hence, looking from a single point while talking about IOT security and trying to produce a solution will not be the right road map. It would be more accurate to move forward with different security solutions in different layers of IOT technology, even though the widespread usage of the IoTs and the various purposes of the devices will make this task harder.

Low Level Security Solutions

Suo et al. refer (2012) to different security measures that can be applied according to the different needs of IOT. The first mechanism is an authentication system to block unauthorized access. Wind River (2015) also discusses about the fact that user-based authentication is insufficient for IoT security. In M2M communications, the backbone of IoT communication, there is often no user to be authenticated. Wind River (2015) suggests applying device-based authentication alongside with user-based authentication in IoT world, where thousands of devices are communicating with each other. Suo et al. (2012) agree that data encryption must be strictly enforced in order to provide confidentiality, one of the three basic principles of cyber security. They approach this subject in terms of cost and security whilst, suggesting two different methods. First is by-hop encryption. The data transferred with this method is encrypted, but is decrypted in each node (at each hop). The data decrypted in a node is encrypted again once the destination of the data is figured, and it is redirected to the next node. In this way, the data is protected against attackers such as MITM (Man in the Middle attacker) while been transferred on the network, but decrypting the data into plain text in each node creates a certain vulnerability. This lightweight encryption can provide the appropriate security for the intended purpose of the device, especially for devices that have relatively low fees. The second mechanism is end-to-end encryption, which is a widely popular method nowadays. Data transmitted by this mechanism is decrypted only on the sender or the receiver. This provides a higher level of security; but the cost of implementing it is also higher than by-hop encryption.

Safety suggestions, the protection and user privacy are the main focuses of sensor data. Sensor technology, like many other technologies, continues to evolve without a break. Speed, heat, motion, sound, etc. sensors are widespread in daily lives. As most of these sensors now has internet connection they can be regarded as IoT devices. Lu (2014) claims that one of the main differences between traditional internet and IoTs, is the amount of personal data collected. The personal data collected by IoT devices is much higher. One of the main reasons behind this the data being collected intentionally/unintentionally through sensors. Atzori et al. (2010) implies that people are often unaware of these sensors around them; and as a result, they are unaware of the information these sensors collect or don't collect about them. Nevertheless, it would be difficult to motivate the sensor manufacturers to conform to this privacy principal as any malicious person can buy these cheap sensors, place them in the same physical environment and collect the same data. Hence, configuring the devices to get data collection under control to respect privacy is an unprofitable activity for the manufacturers. According to the Suo et al. (2012) IoT mechanisms must be re-adapted to protect human privacy and people should be aware when they're data is being collected, They should be able choose whether they prefer to be monitored or not, and remain anonymous whenever they want.

Intermediate Level Security Solutions

The term "Privacy by Design", which was introduced by US Federal Trade Commission (FTC), is examined by Bowman & Blackwell (2018). The purpose of this model proposed by FTC is to design protocols that will enable IoT devices to protect user privacy from the very first stage (authentication, encryption, etc.) and to make sure that the IoT devices have appropriate hardware to support future patches/updates in this context. According to Bowman & Blackwell (2018), IoT devices should be designed so that they can access and adapt to patches or updates that may occur after the date they are introduced to the market.

When considering user privacy, it is vital to inform the user and to collect the data within knowledge and consent of the user. General Data Protection Regulation (GDPR), which released its 3rd version in April 2016 (enforceable since 25 May 2018), attaches great importance to user privacy, not only in IoT world but in every area where user data is being collected. It encourages informing the user about data collection, collecting the data with users consent and following the privacy standards when storing/processing/sharing the data. Thus, GDPR could be a proper motivation in the future, for the manufacturers to consider user privacy when designing their IoT products. Lu (2014) points out the "Simplified User Choice" and "Transparency" principles proposed by FTC alongside with "Privacy by Design". Lu (2014) claims that with these principles as a guide, user privacy will be/can be built from the first stage of design. However, when it comes to applying these policies, which are quite satisfactory in theory, can be quite difficult and costly to implement - especially in IoT devices.

Beecher (2017) suggests that organizations should implement an "authentication chain of trust" which uses cryptographic key exchange alongside with public key infrastructure with x.509 certificates. This is a precaution against firmware compromise and is vital for establishing a trust. Furthermore, Beecher (2017) claims that updating IoT endpoints through cloud systems are also useful in terms of security and reliability.

High Level Security Solutions

Li (2017) states that device interconnection is one of the most critical requirements of IoT world as it provides features such as sensing, communicating, information processing etc. With the wide spread use of IoT endpoints and M2M devices, there are thousands of devices communicating / interacting with each other every second. Kumar & Mallick (2018) argues that as a result of all these interacting devices, a large amount of data is being created and these data are often stored in centralized servers and they believe this causes certain problems such as performance issues. They claim the centralized server concept is not the best suitable solution for handling large-scale systems such as IoT systems.

The increased internet infrastructure needed to process the huge amount of data processed in IoT systems can be achieved through decentralized (distributed) networks. Kumar & Mallick (2018) offers Blockchain (BC) technology to be applied on IoT systems. It can improve the privacy and reliability of IoT systems by providing a solid structure and more effective performance. Dorri et al. (2016) also claims that the use of BC might enhance the security and performance of IoT systems. There are three known and proven features of BC that would aid IoT systems to solve their privacy and security issues:

1. **Decentralization:** Scalability and robustness can be achieved distributed resources instead of a centralized server system.

2.   **Anonymity:** Protecting the identity of the end-users.
3.   **Security:** A secure network is crucial in systems such as IoT where many numbers of devices are in interaction.

Nevertheless, Dorri et al. (2016) are well aware of the fact that employing BC structure on IoT systems is not a straightforward job and that there issues to be handled such as:

1.   Mining, the backbone of BC technology, needs advanced computational power whereas IoT devices often has low resources.
2.   IoT networks are intended to have low latency whereas mining blocks is time consuming.
3.   Some underlying BC protocols create overhead traffic which is often an undesired situation in IoT devices with bandwidth limits.

These solutions had to be dealt with in order for applying BC structure on IoT networks could become a valid solution in IoT privacy and security.

Since it is not possible for each IOT manufacturer to accept, apply and control all these vulnerability possibilities and user privacy issues; with a regulation that can come into effect in Europe initially, it may be possible to make manufacturers increase their focus on this subject and make them invest more fix all (or at least most) of these vulnerabilities. CE (Conformité Européene) regulation realized by European Commission is a good example in this context. It would be unfair to expect every IoT manufacturer to implement protocols such as SSL, since some IoT devices have very limited purposes thus, they are produced in a relatively cheap manner. But with a proper regulation or a guideline, we can at least motivate the manufacturers to take basic precautions such as: Not picking simple usernames and passwords as default, encouraging the user to change the username and password after the first configuration, implementing a machine-based authentication and choosing reliable Cloud services when storing information. These simple measures will aid IoT's self-security while modern protocols to secure IoT communication are being worked on.

Suo et al. admits (2012) that implementing the technology that is used in todays "Network Layer", on IoTs network communication mechanisms can be a really difficult task. The SSL/TLS protocol, - the most common network communication protocol- is the first method that comes to mind. But, as mentioned earlier in this chapter, it is not preferred by the manufacturers because it increases hardware costs. Zhou et al. (2018) argues SSL protocol, which is a measure against "Man in the Middle" aggressors who try to intercept the network communications, is being omitted by manufacturers due to limited resources. The policy to be followed here is giving manufacturers the appropriate motivation to produce devices with hardware that SSL can be implemented on, so that the device could benefit from its certificate verifications and encryption mechanisms. The DDoS attacks that Mirai or other malwares conduct their operations within in the "Network Layer". IoT devices rarely use tunnel mechanisms such as "ipsec" and conduct their communications on the Internet. This increases their vulnerability against DDoS attacks. Kouicem et al. (2018) claim that, instead of trying to overcome this with today's technology, innovative measures and 'disaster recovery' mechanisms must be studied.

CONCLUSION

There is no regulation available regarding IoT's self-security, except for the standard work safety regulations and manufacturers own guidelines on information security and cyber security. In their chapter, we investigate the importance of IoT's self security and its vulnerabilities towards business continuity. As Bosua et al. (2017) points out to the lack of legal regulation concerning IoTs, designers and developers concentrate more on innovation, rather than privacy. Hence, the self-security of the IoTs are at the initiative of the producers while their communication security is at the discretion of the end user. A product can be secure only if the manufacturer wants it to be secure and designs it appropriately. IP cameras, which are sold millions globally, have admin/admin as default username/password combination and the users are not encouraged to change this combination after the initial configuration. Thus, malwares like Mirai can exploit devices for their intended purpose by taking advantage of unchanged default username and password vulnerabilities.

It is inevitable to have a worldwide recognized regulation, at least in Europe, regarding IoT security. Just like electronic good produced in the Far East needs to fulfill certain standards and have certificates in order to enter European market, IoT devices too should have similar control mechanisms, backed with a regulation. The initial state of each regulation is extremely inadequate regarding its goal. For instance; GDPR has released its 3rd version in 2018. It is unlikely that the regulation to be designed regarding IoT security will be fully ready in the first place. IoT self-security can be obtained with a certificate that will be kept mandatory during the European Union IOT import.

As a conclusion of this chapter, the following checks and rules can be expected for ensuring IoT's self security on daily business for business continuity:

- *Updating the Operating System*

The operating system is the heart of all smart devices. Operating systems used by IOT vendors (usually open source operating systems) should be documented on how often updates are made and on their update mechanisms. Manufacturers using cloud services for updating must choose services from the list of safe countries specified in GDPR. Tight resource checks should be applied on every update made; if update servers are seized by malicious people, the devices should be able to cancel the update process and generate alarms. Applications used by the operating systems in the IoTs (openSSH, openSSL etc.), which belong to different developers, should not be delivered to the end user together with the product if not absolutely necessary; and should be removed during the production phase. In this way, possible vulnerabilities that may arise from these applications are avoided.

- *Updating the Applications*

Applications running on IoT operating systems that enable IoT to function properly for its purposes, should also be frequently audited and checked for both feature updates and security updates. It should be ensured that these updates are also made from the correct servers and from the correct update packages.

- *Changing the Default Password*

Users must be encouraged to change the default usernames and passwords that were set by the manufacturer, in the first configuration. The new password may not be too complex (for the sake of easy configuration); but it must be at least five characters long and contain at least one punctuation. Passwords that contain punctuation marks are strong precautions against password guessing attacks such as "Dictionary Attack".

- *Managing Panel and CLI Access Security*

Manufacturers should follow software security regulations while developing IoT management panels, which are often open to Internet or other untrusted/insecure networks. The management panels should be objected to one or more penetration test. Vulnerabilities discovered in these tests should be patched and reported accordingly. Furthermore, these panels should be accessed through HTTPs only, to ensure security of authentication credentials or other sensitive data (SSL encryption). Identical measures should be considered when dealing with IoTs which have their control panel on cloud systems. Regular penetration tests (e.g. every two year) should be mandatory on these systems.

- *Obligation to Inform*

The manufacturers must provide guidelines in printed or electronic media, for the end-users. These guidelines should include basic safety principles to be followed, the precautions to be applied during use and suggestions for keeping the products safe. For instance, encouraging the user to shut down the device or disrupt its network connection when not in use, could be a simple and effective measure. In addition, IoT manufacturers must form a system to inform their users about the updates; describing their necessity and guiding them on how.

REFERENCES

Akatyev, N., & James, J. I. (2017). Evidence identification in IoT networks based on threat assessment. *Future Generation Computer Systems*. doi:10.1016/j.future.2017.10.012

Ammar, M., Russello, G., & Crispo, B. (2018). Internet of Things: A survey on the security of IoT frameworks. *Journal of Information Security and Applications*, *38*, 8–27. doi:10.1016/j.jisa.2017.11.002

Atzori, L., Iera, A., & Morabito, G. (2010). The internet of things: A survey. *Computer Networks*, *54*(15), 2787–2805. doi:10.1016/j.comnet.2010.05.010

Bauer, H., Burkacky, O., & Knochenhauer, C. (2017). *Security in the Internet of Things*. McKinsey Report. Retrieved from: https://www.mckinsey.com/

Beecher, P. (2018). Enterprise-grade networks: The answer to IoT security challenges. *Network Security*, *2018*(7), 6–9. doi:10.1016/S1353-4858(18)30067-9

Bosua, R., Richardson, M., Clark, K., Maynard, S., Ahmad, A., & Webb, J. (2017). *Privacy in a world of the Internet of Things: A Le and Regulatory Perspective*. The University of Melbourne Network Society Institute Research Paper. Retrieved from: https://networkedsociety.unimelb.edu.au

Bowman, B., & Blackwell, H. (2018). *Hurdles in the Internet of Things Must clear for Manufacturers and Providers*. LegalTech. Retrieved from: https://www.bytebacklaw.com/

Chadd, A. (2018). DDoS attacks: Past, present and future. *Network Security, 2018*(7), 13–15. doi:10.1016/S1353-4858(18)30069-2

Cluley, G. (2016). *These 60 dumb passwords can hijack over 500,000 IoT devices into the Mirai botnet*. Retrieved from: https://www.grahamcluley.com/mirai-botnet-password/

Costigan, S. S., & Gustav, L. (2016). Policy and the Internet of Things. *Connections, 15*(2), 9–18. doi:10.11610/Connections.15.2.01

Davies, R. (2018). Apple Becomes World's First Trillion-dollar Company. *The Guardian*. Retrieved from: https://www.theguardian.com/technology/2018/aug/02/apple-becomes-worlds-first-trillion-dollar-company

Dorri, A., Kanhere, S. S., & Jurdak, R. (2016). *Blockchain in internet of things: Challenges and Solutions*. Retrieved from: https://arxiv.org/pdf/1608.05187.pdf

Fildes, J. (2010). Stuxnet worm targeted high-value Iranian assets. *BBC*. Retrieved from: https://www.bbc.com/news/technology-11388018

Fong, K., Hepler, K., Raghavan, R., & Rowland, P. (2018). *rIoT: Quantifying Consumer Costs of Insecure Internet of Things Devices*. University of California Berkeley, School of Information Report. Retrieved from: https://groups.ischool.berkeley.edu/riot/

Gartner. (2014). *4.9 Billion Connected "Things" Will Be in Use in 2015*. Retrieved from: https://www.gartner.com/newsroom/id/2905717

Gartner. (2017). *8.4 Billion Connected Things Will Be in Use in 2017, Up 31 Percent From 2016*. Retrieved from: https://www.gartner.com/en/newsroom/press-releases/2017-02-07-gartner-says-8-billion-connected-things-will-be-in-use-in-2017-up-31-percent-from-2016

IDC Digital Universe. (2012). *The Digital Universe in 2020: Big Data, Bigger Digital Shadows, and Biggest Growth in the Far East*. IDC Report. Retrieved from: http://emc.com

Khan, M. A., & Salah, K. (2018). IoT security: Review, blockchain solutions, and open challenges. *Future Generation Computer Systems, 82*, 395–411. doi:10.1016/j.future.2017.11.022

Kouicem, D. E., Bouabdallah, A., & Lakhlef, H. (2018). Internet of things security: A top-down survey. *Computer Networks, 141*, 199–221. doi:10.1016/j.comnet.2018.03.012

Krebs, B. (2018). Mirai IoT Botnet Co-Authors Plead Guilty. *Krebsonsecurity*. Retrieved from: https://krebsonsecurity.com/2017/mirai-iot-botnet-co-authors-plead-guilty

Kumar, N. M., & Mallick, P. K. (2018). Blockchain Technology for Security Issues and Challenges in IoT. *Procedia Computer Science, 132*, 1815–1823. doi:10.1016/j.procs.2018.05.140

Li, S. (2017). Security Requirements in IoT Architecture. *Securing the Internet of Things*, 97-108.

Lu, C. (2014). *Overview of Security and Privacy Issues in the Internet of Things*. Washington University in St. Louis Computer Science and Engineering Research Paper. Retrieved from: https://www.cse.wustl.edu/~jain/cse574-14/ftp/security.pdf

McKinsey. (2018). *The IoT as a growth driver*. McKinsey Market Analysis Report of 2018. Retrieved from: https://www.mckinsey.com/

Mims, N. (2017). *The Botnet Problem, Computer and Information Security Handbook* (3rd ed.). Cambridge, MA: Morgan Kaufmann.

O'Donnell, L. (2018). Security Glitch in IoT Camera Enabled Remote Monitoring. *ThreatPost*. Retrieved from: https://threatpost.com/security-glitch-in-iot-camera-enabled-remote-monitoring/134504/

Olzak, T. (2017). MQTT is not Evil, Just Not Always Secure. *Csonline*. Retrieved from: https://www.csoonline.com/article/3208325/internet-of-things/mqtt-is-not-evil-just-not-always-secure.html

Omitola, T., & Willis, G. (2018). Towards Mapping the Security Challenges of the Internet of Things (IoT) Supply Chain. *Procedia Computer Science*, *126*, 441–450. doi:10.1016/j.procs.2018.07.278

Pan, X., Ling, Z., Pingley, A., Yu, W., Ren, K., Zhang, N., & Fu, X. (2016). How privacy leaks from bluetooth mouse? *IEEE Transactions on Dependable and Secure Computing*, *13*(4), 461–473. doi:10.1109/TDSC.2015.2413410

Purdy, M., & Davarzani, L. (2015). *The Growth Game-Changer: How the Industrial Internet of Things can drive progress and prosperity*. Accenture Strategy Report. Retrieved from: https://www.accenture.com/

Sha, K., Wei, W., Yang, T. A., Wang, Z., & Shi, W. (2018). On security challenges and open issues in Internet of Things. *Future Generation Computer Systems*, *83*, 326–337. doi:10.1016/j.future.2018.01.059

Shakarian, P., Shakarian, J., & Ruef, A. (2013). *Attacking Iranian Nuclear Facilities*, 223-239. Doi:10.1016/B978-0-12-407814-7.00013-0

Suo, H., Wan, J., Zou, C., & Liu, J. (2012). Security in the Internet of Things: A Review. *International Conference on Computer Science and Electronics Engineering*, *3*, 648-651. 10.1109/ICCSEE.2012.373

Weber, R. (2015). Internet of Things: Privacy Issues Revisited. *Computer Law & Security Review*, *31*(5), 618–627. doi:10.1016/j.clsr.2015.07.002

Wind River. (2015). *Security in the Internet of Things*. Retrieved from: https://www.windriver.com

Woolf, N. (2016). DdoS attack that disrupted internet was largest of its kind in history. *The Guardian*. Retrieved from: https://www.theguardian.com/technology/2016/oct/26/ddos-attack-dyn-mirai-botnet

Zhou, W., Jia, Y., Peng, A., Zhang, Y., & Liu, P. (2018). The Effect of IoT New Features on Security and Privacy: New Threats, Existing Solutions, and Challenges Yet to Be Solved. *IEEE Internet of Things Journal*, 1-1.

Chapter 22
Survey on Various MapReduce Scheduling Algorithms

Vaibhav Pandey
Punjab Engineering College (Deemed), India

Poonam Saini
Punjab Engineering College (Deemed), India

ABSTRACT

The advent of social networking and internet of things (IoT) has resulted in exponential growth of data in the last few years. This, in turn, has increased the need to process and analyze such data for optimal decision making. In order to achieve better results, there is an emergence of newly-built architectures for parallel processing. Hadoop MapReduce (MR) is a programming model that is considered as one of the most powerful computation tools for processing the data on a given cluster of commodity nodes. However, the management of clusters along with various quality requirements necessitates the use of efficient MR scheduling. The chapter discusses the classification of MR scheduling algorithms based on their applicability with required parameters of quality of service (QoS). After classification, a detailed study of MR schedulers has been presented along with their comparison on various parameters.

INTRODUCTION

The amount of data generated by present generation of social networking sites and IoT is very large. For instance, Facebook gets approximately 10 million new photos uploaded every hour; Twitter has approximately 400 million tweets per day and Google processes over 24 petabytes of data every day (Shields, 2014). The scale, diversity, and complexity of such data require new architecture and techniques in order to process data. This, in turn, increases the accuracy of decision-making applications. The optimal solution to handle a large volume of data is to run parallel data tasks which may operate on different data sets.

In existing literature, one of the most popular programming paradigms that process a large volume of data in parallel is MapReduce (MR) programming model (Dean & Ghemawat, 2008). "*MapReduce is a programming model and an associated implementation for processing and generating large data sets with a parallel, distributed algorithm on a cluster.*" In MapReduce model, the program is defined

DOI: 10.4018/978-1-5225-8407-0.ch022

as a sequence of *map* and *reduce* tasks. Both tasks, map and reduce, are processed in a distributed fashion *i.e.,* all map tasks can be performed in parallel provided that each map operation is independent of other. However, in practice, it is limited by the number of independent data sources, number of CPUs near each source etc. The reduce task too has similar limitations. Nevertheless, MapReduce has become popular during last few years due to its better performance in comparison to other parallel programming models. Features like data-local scheduling, application robustness, ease of use and scalability make it more efficient.

Here, MR scheduler plays an important role to fulfill the requirements like response time, data locality, energy efficiency and fairness. Although few performance parameters have been addressed by different MR scheduling algorithms, some other parameters are compromised while meeting the essential one. For example, if a scheduler follows the fair policy to select the task, it may compromise data locality. Therefore, it becomes a challenge to design a single scheduler with all required parameters. Thus, scheduling in MapReduce is an optimization problem with multiple objectives and is NP-Hard (Fischer, Su, & Yin, 2010).

MAPREDUCE BACKGROUND

Hadoop is an open source framework to store and process huge data sets with a cluster of commodity hardware ("Apache Hadoop," 2018). It enables application to work with petabytes of data and a large number of computationally independent computers. The core of Hadoop consists of two components: *Hadoop Distributed File System* (HDFS) and *MapReduce* (MR).

MapReduce is main processing component and is often referred to as heart of Hadoop. It is a framework which is used to execute applications where large data sets are processed on a cluster of commodity hardware. Here, the input is a set of key-value pair and corresponding output is also a key-value pair. Further, there is a single master node running *JobTracker* (JT) process and multiple slave nodes running *TaskTrackers* (TT) processes. The master node is responsible for task scheduling on slave nodes, monitoring those tasks and handling failure by re-executing the task. Slave nodes, on the other hand, follow the instructions of master node and execute the assigned tasks. In addition, slave nodes perform two sets of tasks, namely, *map* and *reduce*. The map function takes *<key, value>* pair as input and produces an intermediate *<key, value>* pair as output. Thereafter, output of map function with same key are grouped together and are given as an input to reduce function. The reduce function, lastly, performs reduce operation and output is appended to a final output file. Figure 1 shows the schematic view of task execution in Hadoop using MapReduce.

CLASSIFICATION OF MAPREDUCE SCHEDULING ALGORITHMS IN HADOOP

Till 2008, Hadoop supported a single scheduler (FIFO) that was integrated within the JT. Although the implementation was good enough for traditional batch jobs of Hadoop, such as log mining and web indexing, it was not flexible as well as customizable. Later, a bug called HADOOP-3412, stating that the scheduler must be independent of JT, was reported (Jones, 2011). Thereafter, new scheduler in Hadoop became pluggable. This, in turn, enabled the efficient design of new scheduling algorithms for a variety of jobs having different characteristics and requirement. A large number of scheduling algorithms have

Figure 1. Task execution in Hadoop MapReduce

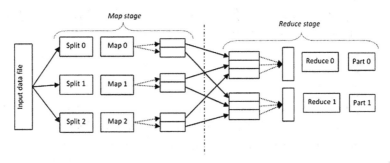

been proposed for MapReduce which focus on different parameters. Also, there are large numbers of parameters on the basis of which schedulers can be classified like preemptive and non-preemptive, adaptive and non-adaptive, task-focused and job-focused. In this chapter, various improvements to Hadoop schedulers have been categorized on the basis of QoS parameters. For example, some schedulers were proposed to improve fairness while some focused on improving response time and others tend to meet deadline constraints. The classification is shown in Table 1 followed with a detailed description.

MAPREDUCE SCHEDULING ALGORITHMS

This section presents the extensive study of various MapReduce scheduling algorithms on the basis of classification framework discussed in the previous section. Strengths and weaknesses of each scheduling algorithm has been discussed in detail. Studied algorithms have been analysed on various parameters in

Table 1. Classification and description of scheduling algorithms

Classification	Description
Fairness-Aware Schedulers	Fairness, in the context of Hadoop MapReduce Scheduler, is to assign resources to jobs and users such that on an average each job and user roughly gets an equal share of the cluster resources. Thus, schedulers focus on assigning an equal number of resources to each job.
Response Time-Aware Schedulers	Speculative Execution is used to improve response time in Hadoop and is responsible to schedule backup tasks for tasks which are extremely slow (also called as straggler tasks). Thus, overall response time of job is not affected. The focus is to design algorithms to correctly identify the straggler tasks in order to launch a backup copy.
Deadline-Aware Schedulers	There are jobs in certain applications which are deadline driven and require completion within a stipulated time. The primary focus is to meet job deadline by minimizing completion time of job.
Throughput-Aware Schedulers	Throughput is measure of the number of jobs or tasks completed in a given time interval. MapReduce scheduling algorithms tend to improve throughput by improving other quality attributes like data locality and energy efficiency. Data locality in Hadoop refers to "proximity" of data with respect to mapper tasks working on the data.
Failure-Aware Schedulers	Failures are common in cloud data centers because of dynamic nature of cloud as well as its scale and complexity. The failure aware scheduling algorithms focus on handling failed tasks or tasks which are most likely to fail are considered.
Resource-Aware Schedulers	Resource utilization is important for both cloud providers and end users. Cloud providers require a high level of resource utilization whereas users want consistency between quality of service and the price being paid. The design of algorithms focuses on maximum resource utilization.

tabular form. Although some other studies of MapReduce schedulers are available in literature (Nimbalkar & Gadekar, 2015; Pandey & Saini, 2018b; Varma, 2013; Yoo & Sim, 2011), this chapter discusses MR schedulers from a new angle of classification.

Fairness-Aware Schedulers

Fairness in context of Hadoop MR Scheduler is to assign resources to jobs and users such that each job and user gets an equal share of the cluster resources. Here, shorter jobs, as well as longer jobs, share resources at the same time which leads to faster execution of shorter jobs and starvation free longer jobs. Facebook developed first scheduler which takes into account the fairness while scheduling jobs (Jones, 2011) ("Fair Scheduler," 2018). Fair Scheduler (FS) is based on three concepts:

- Jobs are placed into pools for selection.
- Each pool can have a guaranteed capacity *i.e.,* each pool has a minimum number of map slots and reduce slots. Any pending job in the pool may use the available slots, however, slots can be used by other pools, in case, there are no pending jobs.
- Any excess capacity is allocated between jobs using fair sharing.

The scheduler selects a job with highest deficit to schedule next. To calculate deficit, it computes the difference between compute time that the job has actually received and the time it should have received when executed with an ideal scheduler. Capacity Scheduler (CS) from Yahoo ("CapacityScheduler Guide," 2018) uses the principle of FS and the concept of named queues where each queue can represent a user (a person or an organization). Capacity Scheduler was designed for a large cluster with multiple independent customers and target applications. Each queue has a configurable number of map and reduce slots and is assigned a guaranteed capacity. Any unused capacity is shared between queues. To achieve fairness, both schedulers compromise data locality. Moreover, both these schedulers fail to handle a large number of queues having varying capacities.

Table 2. Comparative analysis of fairness-aware scheduling algorithms

Scheduling Algorithm	Strengths	Weaknesses	Environment	Type
Fair Scheduler ("Fair Scheduler," 2018)	• Allocates pools to each user • Divides resources equally among pools	• Fails to handle a large number of pools having varying capacity • Compromises data locality	Homogeneous	Non-preemptive
Capacity Scheduler ("CapacityScheduler Guide," 2018)	• Divides resources among queues equally • Additional security measures are built in for access control	• Fails to handle a large number of queues with varying capacity • Compromises data locality	Homogeneous	Non-preemptive
Dynamic Priority (Sandholm & Lai, 2010)	• Prevent users from consuming resources excessively for noncritical jobs at peak time	• The bidding system is not precise • Biased towards small jobs	Heterogeneous	Preemptive
NSA (Peng & Ma, 2011)	• Schedules tasks of different jobs in proportion of their sizes	• The response time for small jobs gets affected due to large jobs	Homogeneous	Preemptive

Dynamic Priority (DP) Scheduler proposed by Sandholm *et al.* (Sandholm & Lai, 2010), allows users to dynamically bid and purchase the capacity and quality of service that they need to meet their requirements. This approach allows users to get the slots (map and reduce) on the basis of proportional share per unit time (allocation interval) and helps scheduler to take decisions about which users and jobs to prioritize. The allocation interval is configurable. The price of slot depends on the load of system *i.e.,* when demand is high, the cost of slot will be high to ensure that users with less critical jobs scale back their jobs and only critical jobs get executed. In each allocation interval, scheduler performs following functions:

1. Each user i sets his spending rate S_i on the basis of his budget b.
2. The scheduler aggregates all spending rates from current users and calculates Hadoop cluster price p.
3. Allocates $(S_i/p)*c$ task slots to user i, where c is aggregate slot capacity of cluster.
4. For user i, deducts $S_i * u_i$ from budget b of user, where u_i is number of slots used by user.

The scheduler is preemptive in nature. It reclaims task slots from users that have been allocated, however, no longer paid for and hence allocates the slots to other users.

A New Scheduling Algorithm (NSA) was proposed by Peng *et al.* (Peng & Ma, 2011) which overcome the limitation of DP Scheduler of being biased towards smaller jobs. The scheduling algorithm creates a resource pool for each user. It calculates unfulfilled tasks *i.e.,* tasks whose status is "not complete", based upon which the percentage of a job's unfulfilled tasks is calculated with respect to total unfulfilled tasks. This ensures a balanced distribution of available slots so that job with a maximum number of unfulfilled tasks may be allotted more number of slots. The algorithm is preemptive and uses delay scheduling for data locality in order to schedule the jobs. However, response time for smaller jobs gets affected because of larger jobs. Table 2 summarises all MR schedulers discussed in this subsection.

Response Time-Aware Scheduling

The Speculative Execution is a technique used to improve response time in Hadoop and is responsible for scheduling backup tasks for tasks that are extremely slow. This technique restricts slower tasks to affect the overall response time of jobs. The default scheduler of Hadoop MR uses speculative execution to improve response time. It divides map task (MT) and reduce task (RT) into different stages and each stage is assigned some weight. Map Task has two stages, namely, *Execute Map Function (M_1)* and *Reorder Intermediate Results (M_2)*. Further, reduce task has three stages, namely, *Copy Data(R_1)*, *Order(R_2)* and *Merge(R_3)*.The weights assigned to these stages in default scheduler are M_1-1.0, M_2-0 and R_1, R_2, R_3-1/3. The default scheduler uses a progress score to determine whether a task is a straggler or not. A task is marked for speculative execution only after it has run for at least one minute and its progress score (PS) is less the average of its category minus 0.2. The following Eq. (1) calculates PS of a particular task where N and M is a number of key-value pairs to be processed and successfully processed in the task respectively. And, K are the number of stages completed by reduce tasks. Further Eq. (2) calculates average PS of a job where *PS[i]* is progress score of ith task, T is total number of tasks to be executed.

$$PS = \begin{cases} M \,/\, N & for\,map\,task \\ \dfrac{1}{3} * \left(K + M \,/\, N \right) & for\,reduce\,task \end{cases} \tag{1}$$

$$PS_{avg} = \sum_{i=1}^{T} PS\big[i\big] \,/\, T \tag{2}$$

The limitation of default speculative execution algorithm is its inherent assumption of homogeneous environment and hence, fails to handle the heterogeneous clusters. Later, to overcome the issue, Zaharia *et al.* (Zaharia, Konwinski, Joseph, Katz, & Stoica, 2008) introduced LATE (Longest Approximate Time to End) scheduler. LATE selects the task for speculative execution that will finish farthest into future. It uses equations 1 and 2 to calculate progress score and then calculates *Progress Rate* (PR) as *PS/T* where *T* is the time for which task has been running. Further, it estimates the time to completion as *(1-PS)/PR*.

It uses a threshold *SlowTaskThreshold* to determine whether a task is slow enough to be executed speculatively. *SlowTaskThreshold* is set to 25th percentile of task progress rate. In order to avoid excessive speculation, it defines a limit (*SpeculativeCap*) on the number of speculative tasks that can run at once. *SpeculativeCap* is set to 10% of available slots. The approach uses a static method to compute progress of a task. The values used for M_1, M_2, R_1, R_2, R_3 are always 1, 0, 1/3, 1/3, 1/3 respectively. Although LATE uses an efficient strategy to find backup tasks, it failed to calculate *time-to-end* for tasks accurately. Moreover, data locality is not considered while launching a backup task on node.

Chen *et al.* (Chen, Zhang, Guo, Deng, & Guo, 2010) introduced SAMR (Self-Adaptive MapReduce) scheduling algorithm which uses a similar idea as that of LATE with following two improvements:

1. It uses historical information stored on every node to calculate the weights at each stage (M_1, M_2, R_1, R_2, R_3) dynamically and accurately.
2. It further classifies the slow nodes as map slow nodes and reduce slow nodes.

The historical information is stored in XML format on every node and is updated after each execution. However, SAMR only considers hardware heterogeneity and ignores the fact that map and reduce stage weights for different types of jobs may be different. Also, for same type of jobs, different datasets may lead to different weights.

HAT (History-based Auto-Tuning) (Chen et al., 2013) was a variation of SAMR. The protocol tunes the value of map and reduce stages based on historical values of these stages in completed tasks. HAT estimates the progress score of running tasks accurately on the basis of values of these stages for current hardware and application features.

ESAMR (Enhanced Self-Adaptive MapReduce) scheduling algorithm was another enhancement of SAMR, proposed by Sun *et al.* (Sun, He, & Lu, 2012), which considers hardware heterogeneity into account while calculating stage weights considering different job types and different job sizes. To identify slow tasks accurately, ESAMR differentiates historical stage weights information on each node and divide them into *k* clusters by using a *k*-means clustering algorithm. *K*-means clustering partitions *n* observations into *k* clusters where each observation belongs to cluster with nearest mean, serving as a prototype of cluster (Macqueen, 1967).

Wang *et al.* (Y. Wang, Lu, Lou, & Wei, 2015) proposed the concept of Partial Speculative Execution (PSE). PSE reduces the cost of re-reading, re-computing and re-copying by introducing checkpoint for the work done by original task (straggler) and restarting from that checkpoint. To achieve the goal, it allows original task and a backup copy to communicate by transferring the checkpointing information. Also, PSE introduced two checkpointing algorithms and corresponding recovery algorithms. PSE automatically degrades to normal speculative execution in case checkpointing consumes more time. The major challenge in the approach is that checkpointing should be as fast as possible to avoid overheads for the overall process. Table 3 summarises all MR scheduling discussed in this subsection.

Deadline-Aware Scheduling

The default scheduler of Hadoop does not guarantee that a job will be completed within a specified deadline. FIFO and other default schedulers work fine for batch processing jobs, however, there are certain applications which are deadline driven and require completion time guarantee. Hence, it is required for improvement over default scheduler that may focus primarily on meeting deadlines. Kc. *et al.* (Kc & Anyanwu, 2010) proposed a scheduling approach to meet deadlines. The authors in the paper focused on performing a schedulability test before actually executing job on Hadoop. The job is executed when it clears the schedulability test (*i.e.,* when cluster has sufficient amount of map and reduce slots available to complete job within a specified deadline). The schedulability test is based on slots availability at a given time or in future. The authors proposed *job execution cost model* and a *constraint-based Hadoop scheduler*. The constraint-based Hadoop Scheduler performs the schedulability test of a job based on

Table 3. Comparative analysis of response time-aware scheduling algorithms

Scheduling Algorithm	Strengths	Weaknesses	Environment	Type
LATE (Zaharia et al., 2008)	• Offers a better approach to select a task for speculative execution which results in reducing the response time of job • Ensures that speculative copy of task is not launched on stragglers	• Uses a static method to compute the progress of a task • Ignores data locality while launching backup tasks	Heterogeneous	Non-preemptive
SAMR (Chen et al., 2010)	• Uses historical information stored on every node to calculate the weights at each stage dynamically • Classifies nodes as fast and slow nodes	• Considers hardware heterogeneity only and ignores the fact that Map and Reduce stage weights for different types of jobs may be different	Heterogeneous	Non-preemptive
HAT (Chen et al., 2013)	• Estimate progress score of running tasks accurately on the basis of the values of these stages for current hardware and application features	-	Heterogeneous	Non-preemptive
ESAMR (Sun et al., 2012)	• Considers different job types, job sizes and hardware heterogeneity while calculating stage weights	• Overhead due to k means clustering algorithm	Heterogeneous	Non-preemptive
PSE (Y. Wang et al., 2015)	• Reduces the cost of re-reading, re-computing and re-copying by introducing checkpoint for the work done by original task and starting from that checkpoint	• Checkpointing is an overhead for overall process	Heterogeneous	Preemptive

proposed job execution cost model. Once the job is found schedulable, it is assigned a minimum number of tasks needed to meet its deadline and hence, empty slots may be available for later jobs submission. The limitation in the approach is that cost model failed to estimate cost correctly because of its assumption that MR runtime parameters are always known. The second drawback is the rejection of a job, in case, job is not schedulable.

Further, in literature, in order to correctly find runtime parameters of MapReduce, Verma *et al.* (Verma, Cherkasova, Kumar, & Campbell, 2012) used the observation that many production jobs are run periodically on new data and thus a job profile can be created that reflects critical performance characteristics of underlying job during all execution phases. The algorithm works as follows. For each job with a specified deadline, estimate and allocate appropriate number of map and reduce slots required to complete the job within specified deadline. The interesting feature of mechanism is that as time progresses and job deadline gets closer, mechanism can dynamically recalculate and adjust the amount of resources required by each job to meet its deadline. The spare resources are unallocated map and reduce slots left when each job had been assigned its minimum resource quota to meet a given deadline. The mechanism uses job profile information to make the prediction. When amount of released resources over time does not guarantee timely completion of newly arrived job, the mechanism will de-allocate spare slots.

Natjam, proposed by Cho *et al.* (Cho et al., 2013), performs schedulability test and also introduces the concept of eviction policies for executing jobs with hard and fixed deadlines by taking up the resources (if not available) from currently executing jobs, *i.e.,* the job is not rejected, rather, resources are taken from currently executing low priority jobs. Natjam proposes policies for three different categories namely Job Eviction, Task Eviction and Job Selection when resources get free. For job eviction, it uses either MDF (Maximum deadline first) or MLF (Maximum Laxity First). For task eviction either SRT (Shortest remaining time first) or LRT (Longest remaining time first) are used. When resources get free, Natjam selects a job from suspended ones and assign resources to it. The possible job selection policies are Earliest Deadline First (EDF) and Least Laxity First (LLF). Natjam uses the concept of checkpointing to preempt and resume jobs, which is an overhead. Moreover, it does not take into account the data locality for scheduling the jobs, though; data locality may improve the performance of Natjam.

The deadline aware scheduling algorithms that have been proposed so far do not consider the heterogeneity of cluster into account. Different nodes in a heterogeneous cluster have different computing capacity, so considering all nodes same while scheduling jobs is not appropriate. Tang *et al.* (Tang et al., 2013) proposed another variation of deadline constraint algorithm, MTSD, that takes heterogeneity into account while making scheduling decisions. The other observation of MTSD is that it is not accurate to take a map and reduce tasks equivalent while calculating average execution time for all tasks because of different nature of tasks. MTSD introduced a node classification algorithm. The classification algorithm classifies the nodes in cluster to multiple levels on the basis of their computing capacity. MTSD then distributes data on these nodes in proportion of the level of that node *i.e.,* node at highest level (fastest node) will get the maximum proportion of data and vice versa.

The approach of data distribution highly improves data locality and thus the execution time. MTSD finds out deadline for map and reduce tasks separately by taking proportion of map and reduce tasks. Further, it estimates the time required for remaining tasks on lowest level node (slowest node) by using the data from partially executed tasks and calculates the number of map and reduce slots required to complete the job. Table 4 summarises all MR scheduling discussed in this subsection.

Table 4. Comparative analysis of deadline-aware scheduling algorithms

Scheduling Algorithm	Strengths	Weaknesses	Environment	Type
Kc. et al. (Kc & Anyanwu, 2010)	• Performs a schedulability test and execute job if it passes the test	• The cost model fail to estimate the cost correctly because of its assumption that mapreduce runtime parameters are always known	Homogeneous	Non-preemptive
Verma et al. (Verma et al., 2012)	• Uses the concept of job profiling which reflects critical performance characteristics of underlying job during all execution phases	• EDF is not effective with dynamically available resources • Do not consider future resource availability	Homogeneous	Non-preemptive
Natjam (Cho et al., 2013)	• Performs schedulability test • Introduces the concept of eviction policies for executing jobs with hard and fixed deadlines by taking up resources from currently executing jobs	• Checkpointing is an overhead • Do not consider data locality for scheduling jobs	Homogeneous	Preemptive
MTSD (Tang, Zhou, Li, & Li, 2013)	• Takes heterogeneity into account while taking scheduling decisions	• The entire focus is on map tasks ignoring the reduce tasks completely	Heterogeneous	Non-preemptive

Throughput-Aware Scheduling

Throughput is the measure of number of jobs or tasks completed in a given time interval. MR scheduling algorithms tend to improve throughput by improving other quality attributes like data locality and energy efficiency. Data locality in Hadoop refers to the "proximity" of the data with respect to the mapper tasks working on the data. Data locality improves the performance to a great extent because it saves the cost of copying data over a network from data node.

Zaharia *et al.* (Zaharia et al., 2010) observed that in order to achieve fairness, data locality is compromised. Moreover, there were two major problems with fair scheduling that were observed: *head of the line scheduling* and *sticky slots*. The authors proposed a Delay Scheduling algorithm which provides a solution to both these problems and at the same time increases the performance due to high data locality. The idea behind delay scheduling is that when a job to be scheduled next according to fairness, and if it is not able to launch a local task, it is skipped for some predefined number of times (*skipcount*) while the other job is allowed to launch the task. Hence, every time the job is skipped, *skipcount* is incremented by one. In case, the *skipcount* reaches a certain threshold and job is not able to launch a local task, the job will be allowed to launch a non-local task. However, in a single heartbeat signal, the algorithm allows a node to launch multiple non-local tasks whenever the local tasks are not found which may degrade its performance in comparison to default scheduler.

Another variation of Delay Scheduling is Matchmaking which was introduced by He *et al.* (Peng & Ma, 2011). The biggest achievement of the approach over Delay Scheduling is that it does not require tuning of a threshold parameter. The approach is called matchmaking because it tries to match a node for a map task that contains input data for that map task. It gives a node a fair chance to obtain a local task, and in case a node fails to find a local task, it will not be assigned a non-local task in that interval. However, when a node fails to get a local task in the second consecutive interval as well, it will be assigned a non-local task to avoid wastage of cluster resources.

Another variation of Delay Scheduler is Coupling Scheduler proposed by Tan *et al.* (Tan, Meng, & Zhang, 2012). The scheduler uses random peeking scheduling approach to improve data locality. At every heartbeat interval, the scheduler randomly selects some nodes K from total nodes of cluster N and checks the number of nodes out of selected nodes K that have local map input and free map slots. Further, the scheduler estimates total number of nodes having free slots N_m and the percentage of nodes having local map tasks P_m. In case, there are many nodes available having local data and free slots, the scheduler skips current heartbeat and delays the scheduling. However, in case, pending map tasks of a job are more as compared to free slots, scheduling is not delayed and a remote map task is launched.

Next-K-Node Scheduling (NKS) approach, proposed by Zhang *et al.* (X. Zhang, Zhong, Feng, Tu, & Fan, 2011), is another variation of the Delay Scheduling algorithm which is based on the concept of probability. NKS predicts the node that will be available next and request a task. The decision is taken on the basis of progress of current task running on that node. To calculate the progress, NKS divides the size of processed input data by total size of input data. The scheduler calculates the probabilities such that tasks that do not have input data on next k nodes have higher probabilities than the tasks with data available on next k nodes. Whenever a node requests a task, NKS will preserve tasks with lower probabilities and schedules tasks with higher probabilities.

The aforementioned algorithms focus on data locality to improve the overall performance of MapReduce. However, Wang *et al.* (W. Wang, Zhu, Ying, Tan, & Zhang, 2016) highlighted the fact that locality is an indirect performance measure and thus, throughput and delay are the more important parameters for measuring the performance. Moreover, too much focus on data locality may lead to an uneven distribution of tasks among machines. Therefore, authors introduced a scheduling algorithm that maintains a balance between data locality and load balancing that, in turn, results in high throughput and heavy traffic optimality. The scheduler introduces a new queuing architecture (join the shortest queue routing policy) and a max weight scheduling technique. The queuing architecture assigns tasks to the appropriate queue and max weight scheduling technique picks the task from queue for scheduling. According to the new queuing architecture, there are three queues associated with three local machines and a common queue to all machines. The algorithm has a very low computation complexity. Table 5 summarises all MR scheduling discussed in this subsection.

Failure-Aware Scheduling

Failures are very common in cloud data centers because of dynamic nature of cloud as well as its scale and complexity. The common failure types include hard drive failures, individual machine failures and power failures in a cloud environment and thus, impact the overall performance of Hadoop running on that cloud. Hence, taking into consideration of such failures, the concept of failure aware scheduling comes into picture. Hadoop handles the individual node failure by re-executing the tasks of failed node on some other healthy node. Although Hadoop gives highest priority to recovery of tasks, still their execution depends on the various factors of cluster nodes like a number of available slots or the time taken by currently executing tasks etc. Moreover, in default Hadoop scheduler, data locality is completely ignored while launching recovery tasks.

A failure aware scheduler Chronos proposed by Yildiz *et al.* (Yildiz, Ibrahim, & Antoniu, 2017) introduces a lightweight, work conserving preemption technique for fast recovery of failed tasks rather than waiting to get free slots. Chronos uses a selection algorithm to select the list of tasks that can be preempted to make room for recovery tasks to execute. The selection algorithm takes into account dif-

Table 5. Comparative analysis of throughput-aware scheduling algorithms

Scheduling Algorithm	Strengths	Weaknesses	Environment	Type
Delay Scheduling (Zaharia et al., 2010)	• Solves two major problems - *head of the line scheduling* and *sticky slots*	• Allows a node to launch multiple non-local tasks in case local tasks are not found which sometimes worsen its performance in comparison to default scheduler	Homogeneous	Non-preemptive
Matchmaking (Peng & Ma, 2011)	• Do not require tuning of a threshold parameter • Tries to match a node for a map task that contains input data for that map task	• Wastage of cluster resources	Homogeneous	Non-preemptive
Coupling Scheduler (Tan et al., 2012)	• Uses random peeking scheduling approach for improving data locality	• Wastage of cluster resources	Homogeneous	Non-preemptive
NKS (X. Zhang et al., 2011)	• Probability based scheduling. • Request a task on the basis of the progress of the task currently running on that node	• Only for homogeneous clusters	Homogeneous	Non-preemptive
Wang et al. (W. Wang et al., 2016)	• Maintains a balance between data locality and the load balancing	• The entire focus is on map tasks ignoring the reduce tasks completely	Homogeneous	Non-preemptive

ferent parameters like progress score of running tasks, the location of the recovery tasks' input data and scheduling objectives. Whenever a failure is detected, the scheduling algorithm will prepare a list of tasks that are running on nodes where the input data for failed tasks is present (to achieve data locality for recovery tasks). The list is then sorted as per job priority in order to decide whether the failed task can preempt any of these tasks or not. The failed task can preempt only low priority tasks. In case, there is some task that can be preempted to free some slots for failed task, then that list is forwarded to pre-emption mechanism. Although Chronos gives better results in comparison to default scheduler, it takes action only on the occurrence of a failure.

ATLAS (AdapTive faiLure Aware Scheduler) proposed by Soualhia *et al.* (Soualhia et al., 2015), on the other hand, predict the failures, in advance, by sharing the information between tasks and reschedule these tasks on appropriate nodes. Thus, the algorithm is proactive and fault-tolerant. There are

Table 6. Comparative analysis of failure-aware scheduling algorithms

Scheduling Algorithm	Strengths	Weaknesses	Environment	Type
ATLAS (Soualhia, Khomh, & Tahar, 2015)	• Predicts the failures in the cluster by sharing the information between tasks in advance and reschedule the tasks on appropriate nodes	• Use of statistical predictive learning techniques is costly • Delay the execution of jobs which are predicted to be failed	Heterogeneous	Non-preemptive
CHRONOS (Yildiz et al., 2017)	• Uses a lightweight, work conserving pre-emption technique for fast recovery of failed tasks	• Do not predict the failure in the cluster	Heterogeneous	Preemptive

two strategies to reschedule the tasks which are predicted as failed: (i) penalty mechanism (ii) multiple speculative executions. The prediction algorithm collects the data about previously executed tasks and jobs by running different jobs on Hadoop. The algorithm, further, analyzes the data to retrieve the main attributes of a job and its tasks. Thereafter, the algorithm establishes the correlation between attributes and the scheduling outcome of the jobs in order to identify the relevant attributes. The prediction model detects the failure using statistical predictive learning techniques. Though, ATLAS has reduced the total number of failures, however, applying statistical predictive learning technique is an expensive operation. Moreover, the execution of jobs is delayed for fail-to-be jobs by assigning them low priority, until the scheduler finds a suitable number of resources to execute the jobs. Table 6 summarises all MR scheduling discussed in this subsection.

Resource-Aware Scheduling

In order to improve resource utilization in Hadoop, resource aware schedulers have been introduced. Polo *et al.* (Polo et al., 2011) proposed RAS (Resource-aware Adaptive Scheduler) for Hadoop. In RAS, a slot is fixed for a specific task in a specific job. RAS uses the profiling information from previous execution of jobs and considers completion goals that are submitted by users as soft deadlines. RAS has three main components: (i) *job time completion estimator* (ii) *placement algorithm* (iii) *Job utility calculator*. The job time completion estimator estimates number of map tasks that have to be allocated simultaneously to meet the deadline of a job. The placement algorithm forms possible placement matrices after examining tasks on different TTs and their resource allocation. The job utility calculator, on the other hand, gives a utility value for a placement matrix. The placement algorithm uses the value to select best placement choice. Afterward, task scheduler enforces the placement decision. The entire focus of RAS is on Memory, I/O and CPU. The scheduling algorithm does not consider storage capacities of TTs and network bandwidth parameters.

COSHH (Classification and Optimization based Scheduler for Heterogeneous Hadoop) was introduced by Rasooli *et al.* (Rasooli & Down, 2014) with the aim of maximizing resource utilization while achieving fairness. In COSHH, Hadoop system assigns a priority to each user. The number of slots assigned to user depends on assigned priority. Whenever a new job arrives in the cluster, task scheduling component of COSHH uses a task duration predictor to estimate the mean execution time of jobs on available resources. Further, estimation is used by queuing process to choose a queue for job. The algorithm uses the classification and optimization technique to classify jobs. Whenever a resource is available, routing process selects a job by searching through classes and forwards it to task scheduling component. The component further selects the task from selected job. The classification and optimization techniques add an overhead to scheduler. Thus, the authors have defined a threshold on the usage of techniques. In order to reduce the overhead, COSHH takes scheduling decisions by using minimum available system information, which, in turn, degrades the performance of scheduler. Moreover, scheduler does not consider resource availability while taking scheduling decisions.

RDS, a Resource and Deadline-aware Scheduler for Hadoop proposed by Cheng *et al.* (Cheng, Rao, Jiang, & Zhou, 2015), consider future resource availability while minimizing the job deadline misses. RDS divides job execution into control intervals and builds performance models for estimating job progress, which, in turn, infers overall job completion time. There are three main components: (i) *fuzzy performance model* (ii) *resource predictor* (iii) *scheduling optimizer*. The fuzzy model performs fine-grained job completion time estimation and self-adaptation at every measurement interval. The resource predictor, on the other hand, takes the history information on resource availability and predicts amount of available resources for next few intervals. Afterward, scheduling optimizer adjusts the number of slots allocated to each running job based on an online receding horizon control algorithm. The receding horizon control algorithm gives a task resource allocation matrix that minimizes job deadline misses while considering future resource availability.

The aforementioned resource-aware scheduling algorithms assume that resource requirements of a task remain stable over its lifetime. PRISM, proposed by Zhang *et al.* (Q. Zhang, Zhani, Yang, Boutaba, & Wong, 2015), on the other hand, introduced the concept of phase level resource aware scheduling. The algorithm divides Map and Reduce tasks into different phases. The map has two phases: *map* and *merge*, and Reduce has three phases: *shuffle*, *sort* and *reduce*. There are three components in PRISM: (i) *phase based scheduler* (ii) *local node* (iii) *a job progress monitor*. Whenever a task finishes execution of a particular phase, it asks permission from node manager to start next phase which, in turn, forwards the request to scheduler. The scheduler uses current progress information and phase level resource requirement to take a decision. The scheduler, on the basis of information, either allows the task to continue its next phase or launches a new task. However, pausing a task at runtime delays the completion of current task as well as all subsequent tasks. Moreover, performance of PRISM is highly dependent on the procedure used to collect the profiling information for job. Table 7 summarises all MR scheduling discussed in this subsection.

RESEARCH DIRECTIONS

The existing schedulers available in the literature for Hadoop MapReduce environment capture much of the aspects. Sometimes they consider one of the QoS parameters, say fairness, and come up with some

Table 7. Comparative analysis of resource-aware scheduling algorithms

Scheduling Algorithm	Strengths	Weaknesses	Environment	Type
RAS (Polo et al., 2011)	• Uses the profiling information from the previous execution of jobs to schedule a job • Dynamic in nature	• The entire focus is on three resource capacities – Memory, I/O, CPU only and ignores storage capacities of the TTs and network bandwidth parameters	Heterogeneous	Non-preemptive
COSHH (Rasooli & Down, 2014)	• Maximizes resource utilization while achieving fairness	• Classification and optimization techniques add an overhead • Do not consider future resource availability while making scheduling decisions	Heterogeneous	Non-preemptive
RDS(Cheng et al., 2015)	• Considers future resource availability when minimizing job deadline misses	• Do not consider different requirements of tasks in different stages	Heterogeneous	Non-preemptive
PRISM (Q. Zhang et al., 2015)	• Introduces the concept of phase level resource scheduling • Considers the difference of resource requirements of different phases of the map and reduce tasks	• Pausing a task at runtime delays the completion of the task • Performance of prism is highly dependent on the profiling procedure	Heterogeneous	Preemptive

heuristics to overcome the problem. While some other time, they consider different QoS parameter. However, there is still some place for improvement. Following are some research trends in field of MR scheduling algorithms.

- Multi-objective scheduling problem is a most trending area of research in the field of cloud and MapReduce scheduling, where more than one QoS parameters are being optimized at the same time. The NP-hard problem of multi-objective MapReduce scheduling becomes even more complex when one parameter is needed to be maximized and other is minimized.
- As the MapReduce scheduling is an NP-hard optimization problem, we often try to find the near optimal solution either through approximation algorithms or nature-inspired meta-heuristic algorithms. The goodness of approximation algorithms is represented as approximation ratio and always has a theoretical proof for it. On the other hand, meta-heuristic algorithms like Genetic Algorithm (GA), Particle Swarm Optimization (PSO), and Ant Colony Optimization (ACO) etc. do not provide any guarantee of the closeness of the optimal solution. Both these techniques are gaining popularity in designing MR scheduling algorithms.
- In Hadoop environment, criteria of energy efficiency have been given very few attention (Li, Ju, Jia, & Sun, 2015; Mashayekhy, Nejad, Grosu, Zhang, & Shi, 2015; Pandey & Saini, 2018a). Heterogeneous hardware can be exploited to conserve energy consumption by allocating a task to a suitable node from the viewpoint of energy consumption. For instance, some nodes consume less power for CPU-intensive and other for I/O-intensive tasks. Scheduling tasks to appropriate nodes will lead to better energy consumption. Further, energy consumption at the job level needs to be revisited.

CONCLUSION

Big data has become an important research issue due to its tremendous growth and associated complexity. Moreover, the analysis of such volume of data and further inference of an optimal decision is a major problem in various applications. Hence, the newly-built architectures, like Hadoop MapReduce and Spark have been adopted to handle the problem. Hadoop MapReduce handles Big Data demand with parallel processing on the cluster of commodity nodes. Thus, scheduling plays an important role. In this chapter, we presented a survey of different MapReduce Scheduling algorithms with varying QoS requirements. All studied scheduling algorithms have been analyzed and compared on the basis of various parameters.

REFERENCES

Apache Hadoop. (2018). Retrieved November 20, 2018, from http://hadoop.apache.org/

CapacityScheduler Guide. (2018). Retrieved November 20, 2018, from https://hadoop.apache.org/docs/r1.2.1/capacity_scheduler.html

Chen, Q., Guo, M., Deng, Q., Zheng, L., Guo, S., & Shen, Y. (2013). HAT: History-based auto-tuning MapReduce in heterogeneous environments. *The Journal of Supercomputing*, *64*(3), 1038–1054. doi:10.100711227-011-0682-5

Chen, Q., Zhang, D., Guo, M., Deng, Q., & Guo, S. (2010). SAMR: A Self-adaptive MapReduce Scheduling Algorithm in Heterogeneous Environment. In *2010 10th IEEE International Conference on Computer and Information Technology* (pp. 2736–2743). IEEE. 10.1109/CIT.2010.458

Cheng, D., Rao, J., Jiang, C., & Zhou, X. (2015). Resource and Deadline-Aware Job Scheduling in Dynamic Hadoop Clusters. In *2015 IEEE International Parallel and Distributed Processing Symposium* (pp. 956–965). IEEE. 10.1109/IPDPS.2015.36

Cho, B., Rahman, M., Chajed, T., Gupta, I., Abad, C., Roberts, N., & Lin, P. (2013). Natjam. In *Proceedings of the 4th annual Symposium on Cloud Computing - SOCC '13* (pp. 1–17). New York: ACM Press. 10.1145/2523616.2523624

Dean, J., & Ghemawat, S. (2008). MapReduce: Simplified data processing on large clusters. *Communications of the ACM, 51*(1), 107. doi:10.1145/1327452.1327492

Fair Scheduler. (2018). Retrieved November 20, 2018, from https://hadoop.apache.org/docs/r1.2.1/fair_scheduler.html

Fischer, M. J., Su, X., & Yin, Y. (2010). Assigning tasks for efficiency in Hadoop. In *Proceedings of the 22nd ACM symposium on Parallelism in algorithms and architectures - SPAA '10* (p. 30). New York: ACM Press. 10.1145/1810479.1810484

Jones, M. (2011). *Scheduling in Hadoop – IBM Developer*. Retrieved November 20, 2018, from https://developer.ibm.com/articles/os-hadoop-scheduling/

Kc, K., & Anyanwu, K. (2010). Scheduling Hadoop Jobs to Meet Deadlines. In *2010 IEEE Second International Conference on Cloud Computing Technology and Science* (pp. 388–392). IEEE. 10.1109/CloudCom.2010.97

Li, P., Ju, L., Jia, Z., & Sun, Z. (2015). SLA-aware energy-efficient scheduling scheme for hadoop YARN. In *Proceedings -IEEE 17th International Conference on High Performance Computing and Communications, 2015* (pp. 623–628). IEEE. 10.1109/HPCC-CSS-ICESS.2015.181

Macqueen, J. (1967). Some methods for classification and analysis of multivariate observations. *5th Berkeley Symposium on Mathematical Statistics and Probability*, 281-297. Retrieved from http://citeseer.ist.psu.edu/viewdoc/summary?doi=10.1.1.308.8619

Mashayekhy, L., Nejad, M. M., Grosu, D., Zhang, Q., & Shi, W. (2015). Energy-Aware Scheduling of MapReduce Jobs for Big Data Applications. *IEEE Transactions on Parallel and Distributed Systems, 26*(10), 2720–2733. doi:10.1109/TPDS.2014.2358556

Nimbalkar, P. P., & Gadekar, D. P. (2015). Survey on Scheduling Algorithm in MapReduce Framework. *International Journal of Science, Engineering and Technology Research, 4*(4), 1226–1230. Retrieved from http://ijsetr.org/wp-content/uploads/2015/05/IJSETR-VOL-4-ISSUE-4-1226-1230.pdf

Pandey, V., & Saini, P. (2018a). An Energy-Efficient Greedy MapReduce Scheduler for Heterogeneous Hadoop YARN Cluster. In *6th International Conference on Big Data Analytics-2018* (pp. 282–291). Springer. 10.1007/978-3-030-04780-1_19

Pandey, V., & Saini, P. (2018b). How *Heterogeneity* Affects the Design of Hadoop MapReduce Schedulers: A State-of-the-Art Survey and Challenges. *Big Data, 6*(2), 72–95. doi:10.1089/big.2018.0013 PMID:29924647

Peng, Z., & Ma, Y. (2011). *A New Scheduling Algorithm in Hadoop MapReduce.* Berlin: Springer; doi:10.1007/978-3-642-24282-3_74

Polo, J., Castillo, C., Carrera, D., Becerra, Y., Whalley, I., & Steinder, M., … Ayguadé, E. (2011). Resource-Aware Adaptive Scheduling for MapReduce Clusters. In *Proceedings of the 12th ACM/IFIP/ USENIX international conference on Middleware* (pp. 187–207). Springer-Verlag. 10.1007/978-3-642-25821-3_10

Rasooli, A., & Down, D. G. (2014). COSHH: A classification and optimization based scheduler for heterogeneous Hadoop systems. *Future Generation Computer Systems, 36,* 1–15. doi:10.1016/j.future.2014.01.002

Sandholm, T., & Lai, K. (2010). *Dynamic Proportional Share Scheduling in Hadoop.* Berlin: Springer. doi:10.1007/978-3-642-16505-4_7

Shields, A. (2014). *Why traditional database systems fail to support "big data."* Retrieved November 20, 2018, from https://marketrealist.com/2014/07/traditional-database-systems-fail-support-big-data

Soualhia, M., Khomh, F., & Tahar, S. (2015). ATLAS: An AdapTive faiLure-Aware Scheduler for Hadoop. In *2015 IEEE 34th International Performance Computing and Communications Conference (IPCCC)* (pp. 1–8). IEEE. 10.1109/PCCC.2015.7410316

Sun, X., He, C., & Lu, Y. (2012). ESAMR: An Enhanced Self-Adaptive MapReduce Scheduling Algorithm. In *2012 IEEE 18th International Conference on Parallel and Distributed Systems* (pp. 148–155). IEEE. 10.1109/ICPADS.2012.30

Tan, J., Meng, X., & Zhang, L. (2012). Coupling scheduler for MapReduce/Hadoop. In *Proceedings of the 21st international symposium on High-Performance Parallel and Distributed Computing - HPDC '12* (p. 129). New York: ACM Press. 10.1145/2287076.2287097

Tang, Z., Zhou, J., Li, K., & Li, R. (2013). A MapReduce task scheduling algorithm for deadline constraints. *Cluster Computing, 16*(4), 651–662. doi:10.100710586-012-0236-5

Varma, R. (2013). Survey on MapReduce and Scheduling Algorithms in Hadoop. *International Journal of Science and Research, 14*(2), 2319–7064. Retrieved from https://www.ijsr.net/archive/v4i2/SUB151194.pdf

Verma, A., Cherkasova, L., Kumar, V. S., & Campbell, R. H. (2012). Deadline-based workload management for MapReduce environments: Pieces of the performance puzzle. In *2012 IEEE Network Operations and Management Symposium* (pp. 900–905). IEEE. 10.1109/NOMS.2012.6212006

Wang, W., Zhu, K., Ying, L., Tan, J., & Zhang, L. (2016). MapTask Scheduling in MapReduce With Data Locality: Throughput and Heavy-Traffic Optimality. *IEEE/ACM Transactions on Networking, 24*(1), 190–203. doi:10.1109/TNET.2014.2362745

Wang, Y., Lu, W., Lou, R., & Wei, B. (2015). Improving MapReduce Performance with Partial Speculative Execution. *Journal of Grid Computing, 13*(4), 587–604. doi:10.100710723-015-9350-y

Yildiz, O., Ibrahim, S., & Antoniu, G. (2017). Enabling fast failure recovery in shared Hadoop clusters: Towards failure-aware scheduling. *Future Generation Computer Systems*, *74*, 208–219. doi:10.1016/j. future.2016.02.015

Yoo, D., & Sim, K. M. (2011). A comparative review of job scheduling for MapReduce. In *2011 IEEE International Conference on Cloud Computing and Intelligence Systems* (pp. 353–358). IEEE. 10.1109/ CCIS.2011.6045089

Zaharia, M., Borthakur, D., Sen Sarma, J., Elmeleegy, K., Shenker, S., & Stoica, I. (2010). Delay scheduling. In *Proceedings of the 5th European conference on Computer systems - EuroSys '10* (p. 265). New York: ACM Press. 10.1145/1755913.1755940

Zaharia, M., Konwinski, A., Joseph, A. D., Katz, R., & Stoica, I. (2008). Improving MapReduce performance in heterogeneous environments. In *Proceedings of the 8th USENIX Conference on Operating Systems Design and Implementation*. USENIX Association. Retrieved from https://dl.acm.org/citation. cfm?id=1855744

Zhang, Q., Zhani, M. F., Yang, Y., Boutaba, R., & Wong, B. (2015). PRISM: Fine-Grained Resource-Aware Scheduling for MapReduce. *IEEE Transactions on Cloud Computing*, *3*(2), 182–194. doi:10.1109/ TCC.2014.2379096

Zhang, X., Zhong, Z., Feng, S., Tu, B., & Fan, J. (2011). Improving Data Locality of MapReduce by Scheduling in Homogeneous Computing Environments. In *2011 IEEE Ninth International Symposium on Parallel and Distributed Processing with Applications* (pp. 120–126). IEEE. 10.1109/ISPA.2011.14

Chapter 23
Software–Defined Networks (SDN):
A Survey

Rabia Bilal
Usman Institute of Technology, Pakistan

Bilal Muhammad Khan
National University of Sciences and Technology Islamabad, Pakistan

ABSTRACT

Software-defined networks (SDN) are a new paradigm shift in the world of network centralized command and control, providing network omniscience and separates control and data planes. Most of the research work till date focuses on increasing efficiency and manageability of computational and storage resources which results in emergence of current virtualization technologies. The feasibility and applications of SDN in current datacenters and network infrastructures is being studied by academia, industry, and the standardization bodies. This chapter explains SDN concepts and its difference from legacy networking, interrelated terminologies, protocols, programming languages, benefits, and shortcomings. Moreover, exploration of current research areas and techniques along with in-depth analysis and future research directions will be presented.

INTRODUCTION

Software Defined Networks concept is not new and have started to evolve since 1998 from Ipsilon's general switch management protocol (Network Working Group, 1998), IETF FORCES (Retana, Atlas & Brungard, 2015), IETF path computational element (Architecture Adrian Farrel), Clean slate 4D (Greenberg *et al.*, 2015), Ethane (Casado *et al.*, 2007)which was full scale research implementation.

Mostly SDN is confused with Network Function virtualization (NFV) terminology; Technically SDN is the architecture of network which separates control plane from data plane, whereas NFV is taking physical networking equipment such as routers, switches, firewalls, load balancers and running them as virtual machines (VM) (Network Function Virtualisation, 2012) as shown in Figure 1.

DOI: 10.4018/978-1-5225-8407-0.ch023

Figure 1. Relationship between NFV and SDN

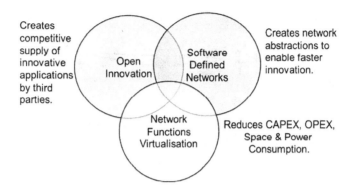

SDN predominantly software based enjoys larger acceptability and ease of deployment; which is not true in case of hardware innovation cycle that may take years to reach market. SDN runs control software on modern multi-core processors resulting in easy updating of control protocols and faster processing. This software based modular approach enables devices in data plane to work without any processing overheads, resulting in simpler and lower cost switches. The approach provides better platform for protocol development as in case of Google which implemented their WAN connectivity in VAHDAT project (Software Define WAN, 2015). This methodology of software define WAN architecture enables Google to successfully improves Network utilization up to 100% as well as time critical traffic get prioritization and remaining bandwidth is filled with bulk data.

SDN ARCHITECTURE

In conventional network, devices comprises of almost all the layers including management, control and data plane which increases touch points in network causing lack of visibility and control. Moreover legacy network works on the basis of Human in loop; this situation makes it more challenging and causes serious degradation of network performance, since humans cannot fix all the problems in real-time and their responses are more reactive rather than pro-active as shown in figure 2.

In case of SDN network, controller serves as a bridge between human in loop and machine. Controller gives real time situation awareness, effect, redirects the flows by sending configuration changes to network devices and modify flow table of network devices as shown in figure 3. Here the North bound and south bound interface are not related to flow of data but instead they are from perspective of SDN Controller in control plane.

- Up (North) to Management Plane
- Down (South) to the Data Plane

Figure 2. Layered Approach of Device

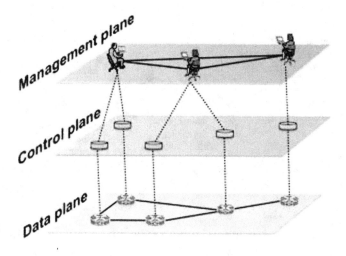

Figure 3. SDN architecture

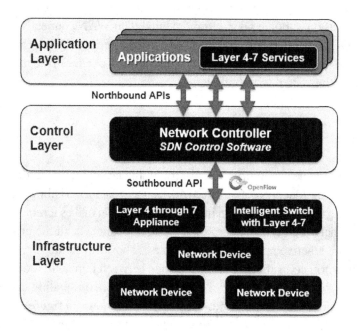

Moreover there is an East/West interface available which enables one logical controller communicate to another logical controller. Currently only south bound interface have standard protocol namely Open flow (ONF Technical Library) however north bound interface still lacks in standardization; moreover SDN controller requires plugins to work with north bound applications. A working group namely 'North-bound API WG' (North Bound Interface) is working towards developing API that adds abstraction and encapsulate implementation complexity of north bound management plane from the SDN controller platform (North Bound Interface).

Figure 4. NBI Standardization

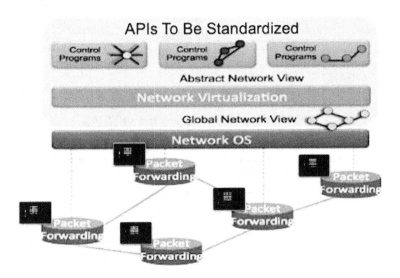

OPENFLOW

Openflow is a standard southbound API for SDN to ensure different vendor interoperability and achieve goal of Vendor independent platform (Bakshi *et al.,* 2016). "OpenFlow" began as an idea about how research networks could be built. There are five versions of openflow and each version is advanced form of its previous version (Isabelle GUIS, 2016). Table 1 summarizes the release dates of these versions.

Version 1.0 of open flow is the first draft of the protocol and thus widely deployed. It has basic packet handling mechanism and quality of service (QoS) features compare to later versions. Version 1.1 introduced multiple flow tables pipeline, MPLS tags, VLAN tags and group table.

Version 1.2 comes with IPv6 support added, switch connectivity with multiple controllers with master-slave role thus failover implementation can be done.

Version 1.3 introduces new feature of OAM, arbitrary auxiliary connections between master controller and the switch can be made which load balance control plane. IPv6 Extension Header handling support and flow counters. Version 1.4 introduces new TLV structures and optical ports configuration is possible. The configuration of optical ports is now possible. Controllers can bundle all control messages sent to switches. In Version 1.5, "Egress table" resolve the issue of post process the packet without chaining another switch after the output port. Table 2 summarizes different versions of open flow along with their features and target problem areas.

Table 1. Open flow Versions

Version	Release Date
1.0	Dec-2009
1.1	Feb- 2011
1.2	Dec -2011
1.3	Jun- 2012
1.4	Oct – 2013
1.5	Dec-2014

Figure 5. Openflow pipelining

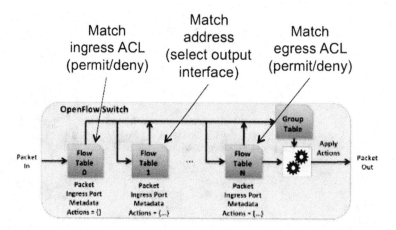

Figure 6. Openflow 1.2

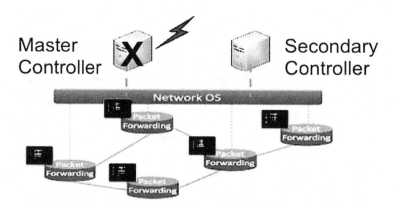

Network Topologies and Design

Traditional network topologies of datacenter and service provider network are divided into three-tier structure namely core, distribution and access layers. This design is more robust and fault tolerant but in case of any equipment or connectivity failures greatly reduced bandwidth of overall system.

SDN use leaf/spine topology which allows for easy scale out and enables network team to extend same architecture to scalable size, increasing its performance without compromise. The idea in this new design is that each spine switches connected to every leaf switche.

Since the controller decides from where the data should flow therefore protocols like spanning tree are no longer required. In (Casado *et al.*, 2012) a proposal to use insight underlying MPLS technology to overcome shortcomings of SDN and enhance simplicity in hardware alongside making controls more flexible is proposed. Furthermore, researchers are also suggesting that modularity should not be discarded in new SDN design. A concept of reliable flooding (Akella & Krishnamurthy, 2014) is presented as a method for communication between controllers and switches to enhance the flexibility and QoS of SDNs.

Table 2. Advancement in open flow protocol

Openflow Version	Features	Challenges Solved
1.0-1.1	Multiple Tables, Group Tables, Vlan & MPLS support	Flow entry explosion, Enable Applying action sets to group of flows
1.1-1.2	OXM Match, Multiple Controller	Extend matching flexibility, High availability
1.2-1.3	Meter Table, Table miss entry.	QoS and DiffServ, flexible configuration
1.3-1.4	Synchronized Table, Bundle	Enhance table scalability, Enhance switch synchronization
1.4-1.5	Egress Table, Scheduled bundle	Further enhance switch synchronization

Figure 7. Three-tier traditional design

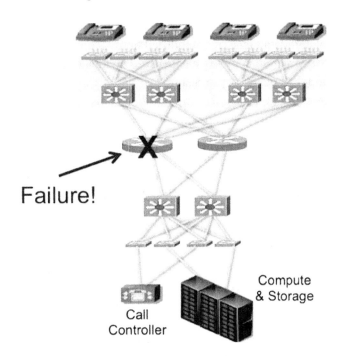

CONTROL PLANE

Control plane involve in all actions of data plane but do not involve end user packets for e.g. packets handling policies such as routing and switching. An abstraction of Consistent Policy Composition (Canini *et al.*, 2013) is defined for Asynchronous environment to deal with the issues of conflicting policies. It

Figure 8. Leaf/spine design

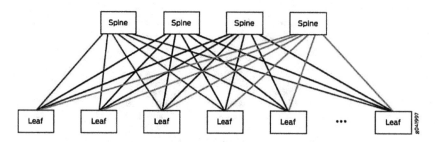

was expected that only policy updates that induce a correct network behavior are allowed to affect the traffic but later on results shows that abstraction cannot tolerate single controller crash.

NOX was built with a concept of Operating system of a Network that provides a programmatic interface. NOX extends earlier SDN controllers work i.e. SANE/Ethane and was designed around multiple applications (Moyano *et al.*, 2017). Facilities such as VINI (Moyano *et al.*, 2017) and Emulab (Hernando *et al.*, 2017) allows multiple simultaneous experiments to test new services over testbed, however the major drawback is that these facilities merely run on software platform using conventional CPU while in real world scenarios algorithms are run on ASIC based devices which are far more superior in terms of processing speed. In order to fill this gap FlowVisor (Sherwood *et al.*, 2010) is introduced. Flow Visor resides in between control and data plane of unmodified hardware which supports Open-Flow turning production network to testbed without any extra expense. The idea of dividing the communication between the control plane and data planes is promising.

Moreover ONIX (Koponen et al, 2010) platform implement distributed network control plane and is considered as first opensource platform based on openflow for large scale production networks. Initial version of NOX was based on cooperative threading and uses single threaded manner to process events while later version of NOX was a multithreaded application.

Beacon (Erickson, 2013) is another OpenFlow controller built on Java language. This system is built in modular approach and is highly scalable. In Openflow Network controller is responsible for managing all flows between devices which can create performance bottleneck. Maestro introduces optimization technique of parallelism to avoid issues of performance bottleneck (Cai *et al.*,2011) and scale throughput of system. Single threaded event loops used in NOX controllers are not capable of using Multi-Core CPU technology to its full potential. In (Heller *et al.*,2012) a mechanism for location and numbers of controller selection mechanism is proposed, the selection depends on latency and the network link quality.

Hyperflow (Tootoonchian, 2010) optimizes control plane by keeping network control logic centralized and decision making is localized by controllers serving that region of network hence minimizing response time of control plane. HyperFlow application is a C++ NOX application runs on each controller to maintain consistent communications with controllers and share network-wide view. Kandoo (Yeganeh *et al.*, 2012) suggested to use multiple layers of controllers which effectively reduces control channel consumptions when compared to normal openflow controller. DIFANE (Minlan *et al.*, 2010) offload partial forwarding decisions from the controller to authority switches which have directory of rules.

Yanc controller (Monaco *et al.*, 2013) platform controllers use existing operating system 'UNIX' in building controller which is different idea compare to other controllers which uses different types of programming language like NOX uses C++, Ryu uses Python, Floodlight uses Java, Nettle uses Haskell e.t.c. Yanc use current operation system of UNIX as Network operating system and proved that if we follow this footstep it leverages innovation in the operating system space.

In SDN network control is centralized logically but there are many factors that also need to be address in order to consider it as distributed system for example HA, scalability, and delay which dictate that a robustness of platform. In SDN, Synchronization of policy is necessary in distributed controller platform. Overlapping policy updates leads to inconsistencies in data plane packet forwarding. A solution was proposed by defining consistency through reduction in a sequential policy architecture (Canini *et al.*, 2013) according to correctness in data structure was done.

Unlike domain specific language proposals Beehive (Hassas *et al.*, 2013) depends on familiar programming with abstraction for storing state of application. Through automatic compilation of applications into their distributed counterparts and sharing state between application functions optimization of functions and designing scalable control applications was done.

In order to SDN system gain popularity and widely adopted each portion of stack is developed by different entities thus encouraging diversity. There are four scenarios in SDN fault model: controller hardware failures, controller crashes due to bugs, network device failures and SDN App crashes. Lego-SDN (Chadrasekaran, 2014) doesn't focus on Controller failure but instead on failures of SDN applications. In controllers like FloodLight and NOX, any component failure in the controller stack results in complete devastation of control plane. If fault in one SDN application is not handled, then it will cause other dependent applications and controller to stop working. Due to lack of isolation between applications of SDN and controller, NOX faces same challenge. LegoSDN prototype works with Flood-Light. Layer of Isolation is provided by AppVisor and NetLog (network-wide transaction system) supports roll backs & atomic.

Switch performance degrades on high traffic load due to limited throughput capability of control agents (Wang *et al.*, 2014). Scotch uses vSwitch based overlay to elastically scales up capacity of control plane capacity. Controller communicates with Openflow switch through secure channel using OpenFlow Agent. Saturation of control channel between switch and controller causes switch not to send updates to controller about new flows. Scoth uses capacity of data plane to increase throughput of control paths and bridges gap between control and data plane by tunneling newly created flows to vSwitches. When congestion is faced on control path of a physical switch is overloaded, so new flows will be tunneled towards may vSwitches, avoiding it to be sent to centralized controller. Scotch utilizes high control plane capacity of vSwitches and the high data plane capacity of hardware switches.

ONOS (Berde *et al.*,2014) is a carrier grade version of SDN focuses on core network traffic engineering and mainly developed by an idea of Onix. In ONOS's architecture is in runtime instance and have multiple failover instances which can take over if one instance fails using leader election among instances. Programming and discovering information is basically responsibilities of master instance. It follows distributed architecture which runs on many servers, a subnet of switches has its own master controller. ONOS prototype was presented at Open Networking Summit in 2013 showed ONOS with hundreds of virtual switches, global network view, capability of adding switches dynamically and cluster of ONOS instance, failover of instances and alternative link selection in response to link failure. Second prototype was focused to remove performance bottleneck in remote data operations.

Multiple network management Apps can work separately showing network performance parameters in Statesman(Sun *et al.*,2014) showing target state (TS) which is yardstick of performance of network and observed state (OS) which is success and failure to achieve TS which reflect OS and proposed state

(PS). Dependency model used ensures safe merging of proposed states. Statesman uses network state to detect conflicts and invariant violations. Statesman is widely used in Microsoft Azure Datacenters.

CoVisor architecture allows multiple controllers to cooperate while handling same shared traffic. CoVisor limit topology view by creating custom virtual topologies and specifying access controls that regulate the packets. Algorithms proposed in CoVisor is for composing policies, compiling virtual networks to OpenFlow rules, and processing rule from upstream controller. CoVisor (Jin *et al.*, 2015) allows the administrator to virtualize the underlying topology and restrict the packet-processing capabilities available to each controller. CoVisor prototype was modification of OpenVirteX with 4000+ lines of Java code and introduces composition and incremental update logic which is different from isolation logic of OpenVirteX.

DATA PLANE

Data plane involve in all actions that are result of packets received from user end for e.g. forwarding packets, fragmentation, reassembly of packets and replication of multicasting. DevoFlow (Curtis *et al.*, 2011) was a modification of openflow and based on assumption that current openflow standard is incapable of handling performance requirement of current and future networks. It was evaluated through simulations and load-balance data center traffic. Devoflow attempts to resolve two issues with openflow setup one is that controller is not invoked on every flow setup and other is that collecting each flow counters increased overhead on controller by making openflow switch smart enough to take responsibility which violates concept of SDN i.e. centralized management.

DIFANE (Minlan *et al.*, 2010) keeps all traffic in the data plane by selectively directing packets through intermediate switches that store the necessary rules hence no need to change functionality of control plane. DIFANE uses wildcard in data plane which enables use of commodity switch hardware which is different from current SDN solutions which directs the first packet of "microflow" to a centralized controller which then decides which rules should be installed. Click-based OpenFlow switch (kernel level) were used for experimentation procedures. DIFANE reduces overhead of caching misses by keeping them in the data plane through caching wildcard rules and uses intermediate switches for "miss" packets. DIFANE uses a link-state routing protocol between the switches which helps in customization of forwarding of traffic between end device.

Another proposal was that CPU of switches should handle both control plane and data plane traffic which overcomes limitation of small forwarding table and shallow packet buffer for which a prototype switch using ServerSwitch platform was made (Lu *et al.*,2012) This Prototype results shows that over 90% traffic was offloaded, without any packet loss it absorb large bursts of traffic, and can be easily used for network security layer against low-rate burst attacks.

OpenFlow have many counters for each flow-table rule which can be avoided by ASIC if the ASIC data plane have fast connectivity CPU with memory, in this way we can replace traditional counters with a streams towards CPU, and then process each stream in the CPU. As a result flexibility can be achieved regarding counter-related information (Jeffery *et al.*,2012). Author insist that a "smart controller, dumb switch" architecture of SDN network is not very convincing with the availability of high performance embedded CPUs which can be place in switches and open doors of new innovation.

There were many new concept of hardware such as NPU and GPU were introduced to support vision of programmable Networks but both of them were far away for performance of switches using ASICs (Bosshart *et al.,*2013). The idea of changing hardware functionality upon software upgrade was focused on RISC based pipelined architecture for switching chips named RMT. It allows the forwarding plane to be changed in the field without modifying hardware. Memory block coupled within or different stages is key for reconfigurable match tables. For matching edibility of flows TCAM can be widely used.

Another idea (Sivaraman *et al.,*2013) was suggested to use data plane for aligning queueing and scheduling using a small reconfigurable hardware such as FPGA. Proposed hardware was made for high density of ports unlike previous implementation i.e. SwitchBlade (Anwer *et al.,*2014), NetFPGA (Lockwood *et al.,*2015) and Chimpp (Rubow *et al.,*2016).

SmartSouth (Schiff *et al.,* 2015) only uses OpenFlow match action and reduce interaction with control plane. Four applications of this concept: topology snapshot, any cast, black hole- and critical node detection was discussed. By using fast failover mechanism of openflow, the data plane functions can be made prune to failures.

CAB (Yan *et al.,*2014) cache Wildcard rules which enables aggregating flows, reusability, policies update and achieves efficient switch memory use. CacheFlow (Katta *et al.,*2014) supports infinite switch abstraction by using hardware-software architecture which supports rewriting, reordering and caching important switch rules. Legacy switches implement rules using TCAM but it is more expensive and power hungry when compare to RAM based storage systems. Cache-Flow logically placed between controller and hardware switch, the system could easily run on the controller resulting a switch with infinite cache.

A new solution for installing rules on switches name as Integer Linear Programming (ILP) (Zhang *et al.,*2014) which optimizes total number of rules and addressing switch TCAM capacity limitations. This solution was modification of Big Switch abstraction. Another paper explores the design of a compiler for switching chips and interaction between ILP and algorithms (Jose *et al.,* 2014).

HYBRID NETWORKS

Although SDN technology have gain significant importance in industry but Network operators have to run both legacy and SDN networks hand in hand until completely transiting to SDN. Incremental deployment will be done so that Network operators can guess reliability and can overcome any issues in their current services. SDN have to Interface with other network and have to support not all but most of network protocols. Hybrid switches can also be used which have both SDN components and traditional networking protocols components. If SDN doesn't know where to forward then it feeds traditional forwarding engine.

For testing the feasibility and judging the efficiency of SDN many testbed experiments have done with hardware switches and through simulation on real network topologies such as Panopticon (Levin *et al.,* 2014) which hides legacy devices acting as a "network hypervisor" that maps the logical SDN abstraction to hardware, HybNET (Lu *et al.,* 2013) based on openstack Neutron, ClosedFlow(Keller *et al.,* 2013) which allow layers on top of OpenFlow thus devices which doesn't support openflow can be used.

PROGRAMMING SDN

Frenetic project (Foster *et al.,* 2013) propose simple high level abstractions for programming namely monitoring network traffic, packet-forwarding policies, and updating policies continuously according to changing traffic pattern which makes programming applications in SDN easier. (Foster *et al.,* 2011). This programming language overcomes limitation of different industry standard languages such as overlapping of decision rules (un)installed by one App or module by other App or modules. address the issue of how to program a collection of interconnected switches instead of single device.

Pyretic's (Monsanto *et al.,*2013) sequential composition allows one module to inspect processed packets of other module for example doing routing of packets after it has been allowed by access control. It provides programmers to focus on their domain expertise and design applications in modular way.

NetCore process packets using arbitrary functions instead of expressing forwarding policies which was used in Frenetic. Compiler of NetCore uses idea of dividing labor and divides run-time system into two parts, one for switches and other that for controller.

Software bugs and misconfiguration are the source of Networks failure. General system for establishing controller correctness that reduces the proof obligation needed. Machine-Verified Network Controllers (Voellmy & Hudak, 2011) gives network programmers robust static guarantees backed by machine-checked and uses Featherweight OpenFlow which formal model of openflow. Architecture is divided into three level of abstraction NetCore, Flow tables and Featherweight openflow.

Procera addresses to the problem of lack of configurable interface and provides declarative policy language which is reactive to dynamic changes of Network. (Rocha & Launchbury, 2011) FRP based language Low level control programs are written on FRP based language in Nettle and embedded in a functional programming language.

Hierarchical Flow Tables (Ferguson *et al.,* 2013) uses a tree structure to take on each packet. HFT uses conflict-resolution operators to address issue of conflicts. Coq proof assistant was used to check policies by newly designed compiler. In Participatory Networking end users/applications can request high-level, abstract network resources, and HFT successfully compiles these requests to configurations.

Isolation is required between different kinds of traffic and is introduced by Splendid Isolation (Gutz *et al.,* 2012) abstraction which supports programming isolated parts of Network i.e. isolation provided at the language level. Compiler ensures that each part is isolated from other part though specifications with respect to packet processing.

Corybantic (Mogul *et al.,*2013) addresses to the problem of multiple controller functions competes for resources design and is based on modular composition of independent controller modules managing different aspects of the network.Corybantic works at a higher layer of the controller stack by consolidating multi-target issue single target issue by communicating goals in a common currency.

NetEgg (Yuan *et al.,*2014) uses algorithm that automatically surmises the state that should be kept up to display the wanted behavior alongside the principles for handling network packet flows and updating state in this manner create executions that are steady with example behavior.

Switch diversity poses two probe first is understanding the challenge for e.g maximum amount of flows that can be inserted depends on match field. Many important behaviors are not reported. Second, diversity results in utilization challenge thus controllers control signals will become complex. Tango (Lazaris *et al.,*2014) introduces probing engine that addresses switch diversity and corresponds to switch capabilities and behaviors using OpenFlow commands. Tango evaluation shows optimal behavior of probing algorithm both on hardware and software/emulated software switches.

Merlin (Soulé *et al.,*2013) utilizes high-level policy making approach by utilizing programs in a declarative programming language for overseeing network resources in SDN. Compiler maps policies into a problem that decide capacity and resource allocation portions utilizing parameterizable. Code is created which can be executed on the network components to uphold the policies. Merlin gives mechanism to designating control of sub-policies and for confirming that alterations made to sub-policies don't disregard global constraint. Tests results shows that network resources to dynamically adjust policies according to their necessities. Single modules of SDN can take larger part of bandwidth pipe accessible in system which can bring about lack of resource accessible for different modules.

Athens (young *et al.,*2014) is a revision of the Corybantic design, but propose different network states and voting mechanisms for non-rulebased conflict resolution. Modules must bolster adaptability in module parity and accuracy. Athen builds up a system with the ideas of parity and accuracy to outline the problem and group. In addition, tests demonstrate that Athens system is ensured to choose a Pareto effective assignment among known candidates, and in a few cases prompts a Pareto superior allocation over simpler procedures that don't consider preferences.

Tools are required by network operators to express how a network's data-plane behavior should respond to events and changing conditions. Kinetic (Kim *et al.,*2015) is a domain specific language and network control system that automatically verifies the correctness of these control programs.

P4 (Bosshart *et al.,*2013) is high-level language for programming protocol-independent packet processors. P4 works in conjunction with SDN protocol like OpenFlow. In its present structure, OpenFlow expressly specifies headers of protocol on which it works. This set has developed from 12 to 41 fields in a couple of year, expanding the intricacy of the specification while still not giving the adaptability to include new headers. P4 programs specify how a switch processes packets, can describes everything from high- performance forwarding ASICs to software switches and allows network engineers to change the way their switches process each packets flows after their installation.

EMULATION AND SIMULATION

Mininet uses OS-level virtualization and can be easily deployed on laptop (Lantz, Heller & McKeown, 2013). Mininet can only be run on a single machine and cannot do emulation wireless network which are its major drawbacks. IMUNES (Moyano *et al.,* 2017) and EMULAB is also OS-level virtualization but faces same issue of un-availability of hardware prototyping.

Current methodologies neglect to represent noteworthy vendor-specific architecture in the SDN switch control path and usage of OpenFlow-capable switches can drastically affect latency and throughput. An approach and emulator extension to replicate these performance of control-path was proposed (Yuxing *et al.,*2013). OVS is not a decent approximaion of genuine OpenFlow equipment, and that basic strides can significantly expand the precision of emulation.

SDN APPLICATIONS

Tremendous number of functions can be used in an SDN, few of the application areas are discussed below:

Big Data

Big Data is the term for information sets so expansive that conventional information processing methods gets to be inadequate. The measure of digital information in 2011 is around 1.8 trillion gigabytes which will increase to 50 times more by year 2020(Bakshi & Kapil, 2012). Thus Network infrastructure should be able to support this huge amount of data. In this section, we focus on recent advancement made on big data using SDN.

A network management design, for example, FlowComb have been presented that helps Big Data processing applications to accomplish high usage and data processing and handling times. A central engine for making decision which utilizes idea of SDN gathers information movement areas from agents and avoid any congestion by scheduling next data streams.

(Monga *et al.,*2012) Monga uses SDN concept for campus environment big-data science-architectural models. (Herodotou & Herodotos, 2011) Proposed a self-tuning system for big data analytics. Bursting data in Transportation SDN was analyzed in recent case study and was presented in (Sadasivara & Abhinava, 2013) which introduces their endeavors on Software-Defined Networking for big data science-design models from campus network to WAN network. To sidestep conventional hotspots in common campus network, the author has built in view of the SC11 SCinet Research Sandbox demonstrator with SDN for purpose of a versatile architecture methodology. The proposed work has been turned out to be basic and all the more imperatively versatile to network structure. General talking, strategy in this work is incremental, yet we are happy to see its framework approval has demonstrated yet another SDN plan.

For Big-data run-time programs is helpful for big data that require successive reconfigurations. (Wang, Guohui & Shaikh, 2012) Introduces their endeavors of run-time network programming in big data applications. In particular, the author consolidated SDN controller and optical switching to acknowledge close coordinated effort of control plane and potential applications. Joint improvements of network control plane and applications have been investigated.

Analysis demonstrates that, at a moderately little overhead of configurations, the proposed combination offers extraordinary possibilities for enhancing applications performance. The efficient design and assessment in this work is motivating. Big data transportation is yet another essential part for SDN data exchange as it guarantees littler transportation delays. Bursting data in Transportation SDN was presented in (Das *et al.,*2013) recently.

The author proposed a SDN-enabled optical transportation design which networks seamlessly inside server farms. A case study with an OpenFlow-capable optical vSwitch dealing with a little optical transport system was accounted for. The author contends that their expansion and inherent programmability brought by SDN are considerable in real world applications. Be that as it may, general effect must be further approved in bigger organizations. In aggregate, real world case studies analyses on SDN and also run-time programming and bursting data transportation has been accounted for and they all demonstrated promising progression contrasted with existing methodologies.

Cloud

General management framework created for SDN, similar to NOX (Bozkurt *et al.,* 2016) can be stretched out to particular situations like the datacenter the paper as a solid occurrence of a general network platform.

VXLAN resolves limitation of 4K limitation of VLAN and is a Layer 2 hybrid network over a Layer 3 Network. IP multicast requires great amount of resources such as IP multicast table and CPU which limits scalability. (Nakagawa, Hyoudou& Shimizu,2012) A new management method using OpenFlow for IP Multicast was proposed which eliminates periodical Join/Leave messages thus increases efficiency in terms of control signaling and achieves more in test Layer 2. This method implements multipath control in LAN network.

NaaS is new service which is getting popularity due to its capability to configure network in current cloud computing environment. (Raghavendra, Lobo & Lee, 2012) Author have proposed instance of pair shortest path algorithm which is versatile lightweight dynamic graph query mechanisms based on TEDI (Wei, 2010) algorithm and can be utilized to empower practical computation times, in presence of network dynamism.

Security

Ethane was implemented for both hardware and software in LAN and WLAN in Stanford University's network (Stewart *et al.,*2017). Ethane follows three fundamental principles i.e. high level Names were used for policy declaration, path declaration policies, and binding of origin of packets. These fundamentals Network Security key principles and makes it easy to manage.

Resonance (Goransson *et al.,*2016) was new security system applied to Georgia Tech's NAC system enforcing policies using flow-level information and real-time monitoring alerts. Lower layers traffic is controlled using programmable switches.

MTD namely Moving target defense changes host IP address and conceals network resources from outer/inside scanners. It wipes out shortcomings of static setup which is favorable position for Network Security attacks.(Jafarian, Ehab & Duan, 2013) OpenFlow Random Host Mutation (OFRHM) utilizes MTD design that allocate virtual IP addresses with high unpredictability and integrity of configurations. This technique can guard against stealthy filtering, worm spread, and other scanning based network attacks.

In legacy network DDOS attacks are mitigated by many procedures of which two are remote triggered Black holing and other is diverting malicious traffic to scrubbing facility/servers. NetFuse (wang *et al.,*2013) is a mechanism to protect against high traffic surge in data center networks which is based on openflow. It collects openflow control messages passively to detect active traffic flows to identify and isolates malicious traffic with minimum wrong alert rate.

FortNOX (Porras *et al.,*2012) is a software augmentation for the NOX OpenFlow controller that gives part based authorization and security requirement enforcement. NOX utilizes FortNOX for real-time checking of flow rules inconsistencies and may acknowledge or dismiss the new rule, contingent upon requester with higher security approval.

Routing

Because of high port density necessity in current server farm, topologies comprise of multi-rooted trees depend on per-flow static hashing and lose data transfer capacity because of collisions.

Hedera (Fares *et al.,*2010) addresses these problems and propose a dynamic flow scheduling system to efficiently utilize network resources. This was implemented using legacy switches and current hosts, and show that it is highly efficient. Data Centers are vital part of Internet services however consumes colossal measures of energy, and the subsequent operational expenses have impelled enthusiasm for enhancing their effectiveness. 70% of a server farm's aggregate force spending plan includes servers and cooling. ElasticTree (Heller *et al.,*2010) is a network wide power supervisor, which powerfully conforms the arrangement of dynamic system to fulfill changing server farm activity in this way can spare portion of the Network Power.

RCP has numerous advantages like adaptable routing, improved security, and ISP network network connectivity tasks. RCPs with regards to datacenter taking into account OpenFlow/SDN (Rothenberg *et al.*,2012) with various use cases, recognizing deployment challenges and advantages. Outline design of the Route-Flow Control Platform (RFCP) is a controller-driven hybrid Network administration model. BGP arrangement is done across numerous routers while RCPs permit AS to effectively deploy services.

SDNs can be adequately utilized for network traffic engineering. Unified controller altogether enhances Network use and additionally to lessen delays and packet loss. (Agarwal, Kodialam & Lakshman, 2013) Fast Fully Polynomial Time Approximation Schemes (FPTAS) was created for solving traffic engineering optimization.

LTE

Easiest way to implement SDN in Mobile Packet core is to do in the EPC because 3rd Generation Partnership Project (3GPP) standards have already identified a control-signaling plane separate from the data plane. But gateways are combined which needed to be distributed to the edge while keeping the control plane and 3GPP interfaces the same.

Industry is facing challenge of exponential growth of increase in data packet which is using majority of Network resources. Many solutions have been proposed, one which is Device to Device communication. (Li *et al.*,2013) Two approach are used to identify candidates of D2D, first is network-controlled approach and other is adhoc.

CHALLENGES

Researchers are criticizing that architecture of SDN i.e. separate control plane and data plane not only have advantages but also have serious issues as well. As application developers will be writing applications for use in SDN, there are great possibility that Apps can be buggy because developers don't know much about Networking. Networking staff are well aware about protocols but have very basic knowledge of software and in most of case they have no knowledge which creates communication barriers between Networking and developers staff. In order to overcome these hurdles extensive training will be required. Apps vendor will require to develop SDN modules which will be validated by Vendors and validated by customer.

Diagnostics tools such as Ping and Traceroutes will not be applicable in SDN thus requires a new set of tools for troubleshooting in SDN. Researchers are working on such tools but are at initial level and will require extensive overhaul before putting it in a production service provider network.

Another challenge is to integrate SDN functions with non-SDN functions for e.g. integrating SNMP for hardware management (fan, temperature, power supplies) which are well managed by SNMP in legacy network. With the help of the service abstraction layer (SAL), work have been done to make a reactive network using bidirectional communication between controller and but still SDN lacks in getting physical parameter of hardware

SDN needs to tools to map error between physical and Virtual environment so that if any error is occurring at physical lever for e.g. duplex mismatch then controller can identify which Virtual machine is affected. Although SDN have resolved a lot of our legacy Network architecture but researchers are criticizing that SDN is not meant to scale up, for e.g if a device has received a unknown destination packet than it have to consult Controller for it which is a potential delay of msec while on the other hand legacy network with embedded design technology it is just a matter of fraction of seconds.While legacy network is deployed all over the world but still we need that our current equipment supports SDN which have hurdles like limited forwarding table size in switches. SDN need a separate control network which increases cost and complexity when run in parallel with legacy network equipment. Research is already in progress to overcome shortcomings of SDN technology.

CONCLUSION

This article presented a brief overview of SDN development, from early promising conceptual phases to recent development. There are many hurdles in SDN technology development and adaptation widely but new technologies always have such detractors. Earlier in Routing and Switching we came to conclusion that in order to speed lookup process we need to "Switch when we can and route when we must", nowadays we never discuss such issues as CPU advancement hence routers are fast enough. Recent development for overcoming TCAM entries limitation lead to development of 64K Wildcard TCAM entries and 128K hash table exact match entries. New Network topologies offer greater resilience avoiding bottleneck of controller performance.

Many issues concerning with the SDN network is under focus of research by researchers in academia and technology industries relating to the distributed controller architecture, interaction of forwarding elements, ICN or information centric networking and APIs. We will be focusing our future research work on Hybrid network model for SDN as SDN have to work in side by side with legacy network.

REFERENCES

Agarwal, Kodialam, & Lakshman. (2013). *Traffic Engineering in Software-defined Networks*. Infocom.

Akella, A., & Krishnamurthy, A. (2014). *A Highly Available Software Defined Fabric*. HotNets. doi:10.1145/2670518.2673884

Al-Fares, M., Radhakrishnan, S., Raghavan, B., Huang, N., & Vahdat, A. (2010). *Hedera: Dynamic Flow Scheduling for Data Center Networks*. NSDI.

Anwer, M. B., Motiwala, M., Tariq, M. b., & Feamster, N. (2014). Switchblade: a platform for rapid deployment of network protocols on programmable hardware. *Proceedings of the ACM SIGCOMM*.

AuYoung, A., Ma, Y., Banerjee, S., Lee, J., Sharma, P., Turner, Y., ... Yu, C. (2013). *Transparent and Flexible Network Management for Big Data Processing in the Cloud*. HotCloud.

Bakhshi, T., & Ghita, B. (2016). User-centric traffic optimization in residential software defined networks. In *2016 23rd International conference on telecommunications (ICT)* (pp. 1–6). Academic Press. 10.1109/ICT.2016.7500389

Bakshi, K. (2012). Considerations for big data: Architecture and approach. In *Aerospace Conference*. IEEE. 10.1109/AERO.2012.6187357

Bavier, A., Feamster, N., Huang, M., Peterson, L., & Rexford, J. (2006). In vini veritas: realistic and controlled Network experimentation. In *SIGCOMM '06* (pp. 3–14). New York: ACM. doi:10.1145/1159913.1159916

Berde, Gerola, Hart, Higuchi, Kobayashi, Koide, … Parulukar. (2014). *ONOS: Towards An Open Distributed SDN OS*. HotSDN.

Bosshart, Daly, Gibb, Izzard, McKeown, Rexford, … Walker. (2015). *P4: Programming Protocol-Independent Packet Processors*. Academic Press.

Bosshart, Daly, Izzard, McKeown, Rexford, Talayco, … Walker. (2013). *Programming Protocol-Independent Packet Processors*. Academic Press.

Bosshart, P., Gibb, G., Kim, H.-S., Varghese, G., McKeown, N., Izzard, M., ... Horowitz, M. (2013). *Forwarding Metamorphosis: Fast Programmable Match-Action Processing in Hardware for SDN*. Sigcomm. doi:10.1145/2486001.2486011

Bozkurt, I. N., & Benson, T. (2018). Contextual router: Advancing experience oriented networking to the Alshnta et al., Cogent Engineering. In *Proceedings of the symposium on SDN research* (p. 15: 1–15:7). Academic Press.

Cai, Cox, & Ng. (2011). *Maestro: A System for Scalable OpenFlow Control*. Academic Press.

Canini, Kuznetsov, Levin, & Schmid. (2013). *The Case for Reliable Software Transactional Networking*. Academic Press.

Canini, Kuznetsov, Levin, & Schmid. (2013). *Software Transactional Networking: Concurrent and Consistent Policy Composition*. HotSDN.

Casado. (2015). *What OpenFlow is (and more importantly, what it's not)*. Academic Press.

Casado, Koponen, Shenker, & Tootoonchian. (2012). *Fabric: A Retrospective on Evolving SDN*. HotSDN.

Casado, M., Freedman, M. J., Pettit, J., Luo, J., McKeown, N., & Shenker, S. (2007). *Ethane: Taking Control of the Enterprise*. Sigcomm.

Chadrasekaran, B., & Benson, T. (2014). *Tolerating SDN Application Failures with Lego SDN*. HotNets.

Curtis, A. R., Mogul, J. C., Tourrilhes, J., Yalagandula, P., Sharma, P., & Banerjee, S. (2011). *DevoFlow: Scaling Flow Management for High-performance Networks*. Sigcomm. doi:10.1145/2018436.2018466

Ethane, M. (2007). Ethane: Taking control of the enterprise. *Computer Communication Review*, *37*(4), 1–12.

Farrel, A. (2015). Path Computation Element (PCE). *Architecture (Washington, D.C.)*.

Ferguson, Guha, Liang, Fonseca, & Krishnamurthi. (2013). *Hierarchical Policies for Software Defined Network*. Academic Press.

Flores Moyano, R., Fernández, D., Bellido, L., & González, C. (2017). *A software-defined networking approach to improve service provision in residential networks. International Journal Network Managed.* doi:10.1002/nem.1984

Foster, N., Guha, A., Reitblatt, M., Story, A., Freedman, M. J., Katta, N. P., ... Harrison, R. (2013). Languages for Software-Defined Networks. *IEEE Communications Magazine, 51*(2), 128–134. doi:10.1109/MCOM.2013.6461197

Foster, N., Harrison, R., Freedman, M. J., Monsanto, C., Rexford, J., Story, A., & Walker, D. (2011). *Frenetic: A Network Programming Language.* ICFP. doi:10.1145/2034773.2034812

Goransson, P., Black, C., & Culver, T. (2016). *Software defined networks: A comprehensive approach.* Cambridge, MA: Morgan Kaufmann.

Greenberg, Hjalmtysson, Maltz, Myers, Rexford, Xie, ... Zhang. (2015). *A Clean Slate 4D Approach to Network Control and Management.* Academic Press.

Gude, N., Koponen, T., Pettit, J., Ben Pfaff, M. C., McKeown, N., & Shenker, S. (2008). *NOX: Towards an Operating System for Networks.* CCR. doi:10.1145/1384609.1384625

Guha, A., Reitblatt, M., & Foster, N. (2013). *Machine-Verified Network Controllers.* PLDI. doi:10.1145/2491956.2462178

Gutz, Story, Schlesinger, & Foster. (2012). *Splendid Isolation: A Slice Abstraction for Software-Defined Networks.* HotSDN.

Hand & Keller. (2013). *ClosedFlow: OpenFlow-like Control over ProprietaryDevices.* Academic Press.

Heller, Sherwood, & McKeown. (2012). *The Controller Placement Problem.* HotSDN.

Heller, B., Seetharaman, S., Mahadevan, P., Yakoumis, Y., Sharma, P., Banerjee, S., & McKeown, N. (2010). *ElasticTree: Saving Energy in Data Center Networks.* NSDI.

Hernando, A. B. G., Fariña, A. D. S., Triana, L. B., Piñar, F. J. R., & Cambronero, D. F. (2017). *Virtualization of residential IoT functionality by using NFV and SDN. In 2017 IEEE International Conference on Consumer Electronics* (pp. 86–87). ICCE.

Herodotou, H. (2011). *Starfish: A Self-tuning System for Big Data Analytics* (Vol. 11). CIDR.

Huang, Yocum, & Snoeren. (2013). *High-Fidelity Switch Models for Software-Defined Network Emulation.* Academic Press.

Jafarian, Al-Shaer, & Duan. (2013). *OpenFlow Random Host Mutation: Transparent Moving Target Defense using Software Defined Networking.* Academic Press.

Jin, X., Gossels, J., Rexford, J., & Walker, D. (2015). *CoVisor: A Compositional Hypervisor for Software-Defined Network.* NSDI.

Jose, L., Yan, L., Varghese, G., & McKeown, N. (2015). *Compiling Packet Programs to Reconfigurable Switches.* NSDI.

Katta, Alipurfard, Rexford, & Walker. (2014). *Infinite CacheFlow in Software-defined Networks.* HotSDN.

Kim, H., Reich, J., Gupta, A., Shahbaz, M., Feamster, N., & Kinetic, R. C. (2015). *Verifyable Dynamic Network Control*. NSDI.

Koponen, T. (2010). *Onix: A Distributed Control Platform for Large-scale Production Network*. OSDI.

Lantz, Heller, & McKeown. (2015). *A Network in a Laptop: Rapid Prototyping for Software-Defined Network*. Academic Press.

Lazaris, A., Tahara, D., Huang, X., Li, L. E., & Voellmy, A. (2014). *Tango: Simplifying SDN Control with Automatic SwitchProperty Inference*. Abstraction, and Optimization, CoNext.

Levin, D., Canini, M., Schmid, S., Schaffert, F., & Feldmann, A. (2014). *Panopticon: Reaping the Benefits of Incremental SDN Deployment in Enterprise Networks*. USENIX ATC.

Li, Wu, Hui, Jin, & Chen. (2015). *Social-Aware D2D Communications: Qualitative Insights and Quantitative Analysis*. Academic Press.

Liang, C., & Mogul, J. C. (2014). *Democratic Resolution of Resource Conflicts BetweenSDN Control Programs*. CoNext.

Lockwood, McKeown, Watson, Gibb, Hartke, Naous, ... Luo. (2015). *Netfpga–an open platform for gigabit-rate network switching and routing*. Academic Press.

Lu, Arora, Zhang, Lumezanu, Rhee, & Jiang. (2013). *HybNET: Network Manager for a Hybrid Network Infrastructure, Middleware (industrial track)*. Academic Press.

Lu, Miao, Xiong, & Guo. (2012). *Using CPU as a Traffic Co-processing Unit in Commodity Switches*. HotSDN.

McKeown, N., Anderson, T., Balakrishnan, H., Parulkar, G., Peterson, L., Rexford, J., ... Turner, J. (2008). *OpenFlow: Enabling Innovation in Campus Networks*. CCR. doi:10.1145/1355734.1355746

McKeown & Anderson. (2008). *OpenFlow: Enabling Innovation in Campus Networks*. Academic Press.

Mogul & Congdon. (2012). *Hey, You Darned Counters! Get off My ASIC*. HotSDN.

Mogul, J. C., AuYoung, A., Banerjee, S., Popa, L., Lee, J., Mudigonda, J., ... Turner, Y. (2013). *Corybantic: Towards the Modular Composition of SDN Control Programs*. HotNets. doi:10.1145/2535771.2535795

Monaco, M., Michel, O., & Keller, E. (2013). *Applying Operating System Principles to SDN Controller Design*. HotNets. doi:10.1145/2535771.2535789

Monga, I., Pouyoul, E., & Guok, C. (2012). Software-Defined Networking for Big-Data Science- Architectural Models from Campus to the WAN. In High Performance Computing, Networking, Storage and Analysis (SCC), 2012 SC Companion. IEEE.

Monsanto, Reich, Foster, Rexford, & Walker. (2013). *Composing Software-Defined Networks*. NSDI.

Moyano, R. F., Cambronero, D. F., & Triana, L. B. (2017). A user-centric {SDN} management architecture for NFV-based residential networks. *Computer Standards & Interfaces*, *54*(Part 4), 279–292. doi:10.1016/j.csi.2017.01.010

Moyano, R. F., Fernández, D., Bellido, L., Merayo, N., Aguado, J. C., & De Miguel, I. (2017). NFV-based QoS provision for software defined optical access and residential networks. In *2017 IEEE/ACM 25th International symposium on quality of service (IWQoS)* (pp. 1–5). IEEE.

Nakagawa, Hyoudou, & Shimizu. (2012). *A Management Method of IP Multicast in Overlay Networks using OpenFlow*. HotSDN.

Nayak, A., Reimers, A., Feamster, N., & Clark, R. (2009). *Resonance: Dynamic Access Control in Enterprise Network*. WREN.

Porras, Shin, Yegneswaran, Fong, Tyson, & Gu. (2012). *A Security Enforcement Kernel for OpenFlow Networks*. HotSDN.

Raghavendra, Lobo, & Lee. (2012). *Dynamic Graph Query Primitives for SDN-based Cloud Network Management*. HotSDN.

Rocha, R., & Launchbury, J. (2011). *Practical Aspects of Declarative Languages - 13th International Symposium, PADL 2011, Austin, TX, USA, January 24-25, 2011. Proceedings, volume 6539 of Lecture Notes in Computer Science*. Springer.

Rothenberg, Nascimento, Salvador, Correa, de Lucena, & Raszuk. (2012). *Revisiting Routing Control Platforms with the Eyes and Muscles of Software-Defined Networking*. HotSDN.

Rubow, E., McGeer, R., Mogul, J., & Vahdat, A. (2016). *Chimpp: A click-based programming and simulation environment for reconfigurable networking hardware*. Chimpp.

Sadasivarao, A. (2013). Bursting Data between Data Centers: Case for Transport SDN. In *High-Performance Interconnects (HOTI), 2013 IEEE 21st Annual Symposium on*. IEEE. 10.1109/HOTI.2013.20

Schiff, L., Borokhovich, M., & Schmid, S. (2014). *Reclaiming the Brain: Useful OpenFlow Functions in the Data Plane*. HotNets. doi:10.1145/2670518.2673874

Sherwood, R., Gibb, G., Yap, K.-K., Appenzeller, G., Casado, M., McKeown, N., & Parulkar, G. (2010). *Can the Production Network Be the Testbed*. OSDI.

Sivaraman, A., Weinstein, K., Subramanian, S., & Balakrishnan, H. (2013). *No Silver Bullet: Extending SDN to the Data Plane*. HotNets. doi:10.1145/2535771.2535796

Soulé, R., Basu, S., Marandi, P. J., Pedone, F., Kleinberg, R., Sirer, E. G., & Foster, N. (2014). *Merlin: A Language for Provisioning Network Resources*. CoNext.

Stewart, C. E., Vasu, A. M., & Keller, E. (2017). CommunityGuard: A crowdsourced home cybersecurity system. In *Proceedings of the ACM International workshop on security in software defined networks & network function virtualization* (pp. 1–6). ACM.

Sun, P., Mahajan, R., & Rexford, J. (2014). *Lihua YuanMing Zhang, Ahsan Arefin: A Network State Management Service*. Sigcomm.

Tavakoli, A., Casado, M., Koponen, T., & Shenker, S. (2009). *Applying NOX to the Datacenter*. HotNets.

Tootoonchian, A., & Ganjali, Y. (2010). *HyperFlow: A Distributed Control Plane for OpenFlow*. INM.

Voellmy, A., & Hudak, P. (2011). *Nettle: Functional Reactive Programming of OpenFlow Networks*. PADL.

Wang, Ng, & Shaikh. (2012). Programming your network at run-time for big data applications. In *Proceedings of the first workshop on Hot topics in software defined networks*. ACM. 10.1145/2342441.2342462

Wang, A., Guo, Y., & Hao, F. (2014). *Scotch: Elastically Scaling up SDN Control-Plane usingvSwitch based Overlay*. CoNext.

Wang, Y., Zhang, Y., Singh, V., Lumezanu, C., & Jiang, G. (2013). *NetFuse: Short-circuiting Traffic Surges in the Cloud*. ICC.

Wei, F. (2010). TEDI: efficient shortest path query answering on graphs. *Proceedings of SIGMOD*. 10.1145/1807167.1807181

White. (2002). An integrated experimental environment for distributed systems and networks. In *Proc. of the Fifth Symposium on Operating Systems Design and Implementation* (pp. 255–270). Boston, MA: USENIX Association.

Yan, Xu, Xing, Xi, & Chao. (2014). *CAB: A Reactive Wildcard Rule Caching System for Software-Defined Networks*. HotSDN.

Yeganeh & Ganjali. (2012). *Kandoo: A Framework for Efficient and Scalable Offloading of Control Applications*. HotSDN.

Yeganeh & Ganjali. (2015). *Beehive: Towards a Simple Abstraction for Scalable Software-defined Networks*. Academic Press.

Yu, M., Rexford, J., Freedman, M. J., & Wang, J. (2010). *Scalable Flow-based Networking with DIFANE*. Sigcomm. doi:10.1145/1851182.1851224

Yuan, Y., Alur, R., & Loo, B. T. (2014). *NetEgg: Programming Network Policies by Examples*. HotNets. doi:10.1145/2670518.2673879

Zec, M., & Mikuc, M. (2004). Operating system support for integrated network emulation in imunes. *Proc. of the 1st Workshop on Operating System and Architectural Support for the on demand IT Infra-Structure (OASIS)*.

Zhang, S., Ivancic, F., Lumezanu, C., Yuan, Y., Gupta, A., & Malik, S. (2014). *An Adaptable Rule Placement for Software-defined Networks*. DSN. doi:10.1109/DSN.2014.24

Compilation of References

Aafer, Y., Du, W., & Yin, H. (2013). Droidapiminer: Mining api-level features for robust malware detection in android. In *International conference on security and privacy in communication systems* (pp. 86–103). Academic Press. 10.1007/978-3-319-04283-1_6

Aazam, M., Khan, I., Alsaffar, A. A., & Huh, E. N. (2014). The cloud of Things: Integrating the g Internet of Things and cloud computing and the issues involved. In *Applied Sciences and Technology (IBCAST), 2014 11th International Bhurban Conference on* (pp. 414-419). IEEE.

Abadi, M., Barham, P., Chen, J., Chen, Z., Davis, A., Dean, J., . . . Isard, M. (2016). Tensorflow: A System For Large-Scale Machine Learning. *Osdi, 16,* 265-283.

Abadi, M., Chu, A., Goodfellow, I., McMahan, H. B., Mironov, I., Talwar, K., & Zhang, L. (2016). Deep learning with differential privacy. In *Proceedings of the 2016 ACM SIGSAC Conference on Computer and Communications Security* (pp. 308–318). ACM. 10.1145/2976749.2978318

Abdelkader, T., Naik, K., Nayak, A., Goel, N., & Srivastava, V. (2016). Goe,l N., Srivastava, V. (2016).A performance comparison of delay-tolerant network routing protocols. *IEEE Network, 30*(2), 46–53. doi:10.1109/MNET.2016.7437024

Abdelshkour, M. (2015, March 27). *IoT, from Cloud to Fog Computing.* Retrieved from https://blogs.cisco.com/perspectives/iot-from-cloud-to-fog-computing

Aboroujilah, A., & Amusa, A. S. (2017). *Cloud-Based DDoS HTTP Attack Detection Using Covariance Matrix Approach.* Journal Comp. Netw. and Communic. doi:10.1155/2017/7674594

Aboudi, N. E., & Benhlima, L. (2017). Parallel and Distributed Population based Feature Selection Framework for Health Monitoring. *International Journal of Cloud Applications and Computing, 7*(1), 57–71. doi:10.4018/IJCAC.2017010104

Abujabal, Yahya, Riedewald, & Weikum. (2017). Automated Template Generation for Question Answering over knowledge graph. *IW3C2.*

Abu-Libdeh, H., Princehouse, L., & Weatherspoon, H. (2010, June). RACS: a case for cloud storage diversity. In *Proceedings of the 1st ACM symposium on Cloud computing* (pp. 229-240). ACM. 10.1145/1807128.1807165

Acer, U., Giaccone, P., Hay, D., Neglia, G., & Tarapiah, S. (2012). Timely data delivery in a realistic bus network. *IEEE Transactions on Vehicular Technology, 61*(3), 1251–1265. doi:10.1109/TVT.2011.2179072

Achlioptas, D. (2003). Database-friendly random projections: Johnson-Lindenstrauss with binary coins. *Journal of Computer and System Sciences, 66*(4), 671–687. doi:10.1016/S0022-0000(03)00025-4

Ad, I., Hubaux, J., & Edward, K. (2008). Impact of denial of service attacks on Ad Hoc networks. *IEEE/ACM Transactions on Networking, 16*(1), 791–802. doi:10.1109/TNET.2007.904002

Agarwal, Kodialam, & Lakshman. (2013). *Traffic Engineering in Software-defined Networks*. Infocom.

Agarwal, T. (n.d.). *How does the Smart Card Works?* Retrieved October 8, 2018, from ElProCus – Electronic Projects for Engineering Students: https://www.elprocus.com/working-of-smart-card/

Agarwal, H., & Sharma, A. (2016). A Comprehensive Survey of Fault Tolerance Techniques in Cloud Computing. In *International Conference on Computing and Network Communications (CoCoNet)*. IEEE.

Ahmadi, M., Vali, M., Moghaddam, F., Hakemi, A., & Madadipouya, K. (2015). A Reliable User Authentication and Data Protection Model in Cloud Computing Environments. *International Conference on Information, System and Convergence Applications*.

Ahmed, K., Omar, M. H., & Hassan, S. (2016). Routing Strategies and Buffer Management in Delay Tolerant Networks, *Journal of Telecommunication. Electronic and Computer Engineering*, *8*(10), 139–143.

Ahmed, M. H., & Rehmani, M. H. (2017). Rehmani, Mobile edge computing: Opportunities, solutions, and challenges. *Future Generation Computer Systems*, *70*, 59–63. doi:10.1016/j.future.2016.09.015

Ahuja, S., & Mani, S. (2013). Empirical performance analysis of HPC benchmarks across variations of cloud computing. *International Journal of Cloud Applications and Computing*, *3*(1), 13–26. doi:10.4018/ijcac.2013010102

Ahuja, S., & Rolli, A. (2011). Survey of the state-of-the-art of cloud computing. *International Journal of Cloud Applications and Computing*, *1*(4), 34–43. doi:10.4018/ijcac.2011100103

Ahuja, S., & Sridharan, S. (2012). Performance evaluation of hypervisors for cloud computing. *International Journal of Cloud Applications and Computing*, *2*(3), 26–67. doi:10.4018/ijcac.2012070102

Aich, S., Younga, K., Hui, K. L., Al-absi, A. A., & Sain, M. (2018). A Nonlinear Decision Tree based Classification Approach to Predict the Parkinson ' s disease using Different Feature Sets of Voice Data. In *International Conference on Advanced Communication Technology*. IEEE.

Akatyev, N., & James, J. I. (2017). Evidence identification in IoT networks based on threat assessment. *Future Generation Computer Systems*. doi:10.1016/j.future.2017.10.012

Akella, A., & Krishnamurthy, A. (2014). *A Highly Available Software Defined Fabric*. HotNets. doi:10.1145/2670518.2673884

Akter, R. (n.d.). *An Improved Genetic Algorithm for Document Clustering on the Cloud*. Retrieved from https://www.igi-global.com/article/an-improved-genetic-algorithm-for-document-clustering-on-the-cloud/213987

Al Noor, S., & Hasan, R. (2015). D-cloc: A delay tolerant cloud formation using context-aware mobile crowdsourcing. In *Cloud Computing Technology and Science (CloudCom), 2015 IEEE 7th International Conference on* (pp. 147-154). IEEE.

Alam, S., Chowdhury, M. M. R., & Noll, J. (2010). SenaaS: An event-driven sensor virtualization approach for Internet of Things cloud. *2010 IEEE International Conference on Networked Embedded Systems for Enterprise Applications*. 10.1109/NESEA.2010.5678060

Alavi, A. H., Jiao, P., Buttlar, W. G., & Lajnef, N. (2018). Internet of Things-enabled smart cities: State-of-the-art and future trends. *Measurement*, *129*, 589–606. doi:10.1016/j.measurement.2018.07.067

Alaya, M. B., Medjiah, S., Monteil, T., & Drira, K. (2015). Toward semantic interoperability in onem2m architecture. *IEEE Communications Magazine*, *53*(12), 35–41. doi:10.1109/MCOM.2015.7355582

Albano, M., Ferreira, L. L., & Delsing, J. (2016). Qos-as-a-service in the localcloud. *Proc IEEE ETFA, SOCNE Workshop*.

Albert Greenberg, Gisli Hjalmtysson, David A. Maltz, Andy Myers, Jennifer Rexford, Geoffrey Xie, Hong Yan, Jibin Zhan, Hui Zhang: A Clean Slate 4D Approach to Network Control and Management,, 2015

Al-Fares, M., Radhakrishnan, S., Raghavan, B., Huang, N., & Vahdat, A. (2010). *Hedera: Dynamic Flow Scheduling for Data Center Networks.* NSDI.

Alliance, S. C. (2011). *Card Payments Roadmap in the United States: How Will EMV Impact the Future Payments Infrastructure?* Smart Card Alliance. Retrieved from www.smartcardalliance.org

Alliance, S. T. (2017). *Blockchain and Smart Card Technology.* Secure Technology Alliance. Secure Technology Alliance.

Alohali, B., Merabti, M., & Kifayat, K. (2014). *A Secure Scheme for a Smart House Based on Cloud of Things (CoT).* Academic Press.

Alomari, E., Manickam, S., Gupta, B. B., Karuppayah, S., & Alfaris, R. (2012). *Botnet-based distributed denial of service (DDoS) attacks on web servers: classification and art.* arXiv preprint arXiv:1208.0403

Alrokayan, M., Dastjerdi, A. V., & Buyya, R. (2015). SLA-Aware Provisioning and Scheduling of Cloud Resources for Big Data Analytics. *2014 IEEE International Conference on Cloud Computing in Emerging Markets, CCEM 2014,* 1–8.

Alsghaier, H., Akour, M., Shehabat, I., & Aldiabat, S. (2017). The impact of big data analytics on business competitiveness. *Proceedings of the New Trends in Information Technology.*

Alvarez, G., & Li, S. (2006). Some Basic Cryptographic Requirements For Chaos-Based Cryptosystems. *International Journal of Bifurcation and Chaos in Applied Sciences and Engineering, 16*(08), 2129–2151. doi:10.1142/S0218127406015970

Alvaro Retana, Alia Atlas, Deborah Brungard:Forwarding and Control Element Separation (Concluded WG), Rtg Area: | 2001-Jul-27 — 2015-Mar-24

Alzain, M. A., & Pardede, E. (2011, January). Using multi shares for ensuring privacy in database-as-a-service. In *2011 44th Hawaii International Conference on System Sciences* (pp. 1-9). IEEE. 10.1109/HICSS.2011.478

AlZain, M. A., Soh, B., & Pardede, E. (2011, December). MCDB: Using multi-clouds to ensure security in cloud computing. In *Dependable, autonomic and secure computing (DASC), 2011 IEEE Ninth International Conference on* (pp. 784-791). IEEE.

Amazon, Amazon Web Services. (2010). *Web services licensing agreement.* Author.

Amazon.com. Inc. (n.d.a). *Elastic Compute Cloud.* Retrieved from http://aws.amazon.com/ec2/

Amazon.com. Inc. (n.d.b). *EC2 Pricing.* Retrieved from http://aws.amazon.com/ec2/pricing/

Amazon.com. Inc. (n.d.c). *EC2 Instance Types.* Retrieved from http://aws.amazon.com/ec2/instance-types/

Amendola, D., Rango, F. D., Massri, K., & Vitaletti, A. (2014). Efficient neighbor discovery in RFID based devices over resource-constrained DTN networks. *ICC 14: Proceedings of the IEEE International Conference on Communications,* 3842–3847. 10.1109/ICC.2014.6883920

Ammar, M., Russello, G., & Crispo, B. (2018). Internet of Things: A survey on the security of IoT frameworks. *Journal of Information Security and Applications, 38,* 8–27. doi:10.1016/j.jisa.2017.11.002

Anagnostopoulos, T., Zaslavsky, A., Kolomvatsos, K., Medvedev, A., Amirian, P., Morley, J., & Hadjieftymiades, S. (2017). Challenges and Opportunities of Waste Management in IoT-Enabled Smart Cities: A Survey. *IEEE Transactions on Sustainable Computing, 2*(3), 275–289. doi:10.1109/TSUSC.2017.2691049

Anderson, H. S., Filar, B., & Roth, P. (2017). *Evading Machine Learning Malware Detection.* Academic Press.

Anderson, R., & Biham, E. (1996). Two Practical and Provably Secured Block Ciphers: BEAR and LION. In *Fast Software Encryption, Third International Workshop Proceedings*. Springer-Verlag.

Anderson, H. S., Kharkar, A., Filar, B., & Roth, P. (2017). *Evading machine learning malware detection*. Black Hat.

Andrew D. Ferguson, Arjun Guha, Chen Liang, Rodrigo Fonseca, Shriram Krishnamurthi: Hierarchical Policies for Software Defined Network,2013.

Ankita & Khatiwala. (2015). Survey on DDoS Attack Detection and Prevention in Cloud. *International Journal of Engineering Technology, Management and Applied Sciences, 3*(2).

Ansa, G., Johnson, E., Cruickshank, H., & Sun, Z. (2010). Mitigating denial of service attacks in delay-and disruption-tolerant networks. *Proc. Int. Conf. Personal Satellite Services*, 221–234. 10.1007/978-3-642-13618-4_16

Antonakakis, M., Perdisci, R., Nadji, Y., Vasiloglou, N., Abu-Nimeh, S., Lee, W., & Dagon, D. (2012). From Throw-Away Traffic to Bots: Detecting the Rise of DGA-Based Malware. In *Security'12 Proceedings of the 21st USENIX conference on Security symposium* (p. 24). ACM.

Antonopoulos, M. (2014). *Mastering Bitcoin: Unlocking Digital Cryptocurrencies* (1st ed.). Sebastopol, CA: O'Reilly Media, Inc.

Anwer, M. B., Motiwala, M., Tariq, M. b., & Feamster, N. (2014). Switchblade: a platform for rapid deployment of network protocols on programmable hardware. *Proceedings of the ACM SIGCOMM*.

Apache Hadoop. (2018). Retrieved November 20, 2018, from http://hadoop.apache.org/

Arjovsky, M., Chintala, S., & Bottou, L. (2017). *Wasserstein Gan*. Arxiv Preprint Arxiv:1701.07875

Armbrust, M., Fox, A., Griffith, R., Joseph, A. D., Katz, R., Konwinski, A., ... Zaharia, M. (2010). A view of cloud computing. *Communications of the ACM, 53*(4), 50–58. doi:10.1145/1721654.1721672

Arnold, J., Williams, J., Srinivasan, R., Kings, K., & Griggs, R. (1994). *SWAT: soil and water assessment tool*. Temple, TX: US Department of Agriculture, Agricultural Research Service, Grassland, Soil and Water Research Laboratory.

Arp, D., Spreitzenbarth, M., Hubner, M., Gascon, H., Rieck, K., & Siemens, C. (2014). DREBIN: Effective and Explainable Detection of Android Malware in Your Pocket. In Ndss (Vol. 14, pp. 23–26). Academic Press.

Ashwini, K., & Amutha, R. (2018). Fast and secured cloud assisted recovery scheme for compressively sensed signals using new chaotic system. *Multimedia Tools and Applications, 77*(24), 31581–31606. doi:10.100711042-018-6112-4

Asokan, N., Kostiainen, K., & Ginzboorg, P. (2007). Applicability of identity-based cryptography for disruption tolerant networking. *Proc. Of Mobi Opp*, 52-56.

Assunção, M. D., Calheiros, R. N., Bianchi, S., Netto, M. A. S., & Buyya, R. (2015). Big Data Computing and Clouds: Trends and Future Directions. *Journal of Parallel and Distributed Computing, 79–80*, 3–15. doi:10.1016/j.jpdc.2014.08.003

Atzori, L., Iera, A., & Morabito, G. (2010). TheInternet of Things: A Survey. *Computer Networks, 54*(15), 2787–2805. doi:10.1016/j.comnet.2010.05.010

AuYoung, A., Ma, Y., Banerjee, S., Lee, J., Sharma, P., Turner, Y., ... Yu, C. (2013). *Transparent and Flexible Network Management for Big Data Processing in the Cloud*. HotCloud.

Auzias, M., Mahéo, Y., & Raimbault, F. (2015). CoAP over BP for a delay tolerant internet of things. *FiCloud 15: Proceedings of the International Conference on Future Internet of Things and Cloud*, 118–123. 10.1109/FiCloud.2015.33

Aven, T. (2006). A unified framework for risk and vulnerability analysis covering both safety and security. *Journal of Reliability Engineering and System Safety, 92*(6), 745–754.

Awad, A., Matthews, A., Qiao, Y., & Lee, B. (2018). Chaotic Searchable Encryption for Mobile Cloud Storage. *IEEE Transactions on Cloud Computing, 6*(2), 440–452. doi:10.1109/TCC.2015.2511747

Awerbuch, B., David, H., Cristina, N., & Herbert, R. (2002). An on-demand secure routing protocol resilient to byzantine failures. In *Proceedings of the 1st ACM workshop on Wireless security* (pp. 21-30). Atlanta, GA: ACM. 10.1145/570681.570684

AWS - Amazon EC2 Instance Types. (2014). Available: http://aws.amazon.com/ec2/instance-types/

Axon, L., & Goldsmith, M. (2017). *PB-PKI: a privacy-aware blockchain-based PKI. SCITEPRESS*. SCITEPRESS.

Ayyub, S., & Kaushik, P. (2015). Securing Images in Cloud using Hyper Chaos with User Authentication. *International Journal of Computers and Applications, 121*(17), 18–23. doi:10.5120/21632-4951

Azarderakhsh, R., Longa, P., Hu, S., & Jao, D. (2013). Efficient implementation of bilinear pairings on ARM processors. *Springer Selected Areas in Cryptography*, 149-165.

B. White and J. L. et al. An integrated experimental environment for distributed systems and networks. In Proc. of the Fifth Symposium on Operating Systems Design and Implementation, pages 255–270, Boston, MA, Dec. 2002. USENIX Association.

Baars, D. S. (n.d.). *Towards self-sovereign identity using blockchain technology.* University of Twente.

Babu, S., Chandini, M., Lavanya, P., Ganapathy, K., & Vaidehi, V. (2013, July). Cloud-enabled remote health monitoring system. In *Proceedings of International Conference on Recent Trends in Information Technology (ICRTIT)* (pp. 702-707). IEEE.

Bae, J., & Lim, H. (2018). Random Mining Group Selection to Prevent 51% Attacks on Bitcoin. In *2018 48th Annual IEEE/IFIP International Conference on Dependable Systems and Networks Workshops (DSN-W)* (pp. 81-82). Luxembourg: IEEE.

Baig, A. R., & Jabeen, H. (2016). Big data analytics for behavior monitoring of students. *Procedia Computer Science, 82*, 43–48. doi:10.1016/j.procs.2016.04.007

Bakhshi, T., & Ghita, B. (2016). User-centric traffic optimization in residential software defined networks. In *2016 23rd International conference on telecommunications (ICT)* (pp. 1–6). Academic Press. 10.1109/ICT.2016.7500389

Bakhshi, T., & Ghita, B. User-centric traffic optimization in residential software defined networks. In 2016 23rd International conference on telecommunications (ICT) (pp. 1–6), 2016.

Bakshi, K. (2012). Considerations for big data: Architecture and approach. In *Aerospace Conference*. IEEE. 10.1109/AERO.2012.6187357

Banafa, A. (2014, August 31). *What is fog computing?* Retrieved from https://ahmedbanafa.blogspot.com/2014/08/what-is-fog-computing.html

Banafa, A. (n.d.). *How to Secure the Internet of Things (IoT) with Blockchain.* Retrieved December 3, 2018, from DATA-FLOQ.COM: https://datafloq.com/read/securing-internet-of-things-iot-with-blockchain/2228

Banerjee, M., Lee, J., & Choo, K. K. R. (2018). A block chain future for internet of things security: A position paper. *Digital Communications and Networks, 4*(3), 149–160. doi:10.1016/j.dcan.2017.10.006

BANKEX. (n.d.). *The First NFC-solution on Blockchain.* Retrieved October 20, 2018, from blog.bankex.org: https://blog.bankex.org/the-first-nfc-decision-on-blockchain-d49692e26ee7

Barbero, C., Zovo, P. D., & Gobbi, B. (2011). A Flexible ContextAware Reasoning Approach for IoT Applications. *IEEE 12th International Conference on Mobile Data Management*, 266–275.

Barreno, M., Nelson, B., Joseph, A. D., & Tygar, J. D. (2010). The Security Of Machine Learning. *Machine Learning*, *81*(2), 121–148.

Barua, K., & Mishra, B. S. P. (2016). Trends in big data. *CSI Communications*, *40*(8), 18-19.

Ba, S., & Joseph, V. R. (2012). Composite Gaussian process models for emulating expensive functions. *The Annals of Applied Statistics*, *6*(4), 1838–1860. doi:10.1214/12-AOAS570

Batallas, D., & Yassine, A. (2006). Information leaders in product development organizational networks: Social network analysis of the design structure matrix. *IEEE Transactions on Engineering Management*, *53*(4), 570–582. doi:10.1109/TEM.2006.883706

Bauer, H., Burkacky, O., & Knochenhauer, C. (2017). *Security in the Internet of Things.* McKinsey Report. Retrieved from: https://www.mckinsey.com/

Bavier, A., Feamster, N., Huang, M., Peterson, L., & Rexford, J. (2006). In vini veritas: realistic and controlled Network experimentation. In *SIGCOMM '06* (pp. 3–14). New York: ACM. doi:10.1145/1159913.1159916

Beecher, P. (2018). Enterprise-grade networks: The answer to IoT security challenges. *Network Security*, *2018*(7), 6–9. doi:10.1016/S1353-4858(18)30067-9

Benamar, N., Singh, K. D., Benamar, M., Ouadghiri, D. E., & Bonnin, J. M. (2014). Routing Protocols in Vehicular Delay Tolerant Networks: A Comprehensive Survey. *Computer Communications*, *48*, 141–158. doi:10.1016/j.comcom.2014.03.024

Bender, A., Adam, B., Neil, S., Bobby, B., & Daniel, S. (2009). Persona: an online social network with user-defined privacy. In *Proceedings of the ACM SIGCOMM 2009 conference on Data communication* (pp. 135-146). Barcelona, Spain: ACM.

Bengio, Y., & Lecun, Y. (2007). Scaling Learning Algorithms Towards AI. *Large-Scale Kernel Machines*, *34*(5), 1–41.

Benner, P., Gugercin, S., & Willcox, K. (2015). A Survey of Projection-Based Model Reduction Methods for Parametric Dynamical Systems. *SIAM Review*, *57*(4), 483–531. doi:10.1137/130932715

Berde, Gerola, Hart, Higuchi, Kobayashi, Koide, … Parulukar. (2014). *ONOS: Towards An Open Distributed SDN OS.* HotSDN.

Bhatt, C., Dey, N., & Ashour, A. S. (Eds.). (2017). Internet of things and big data technologies for next generation healthcare. Academic Press. doi:10.1007/978-3-319-49736-5

Bhattacharjee, N. V., Ranjan, P., Mandal, A., & Tollner, E. W. (2017). *Inverse mapping for rainfall-runoff models using history matching approach.* arXiv: 1709.02907

Bhushan, K., & Gupta, B. B. (2018, February). Detecting DDoS Attack using Software Defined Network (SDN) in Cloud Computing Environment. In *2018 5th International Conference on Signal Processing and Integrated Networks (SPIN)* (pp. 872-877). IEEE.

Bhushan, K., & Gupta, B. (2017). Security challenges in cloud computing: State-of-art. *International Journal of Big Data Intelligence*, *4*(2), 81. doi:10.1504/IJBDI.2017.083116

Bhushan, K., & Gupta, B. B. (2017). Network flow analysis for detection and mitigation of Fraudulent Resource Consumption (FRC) attacks in multimedia cloud computing. *Multimedia Tools and Applications*. doi:10.100711042-017-5522-z

Bhushan, K., & Gupta, B. B. (2018). A novel approach to defend multimedia flash crowd in cloud environment. *Multimedia Tools and Applications*, *77*(4), 4609–4639. doi:10.100711042-017-4742-6

Bhushan, K., & Gupta, B. B. (2018). Distributed denial of service (DDoS) attack mitigation in software defined network (SDN)-based cloud computing environment. *Journal of Ambient Intelligence and Humanized Computing*. doi:10.100712652-018-0800-9

Biggio, B., Corona, I., Maiorca, D., Nelson, B., Šrndić, N., & Laskov, P. … Roli, F. (2013). Evasion attacks against machine learning at test time. In *Joint European conference on machine learning and knowledge discovery in databases* (pp. 387–402). Academic Press.

Biggio, B., Corona, I., Maiorca, D., Nelson, B., Šrndić, N., Laskov, P., ... Roli, F. (2013). (2013). Evasion Attacks Against Machine Learning At Test Time. Paper Presented At The *Joint European Conference On Machine Learning And Knowledge Discovery In Databases*, 387-402.

Biggio, B., Fumera, G., & Roli, F. (2010a). Multiple Classifier Systems For Robust Classifier Design In Adversarial Environments. *International Journal of Machine Learning and Cybernetics*, *1*(1-4), 27–41. doi:10.100713042-010-0007-7

Biggio, B., Fumera, G., & Roli, F. (2014). Security Evaluation Of Pattern Classifiers Under Attack. *IEEE Transactions on Knowledge and Data Engineering*, *26*(4), 984–996. doi:10.1109/TKDE.2013.57

Bingham, D., Ranjan, P., & Welch, W. J. (2014). Sequential design of computer experiments for optimization, estimating contours, and related objectives. In *Statistics in Action: A Canadian Outlook* (pp. 109–124). Chapman & Hall/CRC. doi:10.1201/b16597-8

Bingham, E., & Mannila, H. (2001). Random projection in dimensionality reduction. *Proceedings of the Seventh ACM SIGKDD International Conference on Knowledge Discovery and Data Mining - KDD 01*. 10.1145/502512.502546

Biro, A., & Bartczak, J. K. (2013). Patent No. US9165235B2. United States Patent Office.

Blackledge, J., Bezobrazov, S., & Tobin, P. (2015). Cryptography using artificial intelligence. *2015 International Joint Conference on Neural Networks (IJCNN)*. 10.1109/IJCNN.2015.7280536

Blackledge, J., McKeever, M., Tobin, L., & Tobin, P. (2018). Secrecy and Randomness: Encoding Cloud data Locally using a One-Time Pad. *International Journal on Advances in Security*, *10*(3 & 4), 2017.

Blackledge, J., & Ptitsyn, N. (2011). On the Applications of Deterministic Chaos for Encrypting Data on the Cloud. *Third International Conference on Evolving Internet INTERNET*.

Blei, D. M., Ng, A. Y., & Michael, I. J. (2003). Latent Dirichlet Allocation. *Journal of Machine Learning Research*.

Bo Yan, Yang Xu, Hongya Xing, Kang Xi, H. Jonathan Chao: CAB: A Reactive Wildcard Rule Caching System for Software-Defined Networks, HotSDN 2014

Bob Lantz, Brandon Heller, Nick McKeown: A Network in a Laptop: Rapid Prototyping for Software-Defined Network, 2015

Bohli, J. M., Gruschka, N., Jensen, M., Iacono, L. L., & Marnau, N. (2013). Security and privacy-enhancing multi-cloud architectures. *IEEE Transactions on Dependable and Secure Computing*, *10*(4), 212–224. doi:10.1109/TDSC.2013.6

Boireau, O. (2018). Securing the blockchain against hackers. *Network Security*, *2018*(1), 8–11. doi:10.1016/S1353-4858(18)30006-0

Boneh, D., & Boyen, X. (2008). Short signatures without random oracles and the SDH assumption in bilinear groups. *Journal of Cryptology, 21*(2), 149–177. doi:10.100700145-007-9005-7

Bonneau, J., Miller, A., Clark, J., Narayanan, A., Kroll, A. J., & Felten, W. E. (2015). SoK: Research Perspectives and Challenges for Bitcoin and Cryptocurrencies. In *IEEE Symposium on Security and Privacy* (pp. 104-121). San Jose, CA: IEEE. 10.1109/SP.2015.14

Bonomi, F., Milito, R., Zhu, J., & Addepalli, S. (2012). Fog computing and its role in the internet of things. *Proceedings of the First Edition of the MCC Workshop on Mobile Cloud Computing*, 13–16.

Bonomi, Milito, Natarajan, & Zhu. (2014). *Fog Computing: A Platform for Internet of Things and Analytics*. Springer.

Bonomi, F. (2014). *Fog Computing: A Platform for Internet of Things and Analytics. In Big Data and Internet of Things: A Roadmap for Smart Environments* (Vol. 546, pp. 169–186). SCI.

Booker, A. J., Dennis, J. E. Jr, Frank, P. D., Serafini, D. B., Torczon, V., & Trosset, M. W. (1999). A rigorous framework for optimization of expensive functions by surrogatess. *Structural and Multidisciplinary Optimization, 17*(1), 1–13. doi:10.1007/BF01197708

Bosshart, Daly, Gibb, Izzard, McKeown, Rexford, … Walker. (2015). *P4: Programming Protocol-Independent Packet Processors*. Academic Press.

Bosshart, Daly, Izzard, McKeown, Rexford, Talayco, … Walker. (2013). *Programming Protocol-Independent Packet Processors*. Academic Press.

Bosshart, P., Gibb, G., Kim, H.-S., Varghese, G., McKeown, N., Izzard, M., ... Horowitz, M. (2013). *Forwarding Meta-morphosis: Fast Programmable Match-Action Processing in Hardware for SDN*. Sigcomm. doi:10.1145/2486001.2486011

Bosua, R., Richardson, M., Clark, K., Maynard, S., Ahmad, A., & Webb, J. (2017). *Privacy in a world of the Internet of Things: A Le and Regulatory Perspective*. The University of Melbourne Network Society Institute Research Paper. Retrieved from: https://networkedsociety.unimelb.edu.au

Bou-Harb, E. (2017). On the Impact of Empirical Attack Models Targeting Marine Transportation. *5th IEEE International Conference on Models and Technologies for Intelligent Transportation Systems*. DOI: 10.1109/MTITS.2017.8005665

Boutsidis, C., Zouzias, A., Mahoney, M. W., & Drineas, P. (2015). Randomized Dimensionality Reduction for k -Means Clustering. *IEEE Transactions on Information Theory, 61*(2), 1045–1062. doi:10.1109/TIT.2014.2375327

Bowman, B., & Blackwell, H. (2018). *Hurdles in the Internet of Things Must clear for Manufacturers and Providers*. LegalTech. Retrieved from: https://www.bytebacklaw.com/

Boyes, H. A. (2013). Cyber Security of Intelligent Buildings: A Review. *8th IET International System Safety Conference incorporating the Cyber Security*. 10.1049/cp.2013.1698

Bozkurt, I. N., & Benson, T. (2018). Contextual router: Advancing experience oriented networking to the Alshnta et al., Cogent Engineering. In *Proceedings of the symposium on SDN research* (p. 15: 1–15:7). Academic Press.

Bozkurt, I. N., & Benson, T. Contextual router: Advancing experience oriented networking to the Alshnta et al., Cogent Engineering (2018). In Proceedings of the symposium on SDN research (p. 15: 1–15:7), 2016.

Brandon Heller, Rob Sherwood, Nick McKeown: The Controller Placement Problem, HotSDN 2012

Broch, J., Maltz, D. A., Johnson, D. B., Hu, Y.,Jetcheva, J. (1998). A Performance Comparison of Multi-Hop Wireless Ad Hoc Network Routing Protocols. *ACM Mobicom*.

Brunner, E. M., & Suter, M. (2008). *International CIIP Handbook 2008/2009*. Center for Security Studies, ETH Zurich. Retrieved from http://www.css.ethz.ch/content/dam/ethz/special-interest/gess/cis/center-for-securities-studies/pdfs/CIIP-HB-08-09.pdf

Brzuska, C., Fischlin, M., Freudenreich, T., Lehmann, A., Page, M., Schelbert, J., ... (2009). Security of sanitizable signatures revisited. In *Proceeding of the 12th International Conference on Practice and Theory in Public Key Cryptography* (pp. 317-336). Springer-Verlag Berlin.

Bui, N., & Zorzi, M. (2011), Health care applications: A solution based on the internet of things. In *Proc. of the 4th Int. Symposium on Applied Sciences in Biomed. and Com. Tech., ser.* (pp.1–5). Academic Press. 10.1145/2093698.2093829

Bul, S. R., Biggio, B., & Pillai, I. (n.d.). *Randomized Prediction Games for Adversarial Machine Learning. Academic Press.*

Bulut, E., Wang, Z., & Szymanski, B. K. (2009). Impact of social networks on delay tolerant routing. IEEE GLOBECOM '09. doi:10.1109/GLOCOM.2009.5425860

Burleigh, S., Hooke, A., Torgerson, L., Fall, K., Cerf, V., Durst, B., ... Weiss, H. (2003). Delay-tolerant networking: An approach to interplanetary internet. *Communications Magazine, IEEE, 41*(6), 128–136. doi:10.1109/MCOM.2003.1204759

Büsching, F., Bottazzi, M., Pöttner, W., & Wolf, L. (2013). *DTWBAN: Disruption Tolerant Wireless Body Area Networks in Healthcare Applications*,. In The International Workshop on e-Health Pervasive Wireless Applications and Services (eHPWAS'13), Lyon, France.

Butler, A., Haynes, R. D., Humphries, T. D., & Ranjan, P. (2014). Efficient optimization of the likelihood function in Gaussian process modelling. *Computational Statistics & Data Analysis, 73*, 40–52. doi:10.1016/j.csda.2013.11.017

Buyya, R. (2009). Market-oriented cloud computing: Vision, hype, and reality of delivering computing as the 5th utility. *2009 9th IEEE/ACM International Symposium on Cluster Computing and the Grid, CCGRID 2009*. 10.1109/CCGRID.2009.97

Buyya. (2013). *Mastering cloud computing*. Morgan Kaufman.

Buyya, R., & Barreto, D. (2016). Multi-cloud resource provisioning with Aneka: A unified and integrated utilisation of microsoft azure and amazon EC2 instances. *2015 International Conference on Computing and Network Communications, CoCoNet 2015*.

Buyya, R., Yeo, C. S., Venugopal, S., Broberg, J., & Brandic, I. (2009, June). Cloud Computing and Emerging IT Platforms: Vision, Hype, and Reality for Delivering Computing as the 5th Utility. *Future Generation Computer Systems, 25*(6), 17. doi:10.1016/j.future.2008.12.001

Cachin, C. (2017). *Blockchain, cryptography, and consensus*. IBM Research. doi:10.4204/EPTCS.261.1

Cachin, C., Keidar, I., & Shraer, A. (2009). Trusting the cloud. *ACM Sigact News, 40*(2), 81–86. doi:10.1145/1556154.1556173

Cai, Cox, & Ng. (2011). *Maestro: A System for Scalable OpenFlow Control*. Academic Press.

Calandriello, G., Papadimitratos, P., Hubaux, J. P., & Lioy, A. (2007). Efficient and robust pseudonymous authentication in VANET. In *Proceeding of 4th ACM International Workshop VANET* (pp. 19–28). Montréal, QC, Canada: ACM. 10.1145/1287748.1287752

Calheiros, R. N., Ranjan, R., Beloglazov, A., De Rose, C. A. F., & Buyya, R. (2011, January). CloudSim: A toolkit for modeling and simulation of cloud computing environments and evaluation of resource provisioning algorithms. *Software, Practice & Experience, 41*(1), 23–50. doi:10.1002pe.995

Calleja, A., Martín, A., Menéndez, H. D., Tapiador, J., & Clark, D. (2018). Picking on the family: Disrupting android malware triage by forcing misclassification. *Expert Systems with Applications, 95*, 113–126. doi:10.1016/j.eswa.2017.11.032

Candès, E. J. (2008). The restricted isometry property and its implications for compressed sensing. *Comptes Rendus Mathematique, 346*(9-10), 589–592. doi:10.1016/j.crma.2008.03.014

Canini, Kuznetsov, Levin, & Schmid. (2013). *Software Transactional Networking: Concurrent and Consistent Policy Composition*. HotSDN.

Canini, Kuznetsov, Levin, & Schmid. (2013). *The Case for Reliable Software Transactional Networking*. Academic Press.

Cao, W., Czarnek, N., Shan, J., & Li, L. (2018). Microaneurysm detection using principal component analysis and machine learning methods. *IEEE Transactions on Nanobioscience, 17*(3), 191–198. doi:10.1109/TNB.2018.2840084 PMID:29994317

Cao, Y., & Sun, Z. (2012). Routing in delay/disruption tolerant networks: Taxonomy, Survey and Challenges. *IEEE Communications Surveys and Tutorials*, 1–24.

CapacityScheduler Guide. (2018). Retrieved November 20, 2018, from https://hadoop.apache.org/docs/r1.2.1/capacity_scheduler.html

Carlini, N., & Wagner, D. (2016). *Defensive distillation is not robust to adversarial examples*. ArXiv Preprint ArXiv:1607.04311

Carlini, N., & Wagner, D. (2017). *Adversarial Examples Are Not Easily Detected*. Retrieved From Http://Dl.Acm.Org/Citation.Cfm?Id=3140444

Carlini, N., & Wagner, D. (2018). *Audio Adversarial Examples: Targeted Attacks On Speech-To-Text*. Arxiv Preprint Arxiv:1801.01944

Carlini, N., Katz, G., Barrett, C., & Dill, D. L. (2017). *Ground-Truth Adversarial Examples*. Arxiv Preprint Arxiv:1709.10207

Carlini, N., & Wagner, D. (2017a). Adversarial Examples Are Not Easily Detected: Bypassing Ten Detection Methods. *Proceedings Of The 10th ACM Workshop On Artificial Intelligence And Security*, 3-14.

Carlini, N., & Wagner, D. (2017b). Towards Evaluating The Robustness Of Neural Networks. *2017 IEEE Symposium On Security And Privacy (SP)*, 39-57. 10.1109/SP.2017.49

Casado, Koponen, Shenker, & Tootoonchian. (2012). *Fabric: A Retrospective on Evolving SDN*. HotSDN.

Casado. (2015). *What OpenFlow is (and more importantly, what it's not)*. Academic Press.

Casado, M., Freedman, M. J., Pettit, J., Luo, J., McKeown, N., & Shenker, S. (2007). *Ethane: Taking Control of the Enterprise*. Sigcomm.

Cerf, V., Burleigh, S., Hooke, A., Torgerson, L., Durst, R., Scott, K., Fall, K., & Weiss, H. (2002). *Delay-Tolerant Network Architecture: The Evolving Interplanetary Internet*. draft-irtf-ipnrg-arch-01.txt.

Cerf, V., Burleigh, S., Hooke, A., Torgerson, L., Durst, R., Scott, K., Fall, K., & Weiss, H. (2007). *Delay Tolerant Networking Architecture*. Internet RFC 4838.

Chadd, A. (2018). DDoS attacks: Past, present and future. *Network Security, 2018*(7), 13–15. doi:10.1016/S1353-4858(18)30069-2

Chadrasekaran, B., & Benson, T. (2014). *Tolerating SDN Application Failures with Lego SDN*. HotNets.

Chapman, L., Young, D., Muller, C., Rose, P., Lucas, C., & Walden, J. (2014). Winter road maintenance and the internet of things. *Proceedings of the 17th International Road Weather Conference, 18.*

Chatfield, K., Simonyan, K., Vedaldi, A., & Zisserman, A. (2014). *Return Of The Devil In The Details: Delving Deep Into Convolutional Nets.* Arxiv Preprint Arxiv:1405.3531

Chaudhary, D., Bhushan, K., & Gupta, B. B. (2018). Survey on DDoS Attacks and Defense Mechanisms in Cloud and Fog Computing. *International Journal of E-Services and Mobile Applications, 10*(3), 61–83. doi:10.4018/IJESMA.2018070104

Chaudhary, P., & Gupta, B. B. (2017). A novel framework to alleviate dissemination of XSS worms in online social network (OSN) using view segregation. *Neural Network World, 27*(1), 5–25. doi:10.14311/NNW.2017.27.001

Chen, L., Hou, S., & Ye, Y. (n.d.). *SecureDroid : Enhancing Security of Machine Learning-based Detection against Adversarial Android Malware Attacks.* Academic Press.

Chen, L., Ye, Y., & Bourlai, T. (2017). Adversarial Machine Learning in Malware Detection: Arms Race between Evasion Attack and Defense. In *Intelligence and Security Informatics Conference (EISIC), 2017 European* (pp. 99–106). Academic Press. 10.1109/EISIC.2017.21

Chen, Q., Zhang, D., Guo, M., Deng, Q., & Guo, S. (2010). SAMR: A Self-adaptive MapReduce Scheduling Algorithm in Heterogeneous Environment. In *2010 10th IEEE International Conference on Computer and Information Technology* (pp. 2736–2743). IEEE. 10.1109/CIT.2010.458

Chen, S., Xue, M., Fan, L., Hao, S., Xu, L., Zhu, H., & Li, B. (n.d.). *Automated Poisoning Attacks and Defenses in Malware Detection Systems: An Adversarial Machine Learning Approach.* Academic Press.

Chen, X., Li, B., & Vorobeychik, Y. (2000). Evaluation of Defensive Methods for DNNS Against Multiple Adversarial Evasion Models. In ICLR 2017. doi:10.2507/daaam.scibook.2010.27

Chen, C. H., Lin, J. W., & Kuo, S. Y. (2014). Deadline-Constrained MapReduce Scheduling Based on Graph Modelling. *IEEE International Conference on Cloud Computing, CLOUD*, 416–23. 10.1109/CLOUD.2014.63

Chen, C. P., & Zhang, C. (2014). Data-intensive applications, challenges, techniques and technologies: A survey on Big Data. *Information Sciences, 275*, 314–347. doi:10.1016/j.ins.2014.01.015

Cheng, D., Rao, J., Jiang, C., & Zhou, X. (2015). Resource and Deadline-Aware Job Scheduling in Dynamic Hadoop Clusters. In *2015 IEEE International Parallel and Distributed Processing Symposium* (pp. 956–965). IEEE. 10.1109/IPDPS.2015.36

Cheng, D., Zhou, X., Lama, P., Wu, J., & Jiang, C. (2017). Cross-Platform Resource Scheduling for Spark and MapReduce on YARN. *IEEE Transactions on Computers, 66*(8), 1341–1353. doi:10.1109/TC.2017.2669964

Chen, P., Zhang, H., Sharma, Y., Yi, J., & Hsieh, C. (2017). Zoo: Zeroth Order Optimization Based Black-Box Attacks To Deep Neural Networks Without Training Substitute Models. *Proceedings Of The 10th ACM Workshop On Artificial Intelligence And Security*, 15-26.

Chen, Q., Guo, M., Deng, Q., Zheng, L., Guo, S., & Shen, Y. (2013). HAT: History-based auto-tuning MapReduce in heterogeneous environments. *The Journal of Supercomputing, 64*(3), 1038–1054. doi:10.100711227-011-0682-5

Chen, S., Xue, M., Fan, L., Hao, S., Xu, L., Zhu, H., & Li, B. (2018). Automated poisoning attacks and defenses in malware detection systems: An adversarial machine learning approach. *Computers & Security, 73*, 326–344. doi:10.1016/j.cose.2017.11.007

Chen, Y., Nadji, Y., Kountouras, A., Monrose, F., Perdisci, R., Antonakakis, M., & Vasiloglou, N. (2017). Practical attacks against graph-based clustering. In *Proceedings of the 2017 ACM SIGSAC Conference on Computer and Communications Security* (pp. 1125–1142). ACM. 10.1145/3133956.3134083

Chiappetta, A. (2017). Critical Infrastructure Protection: Beyond the Hybrid Port and Airport Firmware; Security; Cyber-security applications on transport. *5th IEEE International Conference on Models and Technologies for Intelligent Transportation Systems.* DOI: 10.1109/MTITS.2017.8005666

Chiappetta, A. (2017). Hybrid ports: The role of IoT and Cyber Security in the next decade. *Journal of Sustainable Development of Transport and Logistics, 2*(2), 47–56. doi:10.14254/jsdtl.2017.2-2.4

Chin, J., Callaghan, V., & Lam, I. (2017). Understanding and personalising smart city services using machine learning, the internet-of-things and big data. *Industrial Electronics (ISIE), 2017 IEEE 26th International Symposium on, IEEE,* 2050–2055. 10.1109/ISIE.2017.8001570

Chin, J., Callaghan, V., & Lam, I. (2017). Understanding and personalising smart city services using machine learning. *The Internet-of-Things and Big Data. IEEE 26th International Symposium on Industrial Electronics (ISIE), 2050-2055.

Chipman, H., Ranjan, P., & Wang, W. (2012). Sequential design for computer experiments with a flexible bayesian additive model. *The Canadian Journal of Statistics, 40*(4), 663–678. doi:10.1002/cjs.11156

Cho, B., Rahman, M., Chajed, T., Gupta, I., Abad, C., Roberts, N., & Lin, P. (2013). Natjam. In *Proceedings of the 4th annual Symposium on Cloud Computing - SOCC '13* (pp. 1–17). New York: ACM Press. 10.1145/2523616.2523624

Choi, N., Vu, H., Burchfield, R., & Yazd, S. A. (2012). *Introduction to NS-2.* Retrieved from https://www.utdallas.edu/~venky/acn/Handouts/ns2-sara.pdf

Choo, K.-K. R., Lu, R., Chen, L., & Yi, X. (2018). A foggy research future: Advances and future opportunities in fog computing research. *Future Generation Computer Systems, 78*(2), 677–697. doi:10.1016/j.future.2017.09.014

Christian Esteve Rothenberg, Marcelo Ribeiro Nascimento, Marcos Rogerio Salvador, Carlos N.A. Correa, Sidney C. de Lucena, Robert Raszuk: Revisiting Routing Control Platforms with the Eyes and Muscles of Software-Defined Networking,, HotSDN 2012

Chumbley, A., Williams, C., & Duna, A. (n.d.). *Homomorphic Encryption.* Retrieved from https://brilliant.org/wiki/homomorphic-encryption/

Chung, J., Gulcehre, C., Cho, K., & Bengio, Y. (2014). *Empirical Evaluation Of Gated Recurrent Neural Networks On Sequence Modeling.* Arxiv Preprint Arxiv:1412.3555

Clausen, T., & Jacquet, P. (2003). *Optimized link state routing protocol. RFC 3626.* IETF.

Cloud Project. (2014). Retrieved from http://clout-project.eu/

Cloud Security Alliance. (2013, February). The Notorious Nine. Cloud Computing Top Threats in 2013. *Security,* 1–14.

Cluley, G. (2016). *These 60 dumb passwords can hijack over 500,000 IoT devices into the Mirai botnet.* Retrieved from: https://www.grahamcluley.com/mirai-botnet-password/

Coker.com. (n.d.). *Bonnie++.* Retrieved from http://www.coker.com.au/bonnie++/

Columbus, L. (2018). *10 Charts That Will Change Your Perspective Of Big Data's Growth.* Retrieved from http://www.forbes.com/sites/louiscolumbus/2018/05/23/10-charts-that-will-change-your-perspective-of-big-datas-growth/#232420072926

Cong, Z., Jun, S., Wei, G., Xie, M., & Min, J. (2018). CCA-secure ABE with outsourced decryption for fog computing. *Future Generation Computer Systems*, *78*(2), 730–738.

Contagio Mobile. (n.d.). Retrieved December 17, 2018, from http://contagiominidump.blogspot.com/

Corbet, S., Lucey, B., & Yarovaya, L. (2018). Datestamping the Bitcoin and Ethereum bubbles. *Finance Research Letters*, *26*, 81–88. doi:10.1016/j.frl.2017.12.006

Costigan, S. S., & Gustav, L. (2016). Policy and the Internet of Things. *Connections*, *15*(2), 9–18. doi:10.11610/Connections.15.2.01

Covington, M. J., & Carskadden, R. (2013). Threat implications of the Internet of Things. *IEEE 5th International Conference on Cyber Conflict (Cycon)*, 1-12.

Cramer, Rost, Bentley, & AymanShamma. (2011). *2nd workshop on research in the large. using app stores, wide distribution channels and big data in ubicomp research*. Retrieved from http://doi.acm.org/10.1145/2030112.2030244

Croman, K., Decker, C., Eyal, I., Gencer, E. A., Juels, A., Kosba, A., & … . (2016). On Scaling Decentralized Blockchains. In *International Conference on Financial Cryptography and Data Security* (pp. 106-125). Sliema, Malta: Springer. 10.1007/978-3-662-53357-4_8

CrystalE. (n.d.). Retrieved from http://www.crystalinks.com/chaos.html

Cubuk, E. D., Zoph, B., Schoenholz, S. S., & Le, Q. V. (2017). *Intriguing Properties of Adversarial Examples*. ArXiv Preprint ArXiv:1711.02846

Cui, W., Xiao, Y., Wang, H., Song, Y., Hwang, S., & Wang, W. (2017). KBQA: Learning question answering over QA Corpora and Knowledge bases. *Proceedings of the VLDB Endowment International Conference on Very Large Data Bases*, *10*(5), 565–576. doi:10.14778/3055540.3055549

Curtis, A. R., Mogul, J. C., Tourrilhes, J., Yalagandula, P., Sharma, P., & Banerjee, S. (2011). *DevoFlow: Scaling Flow Management for High-performance Networks*. Sigcomm. doi:10.1145/2018436.2018466

Cy, V. O. D. (2017). a novel trinity multimedia social network scheme. *Multimedia Tools and Applications*, *76*(18), 18513–18529. doi:10.100711042-016-4162-z

Da Costa, C. A., Pasluosta, C. F., Eskofier, B., da Silva, D. B., & da Rosa Righi, R. (2018). Internet of Health Things: Toward intelligent vital signs monitoring in hospital wards. *Artificial Intelligence in Medicine*, *89*, 61–69. doi:10.1016/j.artmed.2018.05.005 PMID:29871778

Dabosville, G. (n.d.). *Past & Future Issues in Smartcard Industry*. Retrieved October 5, 2018, from Oberthur Technologies: https://www.cosic.esat.kuleuven.be/ecrypt/courses/albena11/slides/guillaume_dabosville_smartcards.pdf

Dai, H., & Su, S. (2015). Method study on energy performance management of micro-grid under smart energy grid. *Smart Grid*, *3*(10), 895–900.

Dalvi, N., Domingos, P., Sanghai, S., & Verma, D. (2004). (2004). Adversarial Classification. *Proceedings Of The Tenth ACM SIGKDD International Conference On Knowledge Discovery And Data Mining*, 99-108.

Damaševičius, R., Vasiljevas, M., Šalkevičius, J., & Woźniak, M. (2016). Human Activity Recognition in AAL Environments Using Random Projections. *Computational and Mathematical Methods in Medicine*, *2016*, 1–17. doi:10.1155/2016/4073584 PMID:27413392

Dancik, G. M., & Dorman, K. S. (2008). mlegp: Statistical analysis for computer models of biological systems using R. *Bioinformatics (Oxford, England)*, *24*(17), 1966–1967. doi:10.1093/bioinformatics/btn329 PMID:18635570

Daniel, J. A. (2009). Data Management in the Cloud: Limitations and Opportunities. *A Quarterly Bulletin of the Computer Society of the IEEE Technical Committee on Data Engineering, 32*, 3–12.

Danny Yuxing Huang, Kenneth Yocum, Alex C. Snoeren: High-Fidelity Switch Models for Software-Defined Network Emulation, 2013

Darklord. (2008). *Little progress in U.S. airport security. Fly away simulation.* Retrieved Mar. 3, 2008: http://flyaway-simulation.com/article2330.html

Das, D., & Misra, R. (2011). Programmable Cellular Automata Based Efficient Parallel AES Encryption Algorithm. *International Journal of Network Security & Its Applications, 3*(6), 204. doi:10.5121/ijnsa.2011.3615

Dasgupta, S., & Gupta, A. (2002). An elementary proof of a theorem of Johnson and Lindenstrauss. *Random Structures and Algorithms, 22*(1), 60–65. doi:10.1002/rsa.10073

Das, S., & Kalita, H. K. (2016). Advanced Dimensionality Reduction Method for Big Data. *Big Data*, 2388–2400. doi:10.4018/978-1-4666-9840-6.ch108

Davies, R. (2018). Apple Becomes World's First Trillion-dollar Company. *The Guardian*. Retrieved from: https://www.theguardian.com/technology/2018/aug/02/apple-becomes-worlds-first-trillion-dollar-company

Davis, R. (2003). The data encryption standard in perspective. In *Communications Society Magazine* (pp. 5–9). IEEE.

Dean, J., & Ghemawat, S. (2008). MapReduce: Simplified data processing on large clusters. *Communications of the ACM, 51*(1), 107. doi:10.1145/1327452.1327492

Deepali, Bhushan. K. (2017, May). DDoS attack defense framework for cloud using fog computing. In *Recent Trends in Electronics, Information & Communication Technology (RTEICT), 2017 2nd IEEE International Conference on* (pp. 534-538). IEEE.

Deepali, Bhushan., K. (2017, August). DDoS attack mitigation and resource provisioning in cloud using fog computing. In *Smart Technologies For Smart Nation (SmartTechCon), 2017 International Conference On* (pp. 308-313). IEEE.

Degabriele, P. J., Lehmann, A., Paterson, G. K., Smart, P. N., & Strefler, M. (2012). *On the Joint Security of Encryption and Signature in EMV*. Berlin: Springer. doi:10.1007/978-3-642-27954-6_8

Delen, D., & Demirkan, H. (2013). Data, information and analytics as services. *Decision Support Systems, 55*(1), 359–363. doi:10.1016/j.dss.2012.05.044

Delmolino, K., Arnett, M., Kosba, A., Miller, A., & Shi, E. (2016). Step by Step Towards Creating a Safe Smart Contract: Lessons and Insights from a Cryptocurrency Lab. In *International Conference on Financial Cryptography and Data Security* (pp. 77-94). Sliema, Malta: Springer. 10.1007/978-3-662-53357-4_6

Demmer, M., & Fall, K. (2007). DTLSR: delay tolerant routing for developing regions. *Proceedings of the 1st ACM SIGCOMM Workshop on Networked Systems for Developing Regions*, 1–6. 10.1145/1326571.1326579

Demontis, A., Member, S., Melis, M., Member, S., Biggio, B., Maiorca, D., … Roli, F. (n.d.). *Yes, Machine Learning Can Be More Secure ! A Case Study on Android Malware Detection*. Academic Press.

Deng, J., Han, R., & Mishra, S. (2003). *Enhancing base station security in wireless sensor networks. CU-CS-951-03: University of Colorado*. Department of Computer Science Technical Report.

Deng, J., Richard, H., & Shivakant, M. (2006). Decorrelating wireless sensor network traffic to inhibit traffic analysis attacks. *Elsevier Pervasive and Mobile Computing Journal, 2*(2), 159–186. doi:10.1016/j.pmcj.2005.12.003

Deng, R., Lu, R., Lai, C., Luan Tom, H., & Hao, L. (2016). Optimal workload allocation in fog-cloud computing toward balanced delay and power consumption. *IEEE Internet of Things J.*, *3*(6), 1171–1181.

Denis, F. (n.d.). *blogbench - manned.org*. Retrieved from http://manned.org/blogbench/fbdee406

Derhamy, H., Eliasson, J., Delsing, J., & Priller, P. (2015). A survey of commercialframeworks for the internet of things. Emerging Technologies &Factory Automation (ETFA 2015), 1–8.

Diffiee, W., & Hellman, M. (1976). New Directions in Cryptography. *IEEE Transactions on Information Theory*, *IT-22*(6), 644–654. doi:10.1109/TIT.1976.1055638

Directive (EU) 2016/1148 of the European Parliament and of the Council of 6 July 2016 concerning measures for a high common level of security of network and information systems across the Union ["NIS Directive"], Brussels, July 2016.

Distefano, S., Merlino, G., & Puliafito, A. (2012). Enabling the cloud of things. In *Innovative Mobile and Internet Services in Ubiquitous Computing (IMIS), 2012 Sixth International Conference on* (pp. 858-863). IEEE. 10.1109/IMIS.2012.61

Distefano, S., Merlino, G., & Puliafito, A. (2012). Enabling the Cloud of Things. *Proceedings of the 2012 Sixth International Conference on Innovative Mobile and Internet Services in Ubiquitous Computing*, 858-863.

Djahel, S., Doolan, R., Muntean, G.-M., & Murphy, J. (2015). A communications-oriented perspective on traffic management systems for smart cities: Challenges and innovative approaches. *IEEE Communications Surveys and Tutorials*, *17*(1), 125–151. doi:10.1109/COMST.2014.2339817

Do & Pham. (2018). DW-PathSim: a distributed computing model for topic-driven weighted meta-path-based similarity measure in a large-scale content-based heterogeneous information network. *Journal of Information and Telecommunication*, 1-20.

Dobre, F., & Xhafa, F. (2014). Xhafa, Intelligent services for big data science. *Future Generation Computer Systems*, *37*, 267–281. doi:10.1016/j.future.2013.07.014

Dogru, T., Mody, M., & Leonardi, C. (2018). *Blockchain Technology & its Implications for the Hospitality Industry*. Boston University.

Donald, G., John, F. S., James, M. T., & Carl, M. H. (2008). *Fundamentals of queueing theory* (4th ed.). Wiley.

Dong, Y., Liao, F., Pang, T., Su, H., Zhu, J., Hu, X., & Li, J. (2018). (2018). *Boosting Adversarial Attacks With Momentum. The IEEE Conference On Computer Vision And Pattern Recognition (CVPR)*.

Dongyoung, K., & Junbeom, H. (2018). Privacy-preserving deduplication of encrypted data with dynamic ownership management in fog computing. *Future Generation Computer Systems*, *78*(2), 739–752.

Dopico, N., Gutiérrez, A., & Zazo, S. (2011). Performance analysis of a delay tolerant application for herd localization. *Computer Networks*, *55*(8), 1770–1783. doi:10.1016/j.comnet.2011.01.007

Dorri, A., Kanhere, S. S., & Jurdak, R. (2016). *Blockchain in internet of things: Challenges and Solutions*. Retrieved from: https://arxiv.org/pdf/1608.05187.pdf

Dorri, A., Kanhere, S. S., & Jurdak, R. (2017). Towards an Optimized BlockChain for IoT. In *Proceedings of the Second International Conference on Internet-of-Things Design and Implementation* (pp. 173-178). ACM.

Dorri, A., Kanhere, S. S., Jurdak, R., & Gauravaram, P. (2017). Blockchain for IoT security and privacy: The case study of a smart home. In *2017 IEEE International Conference on Pervasive Computing and Communications Workshops (PerCom Workshops)* (pp. 618-623). Kona, HI: IEEE. 10.1109/PERCOMW.2017.7917634

Douceur, J. R. (2002). *The Sybil attack' in Peer-to-Peer Systems*. Berlin, Germany: Springer. doi:10.1007/3-540-45748-8_24

DTNRG. (2005). *Delay tolerant networking research group: dtn-interest mailing list archive*. Available from http://mailman.dtnrg.org/pipermail/dtn-interest/2005-April/

Dube, P., Bhattacharjee, B., & Petit-bois, E. (n.d.). *Improving Transferability of Deep Neural Networks*. Academic Press.

Ebin Deni Raj, L. D. (2014). *Forecasting the Trends in Cloud Computing and its Impact on Future IT Business*. IGI Global.

Egwutuoha, I. P., Chen, S., Levy, D., Selic, B., & Calvo, R. (2014). Cost-oriented proactive fault tolerance approach to high performance computing (HPC) in the cloud. *International Journal of Parallel, Emergent and Distributed Systems*, *29*(4), 363–378. doi:10.1080/17445760.2013.803686

Elias, B. (2008). *National Aviation Security Policy, Strategy, and Mode-Specific Plans: Background and Consideration for Congress*. CRS Reports for Congress, Congressional Research Services, Order Code RL34302.

Emery, X. (2009). The kriging update equations and their application to the selection of neighboring data. *Computational Geosciences*, *13*(3), 269–280. doi:10.100710596-008-9116-8

Emre, S., Riva, O., Stuedi, P., & Alonso, G. (2009). Enabling social networking in ad hoc networks of mobile phones. *Proceedings of the VLDB Endowment International Conference on Very Large Data Bases*, *2*(2), 1634–1637. doi:10.14778/1687553.1687611

EMVCo. (n.d.). *Worldwide EMV® Deployment Statistics*. Retrieved October 10, 2018, from emvco.com: https://www.emvco.com/about/deployment-statistics/

ENISA. (2016). *Smart Airports: How to protect airport passengers from cyber disruptions*. Retrieved from https://www.enisa.europa.eu/news/enisa-news/smart-airports-how-to-protect-airport-passengers-from-cyber-disruptions

ENISA. (2017). *EU strategies to secure the EU cyberspace and critical infrastructure against hackers. Speech by ENISA's Executive Director, Prof*. Dr. Udo Helmbrecht - AECA Round-Table Conference-Luncheon.

Eris Industries. (2016). *Documentation_Blockchains*. Available: https://docs.erisindustries.com/explainers/blockchains/

Erlingsson, Ú., Pihur, V., & Korolova, A. (2014). Rappor: Randomized aggregatable privacy-preserving ordinal response. In *Proceedings of the 2014 ACM SIGSAC conference on computer and communications security* (pp. 1054–1067). ACM. 10.1145/2660267.2660348

Ethane, M. (2007). Casado, M.J. Freedman, J. Pettit, J. Luo, N. McKeown, and S. Shenker. Ethane: Taking control of the enterprise. *Computer Communication Review*, *37*(4), 1–12.

Ethane, M. (2007). Ethane: Taking control of the enterprise. *Computer Communication Review*, *37*(4), 1–12.

Evangelos, A. K., Nikolaos, D. T., & Anthony, C. B. (2011). *Integrating RFIDs and smartobjects into a UnifiedInternet of Things architecture*. Advances in Internet of Things.

Evans, D. (2011). *The internet of things how the next evolution of the internet is changing everything*. Cisco, Tech. Report.

Eyal, I., & Sirer, G. E. (2018). Majority is not enough: Bitcoin mining is vulnerable. *Communications of the ACM*, *61*(7), 95–102. doi:10.1145/3212998

Eykholt, K., Evtimov, I., Fernandes, E., Li, B., Rahmati, A., Xiao, C., ... Song, D. (2018). Robust Physical-World Attacks On Deep Learning Visual Classification. *Proceedings Of The IEEE Conference On Computer Vision And Pattern Recognition*, 1625-1634.

Fair Scheduler. (2018). Retrieved November 20, 2018, from https://hadoop.apache.org/docs/r1.2.1/fair_scheduler.html

Fall, K. (2003). A Delay-Tolerant Network Architecture for Challenged Internets. In *Proc. ACM SIGCOMM '03*. New York: ACM Press. 10.1145/863955.863960

Fall, K., Hong, W., & Madden, S. (2003). *Custody Transfer for Reliable Delivery in Delay Tolerant Networks*. Technical Report IRB-TR-03-030, Intel Research Berkeley.

Fall, K., & Farrell, S. (2008). DTN: An architectural retrospective. *J. IEEE Journal on Selected Areas in Communications*, *26*(5), 828–836. doi:10.1109/JSAC.2008.080609

Fang, K.-T., Li, R., & Sudjianto, A. (2005). *Design and modeling for computer experiments*. Chapman and Hall/CRC. doi:10.1201/9781420034899

Farrel, A. (2015). Path Computation Element (PCE). *Architecture (Washington, D.C.)*.

Farrell, S., Ramadas, M., & Burleigh, S. (2008c). *Transmission ProtocolSecurity Extensions*. Internet RFC 5327. Available: http://www.rfc-editor. org/rfc/rfc5327.txt

Farrell, S., Symington, S., & Weiss, H. (2006). *Delay-Tolerant Networking Security Overview*. draft-irtf-dtnrg-sec-overview-01.txt.

Farrell, S., Symington, S., Weiss, H., & Lovell, P. (2008a). *Delay- Tolerant Networking Security Overview*. draft-irtf-dtnrg-sec-overview-04.txt.

Farrell, S., Symington, S., Weiss, H., & Lovell, P. (2008b). *Bundle Security Protocol Specification*. draft-irtf-dtnrg-sec-overview-04.txt.

Farrell, S., & Cahill, V. (2006). *Delay-and disruption-tolerant networking*. Norwood, MA: Artech House.

Farrell, S., & Cahill, V. (2016). Security considerations in space and delay tolerant network*s. Proc. of SMC-IT'06*.

Fathima, G., & Wahidabanu, R. (2011). Integrating Buffer Management with Epidemic Routing, in in Delay Tolerant Networks. *Journal of Computational Science*, *7*(7), 1038–1045. doi:10.3844/jcssp.2011.1038.1045

Faust, O., Hagiwara, Y., Hong, T. J., Lih, O. S., & Acharya, U. R. (2018). Deep learning for healthcare applications based on physiological signals: A review. *Computer Methods and Programs in Biomedicine*, *161*, 1-13.

Feinman, R., Curtin, R. R., Shintre, S., & Gardner, A. B. (2017). *Detecting Adversarial Samples From Artifacts*. Arxiv Preprint Arxiv:1703.00410

Feld, S., Sch¨onfeld, M., & Werner, M. (2014). Analyzing the Deployment ofBitcoin's P2P Network under an AS-level Perspective. *Procedia Computer Science*, *32*, 1121–1126. doi:10.1016/j.procs.2014.05.542

Ferdous, M. S., Hussein, R., Alassafi, M., Alharthi, A., Walters, R., & Wills, G. (2016). Threat taxonomy for Cloud of Things. *Internet of Things and Big Data Analysis: Recent Trends and Challenges*, *1*, 149–191.

Ferguson, Guha, Liang, Fonseca, & Krishnamurthi. (2013). *Hierarchical Policies for Software Defined Network*. Academic Press.

Ferrag, M. A., Nafa, M., & Ghanemi, S. (2012b). OlsrBOOK: a privacy-preserving mobile social network leveraging on securing the olsr routing protocol. In *Proceeding of The 8 th International Scientific Conference eLearning and Software for Education* (pp. 133-139). Bucharest, Romania: Editura Universitara.

Ferrag, M. A. (2012a). *Study of attacks in ad hoc networks*. LAP Lambert Academic Publishing.

Ferrag, M. A., Derdour, M., Mukherjee, M., Derhab, A., Maglaras, L., & Janicke, H. (2018). *Blockchain Technologies for the Internet of Things: Research Issues and Challenges. IEEE Internet of Things Journal*.

Ferrag, M. A., Maglaras, L., & Ahmim, A. (2017). Privacy-preserving schemes for ad hoc social networks: A survey. *IEEE Communications Surveys and Tutorials*, *19*(4), 3015–3045. doi:10.1109/COMST.2017.2718178

Ferrag, M. A., Nafa, M., & Ghanemi, S. (2013a). A new security mechanism for ad-hoc on-demand distance vector in mobile ad hoc social networks. In *Proceedings of the 7th Workshop on Wireless and Mobile Ad-Hoc Networks (WMAN 2013) in Conjunction with the Conference on Networked Systems NetSys/KIVS*. Stuttgart, Germany: WMAN.

Ferrag, M. A., Nafa, M., & Ghanemi, S. (2013b). Security and privacy in mobile ad hoc social networks. In D. B. Rawat, B. B. Bista, & G. Yan (Eds.), *Security, Privacy, Trust, and Resource Management in Mobile and Wireless Communications* (pp. 223–244). IGI Global.

Ferrag, M. A., Nafa, M., & Ghanemi, S. (2016). EPSA: An efficient and privacy-preserving scheme against wormhole attack on reactive routing for mobile ad hoc social networks. *International Journal of Security and Networks*, *11*(3), 107–125. doi:10.1504/IJSN.2016.078390

Fildes, J. (2010). Stuxnet worm targeted high-value Iranian assets. *BBC*. Retrieved from: https://www.bbc.com/news/technology-11388018

Finextra. (2016, November 15). *Metro Bank tests smartcard payments on the blockchain.* Retrieved October 20, 2018, from finextra.com: https://www.finextra.com/newsarticle/29764/metro-bank-tests-smartcard-payments-on-the-blockchain

Finn, D., & Ummenhofer, K. (2015). Patent No. US8991712B2. United States Patent Office.

Finn, D., Lotya, M., & Molloy, D. (2018). Patent No. US9960476B2. United States Patent Office.

Fischer, V., Kumar, M. C., Metzen, J. H., & Brox, T. (2017). *Adversarial Examples For Semantic Image Segmentation.* Arxiv Preprint Arxiv:1703.01101

Fischer, M. J., Su, X., & Yin, Y. (2010). Assigning tasks for efficiency in Hadoop. In *Proceedings of the 22nd ACM symposium on Parallelism in algorithms and architectures - SPAA '10* (p. 30). New York: ACM Press. 10.1145/1810479.1810484

Fitzgerald, A. M. (2018). The Internet of disposable things: Throwaway paper and plastic sensors will connect everyday items. *IEEE Spectrum*, *55*(12), 30–35. doi:10.1109/MSPEC.2018.8544981

Flores Moyano, R., Fernández, D., Bellido, L., & González, C. (2017). *A software-defined networking approach to improve service provision in residential networks. International Journal Network Managed.* doi:10.1002/nem.1984

Florissi, P. (2012, February). *Emc And Big Data - A Fun Explanation.* Retrieved from http://www.youtube.com/watch?v=eEpxN0htRKI

Foell, Kortuem, Rawassizadeh, Handte, Iqbal, & Marrón. (2014). Micro-navigation for urban bus passengers: Using the internet of things to improve the public transport experience. In *Proceedings of the 1st International Conference on IoT in Urban Space*. Institute for Computer Sciences, Social-Informatics and Telecommunications Engineering).

Folkerts, E., Alexandrov, A., Sachs, K., Iosup, A., Markl, V., & Tosun, C. (2012). Benchmarking in the cloud: What it should, can, and cannot be. *4th TPC Technology Conference (TPCTC)*, 173-188.

Fong, K., Hepler, K., Raghavan, R., & Rowland, P. (2018). *rIoT: Quantifying Consumer Costs of Insecure Internet of Things Devices*. University of California Berkeley, School of Information Report. Retrieved from: https://groups.ischool.berkeley.edu/riot/

Foster, N., Guha, A., Reitblatt, M., Story, A., Freedman, M. J., Katta, N. P., ... Harrison, R. (2013). Languages for Software-Defined Networks. *IEEE Communications Magazine*, *51*(2), 128–134. doi:10.1109/MCOM.2013.6461197

Foster, N., Harrison, R., Freedman, M. J., Monsanto, C., Rexford, J., Story, A., & Walker, D. (2011). *Frenetic: A Network Programming Language.* ICFP. doi:10.1145/2034773.2034812

Franey, M., Ranjan, P., & Chipman, H. (2012). *A short note on Gaussian process modeling for large datasets using graphics processing units.* arXiv:1203.1269

Franklin, J. (2014). *Modelling European red mite population using the inverse approach* (Master's thesis). Acadia University.

Freeman, L. C. (1978). Centrality in social networks: Conceptual clarification. *Elsevier Social Networks, 1*(3), 215–239. doi:10.1016/0378-8733(78)90021-7

Funahashi, K., & Nakamura, Y. (1993). Approximation Of Dynamical Systems By Continuous Time Recurrent Neural Networks. *Neural Networks, 6*(6), 801–806.

Furrer, R., Genton, M. G., & Nychka, D. (2006). Covariance tapering for interpolation of large spatial datasets. *Journal of Computational and Graphical Statistics, 15*(3), 502–523. doi:10.1198/106186006X132178

Galache, Yonezawa, Gurgen, Pavia, Grella, & Maeomichi. (2014). ClouT: Leveraging Cloud Computing Techniques for Improving Management of Massive IoT Data. *Proceedings of the 2014 IEEE 7th International Conference on Service-Oriented Computing and Applications*, 324-327.

Gandhi, A. (2016). Autoscaling for Hadoop Clusters. *Proceedings - 2016 IEEE International Conference on Cloud Engineering, IC2E 2016: Co-located with the 1st IEEE International Conference on Internet-of-Things Design and Implementation, IoTDI 2016*, 109–18. 10.1109/IC2E.2016.11

Gandomi, A., & Haider, M. (2015). Beyond the hype: Big data concepts, methods, and analytics. *International Journal of Information Management, 35*(2), 137–144. doi:10.1016/j.ijinfomgt.2014.10.007

GAO, Government Accountability Office. (2015). Cybersecurity: Actions Needed to Address Challenges Facing Federal Systems. GAO-15-573T. Washington, DC: GAO.

Gao, L., Luan, T. H., Yu, S., Zhou, W., & Liu, B. (2017). FogRoute: DTN-based data dissemination model in fog computing. IEEE Internet Things J., 4(1), 225–235.

Garay, J., Kiayias, A., & Leonardos, N. (2015). The Bitcoin Backbone Protocol: Analysis and Applications. In *Annual International Conference on the Theory and Applications of Cryptographic Techniques* (pp. 281-310). Berlin: Springer. 10.1007/978-3-662-46803-6_10

Garcia Lopez, P., Montresor, A., Epema, D., Datta, A., Higashino, T., Iamnitchi, A., ... Riviere, E. (2015). Edge-centriccomputing: Vision and challenges. *Computer Communication Review, 45*(5), 37–42. doi:10.1145/2831347.2831354

Garcia, T. P., & Marder, K. (2017). Statistical approaches to longitudinal data analysis in neurodegenerative diseases: Huntington's disease as a model. *Current Neurology and Neuroscience Reports, 17*(14), 1–9. doi:10.100711910-017-0723-4 PMID:28229396

Garcia-Teodoro, P., Diaz-Verdejo, J., Maciá-Fernández, G., & Vázquez, E. (2009). Anomaly-Based Network Intrusion Detection: Techniques, Systems And Challenges. *Computers & Security, 28*(1-2), 18–28. doi:10.1016/j.cose.2008.08.003

Gartner Says 6.4 Billion Connected "Things" Will Be in Use in 2016, Up 30 Percent From 2015. (n.d.). Retrieved from http://www.gartner.com/newsroom/id/3165317

Gartner. (2014). *4.9 Billion Connected "Things" Will Be in Use in 2015.* Retrieved from: https://www.gartner.com/newsroom/id/2905717

Gartner. (2017). *8.4 Billion Connected Things Will Be in Use in 2017, Up 31 Percent From 2016*. Retrieved from: https://www.gartner.com/en/newsroom/press-releases/2017-02-07-gartner-says-8-billion-connected-things-will-be-in-use-in-2017-up-31-percent-from-2016

gemalto. (2018). *Smart card basics – A short guide (2018)*. Retrieved October 1, 2018, from gemalto security to be free: https://www.gemalto.com/companyinfo/smart-cards-basics

George, L. (2011). *HBase: The Definitive Guide*. Retrieved from http://books.google.com/books?hl=en&lr=&id=nUh iQxUXVpMC&pgis=1

Ghodsi, A. (2011). Dominant Resource Fairness : Fair Allocation of Multiple Resource Types Maps Reduces. *Ratio*, 24–24. Retrieved from http://www.usenix.org/events/nsdi11/tech/full_papers/Ghodsi.pdf

Ghoshal, D., Canon, R., & Ramakrishnan, L. (2011). IO Performance of Virtualized Cloud Environments. *Proceedings of the DataCloud-SC '11 Proceedings of the Second International Workshop on Data Intensive Computing in the Cloud*, 71-80. 10.1145/2087522.2087535

Github.com. (n.d.). *byte-unixbench - A Unix benchmark suite*. Retrieved from https://github.com/kdlucas/byte-unixbench

Github.org. (n.d.). *Dbench*. Retrieved from https://github.com/sahlberg/dbench

Globerson, A., & Roweis, S. (2006). Nightmare at test time: robust learning by feature deletion. In *Proceedings of the 23rd international conference on Machine learning* (pp. 353–360). Academic Press. 10.1145/1143844.1143889

Gong, Z., Wang, W., & Ku, W. (2017). *Adversarial And Clean Data Are Not Twins*. Arxiv Preprint Arxiv:1704.04960

González-Torres, A., García-Peñalvo, F. J., Therón-Sánchez, T., & Colomo-Palacios, R. (2016). Knowledge Discovery in Software Teams by Means of Evolutionary Visual Software Analytics. *Science of Computer Programming*, *121*(C), 55–74. doi:10.1016/j.scico.2015.09.005

Goodfellow, I. J., Shlens, J., & Szegedy, C. (2014). *Explaining and harnessing adversarial examples*. ArXiv Preprint ArXiv:1412.6572

Goodfellow, I. J., Shlens, J., & Szegedy, C. (2014). *Explaining And Harnessing Adversarial Examples*. Retrieved From Https://Www.Openaire.Eu/Search/Publication?Articleid=Od_____18:2bc05c2b2e804ef575988e1726ae8a5b

Goodfellow, I., Pouget-Abadie, J., Mirza, M., Xu, B., Warde-Farley, D., Ozair, S., . . . Bengio, Y. (2014). Generative Adversarial Nets. *Advances In Neural Information Processing Systems,* 2672-2680.

Google Inc. (n.d.). *App Engine*. Retrieved from https://developers.google.com/appengine/

Gope, P., & Hwang, T. (2015). Untraceable Sensor Movement in Distributed IoT Infrastructure. *IEEE Sensors Journal*, *15*(9), 5340–5348. doi:10.1109/JSEN.2015.2441113

Gopinath, D., Katz, G., Pasareanu, C. S., & Barrett, C. (2017). *Deepsafe: A Data-Driven Approach For Checking Adversarial Robustness In Neural Networks*. Arxiv Preprint Arxiv:1710.00486

Goransson, P., Black, C., & Culver, T. (2016). *Software defined networks: A comprehensive approach*. Cambridge, MA: Morgan Kaufmann.

Grabbe, J. (2003). Data Encryption Standard: The Triple DES algorithm illustrated Laissez Faire city time. Academic Press.

Gramacy, R. B. (2015). *laGP: Local approximate Gaussian process regression*. R package version 1.2-1.

Gramacy, R., Niemi, J., and Weiss, R. (2014). Massively parallel approximate Gaussian process regression. *SIAM/ASA Journal on Uncertainty Quantification*, *2*(1), 564–584.

Gramacy, R. B. (2007). tgp: An R package for Bayesian nonstationary, semiparametric nonlinear regression and design by treed Gaussian process models. *Journal of Statistical Software, 19*(9), 1–46. doi:10.18637/jss.v019.i09 PMID:21494410

Gramacy, R. B. (2016). lagp: Large-scale spatial modeling via local approximate gaussian processes in R. *Journal of Statistical Software, 72*(1), 1–46. doi:10.18637/jss.v072.i01

Gramacy, R. B., & Apley, D. W. (2015). Local Gaussian process approximation for large computer experiments. *Journal of Computational and Graphical Statistics, 24*(2), 561–578. doi:10.1080/10618600.2014.914442

Gramacy, R. B., & Lee, H. K. (2012). Cases for the nugget in modeling computer experiments. *Statistics and Computing, 22*(3), 713–722. doi:10.100711222-010-9224-x

Greenberg, Hjalmtysson, Maltz, Myers, Rexford, Xie, … Zhang. (2015). *A Clean Slate 4D Approach to Network Control and Management*. Academic Press.

Greenberg, D. (1979). A numerical model investigation of tidal phenomena in the Bay of Fundy and Gulf of Maine. *Marine Geodesy, 2*(2), 161–187. doi:10.1080/15210607909379345

Grosse, K., Papernot, N., Manoharan, P., Backes, M., & McDaniel, P. (2016). *Adversarial perturbations against deep neural networks for malware classification*. ArXiv Preprint ArXiv:1606.04435

Grosse, K., Papernot, N., Manoharan, P., Backes, M., & Mcdaniel, P. (2017). Adversarial Examples For Malware Detection. *European Symposium On Research In Computer Security*, 62-79.

Gruebner, O., Sykora, M., Lowe, S. R., Shankardass, K., Galea, S., & Subramanian, S. V. (2017). Big data opportunities for social behavioral and mental health research. *Social Science & Medicine, 189*, 167–169. doi:10.1016/j.socscimed.2017.07.018 PMID:28755794

Grundy, A. (2012). *Congestion control framework for delay-tolerant communications*. University of Nottingham.

Gu, S., & Rigazio, L. (2014). *Towards Deep Neural Network Architectures Robust To Adversarial Examples*. Arxiv Preprint Arxiv:1412.5068

Gubbi, J., Buyya, R., Marusic, S., & Palaniswami, M. (2013, September). Internet of Things (IoT): A vision, architectural elements, and future directions. *Future Generation Computer Systems, 29*(7), 1645–1660. doi:10.1016/j.future.2013.01.010

Gude, N., Koponen, T., Pettit, J., Ben Pfaff, M. C., McKeown, N., & Shenker, S. (2008). *NOX: Towards an Operating System for Networks*. CCR. doi:10.1145/1384609.1384625

Guha, A., Reitblatt, M., & Foster, N. (2013). *Machine-Verified Network Controllers*. PLDI. doi:10.1145/2491956.2462178

Guha, S., Tang, K., & Francis, P. (2008). NOYB: privacy in online social networks. In *Proceedings of the first workshop on Online social networks* (pp. 49–54). Seattle, WA: ACM. 10.1145/1397735.1397747

Gu, J., Sun, B., Du, X., Wang, J., Zhuang, Y., & Wang, Z. (2018). Consortium Blockchain-Based Malware Detection in Mobile Devices. *IEEE Access: Practical Innovations, Open Solutions, 6*, 12118–12128. doi:10.1109/ACCESS.2018.2805783

Guohan Lu, Rui Miao, Yongqiang Xiong, Chuanxiong Guo: Using CPU as a Traffic Co-processing Unit in Commodity Switches, HotSDN 2012

Guo, Y., Rao, J., Jiang, C., & Zhou, X. (2017). Moving Hadoop into the Cloud with Flexible Slot Management and Speculative Execution. *IEEE Transactions on Parallel and Distributed Systems, 28*(3), 798–812. doi:10.1109/TPDS.2016.2587641

Gupta, B. (n.d.). *Assessment of Honeypots: Issues, Challenges and Future Directions*. Retrieved from https://www.igi-global.com/article/assessment-of-honeypots/196190

Gupta, B. B., & Quamara, M. (2018). An overview of Internet of Things (IoT): Architectural aspects, challenges, and protocols. In *Concurrency and Computation: Practice and Experience*. Wiley. doi:10.1002/cpe.4946

Gupta, B. B. (Ed.). (2018). *Computer and Cyber Security: Principles, Algorithm, Applications, and Perspectives*. CRC Press.

Gupta, B., Agrawal, D. P., & Yamaguchi, S. (2016). *Handbook Of Research On Modern Cryptographic Solutions For Computer And Cyber Security*. IGI Global.

Gupta, B., Agrawal, D. P., & Yamaguchi, S. (Eds.). (2016). *Handbook of research on modern cryptographic solutions for computer and cyber security*. IGI Global. doi:10.4018/978-1-5225-0105-3

Gupta, H., Dastjerdi, A. V., Ghoshy, S. K., & Buyya, R. (2017). iFogSim: A Toolkit for Modeling and Simulation of Resource Management Techniques in Internet of Things, Edge and Fog Computing Environments. *Special Issue: Cloud and Fog Computing*, *47*(9), 1275–1296.

Gupta, H., Vahid Dastjerdi, A., Ghosh, S. K., & Buyya, R. (2017, September). iFogSim: A toolkit for modeling and simulation of resource management techniques in the Internet of Things, Edge and Fog computing environments. *Software, Practice & Experience*, *47*(9), 1275–1296. doi:10.1002pe.2509

Gupta, S., & Gupta, B. B. (2017). Detection, avoidance, and attack pattern mechanisms in modern web application vulnerabilities: Present and future challenges. *International Journal of Cloud Applications and Computing*, *7*(3), 1–43. doi:10.4018/IJCAC.2017070101

Gupta, V., Singh, G., & Gupta, R. (2012). Advance cryptography algorithm for improving data security. *International Journal of Advanced Research in Computer Science and Software Engineering, 2*(1).

Gutierrez. (2017). *InsideBIGDATA Guide to Data Analytics in Government*. DELL EMC, Intel.

Guttorp, P., & Gneiting, T. (2006). Studies in the history of probability and statistics xlix on the matrn correlation family. *Biometrika*, *93*(4), 989–995. doi:10.1093/biomet/93.4.989

Gutz, Story, Schlesinger, & Foster. (2012). *Splendid Isolation: A Slice Abstraction for Software-Defined Networks*. HotSDN.

Guyot, V. (2010). Smart Card Security. In G. Pujolle & G. Pujolle (Eds.), *Management, Control and Evolution of IP Networks*. Wiley Online Library.

Haak, D. (2010). *Achieving high performance in smart grid data management*. White paper from Accenture.

Hachem, S., Teixeira, T., & Issarny, V. (2011). Ontologies for the internet of things. In *Proceedings of the 8thMiddleware Doctoral Symposium on - MDS '11*. ACM Press.

Haluza, D., & Jungwirth, D. (2016). ICT and the future of healthcare: Aspects of pervasive health monitoring. *Informatics for Health & Social Care*, *43*(1), 1–12. doi:10.1080/17538157.2016.1255215 PMID:28005444

Hand & Keller. (2013). *ClosedFlow: OpenFlow-like Control over Proprietary Devices*. Academic Press.

Haris, B. C., & Sinha, R. (2014). Exploring Data-Independent Dimensionality Reduction in Sparse Representation-Based Speaker Identification. *Circuits, Systems, and Signal Processing*, *33*(8), 2521–2538. doi:10.100700034-014-9757-x

Hashem. (2015). The rise of big data on cloud computing: Review and open research issues. *Information Systems*, *47*, 98–115.

Hashem, I. A. T., Yaqoob, I., Anuar, N. B., Mokhtar, S., Gani, A., & Khan, S. U. (2015). The rise of "big data" on cloudcomputing: Review and open research issues. *Information Systems*, *47*, 98–115. doi:10.1016/j.is.2014.07.006

Hassan, M. K., El Desouky, A. I., Elghamrawy, S. M., & Sarhan, A. M. (2018). Intelligent hybrid remote patient-monitoring model with cloud-based framework for knowledge discovery. *Computers & Electrical Engineering, 70*, 1034–1048. doi:10.1016/j.compeleceng.2018.02.032

Hayes, M. A., & Capretz, M. A. (2014). Contextual anomaly detection in big sensor data. *Big Data (BigDataCongress), 2014 IEEE International Congress on*, 64–71.

He, K., Gkioxari, G., Dollár, P., & Girshick, R. (2017). Mask R-Cnn. *Computer Vision (ICCV), 2017 IEEE International Conference On*, 2980-2988.

He, K., Zhang, X., Ren, S., & Sun, J. (2016). Deep Residual Learning For Image Recognition. *Proceedings Of The IEEE Conference On Computer Vision And Pattern Recognition*, 770-778.

Heller, Sherwood, & McKeown. (2012). *The Controller Placement Problem*. HotSDN.

Heller, B., Seetharaman, S., Mahadevan, P., Yakoumis, Y., Sharma, P., Banerjee, S., & McKeown, N. (2010). *ElasticTree: Saving Energy in Data Center Networks*. NSDI.

Hemanth, D. J., Anitha, J., & Indumathy, A. (2018). Diabetic Retinopathy Diagnosis in Retinal Images Using Hopfield Neural Network. *Journal of the Institution of Electronics and Telecommunication Engineers, 62*(6), 893–900. doi:10.1 080/03772063.2016.1221745 PMID:30382410

Hendrycks, D., & Gimpel, K. (2016). *Early Methods For Detecting Adversarial Images*. Arxiv Preprint Arxiv:1608.00530

Herbert, J., & Litchfield, A. (2015). A Novel Method for Decentralised Peerto-Peer Software License Validation Using Cryptocurrency Blockchain Technology. ACSC, 159, 27–35.

Hermann, M., & Klein, R. (2015). A Visual Analytics Perspective on Shape Analysis: State of the Art and Future Prospects. *Computers & Graphics, 53*, 63–71. doi:10.1016/j.cag.2015.08.008

Hernando, A. B. G., Fariña, A. D. S., Triana, L. B., Piñar, F. J. R., & Cambronero, D. F. (2017). *Virtualization of residential IoT functionality by using NFV and SDN. In 2017 IEEE international conference on consumer electronics* (pp. 86–87). ICCE.

Hernando, A. B. G., Fariña, A. D. S., Triana, L. B., Piñar, F. J. R., & Cambronero, D. F. (2017). *Virtualization of residential IoT functionality by using NFV and SDN. In 2017 IEEE International Conference on Consumer Electronics* (pp. 86–87). ICCE.

Herodotou, H. (2011). *Starfish: A Self-tuning System for Big Data Analytics* (Vol. 11). CIDR.

Heydon, R. (2013). *Bluetooth Low Energy*. Prentice Hall.

Higdon, D., Swall, J., & J., K. (1999). Non-stationary spatial modeling. *Bayesian Statistics, 6*, 761–768.

Higdon, D., Gattiker, J., Williams, B., & Rightley, M. (2008). Computer model calibration using high-dimensional output. *Journal of the American Statistical Association, 103*(482), 570–583. doi:10.1198/016214507000000888

Hindman, B. (2011). *Mesos: A Platform for Fine-Grained Resource Sharing in the Data Center*. Retrieved from http://static.usenix.org/events/nsdi11/tech/full_papers/Hindman_new.pdf

Hinton, G., Vinyals, O., & Dean, J. (2015). *Distilling The Knowledge In A Neural Network*. Arxiv Preprint Arxiv:1503.02531

Hirai, Y. (2017). Defining the Ethereum Virtual Machine for Interactive Theorem Provers. In *International Conference on Financial Cryptography and Data Security* (pp. 520-535). Sliema, Malta: Springer. 10.1007/978-3-319-70278-0_33

Hira, Z. M., & Gillies, D. F. (2015). A Review of Feature Selection and Feature Extraction Methods Applied on Microarray Data. *Advances in Bioinformatics, 2015*, 1–13. doi:10.1155/2015/198363 PMID:26170834

Hochreiter, S. (1998). The Vanishing Gradient Problem During Learning Recurrent Neural Nets And Problem Solutions. *International Journal of Uncertainty, Fuzziness and Knowledge-based Systems, 6*(2), 107–116.

Hochreiter, S., & Schmidhuber, J. (1997). Long Short-Term Memory. *Neural Computation, 9*(8), 1735–1780. doi:10.1162/neco.1997.9.8.1735

Hossain, M., Muhammad, G., & Abdul, W. (n.d.). *Cloud-assisted secure video transmission and sharing framework for smart cities.* Elsevier. Retrieved from https://www.sciencedirect.com/science/article/pii/S0167739X17305198

Hossain, M. S., Muhammad, G., Abdul, W., Song, B., & Gupta, B. (2018). Cloud-assisted secure video transmission and sharing framework for smart cities. *Future Generation Computer Systems, 83*, 596–606. doi:10.1016/j.future.2017.03.029

Hu, V. C., Ferraiolo, D. F., & Kuhn, D. R. (2006). *Assessment of access control systems.* U.S. Nat. Inst. Standards Technol., Interagency Rep. 7316.

Hu, W., & Tan, Y. (2016). *Generating Adversarial Malware Examples for Black-Box Attacks Based on GAN.* Academic Press.

Hu, W., & Tan, Y. (2017). *Generating Adversarial Malware Examples For Black-Box Attacks Based On GAN.* Arxiv Preprint Arxiv:1702.05983

Huang, R., Xu, B., Schuurmans, D., & Szepesvári, C. (2015). *Learning With A Strong Adversary.* Arxiv Preprint Arxiv:1511.03034

Huang, Yocum, & Snoeren. (2013). *High-Fidelity Switch Models for Software-Defined Network Emulation.* Academic Press.

Huang, A., Hemberg, E., & Reilly, U. O. (n.d.). *Adversarial Deep Learning for Robust Detection of Binary Encoded Malware.* Academic Press.

Huang, G. B., Mattar, M., Berg, T., & Learned-Miller, E. (2008). Labeled Faces. In *The Wild: A Database Forstudying Face Recognition In Unconstrained Environments. Workshop On Faces In'real-Life' Images: Detection.* Alignment, And Recognition.

Huang, L., Joseph, A. D., Nelson, B., Rubinstein, B. I. P., & Tygar, J. D. (2011). Adversarial machine learning. In *Proceedings of the 4th ACM workshop on Security and artificial intelligence* (pp. 43–58). ACM.

Huang, Z., Zheng, Y., Cheng, R., Sun, Y., Mamoulis, N., & Li, X. (2016). *Meta structure: Computing relevance in large heterogeneous information networks.* ACM. doi:10.1145/2939672.2939815

Hua, W., & Xun, Y. (2016). Protecting outsourced data in cloud computing through access management. *Concurrency. Pract. Exp., 28*(3), 600–615. doi:10.1002/cpe.3286

Hui Lu, Nipun Arora, Hui Zhang, Cristian Lumezanu, Junghwan Rhee, Guofei Jiang,: HybNET: Network Manager for a Hybrid Network Infrastructure, Middleware (industrial track) 2013

Hwang, E., & Kim, K. H. (2012). Minimizing Cost of Virtual Machines for Deadline-Constrained MapReduce Applications in the Cloud. *Proceedings - IEEE/ACM International Workshop on Grid Computing*, 130–38. 10.1109/Grid.2012.19

Iansiti, M., & Lakhani, R. K. (2017). The Truth About Blockchain. *Harvard Business Review, 95*(1), 118–127.

Icl.cs.utk.edu. (n.d.). *Cachebench Home Page.* Retrieved from http://icl.cs.utk.edu/llcbench/cachebench.html

IDC Digital Universe. (2012). *The Digital Universe in 2020: Big Data, Bigger Digital Shadows, and Biggest Growth in the Far East*. IDC Report. Retrieved from: http://emc.com

IETF MANET group. (n.d.). Retrieved June 01, 2013, from http://datatracker.ietf.org/wg/manet/

Imes, C., Hofmeyr, S., & Hoffmann, H. (2018). Energy-Efficient Application Resource Scheduling Using Machine Learning Classifiers. In *Proceedings of the 47th International Conference on Parallel Processing - ICPP 2018* (pp. 1–11). New York: ACM Press. doi:10.1145/3225058.3225088

Indian Institute of Technology Kharagpur. (2009, December 31). *NPTEL: Electrical Engineering - Chaos, Fractals & Dynamic Systems*. Retrieved from https://nptel.ac.in/courses/108105054/6

Indian Institute of Technology Kharagpur. (2017, June 8). *NPTEL: Computer Science and Engineering - NOC:Cloud computing*. Retrieved from https://nptel.ac.in/courses/106105167/26

Information Sciences Institute. (2008). Retrieved June 01, 2013, from http://www.isi.edu/nsnam/ns/

Intelligence, C. B. (2008). Disruptive civil technologies. Six Technologies with Potential Impacts on US Interests Out to 2025.

Introduction to Mininet~miniet/mininet Wiki~Github. (n.d.). Retrieved from https://github.com/mininet/mininet/wiki/Introduction-to-Mininet

IOR Benchmark on SourceForge. (n.d.). Retrieved from http://sourceforge.net/projects/ior-sio/

IoT Centric Cloud: A catalyst for innovation in Europe. (2013). *Networking Session, ICT Event 2013*.

IOzone.org. Retrieved from http://www.iozone.org/

Iperf. (n.d.). Retrieved from https://iperf.fr/

Ipsilon's General Switch Management Protocol Specification, Network Working Group 1998

Isento, J., Rodrigues, J., Dias, J., Paula, M. C. J., & Vinel, A. (2013). Vehicular delay-tolerant networks - A novel solution for vehicular communications. *IEEE Intelligent Transportation Systems Magazine*, 5(4), 10–19. doi:10.1109/MITS.2013.2267625

Islam, M. T., Karunasekera, S., & Buyya, R. (2017). DSpark: Deadline-Based Resource Allocation for Big Data Applications in Apache Spark. In *2017 IEEE 13th International Conference on E-Science (e-Science)* (pp. 89–98). Auckland, New Zealand: IEEE. doi:10.1109/eScience.2017.21

J. W. Lockwood, N. McKeown, G. Watson, G. Gibb, P. Hartke, J. Naous, R. Raghuraman, and J. Luo,: Netfpga–an open platform for gigabit-rate network switching and routing, 2015

Jafar Haadi Jafarian, Ehab Al-Shaer, Qi Duan: OpenFlow Random Host Mutation: Transparent Moving Target Defense using Software Defined Networking, 2013

Jafarian, Al-Shaer, & Duan. (2013). *OpenFlow Random Host Mutation: Transparent Moving Target Defense using Software Defined Networking*. Academic Press.

Jain, P., Gyanchandani, M., & Khare, N. (2016). Big data privacy: A technological perspective and review. *Journal of Big Data*, 3(1), 25. doi:10.118640537-016-0059-y

Jain, S., & Chawla, M. (2014). Survey of buffer management policies for delay tolerant networks. *Journal of Engineering*, 7, 1–7.

Jain, S., Fall, K., & Patra, R. (2004). Routing in a delay tolerant network. *Computer Communication Review, 34*(4), 145–158. doi:10.1145/1030194.1015484

Javaid, A., Niyaz, Q., Sun, W., & Alam, M. (2016). A Deep Learning Approach For Network Intrusion Detection System. *Proceedings Of The 9th EAI International Conference On Bio-Inspired Information And Communications Technologies (Formerly BIONETICS),* 21-26.

Jeffrey C. Mogul, Paul Congdon: Hey, You Darned Counters! Get off My ASIC, HotSDN 2012

Jia, R., & Liang, P. (2017). *Adversarial Examples For Evaluating Reading Comprehension Systems.* Arxiv Preprint Arxiv:1707.07328

Jian, Y., Shigang, C., Zhan, Z., & Liang, Z. (2007). Protecting receiver-location privacy in wireless sensor networks. In *Proceedings of 26th IEEE International Conference on Computer Communications* (pp. 1955-1963). Anchorage, AK: IEEE Computer Society. 10.1109/INFCOM.2007.227

Jiang, Q., Ma, J., & Wei, F. (2018). On the Security of a Privacy-Aware Authentication Scheme for Distributed Mobile Cloud Computing Services. *IEEE Systems Journal, 12*(2), 2039–2042. doi:10.1109/JSYST.2016.2574719

Jiang, Y., Willy, S., Yi, M., & Guo, F. (2018). Ciphertext-policy attribute-based encryption against key-delegation abuse in fog computing. *Future Generation Computer Systems, 78*(2), 720–729. doi:10.1016/j.future.2017.01.026

Jian, L., Li, J., Lei, Z., Dai, F., Zhang, Y., Meng, X., & Jian, S. (2018). Secure intelligent traffic light control using fog computing. *Future Generation Computer Systems, 78*(2), 817–824.

Jia, Y., Shelhamer, E., Donahue, J., Karayev, S., Long, J., Girshick, R., ... Darrell, T. (2014). Caffe: Convolutional Architecture For Fast Feature Embedding. *Proceedings Of The 22nd ACM International Conference On Multimedia,* 675-678.

Jin, X., Guo, K., Song, C., Li, X., Zhao, G., Luo, J., . . . Wang, H. (2016). Private Video Foreground Extraction Through Chaotic Mapping Based Encryption in the Cloud. MultiMedia Modeling Lecture Notes in Computer Science, 562-573. doi:10.1007/978-3-319-27671-7_47

Jin, X., Gossels, J., Rexford, J., & Walker, D. (2015). *CoVisor: A Compositional Hypervisor for Software-Defined Network.* NSDI.

Johnson, E., Ansa, G., Cruickshank, H., & Sun, Z. (2010). Access control framework for delay/disruption tolerant networks. *Proc. Int. Conf. Personal Satellite Services,* 249–264. 10.1007/978-3-642-13618-4_18

Johnson, W. B., Lindenstrauss, J., & Schechtman, G. (1986). Extensions of lipschitz maps into Banach spaces. *Israel Journal of Mathematics, 54*(2), 129–138. doi:10.1007/BF02764938

Jones, M. (2011). *Scheduling in Hadoop – IBM Developer.* Retrieved November 20, 2018, from https://developer.ibm.com/articles/os-hadoop-scheduling/

Jones, D. R., Schonlau, M., & Welch, W. J. (1998). Efficient global optimization of expensive black-box functions. *Journal of Global Optimization, 13*(4), 455–492. doi:10.1023/A:1008306431147

Jose, L., Yan, L., Varghese, G., & McKeown, N. (2015). *Compiling Packet Programs to Reconfigurable Switches.* NSDI.

Joseph, V., Hung, Y., & Sudjianto, A. (2008). Blind kriging: A new method for developing metamodels. *ASME. Journal of Mechanical Design, 130*(3), 031102, 031102–031108. doi:10.1115/1.2829873

Jozefowicz, Zaremba, & Sutskever. (2015). An Empirical Exploration of Recurrent Network Architectures. *JMLR: W&CP, 37.*

Juang, P., Oki, H., Wang, Y., Martonosi, M., Peh, L., & Rubenstein, D. (2002). Energy-Efficient Computing for Wildlife Tracking: Design Trade-Offs and Early Experiences with Zebranet. *SIGARCH Comp. Architure News, 30*(Oct), 96–107. doi:10.1145/635506.605408

Jyothi, S. A. (2016). Morpheus: Towards Automated SLOs for Enterprise Clusters. *12th USENIX Symposium on Operating Systems Design and Implementation (OSDI 16)*, 117–34. Retrieved from https://www.usenix.org/conference/osdi16/technical-sessions/presentation/jyothi

Kafle, S. (2017). *Neural Question Answering: the role of knowledge bases*. Academic Press.

Kakkar A., Singh M. L., & Bansal P. K. (2010). Efficient Key Mechanisms in Multinode Network for Secured Data Transmission. *International Journal of Engineering Science and Technology, 2*(5), 787-795.

Kakkar, A., Singh, M. L., & Bansal, P. K. (2012). Comparison of Various Encryption Algorithms and Techniques for Secured Data Communication in Multi-node Network. *IACSIT International Journal of Engineering and Technology, 2*(1).

Kallivayalil, T. & Uddin, M. (2017). A Multifamily Android Malware Detection Using Deep Autoencoder Based Feature Extraction. In *Proceedings of 2017 IEEE Conference on Advanced Computing (ICoAC)*. IEEE.

Kamatchi, V., Rajeswari, M., & Raja, K. (2013). Securing data from black hole attack using aodv routing for mobile ad hoc networks. In *Proceedings of the Second International Conference on Advances in Computing and Information Technology* (pp. 365-373). Chennai, India: Springer Berlin Heidelberg. 10.1007/978-3-642-31552-7_38

Kandukuri, B. R., Paturi, R. V., & Rakshit, A. (2009). Cloud Security Issues. *Proceedings of IEEE International Conference on Services Computing*, 517-520.

Kapritsos, M., Wang, Y., Quema, V., Clement, A., Alvisi, L., & Dahlin, M. (2012). All about eve: Execute-verify replication for multi-core servers. *Proceedings of 10th USENIX Symp. Oper. Syst. Design Implement. (OSDI)*, 237-250.

Karsten, R., McMillan, J., Lickley, M., & Haynes, R. (2008). Assessment of tidal current energy for the Minas Passage, Bay of Fundy. *Proceedings of the Institution of Mechanical Engineers. Part A, Journal of Power and Energy, 222*(5), 493–507. doi:10.1243/09576509JPE555

Karthigai, P.K., & Baskaran, K. (2010). An ASIC implementation of low power and high throughput blowfish crypto algo-rithm. *Microelectron. J., 41*(6), 347-355.

Kate, A., Zaverucha, G. M., & Hengartner, U. (2007). Anonymity and security in delay tolerant networks. *Proc. of SecureComm'07*. 10.1109/SECCOM.2007.4550373

Katsifodimos, A., & Schelter, S. (2016). Apache Flink: Stream Analytics at Scale. *2016 IEEE International Conference on Cloud Engineering Workshop (IC2EW)*, 193–193. Retrieved from http://ieeexplore.ieee.org/document/7527842/

Katta, Alipurfard, Rexford, & Walker. (2014). *Infinite CacheFlow in Software-defined Networks*. HotSDN.

Katz, G., Barrett, C., Dill, D. L., Julian, K., & Kochenderfer, M. J. (2017). Reluplex: An Efficient SMT Solver For Verifying Deep Neural Networks. Paper Presented At The *International Conference On Computer Aided Verification*, 97-117.

Kaufman, C. G., Bingham, D., Habib, S., Heitmann, K., & Frieman, J. A. (2011). Efficient emulators of computer experiments using compactly supported correlation functions, with an application to cosmology. *The Annals of Applied Statistics, 5*(4), 2470–2492. doi:10.1214/11-AOAS489

Kaur, D., Aujla, G. S., Kumar, N., Zomaya, A. Y., Perera, C., & Ranjan, R. (2018). Tensor-Based Big Data Management Scheme for Dimensionality Reduction Problem in Smart Grid Systems: SDN Perspective. *IEEE Transactions on Knowledge and Data Engineering, 30*(10), 1985–1998. doi:10.1109/TKDE.2018.2809747

Kaur, P. D., & Chana, I. (2014). A Resource Elasticity Framework for QoS-Aware Execution of Cloud Applications. *Future Generation Computer Systems*, *37*, 14–25. doi:10.1016/j.future.2014.02.018

Kc, K., & Anyanwu, K. (2010). Scheduling Hadoop Jobs to Meet Deadlines. *Proceedings - 2nd IEEE International Conference on Cloud Computing Technology and Science, CloudCom 2010*, 388–92. 10.1109/CloudCom.2010.97

Kearney, A. T. (n.d.). *The Internet of Things: A New Path to European Prosperity*. Retrieved from https://www.atkearney.com/documents/10192/7125406/The+Internet+of+ThingsA+New+Path+to+European+Prosperity.pdf/e5ad6a65-84e5-4c92-b468-200fa4e0b7bc

Kearns, M., & Li, M. (1993). Learning in the presence of malicious errors. *SIAM Journal on Computing*, *22*(4), 807–837. doi:10.1137/0222052

Khabbaz, M., Assi, C., & Fawaz, W. (2011). Disruption-tolerant networking: A comprehensive survey on recent developments and persisting challenges. *IEEE Commun. Surveys Tuts.*, 1–34.

Khan, R., & Khan, S. (2012). Future Internet: The Internet of Things Architecture, Possible Applications, and Key Challenges. *Proceedings of 10th International Conference on Frontiers of Information Technology.*

Khan, S., & Alam, M. (2016). The changing face of journalism and mass communications in the big data era. *CSI Communications*, *40*(8),16-17.

Khan, M. A., & Salah, K. (2018). IoT security: Review, blockchain solutions, and open challenges. *Future Generation Computer Systems*, *82*, 395–411. doi:10.1016/j.future.2017.11.022

Khan, S., Ansari, F., & Dhalvelkar, H. A. (2017). Computer. Criminal investigation using call data records (cdr) through big data technology. In *International Conference on Nascent Technologies in Engineering Field (ICNTE)*. Mumbai, India: IEEE. 10.1109/ICNTE.2017.7947942

Kiayias, A., Russell, A., David, B., & Oliynykov, R. (2018). Ouroboros: A Provably Secure Proof-of-Stake Blockchain Protocol. In *Annual International Cryptology Conference* (pp. 357-388). Santa Barbara, CA: Springer.

Kim, B.-G., Zhang, Y., van der Schaar, M., & Lee, J.-W. (2016). Dynamic Pricing and Energy Consumption Scheduling With Reinforcement Learning. *IEEE Transactions on Smart Grid*, *7*(5), 2187–2198. doi:10.1109/TSG.2015.2495145

Kim, H., Reich, J., Gupta, A., Shahbaz, M., Feamster, N., & Kinetic, R. C. (2015). *Verifyable Dynamic Network Control.* NSDI.

Kim, S. H., & Kim, D. (2015). Enabling Multi-tenancy via Middleware-level Virtualization with Organization Management in the Cloud of Things. Services Computing. *IEEE Transactions on*, *8*(6), 971–984.

Kim, Y. C., & Lee, K. (2018). Risk Management to Cryptocurrency Exchange and Investors Guidelines to Prevent Potential Threats. In *2018 International Conference on Platform Technology and Service (PlatCon)* (pp. 1-6). Jeju, South Korea: IEEE. 10.1109/PlatCon.2018.8472760

Kindberg, T. (2002). People Places and Things: Web Presence for the Real World. *ACM J. Mobile Networks and Applications, 7*(5), 365–376.

Kirkpatrick, K. (2013, September). Software-defined networking. *Communications of the ACM*, *56*(9), 16–19. doi:10.1145/2500468.2500473

Köhler, Jünemann, & Hartenstein. (2015). Confidential database-as-a-service approaches: taxonomy and survey. Journal of Cloud Computing: Advances, *Systems and Applications*, *4*, 1. doi:10.118613677-014-0025-1

Koponen, T. (2010). *Onix: A Distributed Control Platform for Large-scale Production Network.* OSDI.

Kouicem, D. E., Bouabdallah, A., & Lakhlef, H. (2018). Internet of things security: A top-down survey. *Computer Networks*, *141*, 199–221. doi:10.1016/j.comnet.2018.03.012

Kovacs Eduard. (2015). *Trains Vulnerable to Hacker Attacks: Researchers*. Retrieved from https://www.securityweek.com/trains-vulnerable-hacker-attacks-researchers

Kovatsch, M., Hassan, Y. N., & Mayer, S. (2015). Practical semantics for theinternet of things: Physical states, device mashups, and open questions. *Internet of Things (IOT), 2015 5th International Conference on the*, 54–61.

Krebs, B. (2018). Mirai IoT Botnet Co-Authors Plead Guilty. *Krebsonsecurity*. Retrieved from: https://krebsonsecurity.com/2017/mirai-iot-botnet-co-authors-plead-guilty

Krizhevsky, A., Sutskever, I., & Hinton, G. E. (2012). Imagenet Classification With Deep Convolutional Neural Networks. *Advances In Neural Information Processing Systems,* 1097-1105.

Kshetri, N. (2017). Can Blockchain Strengthen the Internet of Things? *IT Professional*, *19*(4), 68–72. doi:10.1109/MITP.2017.3051335

Kulkarni, A., Bhartiya, V., Kishore, G.H., & Gunturi, S.B. (2016). Data management: backbone of digital economy. *CSI Communications*, *40*(8), 7-13.

Kumar, N., Berg, A. C., Belhumeur, P. N., & Nayar, S. K. (2009). Attribute And Simile Classifiers For Face Verification. *Computer Vision, 2009 IEEE 12th International Conference On*, 365-372.

Kumar, N. M., & Mallick, P. K. (2018). Blockchain Technology for Security Issues and Challenges in IoT. *Procedia Computer Science*, *132*, 1815–1823. doi:10.1016/j.procs.2018.05.140

Kune, R., Konugurthi, P. K., Agarwal, A., Chillarige, R. R., & Buyya, R. (2016). The Anatomy of Big Data Computing. *Software, Practice & Experience*, *46*(1), 79–105. doi:10.1002pe.2374

Kurakin, A., Goodfellow, I., & Bengio, S. (2016). *Adversarial examples in the physical world*. ArXiv Preprint ArXiv:1607.02533

Kurakin, A., Goodfellow, I., & Bengio, S. (2016a). *Adversarial Examples In The Physical World*. Arxiv Preprint Arxiv:1607.02533

Kurakin, A., Goodfellow, I., & Bengio, S. (2016b). *Adversarial Machine Learning At Scale*. Arxiv Preprint Arxiv:1611.01236

Kusiak, A., Zhang, Z., & Verma, A. (2013). Prediction, operations, and condition monitoring in wind energy. *Energy*, *60*, 1–12. doi:10.1016/j.energy.2013.07.051

La Diega, G. N., & Walden, I. (2016). *Contracting for the 'Internet of Things': Looking into the Nest*. Queen Mary School of Law Legal Studies Research Paper No. 219/2016.

Laat, C., Gross, G., Gommans, L., Vollbrecht, J., & Spence, D. (2012). *Generic AAA architecture*. Internet RFC 2903. Available: http://www.rfc-editor. org/rfc/rfc2903.txt

Lakshman, A., & Malik, P. (2010). Cassandra. *Operating Systems Review*, *44*(2), 35. doi:10.1145/1773912.1773922

Lan, M., Samy, L., Alshurafa, N., Suh, M. K., Ghasemzadeh, H., Macabasco-O'Connell, A., & Sarrafzadeh, M. (2012). Wanda: An end-to-end remote health monitoring and analytics system for heart failure patients, In *Proc. of the Conf. on Wireless Health* (pp.1–9). Academic Press. 10.1145/2448096.2448105

Lantz, Heller, & McKeown. (2015). *A Network in a Laptop: Rapid Prototyping for Software-Defined Network*. Academic Press.

Lazaris, A., Tahara, D., Huang, X., Li, L. E., & Voellmy, A. (2014). *Tango: Simplifying SDN Control with Automatic SwitchProperty Inference*. Abstraction, and Optimization, CoNext.

Lazaris, A., Tahara, D., Huang, X., Li, L. E., & Voellmy, A. (2014). *Y. Richard Yang, Minlan Yu: Tango: Simplifying SDN Control with Automatic SwitchProperty Inference*. Abstraction, and Optimization, CoNext.

Lecun, Y., Bottou, L., Bengio, Y., & Haffner, P. (1998). Gradient-based learning applied to document recognition. *Proceedings of the IEEE*, *86*(11), 2278–2324. doi:10.1109/5.726791

Lee, I. (2017). Big data: Dimensions, evolution, impacts, and challenges. *Business Horizons*, *60*(3), 293-303.

Lee, H., Kim, J., Ha, D., Kim, T., & Kim, S. (2015). Differentiating ASK Demodulator for Contactless Smart Cards Supporting VHBR. *IEEE Transactions on Circuits and Wystems. II, Express Briefs*, *62*(7), 641–645. doi:10.1109/TC-SII.2015.2415653

Lee, J., & Hong, C. S. (2011). A mechanism for building Ad-hoc social network based on users interest. In *Proceedings of the 13th Asia-pacific Network Operatens and Management Symposium* (pp. 1-4). Taipei, Taiwan: IEEE Computer Society.

Lenk, A., Menzel, M., Lipsky, J., Tai, S., & Offermann, P. (2011). What are you paying for? Performance benchmarking for infrastructure-as-a-service offerings. *Cloud Computing (CLOUD), 2011 IEEE International Conference on*, 484-491.

Levanti, N. (n.d.). UK railways had four major cyber-attacks in one year. *Infrastructure Intelligence*. Retrieved from http://www.infrastructure-intelligence.com/article/jul-2016/uk-railways-had-4-major-cyberattacks-one-year

Levin, D., Canini, M., Schmid, S., Schaffert, F., & Feldmann, A. (2014). *Panopticon: Reaping the Benefits of Incremental SDN Deployment in Enterprise Networks*. USENIX ATC.

Li Da, X., Wu, H., & Shancang, L. (2014). Internet of Things in industries: A survey. *IEEE Transactions on Industrial Informatics*, *10*(4), 2233–2243. doi:10.1109/TII.2014.2300753

Li, H., Bok, K., & Yoo, J. (2013). Mobile P2P social network using location and profile. In Ubiquitous Information Technologies and Applications (Vol. 214, pp. 333-339). Springer Netherlands. doi:10.1007/978-94-007-5857-5_36

Li, P., Ju, L., Jia, Z., & Sun, Z. (2015). SLA-aware energy-efficient scheduling scheme for hadoop YARN. In *Proceedings -IEEE 17th International Conference on High Performance Computing and Communications, 2015* (pp. 623–628). IEEE. 10.1109/HPCC-CSS-ICESS.2015.181

Li, S. (2017). Security Requirements in IoT Architecture. *Securing the Internet of Things*, 97-108.

Li, Wu, Hui, Jin, & Chen. (2015). *Social-Aware D2D Communications: Qualitative Insights and Quantitative Analysis*. Academic Press.

Li, Y., Yong, Y., & Min, G. (2017). Fuzzy identity-based data integrity auditing for reliable cloud storage systems. IEEE Trans. Dependable Secure Comput., 1-12.

Liang, C., & Mogul, J. C. (2014). *Democratic Resolution of Resource Conflicts BetweenSDN Control Programs*. CoNext.

Liang, X., Li, X., Luan, T., Lu, R., Lin, X., & Shen, X. (2012). Morality-driven data forwarding with privacy preservation in mobile social networks. *IEEE Transactions on Vehicular Technology*, *61*(7), 3209–3221. doi:10.1109/TVT.2012.2202932

Liang, X., Zhang, K., Shen, X., & Lin, X. (2014). Security and privacy in mobile social networks: Challenges and solutions. *IEEE Wireless Communications*, *21*(1), 33–41. doi:10.1109/MWC.2014.6757895

Li, D., Aung, Z., Williams, J. R., & Sanchez, A. (2014). No peeking: Privacy preserving demand response system in smart grids. *International Journal of Parallel, Emergent and Distributed Systems, 29*(3), 290–315. doi:10.1080/17445 760.2013.851677

Lie, K.-A., Krogstad, S., Ligaarden, I., Natvig, J., Nilsen, H., & Skaflestad, B. (2012). Open-source MATLAB implementation of consistent discretizations on complex grids. *Computational Geosciences, 16*(2), 297–322. doi:10.100710596-011-9244-4

Li, J., & Liu, H. (2017). Challenges of Feature Selection for Big Data Analytics. *IEEE Intelligent Systems, 32*(2), 9–15. doi:10.1109/MIS.2017.38

Lim, N., Majumdar, S., & Ashwood-Smith, P. (2014). A Constraint Programming-Based Resource Management Technique for Processing Mapreduce Jobs with SLAs on Clouds. *Proceedings of the International Conference on Parallel Processing*, 411–21. 10.1109/ICPP.2014.50

Limna & Tandayya. (2016). A flexible and scalable component-based system architecture for video surveillance as a service, running on infrastructure as a service. In *Multimed Tools Applications*. Springer. doi doi:10.100711042-014-2373-8

Lindgren, A., & Doria, A. (2012). *Probabilistic Routing in Intermittently Connected Networks*. Internet-Draft, draft-irtf-dtnrg-prophet.

Lin, H., Wen, F., & Du, C. (2015). An Improved Anonymous Multi-Server Authenticated Key Agreement Scheme Using Smart Cards and Biometrics. *Wireless Personal Communications, 84*(4), 2351–2362. doi:10.100711277-015-2708-4

Linkletter, C., Bingham, D., Hengartner, N., Higdon, D., & Ye, K. Q. (2006). Variable selection for gaussian process models in computer experiments. *Technometrics, 48*(4), 478–490. doi:10.1198/004017006000000228

Lin, X., Lu, R., Shen, X., Nemoto, Y., & Kato, N. (2009). SAGE: A strong privacy-preserving scheme against global eavesdropping for ehealth systems. *IEEE Journal on Selected Areas in Communications, 27*(4), 365–378. doi:10.1109/JSAC.2009.090502

Li, P., Hastie, T. J., & Church, K. W. (2006). Very sparse random projections. *Proceedings of the 12th ACM SIGKDD International Conference on Knowledge Discovery and Data Mining - KDD 06*. 10.1145/1150402.1150436

Lipa, C. (n.d.). *Introduction to the Logistic Map*. Retrieved from http://pi.math.cornell.edu/~lipa/mec/lesson3.html

Li, T., Gupta, B. B., & Metere, R. (2018). Socially-conforming cooperative computation in cloud networks. *Journal of Parallel and Distributed Computing, 117*, 274–280. doi:10.1016/j.jpdc.2017.06.006

Liu & Feng. (2018). Deep Learning in Question Answering. In Deep Learning in Natural Language Processing. Springer.

Liu, H., Ong, Y.-S., Shen, X., & Cai, J. (2018). *When Gaussian process meets big data: A review of scalable GPs*. arXiv:1807.01065

Liu, L., Liu, D., Zhang, Y., & Peng, Y. (2016). Effective sensor selection and data anomaly detection for condition monitoring of aircraft engines. *Sensors, 16*(5), 623.

Liu, Ng, Lee, Son, & Stojmenovic. (2014). *Cooperative data dissemination in hybrid vehicular networks: Vanet as a software defined network*. Submitted for publication.

Liu, S., & Dong, R. (2017). Patent No. US9665866B2. United States Patent Office.

Liu, Y., Chen, X., Liu, C., & Song, D. (2016). *Delving Into Transferable Adversarial Examples And Black-Box Attacks*. Arxiv Preprint Arxiv:1611.02770

Liu, Yang, Zhang, & Chen. (2015). External integrity verification for outsourced big data in cloud and IoT: A big picture. *Future Generation Computer Systems, 49*, 58–67.

Liu, J., Xiao, Y., & Chen, C. L. P. (2012). Authentication and Access Control in the Internet of Things. *2012 32nd International Conference on Distributed Computing Systems Workshops*, 588–592. 10.1109/ICDCSW.2012.23

Liu, W., Anguelov, D., Erhan, D., Szegedy, C., Reed, S., Fu, C., & Berg, A. C. (2016). Ssd: Single Shot Multibox Detector. *European Conference On Computer Vision*, 21-37.

Liu, X., & Deng Robert, H. (2018). Hybrid privacy-preserving clinical decision support system in fog–cloud computing. *Future Generation Computer Systems, 78*(2), 825–837. doi:10.1016/j.future.2017.03.018

Liu, Z., Tong, L., Ping, L., Jia, C., & Jin, L. (2018). Verifiable searchable encryption with aggregate keys for data sharing system. *Future Generation Computer Systems, 78*(2), 778–788. doi:10.1016/j.future.2017.02.024

Liu, Z., Zhao, H., Chen, W., Cao, X., Peng, H., & Yang, J. (2017). Communications in Computer and Information Science. In *National Conference of Theoretical Computer Science* (pp. 133-143). Wuhan, China: Springer. 10.1007/978-981-10-6893-5_10

Li, Y., Yong, Y., Bo, Y., Min, G., & Huai, W. (2018). Privacy preserving cloud data auditing with efficient key update. *Future Generation Computer Systems, 78*(2), 789–798. doi:10.1016/j.future.2016.09.003

Lockwood, McKeown, Watson, Gibb, Hartke, Naous, … Luo. (2015). *Netfpga–an open platform for gigabit-rate network switching and routing*. Academic Press.

Lohachab, A., & Karambir, B. (2018). Critical Analysis of DDoS—An Emerging Security Threat over IoT Networks. *Journal of Communications and Information Networks, 3*(3), 57–78. doi:10.100741650-018-0022-5

Loukas, G., & Oke, G. (2010). Protection against denial of service attacks: A survey. *The Computer Journal, 53*(7), 1020–1037. doi:10.1093/comjnl/bxp078

Lowd, D., & Meek, C. (2005). Adversarial Learning. *Proceedings Of The Eleventh ACM SIGKDD International Conference On Knowledge Discovery In Data Mining*, 641-647.

Lu, Arora, Zhang, Lumezanu, Rhee, & Jiang. (2013). *HybNET: Network Manager for a Hybrid Network Infrastructure, Middleware (industrial track)*. Academic Press.

Lu, C. (2014). *Overview of Security and Privacy Issues in the Internet of Things*. Washington University in St. Louis Computer Science and Engineering Research Paper. Retrieved from: https://www.cse.wustl.edu/~jain/cse574-14/ftp/security.pdf

Lu, J., Issaranon, T., & Forsyth, D. A. (2017). Safetynet: Detecting And Rejecting Adversarial Examples Robustly. *Iccv*, 446-454.

Lu, Miao, Xiong, & Guo. (2012). *Using CPU as a Traffic Co-processing Unit in Commodity Switches*. HotSDN.

Luan, T. H., Gao, L., Li, Z., Xiang, Y., Wei, G., & Sun, L. (2015). Fog computing: focusing on mobile users at the edge. *Comput. Sci.*

Lu, J., & Gokhale, S. S. (2013). Hierarchical availability analysis of multi-tiered Web applications. *Software Quality Journal, 21*(2), 355–376. doi:10.100711219-012-9176-9

Lukovnikov, D., Fischer, A., Lehmann, J., & Auer, S. (2017). *Neural Network based Question Answering over knowledge Graphs on Word and Character*. ACM.

Lu, Q., Li, S., Zhang, W., & Zhang, L. (2016). A Genetic Algorithm-Based Job Scheduling Model for Big Data Analytics. *EURASIP Journal on Wireless Communications and Networking, 152*(1), 152. doi:10.118613638-016-0651-z PMID:27429611

Lu, R. (2012). *Security and privacy preservation in vehicular social networks*. University of Waterloo.

Lu, R., Liang, X., Li, X., Lin, X., & Shen, X. (2012a). EPPA: An efficient and privacy-preserving aggregation scheme for secure smart grid communications. *IEEE Transactions on Parallel and Distributed Systems, 23*(9), 1621–1631. doi:10.1109/TPDS.2012.86

Lu, R., Lin, X., Liang, X., & Shen, X. (2012c). A dynamic privacy-preserving key management scheme for location based services in VANETs. *IEEE Transactions on Intelligent Transportation Systems, 13*(1), 127–139. doi:10.1109/TITS.2011.2164068

Lu, R., Lin, X., Zhu, H., Liang, X., & Shen, X. (2012b). BECAN: A bandwidth-efficient cooperative authentication scheme for filtering injected false data in wireless sensor networks. *IEEE Transactions on Parallel and Distributed Systems, 23*(1), 32–43. doi:10.1109/TPDS.2011.95

Lu, R., Li, X., Liang, X., Shen, X., & Lin, X. (2011). GRS: The green, reliability, and security of emerging machine to machine communications. *IEEE Communications Magazine, 49*(4), 28–35. doi:10.1109/MCOM.2011.5741143

MacDonald, B., Ranjan, P., & Chipman, H. (2015). GPfit: An R package for fitting a Gaussian process model to deterministic simulator outputs. *Journal of Statistical Software, 64*(12), 1–23. doi:10.18637/jss.v064.i12

Macqueen, J. (1967). Some methods for classification and analysis of multivariate observations. *5th Berkeley Symposium on Mathematical Statistics and Probability*, 281-297. Retrieved from http://citeseer.ist.psu.edu/viewdoc/summary?doi=10.1.1.308.8619

Mahalle, P., & Anggorojati, B. (2012). *Identity establishment and capability-based access control (IECAC)*. Retrieved from http://ieeexplore.ieee.org/xpls/abs_all.jsp?arnumber=6398758

Maiorca, D., Biggio, B., Member, S., Chiappe, M. E., Giacinto, G., & Member, S. (n.d.). *Adversarial Detection of Flash Malware : Limitations and Open Issues*. Academic Press.

Manogaran, G., Varatharajan, R., Lopez, D., Kumar, P. M., Sundarasekar, R., & Thota, C. (2018). A new architecture of Internet of Things and big data ecosystem for secured smart healthcare monitoring and alerting system. *Future Generation Computer Systems, 82*, 375–387. doi:10.1016/j.future.2017.10.045

Mansuri, S. (2013). *Performance Analysis of Epidemic Routing Protocol for Buffer Management Policies in DTNs using ONE*. Int. J. Eng. Assoc.

Manyika, J., Chui, M., Bughin, J., Brown, B., Dobbs, R., Roxburgh, C. & Byers, A.H. (2017). *Big Data: The Next Frontier for Innovation, Competition, and Productivity*. McKinsey Global Institute.

Mao, Y., Chen, Y., Hackmann, G., Chen, M., Lu, C., Kollef, M., & Bailey, T. C. (2011). Medical data mining for early deterioration warning in general hospital wards. In *IEEE 11th Int. Conf. on Data Mining Workshops*, (pp.1042–1049). Academic Press. 10.1109/ICDMW.2011.117

Mao, W. (2003). *Modern Cryptography: Theory and Practice*. Prentice Hall.

Marco Canini, Petr Kuznetsov, Dan Levin, Stefan Schmid: Software Transactional Networking: Concurrent and Consistent Policy Composition, HotSDN 2013

Marco Canini, Petr Kuznetsov, Dan Levin, Stefan Schmid: The Case for Reliable Software Transactional Networking, 2013

Mariconti, E., Onwuzurike, L., Andriotis, P., De Cristofaro, E., Ross, G., & Stringhini, G. (2016). *Mamadroid: Detecting android malware by building markov chains of behavioral models.* ArXiv Preprint ArXiv:1612.04433

Marinov, M. B., Topalov, I., Gieva, E., & Nikolov, G. (2016). Air quality monitoring in urban environments. *39th International Spring Seminar on Electronics Technology (ISSE),* 443-448.

Maroulis, S., & Zacheilas, N. (2017b). ExpREsS: EneRgy Efficient Scheduling of Mixed Stream and Batch Processing Workloads. *Proceedings - 2017 IEEE International Conference on Autonomic Computing, ICAC 2017,* 27–32. 10.1109/ICAC.2017.43

Maroulis, Zacheilas, & Kalogeraki. (2017a). A Framework for Efficient Energy Scheduling of Spark Workloads. *Proceedings - International Conference on Distributed Computing Systems,* 2614–15.

Martìn Casado, Teemu Koponen, Scott Shenker, Amin Tootoonchian: Fabric: A Retrospective on Evolving SDN, HotSDN 2012

Martìn Casado: What OpenFlow is (and more importantly, what it's not),2015

Martirano, L. (2011). A smart lighting control to save energy. *Intelligent Data Acquisition and Advanced Computing Systems (IDAACS), 2011 IEEE 6th International Conference on,* 132–138. 10.1109/IDAACS.2011.6072726

Mashayekhy, L., Nejad, M. M., Grosu, D., Zhang, Q., & Shi, W. (2015). Energy-Aware Scheduling of MapReduce Jobs for Big Data Applications. *IEEE Transactions on Parallel and Distributed Systems, 26*(10), 2720–2733. doi:10.1109/TPDS.2014.2358556

Massachusetts Institute of Technology. (n.d.). *StarCluster.* Retrieved from http://star.mit.edu/cluster/

Mayer, S., Wilde, E., & Michahelles, F. (2015). A connective fabric for bridging internet of things silos. *Internet of Things (IOT), 2015 5th International Conference on the,* 148–154.

Mayes, K. (2017). An Introduction to Smart Cards. In *Smart Cards, Tokens, Security and Applications* (Vol. 1). Cham: Springer. doi:10.1007/978-3-319-50500-8_1

Mayes, K., & Markantonakis, K. (2008). *Smart Cards, Tokens, Security and Applications* (Vol. 1). New York: Springer Cham. doi:10.1007/978-0-387-72198-9

McCalpin, J. D. (1995). *Memory bandwidth and machine balance in current high performance computers. In IEEE Computer Society Technical Committee on Computer Architecture (TCCA)* (pp. 19–25). IEEE.

McKeown & Anderson. (2008). *OpenFlow: Enabling Innovation in Campus Networks.* Academic Press.

McKeown, N., Anderson, T., Balakrishnan, H., Parulkar, G., Peterson, L., Rexford, J., ... Turner, J. (2008). *OpenFlow: Enabling Innovation in Campus Networks.* CCR. doi:10.1145/1355734.1355746

McKinsey. (2018). *The IoT as a growth driver.* McKinsey Market Analysis Report of 2018. Retrieved from: https://www.mckinsey.com/

Mehdi, R., Paul, R., & Raymond, C. K.-K. (2017). Cloud of things in smart agriculture: Intelligent irrigation monitoring by thermal imaging. *IEEE Cloud Comput., 4*(1), 10–15. doi:10.1109/MCC.2017.5

Mehta, N., & Shah, M. (2014). Performance of Efficient Routing Protocol in Delay Tolerant Network: A Comparative Survey. *International Journal of Future Generation Communication and Networking, 7*(1), 151–158. doi:10.14257/ijfgcn.2014.7.1.15

Meng, D., & Chen, H. (2017). Magnet: A Two-Pronged Defense Against Adversarial Examples. *Proceedings Of The 2017 ACM SIGSAC Conference On Computer And Communications Security,* 135-147.

Meslhy, Abd elkader, & El-etriby. (2013). *Data Security Model for Cloud Computing.* doi:10.13140/2.1.2064.4489

Metzen, J. H., Genewein, T., Fischer, V., & Bischoff, B. (2017). *On Detecting Adversarial Perturbations.* Arxiv Preprint Arxiv:1702.04267

Michael, B., Casassa, M. M., Chen, L., & Siani, P. (2014). End-to-end policy-based encryption techniques for multi-party data management. *Computer Standards & Interfaces, 36*(4), 689–703. doi:10.1016/j.csi.2013.12.004

Microsoft Azure. (2016). *Microsoft Azure Pricing calculator.* Microsoft. Available: https://azure.microsoft.com/en-us/pricing/calculator/

Microsoft. (n.d.). *Windows Azure.* Retrieved from http://www.windowsazure.com/en-us/

Midgley, P. (2009). The role of smart bike-sharing systems in urban mobility. *Journeys, 2*(1), 23–31.

Mims, N. (2017). *The Botnet Problem, Computer and Information Security Handbook* (3rd ed.). Cambridge, MA: Morgan Kaufmann.

Mobile Ad-Hoc and DTN Networks at IPCAS Lab. (n.d.). Available: http://www.ece.gatech.edu/research/labs/WCCL/DTN2.html

Moghaddam, F. F., Alrashdan, M. T., & Karimi, O. (2013). A Comparative Study of Applying Real-Time Encryption in Cloud Computing Environments. *Proc. of IEEE 2nd International Conference on Cloud Networking (CloudNet).* 10.1109/CloudNet.2013.6710575

Mogul & Congdon. (2012). *Hey, You Darned Counters! Get off My ASIC.* HotSDN.

Mogul, J. C., AuYoung, A., Banerjee, S., Popa, L., Lee, J., Mudigonda, J., ... Turner, Y. (2013). *Corybantic: Towards the Modular Composition of SDN Control Programs.* HotNets. doi:10.1145/2535771.2535795

Mohanty, S. P., Choppali, U., & Kougianos, E. (2016, July). Everything You wanted to Know about Smart Cities. *IEEE Consumer Electronics Magazine, 6*(3), 60–70. doi:10.1109/MCE.2016.2556879

Monaco, M., Michel, O., & Keller, E. (2013). *Applying Operating System Principles to SDN Controller Design.* HotNets. doi:10.1145/2535771.2535789

Monga, I., Pouyoul, E., & Guok, C. (2012). Software-Defined Networking for Big-Data Science- Architectural Models from Campus to the WAN. In High Performance Computing, Networking, Storage and Analysis (SCC), 2012 SC Companion. IEEE.

Monga, I., Pouyoul, E., & Guok, C. Software-Defined Networking for Big-Data Science- Architectural Models from Campus to the WAN. High Performance Computing, Networking, Storage and Analysis (SCC), 2012 SC Companion. IEEE, 2012.

Monsanto, Reich, Foster, Rexford, & Walker. (2013). *Composing Software-Defined Networks.* NSDI.

MonsantoChristopherReichJoshuaFosterNateRexfordJenniferNetworksDavid Walker Composing Software-Defined, NSDI 2013

Moosavi Dezfooli, S. M., Fawzi, A., & Frossard, P. (2016). Deepfool: a simple and accurate method to fool deep neural networks. In *Proceedings of 2016 IEEE Conference on Computer Vision and Pattern Recognition (CVPR).* IEEE. 10.1109/CVPR.2016.282

Moosavi-Dezfooli, S., Fawzi, A., Fawzi, O., & Frossard, P. (2017). *Universal Adversarial Perturbations*. Arxiv Preprint.

Moosavi-Dezfooli, S., Fawzi, A., & Frossard, P. (2016). Deepfool: A Simple And Accurate Method To Fool Deep Neural Networks. *Proceedings Of The IEEE Conference On Computer Vision And Pattern Recognition*, 2574-2582.

Mosakheil, J. H. (2018). *Security Threats Classification in Blockchains*. Herberger School of Business, Information Assurance and Information Systems. St. Cloud State University.

Mosola, N. N. (2017). Chaos-based Encryption Keys and Neural Key-store for Cloud-hosted Data Confidentiality. In *Southern Africa Telecommunication Networks and Applications Conference (SATNAC, 2017)*. Royal Caribbean International.

Moura, J. (2015). *Intelligent Management and Efficient Operation of Big Data*. IGI Global.

Moyano, R. F., Fernández, D., Bellido, L., Merayo, N., Aguado, J. C., & De Miguel, I. (2017). NFV-based QoS provision for software defined optical access and residential networks. In *2017 IEEE/ACM 25th International symposium on quality of service (IWQoS)* (pp. 1–5). IEEE.

Moyano, R. F., Fernández, D., Bellido, L., Merayo, N., Aguado, J. C., & De Miguel, I. NFV-based QoS provision for software defined optical access and residential networks. In 2017 IEEE/ACM 25th International symposium on quality of service (IWQoS) (pp. 1–5), 2017.

Moyano, R. F., Cambronero, D. F., & Triana, L. B. (2017). A user-centric {SDN} management architecture for NFV-based residential networks. *Computer Standards & Interfaces*, *54*(Part 4), 279–292. doi:10.1016/j.csi.2017.01.010

Mucci, P. J., & London, K. (1998). *The CacheBench report*. Retrieved from http://www.cs.surrey.ac.uk/BIMA/People/L.Gillam/downloads/publications/Fair%20Benchmarking%20for%20Cloud%20Computing%20Systems.pdf

Nadjaran Toosi, Sinnott, & Buyya. (2018). Resource provisioning for data-intensive applications with deadline constraints on hybrid clouds using Aneka. *Futur. Gener. Comput. Syst.*

Naga Katta, Omid Alipurfard, Jennifer Rexford, David Walker: Infinite CacheFlow in Software-defined Networks, HotSDN 2014

Nair, V., & Hinton, G. E. (2010). Rectified Linear Units Improve Restricted Boltzmann Machines. *Proceedings Of The 27th International Conference On Machine Learning (ICML-10)*, 807-814.

Nait-Abdesselam, F., Bensaou, T., & Taleb, T. (2008). Detecting and avoiding wormhole attacks in wireless ad Hoc networks. *IEEE Communications Magazine*, *46*(4), 127–133. doi:10.1109/MCOM.2008.4481351

Najafabadi, M. M., Villanustre, F., Khoshgoftaar, T. M., Seliya, N., Wald, R., & Muharemagic, E. (2015). Deep Learning Applications And Challenges In Big Data Analytics. *Journal Of Big Data*, *2*(1), 1. doi:10.118640537-014-0007-7

Nakagawa, Hyoudou, & Shimizu. (2012). *A Management Method of IP Multicast in Overlay Networks using OpenFlow*. HotSDN.

Nakamoto, S. (2008). *Bitcoin: A Peer-to-Peer Electronic Cash System*. Available: https://bitcoin.org/bitcoin.pdf

Nambi, S. N. A. U., Sarkar, C., Prasad, R. V., & Rahim, A. (2014). A unified semantic knowledge base for IoT. *2014 IEEE World Forum on Internet of Things (WFIoT)*, 575–580. 10.1109/WF-IoT.2014.6803232

Nayak, A., Reimers, A., Feamster, N., & Clark, R. (2009). *Resonance: Dynamic Access Control in Enterprise Network*. WREN.

Nayak, D. (2015). Adaptive Scheduling in the Cloud - SLA for Hadoop Job Scheduling. *Proceedings of the 2015 Science and Information Conference, SAI 2015*, 832–37. 10.1109/SAI.2015.7237240

Neal, R. (1997). *Monte Carlo implementation of Gaussian process models for Bayesian regression and classification. Technical Report, Deptartment of Statistics*, University of Toronto.

Nelson, B., Barreno, M., Chi, F. J., Joseph, A. D., Rubinstein, B. I. P., Saini, U., … Xia, K. (2009). Misleading learners: Co-opting your spam filter. In Machine learning in cyber trust (pp. 17–51). Springer.

Nelson, B., Barreno, M., Chi, F. J., Joseph, A. D., Rubinstein, B. I. P., Saini, U., ... Xia, K. (2008). Exploiting Machine Learning to Subvert Your Spam Filter. *LEET*, *8*, 1–9.

Nersc.gov. (2013). *IOR*. Retrieved from https://www.nersc.gov/users/computational-systems/cori/nersc-8-procurement/trinity-nersc-8-rfp/nersc-8-trinity-benchmarks/ior/

Nick McKeown, Tom Anderson: OpenFlow: Enabling Innovation in Campus Networks, March 14, 2008.

Nimbalkar, P. P., & Gadekar, D. P. (2015). Survey on Scheduling Algorithm in MapReduce Framework. *International Journal of Science, Engineering and Technology Research, 4*(4), 1226–1230. Retrieved from http://ijsetr.org/wp-content/uploads/2015/05/IJSETR-VOL-4-ISSUE-4-1226-1230.pdf

Niyato, D., Hossain, E. &Camorlinga, S. (2009). Remote Patient Monitoring Service Using Heterogeneous Wireless Access Networks: Architecture and Optimization. *IEEE Journal on Selected Area in Communications*, 412-423.

Noll, L. C., Mende, R. G., & Sisodiya, S. (1996). *U.S. Patent No. US5732138*. Washington, DC: U.S. Patent and Trademark Office.

Ns-3 tutorial, Release ns-3-dev. (2018). Retrieved from https://www.nsnam.org/docs/tutorial/ns-3-tutorial.pdf

Nuevo, L., Valles, D. R., & Pallares, R. M. (2015). OIoT: A platform to manage opportunistic IoT communities. *Proceedings of the International Conference on Intelligent Environments*, 104–111. 10.1109/IE.2015.22

O'Donnell, L. (2018). Security Glitch in IoT Camera Enabled Remote Monitoring. *ThreatPost*. Retrieved from: https://threatpost.com/security-glitch-in-iot-camera-enabled-remote-monitoring/134504/

Odelu, V., Das, K. A., & Goswami, A. (2015). A Secure Biometrics-Based Multi-Server Authentication Protocol Using Smart Cards. *IEEE Transactions on Information Forensics and Security, 10*(5), 1953–1966. doi:10.1109/TIFS.2015.2439964

Olzak, T. (2017). MQTT is not Evil, Just Not Always Secure. *Csonline*. Retrieved from: https://www.csoonline.com/article/3208325/internet-of-things/mqtt-is-not-evil-just-not-always-secure.html

Omitola, T., & Willis, G. (2018). Towards Mapping the Security Challenges of the Internet of Things (IoT) Supply Chain. *Procedia Computer Science, 126*, 441–450. doi:10.1016/j.procs.2018.07.278

Onwunalu, J., & Durlofsky, L. (2010). Application of a particle swarm optimization algorithm for determining optimum well location and type. *Computational Geosciences, 14*(1), 183–198. doi:10.100710596-009-9142-1

OpenStack Cloud Software. (n.d.). *blogbench*. Retrieved from https://review.openstack.org/#/c/97030/

Opsahl, T., Agneessensb, F., & Skvoretzc, J. (2010). Node centrality in weighted networks: Generalizing degree and shortest path. *Elsevier Social Networks, 32*(2), 245–251. doi:10.1016/j.socnet.2010.03.006

Orhean, A. I., Pop, F., & Raicu, I. (2018). New Scheduling Approach Using Reinforcement Learning for Heterogeneous Distributed Systems. *Journal of Parallel and Distributed Computing, 117*, 292–302. doi:10.1016/j.jpdc.2017.05.001

Osanaiye, O., Chen, S., Yan, Z., Lu, R., Choo, K., & Dlodlo, M. (2017). From cloud to fog computing: A review and a conceptual live VM migration framework. *IEEE Access: Practical Innovations, Open Solutions, 5*(99), 8284–8300. doi:10.1109/ACCESS.2017.2692960

Ostermann, S. (2008). *An Early Performance Analysis of Cloud Computing Services for Scientific Computing*. Delft University of Technology Parallel and Distributed Systems Report Series, report number PDS-2008-006. Retrieved from http://www.st.ewi.tudelft.nl/~iosup/PDS-2008-006.pdf

Ottenwälder, B., Koldehofe, B., Rothermel, K., & Ramachandran, U. (2013). MigCEP: operator migration for mobility driven distributed complex event processing. *7th ACM Int. Conf. Distributed Event-based Systems*, 183-194. 10.1145/2488222.2488265

Ott, J., & Kutscher, D. (2004). Drive-Thru Internet: IEEE 802.11b for Automobile Users. *Proceedings - IEEE INFOCOM*.

Ouaguid, A. (2018). *A Novel Security Framework for Managing Android Permissions Using Blockchain Technology*. Academic Press. doi:10.4018/IJCAC.2018010103

Ouf, S., & Nasr, M. (2015). Cloud Computing. *International Journal of Cloud Applications and Computing, 5*(2), 53–61. doi:10.4018/IJCAC.2015040104

Ousterhout, K., Wendell, P., Zaharia, M., & Stoica, I. (2013). Sparrow : Distributed, Low Latency Scheduling. *ACM Symposium on Operating Systems Principles (SOSP)*, 69–84. Retrieved from http://dl.acm.org/citation.cfm?doid=2517349.2522716

Ozturk, C., & Zhang, Y. (2004). Source-location privacy in energy-constrained sensor network routing. In *Proceedings of the 2nd ACM workshop on Security of ad hoc and sensor networks* (pp. 88-93). Washington, DC: ACM. 10.1145/1029102.1029117

Paciorek, C., & Schervish, M. J. (2004). Nonstationary covariance functions for Gaussian process regression. In *Advances in Neural Information Processing Systems 16* (pp. 273–280). Cambridge, MA: MIT Press.

Paharia, B., & Bhushan, K. (2018, July). DDoS Detection and Mitigation in Cloud Via FogFiter: A Defence Mechanism. In *2018 9th International Conference on Computing, Communication and Networking Technologies (ICCCNT)* (pp. 1-7). IEEE. 10.1109/ICCCNT.2018.8493704

Palattell, M., Accettura, N., Vilajonasa, X., Watteyne, T., Grieco, L., Boggia, G. & Dolher M. (2013) Standardized Protocol Stack for the Internet of (Important) Things. *IEEE Communication Surveys & Tutorials*, 1389-1430.

Palazzi, C. E., & Bujari, A. (2012). Social-aware delay tolerant networking for mobile-to-mobile files sharing. *International Journal of Communication Systems, 25*(10), 1281–1299. doi:10.1002/dac.1324

Pal, R., Poray, J., & Sen, M. (2017). Application of Machine Learning Algorithms on Diabetic Retinopathy. In *2nd IEEE International Conference on Recent Trends in Electronics Information and Communication Technology*. IEEE. 10.1109/RTEICT.2017.8256959

Pandey, V., & Saini, P. (2018a). An Energy-Efficient Greedy MapReduce Scheduler for Heterogeneous Hadoop YARN Cluster. In *6th International Conference on Big Data Analytics-2018* (pp. 282–291). Springer. 10.1007/978-3-030-04780-1_19

Pandey, V., & Saini, P. (2018b). How *Heterogeneity* Affects the Design of Hadoop MapReduce Schedulers: A State-of-the-Art Survey and Challenges. *Big Data, 6*(2), 72–95. doi:10.1089/big.2018.0013 PMID:29924647

Pankaj Berde, Matteo Gerola, Jonathan Hart, Yuta Higuchi, Masayoshi Kobayashi, Toshio Koide, Bob Lantz, Brian O'Connor, Pavlin Radoslavov, William Snow, Guru Parulukar: ONOS: Towards An Open Distributed SDN OS, HotSDN 2014

Pantelopoulos, A., & Bourbakis, N. G. (2010). A survey on wearable sensor-based systems for health monitoring and prognosis. *IEEE Transactions on Systems, Man, and Cybernetics, 40*(1), 1–12. doi:10.1109/TSMCC.2009.2032660

Pan, X., Ling, Z., Pingley, A., Yu, W., Ren, K., Zhang, N., & Fu, X. (2016). How privacy leaks from bluetooth mouse? *IEEE Transactions on Dependable and Secure Computing, 13*(4), 461–473. doi:10.1109/TDSC.2015.2413410

Paolicchi, F. (2018). *Benefits for companies which adopt Internet of Things (IoT)*. Retrieved from https://iotlab.tertium-cloud.com/2018/03/21/why-should-enterprises-embrace-internet-of-things/

Paolo Nesi, G. P. (2015). A hadoop based platform for natural language processing of. *Journal of Visual Languages and Computing, 31*, 130–138. doi:10.1016/j.jvlc.2015.10.017

Papa, A., Mital, M., Pisano, P., & Giudice, M. D. (2018). E-health and wellbeing monitoring using smart healthcare devices: An empirical investigation. *Technological Forecasting and Social Change*, 1–10. doi:10.1016/j.techfore.2018.02.018

Papernot, N., Mcdaniel, P., & Goodfellow, I. (2016). *Transferability In Machine Learning: From Phenomena To Black-Box Attacks Using Adversarial Samples*. Arxiv Preprint Arxiv:1605.07277

Papernot, N., McDaniel, P., Jha, S., Fredrikson, M., Celik, Z. B., & Swami, A. (2016). The limitations of deep learning in adversarial settings. In *Security and Privacy (EuroS&P), 2016 IEEE European Symposium on* (pp. 372–387). IEEE. 10.1109/EuroSP.2016.36

Papernot, N., Mcdaniel, P., Wu, X., Jha, S., & Swami, A. (2015). *Distillation As A Defense To Adversarial Perturbations Against Deep Neural Networks*. Arxiv Preprint Arxiv:1511.04508

Papernot, N., McDaniel, P., Wu, X., Jha, S., & Swami, A. (2016). Distillation as a defense to adversarial perturbations against deep neural networks. In *Security and Privacy (SP), 2016 IEEE Symposium on* (pp. 582–597). IEEE. 10.1109/SP.2016.41

Papernot, N., McDaniel, P., Goodfellow, I., Jha, S., Celik, Z. B., & Swami, A. (2017). Practical Black-Box Attacks against Machine Learning. In *Proceedings of the 2017 ACM on Asia Conference on Computer and Communications Security - ASIA CCS '17* (pp. 506–519). New York: ACM Press. 10.1145/3052973.3053009

Papernot, N., McDaniel, P., Goodfellow, I., Jha, S., Celik, Z. B., & Swami, A. (2017). Practical Black-Box Attacks Against Machine Learning. *Proceedings Of The 2017 ACM On Asia Conference On Computer And Communications Security*, 506-519.

Papernot, N., Mcdaniel, P., Jha, S., Fredrikson, M., Celik, Z. B., & Swami, A. (2016). (2016). The Limitations Of Deep Learning In Adversarial Settings. *Security And Privacy (Euros&P), 2016 IEEE European Symposium On*, 372-387.

Park, K., Nguyen, M. C., & Won, H. (2015). Web-based Collaborative Big Data Analytics on Big Data as a Service Platform. *ICACT, 17*th *international conference*.

Park, H. J., & Park, H. J. (2017). Blockchain Security in Cloud Computing: Use Cases, Challenges, and Solutions. *Advanced in Artificial Intelligence and Cloud Computing, 9*(8), 164.

Parkhi, O. M., Vedaldi, A., & Zisserman, A. (2015). Deep Face Recognition. *Bmvc, 1*(3), 6.

Park, J. H. (2011). Inner-product encryption under standard assumptions. *Springer Designs. Codes and Cryptography, 58*(3), 235–257. doi:10.100710623-010-9405-9

Park, S., Moon, S. R., Lee, K., Park, I. B., & Nam, S. (2018). Urinary and Blood MicroRNA-126 and -770 are Potential Noninvasive Biomarker Candidates for Diabetic Nephropathy: A Meta-Analysis. *Cellular Physiology and Biochemistry, 46*(4), 1331–1340. doi:10.1159/000489148 PMID:29689545

Parsi, K., & Sudha, S. (2012). Data Security in Cloud Computing using RSA Algorithm. *International Journal of Research in Computer and Communication Technology, 1*(4), 145.

PassMark Software Inc. (n.d.). Retrieved from http://www.passmark.com/

Pass, R., Seeman, L., & Shelat, A. (2017). Analysis of the Blockchain Protocol in Asynchronous Networks. In *Annual International Conference on the Theory and Applications of Cryptographic Techniques* (pp. 643-673). Paris, France: Springer. 10.1007/978-3-319-56614-6_22

Pat Bosshart, Dan Daly, Glen Gibb, Martin Izzard, Nick McKeown, Jennifer Rexford, Cole Schlesinger, Dan Talayco, Amin Vahdat, George Varghese, David Walker: P4: Programming Protocol-Independent Packet Processors,2015

Pat Bosshart, Dan Daly, Martin Izzard, Nick McKeown, Jennifer Rexford, Dan Talayco, Amin Vahdat, George Varghese, David Walker: Programming Protocol-Independent Packet Processors,2013

Pearson, K. (1901). LIII. On lines and planes of closest fit to systems of points in space. *The London, Edinburgh and Dublin Philosophical Magazine and Journal of Science*, 2(11), 559–572. doi:10.1080/14786440109462720

Pei, K., Cao, Y., Yang, J., & Jana, S. (2017). Deepxplore: Automated Whitebox Testing Of Deep Learning Systems. *Proceedings Of The 26th Symposium On Operating Systems Principles,* 1-18.

Peng, Z., Chen, Z., Liu Joseph, K., Liang, K., & Liu, H. (2018). An efficient access control scheme with outsourcing capability and attribute update for fog computing. *Future Generation Computer Systems*, 78(2), 753–762.

Peng, Z., & Ma, Y. (2011). *A New Scheduling Algorithm in Hadoop MapReduce*. Berlin: Springer; doi:10.1007/978-3-642-24282-3_74

Pentland, A., Fletcher, R., & Hasson, A. (2004). DakNet: Rethinking connectivity in developing nations. *Computer*, 37(1), 78–83. doi:10.1109/MC.2004.1260729

Pereira, P. P., & Eliasson, J. (2015). An Authentication and Access Control Framework for CoAP-based Internet of Things. IEEE.

Perera, C., Zaslavsky, A., Compton, M., Christen, P., & Georgakopoulos, D. (2013). Semantic-Driven Configuration of Internet of Things Middleware. *9th International Conference on Semantics, Knowledge and Grids*, 66–73.

Perera, Zaslavsky, Christen, & Georgakopoulos. (2014). Sensing as a Service Model for Smart Cities Supported by Internet of Things. *Transactions on Emerging Telecommunications Technologies*, 1-12. doi:10.1002/ett

Perera, C., Liu, H. I. H., Jayawardena, S., & Chen, M. (2014). A Survey on Internet of Things from Industrial Market Perspective. *IEEE Access: Practical Innovations, Open Solutions*, 2, 1660–1679. doi:10.1109/ACCESS.2015.2389854

Perkins, C., Belding-Royer, E., & Das, S. (2003). *Ad hoc On-Demand Distance Vector Routing*. Retrieved June 01, 2013, from http://tools.ietf.org/html/rfc3561

Perry, G. (2009). *What are Amazon EC2 compute units? Thinking out cloud*. Retrieved from http://gevaperry.typepad.com/main/2009/03/figuring-out-the-roi-of-infrastructureasaservice.html

Petrakis, E. G., Sotiriadis, S., Soultanopoulos, T., Renta, P. T., Buyya, R., & Bessis, N. (2018). Internet of Things as a Service (iTaaS): Challenges and Solutions for Management of Sensor Data on the Cloud and the Fog. *Internet of Things*, 3(4), 156–174. doi:10.1016/j.iot.2018.09.009

Pham, H. N. A., & Triantaphyllou, E. (2008). The impact of overfitting and overgeneralization on the classification accuracy in data mining. In *Soft computing for knowledge discovery and data mining* (pp. 391–431). Springer. doi:10.1007/978-0-387-69935-6_16

Phillip Porras, Seungwon Shin, Vinod Yegneswaran, Martin Fong, Mabry Tyson, Guofei Gu,: A Security Enforcement Kernel for OpenFlow Networks, HotSDN 2012

Pinheiro, E., Bianchini, R., & Dubnicki, C. (2006). Exploiting redundancy to conserve energy in storage systems. *Performance Evaluation Review*, *31*(1), 15–26. doi:10.1145/1140103.1140281

Plageras, A. P., Psannis, K. E., Stergiou, C., Wang, H., & Gupta, B. B. (2018). Efficient IoT-based sensor BIG Data collection–processing and analysis in smart buildings. *Future Generation Computer Systems*, *82*, 349–357. doi:10.1016/j.future.2017.09.082

Polo, J. (2011). Resource-Aware Adaptive Scheduling for MapReduce Clusters. Lecture Notes in Computer Science, 7049, 187–207. doi:10.1007/978-3-642-25821-3_10

Porras, Shin, Yegneswaran, Fong, Tyson, & Gu. (2012). *A Security Enforcement Kernel for OpenFlow Networks*. HotSDN.

Pratola, M. T., Sain, S. R., Bingham, D., Wiltberger, M., & Rigler, E. J. (2013). Fast sequential computer model calibration of large nonstationary spatial-temporal processes. *Technometrics*, *55*(2), 232–242. doi:10.1080/00401706.2013.775897

Principles of Chaos Engineering. (2018, May). Retrieved from http://principlesofchaos.org/

Priyadarshinee, P. (2018). Cloud Computing Adoption. *International Journal of Cloud Applications and Computing*, *8*(1), 97–116. doi:10.4018/IJCAC.2018010105

Prodanoff, G. Z., Jones, L. E., Chi, H., Elfayoumy, S., & Cummings, C. (2016). Survey of Security Challenges in NFC and RFID for E-Health Applications. *International Journal of E-Health and Medical Communications*, *7*(2), 1–13. doi:10.4018/IJEHMC.2016040101

Purdy, M., & Davarzani, L. (2015). *The Growth Game-Changer: How the Industrial Internet of Things can drive progress and prosperity*. Accenture Strategy Report. Retrieved from: https://www.accenture.com/

Pyyk¨onen, P., Laitinen, J., Viitanen, J., Eloranta, P., & Korhonen, T. (2013). IoT for intelligent traffic system. *Intelligent Computer Communication and Processing (ICCP), 2013 IEEE International Conference on*, 175–179. 10.1109/ICCP.2013.6646104

Qi, L., Xiang, H., Dou, W., Yang, C., Qin, Y., & Zhang, X. (2017). Privacy-Preserving Distributed Service Recommendation Based on Locality-Sensitive Hashing. *2017 IEEE International Conference on Web Services (ICWS)*. 10.1109/ICWS.2017.15

Qin, Z., Yan, J., Ren, K., Chen, C. W., & Wang, C. (2014). Towards Efficient Privacy-preserving Image Feature Extraction in Cloud Computing. *Proceedings of the ACM International Conference on Multimedia - MM 14*. 10.1145/2647868.2654941

Quashie Azasoo, J., & Tweneboah-Koduah, S. (2016). *Cybersecurity architecture in smart metering systems. In Smart living and privacy*. Unpublished paper. CMI Annual Conference, Copenhagen, Denmark.

Quick Facts and Stats on Big Data. (n.d.). Retrieved from http://www.ibmbigdatahub.com/gallery/quick-facts-and-stats-big-data

Quratulain, A., Malik, S. U. R., Adnan, A., Raymond, C. K.-K., Saher, T., & Masoom, A. (2017). A cross tenant access control (CTAC) model for cloud computing: Formal specification and verification. *IEEE Transactions on Information Forensics and Security*, *12*(6), 1259–1268. doi:10.1109/TIFS.2016.2646639

Radenkovic, B. (2017). *From Ubiquitous Computing to the Internet of Things*. IGI Global.

Raghavendra, Lobo, & Lee. (2012). *Dynamic Graph Query Primitives for SDN-based Cloud Network Management*. HotSDN.

Rahman, A., Nakanishi, T., & Fukuda, A. (2013). Delay tolerant network for developing countries. *International Conference on Informatics, Electronics and Vision (ICIEV)*. 10.1109/ICIEV.2013.6572625

Rahmani, A. M., Gia, T. N., Negash, B., Anzanpour, A., Azimi, I., Jiang, M., & Liljeberg, P. (2018). Exploiting smart e-Health gateways at the edge of healthcare Internet-of-Things: A fog computing approach. *Future Generation Computer Systems*, *78*, 641–658. doi:10.1016/j.future.2017.02.014

Rahulamathavan, Y., & Rajarajan, M. (2015). Efficient Privacy-Preserving Facial Expression Classification. *IEEE Transactions on Dependable and Secure Computing*, 1–1. doi:10.1109/TDSC.2015.2453963

Rajkumar, R., Insup, L., Lui, S., & Stankovic, J. (2010). Cyber-physical systems: The next computing revolution. *Proc. 47th ACM/IEEE Des.Autom. Conf. (DAC)*, 731–736.

Ramachandran, S., Chithan, S., & Ravindran, S. (2014). A cost-effective approach towards storage and Privacy preserving for Intermediate data sets in Cloud Environment. *2014 International Conference on Recent Trends in Information Technology*. 10.1109/ICRTIT.2014.6996145

Ramamurthy, B. (n.d.). *Blockchain Basics*. Retrieved September 30, 2018, from coursera.org: https://www.coursera.org/learn/blockchain-basics

Ramya Raghavendra, Jorge Lobo, Kang-Won Lee: Dynamic Graph Query Primitives for SDN-based Cloud Network Management, HotSDN 2012

Ranjan, P., Bingham, D., & Michailidis, G. (2008). Sequential experiment design for contour estimation from complex computer codes. *Technometrics*, *50*(4), 527–541. doi:10.1198/004017008000000541

Ranjan, P., Haynes, R., & Karsten, R. (2011). A computationally stable approach to Gaussian process interpolation of deterministic computer simulation data. *Technometrics*, *53*(4), 366–378. doi:10.1198/TECH.2011.09141

Ranjan, P., Thomas, M., Teismann, H., & Mukhoti, S. (2016). Inverse problem for a timeseries valued computer simulator via scalarization. *Open Journal of Statistics*, *6*(3), 528–544. doi:10.4236/ojs.2016.63045

Rankl, W., & Effing, W. (2004). *Smart Card Handbook* (K. Cox, Trans.). Munich, Germany: John Wiley & Sons.

Rao, B. (2013). The role of medical data analytics in reducing health fraud and improving clinical and financial outcomes. *IEEE 26th International Symposium on Computer-Based Medical Systems*, 3–13. 10.1109/CBMS.2013.6627755

Rashid, S., Ayub, Q., Zahid, M., & Abdullah, A. (2011). E-drop: An effective drop buffer management policy for DTN routing protocols. *Int. J. Computer Applications*, 118-121.

Rasmussen, C. E., & Williams, C. K. (2006). Gaussian processes for machine learning. 2006. The MIT Press.

Rasooli, A., & Down, D. G. (2012). A Hybrid Scheduling Approach for Scalable Heterogeneous Hadoop Systems. *Proceedings - 2012 SC Companion: High Performance Computing. Networking Storage and Analysis, SCC, 2012*, 1284–1291.

Rasooli, A., & Down, D. G. (2014). COSHH: A classification and optimization based scheduler for heterogeneous Hadoop systems. *Future Generation Computer Systems*, *36*, 1–15. doi:10.1016/j.future.2014.01.002

Raveneau, P., & Rivano, H. (2015). *Tests Scenario on DTN for IOT III Urbanet collaboration*. Inria - Research Centre Grenoble – Rhone-Alpes; INRIA, Technical Report RT-0465.

Ravikumar, D. (n.d.). *Role of PSUs for Smart City Ecosystem*. Retrieved from http://smartcity.eletsonline.com/wp-content/uploads/2018/01/Bharat-Electronics-Ravikumar-D.pdf

Ray, P. (2014). Home health hub internet of things (H3IoT): An architectural framework for monitoring health of elderly people. In *Proceedings of Int. Conf. on Science Eng. and Management Research*, (pp.1–3). Academic Press.

Ray, P.P. (2018). A survey on Internet of Things architectures. *Journal of King Saud University - Computer and Information Sciences, 30*(3), 291-319,

Ray. (2016, December). A survey of IoT cloud platforms. *Future Computing and Informatics Journal Volume, 1*(1–2), 35–46.

Raymond, C. K.-K., Junghyun, N., & Dongho, W. (2014). A mechanical approach to derive identity-based protocols from Diffie-Hellman-based protocols. *Inf. Sci., 281*, 182–200. doi:10.1016/j.ins.2014.05.041

Read, J. (2010). Disk IO Benchmarking in the Cloud. *Cloud Harmony.* Retrieved from http://blog.cloudharmony.com/2010/06/disk-io-benchmarking-in-cloud.html

Recommendations on a strategy for space internetworking. (2008). Report of the Interagency Operations Advisory Group, The Space Internetworking Strategy Group (SISG). Retrieved from: https://cwe.ccsds.org/ioag/Final%20Products/SISG%20Report%20v1.4%20FINAL.pdf

Redmon, J., & Farhadi, A. (2017). *YOLO9000: Better, Faster, Stronger.* Arxiv Preprint.

Reichman, O. J., Jones, M. B., & Schildhauer, M. P. (2011). Challenges and Opportunities of Open Data in Ecology. *Science, 331*(6018), 703–705. doi:10.1126cience.1197962 PMID:21311007

Ren, X., Ananthanarayanan, G., Wierman, A., & Yu, M. (2015). Hopper : Decentralized Speculation-Aware Cluster Scheduling at Scale. Sigcomm 2015, 379–92.

Ren, S., He, K., Girshick, R., & Sun, J. (2015). Faster R-Cnn: Towards Real-Time Object Detection With Region Proposal Networks. *Advances in Neural Information Processing Systems*, 91–99.

Reyna, César, Martínez Jiménez, Bermúdez Cabrera, & Méndez Hernández. (2015). A Reinforcement Learning Approach for Scheduling Problems. *Investigación Operacional, 36*(3), 225–31. Retrieved from http://0-search.ebscohost.com.mercury.concordia.ca/login.aspx?direct=true&db=a9h&AN=108651151&site=ehost-live&scope=site

Riggins, F. J., & Wamba, S. F. (2015). Research directions on the adoption, usage, and impact of the internet of things through the use of big data analytics. In *48th Hawaii International Conference* (pp. 1531–1540). HICSS.

Rocha, R., & Launchbury, J. (2011). *Practical Aspects of Declarative Languages - 13th International Symposium, PADL 2011, Austin, TX, USA, January 24-25, 2011. Proceedings, volume 6539 of Lecture Notes in Computer Science.* Springer.

Rocha, R., & Launchbury, J. Practical Aspects of Declarative Languages - 13th International Symposium, PADL 2011, Austin, TX, USA, January 24-25, 2011. Proceedings, volume 6539 of Lecture Notes in Computer Science. Springer.

Rocque, M. (2017). The cybersecurity threat to transportation. *SmartCitiesWorld.* Retrieved from https://www.smartcitiesworld.net/special-reports/special-reports/the-cyber-security-threat-to-transportation

Rodrigo Agerri, X. A. (2015). Big data for Natural Language Processing: A streaming approach. *Knowledge-Based Systems, 79*, 36–42. doi:10.1016/j.knosys.2014.11.007

Rodrigo, R. (2018). *Mobile edge computing, Fog et al.: A survey and analysis of security threats and challenges* (Vol. 78). Future Gener. Comput. Syst.

Rohe, M. (2018). *RANDy -A True-Random Generator Based On Radioactive Decay.* Academic Press.

Rolim, C. O., Koch, F. L., Westphall, C. B., Werner, J., Fracalossi, A., & Salvador, G. S. (2010). A cloud computing solution for patient's data collection in health care institutions. In *Proceedings of International Conference on eHealth, Telemedicine, and Social Medicine*, (pp. 95-99). IEEE. 10.1109/eTELEMED.2010.19

Roman, R., Zhou, J., & Lopez, J. (2013). On the features and challenges of security and privacy the n distributed internet of things. *Computer Networks*, *57*(10), 2266–2279.

Ronald, V. L., & John, P. (2018). *What You Don't Know About the Internet of Things - CloudTweaks*. Retrieved from https://cloudtweaks.com/2016/04/dont-know-internet-things/

Rosenthal, C., Hochstein, L., Blohowiak, A., Jones, N., & Basiri, A. (2017). *Chaos Engineering*. O'Reilly Media, Inc.

Rothenberg, Nascimento, Salvador, Correa, de Lucena, & Raszuk. (2012). *Revisiting Routing Control Platforms with the Eyes and Muscles of Software-Defined Networking*. HotSDN.

Roustant, O., Ginsbourger, D., & Deville, Y. (2012). DiceKriging, DiceOptim: Two R packages for the analysis of computer experiments by kriging-based metamodeling and optimization. *Journal of Statistical Software*, *51*(1), 1–55. doi:10.18637/jss.v051.i01 PMID:23504300

Rozsa, A., Manuel, G., & Boult, T. E. (2018). *Towards Robust Deep Neural Networks with BANG*. Academic Press.

Rozsa, A., Rudd, E. M., & Boult, T. E. (2016). Adversarial Diversity And Hard Positive Generation. *Proceedings Of The IEEE Conference On Computer Vision And Pattern Recognition Workshops*, 25-32.

Rubinstein, B. I. P., Bartlett, P. L., Huang, L., & Taft, N. (2009). *Learning in a large function space: Privacy-preserving mechanisms for SVM learning*. ArXiv Preprint ArXiv:0911.5708

Rubow, E., McGeer, R., Mogul, J., & Vahdat, A. (2016). *Chimpp: A click-based programming and simulation environment for reconfigurable networking hardware*. Chimpp.

Rukhin. (2010). *A statistical test suite for the validation of random number generators and pseudo-random number generators for cryptographic applications*. NIST Special Revised Publication 800-22.

Ryan Hand, Eric Keller: ClosedFlow: OpenFlow-like Control over ProprietaryDevices,2013

Ryan, J., Lin, M., & Miikkulainen, R. (1998). Intrusion Detection With Neural Networks. *Advances In Neural Information Processing Systems*, 943-949.

Sacks, J., Welch, W. J., Mitchell, T. J., & Wynn, H. P. (1989). Design and analysis of computer experiments. *Statistical Science*, *4*(4), 409–423. doi:10.1214/1177012413

Sadasivarao, A. (2013). Bursting Data between Data Centers: Case for Transport SDN. In *High-Performance Interconnects (HOTI), 2013 IEEE 21st Annual Symposium on*. IEEE. 10.1109/HOTI.2013.20

Sadasivarao, A. "Bursting Data between Data Centers: Case for Transport SDN." High-Performance Interconnects (HOTI), 2013 IEEE 21st Annual Symposium on. IEEE, 2013.

Sadeghi, A.-R., Wachsmann, C., & Waidner, M. (2015). Security and privacy challenge in the n industrial internet of things. *Proceedings of the 52nd Annual Design Automation Conference*, 54. doi:10.1016/j.comnet.2012.12.018

Sahu, S. K., Jacintha, M. M., & Singh, A. P. (2017). Comparative Study of Tools for Big Data Analytics: An Analytical Study. In *International Conference on Computing, Communication and Automation*. Greater Noida, India: IEEE. 10.1109/CCAA.2017.8229827

Salah, K., Al-Saba, M., Akhdhor, M., Shaaban, O., & Buhari, M. I. (2011). Performance evaluation of popular cloud IaaS providers. *Internet Technology and Secured Transactions (ICITST), 2011 International Conference for*, 345-349.

Salimans, T., Karpathy, A., Chen, X., & Kingma, D. P. (2017). *Pixelcnn: Improving The Pixelcnn With Discretized Logistic Mixture Likelihood And Other Modifications*. Arxiv Preprint Arxiv:1701.05517

Saltzer, J., & Clark, D. (1984). End-to-end Arguments in System Design. *ACM Transactions on Computer Systems*, *2*(4), 277-288.

Samangouei, P., Kabkab, M., & Chellappa, R. (2018). *Defense-GAN: Protecting Classifiers Against Adversarial Attacks Using Generative Models.* Arxiv Preprint Arxiv:1805.06605

Samuel, H., & Zhaung, W. (2010). Preventing unauthorized messages and achieving end-to-end security in delay tolerant heterogeneous wireless networks. *Journal of Communication*, *5*(2), 152–163.

Sandesara, P. B., O'Neal, W. T., Kelli, H. M., Samman-Tahhan, A., Hammadah, M., Quyymi, A. A., & Sperling, S. S. (2017). The prognostic significance of diabetes and microvascular complications in patients with heart failure with preserved ejection fraction. *Diabetes Care*, *41*(1), 150–155. doi:10.2337/dc17-0755 PMID:29051160

Sandholm, T., & Lai, K. (2010). *Dynamic Proportional Share Scheduling in Hadoop.* Berlin: Springer. doi:10.1007/978-3-642-16505-4_7

Sandhu, R., & Sood, S. K. (2015). Scheduling of Big Data Applications on Distributed Cloud Based on QoS Parameters. *Cluster Computing*, *18*(2), 817–828. doi:10.100710586-014-0416-6

Saneja, B., & Rani, R. (2014). An efficient approach for outlierdetection in big sensor data of health care. *International Journal of Communication Systems*.

Sanguankotchakorn, T., Shrestha, S., & Sugino, N. (2012). Effective Ad Hoc Social Networking on OLSR MANET Using Similarity of Interest Approach. In *Proceedings of 5th International Conference IDCS*, (pp. 15-28). Wuyishan, Fujian, China: Springer Berlin Heidelberg. 10.1007/978-3-642-34883-9_2

Sankar, S. L., Sindhu, M., & Sethumadhavan, M. (2017). Survey of consensus protocols on blockchain applications. In *2017 4th International Conference on Advanced Computing and Communication Systems (ICACCS)* (pp. 1-5). Coimbatore, India: IEEE.

Santana, Chaves, Gerosa, Kon, & Milojicic. (2017). Software Platforms for Smart Cities: Concepts, Requirements, Challenges, and a Unified Reference Architecture. *ACM Computing Surveys*, *50*, 6.

Santner, T. J., Williams, B. J., & Notz, W. I. (2003). *The Design and Analysis of Computer Experiments.* New York: Springer-Verlag. doi:10.1007/978-1-4757-3799-8

Sanzgiri, K., Dahill, B., Levine, B. N., Shields, C., & Belding-Royer, E. M. (2002). A secure routing protocol for ad hoc networks. In *Proceedings of 10th IEEE International Conference on Network Protocols* (pp. 78-87). Paris, France: IEEE Computer Society. 10.1109/ICNP.2002.1181388

Satpathy, Sahoo, & Turuk. (2018). Sensing and Actuation as a Service Delivery Model in Cloud Edge centric Internet of Things. *Future Generation Computer Systems, 86*, 281–296.

Satyanarayanan, M. (2001). Pervasive Computing: Vision and Challenges. *IEEE Personal Comm.*, *8*(4),10–17.

Satyanarayanan, M., Bahl, P., Caceres, R., & Davies, N. (2009). The Case for VM-Based Cloudlets in MobileComputing. *IEEE Pervasive Computing*, *8*(4), 14–23. doi:10.1109/MPRV.2009.82

Saxena, S., & Kishore, N. (2016). Big data:challenges and opportunities in digital forensics. *CSI Communications*, *40*(8), 20.

Schiff, L., Borokhovich, M., & Schmid, S. (2014). *Reclaiming the Brain: Useful OpenFlow Functions in the Data Plane.* HotNets. doi:10.1145/2670518.2673874

Schlechtingen, M., & Santos, I. F. (2014). Wind turbine condition monitoring based on SCADA data using normal behavior models. Part 2: Application examples. *Applied Soft Computing*, *14*(C), 447–460. doi:10.1016/j.asoc.2013.09.016

Schnorr, C. (1991). Efficient signature generation by smart cards. *Journal of Cryptology*, 4(3), 161–174. doi:10.1007/BF00196725

Schonlau, M., Welch, W. J., & Jones, D. R. (1998). Global versus local search in constrained optimization of computer models. Institute of Mathematical Statistics, Hayward, CA, Lecture Notes-Monograph Series, 34, 11–25.

Scott, K., & Burleigh, S. (2007). *Bundle Protocol Specification*. Internet RFC5050.

Scott, M. (2011). On efficient implementation of pairing-based protocols. In *Proceedings of 13th IMA International Conference IMACC* (pp. 296-308). Oxford, UK: Springer Berlin Heidelberg.

Seligman, M., Fall, K., & Mundur, P. (2006). Alternative custodians for congestion control in delay tolerant networks. In *Proc. ACM SIGCOMM Workshop on Challenged Networks*. New York, NY: ACM Press. 10.1145/1162654.1162660

Seo, Y. (2017). Practical Implementations of ECC in the Blockchain. *Journal of Analysis of Applied Mathematics*, 43.

Serban, I. V., Garcıa-Dur, A., Gulcehre, C., Ahn, S., Chandar, S., Courville, A., & Bengio, Y. (2016). Generating Factoid Questions With Recurrent Neural Networks: The 30M Factoid Question-Answer Corpus. *Proceedings of the 54th Annual Meeting of the Association for Computational Linguistics*, 588–598. 10.18653/v1/P16-1056

SESAR. (2017). *Addressing airport cyber-security*. Executive summary report.

Sezer, O. B., Can, S. Z., & Dogdu, E. (2015). Developmentof a smart home ontology and the implementation of asemantic sensor network simulator: An internet of things approach. *Collaboration Technologies and Systems(CTS), 2015 International Conference on, IEEE*, 12–18.

Sezer, O. B., Dogdu, E., Ozbayoglu, M., & Onal, A. (2016). An extended iot framework with semantics, big data,and analytics. In Big Data (Big Data), 2016 IEEE International Conference on, 1849–1856.

Sha, K., Wei, W., Yang, T. A., Wang, Z., & Shi, W. (2018). On security challenges and open issues in Internet of Things. *Future Generation Computer Systems*, 83, 326–337. doi:10.1016/j.future.2018.01.059

Shakarian, P., Shakarian, J., & Ruef, A. (2013). *Attacking Iranian Nuclear Facilities*, 223-239. Doi:10.1016/B978-0-12-407814-7.00013-0

Shamir, A. (1979). How to share a secret. *Communications of the ACM*, 22(11), 612–613. doi:10.1145/359168.359176

Sharif, M., Bhagavatula, S., Bauer, L., & Reiter, M. K. (2016). Accessorize To A Crime: Real And Stealthy Attacks On State-Of-The-Art Face Recognition. *Proceedings Of The 2016 ACM SIGSAC Conference On Computer And Communications Security*, 1528-1540.

Sharples, M., & Domingue, J. (2016). The Blockchain and Kudos: A Distributed System for Educational Record, Reputation and Reward. In *European Conference on Technology Enhanced Learning* (pp. 490-496). Lyon, France: Springer. 10.1007/978-3-319-45153-4_48

Sherwood, R., Gibb, G., Yap, K.-K., Appenzeller, G., Casado, M., McKeown, N., & Parulkar, G. (2010). *Can the Production Network Be the Testbed*. OSDI.

Shi, C., Li, Y., Zhang, J., Sun, Y., & Philip, S. Yu. (2017). A Survey of Heterogeneous Information Network Analysis. *IEEE Transactions on Knowledge and Data Engineering*, 29(1), 17–37. doi:10.1109/TKDE.2016.2598561

Shields, A. (2014). *Why traditional database systems fail to support "big data."* Retrieved November 20, 2018, from https://marketrealist.com/2014/07/traditional-database-systems-fail-support-big-data

Shirey, R. (2007). *Internet security glossary*. Retrieved June 01, 2013, from http://tools.ietf.org/html/rfc4949

Shi, W., Cao, J., Zhang, Q., Li, Y., & Xu, L. (2016). Edge computing: Vision and challenges. *IEEE Internet Things J.*, *3*(5), 637–646. doi:10.1109/JIOT.2016.2579198

Shon, T., Cho, J., Han, K., & Choi, H. (2014, June). Toward advanced mobile cloud computing for the internet of things: Current issues and future direction. *Mobile Networks and Applications*, *19*(3), 404–413. doi:10.100711036-014-0509-8

Shu, Y. (n.d.). *IEC White Paper for "Internet of Things: Wireless Sensor Networks."* Retrieved from http://www.iec.ch/whitepaper/pdf/iecWP-internetofthings-LR-en.pdf

Shvachko, Kuang, Radia, & Chansler. (2013). *The Hadoop Distributed File System*. Academic Press.

Siani, P. (2011). *End-to-end policy-based encryption and management of data in the cloud*. CloudCom.

Sicari, A. S., Rizzardi, L. A., Grieco, L. A., & Coen-Porisini, A. (2015). Security, privacy and trust the n internet of things: The road ahead. *Computer Networks*, *76*, 146–164. doi:10.1016/j.comnet.2014.11.008

Sidhanta, S., Golab, W., & Mukhopadhyay, S. (2016). OptEx: A Deadline-Aware Cost Optimization Model for Spark. *Proceedings - 2016 16th IEEE/ACM International Symposium on Cluster, Cloud, and Grid Computing, CCGrid 2016*, 193–202. 10.1109/CCGrid.2016.10

Simonyan, K., & Zisserman, A. (2014). *Very Deep Convolutional Networks For Large-Scale Image Recognition*. Arxiv Preprint Arxiv:1409.1556

Singh, Pasquier, Bacon, Ko, & Eyers. (2016). Twenty Security Considerations for Cloud-Supported Internet of Things. *IEEE Internet of Things Journal, 3*(3), 269–284. doi:10.1109/jiot.2015.2460333

Singh. (2018). *Source Redundancy Management and Host Intrusion Detection in Wireless Sensor Networks*. Recent Patents on Computer Science.

Sivaraman, A., Weinstein, K., Subramanian, S., & Balakrishnan, H. (2013). *No Silver Bullet: Extending SDN to the Data Plane*. HotNets. doi:10.1145/2535771.2535796

Soheil Hassas Yeganeh, Yashar Ganjali: Beehive: Towards a Simple Abstraction for Scalable Software-defined Networks,2015

Soheil Hassas Yeganeh, Yashar Ganjali: Kandoo: A Framework for Efficient and Scalable Offloading of Control Applications, HotSDN 2012

Song, Y., Kim, T., Nowozin, S., Ermon, S., & Kushman, N. (2017). *Pixeldefend: Leveraging Generative Models To Understand And Defend Against Adversarial Examples*. Arxiv Preprint Arxiv:1710.10766

Song, Z., Cardenas, A. A., & Masuoka, R. (2010). Semantic middleware for the Internet of Things. *Proceeding of 2010 Internet of Things (IOT)*, 1–8.

Soualhia, M., Khomh, F., & Tahar, S. (2015). ATLAS: An AdapTive faiLure-Aware Scheduler for Hadoop. In *2015 IEEE 34th International Performance Computing and Communications Conference (IPCCC)* (pp. 1–8). IEEE. 10.1109/PCCC.2015.7410316

Soulé, R., Basu, S., Marandi, P. J., Pedone, F., Kleinberg, R., Sirer, E. G., & Foster, N. (2014). *Merlin: A Language for Provisioning Network Resources*. CoNext.

Spyropoulos, T., Psounis, K., & Raghavendra, C. S. (2005). Spray-and-Wait: Efficient routing scheme for intermittently connected mobile networks. *ACM SIGCOMM Workshop on Delay Tolerant Network (WDTN)*. 10.1145/1080139.1080143

Spyropoulos, T., Psounis, K., & Raghavendra, C. S. (2008a). Efficient routing in intermittently connected mobile networks: The single-copy case. *IEEE/ACM Transactions on Networking, 16*(1), 63–76. doi:10.1109/TNET.2007.897962

Spyropoulos, T., Psounis, K., & Raghavendra, C. S. (2008b). Efficient routing in intermittently connected mobile networks: The multiple-copy case. *IEEE/ACM Transactions on Networking, 16*(1), 77–90. doi:10.1109/TNET.2007.897964

Stankovic, J. A. (2014). Research Directions for the Internet of Things. *IEEE Internet of Things Journal, 1*(1), 3-9.

Stein, M. L., Chi, Z., & Welty, L. J. (2004). Approximating likelihoods for large spatial data sets. *Journal of the Royal Statistical Society. Series B, Statistical Methodology, 66*(2), 275–296. doi:10.1046/j.1369-7412.2003.05512.x

Stephen Gutz, Alec Story, Cole Schlesinger, Nate Foster: Splendid Isolation: A Slice Abstraction for Software-Defined Networks, HotSDN 2012

Stergiou, C., Psannis, K. E., Kim, B. G., & Gupta, B. (2018). Secure integration of IoT and cloud computing. *Future Generation Computer Systems, 78*, 964–975.

Stergiou, C., Psannis, K. E., Kim, B., & Gupta, B. (2018). Secure integration of IoT and Cloud Computing. *Future Generation Computer Systems, 78*, 964–975. doi:10.1016/j.future.2016.11.031

Stewart, C. E., Vasu, A. M., & Keller, E. (2017). CommunityGuard: A crowdsourced home cybersecurity system. In *Proceedings of the ACM International workshop on security in software defined networks & network function virtualization* (pp. 1–6). ACM.

Stewart, C. E., Vasu, A. M., & Keller, E. CommunityGuard: A crowdsourced home cybersecurity system. In Proceedings of the ACM International workshop on security in software defined networks & network function virtualization (pp. 1–6), 2017.

Stojmenovic, I. (2014). Fog computing: A cloud to the ground support for smart things and machine-to-machine networks. *IEEE Australasian Telecommunication Networks and Applications Conference (ATNAC)*, 117-122. 10.1109/ATNAC.2014.7020884

Stojmenovic, I., & Wen, S. (2014). The fog computing paradigm: Scenarios and Security Issues. *Proceedings of the 2014 Federated Conference on Computer Science and Information Systems, 2*, 1–8. 10.15439/2014F503

Stokes, J. W., Wang, D., Marinescu, M., Marino, M., & Bussone, B. (n.d.). Attack and Defense of Dynamic Analysis-Based. *Adversarial Neural Malware Classification Models.*

Storcheus, D., Rostamizadeh, A., & Kumar, S. (2015). A Survey Of Modern Questions And Challenges In Feature Extraction. *Feature Extraction: Modern Questions And Challenges*, 1-18.

Strauss, T., Hanselmann, M., Junginger, A., & Ulmer, H. (2017). *Ensemble methods as a defense to adversarial perturbations against deep neural networks.* ArXiv Preprint ArXiv:1709.03423

Subashini, S., & Kavitha, V. (2011). A survey on security issues in service delivery models of cloud computing. *Journal of Network and Computer Applications, 34*(1), 1–11.

Suciu, G., Suciu, V., Martian, A., Craciunescu, R., Vulpe, A., Marcu, I., ... Fratu, O. (2015). Big Data, Internet of Thingsand Cloud convergence–an architecture for secure e-healthapplications. *Journal of Medical Systems, 39*(11), 1–8. doi:10.100710916-015-0327-y PMID:26345453

Sugam Agarwal, Murali Kodialam, T.V. Lakshman: Traffic Engineering in Software-defined Networks Infocom 2013

Sun, X., He, C., & Lu, Y. (2012). ESAMR: An Enhanced Self-Adaptive MapReduce Scheduling Algorithm. In *2012 IEEE 18th International Conference on Parallel and Distributed Systems* (pp. 148–155). IEEE. 10.1109/ICPADS.2012.30

Sundarkumar, G. G., Ravi, V., Nwogu, I., & Govindaraju, V. (2015). Malware detection via API calls, topic models and machine learning. *2015 IEEE International Conference on Automation Science and Engineering (CASE)*, 1212–1217. 10.1109/CoASE.2015.7294263

Sun, P., Mahajan, R., & Rexford, J. (2014). *Lihua YuanMing Zhang, Ahsan Arefin: A Network State Management Service*. Sigcomm.

Suo, H., Wan, J., Zou, C., & Liu, J. (2012). Security in the Internet of Things: A Review. *International Conference on Computer Science and Electronics Engineering*, *3*, 648-651. 10.1109/ICCSEE.2012.373

Sutera, M. C. (2014). Patent No. US8640965B2. United States Patent Office.

Sutton, R. S., Barto, A. G., & Bach, F. (1998). *Reinforcement Learning: An Introduction*. MIT Press.

Swanson, T. (2015). *Consensus-as-a-service: A brief report on the emergence of permissioned, distributed ledger systems*. Tech. Rep.

Szegedy, C., Ioffe, S., Vanhoucke, V., & Alemi, A. A. (2017). Inception-V4, Inception-Resnet And The Impact Of Residual Connections On Learning. *Aaai, 4* 12.

Szegedy, C., Zaremba, W., Sutskever, I., Bruna, J., Erhan, D., Goodfellow, I., & Fergus, R. (2013). *Intriguing Properties Of Neural Networks* Retrieved From Https://Www.Openaire.Eu/Search/Publication?Articleid=Od_____18:5d22d1 65a1409152d22f2f7e03072187

Szegedy, C., Vanhoucke, V., Ioffe, S., Shlens, J., & Wojna, Z. (2016). Rethinking The Inception Architecture For Computer Vision. *Proceedings Of The IEEE Conference On Computer Vision And Pattern Recognition*, 2818-2826.

Taft, Lang, & Duggan. (2016). *STeP: Scalable Tenant Placement for Managing Database-as-a-Service Deployments*. SoCC '16, Santa Clara, CA

Taifi, M. (2012). *NPB Benchmark*. Retrieved from https://github.com/moutai/hpc-medley/

Tanay, T., & Griffin, L. (2016). *A boundary tilting persepective on the phenomenon of adversarial examples*. ArXiv Preprint ArXiv:1608.07690

Tang, W., Kannaley, K., Friedman, D. B., Edwards, V. J., Wilcox, S., Levkoff, S. E., ... Belza, B. (2017). Concern about developing Alzheimer's disease or dementia and intention to be screened: An analysis of national survey data. *Archives of Gerontology and Geriatrics*, *71*, 43–49. doi:10.1016/j.archger.2017.02.013 PMID:28279898

Tang, Z., Zhou, J., Li, K., & Li, R. (2013). A MapReduce task scheduling algorithm for deadline constraints. *Cluster Computing*, *16*(4), 651–662. doi:10.100710586-012-0236-5

Tan, J., Meng, X., & Zhang, L. (2012). Coupling scheduler for MapReduce/Hadoop. In *Proceedings of the 21st international symposium on High-Performance Parallel and Distributed Computing - HPDC '12* (p. 129). New York: ACM Press. 10.1145/2287076.2287097

Tavakoli, A., Casado, M., Koponen, T., & Shenker, S. (2009). *Applying NOX to the Datacenter*. HotNets.

TAXTOKEN. (n.d.). *Blockchain accounting solutions*. Retrieved October 20, 2018, from taxtoken.io: https://taxtoken.io/wp-content/uploads/2017/12/TaxToken-OnePager-AccountingSolutions-Website.pdf

Teed, D. (2018, June 21). *The First Blockchain Debit Card*. Retrieved October 20, 2018, from Seeking Alpha: https://seekingalpha.com/article/4183096-first-blockchain-debit-card

Tewari, A., & Gupta, B. B. (2016). Cryptanalysis of a novel ultra-lightweight mutual authentication protocol for IoT devices using RFID tags. *The Journal of Supercomputing*, *73*(3), 1085–1102. doi:10.100711227-016-1849-x

Thanei, G., Heinze, C., & Meinshausen, N. (2017). Random Projections for Large-Scale Regression. *Contributions to Statistics Big and Complex Data Analysis,* 51-68. doi:10.1007/978-3-319-41573-4_3

Thanh Ho, P. D. (2018). Social Network Analysis Based on Topic Model with Temporal Factor. *International Journal of Knowledge and Systems Science*, *9*(1).

The Continuum: Big Data, Cloud & Internet of Things. (n.d.). Retrieved from https://www.ibm.com/blogs/internet-of-things/big-data-cloud-iot/

The Drebin Dataset. (n.d.). Retrieved December 17, 2018, from https://www.sec.cs.tu-bs.de/~danarp/drebin/

Thornton, G. (2017). *The blockchain timeline From inception to maturity.* Retrieved October 10, 2018, from granthornton. global: https://www.grantthornton.global/globalassets/1.-member-firms/global/insights/blockchain-hub/blockchain-timeline_final.pdf

Tootoonchian, A., & Ganjali, Y. (2010). *HyperFlow: A Distributed Control Plane for OpenFlow*. INM.

Toshiyuki, I., Nguyen, M., & Tanaka, K. (2013). Proxy re-encryption in a stronger security model extended from CT-RSA2012. In *Proceedings of The Cryptographers' Track at the RSA Conference* (pp. 277-292). San Francisco, CA: Springer Berlin Heidelberg.

Tramèr, F., Kurakin, A., Papernot, N., Boneh, D., & McDaniel, P. (2017). *Ensemble adversarial training: Attacks and defenses*. ArXiv Preprint ArXiv:1705.07204

Tramèr, F., Kurakin, A., Papernot, N., Goodfellow, I., Boneh, D., & Mcdaniel, P. (2017). *Ensemble Adversarial Training: Attacks And Defenses* Retrieved From Https://Www.Openaire.Eu/Search/Publication?Articleid=Od_____18: 5fc0601651346f3f957eedba1c1435ad

Tramèr, F., Papernot, N., Goodfellow, I., Boneh, D., & McDaniel, P. (2017). *The space of transferable adversarial examples*. ArXiv Preprint ArXiv:1704.03453

Trono, E., Arakava, Y., Tamai, M., & Yasumoto, H. (2015). DTN MapEx: Disaster area mapping through distributed computing over a Delay Tolerant Network. *Eighth International Conference on Mobile Computing and Ubiquitous Networking (ICMU)*, 179–184. 10.1109/ICMU.2015.7061063

Tsai, C., Lai, C., Chao, H., & Vasilakos, A. V. (2015). Big data analytics: A survey. *Journal of Big Data*, *2*(1), 21. doi:10.118640537-015-0030-3 PMID:26191487

Tunstall, M. (2017). Smart Card Security. In *Smart Cards, Tokens, Security and Applications* (pp. 217–251). Cham: Springer. doi:10.1007/978-3-319-50500-8_9

Uchibeke, U. U., Kassani, H. S., Schneider, A. K., & Deters, R. (2018). Blockchain access control Ecosystem for Big Data security. *Computer Science - Cryptography and Security*. arXiv preprint arXiv:1810.04607

Ukis, V., Rajamani, S. T., Balachandran, B., & Friese, T. (2013). Architecture of cloud-based advanced medical image visualization solution. In *IEEE Int. Conf. on Cloud Computing in Emerging Markets*, (pp.1–5). IEEE. 10.1109/CCEM.2013.6684428

Unbehaun, D., Vaziri, D., Aal, K., Li, Q., Wieching, R., & Wulf, V. (2018). MobiAssist - ICT-based Training System for People with Dementia and their Caregivers: Results from a Field Study. In *Proceedings of the 2018 ACM Conference on Supporting Groupwork – GROUP*. Sanibel Island, FL: ACM. 10.1145/3148330.3154513

United States Government Accountability Office. (n.d.). *GAO-16-116T, Maritime Critical Infrastructure Protection.* Retrieved from https://www.gao.gov/assets/680/672973.pdf

University of Virginia. (n.d.). *Stream Benchmark.* Retrieved from http://www.cs.virginia.edu/stream/ref.html

Usama, M., & Zakaria, N. (2017). Chaos-Based Simultaneous Compression and Encryption for Hadoop. *PLoS One, 12*(1), e0168207. doi:10.1371/journal.pone.0168207 PMID:28072850

VAHDAT: Software define WAN Architecture, 2015

Valiant, L. G. (n.d.). *Learning Disjunction of Conjunctions. Academic Press.*

Vaquero & Rodero-Merino. (2014). *Finding your Way in the Fog: Towards a comprehensive Definition of Fog Computing.* HP Laboratories.

Varatharajan, R., Manogaran, G., Priyan, M. K., & Sundarasekar, R. (2017). Wearable sensor devices for early detection of Alzheimer disease using dynamic time warping algorithm. *Cluster Computing*, 1–10. doi:10.100710586-017-0977-2

Varga, P., & Heged, C. (2015). Service interaction through gateways forinter-cloud collaboration within the arrowhead framework. *Proc GWS2015.*

Varma, R. (2013). Survey on MapReduce and Scheduling Algorithms in Hadoop. *International Journal of Science and Research, 14*(2), 2319–7064. Retrieved from https://www.ijsr.net/archive/v4i2/SUB151194.pdf

Vatrapu, R., Mukkamala, R. R., Hussain, A., & Flesch, B. (2016). Social Set Analysis: A Set Theoretical Approach to Big Data Analytics. *IEEE Access: Practical Innovations, Open Solutions, 4*, 2542–2571. doi:10.1109/ACCESS.2016.2559584

Vavilapalli, V. K. (2013). Apache Hadoop YARN. *Proceedings of the 4th annual Symposium on Cloud Computing - SOCC '13, 13*, 1–16. Retrieved from http://dl.acm.org/citation.cfm?doid=2523616.2523633

Vecchiola, C., Chu, X., & Buyya, R. (2009). *Aneka: a software platform for. NET-based cloud computing.* High Speed Large Scale Sci. Comput.

Veluru, S., Rahulamathavan, Y., Gupta, B. B., & Rajarajan, M. (2015). Privacy preserving text analytics: research challenges and strategies in name analysis. In *Standards and standardization: concepts, methodologies, tools, and applications* (pp. 1415–1435). IGI Global. doi:10.4018/978-1-4666-8111-8.ch066

Verma, A., Cherkasova, L., & Campbell, R. H. (2011). Resource Provisioning Framework for MapReduce Jobs with Performance Goals. Lecture Notes in Computer Science, 7049, 165–86. doi:10.1007/978-3-642-25821-3_9

Verma, S., Choubey, R., & Soni, R. (2012). An Efficient Developed New Symmetric Key Cryptography Algorithm for Information Security. *International Journal of Emerging Technology and Advanced Engineering.* Retrieved from www.ijetae.com

Verma, S., Jhajharia, S., & Kumar, R. (2016). Prognosis on wheels: Administrative effort and scope for data science for cancer treatment. *CSI Communications, 40*(8), 28-30.

Verma, A., Cherkasova, L., Kumar, V. S., & Campbell, R. H. (2012). Deadline-based workload management for MapReduce environments: Pieces of the performance puzzle. In *2012 IEEE Network Operations and Management Symposium* (pp. 900–905). IEEE. 10.1109/NOMS.2012.6212006

Vernon, I., Goldstein, M., & Bower, R. G. (2010). Galaxy formation: A bayesian uncertainty analysis. *Bayesian Analysis, 5*(4), 619–669. doi:10.1214/10-BA524

Vernon, I., Goldstein, M., & Bower, R. G. (2014). Bayesian history matching for the observable universe. *Statistical Science, 29*(1), 81–90. doi:10.1214/12-STS412

Violette, M. (2018). IoT Standards. *IEEE Internet of Things Magazine, 1*(1), 6-7.

VirusShare.com. (n.d.). Retrieved December 17, 2018, from https://virusshare.com/

VirusTotal. (n.d.). Retrieved December 17, 2018, from https://www.virustotal.com/#/home/upload

Voellmy, A., & Hudak, P. (2011). *Nettle: Functional Reactive Programming of OpenFlow Networks.* PADL.

Volodina, V., & Williamson, D. (2018). *Nonstationary Gaussian process emulators with kernel mixtures.* arXiv preprint 1803.04906

Vukoli¢, M. (2015). The quest for scalable blockchain fabric: Proof-of-work vs.BFT replication. *Proc. IFIP WG 11.4 Workshop Open Res. Prob-lemsNetw. Secur. (iNetSec),* 112-125.

Vukolić, M. (2017). Rethinking Permissioned Blockchains. In *Proceedings of the ACM Workshop on Blockchain, Cryptocurrencies and Contracts.* Abu Dhabi, UAE: ACM. 10.1145/3055518.3055526

Walker, J. (n.d.). *How HotBits Works.* Retrieved from https://www.fourmilab.ch/hotbits/how3.html

Wang, H., Osen, O. L., Li, G., Li, W., Dai, H. N., & Zeng, W. (2015). Big data and industrial internet of thingsfor the aritime industry in northwestern Norway. TENCON, IEEE Region 10 Conference, 1-5.

Wang, J. (2004). *ns-2 Tutorial (1).* Multimedia Networking Group, The Department of Computer Science, UVA. Retrieved from http://www.cs.virginia.edu/~cs757/slidespdf/cs757-ns2-tutorial1.pdf

Wang, K., & Mohammad, M. H. K. (2015). Performance Prediction for Apache Spark Platform. *Proceedings - 2015 IEEE 17th International Conference on High Performance Computing and Communications, 2015 IEEE 7th International Symposium on Cyberspace Safety and Security and 2015 IEEE 12th International Conference on Embedded Software and Systems, H,* 166–73. 10.1109/HPCC-CSS-ICESS.2015.246

Wang, Ng, & Shaikh. (2012). Programming your network at run-time for big data applications. In *Proceedings of the first workshop on Hot topics in software defined networks.* ACM. 10.1145/2342441.2342462

Wang, W., De, S., Cassar, G., & Moessner, K. (2013). Knowledge Representation in the Internet of Things: Semantic Modelling and its Applications. *Automatika Journal for Control, Measurement, Electronics, Computing and Communications, 54*(4).

Wang, A., Guo, Y., & Hao, F. (2014). *Scotch: Elastically Scaling up SDN Control-Plane usingvSwitch based Overlay.* CoNext.

Wang, A., Guo, Y., & Hao, F. (2014). *T.V. Lakshman, Songqing Chen: Scotch: Elastically Scaling up SDN Control-Plane usingvSwitch based Overlay.* CoNext.

Wang, G. T. S. Ng, and Anees Shaikh. "Programming your network at run-time for big data applications." *Proceedings of the first workshop on Hot topics in software defined networks.* ACM, 2012.

Wang, H., Wang, Z., & Josep, D.-F. (2018). Anonymous and secure aggregation scheme in fog-based public cloud computing. *Future Generation Computer Systems, 78*(2), 712–719. doi:10.1016/j.future.2017.02.032

Wang, Q., Guo, W., Zhang, K., Ororbia, A. G. II, Xing, X., Liu, X., & Giles, C. L. (2017). Adversary resistant deep neural networks with an application to malware detection. In *Proceedings of the 23rd ACM SIGKDD International Conference on Knowledge Discovery and Data Mining* (pp. 1145–1153). ACM. 10.1145/3097983.3098158

Wang, T., Cai, Y., Jia, W., Wen, S., Wang, G., Tian, H., ... Zhong, B. (2015). Maximizing real-time streaming services based on a multi-servers networking framework. *Computer Networks*, *93*(1), 199–212.

Wang, T., Zhou, J., Huang, M., Zakirul Alam Bhuiyan, M. D., Liu, A., Xu, W., & Xie, M. (2018, June). Fog-based storage technology to fight with cyber threat. *Future Generation Computer Systems*, *83*, 208–218. doi:10.1016/j.future.2017.12.036

Wang, W. J., Chang, Y. S., Lo, W. T., & Lee, Y. K. (2013, February). Adaptive scheduling for parallel tasks with QoS satisfaction for hybrid cloud environments. *The Journal of Supercomputing*, *66*(2), 783–811. doi:10.100711227-013-0890-2

Wang, W., & Lu, Z. (2013). Cyber security in the Smart Grid: Survey and challenges. *Computer Networks*, *57*(5), 1344–1371. doi:10.1016/j.comnet.2012.12.017

Wang, W., Zhu, K., Ying, L., Tan, J., & Zhang, L. (2016). MapTask Scheduling in MapReduce With Data Locality: Throughput and Heavy-Traffic Optimality. *IEEE/ACM Transactions on Networking*, *24*(1), 190–203. doi:10.1109/TNET.2014.2362745

Wang, X., Cai, Y., & Li, Z. (2014). A novel hybrid incentive mechanism for node cooperation in mobile cyber-physical systems. *International Journal of Parallel, Emergent and Distributed Systems*, *29*(3), 316–336. doi:10.1080/1744576 0.2013.852194

Wang, Y., Lu, W., Lou, R., & Wei, B. (2015). Improving MapReduce Performance with Partial Speculative Execution. *Journal of Grid Computing*, *13*(4), 587–604. doi:10.100710723-015-9350-y

Wang, Y., Zhang, Y., Singh, V., Lumezanu, C., & Jiang, G. (2013). *NetFuse: Short-circuiting Traffic Surges in the Cloud*. ICC.

Wan, J., O'Grady, M. J., & O'Hare, G. M. P. (2015). Dynamic sensor event segmentation for real-time activity recognition in a smart home context. *PersUbiquitComput*, *19*, 287–301.

Wan, S., Liang, Y., & Zhang, Y. (2018). Deep convolutional neural networks for diabetic retinopathy detection by image classification. *Computers & Electrical Engineering*, *72*, 274–282. doi:10.1016/j.compeleceng.2018.07.042

Want, R. (2014). RFID: The Key to Automating Everything. *Scientific American*, 56–65.

Ward, M. (2006). EMV card payments – An update. *Information Security Technical Report*, *11*(2), 89–92. doi:10.1016/j.istr.2006.03.001

Warthman, F. (2012). *Delay-and Disruption-Tolerant Networks (DTNs) Version 2.0*. Warthman Associates.

Weber, R. (2015). Internet of Things: Privacy Issues Revisited. *Computer Law & Security Review*, *31*(5), 618–627. doi:10.1016/j.clsr.2015.07.002

Wei, C., Fadlullah, Z., Kato, N., & Stojmenovic, I. (2014, July). On optimally reducing power loss in micro-grids with power storage devices. *IEEE Journal on Selected Areas in Communications*, *32*(7), 1361–1370. doi:10.1109/JSAC.2014.2332077

Wei, F. (2010). TEDI: efficient shortest path query answering on graphs. *Proceedings of SIGMOD*. 10.1145/1807167.1807181

Wei, L., Kumar, N., Lolla, V., Keogh, E., Lonardi, S., Ratanamahatana, C. A., & Van Herle, H. (2005). A practical tool for visualizing and data mining medical time series. In *Proc. 18th IEEE Symposium on Computer-Based Med. Sys.*, (pp.341–346). IEEE.

Weston, Bordes, Chopra, Rush, van Merrienboer, Joulin, & Mikolov. (2015). *Towards AI-complete Question Answering: A set of perquisite toy tasks*. Academic Press.

White. (2002). An integrated experimental environment for distributed systems and networks. In *Proc. of the Fifth Symposium on Operating Systems Design and Implementation* (pp. 255–270). Boston, MA: USENIX Association.

Wind River. (2015). *Security in the Internet of Things*. Retrieved from: https://www.windriver.com

Wood, L., Ivancic, W., Eddy, W., Stewart, D., Northam, J., & Jackson, C. (2008). Investigating operation of the Internet in orbit: Five years of collaboration around CL EO. *IEEE Communications Society Satellite and Space Communications Technical Committee Newsletter*, *18*(2), 10-11.

Woolf, N. (2016). DdoS attack that disrupted internet was largest of its kind in history. *The Guardian*. Retrieved from: https://www.theguardian.com/technology/2016/oct/26/ddos-attack-dyn-mirai-botnet

Wu, M. (2012). Research on the architecture of the Internet of things. *Proceedings of 3rd International Conference on Advanced Computer Theory and Engineering*, 20-22.

Wu, H., Zhang, W., Zhang, J., Wei, J., & Huang, T. (2013). A benefit-aware on-demand provisioning approach for multitier applications in cloud computing. *Frontiers of Computer Science*, *7*(4), 459–474. doi:10.100711704-013-2201-8

Wu, W.-C., & Hung, S.-H. (2014). Droiddolphin: a dynamic android malware detection framework using big data and machine learning. *Proceedings of the 2014 Conference on Research in Adaptive and Convergent Systems*, 247–252. 10.1145/2663761.2664223

Xianghui, C., Peng, C., Jiming, C., & Youxian, S. (2013). An online optimization approach for control and communication codesign in networked cyber-physical systems. *IEEE Transactions on Industrial Informatics*, *9*(1), 439–450. doi:10.1109/TII.2012.2216537

Xiao, L., Li, Q., & Liu, J. (2016). Survey on secure cloud storage. *J. Data Acquis. Process.*, *31*(3), 64–472.

Xiao, L., Wei, W., Yang, W., Shen, Y., & Wu, X. (2017). A protocol-free detection against cloud oriented reflection DoS attacks. *Soft Computing*, *21*(13), 3713–3721. doi:10.100700500-015-2025-6

Xiao, Z., & Xiao, Y. (2013). Security and privacy in cloud computing. *IEEE Communications Surveys and Tutorials*, *15*(2), 843–859. doi:10.1109/SURV.2012.060912.00182

Xie, Zeng, Zhou, & He. (2016). Knowledge Base Questions Answering based on Deep Learning Models. *Natural Language Understanding and Intelligent Applications: ICCPOL 2016,* 300-311.

Xie, C. A. W., Zhang, J. A., Zhou, Z. A., Xie, Y. A., & Yuille, L. A. (2017). Adversarial Examples For Semantic Segmentation And Object Detection. *2017 IEEE International Conference On Computer Vision (ICCV)*. 10.1109/ICCV.2017.153

Xie, H., Li, J., Zhang, Q., & Wang, Y. (2016). Comparison among dimensionality reduction techniques based on Random Projection for cancer classification. *Computational Biology and Chemistry*, *65*, 165–172. doi:10.1016/j.compbiolchem.2016.09.010 PMID:27687329

Xu, W., Qi, Y., & Evans, D. (2016). Automatically Evading Classifiers. *Proceedings Of The 2016 Network And Distributed Systems Symposium*.

Xu, W., Qi, Y., & Evans, D. (2016a). Automatically Evading Classifiers: A Case Study on PDF Malware Classifiers. *NDSS*. Retrieved from https://www.semanticscholar.org/paper/Automatically-Evading-Classifiers%3A-A-Case-Study-on-Xu-Qi/5e4fa9397c18062b970910f8ee168d3297cf098f

Xu, W., Qi, Y., & Evans, D. (2016b). *Automatically evading classifiers*. Academic Press.

Xu, Y., Mahendran, V., & Radhakrishnan, S. (2016). *Internet of hybrid opportunistic things: a novel framework for interconnecting IoTs and DTNs*. IEEE Conference on Computer Communications Workshops (INFOCOM WKSHPS), San Francisco, CA.

Xue, Y., & Lu, R. (2017). Achieving efficient and privacy-preserving cross-domain big data deduplication in cloud. IEEE Trans. Big Data, 1-12.

Xun, Y., Athman, B., Dimitrios, G., Andy, S., & Jan, W. (2016). Privacy protection for wireless medical sensor data. *IEEE Transactions on Dependable and Secure Computing, 13*(3), 369–380. doi:10.1109/TDSC.2015.2406699

Xuyun, Chang, Nepal, Pandey, & Jinjun. (2013). A Privacy Leakage Upper Bound Constraint-Based Approach for Cost-Effective Privacy Preserving of Intermediate Data Sets in Cloud. *Parallel and Distributed Systems, IEEE Transactions on, 24*, 1192–1202.

Yadav, R. (2015). *Spark Cookbook*. Packt Publishing.

Yan, Xu, Xing, Xi, & Chao. (2014). *CAB: A Reactive Wildcard Rule Caching System for Software-Defined Networks*. HotSDN.

Yang, C., Wu, Q., Li, H., & Chen, Y. (2017). *Generative poisoning attack method against neural networks*. ArXiv Preprint ArXiv:1703.01340

Yang, W., Kong, D., Xie, T., & Gunter, C. A. (2017). Malware detection in adversarial settings: Exploiting feature evolutions and confusions in android apps. In *Proceedings of the 33rd Annual Computer Security Applications Conference* (pp. 288–302). Academic Press. 10.1145/3134600.3134642

Yang, W., Xiao, X., Andow, B., Li, S., Xie, T., & Enck, W. (n.d.). *AppContext: Differentiating Malicious and Benign Mobile App Behaviors Using Context*. Retrieved from http://taoxie.cs.illinois.edu/publications/icse15-appcontext.pdf

Yang, R., Xu, Q., Ho, A. M., Yu, Z., Hao, W., & Lu, Z. (2018). Position based cryptography with location privacy: A step for Fog Computing. *Future Generation Computer Systems, 78*(2), 799–806. doi:10.1016/j.future.2017.05.035

Yanyong, Z., & Celal, O. (2005). Enhancing source-location privacy in sensor network routing. In *Proceedings of the 25th IEEE International Conference on Distributed Computing Systems* (pp. 599-608). Genova, Italy: IEEE Computer Society.

Yeganeh & Ganjali. (2012). *Kandoo: A Framework for Efficient and Scalable Offloading of Control Applications*. HotSDN.

Yeganeh & Ganjali. (2015). *Beehive: Towards a Simple Abstraction for Scalable Software-defined Networks*. Academic Press.

Yermack, D. (2015). Is Bitcoin a Real Currency? An Economic Appraisal. In D. Lee, & K. Chuen (Eds.), Handbook of Digital Currency Bitcoin, Innovation, Financial Instruments, and Big Data (pp. 31-43). Elsevier. doi:10.1016/B978-0-12-802117-0.00002-3

Yeung, C. A., Liccardi, I., Lu, K., Seneviratne, O., & Berners-lee, T. (2009). Decentralization: The future of online social networking. *W3C Workshop on the Future of Social Networking Position Papers*.

Yildiz, O., Ibrahim, S., & Antoniu, G. (2017). Enabling fast failure recovery in shared Hadoop clusters: Towards failure-aware scheduling. *Future Generation Computer Systems, 74*, 208–219. doi:10.1016/j.future.2016.02.015

Yildiz, O., Ibrahim, S., Phuong, T. A., & Antoniu, G. (2015). Chronos: Failure-Aware Scheduling in Shared Hadoop Clusters. *Proceedings - 2015 IEEE International Conference on Big Data, IEEE. Big Data, 2015*, 313–318.

Yipin, S., Lu, R., Lin, X., & Shen, X. (2010). An efficient pseudonymous authentication scheme with strong privacy preservation for vehicular communications. *IEEE Transactions on Vehicular Technology, 59*(7), 3589–3603. doi:10.1109/TVT.2010.2051468

Yong Li, Ting Wu, Pan Hui, Depeng Jin, and Sheng Chen: Social-Aware D2D Communications: Qualitative Insights and Quantitative Analysis, 2015

Yoo, D., & Sim, K. M. (2011). A comparative review of job scheduling for MapReduce. In *2011 IEEE International Conference on Cloud Computing and Intelligence Systems* (pp. 353–358). IEEE. 10.1109/CCIS.2011.6045089

Yuan, X., He, P., Zhu, Q., & Li, X. (2017). *Adversarial Examples: Attacks And Defenses For Deep Learning*. Retrieved From Https://Www.Openaire.Eu/Search/Publication?Articleid=Od_____18:F09505f95ca22264d0b6a5700fb27f84

Yuan, X., He, P., Zhu, Q., Bhat, R. R., & Li, X. (2017). *Adversarial Examples: Attacks and Defenses for Deep Learning*. ArXiv Preprint ArXiv:1712.07107

Yuan, Y., Alur, R., & Loo, B. T. (2014). *NetEgg: Programming Network Policies by Examples*. HotNets. doi:10.1145/2670518.2673879

Yukihiro Nakagawa, Kazuki Hyoudou, Takeshi Shimizu: A Management Method of IP Multicast in Overlay Networks using OpenFlow, HotSDN 2012

Yu, M., Rexford, J., Freedman, M. J., & Wang, J. (2010). *Scalable Flow-based Networking with DIFANE*. Sigcomm. doi:10.1145/1851182.1851224

Yu, Z., Ho, A. M., Xu, Q., Yang, R., & Han, J. (2018). Towards leakage-resilient fine-grained access control in fog computing. *Future Generation Computer Systems, 78*(2), 763–777. doi:10.1016/j.future.2017.01.025

Zaccone, Karim, & Menshawy. (2017). Deep Learning with TensorFlow. Packt Publishing.

Zacheilas & Kalogeraki. (2016). ChEsS: Cost-Effective Scheduling Across Multiple Heterogeneous Mapreduce Clusters. In *2016 IEEE International Conference on Autonomic Computing (ICAC)*. IEEE. Retrieved from http://ieeexplore.ieee.org/document/7573117/

Zaharia, M., Chowdhury, M., Das, T., & Dave, A. (2012). Resilient Distributed Datasets: A Fault-Tolerant Abstraction for in-Memory Cluster Computing. *Nsdi*, 2–2. Retrieved from https://www.usenix.org/system/files/conference/nsdi12/nsdi12-final138.pdf

Zaharia, M., Konwinski, A., Joseph, A. D., Katz, R., & Stoica, I. (2008). Improving MapReduce performance in heterogeneous environments. In *Proceedings of the 8th USENIX Conference on Operating Systems Design and Implementation*. USENIX Association. Retrieved from https://dl.acm.org/citation.cfm?id=1855744

Zaharia, M., Borthakur, D., Sen Sarma, J., Elmeleegy, K., Shenker, S., & Stoica, I. (2010). Delay scheduling. In *Proceedings of the 5th European conference on Computer systems - EuroSys '10* (p. 265). New York: ACM Press. 10.1145/1755913.1755940

Zaharia, M., Franklin, M. J., Ghodsi, A., Gonzalez, J., Shenker, S., Stoica, I., ... Venkataraman, S. (2016). Apache Spark. *Communications of the ACM, 59*(11), 56–65. doi:10.1145/2934664

Zainab Hassan Ali. (2017). *A New Proposed the Internet of Things (IoT) Virtualization Framework Based on Sensor-as-a-Service Concept*. Wireless PersCommunication. doi:10.100711277-017-4580-x

Zanella, A., Bui, N., Castellani, A., Vangelista, L., & Zorzi, M. (2014). Internet of things for smart cities. *IEEE Internet of Things Journal, 1*(1), 22–32.

Zantedeschi, V., Nicolae, M.-I., & Rawat, A. (2017). Efficient defenses against adversarial attacks. In *Proceedings of the 10th ACM Workshop on Artificial Intelligence and Security* (pp. 39–49). ACM.

Zaslavsky, A., Perera, C., & Georgakopoulos, D. (2013). Sensing as a service and big data. *Proceedings of the International Conference on Advances in Cloud Computing (ACC).*

Zec, M., & Mikuc, M. (2004). Operating system support for integrated network emulation in imunes. *Proc. of the 1st Workshop on Operating System and Architectural Support for the on demand IT InfraStructure (OASIS).*

Zeng, Garg, Strazdins, Jayaraman, Georgakopoulos, & Ranjan. (2017). IOTSim: A simulator for analysing IoT applications. *J. Syst. Archit.*

Zeng, X. (2017). Cost Efficient Scheduling of MapReduce Applications on Public Clouds. *Journal of Computational Science.* Retrieved from https://www.sciencedirect.com/science/article/pii/S1877750317308542

Zguira, Y., Rivano, H., & Meddeb, A. (2018). *IoB-DTN: a lightweight DTN protocol for mobile IoT Applications to smart bike sharing systems. WD2018, 10th IFIP Wireless Days, April 2018*, Dubai, UAE.

Zhang, R., Lin, C. D., & Ranjan, P. (2018a). *DynamicGP: Local Gaussian Process Model for Large-Scale Dynamic Computer Experiments.* R package.

Zhang, R., Lin, C. D., & Ranjan, P. (2018c). *A sequential design approach for calibrating a dynamic population growth model.* arXiv:1811.00153

Zhang, W., Rajasekaran, S., Wood, T., & Zhu, M. (2014). MIMP: Deadline and Interference Aware Scheduling of Hadoop Virtual Machines. *Proceedings - 14th IEEE/ACM International Symposium on Cluster, Cloud, and Grid Computing, CCGrid 2014*, 394–403. 10.1109/CCGrid.2014.101

Zhang, Y., & Wen, J. (2015). An IoT electric business model based on the protocol of bitcoin. ICIN. IEEE, 184–191.

Zhang, Z., Cherkasova, L., & Loo, B. T. (2013). Performance Modeling of MapReduce Jobs in Heterogeneous Cloud Environments. *2013 IEEE Sixth International Conference on Cloud Computing*, 839–46. Retrieved from http://ieeexplore.ieee.org/document/6740232/

Zhang, F., Cao, J., Tan, W., Khan, S. U., Li, K., & Zomaya, A. Y. (2014). Evolutionary Scheduling of Dynamic Multitasking Workloads for Big-Data Analytics in Elastic Cloud. *IEEE Transactions on Emerging Topics in Computing, 2*(3), 338–351. doi:10.1109/TETC.2014.2348196

Zhang, F., Member, S., Chan, P. P. K., Biggio, B., Yeung, D. S., & Roli, F. (2015). Article. *Evasion Attacks, 46*(3), 1–12. doi:10.1109/TCYB.2015.2415032

Zhang, K., Liang, X., Shen, X., & Lu, R. (2014). Exploiting multimedia services in mobile social networks from security and privacy perspectives. *IEEE Communications Magazine, 52*(3), 58–65. doi:10.1109/MCOM.2014.6766086

Zhang, P., Sadler, C. M., Lyon, S. A., & Martonosi, M. (2004). *Hardware design experiences in ZebraNet. In Proc of the 2nd IntConf on Embedded Networked Sensor Systems* (pp. 227–238). New York: ACM.

Zhang, P., White, J. C. D., Lenz, G. S., & Rosenbloom, T. S. (2018). FHIRChain: Applying Blockchain to Securely and Scalably Share Clinical Data. *Computational and Structural Biotechnology Journal, 16*, 267–278. doi:10.1016/j.csbj.2018.07.004 PMID:30108685

Zhang, Q., Zhani, M. F., Yang, Y., Boutaba, R., & Wong, B. (2015). PRISM: Fine-Grained Resource-Aware Scheduling for MapReduce. *IEEE Transactions on Cloud Computing, 3*(2), 182–194. doi:10.1109/TCC.2014.2379096

Zhang, R., Du, T., & Qu, S. (2018). A Principal Component Analysis Algorithm Based on Dimension Reduction Window. *IEEE Access: Practical Innovations, Open Solutions, 6,* 63737–63747. doi:10.1109/ACCESS.2018.2875270

Zhang, R., Lin, C. D., & Ranjan, P. (2018b). Local Gaussian process model for largescale dynamic computer experiments. *Journal of Computational and Graphical Statistics, 27*(4), 798–807. doi:10.1080/10618600.2018.1473778

Zhang, S., Ivancic, F., Lumezanu, C., Yuan, Y., Gupta, A., & Malik, S. (2014). *An Adaptable Rule Placement for Software-defined Networks.* DSN. doi:10.1109/DSN.2014.24

Zhang, T., & Yang, B. (2018). Dimension reduction for big data. *Statistics and Its Interface, 11*(2), 295–306. doi:10.4310/SII.2018.v11.n2.a7

Zhang, X., Wuwong, N., Li, H., & Zhang, X. J. (2010). Information Security Risk Management Framework for the Cloud Computing Environments. *Proceedings of 10th IEEE International Conference on Computer and Information Technology,* 1328-1334. 10.1109/CIT.2010.501

Zhang, X., Zhong, Z., Feng, S., Tu, B., & Fan, J. (2011). Improving Data Locality of MapReduce by Scheduling in Homogeneous Computing Environments. In *2011 IEEE Ninth International Symposium on Parallel and Distributed Processing with Applications* (pp. 120–126). IEEE. 10.1109/ISPA.2011.14

Zhang, Y., Yang, X., Wei, W., & Abdulhameed, A. (2018). A variant of password authenticated key exchange protocol. *Future Generation Computer Systems, 78*(2), 699–711. doi:10.1016/j.future.2017.02.016

Zhang, Z. (2014). Fuxi: A Fault-Tolerant Resource Management and Job Scheduling System at Internet Scale. *Proc. VLDB Endow., 7*(13), 1393–1404. 10.14778/2733004.2733012

Zhao, Y. (2015). SLA-Based Resource Scheduling for Big Data Analytics as a Service in Cloud Computing Environments. *2015 44th International Conference on Parallel Processing,* 510–19. Retrieved from http://ieeexplore.ieee.org/document/7349606/

Zhao, Z., & Cheng, X. (2014). *IEEE 802.11 p for vehicle-to-vehicle (v2v) communications.* IEEE.

Zheng Cai, Alan L. Cox, T.S. Eugene Ng: Maestro: A System for Scalable OpenFlow Control, 2011

Zheng, Q., Wang, X., Khan, M. K., Zhang, W., Gupta, B. B., & Guo, W. (2018). A Lightweight Authenticated Encryption Scheme Based on Chaotic SCML for Railway Cloud Service. *IEEE Access: Practical Innovations, Open Solutions, 6,* 711–722. doi:10.1109/ACCESS.2017.2775038

Zheng, W., Yu, J. X., Zou, L., & Cheng, H. (2018). *Question Answering over knowledge graphs: Question Understanding Via Template Decomposition.* VLDB Endowment. doi:10.14778/3236187.3236192

Zheng, Z., Xie, S., Dai, H., Chen, X., & Wang, H. (2017). An Overview of Blockchain Technology: Architecture, Consensus, and Future Trends. In *2017 IEEE International Congress on Big Data (BigData Congress)* (pp. 557-564). Honolulu, HI: IEEE. 10.1109/BigDataCongress.2017.85

Zhou, W., Jia, Y., Peng, A., Zhang, Y., & Liu, P. (2018). The Effect of IoT New Features on Security and Privacy: New Threats, Existing Solutions, and Challenges Yet to Be Solved. *IEEE Internet of Things Journal,* 1-1.

Zhou, Y., Jiang, X., & Nazish, A. (2011). Dissecting Android Malware : Characterization and Evolution Summarized by : Nazish Asad. *Proceedings - IEEE Symposium on Security and Privacy,* (4), 95–109. 10.1109/SP.2012.16

Zhou, J., Cao, Z., Dong, X., & Vasilakos, A. V. (2017). Security and privacy for cloud-based IoT: Challenges. *IEEE Communications Magazine, 55*(1), 26–33. doi:10.1109/MCOM.2017.1600363CM

Zhou, T., Fang, Y., & Zhang, Y. (2008). Securing wireless sensor networks: A survey. *IEEE Communications Surveys and Tutorials, 10*(3), 6–28. doi:10.1109/COMST.2008.4625802

Zhu, H. (2009). *Security in Delay Tolerant Networks* (PhD Thesis). University of Waterloo.

Zhu, Y., Yan, E., & Song, I.-Y. (2017). The use of a graph-based system to improve bibliographic information retrieval: System design, implementation, and evaluation. *Journal of the Association for Information Science and Technology, 68*(2), 480–490. doi:10.1002/asi.23677

Zikopoulos, P. (2012, March). *IBM Big Data: What is Big Data Part 1 and 2*. Retrieved from http://www.youtube.com/watch?v=B27SpLOOhWw

Zikratov, I., Kuzmin, A., Akimenko, V., Niculichev, V., & Yalansky, L. (2017). *Ensuring data integrity using Blockchain technology. In Proceeding of the 20th Conference of Fruct Association* (pp. 534–539). IEEE.

Zong, Z., Ge, R., & Gu, Q. (2017). Marcher: A Heterogeneous System Supporting Energy-Aware High Performance Computing and Big Data Analytics. *Big Data Research, 8*, 27–38. Retrieved from http://linkinghub.elsevier.com/retrieve/pii/S221457961630048X

Zorzi, M., Gluhak, A., Lange, S., & Bassi, A. (2010). From today's INTRAnet of things to a future INTERnet of things: A wireless- and mobility-related view. *IEEE Wireless Communications, 17*(6), 44–51. doi:10.1109/MWC.2010.5675777

About the Contributors

Brij B. Gupta received PhD degree from Indian Institute of Technology Roorkee, India in the area of Information and Cyber Security. In 2009, he was selected for Canadian Commonwealth Scholarship award by Government of Canada. He has published more than 150 research papers (including 04 books and 18 book chapters) in International Journals and Conferences of high repute including IEEE, Elsevier, ACM, Springer, Wiley, Taylor & Francis, Inderscience, etc. He has visited several countries, i.e. Canada, Japan, Australia, China, Spain, Hong-Kong, Italy, Malaysia, Macau, etc. to present his research work. His biography was selected and published in the 30th Edition of Marquis Who's Who in the World, 2012. In addition, he has been selected to receive 2017 Albert Nelson Marquis Lifetime Achievement Award' by Marquis Who's Who in the World, USA. Dr. Gupta also received Sir Visvesvaraya Young Faculty Research Fellowship Award in 2017 from Ministry of Electronics and Information Technology, government of India. Recently, he has been awarded with '2018 Best Faculty Award for research activities' and '2018 Best Faculty Award for Project and Laboratory Development' from National Institute of Technology Kurukshetra, India. He is also working as principal investigator of various R&D projects sponsored by various government of India funding agencies. He is serving as Associate editor of IEEE Transactions on Industrial Informatics, IEEE Access, and Executive editor of IJITCA, Inderscience, respectively. Moreover, Dr. Gupta is also leading International Journal of Cloud Applications and Computing (IJCAC), IGI Global, USA as Editor-in-Chief. He is also serving as reviewer for various Journals of IEEE, Springer, Wiley, Taylor & Francis, etc. He also served as TPC Chair of 2018 IEEE INFOCOM: CCSNA, USA. Moreover, he served as publicity chair of 10th NSS 2016, 17th IFSA-SCIS 2017 which were held in Taiwan and Japan, respectively. He is also founder chair of FISP and ISCW workshops which organize in different countries every year. Dr. Gupta is serving as organizing Chair of Special Session on Recent Advancements in Cyber Security (SS-CBS) in IEEE Global Conference on Consumer Electronics (GCCE), Japan every year since 2014. Dr. Gupta received outstanding paper awards in both regular and student categories in 5th IEEE Global Conference on Consumer Electronics (GCCE) in Kyoto, Japan during Oct. 7-10, 2016. Dr. Gupta is Senior member of IEEE, Member ACM, SIGCOMM, SDIWC, Internet Society, Institute of Nanotechnology, Life Member, International Association of Engineers (IAENG), Life Member, International Association of Computer Science and Information Technology (IACSIT). He was also visiting researcher with Yamaguchi University, Japan, with Deakin University, Australia and with Swinburne University of Technology, Australia during 2015 and 2018, 2017, and 2018, respectively. At present, Dr. Gupta is working as Assistant Professor in the Department of Computer Engineering, National Institute of Technology Kurukshetra India. His research interest includes Information security, Cyber Security, Mobile/Smartphone, Cloud Computing, Web security, Intrusion detection, Computer networks and Phishing.

Dharma P. Agrawal is the Ohio Board of Regents Distinguished Professor and the founding director for the Center for Distributed and Mobile Computing in the Department of Electrical Engineering and Computing Systems. He has been a faculty member at the ECE Dept., Carnegie Mellon University (on sabbatical leave), N.C. State University, Raleigh and the Wayne State University. His current research interests include applications of sensor networks in monitoring Parkinson's disease patients and neurosis, applications of sensor networks in monitoring fitness of athletes' personnel wellness, applications of sensor networks in monitoring firefighters physical condition in action, efficient secured communication in Sensor networks, secured group communication in Vehicular Networks, use of Femto cells in LTE technology and interference issues, heterogeneous wireless networks, and resource allocation and security in mesh networks for 4G technology. His recent contribution in the form of a co-authored introductory text book on *Introduction to Wireless and Mobile Computing, 4th edition,* has been widely accepted throughout the world. The book has been reprinted both in China and India and translated in to Korean and Chinese languages. His co-authored book on *Ad hoc and Sensor Networks, 2nd edition,* has been published in spring of 2011. A co-edited book entitled, *Encyclopedia on Ad Hoc and Ubiquitous Computing,* has been published by the World Scientific and co-authored books entitled *Wireless Sensor Networks: Deployment Alternatives and Analytical Modeling,* and *Innovative Approaches to Spectrum Selection, Sensing, On-Demand Medium Access in Heterogeneous Multihop Networks,* and *Sharing in Cognitive Radio Networks* have being published by Lambert Academic. He is a founding Editorial Board Member, I*nternational Journal on Distributed Sensor Networks, International Journal of Ad Hoc and Ubiquitous Computing (IJAHUC), International Journal of Ad Hoc & Sensor Wireless Networks* and *the Journal of Information Assurance and Security (JIAS)*. He has served as an editor of the IEEE *Computer magazine*, and the *IEEE Transactions on Computers, the Journal of Parallel and Distributed Systems and* the *International Journal of High Speed Computing*. He has been the Program Chair and General Chair for numerous international conferences and meetings. He has received numerous certificates from the IEEE Computer Society. He was awarded a *Third Millennium Medal,* by the IEEE for his outstanding contributions. He has delivered keynote speech at 34 different international conferences. He has published over 655 papers, given 52 different tutorials and extensive training courses in various conferences in USA, and numerous institutions in Taiwan, Korea, Jordan, UAE, Malaysia, and India in the areas of Ad hoc and Sensor Networks and Mesh Networks, including security issues. He has graduated 72 PhDs and 58 MS students. He has been named as an ISI Highly Cited Researcher, is a Fellow of the IEEE, the ACM, the AAAS and the World Innovation Foundation, and a recent recipient of 2008 IEEE CS Harry Goode Award. Recently, in June 2011, he was selected as the best Mentor for Doctoral Students at the University of Cincinnati. Recently, he has been inducted as a charter fellow of the National Academy of Inventers. He has also been elected a Fellow of the IACSIT (International Association of Computer Science and Information Technology), 2013.

* * *

G. Aghila received her B.E degree in Computer Science and Engineering from Thiagarajar College of Engineering, India, M.E degree in Computer Science and Engineering from College of Engineering Guindy, India and Ph.D. in knowledge representation and reasoning from College of Engineering Guindy, India. She has 30 years of teaching experience for both U.G and P.G. Her research interests includes Artificial Intelligence, Chem-informatics, Image and Audio Steganography, Big data analytics, Edge computing, Block chain in banking and Smart & Secure environment.

Sanjay P. Ahuja has a M.S. and Ph.D. in Computer Science and Engineering from the University of Louisville. He is a Full Professor and the Fidelity Distinguished Professor in Computer and Information Sciences in the School of Computing at the University of North Florida. He is a Senior Member of the IEEE and a member of the SPEC Research Group (RG) and the SPEC RG Cloud Working Group. He is the faculty advisor to the Upsilon Pi Epsilon Computer Science Honor Society. His research interests include Cloud Computing, Fog Computing, IoT, performance evaluation and benchmarking, modeling, and simulation of Networks, Distributed Systems, and Cloud Platforms.

Abdelaziz Amara Korba is an assistant professor in the department of computer science, Badji Mokhtar University, Algeria. His research focuses on security issues in Internet of things, Smart Grid, and wireless ad hoc networks. He received his PhD degree from Badji Mokhtar University. He is currently a researcher at Networks and Systems Laboratory.

Ayan Banerjee is a research assistant in Computer Innovative Research Society, India. He also received his Master of Computer Application degree from West Bengal University of Technology (2016), and Bachelor of Computer Application degree from West Bengal University of Technology (2013).

Kriti Bhushan received his PhD in Computer engineering from National Institute of Technology Kurukshetra, India and M.Tech degree in Computer Science & Engineering from National Institute of Technology Rourkela, India. Currently, he is working as an assistant professor with the department of Computer Engineering, National Institute of Technology Kurukshetra, India. He is a professional member of IEEE, and ACM. His research interest includes Cloud Security, Mobile Security, Network Security, and Cyber Security.

Rabia Bilal holds an Assistant professor position in the Department of Electrical Engineering at Usman Institute of Technology, Karachi, Pakistan. She has an MPhil in Engineering from the University of Sussex, UK, and a BS degree in Electronic Engineering and MS degree in Electronic with specialization in Telecommunication from Sir Syed University of Engineering and Technology, Karachi, Pakistan. She has decade of experience in engineering universities and industry where she was involved in teaching engineering undergraduates, research and publications. Her publications include refereed journal, conference papers, book chapters and books. She is a lifetime member of Pakistan Engineering Council (PEC).

Rajkumar Buyya is a Redmond Barry Distinguished Professor and Director of the Cloud Computing and Distributed Systems (CLOUDS) Laboratory at the University of Melbourne, Australia. He is also serving as the founding CEO of Manjrasoft, a spin-off company of the University, commercializing its innovations in Cloud Computing. He served as a Future Fellow of the Australian Research Council during 2012-2016. He has authored over 625 publications and seven text books including "Mastering Cloud Computing" published by McGraw Hill, China Machine Press, and Morgan Kaufmann for Indian, Chinese and international markets respectively. He also edited several books including "Cloud Computing: Principles and Paradigms" (Wiley Press, USA, Feb 2011). He is one of the highly cited authors in computer science and software engineering worldwide (h-index=118, g-index=255, 72,200+ citations). Microsoft Academic Search Index ranked Dr. Buyya as #1 author in the world (2005-2016) for both field rating and citations evaluations in the area of Distributed and Parallel Computing. "A Scientometric Analysis of Cloud Computing Literature" by German scientists ranked Dr. Buyya as the

World's Top-Cited (#1) Author and the World's Most-Productive (#1) Author in Cloud Computing. Dr. Buyya is recognized as a "2016 Web of Science Highly Cited Researcher" by Thomson Reuters, a Fellow of IEEE, and Scopus Researcher of the Year 2017 with Excellence in Innovative Research Award by Elsevier for his outstanding contributions to Cloud computing. Software technologies for Grid and Cloud computing developed under Dr. Buyya's leadership have gained rapid acceptance and are in use at several academic institutions and commercial enterprises in 40 countries around the world. Dr. Buyya has led the establishment and development of key community activities, including serving as foundation Chair of the IEEE Technical Committee on Scalable Computing and five IEEE/ACM conferences. These contributions and international research leadership of Dr. Buyya are recognized through the award of "2009 IEEE Medal for Excellence in Scalable Computing" from the IEEE Computer Society TCSC. Manjrasoft's Aneka Cloud technology developed under his leadership has received "2010 Frost & Sullivan New Product Innovation Award". Recently, Dr. Buyya received "Mahatma Gandhi Award" along with Gold Medals for his outstanding and extraordinary achievements in Information Technology field and services rendered to promote greater friendship and India-International cooperation. He served as the founding Editor-in-Chief of the IEEE Transactions on Cloud Computing. He is currently serving as Co-Editor-in-Chief of Journal of Software: Practice and Experience, which was established over 45 years ago. For further information on Dr.Buyya, please visit his cyberhome: www.buyya.com.

Andrea Chiappetta (M) graduated in International Economics, PhD in Economy and Institution, act as (contract) professor in Geopolitcs Economy at Marconi International University being also the Director of the Cyber Security Observatory on Critical Infrastructure Protection of the Marconi International University (CSOCIP). Andrea is the Executive Director of ASPISEC, company specialized in Cyber security.

Phuc Do is currently an Associate Professor of the University of Information Technology (UIT), VNU-HCM, Vietnam. His research interests include data mining, text mining, information network analysis, big data analysis and applications.

M. Fevzi Esen has received his M.A. and Ph.D. in quantitative sciences from Istanbul University. He now works at İstanbul Medeniyet University, Faculty of Tourism, as assistant professor. His main interest fields are: data mining, statistics and big data applications in tourism industries.

Mohamed Amine Ferrag received the bachelor's, master's, and Ph.D. degrees from Badji Mokhtar–Annaba University, Algeria, in 2008, 2010, and 2014, respectively, all in computer science. Since 2014, he has been an Assistant Professor with the Department of Computer Science, Guelma University, Algeria. He has edited the book Security Solutions and Applied Cryptography in Smart Grid Communications (IGI Global). His research interests include wireless network security, network coding security, and applied cryptography. He is currently serving in various editorial positions such as Editorial Board Member with Computer Security Journals like the International Journal of Information Security and Privacy (IGI Global), the International Journal of Internet Technology and Secured Transactions (Inderscience Publishers), and the EAI Endorsed Transactions on Security and Safety (EAI). He has served as an Organizing Committee Member (the Track Chair, the Co-Chair, the Publicty Chair, the Proceedings Editor, and the Web Chair) in numerous international conferences.

Ratneshwer Gupta is working as an Assistant Professor in School of Computer and Systems Sciences, Jawaharlal Nehru University, New Delhi,, India. He has done his Ph.D. In Component Based Software Engineering at Department of Computer Science and Engineering, Indian Institute of Technology, Banaras Hindu University (IIT-BHU), Varanasi (India). He has 11 years of teaching experience of UG and PG students. He is currently working on Computer networks and software engineering. He has 22 papers in international journals and 16 papers in international/national conference proceedings. He has 1 book chapter (from IGI Global Publisher) and one monologue (from LAP Germany) in his credit.

M. Harshvardhan is a third-year student in the Integrated Programme in Management (IPM) at Indian Institute of Management Indore, and expected to graduate in March 2021. He is also the Coordinator of Information Technology interest group at IIM Indore.

Muhammed Tawfiqul Islam is an experienced Lecturer with a demonstrated history of working in both academia and industry. Currently, he is pursuing Doctor of Philosophy (Ph.D.) focusing on Cloud Computing, Distributed Systems, Big Data at Cloud Computing and Distributed Systems (CLOUDS) Lab in the School of Computing and Information Systems (CIS) at The University of Melbourne, Australia. He is also a Lecturer (on study leave) at the Department of Computer Science & Engineering, University of Dhaka. He has completed his BS and MS degrees from the same department at the University of Dhaka in 2010 and 2013, respectively. He also worked as a software developer for Internet Society and REVE Systems. Tawfiqul published numerous research papers in various renowned international journal and conferences. His research interests fall mainly into Big Data, Cloud Computing, Distributed Systems, Network Performance, and Measurements.

Teenu S. John is a Research Scholar at the Indian Institute of Information Technology and Management - Kerala (IIITM-K), India. She has completed her Masters in Cybersecurity from TOC-H Institute of Science & Technology, Piravom, Kerala, India. She has completed her Bachelors in Engineering from College of Engineering, Perumon, Kollam, Kerala, India. She has 3 years of teaching experience working at Thejus Engineering College, Thrissur, Kerala & Axis Engineering College, Kodakara. Her area of interest includes Malware detection, Machine learning in Cybersecurity, etc.

Bilal Muhammad Khan holds PhD and Post Doc in wireless communication networks from the University of Sussex UK. He was affiliated with Sussex University UK as Teaching Fellow and Visiting Research Fellow. Currently he is working as Assistant Professor at National University of Sciences and Technology. He is involved in various projects on design of wireless sensor networks, programmable logic controllers, Microcontrollers, Systems administration and Software training. He has published number of journal papers and written many book chapters and also serving in the editorial boards of journals. His research interests are in the area of wireless sensor networks, wireless local area networks.

Rajalakshmi Krishnamurthi obtained her Ph. D in Computer Science and Engineering from Jaypee Institute of Information Technology Noida, India. She did her M. E (CSE), and B. E (EEE) from Bharathiar University, Coimbatore, India. She is currently an Assistant Professor (Senior Grade) with the Department of Computer Science and Engineering, Jaypee Institute of Information Technology, Noida. Her current research interests include Mobile computing, Wireless networks, Cloud Computing, Pervasive Computing.

Anirban Kundu is an Associate Professor in Information Technology Department of Netaji Subhash Engineering College, Kolkata, India. Dr. Kundu is associated with Computer Innovative Research Society, West Bengal, India. Previously, he worked as Post Doctoral Research Fellow at Kuang-Chi Institute of Advanced Technology, Shenzhen, P. R. China. Dr. Kundu also worked as foreign expert under Municipality Government of Shenzhen during 2011 to 2014. Earlier, he worked as an Assistant Professor in Information Technology Department of Netaji Subhash Engineering College, India. He was also a Research Fellow in the Web Intelligence and Distributed Computing Research Lab (WIDiCoReL). He received his BE Mechanical from Bangalore University (1999). He also received his Post Graduate Diploma in Financial Management from Management Studies Promotion Institute (2001), an MTech (IT) from Bengal Engineering and Science University (2004), and PhD (Engineering) in Computer Science from Jadavpur University (2009). His research interests include search engine oriented indexing, ranking, prediction, web page classification, semantic web (ontology-based) and natural language processor with the essence of cellular automata. He is also interested in multi-agent-based system design, fuzzy controlled systems and cloud computing. He has presented his research work in England, Russia, Thailand, China, and India at various international conferences. He is a technical committee member of IEEE Transactions on Services Computing, IEEE Computer Society, since 2018. He has published 105 international research publications (published/accepted) till date within which 45 journals, 51 conferences (among which 19 conference papers have been selected as Book Chapters) and 9 Book Chapters. He has also 2 book publications, and 1 patent. Dr. Kundu has participated in 24 international journals, and 152 international conferences till date.

Vandana Kushwaha is working as an Assistant Professor in Department of Computer Science, Institute of Science, Banaras Hindu University, Varanasi (India). She has 11 years of teaching experience of UG and PG students. She has done her Ph.D. in Computer Science at the Department of Computer Science, Institute of Science, Banaras Hindu University, Varanasi (India). Her research interests include High Speed Network, Wireless Sensor Network, Network algorithms and Congestion control protocols. She has 6 papers in international Journals and one paper in international conference. She has 1 book chapter (from CRC Press) in her credit.

Ankur Lohachab received his Master of Technology (M. Tech.) degree in Computer Science and Engineering from University Institute of Engineering and Technology (UIET), Kurukshetra University, India, in 2018, and Bachelor of Technology (B. Tech.) degree in Computer Science and Engineering from Kurukshetra University, India, in 2015. His research interests broadly include Internet of Things (IoT), Blockchain Technology, Quantum Computing, and Applied Cryptography.

R. S. Mangrulkar has done his PhD in Computer Science and Engineering from SGBAU Amravati in 2016. He has done his B.E (Comp sci. & Engg) from B.N.C.O.E Pusad in 2001 and M.Tech (CSE) from National Institute of Technology, Rourkela, Orissa in 2008. Currently, he is working as Associate Professor, SVKM's D.J. Sanghvi College of Engineering, Vile Parle, Mumbai. Before to this, he worked as Associate Professor and Head, department of Comp. Engineering, Bapurao Deshmukh College of Engineering Sevagram. He has total 16 years of teaching experience to UG and PG level. He has total 14 research publication in international journal and 29 research paper in National and International Conferences. He is reviver of IJCA, Elsevier and AIRCSE journal. He evaluated 9 dissertation report of M.E / M.Tech candidate in RTMNU Nagpur and SRTMNU Nanded. He received gold medal on securing Merit position in SGB Amravati University. He also delivered 28 guest lecture / Expert lectures in Research oriented programs at SGGS Nanded, PIET Nagpur, RCERT Chandrapur and SKNCOE Pune, PVPIT Pune, COE Ambojogai, MGM Nanded, Anjuman COE Nagpur and BDCE Sevagram on "Latex and Its Importance in Manuscript Preparation" and "Network Simulator Programming" and trained almost 700 students of PG and Faculty Members. He also chaired 25 sessions in various national level conference and technical symposium. He also received certification of appreciation from DIG Special Crime Branch Pune and Supretendant of Police and broadcasting media gives wide publicity for the project work guided by him on the topic "Face Recognition System". He received certification of achievement from IIT Kanpur for ACM Programming Context. He is life member of ISTE,CSI,IACSIT and IAENG. He is highly motivated towards research and always promotes use of recent technology for presenting and promoting open source research. His area of interest is Adhoc Network specially design of Routing Protocols. He also received 3.5 lakhs grant under Research Promotion Scheme of AICTE for the project "Secured Energy Efficient Routing Protocol for Delay Tolerant Hybrid Network". Under his leadership, Department of Computer Engineering also received grant of Rs. 1.29 lacs from UGC, AICTE and CSIR for conduction of STTP/Workshop. He is active member of BOS, RTMNU and handed responsibility of framing new syllabus to B.E. Computer Engineering(CBS) and M.Tech Computer Science & Engineering(CBS).

Melody Moh obtained her MS and Ph.D., both in computer science, from Univ. of California - Davis. She joined San Jose State University in 1993, and has been a Professor since Aug 2003. Her research interests include cloud computing, mobile, wireless networking, machine learning applications for cloud, networked systems and their security/privacy issues. She has received over 500K dollars of research grants from both NSF and industry, has published over 150 refereed papers in international journals, conferences and as book chapters, and has consulted for various companies.

R. Murugan was born in Ramanathapuram, Tamilnadu, India, in 1983. He received the B.E. degree in Electronics and Communication Engineering, the M.E. degree in Embedded System Technologies from Anna University, Chennai, Tamilnadu, in 2005, 2010, respectively, and Ph.D. degree from Information and Communication Engineering, Centre for Research, Anna University, Chennai, Tamilnadu, India. He worked as Assistant Professor, in the Department of Electronics and Communication Engineering, Aalim Muhammed Salegh College of Engineering, Chennai from 01st August 2010 to 15th December 2017. He worked as Assistant Professor, in the Department of Electronics and Communication Engineering, St. Peter's Engineering College, Hyderabad from 08th January2018 to 30th May 2018. He is working as Assistant Professor, in the Department of Electronics and Communication Engineering, National Institute of Technology (NIT), Silchar Assam, India, since 15th June 2018.

Nag Nami has been a master student at San Jose State University since 2017, majoring in Computer Science, with research interests in applications of Deep Learning/Machine Learning in the field of security. He had worked for close to 5 year with DELL EMC, and Deloitte as Data Scientist after earning his Bachelor in Technology in Computer Science from KIIT University, India.

Karthikeyan P. is currently working as an Associate Professor in Thiagarajar College of Engineering, Madurai. He has completed the PhD program in Information and Communication Engineering under Anna University, Chennai, Tamilnadu, India in the year 2015. He has received SAP Fellowship award from IIT Bombay for his best performance in the year 2016. He published many papers in refereed international journals and conferences. He is a reviewer in various international journals. His research interests include evolutionary algorithms, mobile ad hoc networks, engineering education and mobile applications.

Vaibhav Pandey is pursuing Ph.D. from Department of Computer Science & Engineering at Punjab Engineering College (Deemed to be University), Chandigarh, India. He received his M.Tech. degree from NIT Hamirpur, HP, India in 2010. He received B. Tech. degree in Computer Science & Engineering stream from UPTU, Lucknow, India in 2008. His research interest includes Distributed Computing Systems, Cloud Computing, Theoretical Computer Science and Wireless Sensors Networks.

Ramesh C. Poonia has rich experience of 14+ years as an academician. At present he is an Associate Professor of Computer Science at Amity Institute of Information Technology, Amity University Rajasthan. Postdoctoral Fellow at Cyber-Physical Systems Laboratory (CPS Lab), Department of ICT and Natural Sciences, Norwegian University of Science and Technology (NTNU), Alesund, Norway. He has received his PhD in Computer Science from the Banasthali University - Rajasthan. His research interests include Vehicular Networks, Wireless & Mobile Networks, Network Protocol Evaluation, Network Simulation & Modeling, and Internet Congestion Control. He has published more than 22 papers and books; some of them have been published in referred journals/conference proceedings as: IEEE Trans. on Computers, IEEE International Conference on Signal Processing and Communication Engineering Systems, ACM - International Conference Proceedings Series (ICPS), International Journal of Wireless & Mobile Networks – AIRCC, IGI Global, Elsevier, Springer and Inderscience. Dr. Poonia is serving as senior member, technical program committee member, member of editorial board/reviewer board of various renowned national and international conferences/journals.

Siddharth R. received B.E degree in Computer Science and Engineering from Karpagam University, India and M.Tech Degree in Information Technology from Madras Institute of Technology, India. He is currently working towards the Ph.D. Degree at Department of Computer Science and Engineering, National Institute of Technology Puducherry, India. His current research interests include Big data analytics, Cloud computing and Feature Extraction techniques.

Linesh Raja is currently working as Assistant Professor at Amity Institute of Information Technology, Amity University Rajasthan, India. He earned the Ph.D. in computer science from Jaipur National University, India Before that he has completed his Masters and Bachelor degree from Birla Institute of Technology, India. Dr. Linesh has published several research papers in the field of wireless communication, mobile networks security and internet of things in various reputed national and international journals. He has chaired various sessions of international conferences. Currently he is the editor of Handbook of Research on Smart Farming Technologies for Sustainable Development, IGI Global. At the same time he is also acting as a guest editor of various reputed journal publishing house, such as Taylor & Francis, Inderscience and Bentham Science. He is the member of ACM and founder member of ACM Jaipur chapter.

Pritam Ranjan is an Associate Professor in the Operations Management and Quantitative Techniques area at IIM Indore. He joined IIM Indore in June 2015, before which he was an associate professor in the department of Mathematics and Statistics at Acadia University, Nova Scotia, Canada. He obtained B.Stat. and M.Stat. degrees from the Indian Statistical Institute, Kolkata, and a Ph.D. degree in statistics in 2007 from Simon Fraser University, BC, Canada. His research areas include statistical modeling, design and analysis of computer experiments, sequential designs for feature estimation, and multi-stage fractional factorial designs with randomization restrictions. Dr. Ranjan has received several research grants from NSERC Canada, MITACS Canada and DST India. He has also served as the editorial board member for several top statistical journals.

Poonam Saini is currently working as Assistant Professor in Department of Computer Science & Engineering at Punjab Engineering College (Deemed to be University), Chandigarh, India. She received her Ph.D. degree in Computer Engineering from National Institute of Technology, Kurukshetra, India in 2013.She has received B. Tech. and M.Tech degrees from Kurukshetra University, Kurukshetra, India in 2003 and 2006 respectively. Her research interest includes Fault-Tolerant Distributed Computing Systems, Mobile Computing, Ad hoc Networks, Wireless Sensors Networks, Cloud Computing and Big Data Analytics.

Nitigya Sambyal is pursuing Ph.D. from Department of Computer Science & Engineering at Punjab Engineering College (Deemed to be University), Chandigarh, India. She received her B.Tech and M.Tech. degree from University of Jammu, Jammu, India in 2013 and 2016 respectively. Her research interest includes Data analytics, Image processing, Machine Learning and Data Mining.

Rajinder Sandhu is currently working as Assistant Professor (Senior Grade) in the Department of Computer Science & Engineering at Jaypee University of Information Technology (JUIT) Waknaghat, Solan, Himachal Pradesh-India since November, 2016. He has obtained his Ph.D. from Guru Nanak Dev University, Amritsar in 2017 and M.E. with honours from Thapar University, Patiala in 2013. He was research fellow in CLOUDs Laboratory, University of Melbourne, Australia in 2016-17. He has published his research work in Scientific Citation Index journals of Elsevier, John Wiley and Springer. He also filed two patents in Indian Patent Office. He is also consultant to Gigabyte Pvt. Ltd. and Nihon Communication, Bangalore for Cloud Computing and Big Data. He is reviewer of many reputed SCI journals of Elsevier, Wiley and Springer. Starting from his M.E., he has delivered multiple expert talks on cloud computing for various workshops and FDPs of reputed universities like JNU-Delhi, PEC-Chandigarh and IIT-Kharakpur. His current working research areas are cloud computing, Big Data and Internet of Things (IoT). Currently, He is working with Prof. Rajkumar Buyya from Australia and Dr. Victor Chang from China on various projects and research papers.

Niti Shah is an undergrad student at Dwarkadas J. Sanghvi College of Engineering pursuing Computer Engineering (B.E. 2019).

J. John Shiny is currently working as an Assistant Professor in the Dept of Information Technology, Thiagarajar College of Engineering, Madurai. She completed her B.Tech (Information Technology) in Hindustan College of Engineering, affiliated to Anna University-Chennai in 2011. She then joined SSN college of Engineering, Chennai to pursue her Masters in Engineering in Computer science and completed in 2013. Thereafter she joined Thiagarajar College of Engineering as an Assistant Professor and currently she is in that designation. She has five years of teaching experience especially in Cloud computing, Network security and Distributed Systems for both UG and PG degrees. She is pursuing Ph.D in the cloud resource allocation area. She has organized one credit courses in the college in association with Dell, Bangaluru.

Vijander Singh working as academician since last 12+ years. Currently, he is serving at Amity University Rajasthan, Jaipur as Associate Professor in the Computer Science Department. He has qualified NET, GATE with Computer Science Subject. He has published more than 20 research papers in reputed international journals. At the same time he is also guest editor of various reputed journals. He is the member of ACM and founder member of ACM Jaipur chapter.

Altan Sirel is a cyber security analyst and researcher. He studied computer engineering in Koc University. He started to work at Solid Information Security in late 2017 as a cyber security researcher. As of November 2018 he is in the cyber security team of BTCTurk.

Rupali Syal received B.Tech in Computer Science from Panjab Technical University, India in 2001; M.E in Computer Science (IT) from Panjab University in 2005, and PhD in Computer Science from Panjab University in 2016. She is currently working as Assistant Professor in Computer Science department in Punjab Engineering College, India. Her research interests are Cryptography, Algorithms and Data Analytics.

Tony Thomas is an Associate Professor at the Indian Institute of Information Technology and Management - Kerala (IIITM-K), India. He received his masters and Ph.D degrees from IIT Kanpur, India. After his Ph.D, he carried out his postdoctoral research at the Korea Advanced Institute of Science and Technology, Daejeon, South Korea. After completing his postdoctoral studies, he joined as a researcher in the Vehicular Communication Group at the General Motors Research Lab, Bangalore, India. He later moved to the School of Computer Engineering, Nanyang Technological University, Singapore as a Senior Researcher Fellow and worked in the domains of multimedia security and video surveillance. His current research interests are malware analysis, biometrics, cryptography, machine learning approaches in cyber security, cyber threat prediction and visualization, and digital forensics. He has published several research papers and book chapters in these domains. He has been a Governing Council Member of the Cyberdome of Kerala Police and an Adjunct Faculty at IISER Thiruvananthapuram. He is a Ph.D research guide in the Faculty of Technology, CUSAT. He has been an editor and reviewer for several journals and conferences as well as a Technical Program Committee Member for several international conferences in the domain of Cyber Security.

Adel Nadjaran Toosi has joined Faculty of Information Technology at Monash University in May 2018. Before, he worked as a Research Fellow in the Cloud Computing and Distributed Systems (CLOUDS) Laboratory in the School of Computing and Information Systems (CIS) at the University of Melbourne for more than three years. He received his Ph.D. degree in Computer Science and Software Engineering from the University of Melbourne in 2015. His thesis was one of the two theses nominated for the Chancellor's Prize for Excellence in the Ph.D. Thesis and John Melvin Memorial Scholarship for the Best Ph.D. Thesis in Engineering. Adel has made significant contributions to the areas of resource management and software systems for cloud computing. His research interests include Distributed Systems, Cloud Computing, Software-Defined Networking (SDN), Green Computing, and Soft Computing. He is currently working on resource management for Software-Defined Networking (SDN)-enabled cloud computing environments.

H. Emre Yilmaz is an information security executive. He is currently working as an Information Security Manager at BTCTurk.com. He's been active in cyber security field in Turkey for more than 20 years and has been involved in developing and marketing phases of several UTM and APT products. He started his career as a network and security expert at Toprakbank A.Ş. and kept working on developing native products at several different organizations. In 2013, he continued his work on cyber security at a firm which he was one of the co-founders of and which operated in Tubitak Teknopark (The Scientific and Technological Research Council of Turkey). As of 2018, he decided to continue his career in BTCTurk.

Kanksha Zaveri is a Computer Engineering (B.E. 2019) student at Dwarkadas J. Sanghvi College of Engineering.

Index

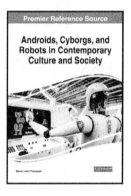

Ensure Quality Research is Introduced to the Academic Community

Become an IGI Global Reviewer for Authored Book Projects

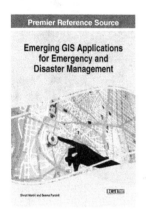

Premier Reference Source

Emerging GIS Applications for Emergency and Disaster Management

Premier Reference Source

Managerial Strategies and Green Solutions for Project Sustainability

Premier Reference Source

Comparative Approaches to Using R and Python for Statistical Data Analysis

Premier Reference Source

Solutions for High-Touch Communications in a High-Tech World

The overall success of an authored book project is dependent on quality and timely reviews.

In this competitive age of scholarly publishing, constructive and timely feedback significantly expedites the turnaround time of manuscripts from submission to acceptance, allowing the publication and discovery of forward-thinking research at a much more expeditious rate. Several IGI Global authored book projects are currently seeking highly qualified experts in the field to fill vacancies on their respective editorial review boards:

Applications may be sent to:
development@igi-global.com

Applicants must have a doctorate (or an equivalent degree) as well as publishing and reviewing experience. Reviewers are asked to write reviews in a timely, collegial, and constructive manner. All reviewers will begin their role on an ad-hoc basis for a period of one year, and upon successful completion of this term can be considered for full editorial review board status, with the potential for a subsequent promotion to Associate Editor.

If you have a colleague that may be interested in this opportunity, we encourage you to share this information with them.

Printed in the United States
By Bookmasters